POLITICAL ANALYSIS

Sara Miller McCune founded SAGE Publishing in 1965 to support the dissemination of usable knowledge and educate a global community. SAGE publishes more than 1000 journals and over 800 new books each year, spanning a wide range of subject areas. Our growing selection of library products includes archives, data, case studies and video. SAGE remains majority owned by our founder and after her lifetime will become owned by a charitable trust that secures the company's continued independence.

Los Angeles | London | New Delhi | Singapore | Washington DC | Melbourne

Matthew Loveless
POLITICAL ANALYSIS

A Guide to Data & Statistics

Los Angeles | London | New Delhi
Singapore | Washington DC | Melbourne

Los Angeles | London | New Delhi
Singapore | Washington DC | Melbourne

SAGE Publications Ltd
1 Oliver's Yard
55 City Road
London EC1Y 1SP

SAGE Publications Inc.
2455 Teller Road
Thousand Oaks, California 91320

SAGE Publications India Pvt Ltd
B 1/I 1 Mohan Cooperative Industrial Area
Mathura Road
New Delhi 110 044

SAGE Publications Asia-Pacific Pte Ltd
3 Church Street
#10-04 Samsung Hub
Singapore 049483

Editor: Andrew Malvern
Editorial assistant: Rhoda Ola-Said
Production editor: Victoria Nicholas
Marketing manager: Lorna Patkai
Cover design: Francis Kenney
Typeset by: C&M Digitals (P) Ltd, Chennai, India
Printed in the UK

© Matthew Loveless 2023

Apart from any fair dealing for the purposes of research, private study, or criticism or review, as permitted under the Copyright, Designs and Patents Act, 1988, this publication may not be reproduced, stored or transmitted in any form, or by any means, without the prior permission in writing of the publisher, or in the case of reprographic reproduction, in accordance with the terms of licences issued by the Copyright Licensing Agency. Enquiries concerning reproduction outside those terms should be sent to the publisher.

Library of Congress Control Number: 2022944849

British Library Cataloguing in Publication data

A catalogue record for this book is available from the British Library

ISBN 978-1-5297-7484-9
ISBN 978-1-5297-7483-2 (pbk)

At SAGE we take sustainability seriously. Most of our products are printed in the UK using responsibly sourced papers and boards. When we print overseas we ensure sustainable papers are used as measured by the PREPS grading system. We undertake an annual audit to monitor our sustainability.

CONTENTS

Discover this Textbook's Online Resources		vii
About the Author		viii
A Prologue		ix

An Introduction — 1

1 The Scientific Method and Statistics — 9
2 Theory and Hypotheses — 27
3 Data and Variables — 47
4 Research Design — 65
5 Statistics and the Scientific Study of Politics — 85

PART I   DESCRIPTIVE STATISTICS — **105**

6 Univariate Descriptive Statistics — 107
7 Measures of Association I: Nominal- and Ordinal-level Variables — 137
8 Measures of Association II: Means Comparison and Correlation — 161
9 Measures of Association III: (Bivariate) Regression — 189

PART II   INFERENTIAL STATISTICS — **217**

10 An Introduction to Inference — 219
11 Inference for Nominal- and Ordinal-level Variables — 239
12 The Central Limit Theorem — 261
13 Inference for Interval-level Variables — 289

PART III MULTIPLE REGRESSION   **315**

14 Multiple Regression   317

15 Extensions to Multiple Regression   341

16 Issues with Multiple Regression   371

17 Binary Logistic Regression   393

18 Categorical and Limited Dependent Variables   419

PART IV CURRENT DEBATES   **441**

19 Big Alternatives   443

20 The Ethics of Data Analysis   463

Index   482

DISCOVER THIS TEXTBOOK'S ONLINE RESOURCES

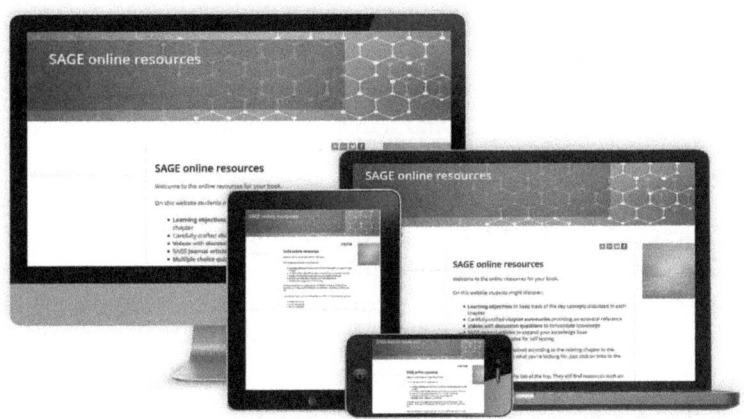

Political Analysis is supported by a wealth of online resources for lecturers to aid study and support teaching, which are available at **www.study.sagepub.com/loveless**

For instructors

Teaching guides outline the key learning objectives covered in each chapter and provide suggested activities/examples to use in class or for assignments.

PowerPoint slides featuring figures and tables from the book, which can be downloaded and customized for use in your own presentations.

Testbanks containing questions related to the key concepts in each chapter can be downloaded and used in class, as homework or in exams.

Datasets for you to share with your students in class or for assignments, which will support their mastery of data analysis and statistics.

ABOUT THE AUTHOR

Matthew Loveless is an Associate Professor in the Department of Political and Social Sciences at the University of Bologna (Italy). He is also co-founder of the Center for Research and Social Progress (cersp.org). He has taught quantitative methods to undergraduate and graduate students since 2003. He has held academic positions in the United States (Georgetown University; University of Mississippi), the United Kingdom (Nuffield Fellow, Oxford; University of Kent), and Italy (Jean Monnet Fellow, European University Institute, Florence; University of Bologna) in addition to visiting positions at Sciences Po – Institut d'Etudes Politiques de Grenoble (France), the University of Georgia (USA), Davidson College (USA), St. Antony's College (Oxford, UK), Mannheimer Zentrum für Europäische Sozialforschung (Germany), and the University of Debrecen (Hungary). His research interests include the field of Political Behavior in Europe, particularly as it relates to how individuals perceive and make sense of politics (recent examples focusing on political attitudes include *International Political Science Review*, *Political Studies*, the *Journal of European Public Policy*). Recent publications also include co-authored work that incorporate party competition with recent publications in *Government and Opposition*, *Electoral Studies*, and the *Journal of Common Market Studies*. He lives with his family in Italy.

A PROLOGUE

This book is only nominally about statistics. It is substantively about empowering you. Learning statistics is just like learning any skill. In this case, statistical skills can help you with the consumption and execution of quantitative analysis. However, these skills can also equip you with the power of logical thinking, thoughtful analysis, and proper interpretation. That is, the practice of critical and clear thinking can be used as a shield and sword against unclear logic, specious arguments, and deception. I want you to have the confidence to interact with statistics and in doing so, make you a more formidable student and citizen. During your study, I invite you to return to this paragraph if you start losing motivation or feeling overwhelmed to remind yourself of the real value of being an educated person.

AN INTRODUCTION

The Aim of this Book

This book was designed to help you pass through unfamiliar territory. This is one of the reasons 'guide' is in the title. However, your destination – the aim of the journey – can be any number of things. It could be simply to pass this class, move on, and put it behind you. Or it could be gaining a sense of what statistics can do – and not do – so that you are not excluded from areas of research and debate. Or it could be the first of many steps toward a more advanced study of statistics and other quantitative methods. Each of these is perfectly understandable and reasonable to the extent it is appropriate to your own direction. I hope this book helps you achieve your goal.

My aim with this book is to help the reader – before the numbers and formulas and computations – to understand *what it is we want to know* and *why we want to know it*. Then, the computation of *how we go about finding it* becomes more intuitive and practical. Thus, I have tried to introduce the basic elements of statistical analysis for political analysis in an intuitive and useful way. Alan Watts was a student of philosophy and attracted substantial attention in the 1960s and 1970s as an interlocutor of eastern religions and philosophies. He wrote and spoke about Taoism, Buddhism, and the later manifestation Zen Buddhism for Western audiences, primarily in the US and UK. His unique appeal was the ability to offer an attainable appreciation of the context and mind necessary to comprehend – and thus, begin to enjoy – oriental philosophies, ideas, and approaches. At the core of his presentations was the superficially humorous but fundamental command to the audience members to 'get out of your own way'!

He maintained that Western minds were over-intellectualized and disincentivized from the 'intuitive mind'. This disincentivized position, in turn, blocked listeners' and readers' ability to see the startlingly obvious and profound insights just waiting, like a cat standing on a counter, to be picked up and enjoyed. Simply, he argued that there are two sides of the mind that must move together, the intellectual mind – to understand and remember the ideas correctly – and the intuitive mind – knowing when and how they are appropriate. This 'feel' for eastern ideas, in Watts's mind, was the challenge to appreciating these approaches.

This has clear analogue to learning statistics. Statistics can be technically difficult and feel foreign. If one were to progress beyond this book, the techniques and estimation procedures become significantly more challenging. This includes the expanding universe of necessary assumptions, the correct choice of technique, drawing valid conclusions, and what we can and cannot say. However, it all comes back to understanding what we are doing with data. What is our goal? What do we want to know from these data and our analysis of it? Why is it important?

Many of these considerations take place long before we sit down with the data. And take place beyond the sphere of statistics itself. This is one of the reasons that some statistics textbooks start off – as I do here – with talking about its use in the broader context of political analysis and the scientific method. Simply using a hammer is not hard: bang, bang, bang. Knowing when best to use a hammer is the trick.

Despite promises, we do not have the ability to fully assess reality, as it exists. As Poincaré reminds us, **science** is a convention, one chosen means to understand the world. There is no one comprehensively optimal means to do so. Thus, the art of science, being a craftsman of science, is knowing when to reach for the tool of statistics as the best means to analyse a problem. And this knowledge will include the incumbent advantages and disadvantages of doing so. However, knowing the most correct – or least-worst – thing to do is vastly superior to any amount of mindless number crunching or flashy techniques.

Why Study Statistics at All?

Whether you just want to be done with a statistics class, sated with this much statistics, or are thirsting for more, there are three really good reasons to study statistics: statistical literacy, statistical abilities, and research skills.

Statistical Literacy

Statistical literacy is reading, understanding, and critically assessing quantitative research. I would argue that whether you like statistics (or see some value in having been exposed to it) or not, you benefit from a statistics course. If you like statistics ('statistics-curious,' perhaps), an introductory course is a good place to start. Understanding core concepts that underpin the modern use of statistics is in itself valuable and serves as a solid basis for exploring more advanced applications. If you don't like statistics, then this is the opportunity to get to know your enemy. If you think that statistics are a waste of time or, worse, obscuring real relationships and findings, understanding where statistics does in fact stand on thin ice or rely on strong assumptions can only empower your position. That is, instead of saying, 'You're wrong to use statistics,' it would be more powerful to say, 'You're wrong to use statistics *because*…'.

In a phrase loosely attributed Pablo Picasso, 'Learn the rules like a pro, so you can break them like an artist.' Learn statistics to be a better critic because throwing uninformed insults is gauche and lazy. In any case, both groups can further benefit – in different ways – from understanding what statistics can do as well as understanding what statistics cannot do.

In addition, a lot of what we know about the world is discovered and often explained in the language of science and the use of statistics. A great deal of what you are hearing about in your other classes comes from the cumulative efforts of scientists using various tools to advance our collective knowledge.

Consider when your other professors say:

- Citizens with socio-economic characteristics A, B, and C in institutional contexts of Y and Z are more likely to vote.
- Initial conflicts with characteristics D, E, and F in regions S and T are more likely to escalate in violence.
- Countries with characteristics M and N are more likely to be democracies.

These results are summarizing predominantly scientific – and very often statistical – analyses. We have identified these patterns derived from the literature of accumulated studies that have been conducted empirically and have drawn conclusions based on those findings. Simply, a lot of what we know about politics, about the world more generally, is the summary of scientific research. And a lot of that research uses statistics.

And, regardless of what you do next, you will be confronted by statistics. This can be in the garden variety form of the news reporting on a legislative outcome, election, or level of support; in an article online; or even in advertising. Or perhaps you will be confronted more substantially and importantly. Imagine confronting some research, a policy paper, white paper, or report for your work. Which position would you rather be in: passing it to a colleague because you can't understand it or engaging with it, asking questions like:

- How appropriate are the data to answering the question?
- Are the chosen statistical techniques appropriate?
- What assumptions have been made?
- What can we conclude about the empirical relationships?
- Have the limitations been acknowledged and addressed?

This would make you a formidable employee. And, even more importantly, this would also make you a formidable democratic citizen. Thus, statistical literacy is not about running around and analysing everything statistically, it is about not being pushed around.

Why let other people explain the world to you?

Statistical Abilities

Statistical abilities include generating descriptive and inferential statistics using statistical software, and interpreting and analysing the output. Not only can being statistically literate help immunize us from bad arguments, questionable correlations, and poor inference, we can also use our abilities to identify and use the most appropriate techniques as well as to recognize inherent limitations.

The ultimate responsibility of an instructor is not to tell you how to do something or give you the answers, it is instead to empower you to take command of your education.

I refer to education not only as the formal form but also what happens to us after university. The most important value of education is not simply being exposed to more books or better teaching; a good education is becoming responsible for your own learning.

As we will see in the later chapters of this book, the most advanced techniques are mere complications on a small set of fundamental concepts. Once you ingest those fundamentals, the rest will flow naturally. I encourage you not to be intimidated by the formulas, and letters, and mathematics. Statistical software has become nearly ubiquitous and so easy to use that the challenge of calculation is not of any grave concern. The challenge of statistics – true also of most things – is learning what to put in, what is happening, and what to do with what comes out. Statistical abilities are recognizing the most effective means to represent relationships among data; to understand the utility of statistics ('What we can do with statistics') and the limitations of statistics ('What we can't do with statistics').

And crucially, in this way, the student becomes the master.

Research Skills

Research skills are the rigorous use of statistics to address a research question and present your choices and results in a clear, informative, and effective manner. Simply, to use statistical techniques to inform and/or support an argument.

It may be becoming increasingly apparent to you that fewer and fewer people, certainly ones that we don't know personally, care very little about what you think, or what you feel, or what you believe. That is not to say that these are not important to you as a person. However, in writing persuasively and convincingly, people are primarily moved by what you can demonstrate. In contrast to opinions and assertions *ipse dixit* ('he asserts without proof'), statistical abilities can be used to support and advance an argument. However, it is not merely using statistics that is sufficient. Statistics is an analytical tool grounded in the scientific method.

As an academic, I find it both amazing and startling to see the number of highly trained quantitative students coming out of advanced programs using wizard-like regressions and techniques. At the same time, I am rejecting more and more submitted papers for a lack of a basic understanding of what these fancy things are assuming and doing to the analysis. It feels as though there have become two groups. Those who wield a heavier hammer and those – a greater majority – who receive the 'traditional' form of statistical training embedded in the crucial context of scientific research. Despite its intimidating size and terrifying power, a heavier hammer *still* does not make everything a nail. We are served better by people who can understand what can be done with a statistical approach as well as what can't be done to produce the research we want – and the research we need.

Math Skills

Quickly, it may surprise you but if you can do the following, you have more than sufficient math skills to do statistics.

3 + 2 = 5

8 − 5 = 3

4 * 5 = 20

30 ÷ 10 = 3

81 > 74 = true

The Data in this Book

One choice that was important in creating this book was making the conscious and time-consuming decision to use actual, publicly available data. Except in a few cases, the data – and subsequent results – in the exercises and examples are available to you. Available to anybody.

The primary reason is that I want you to do it. I want you to be able to use real data and use these techniques to show you that there is no hokey-pokey going on. You can use the things that you have learned here on real data to examine real people and events. You can answer and address real questions. I want you to stay close to an actual analysis of reality.

I will admit that it was tempting to include constructed examples that would perform precisely and cleanly. However, the cloudy answers the academics and researchers are familiar with are the norm. It is uncommon to find convincing, overwhelming, and clear-cut evidence. Sometimes, (statistical) results are not obviously one thing or another. There is the nagging feeling that while the answer may be sufficient, it is not satisfying. For the open-minded and patient scientist, however, these cloudy answers are not necessarily a setback but rather an opportunity, an opportunity to reflect on the nature of the results.

Are we asking the right question? Perhaps the results are cloudy and underwhelming because we have approached our phenomenon of interest hindered by unclear or lazy thinking, scant understanding of previous work, or with a rigid over-attention to these same previous works. If not our question, perhaps it is our method of inquiry. Remember, the phenomenon in which we are interested – as some subset of nature or reality – is simply responding to the question in the manner that you asked it (i.e., in the same way, a statistical software package will give you an answer regardless of how boneheaded the question).

These are not statistical questions *per se* or even scientific questions, they are broader, more philosophical questions to improve the likelihood that both question and method will produce the highest quality synergy for your research. That is to say, be prepared to reflect on what it is you have really found statistically, empirically, epistemologically, even ontologically.

Finally, pedagogically, from my two decades of teaching statistics, I have found that the real data approach empowers students. Why should we tinker around the edges of real political analysis? Pick it up and do it.

Statistics are a Tool

Data can become information which then can become knowledge. Converting data into information is assembling observations into a coherent form. Statistics is one of many ways of doing this. However, statistics is not the answer. It is not the question. It is simply a tool. In its service to science, statistics is popular because it provides a straight-out-of-the-box utility.

Statistics can only help us with what we can measure, and data are nearly always incomplete. Incomplete does not mean lacking (although this is also a problem) but rather the gap between what we want to measure and what we have with which to measure it.

Think about a person that you kind of know, a friend of a friend. How would you quantify the following attributes: age, income, gender, vote in last election, political participation, trust in government, ideology? How would you measure and record these? What if you had to collect the same data on 10 other people, 100 other people, a thousand, ten thousand? Would this change your strategy in collecting these data? In trying to find some way to compare large numbers of things, we are forced to make some concessions. That is, at some point we make our peace with imperfect measures in order to get, however imprecisely, at 'something'.

This is the first partition from reality.

The second partition is that statistics is just a way that we have developed to identify patterns in data. We have done so by exploiting mathematics (which is a very good way at getting at patterns). Werner Heisenberg – yeah, that guy – noted that 'what we observe is not nature in itself but nature exposed to our method of questioning' (2007: 24–5). If we ask statistical questions, we will get statistical answers. If we seek to summarize with patterns, we will get summaries of patterned answers.

What we want to do is to be able to identify patterns in a sensible way and to strengthen our understanding of the world. Yet, patterns are summaries. Some of them will provide more evidence, some less evidence. Some will be complex and some will be less complex. Yet, in the same way that we come to take for granted that there is a constellation called Big Bear (*Ursa Major*) in the distribution of stars in the sky, a pattern that fits our expectation of a pattern that should be there doesn't necessarily mean that it is actually there (Pearl and Mackenzie, 2018). That is, understanding these patterns become how we understand something but the patterns are not *understanding* itself. That comes from a different process of turning information into knowledge.

As the old joke goes, information is knowing that a tomato is a fruit and knowledge is not putting a tomato in fruit salad. In precisely the same way, statistics are a cold, inert tool. We must separate what statistics can do for our analysis as well as what it cannot do, such as come up with good research questions, survey the literature, derive appropriate hypotheses, or correctly interpret the results. Which leads to the biggest surprise: statistics is really subjective.

The English figure of speech 'a jack of all trades, master of none' is often meant derogatorily to describe someone good a several things but not great at any one thing. However, this phrase originally had the opposite intention as the full quote is, 'A jack of all trades, master of none is oftentimes better than a master of one.' That is, expertise in one area only can also lead us to view all problems through that single lens or ascribe only one solution to any problem. Perhaps in this way the study and use of statistics to analyse data as part of a larger, scientific approach can go well beyond merely using statistics and serve you well in any situation that requires rigorous, analytical thinking.

Finally, I include a quote I once heard only once from an unseen speaker many years ago: 'Catch the vigorous horse of your mind.' That seems like the right mindset for acquiring a new skill.

A Parting Note

I will assume by the fact that you are reading this sentence that you have to take a statistics course (or you have a strange sense of what fun is). Well, things could be worse. You could have to write a statistics textbook. So, swings and roundabouts, silver linings and all that. This book was started during the second European wave of the Coronavirus outbreak (January 2021), coinciding with some of Europe's harshest lockdowns, and was written entirely at night. After having (been) woken up at 6am by new baby, home-schooling the other two, full-spectrum parenting, online teaching, online administration meetings, getting everyone to bed, and preparing to do it all again tomorrow, this book grew word by word, sentence by sentence in the dark of the night. It took almost exactly two years.

Perhaps ironically, I hope that you will discover that even though having written a textbook on statistics, I am not dogmatic about it. Statistics is an analytical research tool. Common, but one of many empirical techniques. Science is a framework of understanding. Common, but one of many branches of philosophy. And both, often found together, provoke much larger philosophical questions, ontological questions, epistemological questions. If this is interesting to you, and I hope that it is, ask your instructor for further discussions on these topics.

Acknowledgements

They say that a book is never written alone. That is profoundly true. I want to deeply thank the team at Sage, with a particular mention of Andrew Malvern for convincing me to actually do this. He, Rhoda Ola-Said, and Victoria Nicholas walked and/or dragged me through the process using mostly carrots, some stick. I add a warm thanks to Lorna Patkai, Francis Kenney, and Daniel Price for their professional patience with my novice ideas.

I want to thank the reviewers. Each reviewer of this book (of which there were 6) was not only finding typos, incongruencies, inconsistencies, and flat-out errors but also – from their vantage points outside this project – providing perspectives desperately needed by the author caught in the weeds of word count, coverage, illustrations, techniques, and tables. As the reviewers themselves know, the choice of integrating comments is often a choice of constraint rather than a pure value choice. Comments can be extremely helpful but simply undoable within the constraints of the book. However, each reviewer offered numerous and substantial improvements, and inasmuch as it was possible, many of which were incorporated as they were clear and beneficial improvements to my own thinking, knowledge, and writing.

The process of peer-review is a funny one not understood by many. Having what you intended to write voiced back to you from someone who read it is a process which requires a thick skin (as I am sure the reviewers, as authors themselves, know). But taken in the intended manner, among professional colleagues, it qualifies our discipline to be taken seriously. The peer-review system underpins the confidence we can have in the debates that take place in various disciplines.

Having said that, all academics have a different strategy for reading reviews. Mine is to get a cup of coffee and read all of them at once. Then, I put on my walking shoes and go for a 2- or 3-hour walk in the woods. It usually starts with me saying lots of bad words and explaining to the flora and fauna along the way how stupid the reviewers are but invariably ends with me returning home, recording on my phone, saying, 'Here's where the reviewers were absolutely right and I was absurdly wrong. Implement the following comments to improve the quality, impact, and reach of my project. First, …'

Finally, my greatest appreciation goes to my family. Per il mio amore, non sono sicuro di poterti ringraziare abbastanza per il tuo aiuto, il tuo contributo e il tuo sostegno. Ne'er a truer sentence could be written: I could not have written this book without you. For you other three, I hope you enjoy getting a statistics textbook for your birthdays this year.

All errors remain my own, even the ones I made when I was really, really tired.

Annotated References and Further Reading

King, Gary. 1986. 'How not to lie with statistics: Avoiding common mistakes in quantitative political science' ***American Political Science Review*** **30(3): 666–687.**
A helpful guide by one of the premier methodologists in Political Science.

Pearl, Judea and Dana Mackenzie. 2018. ***The Book of Why: The New Science of Cause and Effect.*** **New York: Basic Books.**
Data alone are hardly a science, regardless how big they get and how skilfully they are manipulated.

Heisenberg, Werner. 1958. ***Physics and Philosophy: The Revolution in Modern Science.*** **New York: Harper.**
Heisenberg provides for scientists of all stripes lessons in our shared form of thinking as well as its undeniable shortcomings common across all fields of inquiry. A seminal work of scientific thought.

1
THE SCIENTIFIC METHOD AND STATISTICS

> **LEARNING OUTCOMES**
>
> In this chapter, you will be able to
>
> - Critically engage the use of science as a means to understand political phenomena.
> - Identify key elements of the Scientific Method.
> - Assess how statistics can be used to achieve many of the aims of scientific research.
> - Articulate the points of alignments between the Scientific Method and the statistical approach to data analysis.
> - Recognize the difference between 'doing statistics' and 'doing science'.
> - Situate the role of statistics and the Scientific Method within the wider discipline of Political Science and International Relations (IR).

Introduction

The goal of this book is to present an understanding of how statistics come to represent relationships among data and, in turn, why this is useful to the scientific study of politics. To do so, we must engage what it means to do science at all. This chapter is an introductory discussion of what the scientific method is and how statistics can aid scientific study. Key characteristics of scientific study are mapped onto the use and techniques of statistical analysis. It also highlights the distinctive power of statistical analysis including the abilities of description, inference, and control.

Why Science?

Science is one of several ways to understand the world. This is a fairly broad definition but underpinning this definition is the assumption that the world is ultimately knowable and that we are able to converge on that knowledge through the application of an agreed-upon and rigorous methodology, called the scientific method. The **Scientific Method** – capital S, capital M – is an objective and replicable analysis of data which results in evidence which can be used to assess proposed explanations for a relationship and whether we can export the resultant explanation to other phenomena. The use of the scientific method progresses collective knowledge by replicating, challenging, and advancing the body of theoretical knowledge of a discipline.

The actual methods and tools used in pursuit of the Scientific Method, within and across disciplines, may differ. Social scientists don't stuff people in test tubes and chemists don't ask molecules how they feel about democracy as a form of government. However, they share key design and analytical elements. At its simplest, in order to achieve a scientific understanding of the world, the scientific method includes a transparent and replicable description of the research design and analysis, a rigorous attempt to identify and explain the relationship under investigation, and a means to assess the appropriate inferences from the results.

What Makes Scientific Research Scientific?

What are these characteristics and practices of applying science that provide access to this specific 'scientific' understanding of the world? Within the disciplines of the social sciences, and Political Science in particular, what made our study more scientific or rigorous has been formally questioned and discussed in the literature several times.

Taking one prominent example, in 1994, leading scholars in the Political Science fields of Political Methodology, International Relations, and Comparative Politics argued that both empirical qualitative work and quantitative work aligned with the core tenets of the scientific method. Gary King, Robert Keohane, and Sidney Verba (KKV), respectively, argued that, done correctly, these disparate approaches (in their various modes) could contribute meaningfully to the scientific advancement in Political Science. That is, using empirical qualitative methods – like document analysis, interviews, or case studies – or quantitative methods – like statistics and experiments – were indistinguishable from one another as scientific endeavours as long as they exhibited core characteristics of the scientific method.

Frankly, science is analytically promiscuous. All forms of empirical work, whether qualitative or quantitative, can adhere to the methods and choices necessary for scientific results. In this way, the authors were trying to reconcile adherents of various approaches by asserting that scientific research has the following characteristics: the content is the method, the conclusions are uncertain, the procedures are public, and the goal is inference. All achievable in many different ways.

Since then and continuing on to today, there has been a lot of discussion about the comprehensiveness and correctness of their criteria. What has remained unassailable are three bedrock principles of scientific research:

1. A transparent and replicable description of the research design and analysis.
2. An attempt to identify and explain the relationship under investigation.
3. The ability to make appropriate inferences from the results of the research.

This applies to research in Political Science just as it does for the physical sciences. For example, Political Scientists may use an experimental approach to isolate the impact of a key variable. The design and implementation of that experiment will differ only in the choice of tools from astrophysicists' experiments in the Large Hadron Collider. The design rules and analytical rigors of experimentation are precisely the same. Thus, for all approaches, the three principles of scientific research, if adhered to as closely as possible, offer the greatest opportunity in creating a greater scientific understanding of the world.

The ultimate goal of scientific research is to understand and even explain as much as we can with as little as we can. The scientific method is the means to do that, by creating research that produces results we can be confident about and use to explain even more. Or put another way, while scientists are interested in their research question, they are more interested in what their questions can tell us about phenomena just beyond their question. We seek to generalize – to explain a class of event – from the objective analysis of what we can observe. And in order to achieve the ability to make such inferences – Principle Number 3 – we must first pass through Principle Numbers 1 and 2. This is the demanding part of science. With the goals of explanation and even generalization, our ability to be confident in our conclusions is predicated on our practice of science.

KKV said it best, 'the content is the method'. Perhaps unintentionally echoing Marshal McLuhan's famous 'the medium is the message', it means that reliable and valid results suitable for inference are achieved in a systematic way. Science is the *method* of inquiry. Science is the scientific method. As the saying goes, science is as science does.

Principle Number 1: The scientific method requires a transparent and replicable description of the research design and analysis

There's a lot to unpack here. First, whatever approach or method one chooses – by which we are talking about examples such as web scraping, document analysis, interviews, large-N statistics studies, case studies, experiments, quasi-experiments, surveys, and on and on – the choices that we make in what to research, what to measure, what to control for, what to include, what to exclude, and how to estimate the relationships we are interested in, not only shape what we will find (a larger question) but also require an accurate, comprehensive, and objective description of all the steps of your analysis. Many of these elements of research will be discussed in the subsequent chapters. However, the motivation for transparency and replication are distinguishing characteristics of the scientific method.

Scientific study is a public procedure. A scientific study outlines the means for others to replicate the work. That is, the methodology for attaining the results must be detailed to the extent that that replication is possible. Why is **replication** (and its **transparency**) so important to the character of science? While research can be guided by previous work and the constraints of the data, ultimately, how a researcher chooses to investigate a question is up to him/her. These choices – as we will see in the following chapters – have a profound effect on the results. Therefore, a replicable description of the methodology allows for others to critique or reproduce them (often in order to find out why they are so good or, sometimes, so bad).

For example, when two scientists are studying the same thing and come to different conclusions, their peers investigate the method for arriving at the competing explanations and determine which appeals to rigorous science. When scientists – not interpretivists – reach a disagreement about a conclusion, they set about the task of finding out who is wrong (or less wrong, in any case). Further rigorous testing produces more evidence in which to determine the fitter of the two explanations (or not!). It is an attempt to approach 'truth'. Not 'The Truth' but, as Dennett calls it, the '...ho hum truth about this particular factual disagreement' (2006: 262).

Published scientific findings are given a great deal of weight and importance. The reason is that for an academic article to be published, it must pass through the process of 'peer-review' in which several experts anonymously read and review every aspect of a potential article. These academic 'peers' poke and prod all of the methodological, theoretical, and stylistic elements in the article and – if they unanimously agree that the article has potential – suggest ways that the author must strengthen the article before being published. This process is necessarily difficult and demanding and in being so, creates better, more replicable, and transparent research. What nearly all forms of peer-review have in common is that the results of research are nearly secondary to how you arrived at them. Science is not advanced by secrecy, sabotage, or trickery. It is advanced by openness, honesty, and transparency (as ideals).

A secondary effect of transparency and replicability is holding the researcher themself to a high standard. Science is sometimes defended as being **objective**. It is not. Efforts are made, however, to try to make it the least **subjective** (if that helps). That is, we seek to eliminate or, more accurately, minimize the influence of our own prejudices and biases. As Max Weber points out, there is no objective science, but the conscious effort to adhere to an agreed-upon method of inquiry as well as the exposure to the strong light of public procedure has the effect of attenuating any overt or unintended subjective bias that might get introduced into our research.

The subjectivity of the formal scientific method is akin to a pilot flying a plane. There are a lot of rules designed to guide a plane in the most efficient but safest route to our destination that each pilot must follow. For example, when the pilot is ready for take-off, s/he doesn't just slam the throttle forward and careen across the tarmac willy-nilly. Take-off procedures, exit patterns, altitudes, landing procedures, and even ground manoeuvres are all tightly controlled to produce an individual and collective success in moving people around by airplane. At the same time, each of the hands that are on the yoke, those in control of each individual plane following these rules, are individual pilots who make crucial adjustments and decisions as well as take key actions that affect the journey (as well as collective outcome). As with pilots, the likelihood of our success as scientists – individually and collectively – is served by adherence to the rules originating from conscious design and experience.

Supporting the demand for objectivity, the scientific approach is a positivist approach – as opposed to a normative approach. **Normative** approaches are concerned with whether things are as they should be or whether they ought to be different (read: better). A **positivist** approach focuses on what *is*, not what we want something to be. To say that normative studies – often found in political theory or philosophy – are 'not scientific' is not to diminish this enormously valuable area of research, both independent of and complementary to empirical studies. Rather it is to highlight the importance, in pursuing objectivity, of forcing us to maintain eye contact with facts.

We can be motivated by our normative concerns but ask non-normative questions for the reason of producing convincing evidence. That is, Political Scientists' own values can lead them to study particular phenomenon. For example, in studies of voter turnout, our research often focuses on what policies *increase* turnout, not *decrease* turnout. We study turnout because higher turnout seems 'better' for democracy. In International Relations, the study of conflict, war, and diplomacy is (hopefully) normatively guided by the notion that less war and conflict is preferred. This doesn't necessarily affect our conclusions, but it can affect what researchers choose to study.

In this way, a positivist approach appeals to objectivity in our research as the scientific method peddles in facts. A country with fair elections is a democracy. In Italy, 39% of the citizens voted for the Communist Party. Income inequality in the United States, as measured by the Gini coefficient, is 0.48 (in 2019). 'Normative', on the other hand, is evaluative and value-laden and describes 'how things *should* be'. All countries should be democracies. Too many Italians voted for the Communist Party. The level of income inequality in the United States is unacceptable. While the distinctions are fairly obvious with these examples, as we will see in the scientific study of politics, this distinction can be hard to maintain, even if we want to.

Principle Number 1 leads us to the revelation that the scientific method doesn't describe what we study, it describes how we study it.

Principle Number 2: The scientific method attempts to identify, isolate, and explain the relationship under investigation

Principle Number 2 is the irreplaceable bridge linking Principle Number 1 to Principle Number 3. Scientific knowledge seeks to move beyond mere description to explanation. We do so in two complementary ways.

One, scientific knowledge tries to – if only partially – explain how the world works through the use of theory. The scientific method relies on the body of theoretical knowledge to advance our collective knowledge by developing, testing, and, when necessary, abandoning theories. Theory explains. The use of theory in scientific study cannot be overstated, and to give it sufficient attention we will investigate the contribution and use of theory in the next chapter.

Let's say that we are interested in whether citizens' education levels affect their propensity to vote in national parliamentary elections. You have been studying this relationship and identify a theory that suggests it is easier for educated citizens to gather and process information about politics and therefore they are more likely to vote because the costs of voting are lower for them (as an information-seeker).

One way to bring some evidence to bear on this question is to analyse some data. So, before the last Bundestag elections in Germany, we ask 1,000 Germans about their education and voting and determine that within this group of German citizens, people with higher levels of education voted more often. We might *describe* the results this way: In this group of Germans in the past national election, the more highly educated voted more often than less educated ones. However, we might *explain* the results this way: The evidence supports our theoretical expectation that more educated Germans are more likely to vote because it is easier for them to gather and process information about politics, in turn lowering the costs of voting.

The second means to identify and explain a relationship is through control. While description represents a step in the explanatory process, explanation is predicated on the ability to not only identify the relationship in which we are interested but to also isolate in order to evaluate the nature of that relationship, controlling for potential intervening or moderating influences. That is, the goal of control is to be able to distinguish between the essential – the 'signal' of the relationships in which we are interested – and non-essential – the noise of the buzzing, complex world around it.

Here, in the attempt to identify and explain the relationship under investigation, we are challenged to determine whether this relationship exists and whether it continues to exist even when we consider all of the other possible explanations for why a German citizen may choose to vote (age, gender, income, political apathy, etc.…). Exerting control over any number of other explanations (ahem, theories) allows us to determine whether the relationship exists – even in the presence of competing explanations. This imperative of the scientific method allows us to weight our explanation in accordance with how well it explains. Therefore, Principle Number 2 – attempts to identify, isolate, and explain the relationship under investigation – increases the confidence that we are describing and explaining the relationship in which we are interested by the formal process of testing of competing explanations.

The demanding principle of transparency and replicability (Principle Number 1) as well as the often-challenging methodological principle of control (Principle Number 2) are steps to the final and definitive goal of scientific research.

Principle Number 3 – The scientific method seeks to derive and make appropriate inferences from the results of our research

If we have adhered to the first two Principles and conducted our research as best we can, we should arrive at results that we can have confidence in. This is the prized opportunity to speak beyond the evidence at hand. We can make inferences; to infer the results of our study to a larger class of events.

Inference is not the same as prediction. Recall our educated German voters above. I might make *predictions* from the results in a number of ways. If I wanted to make a low-risk prediction, I might stick with the same group and same event and argue that in the next Bundestag election, more educated Germans will vote at a higher rate than less educated Germans. I might, based on the confidence I have in my results, aim a little farther by making a prediction about a *similar* event. For example, I might argue that in the upcoming *Bundesrat* election, more educated Germans will vote at a higher rate than less educated Germans. Again, depending on the confidence I have in the results, I might even make a prediction beyond this group of German voters and argue that, for all European countries' national parliamentary elections or European parliamentary elections, more educated Europeans will vote at a higher rate than less educated European voters in that same country. These are a small sample of several predictive statements we could make and represent **descriptive inference**, a projection of what to *expect* from what we know onto new events.

GENERALIZATION AND INFERENCE

In Social Science, the words 'inference' and 'generalization' are sometimes used interchangeably. For casual use, the main idea is similar enough not to create a problem. However, technically, inference refers to the estimation of population parameters from sample data. Generalization is part of the process of theory-building, determining how far what we have learned can be extended to explain a class of events.

Perhaps visually:

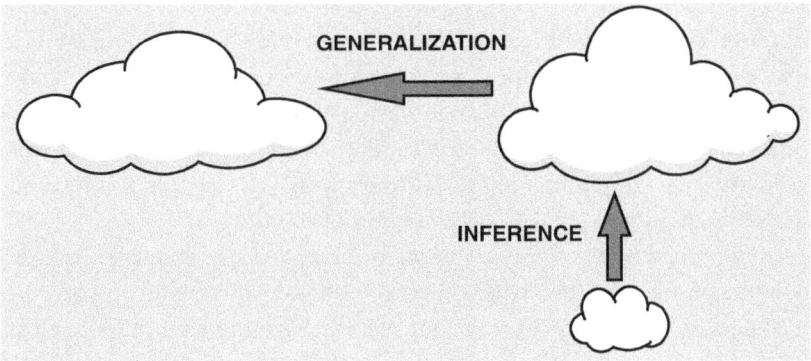

Figure 1.1 Generalization and Inference

For consistency throughout this textbook, inference will be a technical term relating samples to populations and generalization will refer to the (theoretical) process of seeking to explain related phenomena between populations.

However, our goal of scientific research is to be in the position to make inferences beyond the cases under investigation. What we would infer is not an expectation of an outcome (i.e., a prediction) but rather the explanation itself. That is, any inference that we make would carry with it the causal implication embedded in our explanation (our theory). Thus, if we have a great deal of confidence in our study of voting Germans, we might infer that more educated Germans will vote more in the next Bundestag or Bundesrat election than less educated Germans, or even that higher educated EU citizens will vote more in the next European national parliamentary elections than less educated ones *because* it is easier for educated citizens to gather and process information about politics and they are therefore more likely to vote because the costs of voting are lower for them. This projection of what *explains* the relationship we have observed onto new events is called **causal inference**.

Thus, both types of inference involve generalizing the results of our study to a larger class of events. This involves both what we expect to see – i.e., a prediction – and why we would expect to see it – i.e., the causal explanation. Our ability to make inferential claims rests not on any specific action we take at this stage, but rather on our adherence to the rigors of the scientific method up to this point and drawing appropriate conclusions from our empirical analysis. And the ability to derive and make appropriate inferences from the results of our research also improves our theoretical knowledge. In fitting pieces to the collective process of understanding, bit by bit, more and more phenomena, our incremental steps advance scientific knowledge.

A Quest for Certainty

There is, however, a thorny difference between prediction and inference. While we can observe an outcome to confirm or disconfirm a prediction, we cannot reliably observe an inferred causal mechanism in the same way. Scientifically, methodologically, we strive for having confidence in the results of our study. Unfortunately, our confidence in our ability to make such strong inferential claims rests on a debate that has resisted consensus. This debate might be called an elusive quest of certainty.

There are fundamentally two types of scientific knowledge about the world. To compare them, imagine a black box with a lever on one side and a hole on the other. When you pull the lever, a little red ball rolls out. We can imagine a more sophisticated black box, for example, one in which you must pull the lever twice quickly to produce the little red ball, but for simplicity, we know that pulling the lever produces the little red ball. What more do you need to know? If you want a little red ball, pull the lever. Scaling this up, as long as we can predict political, social, and economic relationships, knowing the intricacies of the exact causal link is not all that important.

The other approach wants a fuller answer. *How* does pulling the level produce the little red ball? This approach wants to open the box and articulate the mechanism. It wants to see the dials, levers, knobs, and teethed wheels that link the lever to the red ball. For this approach, in order to decipher the 'real' world, we need to know the 'real' reason things happen.

Which one is best? While there are persuasive arguments on both sides (for space and sanity, we will not take these up here), there is no consensus. And for the day-to-day activity of doing science, it doesn't really matter. However, one's response to this question may depend on your level of comfort with uncertainty. And in a bigger sense, it does kind of matter.

Why do we bring up a quest for certainty here? It is important – blinking red light important – to distinguish between a statement 'proved' true and a statement that we have a great deal of confidence in. The former, more formally known as **deterministic confirmation**, is the conclusion that, given the right set of explanatory variables, the world is entirely predictable. The latter, more formally known as **probabilistic confirmation**, takes the stance that random variation exists in the world and there is nothing you can do about it.

> Deterministic confirmation according to Pierre-Simon Laplace: 'We may regard the present state of the universe as the effect of its past and the cause of its future. An intellect which at a certain moment would know all forces that set nature in motion, and all positions of all items of which nature is composed, if this intellect were also vast enough to submit these data to analysis, it would embrace in a single formula the movements of the greatest bodies of the universe and those of the tiniest atom; for such an intellect nothing would be uncertain and the future just like the past would be present before its eyes.' (1951: 4)

Impressive! Deterministic confirmation would then be big-t True! It is this way – and no other! Such knowledge is undoubtedly a great deal for a scientist to get excited about. It may not, however, be unfair to point out that we do not have Laplace's knowledge of 'all forces that set nature in motion, and all positions of all items of which nature is composed'. And it would be a challenge to do so.

Lest you despair, the scientific method allows us to inch toward deterministic confirmation. We can shrink our orbit toward the ideal state of perfect knowledge through probabilistic confirmation of our research. Probabilistic confirmation – the ability to obtain results that we can have a high degree of confidence in – is also 'true'. Small-t true. True in a qualified manner. That is, although we don't know the motion and positions of all forces, we can – with a rigorous design and analysis – derive a level of confidence from our results to forward scientific research. There is little doubt that a rigorous methodology takes us closer to this final goal. However, even if we were to design the perfect research and make no mistakes, the best that we could reasonably be is quite certain.

You may have noticed a distinguishing hallmark of scientific inquiry is its sometimes frustrating temerity. This is why a professor, cornered at a cocktail party and asked about something related to his/her research, will invariably respond, 'Well, you see, it depends….'. That we cannot control for everything underpins the natural and cultivated hesitancy that many scientists share. For these scientists, 'prove' is not how to think about theory and theory testing. It is what the leading prosecutor does during a courtroom drama on television using corroborating video, audio, eye-witness reports, and DNA evidence to show that the defendant was at the scene of the crime. We test, we update, we precise, we improve, but never 100% prove.

Scientific research must qualify its conclusions with how certain we are that what we are saying is correct (or more accurately, it is often reported as how *unlikely* that our answer is *incorrect*). In a sense, this is the humility of a scientific worldview. Certainty in the complex, interactive world is unattainable for myriad reasons. Yet, if we strive in the direction of certainty, we improve the reliability, validity, honesty, and certainty of our conclusions. It is the embrace of uncertainty that both requires scientists to acknowledge the limitations of every study as well as allows them to make inferential claims. Thus, uncertainty is to be taken seriously. We want to have a great deal of confidence in our findings – achieved primarily through a rigorous, scientific approach. But what we really end up hoping for is the ability to be more right than wrong.

'To be uncertain is uncomfortable, but to be certain is ridiculous' – Chinese proverb

ON KNOWING

There is a larger debate looming in the background. In fact, there are two larger debates, one nested in the other.

The discussion in this chapter centres on science and its attempts to decode and understand the world. Despite popular perception, the Scientific Method can encompass both quantitative methods – such as statistics – and qualitative methods. As long as the design, analysis, and interpretation adhere to the core principles of science, a wide variety of analytical approaches qualify as 'scientific'. Yet, there are some key qualitative methodologies, such as ethnography and discourse analysis, that represent a branch of inquiry at odds with science.

Scientific inquiry is a positivist approach. This is an epistemological term. **Epistemology** asks 'What do you know?' and 'How do you know it?'. Or, more pointedly, 'What is the nature of knowledge and the methods of gaining such knowledge?'. Therefore, a **positivist** epistemological position is one in which the world is 'out there' and can be understood through rigorous examination. Not unsurprisingly, this sounds a lot like our definition of the scientific method in which the world is knowable and the most effective means to do so is science using rigorous, quantitative methods.

The alternative to a positivist epistemological position is an interpretivist epistemological position. Unlike positivists – who see reality as ultimately knowable and converging on a singular truth – **interpretivists** insist that objectivity is impossible as individuals are complex, and what we observe requires an interpretation of the motivations and beliefs of individuals that constitute social reality. That is, reality – rather than being something 'out there' to decode – is created by individuals in a society that must be reveal its underlying significance. Simply, reality cannot be measured, it must be interpreted. This approach requires a dramatically different methodology to go about finding out what is happening. Theoretical approaches such as feminism, Marxism, and queer theory assert that reality as well as knowledge are both constructed by social conflicts.

Is there tension between these groups? A bit, perhaps.

And this contest goes even further back, not in time, but in our thinking about knowing. The central debate in **ontology** precedes even this contest to ask, 'What is the nature of existence? What is real? What is true?'. That is, how do we know anything at all? On one side of this ontological debate, is a simple observation that the world waits to be understood. What is real and what is true are observable and manifest in the world before one's eyes. This is the foundation for the objectivists/positivists who not only think this is not only obvious but are also determined to find the means to do so.

On the other side, the notion that the world is just 'out there', observable and manifest, to be understood, is dismissed entirely. Instead, reality (and any attempted knowledge of it) originates from social and individual construction and cannot be understood otherwise – outside our subjective experience. Here we find the postmodernism, structuralists (and post-structuralists), and even post-positivists (and critical realists). Thus, unlike a scientific approach of systematic search for an underlying and objective order, reality is entirely subjective.

This ontological, epistemological, and methodological debate continues to resist resolution.

Science as a Way of Knowing

There are other ways of understanding the world. Science takes a clear stance that the world is discoverable – at least to the extent of our best understanding of it. The scientific approach, however, is not alone. In addition to – or even in place of – a scientific worldview, one can have, for example, a mystic or religious understanding of the world. Or one can insist that objectivity in discovery overlooks crucial animating features of the world. Or one can dismiss our ability to know anything at all about the world, placing it off limits to any feeble attempts to do so. Each approach has its own methodology and beliefs in pursuit of truth.

But, stepping out of the academic mindset for just a second, let's back up even further. Before methods and before approaches, let's ask, what's wrong with common sense?

Imagine the first time someone sees the moon. Unaided common sense is unlikely to lead us to the knowledge that the moon is a rock that is in a near perfect orbit around this planet – which is also round – and is held in place by the same invisible distortion of spacetime that holds your feet to the ground. That is, while common sense appeals to logic – inasmuch as it makes some sense – and may even be empirical as it does not contradict actual observation, there is a limit to the testable validity of common sense. Without the rigors of the scientific investigation of data, common sense is *more likely* to be subject to the errors of inaccurate or selective observation, overgeneralization, and illogical reasoning. In other words, it has been the characteristics and – admittedly imperfect – practice of obtaining a scientific understanding of the world that has allowed us to understand and even appreciate it even more.

Coming back to the realm of study, at the starting line of even thinking about understanding the world sits the post-modernist. He radically dismisses any epistemological assumptions in the use of science with the goal, not to formulate an alternative set of assumptions but, to register the impossibility of establishing *any* such underpinning for knowledge and to become comfortable with the absence of certainty. A post-modernist approach seeks to avoid judgment and locate – rather than discover – meaning focusing on the unique aspects rather than science's objective appeal to generalization (trying to understand and even explain the world with the little part we actually observe). This is a healthy and vigorous debate.

> **CHECK OUT POSTMODERNISM**
>
> Dickens, David R. and Andrea Fontana. 2015. *Postmodernism and Social Inquiry.* Routledge.

At the same time, prominent methodological alternatives to a strict scientific methodology have also arisen in Political Science and International Relations in particular. One is constructivism, originating from a largely interpretivist approach, which evaluates the world as socially constructed. In constructivism, agency and structure are mutually constituted, in turn viewing the international system as a composition of both material and ideational elements. That is, in order to understand or evaluate phenomena in the study of International Relations, we must take into account the social context (i.e., what lies beyond mere material reality) including the dynamic effect of ideas and beliefs in world politics. Such a method clearly challenges the strict scientific view of the nature of both reality and knowledge in International Relations.

> **CHECK OUT CONSTRUCTIVISM**
>
> Hay, Colin. 2015. 'Social Constructivism' in M. Bevir and R.A.W. Rhodes (eds) *The Routledge Handbook of Interpretive Political Science.* Routledge, pp. 99–112.

Another notable alternative is gender theory. The primary intervention these approaches offer is the direct confrontation with objectivity, particularly in terms of methodology in which knowledge-making is open to myriad voices and inputs. These approaches ask whether the evaluation of political phenomena through the lens of gender reveal a deeper embeddedness of inequality. What do categories of gender (such as masculinity and femininity) offer us when thinking about issues like diplomacy, economic relations, or warfare? Are there institutional hierarchies structured around gender? How do men's and women's distinctive experiences inform our understanding of politics? For example, to what extent do gendered leadership differences manifest different political outputs? Does the gendering of political institutions shape their implications in choices and outcomes? And ultimately, what is the value of using gendered identity as a dimension, versus a separate intersectionality that may arise from alignments that traverse other socio-demographic dimensions or experiences?

These three examples are challenges to how science approaches understanding. Although unlike the somewhat antagonistic stance of postmodernism, both constructivism and feminist political theory overlap in some areas with scientific methodology but also retain unique knowledge elements that distinguish their approach. In one way or another, each of these paradigms share the belief in the discovery of truth (for the post-modernist, it is simply a null set). Here, we take the scientific method not as the only approach, only as the most common one.

> **CHECK OUT FEMINISM**
>
> Ferguson, Michaele L. 2017. 'Neoliberal feminism as political ideology: Revitalizing the study of feminist political ideologies' *Journal of Political Ideologies* 22(3): 221–235.

Statistics: Description, Inference, and Control

Statistics is the mathematical management and handling of data for analysis and provides three key analytical tools: description, inference, and control. These tools allow for the rigorous testing of theory and thus larger claims about the nature of the relationship under investigation.

Description: Unlike other empirical – often qualitative – approaches, statistics can force researchers to make some concessions in order to make concepts measurable. For statistical analysis, the data to be analysed must be to some extent mathematically tractable. This presents us with some issues with which to contend. However, statistics does offer something other methods do not: uncertainty, or more specifically, a measure of uncertainty. Statistics takes uncertainty seriously by providing indicators of how certain (or uncertain) we, unlike our qualitative counterparts, can be that our result is likely to be 'The Result'. *Hint:* There is always some uncertainty. However, a low level of uncertainty means that we can have a high degree of confidence in the results. This power to have confidence in our descriptions (and ultimately, inferences) distinguishes statistics as a powerful analytical tool.

Inference: As a direct function of the abilities to provide measures of uncertainty as well as control for competing explanations, we are offered enormous power to make inferences, that is, more general claims based on the results of our research. We are able to speak to a class of events rather than only the ones in our sample.

Control: Statistics allow the research to impose upon the data techniques with which we can control for competing explanations (think: competing explanations/theories). In doing so, we can isolate and assess the relationship in which we are interested. Statistical control not only most closely resembles the gold standard of experimental control, it can control for a great deal more than other approaches.

Together, the Illustrious Triumvirate of description, inference, and control imbue statistical analysis with a difficult-to-compete-with analytical power at achieving the core aims of the Scientific Method and the scientific study of politics.

Doing Statistics is Not Doing Science

Statistics are seemingly ubiquitous in Political Science research. Scientific reports, publications, and books brim with statistics and appendices filled with even more frightening statistics. Statistics as a tool of scientific research do have a large role. Some might argue an oversized role. However, while this book is about statistics and supports the proper use of statistics, the use of statistics is not, for Political Science or other disciplines, an all-powerful technique that allows us to easily, completely, and perfectly answer every question. Nor is it, and this is the entire point of this opening chapter, a replacement or proxy for science (itself not an all-powerful means to definitively prove things).

It is undeniable that statistics are one of the most well-known and visible investigative tools. While impressive and visible, statistics only reflect key elements of the vastly more impressive foundation of the scientific method. *Doing statistics is not doing science.* Neither does it make you a scientist. Statistics can be a very effective tool in bringing scientific research to fruition but it does not – and cannot – replace the necessary elements of scientific inquiry. Conflating the two can lead to misconceptions about what it is we are trying to achieve. That is, again, if the only tool you have is a hammer, you tend to see every problem as a nail.

The goal of this book is to offer an understanding of *how statistics come to represent relationships among data* and in doing so, inform your understanding of their place in the long line of necessary elements of the scientific method. Also, using statistics looks cool.

Allow me to re-phrase.

To a certain audience, using statistics has an undeniable aesthetic and analytical appeal. They look complex and important. They have been and will be around for a long time. Everything you will learn in this book is unlikely to change in your lifetime (if there will be any developments, they will occur somewhere beyond the neighbourhood of Chapter 18).

More importantly, using statistics in a vacuum is a waste of time. On its own, devoid of context, statistics is a math game. Put in some numbers, pull the handle, see what comes out. The techniques are useful only in that we employ them both correctly and well. This is precisely what the discussion about science and the scientific method is about. Without a reason to use statistics, whether it is to explain a change in wheat futures, the origins of roller skates, or faked UFO sightings, is to be flipping a coin. Forever.

Or maybe it makes more sense to think of statistics as just a woodchipper. It is a tool. If you put something in it, it will give you a result. If you want wood chips, put wood in the woodchipper. If you want soap chips, put in soap. If you want confetti, put in paper. However, if you want to landscape your garden and you need to clear a fallen tree, all of a sudden, a woodchipper just got a lot more useful to achieve the specific goal of clearing the fallen tree which services the larger goal of the landscaped garden. This is the relationship of statistics to the Scientific Method – capital S, capital M.

Statistics are used in service of scientific research. It is the scientific methods that insists on how you define and intend to measure something. Statistical analysis merely reveals what the method has assembled. In other words, what you find has a great deal more to do with what you do before you open your first dataset.

Why Do We Confuse Statistics for Science?

So, why are they so often confused for one another? Doing statistics is confused for doing science because doing statistics looks similar to the three Principles of scientific research. That is, they look like each other. If our goals of the scientific method are to develop and test theories that can explain a class of events and well as to achieve inference – not only the descriptive inference of prediction but also the causal inference of 'scientific' explanation, that is, to explain beyond our results, then statistics provide the most compelling approach.

Table 1.1 The Scientific Method and Statistics

	The Scientific Method	**Statistics**
Principle Number 1	A transparent and replicable description of the research design and analysis.	Statistics has an internal formal rigor grounded in the use of mathematics as its language which eases the handling of assumptions and estimating results. As such, statistics techniques follow a formal methodology specifically to enable replicability.
Principle Number 2	To identify, isolate, and explain the relationship under investigation.	Statistics exposes patterns. It summarizes data, variables, and relationships between variables. Crucially, outside the laboratory, statistics is the most effective method for exerting control of large arrays of competing explanations in scientific studies.
Principle Number 3	Steps to assess the appropriate inferences from the results.	Statistics has an explicit use for and reporting of variance which, in its most advanced form, is a measure of (un)certainty. Using this, we have the ability to make qualified inferences about unobserved phenomena.

Hence, it is a lot easier to see the element of the Scientific Method as statistics formalizes key elements of the scientific method, its power of description, inference, and control. Thus, outside of a laboratory, statistics, used correctly, can provide us with the ability to make strong scientific claims. But it is just one of many tools of the social scientist. Statistics are very good at helping us strive to attain specific and rigorous standards of the scientific method but cannot be treated as a replacement.

Statistics is classically divided into two complementary and essential parts, both covered in this book, called Descriptive Statistics and Inferential Statistics. **Descriptive statistics** allow us to describe and summarize data for consumption and analysis. **Inferential statistics** allow us to know is whether the relationship (i.e., the observed pattern in the data) can be inferred to apply more generally to the population (from which the sample was drawn). Both forms introduce and use methods of control in order to achieve these outcomes. As we progress through the book, it will become obvious that while Descriptive statistics has a great deal to offer, Inferential statistics is the workhorse of modern research.

Now, let's get on with it.

End of Chapter Summary

- Science, as a method of inquiry, is one way to understand the world. It is popular but not the only one.
- The scientific method – a.k.a. the Scientific Method – is an objective and replicable analysis of data which results in evidence which can be used to assess proposed explanations for a relationship and whether we can export the resultant explanation to other phenomena.

- The scientific approach is a positivist – or non-normative – approach such that it appeals to objective facts rather than how things should be.
- Inference can take two forms: descriptive inference or causal inference.
- Science provides probabilistic confirmation rather than deterministic confirmation.
- Statistics provide three key analytical tools – description, inference, and control – which allow for the rigorous testing of theory and thus larger claims about the nature of the relationship under investigation.
- Doing statistics is not doing science. Neither does using statistics make you a scientist.
- Statistics has two complementary and essential parts: Descriptive statistics and Inferential statistics.
- Science doesn't describe what we study, it describes how we study it.

Glossary

- **Science** is one of several ways to try to understand the world.
- **Scientific Method** is an objective and replicable analysis of data which results in evidence which can be used to assess proposed explanations for relationships and whether what we find can be exported to explain other related phenomena.
- **Replication:** The methodology can be performed by someone else, following instructions, and produce the same results.
- **Transparency:** A clear and comprehensive reporting of our methodology including variables, data, conceptual and operational choices, and analytical approach.
- **Objective:** The factual, unfeeling, undistorted intellectual grasp of an object or event that exists.
- **Subjective:** The perception of an object or event that emanates from ourselves: our perspectives, biases, and preferences.
- **Epistemology** is a branch of philosophy concerned with how we come to know things.
- **Ontology** is a branch of metaphysics that is concerned with the state of being or the nature of existence.
- **Positivist** (a.k.a. *non-normative*) refers to the empirical description or investigation of 'how things are'.
- **Interpretivist:** Focuses on intentionality of the actors by interpreting motives, beliefs, and/or reasons of actors and institutions as a means to understand political realities.
- **Normative** refers to the orientation of 'how things should or ought to be'.
- **Descriptive inference** is the projection of what we have observed toward what we can expect from new or unobserved events.
- **Causal inference** is the projection of our *explanation* of what we have observed toward an *explanation* for new or unobserved events.

- **Deterministic confirmation** is the conclusion that, given the complete set of explanatory variables, the world is entirely predictable.
- **Probabilistic confirmation** is the result of making our best guesses about how the world works, with a high – albeit unavoidably *partial* – level of control of a complex, dynamic reality.
- **Statistics** is the mathematical manipulation of data for analysis.
- **Descriptive statistics** allow us to describe and summarize data on hand for consumption and analysis.
- **Inferential statistics** allow us to know whether the observed pattern in the data on hand can be inferred to apply to the population (from which our data was drawn).

Questions

1. Another textbook might describe scientific knowledge as *subject to empirical verification, non-normative, transmissible, general,* and *explanatory*. Take two of these concepts, provide a definition for each of them, and explain why they are important for the development of knowledge in the social sciences.
2. Briefly explain the jump from descriptive to causal inference.
3. Explain why we need to point out that doing statistics can be a part of, but cannot replace, doing science.
4. Werner Heisenberg wrote in *Physics and Philosophy: The Revolution in Modern Science* (1958: 38), '…what we observe is not nature in itself but nature exposed to our method of questioning.' This refers to many aspects of scientific investigation. However, one might interpret this as meaning that the subjective choices we make, no matter how strict our adherence to the objective application of the scientific approach, are crucial to what we find. How does this apply to our discussion of the Scientific Method above?
5. Do adherents of deterministic confirmation watch the weather forecast before leaving the house? Less sarcastically, our ability to predict one aspect of reality – the weather – is at best probabilistic and such 'inferior knowledge' is of no use to someone requiring absolute certainty. Can we live – and even progress our knowledge – with only best guesses about how reality really works?
6. Take a look at the end of this article: Peffley, Mark and Robert Rohrschneider. 2003. 'Democratization and Political Tolerance in Seventeen Countries: A Multi-level Model of Democratic Learning' Political Research Quarterly 56(3): 243–257.
7. Do the authors include a normative discussion in the conclusion or the final few paragraphs? If so, briefly summarize this discussion.
8. Given the three Principles for the Scientific Method above, which is the most important? The least important? Why?

Annotated References and Further Reading

Durkheim, Emile. 1895. *The Rules of Sociological Method* [Règles de la méthode sociologique].
After more than one hundred years, this book continues to serve as a cornerstone for empirical research in the social sciences.

Heisenberg, Werner. 1958. *Physics and Philosophy: The Revolution in Modern Science.* **New York: Harper.**
Heisenberg provides for scientists of all stripes lessons in our shared form of thinking as well as its undeniable shortcomings common across all fields of inquiry. A seminal work of scientific thought.

Kuhn, Thomas. 1962. *The Structure of Scientific Revolutions.* **Chicago: Chicago University Press.**
If you wanted to know more about how science progresses to accumulate knowledge across different scientific disciplines.

Popper, Karl. 1959. *The Logic of Scientific Discovery.* **London: Hutchinson & Co.**
Like Durkheim, a classic that has application even though written in the middle of last century. Nearly as good as anything on the market today.

Signposts to Research and Empirical Examples

Brady, Henry E. 2008. 'Causation and Explanation in Social Science' in Robert E. Goodin (ed.) *The Oxford Handbook of Political Science*. Oxford: Oxford University Press, pp: 217–270.
Dennett, Daniel. 2006. *Breaking the Spell: Religion as a Natural Phenomenon*. New York: Penguin.
Hay, Colin. 2002. *Political Analysis: A Critical Introduction*. Basingstoke: Palgrave Macmillan.
King, Gary, Robert O. Keohane, and Sidney Verba. 1994. *Designing Social Inquiry: Scientific Inference in Qualitative Research*. Princeton: Princeton University Press.
Laplace, Pierre-Simon. 1951. *A Philosophical Essay on Probabilities*, translated into English from the original French 6th ed. by Truscott, F.W. and Emory, F.L. New York: Dover Publications.
Randall, Vicky. 1991. 'Feminism and Political Analysis' *Political Studies* 19(3): 513–522.
Rosenau, Pauline M. 1991. *Post-Modernism and the Social Sciences: Insights, Inroads, and Intrusions*. Princeton: Princeton University Press.

2
THEORY AND HYPOTHESES

> **LEARNING OUTCOMES**
>
> By the end of this chapter, you will be able to:
>
> - Explain why theories and hypotheses are essential elements in the Scientific Method.
> - Compare the contributions of inductive and deductive reasoning.
> - Articulate the core characteristics of strong theories.
> - Discuss the importance and role of causality in theoretical development.
> - Identify and evaluate hypotheses.

Introduction

This chapter explains why we do – and should – use theories and hypotheses in Political Science. Crucial to this chapter is the discussion of how we use hypotheses and causal inference to incrementally accumulate evidence rather than 'prove' theories. We will also be introduced to the core qualities as well as methods to evaluate the validity and utility of both theory and hypotheses. For some hands-on experience, we will evaluate a well-known theory in political communication.

It is nearly impossible to summarize the importance and dimensions of using theory in Political Science – and the social sciences more broadly.

We need to answer such difficult questions as:

Q1: What is a theory?

Q2: What makes a strong theory?

Q3: How do we test theory?

A1: Theory explains the relationship between our variables of interest.

A2: Strong theories are testable, fertile, parsimonious, and falsifiable.

A3: We don't test theories. We test their real-world implications, hypotheses.

Ok, so the answers are pretty clear (if mildly surprising) but the use of the theory is an essential part of the scientific method and guides our choice and use of statistical techniques to study Political Science. As such, theory requires some attention.

The most effective way to study political phenomena scientifically – to generalize from objective and rigorous observation and analysis – is the creation, development, and testing of theory. The use of theory allows for scientific research by maintaining an adaptable and cumulative core of scientific knowledge. In this core of knowledge, theories can be revised, updated, and even discarded. This theoretical core allows for many people to work on the same topic and simultaneously improve our understanding. In this way, theories are weapons for the battlefield of scientific debate. Theories are constantly being challenged by Political Scientists with competing theories, new data or techniques, and fresh ideas. As such, theories are both the essential building blocks of our core knowledge – and at the same time completely provisional as their explanatory power weakens, becomes inadequate, or is supplanted.

What is the Role of Theory in Political Science?

A **theory** systematically relates possible explanations for a phenomenon or set of phenomena. It explains the reason one variable affects another. Simply, a theory explains why.

The essential role of theory in Political Science, and social sciences more broadly, is trifold. One, theory identifies *relationships about the phenomena* in which we are interested. Theory guides our expectations about designing research and suggests important considerations in our modelling process. Two, theory organizes and summarizes the *work that has been done* on our subject. Theories in your field can tell you a great deal about the state of research, what has been tried, and what is working. Three, theory suggests *where to look* for future testing. The flipside of summarizing the work that has been done is that theory can lead us to potentially fertile or unexplored areas of new research.

Together, these functions guide the design of our research, establish the state of the discipline, and suggest important – and often new – considerations in our research. A strong theory or set of theories is like having an older brother or sister who can help you navigate your parents. They can tell you which rules to follow, which things you can get away with, which parent to ask which question, and identify potential areas of 'future research' (the trouble you intend to get into).

Another way to think about theory and its role in Political Science is that we sometimes talk about theories as 'theoretical models' (as the basis for statistical models) or just 'models'. A model of the world and a theory about the nature of a relationship in that world are necessarily simplified versions of reality. This is not a shocking or even particularly interesting element of scientific research. In order to identify and understand the most important elements in a process or relationship, we don't need to know every single little detail.

A MODEL

Think of a plastic airplane model. If we buy and assemble a 1:48 scale RAF Spitfire MK IX, it is not relevant to someone trying to identify which plane it is a model of whether we painted the dials on instrument panel or the pilot's socks. The most important elements of the Spitfire are represented – the elliptical shape of the wings, the flush cockpit, and two cannons and two machine guns rather than four machine guns. The model provides sufficient information to not only distinguish the Spitfire MK IX from other planes – such as its dangerous counterparts, Messerschmitt Bf-109 or Focke-Wulf FW190 – but also from earlier and later variants of Spitfires themselves. That is, the model – the simplification – contains sufficient detail on the elements most necessary to identify and make conclusions about differences and similarities in which we may be interested.

Image 2.1 Spitfire

Source: Biggin Hill Heritage Hangar (Kent, UK)

Thus, modelling is in a sense a search for the essential patterns such that observations are sufficiently coherent within a group as well as sufficiently distinguishable from other groups. The trick to scientific explanation and the use of theory is not merely simplification – but the correct simplification.

Why all the talk of models? Because theories are simplified explanations of relationships. They are models of a part of the world in which we are interested in investigating. Although, before we go any farther, let's be clear on one thing. All theories – as models of relationships – are wrong. They are wrong *because* they are simplifications. This process of simplification is shaped by the assumptions we make, the inability to contain all the information, any error in our measurements, and a change in the (true/real) process in which we are interested. This is a variant of the famous, 'all models are wrong, but some are useful' (Box, 1976). We necessarily leave stuff out making them diminished – thus incomplete – versions of reality.

But used correctly, they are an adaptable and updateable means to progress our knowledge. Thus, theories are enormously helpful in advancing scientific knowledge.

Inductive and Deductive Reasoning

The scientific method – and I tell you all this so you can impress your friends at parties – is a derivative of the *hypothetico-deductive method*. This method tests theory on observable data with an *a priori* unknown outcome. Although the name – *hypothetico-deductive* method – might provide a clue, which do you imagine is the most common origin of theory, inductive or deductive reasoning?

As it turns out, theories very often originate from inductive reasoning. **Inductive reasoning** moves from specific observations to general principle. That is, observation precedes theory. We observe something and think, 'Self, why did that happen?' and try to imagine a more general pattern or explanation of this and related events. For example, we might ask ourselves, 'Self, certain countries don't go to war with each other. Do they share something in common that might explain this?'. Reflection on such spontaneous observations or insights often results in a process of assembling similar events or observations that we can attempt to explain. This is the process of *theory developing*. We are developing an idea to explain the observed phenomenon – and ones like it. This has the additional bonus of creating space in scientific inquiry for innovation, inventiveness, spontaneity, and flair.

Deductive reasoning – on the other hand – moves from general to specific. This is the process of applying theory to new situations or potential data. In this case, theory precedes observation such that we use our current (theoretical) knowledge to create a set of expectations about something specific we have yet to observe. We then test to see whether our expectation is verified. Together, these steps constitute the process of *theory testing*. This is why the deductive theory testing process is the core of the scientific method (a.k.a. hypothetico-deductive method).

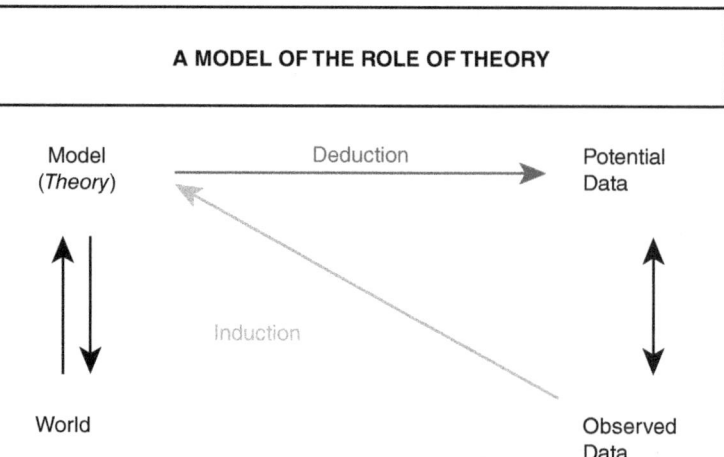

Figure 2.1 A Model of the Role of Theory

In Political Science, our common knowledge is progressed by both the testing of existing theory and the development of new theories to accommodate the attenuation of weak theories and new developments. While novel observations are important as the basis for developing new ideas, stimulating discussions, and proposing potential explanations, progress in our cumulative knowledge is forwarded by theory testing.

A model of theory development in the figure illustrates the use of both inductive and deductive thinking in linking theory (and data) to the analysis of the real world.

The Characteristics of Theory

For such an important element of scientific research, theories are not super complex. A theory is the reason why one variable shapes another. A theory tells us why something had to occur. It tells us what to look at, and because it explains the relationship, tells us what to expect. Perhaps you might have thought it would be more complicated, but that's it.

$$X \rightarrow Y$$

In this illustration, given a relationship between one variable 'X' and another variable 'Y', theory is the arrow.

There are four essential and unique characteristics that are consistent with strong theories. **Strong theories** provide a plausible explanation for the relationship in which we are interested, they are good at explaining, are fit, and tell us when they work and when they don't work. These characteristics can help us to identify potential strengths (or points of weakness) in current theories.

While these characteristics do not ensure the success of any one theory, they can guide our thinking about potential and existing theories. In practice, theories are evaluated by the rough and tumble of rigorous and repeated empirical testing. In this repeated testing, theories either grow stronger by the accumulation of corroborating evidence or weaken by the failure to explain outcomes (i.e., they do not accumulate evidence). Recall from above, we don't prove theories. We don't even set out to prove theories. In this way, it is helpful to avoid thinking of theories as right or wrong. Theories, after repeated testing, become **weak** or **strong**. So, write this down, photocopy this page, carve this in your desk or a friend, email it to yourself, print it out and tape it to your bathroom mirror, or get a tattoo, but commit it to memory: *Theories are not right or wrong. Theories are weak or strong.*

(1) A Strong Theory is a Plausible Explanation for the Relationship in Which We are Interested

Plausible, in this characteristic of theory, refers to the theory being consistent with reality in two senses. One, the plausibility of a strong theory requires that it makes sense – it is logically sound and internally coherent that the 'X' and 'Y' are in a relationship.

We need to ask, is there any reason to suspect that the relationship we propose is internally inconsistent or out of synch with reality? For example, taller candidates for Prime Minister win more often. While height and winning elections both vary, is this a compelling argument, among all other existing explanations, for Prime Ministerial electoral success? Or perhaps, 'Incumbents who are better dressers are more likely to win election' may test the limits of our Political Science audience's patience. Strong theories do well not only to satisfy the need for plausibility but credibility as well. So, out with aliens, the ether, and magic wands.

It feels a bit forced to mention this but the elements included in the theory should also vary. Theories are about relationships; therefore, the elements in the theories should move, preferably with one another. This not only excludes relationships in which the changes in the elements move out of synch with one another but also serves as a reminder that the elements themselves should vary. We should be hesitant to propose a theory that attempts to explain variation with a constant. Or tries to use variation to explain constancy. The name 'variables' is a not-so-subtle reminder that that the elements of our theory should, in fact, 'vary'. For example, recall whether educated Germans were more likely to vote. The level of education for German citizens varies, some have high educational training, some medium, some low. The act of voting also varies as one can vote or not. If, however, the educational level of all Germans was the same, it would be difficult to connect that constant state to the dynamic state of having voted or not. Similarly, if everyone voted, variation in education levels wouldn't be able to explain something that doesn't change (i.e., everybody voting).

The second sense of the plausibility of a strong theory requires that all parts of the theory are consistent with observable reality in that we can conceive of real-world empirical referents. This characteristic takes the longer view. Namely, when we finally bring our theory to the data, we want to be able to test, it as being able to test the theory will be enormously helpful in determining whether the theory is, in fact, weak or strong.

The elements of theory need to be something we can potentially measure. One way to avoid this is for theories to offer clearly defined concepts. This is less about the concreteness or measurability of the elements – this step comes later. Rather, there should be something in the world that we can reasonably point at or think of that could represent 'X' and 'Y'. That is, we should have some reasonable expectation of eventually finding empirical referents for the elements in our theory. Revising the earlier example, 'candidates for Prime Minister who have abundant *je ne sais quoi* are more likely to win', while we might jokingly say this to colleagues, this theory will prove to be problematic to test. The connective tissue of measurement linking the elements of theory to data are discussed in the following chapter and represent a crucial step in our scientific study. However, even at the theoretical level, strong theories constrain what we intend to investigate with reasonable consideration of what we can measure. Any looseness in this connection reduces the confidence we can have in the ultimate results. Unclear theorizing leads to hazy hypothesizing – leading to a lack of clarity, redundancy, and stagnation in the discipline.

This is not an easy characteristic to satisfy. Political Science is full of theories that teeter on the boundary between strong and weak theory precisely for this difficulty. It's not that Political Science is full of fairies, crystal power, or ghosts but many of the concepts in which we are interested resist easy empirical capture. An armchair survey of topics: power, trust, legitimacy, representation, social capital, party identification, inequality, negative media coverage, or sovereignty, reveal this to be widespread. In many literatures, tenacious battles have been fought for years to define what core concepts refer to and can be measured with.

These literatures continue to struggle with the challenge of theorizing such difficult or ambiguous concepts. But they continue to do so as how we think about and how we will measure these will shape what we find. Thus, a strong theory requires both that it makes sense and that observable elements in the real world correspond to all parts of the theory.

(2) A Strong Theory is Fertile

A strong theory does a good job of explaining what we are interested in and keeps on explaining.

It is a colloquial habit (and frankly, a Neanderthal one) to dismiss an idea one disagrees with by using 'well, that's just a theory'. To which we would reply, join us here in the future, you knuckle-dragging mouth-breather, because, as it turns out, most of our knowledge is theoretical. Many think of theories as being correct or incorrect when in fact theories are weak or strong. They become weak by failing to explain, by failing to accumulate evidence. They become strong by accumulating evidence and getting better at explaining. Strong theories tend to generate as many observable implications as possible. In our search for relationships to investigate and understand, we should be mindful of how our concepts can serve us to increase the number of potential data against which we can test our theory. In other words, the more ways you can meaningfully accumulate support or evidence for your theory, the stronger your theory might potentially become.

For example, we might theorize that 'Incumbents win re-election more often because they tend to have *more money*.' Using our characteristics from above, this theory is a testable, logically sound, parsimonious theory. But is it fertile? That is, is it possible to enlarge or expand the concept of 'more money' to increase the theory's applicability to a larger set of cases? We might replace 'more money' with 'greater name recognition' or 'more campaign workers'. Alternatively, we might search for a concept that would bring together the elements in a conceptually coherent way that allows for some conceptual fertility such as, 'Incumbents win re-election more often because they tend to have more *resources*.' In this case, resources include 'more money', 'greater name recognition', 'more campaign workers', and other potential advantages that incumbents may have in elections. Therefore, this strategic change in concept helps us to spiral closer to the characteristics of a good theory. It also creates more ways to test our theory while at the same time not affecting the concreteness of potential alternative measures.

To this characteristic, like so many things in science, we must apply some nuance, some subtlety, some panache to our choices. Seeking concreteness in our concepts but also an expansion of the number of things that can be included is not an easy equilibrium to find. And it is not guided by strict rules. What guides this balance between the tug of concreteness and pull of conceptual breadth is the theory's ability to withstand rigorous testing. Again, theorizing is not all that difficult. Getting a theory to explain something is not all that difficult. However, getting your theory past repeated empirical tests is.

(3) A Strong Theory is Parsimonious

I am bound by textbook law to include the obligatory Albert Einstein quote about science, 'everything should be made as simple as possible, but not simpler'. **Parsimony** is (another) example of this difficult balancing act. It represents the convergence of the ability for a theory to explain as much as it can as efficiently as it can. Building from the previous characteristic, theories must be fertile but with as little as possible. One might imagine this as a fitness check on our thinking. Or as a perhaps more quotidian conundrum, how much weight do I think I need to lift in order to attract a sufficient number of quality suitors? The equilibrium here is a subtle but crucial one.

In precisely this way, parsimony is sometimes referred to as 'leverage'. Just as a well-placed lever can move a substantial large object with something comparatively smaller, we want to leverage greater explanatory power with a relatively simple explanation. Others refer to this as fit. We are searching for the right size. We are best served by theory that doesn't try to explain too much but does not leave us with limited applicability. In other words, in practice improving a theory's parsimony can potentially be the location of real academic contribution.

In a sense, parsimony is the 'model' part of theory. We need *all* of the necessary parts to correspond with the phenomena we are interested in *but not more*. Or we can think of parsimony as a concept like tolerance. We know that too much – or too little – is less than ideal. At the same time, there is no optimal point except between too much and too little (see also 'everyone wants to be noticed but no one wants to be stared at'). Crafting theoretical parsimony is, like theoretical fertility, the subjective, even artistic, part of the scientific approach. There is not a unanimous right answer, but it is fairly obvious when a theory is *not* parsimonious.

- *A theory of questionable parsimony:* Members of Parliament (MPs) who are already in office, are well-liked by their constituents, and face a challenger who has not held office are more likely to win re-election.
- *A more parsimonious version*: Incumbent MPs are more likely to win re-election than challengers.

Like many things, once you start working with theories, their parsimony will become apparent. Some theories are broad and leave too much room in their causal explanations or to what they are referring. Other theories are precise but don't allow us to explain more than a few phenomena.

Why do we set as a characteristic for good theory something that is so difficult to find? In the words of William James, 'the art of being wise is knowing what to overlook'. As a characteristic of strong theory, parsimony, like fertility, appeals to simplicity as a foundation for accumulating knowledge. In the broader scheme of the scientific method, this corresponds to theory's heuristic function – the efficient use of knowledge. Understanding this, recognizing this, is a step toward expertise.

(4) A Strong Theory is Falsifiable

One way to achieve parsimony – to trim and tone our theory – is **falsifiability**. At the heart of evaluating theories is a notion that is often misunderstood: We seek to make theories fail. It is far less interesting to know where theory succeeds in explaining an outcome than to know when it fails. Recall, theories are not right or wrong, they are weak or strong. In addition to accumulating evidence, theories become strong via a process of refinement which discards the parts that do not work. Strong theories can tell us when something is going to happen *and* when something is not going to happen. Discovering this is a process called falsification. Falsifiable does not mean false; instead, it refers to the process of refining theory through repeated testing.

In 1959, Karl Popper argued that theories are not verifiable because we can never test all observable implications of a theory. So rather than seek out all of the implications of a theory, he argued it was more effective – in terms of testing the strength of a theory – to find out where it failed. In doing so, we begin to define the extent of a theory's capability. In other words, we test to falsify as a means to find the edges of a theory's ability to explain.

You are probably familiar with the Black Swan example Popper offers. Upon seeing a white swan, one might comment, 'Ah, what a lovely day walking along the Thames River in Oxford, when what do I see, a white swan! From this single experience, I suppose all swans are white.' First, little imagination is needed to realize – as he argued – that it would be quite difficult to find each and every swan in order to determine whether this was the case. However, and at the same time, while one might also mention that it is a perfect example of the inductive fallacy: a single fact cannot become a universal statement; a single fact *can*, however, be used to show that a universal statement, 'All swans are white,' is not, in fact, universal. That is, as Popper subsequently argued, it is possible to falsify our White Swan theory by the sighting of a single black swan. This does not make the White Swan theory 'false'. Quite the contrary, it improves the theory by improving its accuracy.

> ### SOPHISTICATED METHODOLOGICAL FALSIFICATION
>
> Falsification was such an important step in the development of theoretical science, others augmented Popper's original falsification process. Others built on the idea. Imre Lakatos prominently proposed 'sophisticated methodological falsification' which argued that theories had a hard core (called, the negative heuristic) and a protective belt or periphery (called, the positive heuristic) where 'anomalies' – or attacks on the theory – were handled. There's a surprisingly great deal more on the development of falsification. It was a big deal.

In concrete terms, one might hear of swans on other continents (*Hint:* Australia) and begin to better articulate the White Swans theory. If we did this, and discovered that black swans could be found, for pure example, on every continent but Europe, we might propose:

'All European swans are white.' Now, despite the failure of our White Swan theory to be *universal*, the theory does a better job of *correctly explaining* where we are likely to find white swans. In other words, falsifying our theory improves our theory by improving its predictive accuracy. When we encounter European and Non-European swans, our improved theory is now better at telling us which swans are more or less likely to be white.

Falsification is one of the more effective methods in developing theories: improving their testability, improving their fertility, and maintaining their parsimony. In other words, it helps to define what is and is not permitted by the theory. Falsification draws our attention again to the deeply important idea that theories are not right and wrong, theories are weak or strong. They are constantly being tested, improved, refined, and even discarded.

In the same way that theories are used to progress our cumulative knowledge, one way to identify a real scientist is by that researcher's willingness to be wrong. While each researcher strives to provide the best argument and most support for their research, if they can't produce the evidence needed or others can, one can concede. In this way, falsification potentially separates scientific from non-scientific study.

If the Black Swan example is a bit tired, perhaps we could have a more sublime metaphor for falsification.

One day, in Srikakulam (India), an older sculptor was working in his little garden at the back of the house where he stayed. He had arranged for a large boulder to be brought and placed in the centre of the garden. He looked at it for a few days, thinking about the figure he would sculpt, and after about a week, he started to work. Using a chisel and a hammer, he chipped away bits of the boulder. One day, a younger sculptor happened along the street and caught sight of the big boulder in the back garden. He went to the fence, leaned over and called out to the older sculptor, 'What are you sculpting?' The man replied, 'An elephant with a beautiful howdah (Hindi: हौदा).' The younger sculptor asked, 'Well, have you ever sculpted an elephant with a beautiful howdah before?' 'No,' replied the man who continued with his work, chipping away at the boulder bit by bit. The younger sculptor thought for a moment and then asked, 'Then how are you going to sculpt the elephant with a beautiful howdah?' 'Easy,' said the older sculptor, 'I'll just chip away all the parts of the boulder that don't look like an elephant with a beautiful howdah!' And he laughed and laughed. Finally, the young man joined in. And they laughed together for a long time.

In precisely this way, theories must be falsifiable. They must tell us what the theory can explain and what it cannot explain. What is in, and what is out. What it can and cannot do. Or more prophetically, we seek to make our theories fail as this is the most substantive means to improve them.

So what tells us if a theory is any good, whether it is strong or weak? Strong theories provide a plausible explanation for the relationship in which we are interested, they are good at explaining, are fit, and tell us when they work and when they don't work. A good theory should look like a great white shark with lots of scratches and scars. Still swimming but seen some stuff. Again, the scientific method welcomes challenges as a means to improve its understanding. However, when we arrive as brass tacks, ultimately, a theory has to work, it has to explain. And, while we can theorize a wide range of things, only the greatest of the great white sharks remain. Like the Mad Max's Thunderdome or the Ultimate Fighting Championship: easy to enter, hard to stay in. In all fields of Political Science, there are many challenger theories but fewer mainstay core theories that have stood the hardest test of all, the test of time.

Causation and the Use of Theory

If we see science as a way of understanding the world, the use of theory is one of the necessary tools of the scientist to do so. Inherent in looking at, thinking about, and searching for explanations for why some relationships work and others do not, we invariably engage causality.

Undoubtedly, you have heard the phrase, 'correlation is not causation'. This is accurate although not universally true. Correlation is an actual statistical measurement that describes the nature of a relationship between two interval-level variables (as we will see in Chapter 8). The phrase, for the brigand who said it, is supposed to mock the idea that just because things move together it doesn't mean they are causally related ('Take that, nerd!'). While it pays to agree with someone saying this in order to avoid embarrassing them outright, you could instead offer 'correlation is not *necessarily* causation' implying that correlation is a necessary but insufficient component of a causal relationship. That is, correlation *could be* causation, given the right set of circumstances.

> ### CAUSALITY
>
> Causality, in a (David Hume or J.S. Mill-shaped) nutshell, is essentially:
>
> (1) Contiguity between cause and effect (X and Y covary)
> (2) Temporal precedence (a change in X precedes a change in Y)
> (3) Constant conjunction (when Y changes, X is there; a.k.a. non-spuriousness).

Why is this discussion relevant in a chapter about theory (in a book about statistics)? Causation is a working assumption of theoretical thinking. When we make the theoretical proposition: X → Y, we are making that argument that our 'X' is important in shaping 'Y'. That is, it is clearly an implication of X → Y that they are causally related, i.e., a change in 'X' produces – or *causes* – a change in 'Y'. Simply, theory – as a statement explaining a relationship – is an inherently causal argument.

At the same time, what our brigand from above is inadvertently referring to is the undeniable reality that statistical relationships can show up simply because the estimating procedure of correlation *can* summarize a bunch of dots as a line when in fact the variables have nothing to do with one another. If, for example, we discover that the amount of daily rain in Beijing highly correlates with the price of an Apple Fritter at a

Tim Hortons in downtown Toronto, we are statistically savvy enough to recognize this as a **spurious correlation.** That is, there is not sufficient or evident reason to suspect these are related in a *causal* way.

For now, causality is a necessary implication of theoretical thinking: X → Y. This simply means that it is helpful to *think* causally and to develop models that have causal implications (even if only indirectly testable). Causality is a working assumption tool of the scientist rather than a verifiable statement about reality.

Hypotheses

Ok, back up a second. Let me get this straight, ultimately theories are just simplified guesses about how the world *might* work that we often try to make fail.

Yep. And I imagine that might sound really different than what you were expecting theory to mean. Now, I'm going to tell you how we test theory (you might want to sit down).

We don't. We test the implications of theory. We call these implications **hypotheses**.

The ability to determine if our theory is weak or strong, if we are on the right track or not, comes from deriving concrete examples of the theory and testing those. This is the role of hypotheses. A good hypothesis allows us to take our theory to the data by evaluating how it performs in the 'real world'. Note, this is what non-scientists say in an attempt to diminish scientific results that don't comport with their worldview: 'Yeah, but in the real world...' please see the Common Sense discussion in the previous chapter.

First, we must be introduced to two of the main characters of the scientific inquiry: The **independent variable** and the **dependent variable**. Remember variable 'X' and variable 'Y' in our discussion above? Variables represent what we are interested in studying as the conceptual elements of theories and hypotheses. The independent variable is what we think causes the dependent variable to change.

In the following hypotheses, which elements are the independent variables? Which are the dependent variables?

- Hypothesis 1: More educated citizens are more likely to turn out to vote.
- Hypothesis 2: Incumbent MPs are more likely to win re-election than challengers.
- Hypothesis 3: Nations with higher levels of economic development are more democratic.

The *independent* variables are:

- (H_1) individuals' levels of education
- (H_2) incumbency or challenger status of MPs
- (H_3) nations' levels of economic development.

The *dependent* variables are:

- (H_1) likelihood of an individual voting
- (H_2) election outcomes
- (H_3) whether a country is democratic or not.

Therefore, a hypothesis is an explicit statement that indicates *how* (not *why*, that's for the theory to do) the independent variable affects the dependent variable. It is a declarative statement of the *expected theoretical relationship* between the independent variable and the dependent variable. The explicitness of hypotheses takes theory's appeal to reality toward concreteness, toward measurability.

Recall the example from above in which we want our theory to be fertile. We opted for the more general, 'Incumbents win re-election more often because they tend to have more *resources*,' which allowed us to include 'more money', 'greater name recognition', 'more campaign workers', and other potential advantages that incumbents may have in elections. Hypothesis demand explicitness. So, it is at this point that we replace 'resources' in the theory with 'more money', 'greater name recognition', 'more campaign workers'. That is, we make the general theory 'real world' specific. In this way, we merge our model of the phenomena in which we are interested – our theory – with a direct empirical test of data which will provide information on the quality of our theoretical model.

This, my dear reader, is the central load-bearing column for the scientific method. The effective use of theories and hypotheses prepares the foundation on which we build our research design – including and measuring variables, our analytical strategy – and statistics can do their most impressive work.

THE NULL HYPOTHESIS

I don't want to alarm you or make this worse (you might want to lie down), but we don't actually test hypotheses either. We actually construct the 'null hypothesis' that is the exact opposite of your hypothesis and we test that hypothesis. This advancement in testing was given the moniker Neyman–Pearson hypothesis testing from its originators. In other words, the scientific method requires that we construct simplified versions of reality (theory), make statements about what it would look like in reality (hypothesis), and test the veracity of the exact opposite of this (the null hypothesis).

Again, the colloquial use of hypothesis – in films and conversation – is often mistaken for the work that theory does. Hypotheses are what we expect to see – based on the theory – in our analysis of the 'real world'. Hypotheses do not explain why we see what we see, that's theory's job, only that the relationship behaves as expected. Inasmuch as it does, we find support for the theory. Inasmuch as it doesn't, we fail to find support for our theory. And again, either of these outcomes is welcome. In the first, we find confirmation that the theory predicts what we are trying to explain. In the second, often as usefully, we find out where our theory fails (chip chip goes the non-elephant part of the boulder). We will discuss the process of hypothesis *testing* in greater detail in a later chapter when we need it, but for now, let's see how to spot a good hypothesis in the wild.

Characteristics of Hypotheses

A good hypothesis derives from a strong theory. If we are testing a strong theory, our hypothesis will reflect that theory's appeal to logic, coherency, and correspondence with reality. However, even with this, our hypothesis is not fully ready to meet the data. A good hypothesis has additional characteristics specific to the nature of hypotheses testing.

A hypothesis is a general, non-normative, directional statement of a relationship.

As we talked about in the previous chapter, and like all of our scientific brethren and sistren, we aim to be objective. Being objective requires us to try to minimize the normative nature of research (thanks for the slack, Weber). We have touched on the topic of non-normativeness before. A non-normative statement avoids stating or implying what ought to be. Rather *it is a statement about what is*. A simple example:

- The more resources incumbents have, the more likely they are to win an election.
- Incumbents are more likely to win an election because they are better for the country than their opponents.

In the first, we explicitly state our expectation of the relationship between political actors vying for office and their resources. We know that why this is the case – what is the role of 'more resources' – would be spelled in the theory.

The second hypothesis is a preferred ranking of incumbents' and opponents' value in service to the country. Now, this specific hypothesis is not entirely without merit. There are certainly ways to measure 'better' in a meaningful way – e.g., candidates' representativeness, their preferences for particular policies, or their adherence to the norms and institutions of democracy – to examine incumbents and their opponents. However, stated this way (above), this is not it.

In congruence with an appeal to objectivity, good *hypotheses also seek to be general*. That is, they should explain general occurrences rather than specific ones. Hypotheses are used to help test and thus improve theory. Theories seek to explain a class of events. If our goal in science is to seek probabilistic, general knowledge about political and social phenomena, our research is guided by theory as a means to generalize.

Generally, this is not a demanding requirement. A simple rule is to check that the hypothesis is in plural form.

A simple example:

- Manuel Fernandez, the incumbent, is more likely to win the election because he has more resources than his opponent.
- The more resources incumbents have, the more likely they are to win an election.

In concordance with the larger scientific goal of inference – of explaining a class of events rather than a single event – we design our hypotheses thusly.

In addition to being both objective (non-normative) and general, *a good hypothesis is also directional.* In the hypothesis, the change in the dependent variable moves with a change in the independent variable. If the variables move together – i.e., they both increase or both decrease simultaneously – the hypothesis represents a positive relationship. If, on the other hand, they move in opposition to one another – i.e., as one increases the other decreases – the hypothesis represents a negative relationship.

Look at the following hypotheses:

- People with (more) children are less likely to vote.
- As a non-democratic country's GDP per capita grows, that country is more likely to become a democracy.
- An increased use of de-humanizing language on public airwaves increases the likelihood of civil unrest.

In the first one, as the number of children increases (most consequentially from 0 to 1), the likelihood of voting decreases (a negative relationship). In the second, as national GDP per capita increases, democracy becomes more likely (a positive relationship). In the final example, as a type of language is more prevalent, civil unrest increases (a positive relationship). Simply, for the relationship stated in the hypothesis to be evaluated, we must know about the direction of the relationship. That's it.

Hypotheses: An Example

In the field of political communication, there are a number of exciting theories. However, one well-known and long-standing theory has demonstrated itself to be strong: Agenda Setting (McCombs and Shaw, 1972). The theory states that the issues most prominent in the news are also the issues most important in public opinion. Or – and, yes, you can use this at parties to impress others – 'Media do not tell people what to think, but what to think about.'

In terms of the essential characteristics of theory – strong theories provide a plausible explanation for the relationship in which we are interested, they are good at explaining, are fit, and tell us when they work and when they don't work – let's assume, given that you know about Agenda-Setting theory and it is over 50 years old and still around, that it is has stood the test of time.

Instead, let's focus on deriving a good hypothesis or two. We need a general, non-normative, directional statement of a relationship. First, what are the independent and dependent variables? In the Agenda-Setting theory, what is theorized to cause what?

- Do 'the media' form viewers' opinions?
- Does the news change viewers' values and morals?
- Does the news cause viewers' opinions to change?
- Does the salience of reported issues cause viewers to give more attention to those issues?

While the development of the Agenda-Setting theory since its inception has included many manifestations and various forms, the original *independent* variable is the 'prominence of issues in the news' (in the legacy media: broadcast and print) and the *dependent* variable is the 'public's reported salience given to these same issues'. As such, we might propose the following two hypotheses as a means to test the theory of Agenda Setting:

- *Hypothesis 1:* In a year, BBC viewers will post (or re-post) on Facebook topics that reflect the topics given the largest amounts of time in the BBC news.
- *Hypothesis 2:* Over a one-month period in [*your country*], greater diversity in the headline news stories of each night broadcast will correspond to less convergence in the opinions of viewers on the most important problem facing the country.

These do not represent the only hypotheses that we might make based on Agenda Setting and I imagine that you can think of several alternative hypotheses to these. They do, however, correspond to our criteria for a good hypothesis: a general, non-normative, and directional statement of a relationship.

A Final Note

The use of theory in scientific studies spans an epistemological divide by simultaneously maintaining the scientific aims of seeking to generalize – to explain a class of events – as well as the malleability and adaptability necessary to accommodate new information or better evidence. As a common core of knowledge, the use of theory binds researchers together in the pursuit and advancement of our collective knowledge. If we are proud of science's willingness to be wrong and be revised and updated, theory is that part of science of which we should be the proudest. This brings us to the end of our discussion on the use of theories and hypotheses in the scientific study of politics.

End of Chapter Summary

- The use of theory and hypotheses are the primary means to advance scientific advancement through the testable and adaptable nature of the accumulation of scientific knowledge.

- Theory identifies relationships about the phenomenon in which we are interested; organizes and summarizes the work that has been done on our subject; and suggests where to look for future testing.
- Theories are not right or wrong. Theories are weak or strong.
- Strong theories provide a plausible explanation for the relationship in which we are interested, they are good at explaining, are fit, and tell us when they work and when they don't work.
- The validity of a theory is determined through competing with other theories, which – over time – makes one explanation a more probable explanation than others.
- All theories, as simplifications of reality, are wrong.
- Inductive reasoning moves from specific observations to general principle. Deductive reasoning moves from general to specific.
- Correlation is not necessarily causation.
- Changes in the Independent Variable are theorized to cause changes in the Dependent Variable.
- Hypotheses are about how, not why, two variables are related.

Glossary

- **Theory** explains the reason one variable affects another variable.
- **Hypotheses** are declarative statements of the expected theoretical relationship between the independent variable and dependent variable.
- **Inductive reasoning** moves from specific observations to general principle.
- **Deductive reasoning** moves from general principle to specific observation.
- Theories are **weak or strong**, not right or wrong.
- **Strong theories** provide a plausible explanation for the relationship in which we are interested, they are good at explaining, are fit, and tell us when they work and when they don't work.
- **Parsimony** is the delicate equilibrium of a theory to be able to explain as much as it can with as little as it can. You can think of it as maximizing explanatory leverage.
- **Falsifiability** is a characteristic of theory that tells us when the theory does not work.
- **Independent Variable** is the variable that causes the Dependent Variable to change.
- **Dependent Variable** is the variable changes by the Independent Variable.
- **Spurious correlation** is the seeming relationship between two variables that is, in fact, a function of chance – and thus unreal.

Questions

1. All languages are models in that each is an approximation of reality used by the speakers of that language to communicate with one another. This is never so clear as when we learn a new language and discover its sometimes similar – sometimes

different – words and phrases used to represent the same universe. In fact, it may be possible to think of competing theories as different languages striving to explain the same event. With this in mind, describe how the simplification of reality – for example, with the use of theory – doesn't necessarily limit us and can even help us better understand it.
2. Explain why inductive reasoning is a common source for developing theories and deductive reasoning is more commonly associated with theory testing.
3. Strong theories:

    a. provide a plausible explanation for the relationship in which we are interested
    b. are good at explaining
    c. are fit and
    d. tell us when they work and when they don't work.

Which of these is the least important? Most important? Why?

4. Why (and how) do we use hypothesis to link theory and the real world?
5. Falsifiability is a strange concept: we try to find out where our theory doesn't work in order to make it a better theory. Explain.
6. How does thinking about theories as weak or strong – rather than theories as right or wrong – improve our shared knowledge?
7. Why are theories not right or wrong?

Annotated References and Further Reading

Geddes, Barbara. 2003. *Paradigms and Sandcastles: Theory Building and Research Design in Comparative Politics*. Ann Arbor: University of Michigan Press.

Based to some extent on her own compelling work, Geddes presents strategies of research designs that bring researchers to the important task of engaging the theory.

Kohli, Atul, Peter Evans, Peter Katzenstein, Adam Przeworski, Susanne Rudolph, James Scott, and Theda Skocpol. 1995. 'The role of theory in comparative politics: A symposium' *World Politics* 48: 1–49.

The compiled lectures of a symposium at Princeton from sub-field experts (in 1993–94) that debates the role of theory in Political Science and Comparative Politics in particular.

Signposts to Research and Empirical Examples

Box, G.E.P. 1976. 'Science and statistics' *Journal of the American Statistical Association* 71(356): 791–9. https://doi.org/10.1080/01621459.1976.10480949

Gavroglu, K., Yorgos Goudaroulis, and P. Nicolacopoulos. 1989. 'Imre Lakatos and theories of scientific change' *Boston Studies in the Philosophy of Science*. Boston: Kluwer Academic Publishers. pp. 169–87. https://doi.org/10.1007/978-94-009-3025-4

McCombs, Max. and Donald Shaw. 1972. 'The agenda-setting function of mass media' *Public Opinion Quarterly* 36(2): 176–87. https://doi.org/10.1086/267990

Popper, Karl 2002 [1959]. *The Logic of Scientific Discovery*. Abingdon-on-Thames: Routledge.

Weber, Max. 1904a [1949]. 'Objectivity in social science and social policy' in *The Methodology of the Social Sciences*. Glencoe, IL: Free Press. pp. 50–112.

Cartwright, Nancy. 2004. 'Causation: One word, many things' *Philosophy of Science* 71(5): 805–19. https://doi.org/10.1086/426771

3
DATA AND VARIABLES

> **LEARNING OUTCOMES**
>
> By the end of this chapter, you will be able to
>
> - Describe the importance of data to Political Science research.
> - Critically assess the relationship between data and variables.
> - Identify the crucial importance of the conceptual basis of variables.
> - Evaluate the process of operationalizing variables.
> - Articulate the challenges – such as concept validity and measurement reliability – to both the definition and choice of indicators for variables.

Introduction

Data and variables are the building blocks of scientific research. How we define the elements of our research and select the measures of those concepts are often overlooked steps in the research process. While theory may guide our choices, what to include and exclude in our research will shape our results in important ways.

Data

There is a lot of discussion about data these days. Big data, the availability of data, data collection, data on elections, data on GDP per capita growth, download the data, send me the data, data on manifestos, data on conflict, here's the data, data, data, data.

So, what are data? Data, a collection of singular **datum** combined in the form of a **dataset**, are merely systematically collected, codified observations or information. Codified observations are observations rendered mathematically tractable or, at a minimum, discretely categorized. 'Discretely categorized' is being able to separate observations into a set of comprehensive and exclusive categories.

Frankly, what data are is far less important than what data can do for scientific research. The purpose of data to the statistical analysis of a research question is to provide observations on all the relevant elements to help determine if one explanation is better than another. That is, data are nice to have – but ultimately they are inert. Left alone, they will literally just sit there taking up space on your hard drive or cloud. So, how do data become useful to research?

Data become useful when we press them into service of our research. Data provide us with the material for the building blocks of scientific research: samples and variables. Samples allow us to efficiently study large processes and variables connect the ideas under investigation with the 'real world'. Data render research ideas, theories, and hypotheses into things that can be measured, compared, and tested. They are the proverbial rubber that meets the road. Thus, when we talk about data, we are talking about the elementary components of all research. Data are the quarks to matter, the clay to bricks, the grain to pasta.

In order for the use of statistics to have any power at all, we must consider two things. One, we must consider the actual techniques in statistics, which is what the vast majority of any book on statistics is about: the selection of the most appropriate techniques, the formulas, and drawing conclusions. We will get to this shortly.

The other part to consider is the grist for the (statistics) mill. That is, while statistical techniques can do myriad simple and amazingly complex transformations, if you feed them slop, you will get slop (think of jamming 200 Barbie dolls, two jars of green olives, and homemade prune jam, and a goosedown duvet into a woodchipper). Simply, the most sophisticated mathematical handling of data is moot if in fact the data are garbage.

GIGO

Spanning back to the earliest days of computer programming (the 1950s!), the 'GIGO' concept – garbage in, garbage out – is the origin of this sentiment. Simply, no matter the technique, the quality of output is highly contingent on the quality of the input.

So, let's look at how data become useable to the statistical techniques we will learn later in the book.

For any research project, the quality of data is of utmost importance. Assuming that the data come from a reliable source and is sufficient, e.g., that there is enough of it to answer our question and control for others' explanations, data are transformed into elements of scientific research if they meet the following two demanding criteria when pressed into service. Data must:

(1) be representative of what we are trying to study
(2) be what we want to measure.

One: Data Must be Representative of What We are Trying to Study

Data must be representative of the population they are meant to refer to. If you are interested in European voters, we need data representative of European voters. If you are interested in conflicts in sub-Saharan Africa, you need data representative of conflicts in sub-Saharan Africa. If you are interested in environmental legislation in the European Union Parliament, you need data representative of environmental legislation in the European Union Parliament. *Ad infinitum*. In order to achieve our scientific goal of inference, we need a valid – i.e., representative and sufficient – sample of the unobservable total population that we are interested in. So, let's talk about samples and populations.

Samples and Populations

A **population** is the entire set of what you wish to draw conclusions about. If you are interested in why some citizens vote for Green parties or radical right parties in a country (or a region, like Europe), it would be very difficult to ask everyone in that country (or region) in a systematic and timely manner about their support or vote for these parties. In order to understand such a phenomenon, a researcher can instead take a **sample** of the population in which s/he is interested.

A sample is a subset of units in the population of interest. This is not laziness, this is necessity. In other words, because it is nearly always impossible to collect data on an entire population, we take a sample of that population on which to conduct our investigation. If the sample is valid (that is, it 'looks like' the population from which it was drawn), the conclusions that we reach can be exported to our understanding of the population from which the sample was drawn. The degree of confidence we can have exporting the findings from the sample to the population will be given to us by the statistical techniques we will learn. That is possibly the superpower of statistics: conferring the possibility of making confident inferences from samples to populations.

Clearly, samples – valid and sufficient samples – are crucial to our ability to make confident inferences. While sampling procedures vary between how we conduct surveys or collect data on countries, one thing underpins the collection process: randomization. Our ability to make confident inference is made possible by the assumption that we have a random sample of the population (technically this assumption allows us to estimate the probability that a sample result could be due to chance). With randomized samples, inferential statistics will tell us *exactly* how confident we can be to make such claims. At this point, you can see how this power might be useful to scientific research (think Principle 3).

However, we will take up randomization in Chapter 9 where we can give it the space it deserves. For now, samples are collections of data that hinge on their representativeness of the population.

ORGANIZING DATA

Datasets order observations and variables in the form of rows (observations) and columns (variables). This is often referred to as the **N×K design** where 'N' refers the number of observations and 'K' refers to the number of variables.

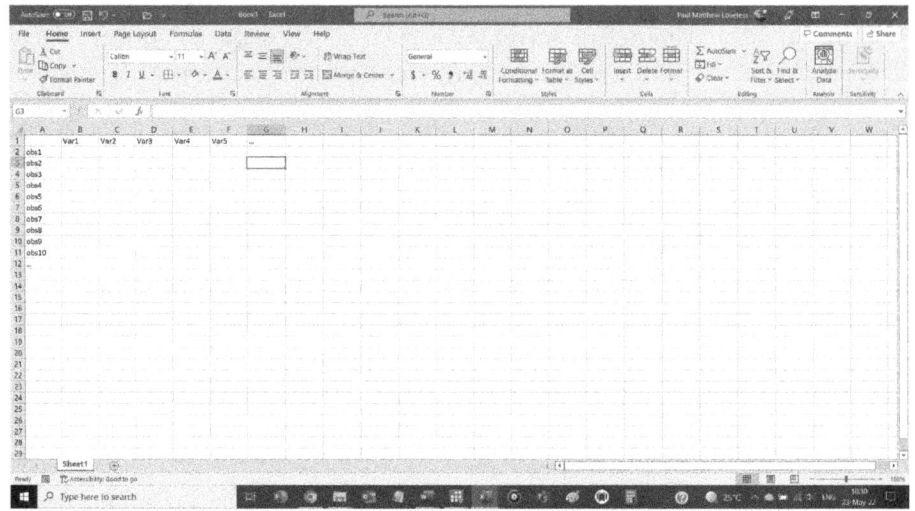

Figure 3.1 A Dataset

Source: Microsoft Excel Spreadsheet (for more information: microsoft.com). Used with permission from Microsoft

In this dataset, for example, Observation 1 (in Figure 3.1, 'obs1') is what we are interested in investigating: for example, a person, a business, a group, or a country. Then the value of the first variable ('Var1') for Observation 1 goes in the row for 'obs1' and column for 'Var1'. Then the value of the second variable ('Var2') for Observation 1 goes in the row for 'obs1' and the column for 'Var2'. And on until we have completed the row of Observation 1. We have input data into the dataset. We can continue to do the same for Observation 2. And repeat until we have as finished (usually because we have run out of observations).

Voilà, a dataset!

Two: Data Should Be What We Want to Measure

How are data transformed into useable elements of scientific research and even statistical analysis? Data must be transformed into meaningful representations of what we intend to study, managed and handled to serve our analytical approach with the ultimate goal of satisfying the demands of our research design. The data that we intend to use must conceptually and operationally capture the phenomena that we are interested in. That is, data become useful to research by being transformed into variables. **Variables** are collections of data that represent concepts in which we are interested. Variables will need to represent what we are interested in, that is, they will need to connect the concepts under investigation with 'real-world' empirical referents. Some concepts offer clear, easy to observe indicators such as the number of votes a party got in an election, GDP per capita-*per capita*, or the number of military bases. In this case, compiling and aligning data with the intended variable is often straightforward. However, variables must also represent abstract concepts we are interested in such as force, justice, power, or inequality. Unlike before, researchers may struggle to convert data into the variables necessary to test and control in their analysis. In addition to the necessary debates over what we are referring to, we must also take the final step of locating a reasonable empirical measurement.

At the same time, social scientists are also, in a sense, overrun with variables that must be contended with. The complexity of world, whether the social reality of influences on vote choice for individuals or the international contexts of the emergence of democracy, is subject to several potential influences. At the same time, the data should be ample enough to contain the information we need on all relevant variables to answer the research question. Not only is it important to have correctly collected, measured, and codified the phenomena that you are interested in, but also everything else that might impose upon that relationship. This is often the hardest criterion.

Fortunately, there are meaningful solutions to each of these challenges. The complexity of variables explains the attractiveness of statistics, namely, its ability to deal with complexity quite handily (Chapter 4). And despite the contests over definitions and 'real-world' indicators, the process of identifying and measuring the phenomena in which we are interested is fairly straightforward.

Let's start from here.

> NOT YOUR CONCEPT
>
> Data are not your concept. How you define (*conceptualize*) and measure (*operationalize*) your variable has a profound effect on what you will find.
>
> – Every statistics textbook ever

Conceptualization and Operationalization

Let's assume that we want to tackle a difficult and timely issue in Political Science. We decide to study the effect of inequality on democracy. Big bite, lots going on here. But, please note, when we say that we are studying inequality and democracy, we aren't really. At least not very well.

You and I and everyone who does Political Science aren't evaluating actual inequality or probing the guts of democracy. We instead are evaluating the best indicators – derived from the available data – of the concepts of inequality and democracy. Instead of putting inequality and democracy into a laboratory, we devise a concept of what we are interested in and explicitly define what we intend to study. Then, we find an indicator that most closely captures this definition.

These two ideas – defines and captures – are possibly the most important steps in the scientific method. **Conceptualization** – the process of defining – and **operationalization** – the process of capturing – constitute the link between our ideas and the real world and thus crucial elements in the research process. Note: the processes of conceptualization and operationalization are not perfect and are rarely fixed.

Recall the pilot metaphor in which subjective inputs not only take place in the objective process of the scientific method but also *must* take place as key elements in the quality and safety of the flight. The (subjective) choices made here will literally determine (1) which analytical techniques are available to your research, (2) the results of your research, and (3) your ability to make (inferential) claims beyond the analysed data of your research.

So, as they say in the pickle industry, kind of a big dill.

For our study on inequality and democracy, making these choices makes practical and analytical sense. Not only has it proven quite difficult for everyone working on inequality to agree on the most appropriate definition of inequality or democracy, but it has also been difficult to then create (or find) a measure that satisfies these definitions.

Yet, research on the relationship between democracy and inequality continues apace. How? Remember the theory as model discussion? We don't need every bit and bob on the model to distinguish it from similar and dissimilar models. We need what are essential to the identification of that concept. And then we just need something to measure that.

As an aside, I am still assuming you want to impress potential new friends at parties – so just drop 'conceptualization' and 'operationalization' casually into conversation to raise the bar for any competitors. You can borrow this from me: 'Hey, how you doin'? Wouldn't you agree that the difficulty of operationalization is problematized by weak conceptualization?' (This can also be used to deflect half-soaked, smart-ass uncles at a family dinner who don't think much of you going to university.)

Let's try our hand at conceptualizing and operationalizing.

Conceptualization

Conceptualization is defining the concepts in which we are interested (or will be needing for control). It is the necessary but unfortunate step of upsetting the smooth integration of the complex world of sensory stimulation into discrete, definable observations. 'Unfortunate' only in that our minds are so adept at attending to a vastly complex and wiggly reality without so much as a sweat, it seems almost a shame to interrupt this seamless flow by imposing something so clumsy as separate categories. However, in order to converge on a common perception of reality, the process of conceptualization – defining what we are interested in examining – is necessary.

This process has two competing demands that simultaneously stretch and constrain our concept. First is *connotation*. What do you mean by the word you are using? What are the defining characteristics or properties? Connotation challenges us to identify and remedy any ambiguity we might have about what we are studying. We want to minimize the distance between the word and what we intend. This is the stretch of our defining process. We want to be sure that everything we intend to study is included.

The second demand, *denotation*, refers to objects themselves. What are you referencing? How far can we extend the definition? We should confront any vagueness between our meaning and what defines the extension of the definition. Denotation constrains our definition to only those things we want to study.

Like theoretical parsimony, the competing demands of connotation and denotation force us to confront what we intend to include and exclude from our concept. This process is a refinement process, carefully inspecting our own ideas about what we intend to study and what that includes. And excludes, so that we are not referring to things we didn't intend to include. Precise conceptualization is a step no research can afford to overlook in seeking the Holy Grail of inference. Take a simple example. If I ask you what a chair is, you likely respond, 'Well, it is something with four legs and you can sit on it'. I reply, 'That is not incorrect' as I sit on the edge of the desk. Ah! In starting to define 'chair', we can see right away that it requires some attention to what makes a chair *specifically* a chair and the definition should include all chairs as well as exclude all non-chairs.

Now, recall that we are doing research on inequality and democracy. Or economic development, poverty, justice, political apathy, partisanship, conflict, party competition, or power. How do we unambiguously move from these words to confront what we intend to include and, again, exclude from our concept? For precisely this reason, conceptualization often takes up lots of space in the design of a research project. Literal space, as articles and books and other publications often spend a great deal of time articulating what it is the research will examine and how we will measure it.

A Political Scientist took this process seriously – motivated by what he perceived was weak conceptualizing – and proposed a rubric for remedying such issues. In 1970, Giovanni Sartori published an article in the *American Political Science Review* in which he highlighted the importance of thinking about our concepts, reminding researchers – as I have pointed out above – that what one measures shapes the outcomes of one's research. He added, what one claims to measure does as well. Or, in one of the most-cited lines in Political Science, 'We are deluding ourselves if we really believe that by saying a variable, we have a variable' (Sartori 1970: 1037).

He advised researchers to be attentive to proper conceptualization in order to avoid 'conceptual stretching', the inadvertent misuse of concepts to include or exclude and thereby undermine the results. As a guide to proper conceptualization, Sartori's suggested using a 'Ladder of Abstraction'. A ladder, in perspective, is wider at the end closest to you and narrower at the far end. With these inverse proportions in mind, he argued that as the attributes assigned to a concept increase (an increase in the number of rungs in the ladder), its extension (the other end) narrows. That is, the more specificity – the more dimensions or characteristics – we include in our concept, the more objects we exclude. While an imperfect guide – but killer metaphor – he was suggesting researchers to attempt to make extensional gains (denotation) without losing the precision and empirical testability (connotation). Or simply, to extend as far as the concept will go, but not farther. In a sense, Sartori's conceptualization is a Goldilocks equilibrium. And like Goldilocks, we may have to try concepts too big and too small before alighting on the one that is just right.

Operationalization

Once we have satisfactorily defined our concept, the second step is operationalization. Operationalization is the process of matching our concept to useable, empirical referents. What is the actual evidence? What is it we are going to look at? Where's the beef?

Imagine if you had designed a wonderful research project, and even gotten as far as conceptualizing all of the relevant variables. Then, you fell ill and couldn't leave the house (which mysteriously has no internet in this story). You call your friend who runs to the window outside your house and you shout down from the window to ask her to help with operationalizing your concepts for your research project. You tell her, 'Bring me X, a list of Ys, and a dataset with Zs.' Operationalization is the process of naming X, Y, and Z. It is the specific, tangible, precise thing that you will actually measure. It is what will be in your friend's hands when she returns.

Operationalization is limited by two things: the quality of conceptualization and the availability or suitability of indicators. The process of conceptualization will do a great deal of the operational work for you. The better the definition, the greater the likelihood of a better choice of indicator. Second, is the choice of actual indicator from what is available.

Data Availability

Operationalization is naturally constrained by the availability (or limitation) of data. In the material sense that we must select from what is best available to capture our concept. The best available can be thought of as having been sent to the store by your mom to get bananas but all the bananas at the store are meh (sage advice suggests to return with the best meh bananas rather than arrive home empty-handed). Thus, in terms of operationalization, 'best available' is having a sense of how well an empirical referent in the real world matches your definition.

There are two strategies. One, you can use what is common to the literature (i.e., what is agreed upon). While this seems the path of least resistance, there remains the practical constraints of doing so. Note that existing measures are often used for their convenience (and acceptable level of problems). That is, the one you choose will probably be determined less by the most appropriate data and more by the one most common to your literature. This does not mean it is incorrect, it just means that you'll need to be aware of the limitations of doing so.

As a quick example, in our inequality and democracy research, the availability of commonly used measures of democracy are multitude.

- The *World Governance Indicators* (https://info.worldbank.org/governance/wgi/) from the World Bank in over 200 countries spanning nearly 25 years. You can choose from indicators of Voice and Accountability; Political Stability and Absence of Violence; Government Effectiveness; Regulatory Quality; Rule of Law; and Control of Corruption. Governance includes the process by which governments are selected, monitored, and replaced; the capacity of the government to effectively formulate and implement sound policies; and the respect of citizens and the state for the institutions that govern economic and social interactions among them.
- *Freedom House's* measures of Political Rights and Civil Liberties (now called 'Global Freedom Scores'; https://freedomhouse.org/countries/freedom-world/scores) in more than 200 countries for nearly 50 years. The surveys measure *individual freedom* – the opportunity to act spontaneously in a variety of fields outside the control of the government and other centres of potential domination – in two broad categories: political rights and civil liberties.
- *The Polity IV Project* (www.systemicpeace.org/polity/polity4.htm), which ranks countries on a scale from −10 (hereditary monarchy) to 10 (fully democratic) for more than 150 countries since the end of the Second World War. The Polity scheme consists of six component measures that record key qualities of executive recruitment, constraints on executive authority, and political competition. It also records changes in the institutionalized qualities of governing authority.

All of these take as a starting point the concept of democracy. Where they begin to differ is the inclusion of the salient attributes. What is it about democracy that we intend? What do we mean when we say 'democracy'? In terms of operationalization, this means that because these data capture various aspects of democracy, they will move together in a coherent fashion but remain *different* as they represent – at the choice of 'what they are each choosing to measure' level – different measurements of democracy. See again: 'Your choice will impact what you ultimately find.'

Another version of data availability is *sufficient* operationalization. That is, unless you are designing the precise process of data collection down to the last question (which is not impossible!), you are at the whim of those that came before you. The measures that we choose from the available existing data should reflect the full range of possible values of that concept so that observations are not inadvertently ignored or suppressed.

Perhaps you want to study attitudes about the role of women in society. You could use the question from the World Values Survey in which respondents are asked about how 'free' women should be to participate in work and politics. The responses range from 0 'a woman's place is at home' to 12 'women should be equal to men in work and politics' (see, for example, Scarborough et al., 2019). While initially an appealing question, this range of responses precludes respondents from being able to register their support for another *greater* than gender equality. What of those who would prefer to see women take a more prominent role in work and politics than men or support the return of the

Amazons of Themyscira? The data are available to study the role of women in society in a large, cross-national survey but the question is potentially limited. Thus, using existing data shapes the process of operationalization is subtle ways.

A final alternative to using existing data or common measures is to propose your own, whether by using a different measure or originating one. To do so, we need to confront two crucial attributes of potential measures: **Validity** and **Reliability**

Validity and Reliability

The indicators that are available to us are, as we started this chapter with, the data that exist or can be gathered. The ones that we choose should satisfy two criteria. One, it is important that the indicator you choose makes intuitive sense. If you intend to find an indicator of inequality (or democracy), the indicator you choose should be a reasonable measure of inequality (or democracy). This intuitive sense refers to whether the indicator is *valid* in the Sartorian sense: does it actually measure the concept you say it does? Two, our indicator must be *reliable*. Reliability is the expectation that the indicator you choose will give you consistent results. That, measured again and again, the indicator isn't capricious, unstable, or unpredictable. This is the same as the advice to be careful not to put your outdoor thermometer in the sun. You will get a reliable indicator of the temperature in the sun, but it will not be a valid measure of the outside ambient temperature (assuming that's what you really want to know).

One approach to establishing operational validity is to argue that it is. That is, one can make a case for why this indicator should be valid 'on its face' (sometimes called, creatively, *face validity*). This is not an easy approach but it is not a wrong approach, especially in the context of a change in concept, something novel, or the discovery of something unexpected.

Another approach, perhaps more convincing than the previous, is to provide *construct validity*. If two concepts are related, then it stands to reason that the measures of those concepts should also be related. Demonstrating that the two measures are in fact related underscores the claim that we are measuring what we intend to measure.

Establishing indicator reliability can be simpler although for new indicators, it can be a challenge. One approach is to *test/re-test*. That is, in repeated measures of the same phenomenon, we should get more or less the same thing time after time. Time after time. This is a common approach for measures found in over-time datasets or repeated samples. Another approach is a *split test*. In random subsets of your sample, our indicator should look more or less the same. That is, if we repeatedly measure our indicator on groups of our data, we should get roughly similar results. Both of these approaches are not rules but rather 'rules of thumb'.

While validity and reliability are closely related, they do bring separate pieces of information to the table. One could substitute accuracy – hitting the correct target – for validity; and precision – returning the same results again and again – for reliability.

Below are illustrative representations of validity and reliability. Let's assume that we are aiming for the bullseye – our intended concept – and the darts represent an indicator or operationalization of that concept. In Figure A (of Figure 3.2), the darts are reliable but not valid. The darts congregate consistently – reliably – in the same place but miss the intended target (i.e., are invalid). In Figure B, our indicator is neither valid nor reliable as it has missed completely. Finally, in Figure C, our indicator is both reliable and valid. This is the indicator we need.

A

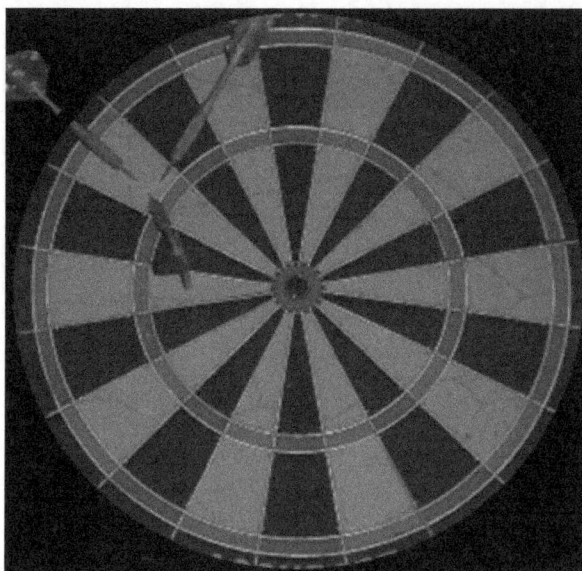

B

C

Figure 3.2 Validity and Reliability

Example: Validity and Reliability

One of the most challenging questions in Political Science is to locate parties along the ideological continuum. One approach has been to ask country experts to rank each party in their countries. But, one is left wondering, how good are these expert placements? How valid and how reliable are these expert placements on the location of parties along the ideological continuum?

One approach for reliability, taken from above, is test and re-test. Ask the experts to place the parties along the continuum. And then – later – literally ask them to do it again. Similar results suggest reliability. Alternatively, one could have *more* experts make placements. High similarity in party placements along the ideological continuum suggests a high level of *inter-coder – thus indicator – reliability*. This is a common approach in political communication or document and content analysis.

Other means to establish validity and reliability are constructing an independent (or at least, alternative) means to measure them. To the extent that these multiple measures align, the indicator you choose is likely a valid one. In this example of placing parties along the ideological continuum, if we assume that people will most likely vote for parties more or less located near their own ideological positions (hotly debated!), one could look at the ideological alignment of the positions of parties and the citizens that voted for them. If extreme left parties' ideological positions are aligning with far-right voters' ideological positions, there may be an issue with the validity of your indicator. If, however, voters' ideological locations align more or less with parties' ideological locations, your placements gather greater support for their validity.

Measurement Error

The frequency or intensity of wars, the percentage of parliamentary seats, or the number of electorally competitive parties can provide some minor conceptual challenges but can be sufficiently defined and operationalized. Yet, in aligning the concepts under investigation with empirical referents from the real world, there is always some slippage. We looked at democracy and attitudes toward the role of women without even accounting for newer and more accurate forms of gender identification or partisan intensity for which conceptualization and operationalization present a challenge. Think of it as a feature not a bug.

At the same time, we seek to avoid any own goals. We seek to minimize any potential bias in our indicators introduced by measurement bias. While we do not engage data collection methods in this book, operationalization poses one particular problem worth mentioning here. **Systematic measurement error** is often a slight deviation in our data collection that affects all of the observations systematically, i.e., all units in more or less the same way. A common systematic error occurs in survey data. It is well-known that respondents tend to 'round up' on their income and 'round down' on their age. The increments are usually quite small and are, importantly, largely inconsequential to any of the statistical techniques. It would, of course, be good to know the correct number, but again, overwhelmingly the deviations are relatively small and have few substantial downstream impacts and thus can be ignored.

In statistics, would we rather have a measurement that is reliable but not valid (although the difference between the not valid and valid measure is more or less known) or valid but not reliable? For the purpose of doing statistics, the former is strongly preferred as we can remedy the systematic measurement error in the former (or ignore it as it has little downstream effect on the results) but there is little we can do with the unreliable measures in the latter.

In contrast to systematic measurement error, there is **non-systematic measurement error**. This is a problem. The indicator measurements are not slightly biased in one direction or another but rather unpredictable. In this case, we know that the measurement of our indicator is off but 'in what direction' and 'by how much' is not an obvious pattern – or is unknown. It doesn't take a lot of imagination to see how measurements that are, well, wrong – and we don't know by how much – are going to produce results that we can't have a lot of confidence in. You are going to want to stop what you are doing and figure out how to get better data.

Example: Conceptualization and Operationalization

It is not possible to overstate the consequence of these two steps in our research. Conceptualization and operationalization represent our selection of the variables that will be analysed to produce the results from which we will draw our conclusions and inferences. Errors at this stage undermine the goal of our scientific endeavour.

The good news is that most of the time, conceptualization and operationalization of the key variables have already been done for you. The literature to which you are writing very likely has fought and settled on agreed-upon concepts and indicators for what you want to analyse. Your contribution to this literature will more than likely be somewhere else. However, in some cases, one stumbles upon a question or literature that might be shaken up with a slight change of concept or slight change in indicator.

There is no one answer for a problem of conceptualization and operationalization. What is one to do when faced with a conceptualization challenge or one recognizes the possibility of conceptual stretching? Argue for a new definition? Search for another concept? Ignore it? Research something else, something more concrete? Clearing that hurdle, what do we do when searching for an indicator? Which indicator do we choose? Do we create our own? Do we measure something else to include or exclude different characteristics?

This is not a moot question in Political Science. Let's revisit political participation. The typology, on which the edifice of the study of political participation is built, derives from a series of articles in the late 1970s and early 1980s. These contributions shared a generic definition – or conceptualization – of political participation as the actions of individuals (either individually or in groups) to affect the policy-making bodies through conventional and unconventional political methods.

Among these, a seminal article articulated the shared conceptual premise of political participation in advanced industrial democracies as a typology of actions. Verba et al. (1978) argued for a typology of 'conventional' political participation – including voting, working in an election campaign, and attending rallies; 'unconventional' political participation – including legal boycotts, picketing, strikes, etc.; and 'illegal acts' – including rioting, unauthorized demonstrations, etc.

These examples became the operational basis for subsequent studies of political participation in the West. That is, for the vast majority of studies of political participation, data was collected on individuals' choices of conventional and unconventional political actions (usually in the form of surveys that asked respondents to report their having done something or willingness to do so). For example, information about individuals' participation in illegal acts were hard to elicit in surveys ('Next question, would you firebomb a city council building? Yes or no? And please answer honestly.') and thus set aside.

The nature of political participation however is changing. One can choose to make sitting down to dinner a political act by the choice to be a vegetarian in opposition to industrial farming. Not wearing fur, reclaiming urban public space, flash mobs, working at a food shelter, hosting a podcast, participating in political theatre, wearing – or not wearing – a mask are all modern equivalents of political protest (read: participation). This is what Theocharis and Van Deth (2018) argue.

Unexpectedly, in updating our thinking about political participation, they offer a new taxonomy of political participation that isn't, 'Yeah, online counts, too, you know.' While digitally networked participation is part of the new forms of political engagement, Theocharis and Van Deth suggest that the internet is just the extension of old forms in a new platform. What is new, or transformative, in their words, are the creative, expressive, and individualized modes of protest activities. These newer forms share the key conceptual dimensions of conventional and unconventional participation, but appeal to younger, more politically disaffected citizens seeking non-institutional participation on their own terms.

This new taxonomy presents us with challenges to the decades-old definitions and measures – the conceptualization and operationalization – of political participation. Given that our choice of definitions and indicators dictate what we will find, what should we do with political participation? While there is no one answer, it behoves us to engage the potential changes to conceptualization and operationalization. Do we need to change the definition or the measures or both?

We can ask, has the definition of political participation changed? Are the newer forms of political actions 'actions of individuals (either individually or in groups) to affect the policy-making bodies through conventional and unconventional political methods'? Well, perhaps, yes. The concept of individuals acting in a manner to impact, affect, or influence the outcome of a political process applies to these newer forms nearly as neatly as the older examples of conventional and unconventional acts do. Oh, that wasn't so hard.

How do we then measure political participation? Or more precisely, in addition to the original indicators, how do we include the array of 'creative, expressive, and individualized modes of protest activities'? This poses a more difficult challenge. How do we know if someone's vegetarianism, mediocre one-man political comedy show, homemade sign pointing at an unfixed pothole, delivering food to a poor neighbourhood, not getting vaccinated are political actions intending to 'influence the outcome of a political process'? Should they be included? Do they need to be impactful? Intentional? Authentic? How will we know? Can we find valid and reliable measures to include? And, most importantly, how will including/excluding them change the outcome?

No pressure.

This case of political participation presents us with a pretty serious challenge. Good. If times are a-changing, we should learn how to adjust our research as well. Here, as in so many aspects of scientific study, there is no one answer, no uniformly best answer. The answer will be up to the researcher(s) who choose to take up this challenge. Fortunately, Political Science is cautiously open to new concepts and new indicators.

Clumsy Segue to Concluding

This chapter has confronted the basics elements of the data-generating process and data quality. We focused on a discussion about the measurement of variables including the key issues of conceptualization and operationalization, reliability, and validity. Ultimately, while we should take them seriously, difficulties in conceptualization and operationalization are not fatal flaws. They do not invalidate the research. These choices, however, do need to be clearly presented as a means to seek to improve the body of knowledge. It is in this scrum that we refine our concepts, their measures, and the resulting analysis.

Data should be comprehensive and sufficient. Comprehensive means that the data are available to include all of the necessary variables as set out in the literature. Sufficient refers to the amount of data necessary to allow for a complete test of competing theories. Both of these are not insubstantial limits to potential research as many topics have literatures that are both deep and wide. In any case, this is an excellent transition to the next chapter on Research Design, in which we are asked to make design choices in order to minimize our potential limitations.

At some point, researchers have tried their best to identify the key elements of core concepts and draw together what is available to create these indicators. So, first a word of thanks. Second, it *is* a matter of choice. Here, the scientific method converts the researcher into the research itself. Your research will always be a blend of rules to follow and subjective choices. Hence, the emphasis on rigor, control, and transparency. Then others can evaluate how closely you have followed the rules and which choices you have made.

So far, we have talked about the scientific method, theories, hypothesis, data, and variables. How does this all fit together? Most of what you will find will come from asking a good question and designing your analysis correctly. This is done through a Research Design.

We take this up next.

End of Chapter Summary

- Data are codified observations.
- Data must be representative of what we are trying to study and be what we want to measure.
- Data are not your concept. How you define and measure your variable has a profound effect on what you will find.
- Conceptualization is the process of defining what we want to study.
- Operationalization is the process of finding an appropriate, 'real-world' measure for that concept.
- Avoid 'conceptual stretching' and measurement bias.
- The validity of a measure refers to whether we are actually measuring what we say we are measuring.
- The reliability of a measure refers to whether our indicator is a consistent measure of what we want to capture.
- Do you have data? Ask yourself, can it be observed and codified? If yes and yes, then yes.

Glossary

- **Data** are codified observations. **Datum** is singular. **Dataset** is a collection of data.
- **N×K design** is the most common form of a dataset where 'N' is the number of observations and 'K' is the number of variables.
- A **population** is the entire set of what you wish to draw conclusions about.
- A **sample** in a subset of units in the population of interest.

- A **variable** is a collection of data that represent a concept in which we are interested.
- **Conceptualization** is the process of defining the concepts in which we are interested.
- **Operationalization** is the process of measuring our concepts with empirical referents in the real world.
- **Validity** is how well the indicator aligns the concept you intend to measure with the measure you have chosen.
- **Reliability** is the expectation that the indicator you choose for your concept will give you consistent results.
- **Systematic measurement error** is a deviation in our data collection that affects all of the observations in more or less the same way (i.e., systematically).
- **Non-systematic measurement errors** are measurements perturbed unpredictably.

Questions

1. Why do we take samples and what kind of problems affect samples?
2. How does the 'competition' between connotation and denotation help us avoid *conceptual stretching* in the process of conceptualization?
3. What is meant by sufficient operationalization?
4. We propose a measure for individuals' views on climate change. We argue that the measure is valid but not reliable. Why is this difficult to imagine?
5. One of the major limitations to studying human rights abuse is the difficulty of obtaining data that is not affected by non-systematic measurement error. Why might this be the case?
6. Some have argued that the problems associated with conceptualization, operationalization, validity, and reliability in Political Science are often overstated. To what extent should we embrace the notion 'Don't let the perfect be the enemy of the good'?

Annotated References and Further Reading

Adcock, Robert and David Collier. 2001. 'Measurement validity: A shared standard for qualitative and quantitative research' *American Political Science Review* **95(3): 529–45.**
Takes a heads-on approach to remedying some of the most common measurement issues in both qualitative and quantitative research, particularly reaching a consensus and speaking across methodological divides.

Jackman, Simon. 2008. 'Measurement' in Robert E. Goodin (ed.) *The Oxford Handbook of Political Science.* **Oxford: Oxford University Press, pp: 119–128.**
Jackman presents a more detailed discussion of the issue of measurement. His approach asks a great deal of the reader and spares little in making the case for its importance to the study of politics.

Signposts to Research and Empirical Examples

For a great example of country experts ranking each party in their countries, see the Chapel Hill expert survey (CHES): www.chesdata.eu/. Bakker, Ryan, Liesbet Hooghe, Seth Jolly, Gary Marks, Jonathan Polk, Jan Rovny, Marco Steenbergen, and Milada Anna Vachudova. 2020. '1999–2019 Chapel Hill Expert Survey Trend File.' Version 1.2. Available on chesdata.eu

Collier, David and Steven Levitsky. 1997. 'Democracy with adjectives: Conceptual innovation in comparative research' *World Politics* 49(3): 430–451.

Corge, P.J. 1988. 'The concept of political participation: Toward a definition' *Comparative Politics* 20(2): 241–249.

Inglehart, Ronald. 1997. *Modernization and Postmodernization: Cultural, Economic, and Political Change in 43 Societies*. Princeton: Princeton University Press.

Munck, Gerardo L. and Jay Verkuilen. 2002. 'Conceptualizing and measuring democracy: Evaluating alternative indices' *Comparative Political Studies* 35(1): 5–34.

Sartori, Giovanni 1970. 'Concept misinformation in comparative politics' *American Political Science Review* 64(4): 1033–1053.

Scarborough WJ, Sin R, Risman B. 2019. 'Attitudes and the stalled gender revolution: Egalitarianism, traditionalism, and ambivalence from 1977 through 2016' *Gender and Society* 33(2):173–200.

Theocharis, Y., and Van Deth, J.W. 2018. 'The continuous expansion of citizen participation: A new taxonomy' *European Political Science Review*, 10(1), 139–163.

Verba, Sidney, Norman Nie, and Joe-on Kim. 1978. *Participation and Political Equality: A Seven-Nation Comparison*. Cambridge: Cambridge University Press.

4
RESEARCH DESIGN

> **LEARNING OUTCOMES**
>
> In this chapter, you will be able to
>
> - Articulate how a well-constructed research design guides empirical analyses.
> - Recognize the importance of well-formed research questions and how they speak to the current state of knowledge
> - Critically assess the choice of analytical approach – that is, how we will find out.
> - Distinguish various forms of empirical research: experiments, case studies, statistics.
> - Identify common problems in research design.

Introduction

A **research design** draws together the scientific approach, theory, and hypotheses as we develop a step-by-step plan for a research project. It states the logic and basic concepts and techniques of empirical research. Research methods and research design in Political Science belong in a bigger book. Both require a great deal more attention than we can sufficiently provide here. This chapter offers an abbreviated but nonetheless substantive discussion of the nature of key analytical concepts, the design and quality of research questions, the importance of literature reviews, and the most common research method approaches. In short, it is a (short) chapter designed to give you an essential guide to conducting a research project.

One reason for presenting the broad strokes and basic structure of a research project, specifically the commonalities and differences in approaches, is that the choices that go into designing research and choosing the appropriate **method** are crucial to what we ultimately find. In addition, and as importantly here, a comparative discussion is enormously informative about the advantages and limitations of using statistics as our analytical tool. While this book introduces you to the power of statistics, keep this chapter in mind as it illustrates the questions statistics can be useful in answering, but also the limitations in using statistics alone. Statistics aren't suitable for answering every research question.

So, a research design specifies what we are going to investigate (a well-formed research question) and what will guide our investigation (the current state of knowledge as well as theories and hypotheses) and how we will find an answer (the **methodology** of investigation). A research design, simply, puts it all together. If you are keeping tabs on each step of the scientific method, this is the *transparent and replicable* part of doing science.

As always, let's start at the beginning.

Research Question

A well-formed **research question** identifies what we are going to investigate. Maybe more precisely, it points out where we are having trouble. There may be a gap in our knowledge. As you read about your topic you will become better oriented to the landscape of the work that has been done. Thus, your experience, training, or insight sees something that others have overlooked, assumed, or just swept under the carpet. Second, knowing the landscape is also helpful for identifying when something isn't behaving as it should. Your research question could, in turn, seek to resolve an observed anomaly or unexpected outcome. Or, finally, your research question might try to explain something novel. In order to do this, it is grounded in what we already know and, if we find an answer, can contribute to our theoretical knowledge. Therefore, our research question, in addition to identifying the phenomenon to be investigated and leading us in the direction of a potentially novel explanation, also demonstrates our familiarity with the landscape, thus qualifying us to conduct this research.

> ### DON'T MISTAKE YOUR DATA FOR YOUR RESEARCH QUESTION
>
> A common mistake in formulating a research question is to substitute your data – or the evidence you will look at – for your question. For example, one might write, 'I am using Round 9 of the European Social Survey in 19 countries to investigate whether Europeans' levels of education are related to their choice to vote or not in national parliamentary elections.' One could simply remove the 'data' part, 'I am investigating whether Europeans' levels of education are related to their choice to vote or not in national parliamentary elections.' However, a research question is a problem you want to investigate in broad terms. Our research question should make this clear.
>
> Therefore, based on our example here, perhaps a better research question might be: 'In Europe, individuals' education levels have long been associated with voting. However, in the context of more urgent issues such as climate change or democratic backsliding, my research question is: "To what extent does education remain a part of the explanation of why Europeans choose to vote or not in national parliamentary elections?" In order to provide a partial answer to this question, I will use Round 9 of the European Social Survey in 19 countries to examine this relationship.'

A research question must meet two conditions. One, can our question produce at least some form of an answer? And two, can it answer the troll guarding the bridge, 'So what?' Why do we care about an answer to our question at all? To the first, broadly surveying what you will need to answer this question, is most of it available, attainable, measurable, and analysable? At the outset of this research project, does it appear that what you need to complete this research is within your reach? You should aim for an optimistic yes. To the second, why is our question worthy of investigation? Why would it be important to someone apart from our field of study? What exactly is the contribution to our collective knowledge? Not easy questions to answer. But necessary questions to answer.

Essentially, your research question is the aiming mechanism for your research project. If you take care and time getting your aim just right, when you set off in pursuit of your research efforts (see below), they will bring you, like a well-loosed arrow, directly to that which you have aimed.

Current State of Knowledge

When devising any new research project, we want to check how our question has been answered before and build on existing knowledge. We must not only know but demonstrate that we have a sense of the landscape of research around our question.

First, a **literature review** will summarize the work that has been done on our topic, including the most substantive works that have altered the landscape of the thinking about our topic. This will likely be an assemblage of classic works and newer contributions that have and continue to shape the debate. Newer works will be an excellent source for a literature review as they will also have reviewed the same literature (although perhaps summarized differently). It answers the questions: what do we know about the performance of each theory and what is still missing? Done well, the literature review not only brings the reader to the inexorable conclusion that your research question is vastly important, but also creates a need for your research's outcome.

A literature review is a demanding request. It may come as a surprise but your interest in a topic is unlikely yours alone. But, standing on the shoulders of giants, perhaps we should be grateful. Those that have come before you have fought the battles that have defined crucial contours of the debate. While this may leave less room for acrobatic fighting techniques, current contributions are no less important. In fact, it is at this point – now that the hardest battles having been fought – that we are able to contribute the most.

Second, our theory section will identify the theories related to our variable of interest as well as any theoretical contribution we hope to make. This section is a comprehensive discussion of the competing explanations – the competing theories – and how they are related. This section clearly defines the variables of interest – the dependent and independent variables, as well as potential hypotheses.

The theory section and literature review should lead us to the opportunity to reckon with theories relevant to your research, derive key hypotheses, and prepare us to engage the data. To do so, we must define and operationalize the central concepts in our analysis: defining our concepts and indicating how will they be measured. We discussed this in the previous chapter.

Now, your command of each step up to this point – research questions, theory, literature review, hypotheses, conceptualization, and operationalization – qualifies you as someone who understands the landscape and particulars of your research area, it demonstrates your expertise. And having set it all up, you must now show how you will find an answer to your research question.

The Analysis: Choosing the Method of Investigation

The method of investigation is how the researcher intends to empirically satisfy the questions of the study. The scientific method requires that we identify, isolate, and assess a relationship between two or more variables relating to a specific case, in order to make inferential claims to explain a class of events. There is a tension here between on the one hand looking to devise a watertight explanation for the causal connection between two variables in a specific example and, on the other hand, looking to generalize from this case to make a universal rule. In our search for the most appropriate analytical method, we must consider – and weigh – our desire to investigate our proposed X->Y and our desire to produce generalizable results. These are not the same thing and, again, there is no one answer. This is another example of subjectivity in the Scientific Method. It is your hands on the controls.

Data Collection

Data collection – also sometimes called a 'measurement strategy' – is the systematic gathering of information on our variables of interest that allows us to answer our research questions by testing the hypotheses derived from relevant theories and determining the outcomes. Depending on the method of inquiry you choose, methods of data collection on political phenomena can include, to mention the most common, the use of existing data such as surveys, natural or quasi-experiments, macro-economic or political data, party manifestos, datasets on parties, conflict, or International Relations; as well as data drawn from texts, speech, documents, websites, video, and other formats; and even original data including interviews, experiments, various forms of first-person participation, and original datasets or surveys. While the process of data collection could be a book on its own; we can consider core components of data collection.

Levels of Analysis and Units of Analysis

The **levels of analysis** refers to the stratum or location of the subject of your study. In Political Science, there are ostensibly three levels of analysis: individuals (or micro-level), actors in the strata between states and persons (meso-level), nation-states, and supranational institutions or organizations (macro-level). While these definitions are not set in stone, they are very common.

These are not to be confused with units of analysis.

Units of analysis are the subject of your study. We want to correctly identify what it is you intend to study. What is the commonality of what you are studying? Individuals? Parties? Parliaments? Countries? International Organizations? Or another way, in investigating various attributes of your unit of analysis, to what do those attributes belong in general? Recall the hypotheses in which we identified the independent and dependent variables.

What are the units of analysis in the following hypotheses?

- More educated citizens are more likely to turnout to vote.
    - *Citizens* are the unit of analysis.
- Incumbent MPs are more likely to win re-election than challengers.
    - *Candidates* for parliament are the unit of analysis.
- Nations with higher levels of economic development are more democratic.
    - *Nations* are the unit of analysis.

Finally, as a form of data consistency, we must acknowledge whether we lack sufficient data to test a hypothesis. For example, it might be interesting to know whether UK voters would not have voted for Brexit if they knew that the coronavirus was going to happen. While a potentially fascinating question, there is simply no data that allows us to test such a historical counterfactual. Or put differently, you would have to build a time machine to find this out. And, let's be clear, if you built a time machine and used it to ask this question, I only have one thing to say to you. Dinosaurs. Are you mad? Go see the dinosaurs. Or Helen of Troy, most beautiful woman in history, launched a thousand ships? Got to check that out. I'll also accept Jimi Hendrix at the 1970 Isle of Wight festival.

Otherwise, insanity.

If you recall from all the way back to Chapter 2, we talked about the Agenda-Setting theory. The theory states that the issues most prominent in the news are also the issues most important in public opinion. What are the units of analysis? While it is tempting to say people, Agenda Setting does not say that *you* watching the news makes *you* supplant your mind with what they broadcast but rather, in the aggregate, greater news attention to specific issues tends to drive the salience of those same issues on the public agenda, a relationship we would expect to see in the aggregate, whether a city, region, or country (or other aggregation).

Case Selection

Case selection is the choice of what to include in a sample. Statistical analyses of large datasets generally have less of an issue of case selection than, for example, studies that focus on one or two cases chosen to stand in for an institutional, economic, or cultural variable (see below). However, even using large datasets, statistical analysis can be affected by case selection. In one way, while we may have several thousand survey responses from citizens of three countries, like small-n studies, the choice of which three countries is crucial to make meaningful comparisons or at a minimum control for macro-level (i.e., country) effects.

In another way, a more refined problem is (Sir Francis) *Galton's Problem*. The observable pool of macro-social units ('countries') are shaped by similar if not related historical social processes. Thus, the study of countries as 'independent observations' is a violation of the assumption that observations of a study are independent and thus autonomous. This has not insubstantial implications for cross-national studies in Comparative Politics as well as International Relations.

Data Suitability

The 'data we are seeking' should match the 'question we are asking'. This is sometimes called 'data consistency'. Simply, we must match data to our theory/hypotheses.

Maintaining consistency between a theory/hypothesis and the data is a common challenge, particularly when individual attributes and behaviours are 'explained' by aggregate patterns. A recognizable example is a television news reporter says some variation of the following: 'Regions in which Candidate X won a greater percentage also have larger amounts of downloads of recipes for deep-fried ice cream sandwiches,' the implication being that those who voted for Candidate X are the same people downloading recipes for deep-fried ice cream sandwiches ('Look at me, I didn't take a stats class but I'm telegenic!').

We – you and me, on the other hand – cannot know whether this is accurate unless we look at data on individual voters which include information both about their vote and online activities. It could very well be that those who voted for Candidate X are the same people downloading enormous numbers of recipes for deep-fried ice cream sandwiches, but these data do not align with what we are trying to conclude.

Drawing conclusions about individual behaviour based on aggregate-level data is called the **ecological fallacy**. What the ecological fallacy means for our fifth characteristic of a good hypothesis is that in order to maintain consistency between the hypothesis and the data, we need to be sure that the hypothesis is answerable by the data that we have. Let's say that you have regional-level education data and regional-level election turnout data, which of the following hypotheses is consistent with the data?

- Turnout is higher in regions with more educated citizens.
- More educated citizens are more likely to vote.

With the regional data, we can only use the first one. In order to properly test the second one, we would need data on individual voters which include information both about their vote and education levels. We cannot test a hypothesis (or draw conclusions) at a level of data that we do not have.

Internal and External Validity

The above issues shape and constrain our abilities to measure and assess the relationship in which we are interested. They are important considerations of our research so that we match our 'level' of research question with the correct 'level' of data collection. However, in determining which research approach is most appropriate for our research question, we need to consider the ability of various empirical approaches to both assess the relationship in which we are interested as well as make generalizations from the results of our study (inference). These abilities are contingent on the internal and external validity of your chosen analytical method.

- **Internal validity** is the extent to which the independent variable can be shown to cause a change in the dependent variable in the data being studied.
- **External validity** is the extent to which the relationship between the independent variable and dependent variable can be generalized to a larger population or a class of events.

All approaches have different levels of internal and external validity and these validities constitute a large part of the reason why we choose one approach over another. In order to show you how different analytical choices shape what we will find and be able to do with those findings, the next sections survey the broad categories of methods you can use in research. In doing so, we will come to appreciate why statistics makes a strong case for itself as an analytical choice in the light of the mix of abilities other approaches offer.

Empirical Approaches in Political Science

Essentially, empirical approaches to the study of politics come in two forms: one, qualitative studies and two, quantitative studies. The qualitative ones refer to the common approach of 'small-n' studies and case studies. The quantitative ones separate into, broadly, experiments, statistical approaches, and formal modelling (Lijphart, 1971). Experiments and quantitative methods are fundamentally *nomothetic* analytical approaches, which refers to their use of statistics, formal logic, or other computational solutions to analyse codified observations to explain a class of problems. Small-n and case studies are *ideographic* analytical approaches in which similar cases are grouped and dissimilar cases are separated by qualities or attributes in order to identify and explain relationships.

Recall from Chapter 1, that King et al. (1994) made an explicit determination that, if science is a method, the debate between the superiority of qualitative methods and quantitative methods is meaningless. The difference above is not science vs not-science, it is the level and complexity of information and the selection of analytical capabilities that each approach offers. Stated differently, empirical qualitative research and experimental and quantitative studies are attempts to identify, isolate, and assess a relationship in order to make inferential claims to explain a class of events. The primary difference is scale. And this is not an insignificant problem.

As scientists, the ability to exert control over the relationship under investigation in our analysis (internal validity) and infer to a larger class of events (external validity) constitute essential criteria by which to assess empirical approaches. In other words, as all approaches have different levels of internal and external validity, we must consider how different approaches resolve these demands as part of the reason why we chose one approach over another. And this, like many choices we have made up to this point, is again part of what we choose will determine the extent of what we can find. We will also see how different methods of data collection and data analysis each have their own strengths and limitations: case studies offer rich detail in the cases we choose; statistics have as a core strength an ability to generalize findings.

Perhaps we should have a quick look at this uncomfortable state of affairs. Broadly conceived, Political Science makes use of three main methods of research: case/small-n studies, experiments, and large-n quantitative studies.

Case Studies and Small-n Studies

For Political Scientists, empirical qualitative work – case/small-n studies – has a rich and productive history in the field. Small-n and case studies offer rich, loamy explanation in contrast to the highly qualified capacities of inference offered by quantitative methods. Qualitative empirical work takes seriously the context in which politics occurs, assuming that meaning is integral to understanding action, and it is this link between individuals and their collective identities (or shared norms) that leads to outcomes. How do these approaches perform in terms of internal and external validity? The goal of case and small-n studies is not to achieve experimental level control but, by choices that shape its design, to be able to control for (or eliminate) competing explanations and at the same time to provide evidence for our theory. In other words, the results of a small-n study will not provide the overwhelming evidence to crown a winning theory but the analysis will align with what you are arguing for and against.

Case Studies and Small-n Studies: Internal Validity

If we are interested in identifying, isolating, and assessing a relationship, one central problem that we have is how to contend with any number of explanations to manage. That is, investigating a small number of cases – whether they are countries, regions, events, or populations, we are confronted with the difficulty of controlling for *all* potential explanations. For case and small-n studies, this is referred to as the 'many variables, small-n' problem. Simply, few cases allow us few opportunities to impose sufficient control to test theories, develop concepts, and generate reasonable external validity.

Przeworski and Teune (1970) proposed two strategies to counterbalance a low number of observations. They suggested, for small-n studies, the Most Similar Design and Most Different Designs.

In the Most Similar Design strategy, if we are interested in the relationship between X and Y, we choose cases in which Y – the outcome – is different yet the other variables to explain Y are the same in all cases except X.

- Country 1: abcX → Y
- Country 2: abcx → y

Again, to examine the relationship between X and Y, both must be different for both countries. Above, X and Y are big in country 1 and small in country 2. Crucially, other potential explanations of Y – a, b, or c – must remain the same (a is small, b is small, and c is small). Therefore, the difference in X potentially explains the difference in Y ($\Delta X \rightarrow \Delta Y$).

This is an enviable design that allows the researcher to make strong claims given the control achieved by the selection of cases. For example, we could look at countries that were similar in many ways yet have a crucial difference. If one country decides to go to war ('Y') and the other does not ('y'), perhaps the crucial difference – x, X: one has a contested border or a coming election and the other does not – can serve as potential explanation for this different outcome.

In the Most Dissimilar Design strategy, we choose cases with the same Ys and are dissimilar in as many ways as possible *except* for the Xs:

- Country 1: AbCX → Y
- Country 2: aBcX → Y

Although there is less dynamism in the relationship in which we are interested, other explanations are eliminated. Expanding on our example above, we can examine countries that both go to war ('Y') yet differ in myriad ways except one (X, X: both have a strong presidential system or high defence budgets).

Nonetheless, while these strategies help to improve our ability to identify, isolate, and ultimately assess a relationship, they often fail to resolve the 'many variables, small-n' problem. A fancier name for this problem that we will use in the study of statistics is **degrees of freedom**. Simply, we must avoid more potential explanations than observations in order to offer sufficient control. In order to eliminate rival explanations, we must have more observations than you have explanations otherwise you will not be able to separate effects.

The degrees-of-freedom problem can be seen in a simple example of studying simultaneous national voting. In Table 4.1, we can compare three studies on the turnout for executive and legislative elections in both Germany and the US to the combined executive and legislative elections in France.

Table 4.1 Studies on Electoral Turnout

	Electoral turnout		
Country	Executive	Legislative	Combined
German study	47%	51%	
US study	52%	44%	
French study			63%

In terms of simultaneous voting, we are tempted to conclude the higher turnout is achieved in combined elections. Or maybe it's just a French thing, such as its strong presidential system or Council of Ministers. Without sufficient observations, we are unable to unravel which conclusion is more correct. We lack the degrees of freedom – the ability to control for rival explanations and provide compelling evidence – to do so.

Case Studies and Small-n Studies: External Validity

The advantages of case and small-n comparisons are clear. Detailed knowledge and 'thick description' (Geertz, 1973) provide a robust and detailed narrative of the path of influence and relation between the variables of interest. Yet, at the same time, while often a compelling narrative, we remain unable to control for all the potentially relevant variables (i.e., alternative explanations/theories). This limits our ability to lend evidence to our own theory (and much less, causal relationships) and in turn substantially curtails the ability of generalizing from the results.

One might argue that this is a strength. Qualitative research is more concerned with interpretation, understanding, and deeper structures of meaning. Perhaps it is this focus that limits its overall appeal as an analytical approach (i.e., often greater content knowledge and regional expertise), although such elements of understanding may often complement, rather than compete, with quantitative explanations. Yet, in the context of the scientific method, the empirical qualitative approaches struggle to provide the internal and external validity we seek.

Experimental Approach

The experimental approach is composed of two essential forms, randomized (or controlled) experiments and quasi- or natural experiments. The former is an analytical design in which researcher has control over exposure of the independent variable in a highly controlled setting (often a literal laboratory). This allows for a systematic collection of data under different, if tightly controlled, conditions for randomly assigned treatment and control groups. If one needed further appeal beyond this level of control, experiments are the result of design rather than *post hoc* manipulation used in statistics and, given attention to the composition of control and treatment group assignment, experiments provide the type of evidence that underpins the highly prized identification of causal mechanisms.

In the latter, quasi- or natural experiments, the independent variable is imposed naturally on comparable groups ('as if' randomly assigned). These groups resemble control and treatment populated groups in much the same way as the Most Similar Design controls for competing explanations (recall: abcX → Y; abcx → y). In such cases, although the researcher does not control the introduction of the stimulus, the similarity creates naturally occurring control and treatment groups. Often, quasi- or natural experiments take the form of a division across cities, states, or nations.

The year 1993 offered two such opportunities: one was the 'Velvet Divorce' of the Czech Republic and Slovakia and the other was the institutional change from a majoritarian to multi-party system in New Zealand. The former allowed for a 'between-group' comparison of a nation state taking separate paths to post-Communist reform – hugely helpful for studies of culture and institutional change – while the latter 'within-group' comparison allowed for the testing of several theories of voting, party competition, and party politics under different contexts in the same country. In most cases of quasi-experiments, internal validity remains high and external validity – by exiting the laboratory – increases. Yet, however potentially potent these naturally occurring quasi-experiments might be, we must wait for them. And twiddling our thumbs is far from an ideal research design.

Experimental Approach: Internal Validity

The level of control achievable with experiments to identify, isolate, and assess relationships also eliminates the possibility of other explanations, thus providing the researcher with powerful evidence of a relationship. With such control, any observed change in the dependent variable can be associated with change in the independent variable. Therefore, the independent variable can be shown to cause a change in the dependent variable. The internal validity of experiments in which the independent variable can be shown to cause a change in the dependent variable makes experiments the gold standard.

There are challenges to the internal validity of experiments. Implementing the artificial environment of experiments can shape how subjects perform knowing that they are being observed (observation bias). Randomized assignment to treatment and control groups attenuates many of the issues related to probability but it does not resolve it completely. Experimental focus on mechanisms can be less relevant to capturing individuals' long-term habitual behaviours or long-term processes such as 'political socialization'. Finally, no matter the sophistication of the design, experimental approaches are not immune to the myriad other challenges to analysis in Political Science. For example, despite the degree of accuracy to which a relationship can be evaluated, if the variables are poorly conceptualized or poor indicators used (or worse still, both), we are not providing evidence of what we think we are.

Experimental Approach: External Validity

If, however, we prioritize on the generalizability of the results – the extent to which the relationship between the independent variable and dependent variable can be generalized to a larger population or a class of events – experiments move to last place. While experimental primacy among analytical approaches is based on their ability to confer causal power, they are woefully limited in offering much for making inferences. Data collection is often costly and experiments are no exception. Because of this, experiments can over-represent WEIRD respondents: **W**estern, **E**ducated, **I**ndustrialized, **R**ich, **D**emocratic societies. Thus, results can be limited in export. Experimental control is the suppressing of other influences, in a sense, turning down the 'noise' of real world. As such, control – as the heir apparent to bestowing causality – may at the same time undermine our ability to know when the relationship under investigation *doesn't* work (i.e., falsifiability). Experiments heavily favour investigating people. While countries – as one important unit of analysis in Political Science – can be subjected to quasi-experiments, as pointed out above, this reduces the desirable internal validity. Experiments are good at theory testing by identifying empirical (ir)regularities but, because of their limited external validity, less useful in theory generating. Again, innovative uses of experimental control embedded in other research approaches offer some counterbalance to these critiques but remain difficult to design, costly, and narrowly focused.

Quantitative Methods: Statistics

The appeal of statistics is (1) its resemblance to the scientific method, (2), ability to handle a great number of competing explanations simultaneously, (3) its impressive approximation of experimental control, and (4) its ability to confer confidence in inferential claims from the extant results. In terms of achieving the goals of the scientific method, statistics appears like a clear winner. However, the ability of statistics to provide these advantages is reliant on the quality and quantity of the data. That is, the data should be what we intend to examine, conceptually and operationally, and numerous enough to provide both sufficient variables to control for competing explanations as well as a meaningful, random, and representative sample of the population in which you are interested.

Statistics: Internal Validity

With sufficient data, statistical analysis allows us to make and test strong empirical claims and test competing theories. The nature of statistical work also rewards replication and transparency. That is to say, fairly consistent and stable estimates of the relationships in which we are interested – even with different datasets – confer substantial confidence in the results and are thus thought to reasonably approximate 'reality'.

Again, the ability to make such claims is based on the researcher's ability to include all plausible or theorized variables according to the literature. This is increasingly a difficult feat as many literatures have become quite complex and demanding in terms of what should be included in the analysis. At the same time, the results of statistical analysis are crucially dependent on the quality of data – and our ability to render that data useful as concepts and indicators – in order to distinguish the salient signal from the noise in a *post hoc* manipulation of the data. Further, inasmuch as variables included in the analysis proxy, approximate, or in other ways reduce the complexity or nuance of concepts, this casts greater suspicion on the confidence in our results. Finally, as we will discover in the rest of this book, statistics can be a powerful tool of description, inference, and control. We can still be tricked by the inevitabilities of probability and chance to pure coincidence in having discovered something that was not there (i.e., spuriousness).

Statistics: External Validity

Beyond all other approaches, the external validity of statistics – the ability to infer both descriptive and causal implications to cases outside of the analysis – is to be envied. This ability rests on the same foundational assumptions of internal validity, in particular, the quality, sufficiency, and precision of the data, but includes an explicit ability to generalize to the population from which the sample was drawn. However, the weakness of the external validity of statistics reflects the weakness of the internal validity of statistics. Inasmuch as we exclude or use poorly measured variables, external validity is undermined. In this book, we will confront other limitations as we progress through our study of statistics.

Despite these concerns, if we are interested in adhering to and achieving the rules and goals of the scientific method, statistics can be a strong choice of analytical approach. That is, while statistics is not always the best or most appropriate choice for our research design, it simultaneously delivers the desirable results of being able to identify, isolate, and assess a relationship in order to make inferential claims to explain a class of events.

Table 4.2 Empirical Approaches: Internal and External Validity

	Internal validity	External validity
Case/small-n studies	Medium	Low
Experiments	High	Low
Large-n quantitative studies	Medium/High	Medium/High

The goal here is not to persuade you that statistics is the best approach to study politics. It is not. It has its own advantages and disadvantages. The goal is to present a broad categorical summary of the most common **analytical approaches** in order to highlight their ability to satisfy our goals for the research we want to conduct.

RESEARCH DESIGN CHECKLIST

The first part of a Research Design should include what you are studying and why.

1. What is your research question?
2. How does this contribute to our knowledge?
3. What will you demonstrate?
4. What makes the subject important? [this is technically known as the 'So What?' question]

(Continued)

The second part is a **Theory Section**:

1. What theories are relevant and included?
2. Which theory are you using or proposing?
3. What are the dependent, key independent, and control variables?
4. Have you provided good hypotheses derived from the theory?
5. Under what conditions does your theory work and not work?

The third part is the **Literature Review**, which explains the landscape and distribution of evidence of the relevant theories from the previous section.

1. What is the current state of our knowledge?
2. What is settled or agreed upon? What is up for debate or still unknown? [theoretically or methodologically]
3. Where does your research fit? And how will it resolve a problem?

The fourth and final part is the **Methods Section**.

1. How will you answer the question(s) that you have posed?
2. What is your choice of analytical approach?
3. How will you conceptualize and operationalize the variables necessary to fully address your question?
4. What are the data you will use?
5. What results will allow you to eliminate rival explanations/support your theory?

Choice of Analytical Approach (Also) Shapes What We Will Find

At this point, you might notice that there are a great deal of subjective considerations in scientific study. This choice of approach just happens to be one of the big ones to which we sometimes give the least consideration. A premier example of this can be found in the study of social movements and resistance.

Summarized by McAdam et al. (2012), people become socially mobilized (primarily in advanced industrial societies) by an interaction of people, opportunity structures, and group-level mobilization. Political opportunity structures do not incite contentious action unless there exists some level of discontent. Discontent is not a sufficient impetus for action unless existing modes of formal and informal communication are deficient. Structural (or institutional) repression does not insure contentious action without clear disparity (or clearly perceived disparity) between groups.

In other words, it is not sufficient to be aggrieved to join a protest. While protest movements require that we are disgruntled, we must perceive some chance in the probability of success. This is contingent on the balance between challengers and authority – through a fissure in elites' alignments, breakdowns or regime changes, or the state's capacity for repression – aligning with groups which are able to utilize these opportunities to exploit these moments via their organizational nature to coordinate, sustain, and give meaning to grievance and resource mobilization. This understanding of individual participation in protest movements derives from both qualitative and quantitative empirical studies conducted over a span of many years in several countries.

James Scott (1990) took another approach to understanding protest and resistance. He argues that culture informs social movements as carriers of meaning and makers of meaning. Specifically, overlooked by quantitative analysis, discourses and practices of class conflict take the form of 'everyday peasant resistance' in which the poor and the well-to-do abide by different norms and rules. In this framework, visible contests are called 'public transcripts' and the unseen forms and multitudes of resistance are called, 'hidden transcripts'. These 'arts of resistance' are the 'infrapolitics' of the oppressed, frustrated by a lack of reciprocal action. Thus, assessing public demonstrations, strikes, and boycotts does not provide a complete picture of the relationship between dominators and their subjects. They are not indicative of the nature and extent of that system of domination. It is the infrapolitics of private (non-authority) networks that serve as an undetected, and potentially powerful, source of resistance (see also Scott, 1985).

McAdam's and Scott's research projects are not aimed at precisely the same thing. Scott's approach required a great deal more involvement and nuance, with results that reflect that choice. McAdam's summary of the empirical work belies a distance, eyes set on the horizon, approach. Both approaches offer useable and important results, *but the results are different*, reflecting to some extent the difference in approach.

Perhaps, more generally, there is no perfect research design. Thus, careful consideration must be given to the choice of approach so that you are testing and finding what you intend to test and find. The best we can do is survey the applicable approaches, evaluate the limitations, make a choice, anticipate and contend with threats to validity, identify limitations and what you can reasonably do to address them, and move forward.

New Methods?

Newer approaches have started to merge the internal and external validity capabilities of different approaches in order to strengthen standalone traditional approaches. One means is mixed method analysis in which different approaches are used to complement or improve on the shortcomings of the other approach. For example, one might use statistics to analyse cross-national survey data on climate-change perceptions. The findings might be supportive of a particular theory but lack sufficient observations (e.g., cross-temporally) to make a convincing causal conclusion. One could add an experiment that tests the implied mechanism identified in the surveys. While not conclusive, it can provide some evidence that the proposed causal relationship does perform consistently under different analytic procedures.

Alternatively, more innovative approaches have sought to integrate rather than merely combine different approaches in an attempt to coax the advantages of both approaches simultaneously. It will not surprise you to discover that the most common attempt is to embed the internal validity of experiments in other approaches such as randomized field experiments and survey experiments. These approaches, depending on your perspective, increase the external validity of the embedded experiments or increase the internal validity of the other approach.

Remaining Issues

Our research design must not only play offense – asking a good question, reviewing the state of the field, stating the goals and expectations, and laying out the plan of analysis – but also defence. As no research design is perfect, there will be problems. Identifying these explicitly demonstrates your expertise not your shortcomings.

Therefore, a research design forces us to contend with the questions of:

- Establishing, to some extent, cause and effect in the empirical relationships
- Eliminating plausible and rival explanations
- Deriving conclusions from the analysis of data
- Answering the questions we have posed.

But, perhaps, our research should offer something that others want to know. Guiding our choices can also be our own sense of what is important to know, as an individual but also in a larger collective sense. We are driven by a sense of fullness or completeness for its own sake. Yet, what is the larger relevance of your efforts? What will others learn from the results of our research? Is this valuable to know? Are we addressing the important concerns of others in the field?

And just as importantly, where do your potential research strengths lie? Different methods may be chosen for different reasons, regional expertise, cultural or linguistic skills, normative concern. Perhaps you feel a propensity toward one approach over another. These are not trifling matters. What we know about what we want to find, the manner in which to find out, and our own strengths and interests, can create a powerful synergy of knowledge, intuition, and skills. And it is the research design in which our subjectivity finds the most – and most important – input. The use and utility of a research design is to recognize and improve the questions that we ask as well as what constitutes evidence in answering our question.

This is doing science.

End of Chapter Summary

- A research design is a step-by-step plan for a research project.
- A research question defines the contours of the research inquiry.
- A literature review reveals the landscape of the existing work on your topic. Done well, it will lead your reader to the obviousness and importance of your research

question by highlighting gaps in our existing knowledge that your project looks to fill.
- Data collection is the systematic gathering of information on our variables of interest.
- The units of analysis are the subject of your study.
- We must strive to maintain consistency between a theory/hypothesis and the data.
- The advantages and disadvantages of research methods can be compared in many ways, but it mostly depends on what you want to find and how you want to find out.

Glossary

- An **analytical approach** is the empirical means – each with their own methods – through which you will try to answer your question. Examples include document analysis, case studies, statistics.
- **Methods** are the tools of the analytical approach to conduct data collection and analysis.
- **Methodology** is our broader philosophy of science beliefs, around what is it we want to know, and what's the best source of knowledge
- A **research design** draws together the key elements of the scientific method – theory, hypotheses, defining and identifying variables, and gathering data – to develop a step-by-step plan for finding the best results for a research project. A **research question** identifies what we are going to investigate.
- A **literature review** provides readers a survey of the current research and how it is related to your research project.
- **Data collection** is the systematic gathering of information on our variables of interest that allows us to answer our research questions by testing the hypotheses derived from relevant theories and determining the outcomes.
- **Internal validity** is the extent to which the independent variable can be shown to cause a change in the dependent variable of the given case/relationship under investigation.
- **External validity** is the extent to which the relationship between the independent variable and dependent variable can be generalized to a larger population or a class of events.
- **Levels of analysis** (in Political Science) includes three basic levels: Micro- (individuals), Macro- (nations or groups of nations), and Meso- (whatever falls between such as regions, cities, neighbourhoods, *inter alia*).
- **Degrees of freedom:** We must have more observations than explanations.
- **Units of analysis** are the subject of your study.
- The **ecological fallacy** is the attempt to draw individual-level conclusions from aggregate-level data.

Questions

1. What are the key differences in what we expect to learn from a case study of Benin's political institutional evolution and a seven-country, cross-national study of sub-Saharan west Africa's political institutions?
2. Does the number of observations matter? If so, how and why? Use 'degrees of freedom' in your answer.
3. Statistics, as a single approach, seems to have the best balance between internal and external validity. Why don't we use them all the time to study political phenomena?
4. Recent critics of quantitative methods have pointed out that the increasing sophistication of statistics over the past two or three decades has led to more research with less long-term value to Political Science. Is this just sour grapes or is there a meaningful criticism here?
5. 'The differences between quantitative and qualitative traditions are methodologically and substantively unimportant. All good research can be understood to derive from the same underlying logic of inference. Both quantitative and qualitative research can be systematic and scientific.' Do you agree with this statement? Why?
6. The internal validity and external validity of analytical approaches resemble Principles 2 and 3 of scientific study. Is this a coincidence? If not, why not?

Annotated References and Further Reading

Bates, Robert H. 1997. 'Area studies and the discipline: A useful controversy' ***Political Science and Politics*** **30(2): 166–169.**

Area-specific knowledge was once the domain of groups of experts of particular regions and countries. Once revered (particularly in Comparative Politics), regional or area experts have been sidelined by the increasing sophistication of statistical methods to incorporate country and regional context.

Box-Steffensmeier, Janet M., Henry E. Brady, and David Collier. 2008. 'Political science methodology' in Robert E. Goodin (ed.) ***The Oxford Handbook of Political Science.*** **Oxford: Oxford University Press, pp: 3–31.**

This is a comprehensive chapter that describes in greater detail the core techniques, challenges, and opportunities for the scientific study of political phenomena.

Morton, Rebecca B. and Kenneth C. Williams. 2010. ***Experimental Political Science and the Study of Causality.*** **Cambridge: Cambridge University Press.**

This is the premier book on the use of experimental approaches in Political Science. Although a demanding and sometimes intimidating read, Morton and Williams explain why experiments sit at the throne of causality but also still struggle.

Signposts to Research and Empirical Examples

Geertz, Clifford. 1973. *Thick Description: Towards an Interpretive Theory of Culture in The Interpretation of Cultures*. New York: Basic Books. Chapter 1.

Lijphart, Arend. 1971. 'Comparative politics and the comparative method' *American Political Science Review* 65: 682–693.

McAdam, Doug, Sidney Tarrow, Charles Tilly. 2012. 'Comparative Perspectives on Contentious Politics' in M.I. Lichbach and A.S. Zuckerman (eds) *Comparative Politics*. Cambridge: Cambridge University Press. 2nd edn. pp. 260–290.

Przeworski, Adam and Henry Teune. 1970. *The Logic of Comparative Social Inquiry*. New York: Wiley.

Ross, Marc Howard and Elizabeth Homer. 1976. 'Galton's problem in cross-national research' *World Politics* 29(1): 1–28. https://doi.org/10.2307/2010045

Scott, James. 1985. *Weapons of the Weak: Everyday Forms of Peasant Resistance*. New Haven and London: Yale University Press.

Scott, James. 1990. *Domination and the Arts of Resistance: Hidden Transcripts*. New Haven and London: Yale University Press.

5
STATISTICS AND THE SCIENTIFIC STUDY OF POLITICS

> **LEARNING OUTCOMES**
>
> In this chapter, you will be able to
>
> - Critically evaluate the use of statistics to study of Political Science.
> - Identify key elements of the Scientific Method in the study of political phenomena.
> - Engage the current debates within Political Science over the use of statistics.
> - Identify problems with the use of statistics in Political Science.

Introduction

Ernest Rutherford, the father of nuclear physics, once famously quipped, 'All science is either physics…or stamp collecting.' Perhaps Ernest needs to have a juice box and to cool his jets. In the first chapter, we asked, what makes scientific research scientific? In the previous chapters, we broke the process down into its constituent parts. In this chapter, we ask, how does the scientific method help us answer our questions in Political Science?

The Use and Importance of a Scientific Approach in Political Science

Politics is Worth Knowing About

We know that specific methods of the scientific approach are discipline-dependent. What we have also seen from previous chapters is that while our analytical approach – from statistics to case studies – can vary widely based on what we are trying to examine, the answers we seek, data availability, units of analysis, the quest for generalization, *yadda yadda yadda*, it is in fact our research question, our choice of theory, our skilful derivation of hypotheses, and our careful attention to the definition and measure of our variables that align our study of Political Science with the scientific method. A conscientious Political Scientist is constantly pushing all elements of her research toward these ideals.

But the question remains, why? Is the scientific method, the appeal to science, appropriate for the study of political phenomena? Yes. As a famous English Political Scientist, who shall remain nameless, once remarked to me in a noisy pub, 'Prediction and polls are for plonkers.' In other words, guessing election outcomes and sticking our fingers in the air with polls are small game. We want to be in the big hunt alongside the big hunters. It is not a question of can, it is a question of should.

Ok, then, should we study politics scientifically?

Absolutely. We want to have something to say about a class of events, to develop the cumulative theoretical knowledge of a wide range of political phenomena, to demonstrate scientific ability not through the wanton use of sophisticated analytical techniques but rather by having something to show for having done so. Put more confrontationally, among the alternatives, the scientific method is the best means to achieve worthwhile goals in Political Science: analytical comparability and consistency as well as the ability to make cumulative progress in our understanding of political phenomena. Thus, with broad adherence to the scientific method, Political Scientists seek and create probabilistic, general knowledge about political and social phenomena.

Perhaps more importantly to the question of why to study politics scientifically is that politics is worth knowing about. Politics is – like many of the social sciences – provocative: it is hot button issues, it is about choices at the individual level but also at the national level, and political outcomes can have serious consequences, it is unavoidable. International Relations is the study of, among many things, migration, war, and poverty. Political behaviour includes a wide array of attitudes and behaviours including voting for extreme parties, demonstrations, support for democracy, political sophistication, and tolerance. Other comparativists look at party competition, polarization, and coalition breakdown.

Consider these research questions:

- Why do citizens seem to be trusting their own governments less and less?
- Are the post-war institutions of democracy in the West failing?
- How does income inequality make voters more politically active?
- Why are there so many new parties – left and right?
- Why do political party systems seem to be polarizing?
- Why are there more 'less deadly conflicts' and fewer 'more deadly conflicts'?
- To what extent is international power shifting from multi-polarity to uni-polarity?
- What are the alternatives to popular democracy?
- Why do we see a rise in entrepreneurial elites?
- Can political culture provide partial explanation for the relative success in the fight against Covid-19?
- Will there be a fourth wave of democracy?
- What would happen to presidential and congressional elections in the US if it replaced its majoritarian electoral system with proportional representation?
- Can supra-national human rights legislation and action increase the protection of human rights?

None of these can be viewed insensitively. Clearly, applying the scientific method to the study of political phenomena is not a small task but it is achievable and necessary. The Scientific Method relies upon abstraction, specifically theories as models and the processes of conceptualization and operationalization. We can think of this as the difference between a reasonably detailed map and the actual landscape. There is no substitute for reality. However, in order to link our understanding of this area to the understanding of other areas, we use a common if simplified language of topographical and cadastral mapping, as well as planimetric and hydrogeological features. While not complete, a good map conveys the essential elements to assist your passage across the landscape.

Thus, a scientific approach to the study of politics is a natural extension of the scientific approach to understanding the world. It grows by the repeated overthrow of theories with the help of evidence in an attempt to decode the (political) world by seeking to make inferences on the basis of empirical information and probabilistic regularities about the world.

We seek to explain observed political phenomena so as to build toward the ability to generalize from those explanations and in turn predict outcomes outside of our direct observation (i.e., outside our sample or in the future). As discussed in the first chapter, the scientific study of politics shares the same goals as the hard scientist. We need a system to collect data, a means to formally evaluate the evidence against competing explanations, a manner of maximizing inferential conclusions, and a clear application of our findings to improve our collective theoretical knowledge.

> The '…object of political science…is the creation of knowledge, defined as inferences or generalizations about politics drawn from evidence.' – G. Almond (1996: 52)

Objectivity in the Use of the Scientific Method in Political Science

One of the distinguishing characteristics of scientific knowledge is its appeal to objectivity. Remember, objectivity and subjectivity are not the same as normative and non-normative. Objectivity is trying to remove our biases and preferences (i.e., our subjectivity) from our research. We all have biases and preferences. I mean, it's weird but, admit it, you have a favourite burner on the stove (read: you bias it). As such, biases are normal and natural. They are an evolutionary strategy that allows us to organize information and use shortcuts rather than having to store enormous amounts of discrete content. While such biases might improve our evolutionary propensity to survive, biases can be a problem for (social) scientists.

Setting aside the obvious question of whether social scientists are fit to evolve, in the case of Political Science, recall the pilot metaphor (yes, again). The subjectivity of the formal scientific method is akin to a pilot flying a plane. In addition to the rules that exist for all varieties of reasons, individual pilots make constant, crucial adjustments and decisions that shape the quality of the journey.

Objectivity is a challenge to Political Science. Politics is inherently value-laden. Political phenomena often represent an event *and* its significance. This is made apparent to anyone who mentions that they are studying Political Science. Politics is *loaded*. How neutrally can we investigate inequality, war, poverty, polarization, class, corruption, ethnic conflict, gender disparity? These are not simply academically nuanced, contestably defined concepts. As both scientists and citizens, we are well aware of the strong centrifugal pull of the visceral nature of politics: the intensity, apathy, passion, enthusiasm, disdain, unexpectedness, division, joy, and madness of politics. Not only are there few political events without broader significance, they represent fiercely competing visions of what constitutes a 'better' or 'worse' way of doing things.

Because of this, a primary motivation for adhering to the scientific method is that, in the scientific community, *no one cares what we think, feel, or believe; others only care what we can demonstrate*. Researchers therefore (must) embrace objectivity and a readiness to replace ideas with better performing ones. They (must) recognize that, as possible explanations for the phenomena in which we are interested, a given theory's strength is measured by its empirical utility. Any means to improve the reliability, validity, certainty, and honesty of our conclusions is to our collective and individual benefit. This is supported by the growing attention to the transmissibility and replicability of Political Science work – in the form of replication datasets and intricately detailed description of the methodology – which is key to finding the most objective approaches and best measures possible.

To be objective in Political Science is to apply a ruler to an individual's trust in government, a thermometer to the assessment of democratic institutional performance, a scale to national budget allocations. Each of these has a moral, ethical, or (at least a) philosophical facet that goes beyond 'some trust', 'very good', and 32.5%. In other words, Political Scientists can talk of the 'fact' of the level of national-level income inequality but must choose to ignore citizens' perception that income inequality is too high; they can talk of election outcomes but must be silent on who should win (given what they know about the resultant politics); or they can debate the criteria for full-scale conflict to require a minimum of 1000 killed but not whisper under their breath, 'So glad that's not me.'

The challenge of objectivity remains.

The Use and Importance of a Theoretical Approach in Political Science

The reasonable regularities of political phenomena make Political Science an excellent location for deductive theory testing. Elections happen, parties compete for votes, protests take place, countries vie for diplomatic supremacy, conflicts break out, voting turnout increases or decreases, etc.... With such minimally disruptive ebb and flow of events, we are able to develop, test, improve, and discard theories seeking to explain all of these events.

At the same time politics is at the heart of the unexpected. An assassination, a plane crash, an explosion, a calamity, unexpected violence, an election upset, a pandemic, or a natural disaster. Each create the potential for politics to respond or not. When does our collective knowledge work, and when does it fail?

The use of theory as a tool of the scientific method is predicated on the notion that the world can be de-coded to some extent. The things and topics that Political Scientists like to study are messy. While both classic experiments such as subjects in a laboratory – and their newer versions, randomized field experiments, embedded survey experiments – offer clean lines and enviable results, a great deal of what Political Scientists aim to study simply cannot be subjected to the controls needed to make confident causal claims. Whether we study democratization, policy effectiveness, regime change, conflict, political participation, or political attitudes, we are confronted by a landscape of both uncertainty and contestability. Simply, many phenomena have potentially many correct answers.

And we're fine with that.

The Use and Importance of a Research Design in Political Science

Taking the time and effort to think about, investigate, and create a means to assess a relationship in which we are interested, signals to others that we are serious. The research design indicates the variables we are interested in, how they should be related, and what this means (Chapter 4). In doing so, we demonstrate our informed or even expert choices, in turn providing a transparent, replicable plan of research action grounded in the basics of the scientific method. The research method includes the theories which create expectations for relationships, hypotheses which animate these relationships with measurable indicators, and provides preliminary expectations about how the results will support (or not) the theory (Chapter 2). Such designs are not unique to Political Science and reflect the broader and common process of setting up a research project.

This leaves us with how we treat the data. That is, in the context of this book, statistical analysis is how we change data into evidence. Data quality, and specifically the process of conceptualization and operationalization (Chapter 3), are crucial steps necessary for statistics to perform. How observations become codified for mathematical analysis is not unique to Political Science but is the problem for the scientific – and particularly, statistical – study of Political Science. We take this up in the section below.

The Use and Importance of Statistics in Political Science

Developing our cumulative knowledge is a collective project. What we know about political phenomena is the result of a quilt of knowledge derived from many different approaches, of which statistics is a popular and widespread one. We can exploit elements of statistical analysis to adhere very closely to the core tenets of the scientific method (e.g., design, conceptualization, operationalization, the choice of technique, etc....). Thus, outside of a laboratory, statistics, used correctly, can provide the ability to make strong scientific claims.

The appeal of statistics is (1) its resemblance to the scientific method, (2) its ability to handle a great number of competing explanations simultaneously, (3) its impressive approximation of experimental control, and (4) its ability to confer confidence in inferential claims from the extant results. The study of political phenomena is a dynamic, value-filled world, and the ability to harness statistics' powers of description, inference, and control is hard to resist. Despite the sometimes intimidating language of statistics, its popularity in Political Science is underpinned by its wide acceptance in the discipline, abundant availability (and often requirement) of training, ease of teaching (compared to often laborious interpretivist or qualitative methods), and the patina of scientific legitimacy.

Problems for the Use of Statistics in Political Science

The study of politics is a scientific endeavour which is fruitfully oriented to the use of statistics in many ways. Nonetheless, the challenge of using statistics in Political Science is also real. As the previous chapters have set out, the most significant limitations to using statistics to analyse political phenomena starts before we actually do statistics.

Definitions and Measurement

The two most crucial steps for statistics to provide the best results are the processes of conceptualization and operationalization. As discussed above in Chapter 3, how we define what we want to investigate and what we use to assess that concept will affect everything that comes after it, the analysis, the results, the conclusions, and the inferences. No amount of methodological sophistication is able to overcome significant conceptual or operational issues common to Political Science. And if our goal is to demonstrate a causal relationship between two variables, we need to have an extraordinary level of confidence in our indicators. They should be definitionally what we want to measure and are measured accurately with little known or unknown error (note, this isn't the 'garbage in, garbage out' argument). Instead, it is not a provocation to say that Political Science deals with phenomena that tenaciously resist clear conceptualization and operationalization. And there is little that statistical analysis can do to mitigate the effects of a poorly thought-out variable or a poorly measured one.

Conceptual Congruence

Finding the right definition for what we want to examine can be a difficult task. This is made harder in Political Science as we often want to compare concepts across contexts differentiated not only by political institutions or economic systems but also political cultures and societies. How universal is our concept for comparison across our units of analysis? This is called conceptual congruence.

Conceptual congruence takes conceptualization and operationalization on vacation. In statistical studies that very often include an aggregate of groups, whether groups of voters, groups of citizens, or groups of countries, is what we want to measure and how we are measuring it consistent across all groups? How universal is our concept under investigation? Can we assume that what we are measuring has some level of cross-unit consistency? If not, we may be given results that fail to provide a clear picture of the nature of what you are studying.

A good example of conceptual congruence is political participation. Many studies on political participation use four questions from the World Values Survey (or for a regional example, the European Values Study) to construct a variable of non-traditional political participation. The surveys ask respondents to report whether they have actually done any of these things, whether you might do it or would never, under any circumstances, do it. The four activities are signing a petition, attending lawful demonstrations, joining in boycotts, and joining strikes. This seems simple enough.

Yet, joining strikes is deeply culturally driven and very often distinct. In the UK, some strikes call for 'working to contract' or 'work-to-rule' strikes. This is similar – although only similar – to the Italian 'white strike' ('sciopero bianco'). In both, workers do no more than what they are contractually obliged (although UK workers are often forced to make up this work). It is meant to show how much of their job, the quality of their job, is related to the 'extra' they put in by enjoying the work, their colleagues, or other elements of their workplace. By contract, this concept – along with striking in general – does not exist or is not widespread in the US. One might argue that striking at all is so uncommon as to attract national attention versus the commonplace British and Italian strikes.

I remind you of Galton's problem – from the previous chapter – as a similar challenge to conceptual congruence.

Is Political Science Too Quantitative?

This raises a larger issue of using statistics in Political Science, namely the core concern that quantification – or 'over-quantification' – obscures our understanding. There are debates in Political Science that the expansive use of statistics has introduced a 'mathematization' of the study of politics. That is, rather than going through the process of considering the elements of our research questions, conceptualization and operationalization, and weighing different approaches' advantages and disadvantages, too many Political Scientists enter into research with only a hammer.

> ### ПЕРЕСТРОЙКА
>
> This is not a small issue. In 2002, an anonymous email was sent to the editors of the leading Political Science journal the *American Political Science Review*. It lamented the ascent (and perceived hegemony) of quantitative methods in Political Science (by crowding out other methods, particularly in publication). This became known, given the timing, as the *Perestroika Movement*.

This was (and continues to be) a shared concern across all social sciences. It is not a surprise that economists were fast adopters and continue to be strong adherents and developers of statistical analysis. Many of the topics in Economics lend themselves easily to quantification: money, rates, taxes, finance, institutions, *inter alia*. For Political Science, like other Social Science disciplines, this is trickier. There are a number of topics that quantify easily: number of votes, budget spending, seat share, etc....but like other social sciences such as close friends Sociology and Psychology, we also have a large number of important things that don't 'quantify' well. That is, as we move away from aggregate analyses of relatively uncontroversial measures of national economic and political performance (*note*: relatively), we descend toward the messier but also more interesting political behaviours (and opinions, values, and attitudes); parties' strategies, ideological positions, and issue saliences, as well as intra-national diplomacy, negotiating, and positioning – to mention only some of the most common examples.

If you read the Introduction, this is a twist on the example of describing someone you know. If you didn't read, not a problem, just think about someone you kind of know. How would you assess the following attributes: gender, age, income, vote in the last parliamentary election, political participation, trust in government, or ideology? Or let me ask it a bit more precisely, how would you *quantify* the attributes of your friend: gender, age, income, vote in the last parliamentary election, political participation, trust in government, or ideology? It is the shift from assessment to quantification that makes the difference appreciable. We want to quantify these things so that we can do statistics on them. We do so in order to summarize, get results that we have confidence in, make inferences with them, and develop theory. Yet, the distance between what we want to measure and what we can meaningful quantify is not simply an inconvenience. It is the primary challenge to the scientific approach, using statistics, and for many in Political Science.

Such problems are not limited to the study of individuals' attitudes or values or concepts such as political culture. In 1990, the United Nations Development Programme (UNDP) embraced a new type of measurement for 'human development'. While the previous indicator, *Gross National Product* per capita, may have represented a reasonable proxy for several dimensions of human welfare, the UNDP wanted to measure development in a means that captured 'the process of enlarging people's choices' (Sen, 1995). So, the UNDP started including adult literacy and combined enrolment ratios, life expectancy at birth, and an adjusted GNP. They argued that these were essential for people to lead a long and healthy life, to acquire knowledge and have access to resources for a decent standard of living. This change to the conceptualization and operationalization of human development has non-trivial impacts on not only how we think about human development but also where assistance is assigned.

EMPIRICISM

Forcing the world to conform to mathematics has its attractions. We have heard – and probably even repeated – some version of 'the language of nature is mathematics' in reference

> to some example from astronomy or biology. Yet, keep in mind, imaginary numbers [$i = \sqrt{-1}$] now serve as the most accurate way to connect mathematics to how we understand the universe to function. But these numbers do not exist, they are imaginary. So, we have had to disconnect mathematics from reality in order to better understand that same reality. Thus, while the precision and formality of mathematics impose a deeply desired order, it may, at the same time, misrepresent what it is we seek to understand in the manner in which it is meant to be understood. Or at least as far as we can understand reality.

Quality of Data

These challenges are amplified by another regular problem in Political Science, namely, the availability of quality data (this is the GIGO argument, btw). As an analytical method, statistics are used to find patterns. This is particularly useful when we have a large amount of data. However – and here is the second tripwire – the quality and sufficiency of data also shape the results in unintended and even unobservable ways. Even well conceptualized and operationalized variables cannot counteract poor quality of data or a lack of them.

Recall, data are not your concept. However, well conceptualized and operationalized variables drawn from quality data allow statistics to convert these data into information. This does not replace or supplant the necessity to ask better questions or to think *critically* or *creatively* about a problem. However, statistics can prod us to *better thinking* about the topic by leading toward better questions *via* better conceptualization and better measures. A great deal of effort must be given to considering the origin, collection, assembly, sufficiency, and reliability of data.

Thus, questions of definitions and measurement, conceptual congruence, and quantification refer to the elements necessary to perform statistical analysis. These challenges are about transforming important ideas, attitudes, notions, concepts, tendencies, perceptions, dimensions, facets, and other things of interest that have difficult conceptual shapes or elude easy definition into conveniently manageable data. This underscores the necessary relationship between statistics as a tool and the scientific method as means to understand political phenomena.

Causation, Statistics, and Political Science

Causality has taken on new life as a debate in Political Science as statistics have been increasingly argued to square the circle of providing sufficient evidence of causal relationships. On one hand, there are those who subscribe to the traditional scientific approach – causation is part of theory that is supported (or not) by empirical testing. On the other hand, others have increasingly embraced what they see as the ability of the newest techniques in statistics to measure directly the causal relationship in the theory. So, what's the problem?

> **SQUARE THE CIRCLE**
>
> Colloquially this means to do something seemingly impossible. This phrase refers to the difficulty of constructing a square with the same area as a circle using straightforward (read: Euclidean) steps. Mathematically, this was proven impossible as pi (π) was identified as a transcendental number (i.e., neither rational nor irrational).

In the latter half of the 20th century, the widespread application of the scientific method to the study of the social sciences began. The use of theory meant that it was helpful to *think* causally and to develop models that have causal implications, even if only indirectly testable. Theories were to tell us why something 'had to happen'. And, for the most part, causal thinking belonged completely on the theoretical level and supported through rigorous and repeated empirical testing. This is what underpins the notion that theories are weak or strong based on the evidence that they are able to accumulate.

This wasn't some form of academic subterfuge in which researchers developed theories, tested them, and presented to their colleagues saying, 'Oh, look what I've again found, more empirical support for my theory. I guess "X" really does cause "Y" although, of course [*nudge, nudge, wink, wink*], I only mean that theoretically.' Systematically in Political Science, there was a taught and practiced reporting of results that was not only more cautious and hesitant to make such explicit causal claims but also made an effort to list the potential limitations to the data, the method, and any other elements in one's research (of which there are many) that might weaken any serious causal claim about X and Y. Simply, it is understood that rigorous scientific study provides the 'if', theory provides the 'why'. Thus, causality is a theoretical construct and nothing more.

However, more recently, the exponential growth in – and individual access to – computing power has upset the notion that causality is a working assumption of the scientist. That is, treating causation as a part of theory that can be supported (or not) by empirical testing has started to give way to, what some argue is, a direct empirical test of causality. In some disciplines, the causal assumption became seen as a verifiable statement about reality. This methodological leap is exploiting the analytical advantages of different methods such as experimentation, advanced statistical techniques, and innovative research designs. Such increasingly analytical sophistication is a positive development as it improves our abilities to provide more robust results. However, the increased robustness of results challenges the border between where we talk about a causal relationship (theory) and where we actually measure a causal relationship (methods). Simply, some Social Scientists have been increasingly eager to merge these and claim an explicit causal mechanism.

> Believe those who are seeking the Truth.
> Doubt those who find it. – A. Gide (1959: 146)

There are undoubtedly several explanations why causality has become increasingly important in the social sciences and in Political Science in particular. Possibly some felt that the work in their field was vitally important as a means to understand the world with an eye toward improving it (e.g., policy implications). Maybe it was an inevitable outcome to the massive jump in computational capabilities (of both man and machine) converging with a substantial and widespread new availability of data. Some of the attractiveness of presenting causal solutions is offering precise amounts by which the dependent variable will be 'caused by' the independent variable, e.g., for every dollar spent, 16 children will return to school. To non-experts, that attracts attention (spelled: f-u-n-d-i-n-g). To some, perhaps, there seemed to be the possibility of being able claim to have *proved* theories rather than merely test them and thus grow in stature as a discipline (sometimes called 'physics envy'). In any case, causality seems poised to become the true Holy Grail – the understanding the mechanics of the world – versus the false idols of mere inference or quisling prediction.

The use of statistics to 'prove' causal relations rather than provide strong empirical evidence for the causal implications in a theory is still new but expanding rapidly. You may be increasingly seeing this discussion in other courses. Forged in the crucible of the traditional *hypothetico-deductive* scientific approach, many remain comfortable with the position that some explanations are simply more probable than others. That is, if there is to be any search for certainty, we tighten our orbit of the planet of small-t truth by allowing rigorous testing to reveal which theories are *more* 'more likely'. This is an agnostic position about the ability of methodological or analytical techniques to render a causal certainty.

There are a number of issues related to causality and its growing popularity and influence in Political Science, particularly with the use of statistics. We look at a few key debates.

Causation and the Problem of Measurement

One limitation on the focus of a methodological solution to causation is that it focuses on the relationship, the validity of the causation, and ignores the issue that in Political Science, both the X and Y often struggle with substantial conceptual and operational issues. In other words, even if we were able to demonstrate that causation is certain, what is being linked is less certain. And thus, causation as well. Put differently, the debate in Political Science about definitions and measurement of independent and dependent key variables undermines the nature of the linkage between them, i.e., the ability to make causal inferences. In other words, if the definitions and ways to measure our variables are so contentious, it's a challenge to demonstrate universally causality.

Recall our research on inequality and democracy. We have seen a number of indicators for democracy (Chapter 3) and there are almost as many for inequality. Assuming we are talking about national-level income inequality, we would need to decide whether we were primarily interested in the internationally comparable distribution of income by country (Gini), the willingness by individuals to accept smaller incomes in exchange for a more equal distribution decomposable by sub-national groups (Atkinson), or one that has some features of each (Theil) – not to mention other General Entropy measures.

We already know that we are constrained by the availability of data, so why is this important for causality? It is possible to argue that we never actually assess the relationship between inequality and democracy. We can only summarize the relationship between our measure of inequality – e.g., the Gini Index, the Theil, the Atkinson, or some ratio – and our measure of democracy – e.g., the World Governance Indicators (World Bank), Freedom House, or Polity IV measures. These measures have a lot to do with inequality and democracy, respectively, but they are not *in fact* inequality and democracy. As such, any relationship we identify between these measures cannot be said to causally connect inequality and democracy as we are don't actually measure inequality and democracy.

And we cannot ever do so.

In order to determine whether our correlation is causation, while correlation is a necessary but not sufficient condition, we need more evidence. Determining a causal relationship is not the function of a statistical test but rather the coordinated methodology of science: theoretical reasoning, testing, and accumulation of support. Statistics is a mathematical procedure ignorant of the content of the numbers subjected to manipulation. Given that theory must be *a priori* plausible, it acts as a threshold for statistical results, not the other way around.

Universal Causal Mechanisms

Causal mechanisms have a problem with inference. If we can identify causal mechanisms, how far can causal findings extend? What are their limits in time and space? In other words, the desire to infer causal relationships ends where exactly? How universal is causality?

A clear example of this is the early studies of post-communist media systems. As media experts tried to make sense of the wild west of media reform in the former Soviet satellite states of Eastern Europe, many struggled to publish their findings. There was substantial resistance in the field of Political Communication even though the basic assumptions and conditions under which modern theories of media effects had little congruency with the rapid and contentious privatization of former state media apparatuses, revision of media laws, and redesign of media regulations. The process of media democratization did not reflect the warm tidal influx of expanding broadcast and print media in the US and Western Europe in the 1940s, 1950s, and 1960s in which those citizens embraced the wide and easy acculturation of mass media. That is, there were many who argued that the theories generated from inquires on Western/American responses to Western/American media about Western/American political concerns in a Western/American political setting were expected to have no trouble mapping easily onto the massive process of democratization in which states, institutions, and citizens undergoing tectonic shifts unlike any since the end of the second World War. The theories – and their causal implications – were proven, and unimpeachable.

Those that claim to have identified causal relationships must also contend with external validity. Not merely reporting accuracies and deriving appropriate inferences but the temporality of the discovery. Is this now a law on par with Newtonian laws, i.e., it is universal? Have we solved the problem? Or do we need to revisit it? When? What are the generalizable ends of its causal power (more technically, how will we identify when the (true) data-generating process changes? Without this, how can we use the causal mechanism without knowing where it can and can't be used? The onus is on those who claim causality to define the extent and limits of their claims in a reasonable and unbiased manner.

Causation as a Limit on Discovery

It is not sufficient to merely have a high degree of confidence in our findings, causation requires certainty. In Political Science, while we can have greater confidence in some – albeit, fewer – findings, a criteria of causal-only research forces us to ignore culture, big stuff, slow stuff, hard to measure stuff, the messy stuff. Political Science stuff. Causality is useful for observable mechanisms but less good with latent or gradual changes such as learning or socialization. Or bigger processes like culture and society. A narrow focus on causation encourages us to overlook 'messier' topics and potentially miss processes that are fundamental to Political Science. That is, the search for The Arrow of Causality may in fact obscure a greater understanding of 'how things work'.

The difficulty of prioritizing on causality is that identifying a relationship as casual isn't *necessarily* 'more informative' at the cost of learning something else. A myopic focus on producing a 'causal result' can miss the forest for the trees. That is, not all important processes in Political Science are the identifiable relationships between variables. As mentioned above, some of most significant contributions in the study of political culture are woefully lacking in precision, yet are both well-known and influential even outside of the narrow world of academia. Two examples include Ronald Inglehart's materialism and post-materialism and Robert Putnam's social capital.

Ronald Inglehart argued that economic modernization, political institutions, and individuals' values move together in a coherent and – to some extent – predictable pattern (1997). He asserted that economic modernization shifted what people want out of life, what they valued, in turn transforming the basic norms of government, work, religion, family, and sexual behaviour. These are not mere consequences of economic or social changes but shape the socio-economic conditions and are shaped by them in reciprocal fashion. This line of research did little to resolve the causal chicken-or-egg problem of which comes first, whether culture reinforces institutions or institutions reinforce culture. But this work has advanced our understanding of patterns of institutional and political culture change, speaking directly to wide swaths of research on political behaviour, democratization, and modernization.

Robert Putnam inserted the words 'social capital' into conversations of most Social Scientists and every civil servant, NGO employee, and citizen of DC, London, and Brussels. He posited that features of non-political social organization such as trust, norms, and networks can improve the efficiency of society by facilitating coordinated actions, in turn producing better performing democratic institutions (1993, 2000). A subsequent legion of researchers fought ferociously to measure such norms of reciprocity, networks of civic engagement, participation in voluntary social groups, and trust in people and institutions. No one came close. But the work associated with social capital consistently supported the 'congruence postulate' of the relationship between core elements of democratic political culture and the performance of democratic political institutions. Putnam's contribution did little to unravel the causal relationship between culture and institutions but advanced our collective understanding of the importance and nuance of this relationship in myriad ways.

Both of these fertile contributions would have been overlooked or ignored by those insisting on the identification of a causal mechanism. Insistence on causal identification neglects other types of 'necessary but not sufficient' relationships. A simple example comes from my more idealistic years of teaching mathematics in secondary school. At the end of every year, I would ask all of the student whether they played with Lego™ or not. What I found was that most – but not all – of those who performed well responded 'yes'. However, none of those who performed poorly did. Now, when I give gifts to friends' children, I give Lego™. It will not (causally) make them perform well in mathematics, but *not* having them is conspicuously related to *not* performing well mathematically. Lego™ is a 'necessary but not sufficient' explanation for mathematics success.

The debate over causality comes down to one of two positions:

- Causal thinking is a tool of theoretical development. Evidence can accumulate but the actual causal mechanism is never directly assessed.
- Causation can be identified by the application of the correct techniques (research design, analytical tools).

As the Nobel prize winning physicist, Stephen Hawking, wrote, 'what would it mean if we actually did discover the ultimate theory of the universe? ...we could never be quite sure that we had indeed found the correct theory, *since theories can't be proved*. But if the theory was consistent and always gave predictions that agreed with observations, we could be reasonably confident that it was the right one' (1990: 167; *emphasis mine*). In other words, theories are not right or wrong, theories are weak or strong.

> Penetrating so many secrets, we cease to believe in the unknowable.
> But there it sits nevertheless, calmly licking its chops. – H.L. Mencken (1956: 241)

Last Stop for 200 Miles

Image 5.1 Last Stop
Source: Chris Scott

Using the scientific method to study political phenomena originates in the desire to do it well in order to understand things as best we can. Using statistics in political analysis is an attempt to increase our precision in measurement, converge on identifying observable relationships, and make inferences beyond our individual studies.

Political Scientists are forced to make concessions in rigor given the units and contexts of study but share the same commitment to the logic of inference that underpins all scientific endeavours. It is primarily because of the ability of statistics to impose control outside the experimental setting, offer rigorous empirical testing of hypothesis, and provide estimates of the certainty in the conclusions that statistics has become so widely used.

Political Scientists are growing in their confidence that their approaches and research designs are zeroing in actual causal relationships. The motivation of thinking causally gives a clear guide on how to think about the theoretical relationship between our independent and dependent variables, as it should. Whether or not this is being estimated remains a heated debate. However, many designs can provide substantial empirical control and thus tests of causality of a relationship that leave little wiggle room for alternative explanations. So, perhaps we are seeing the light of a new day.

While the things you will learn in this book can help you quite a lot, the use of statistics is only part of the analysis of political phenomena. Recall our discussion of probabilistic and deterministic confirmation in the first chapter. In Political Science, we rely on probabilistic explanations rather than statements that are 100% certain. A natural scientist can demonstrate that water boils at 100 Celsius by direct observation in a controlled environment (at sea level). For Political Scientists, we can provide evidence that voters *tend* to have higher education levels than non-voters. Thus, while water will always boil at 100 Celsius (in standard conditions) not *every* voter will be more educated than *every* non-voter. The scientific method allows us to forgo statements of certainty and use statements that we have a great deal of confidence in to advance our knowledge. That is, probabilistic confirmation is tremendously useful when understood and used correctly.

Finally, causality is a crucial part of theoretical research in Political Science, but the attention it receives is starting to look embarrassingly like a drunk searching for his keys. As the story is variably relayed, walking home from the pub, we see a very drunk person looking for something under a streetlight. We ask what they are looking for, and he replies, 'My keys!' You try to help and after a few minutes ask, 'Are you sure they are around here'? and he replies, 'No! I lost them in the park'. You ask, 'Then why are you looking here'? He replies, 'This is where the light is.'

A Statistics Textbook

A book on statistics can give you the impression that this is *the way* political analysis is done. It is important you keep in mind that quantitative methods are not the superior way of analysing data (albeit prominent) but rather just one of many ways of doing so. Useful for somethings, less useful for others.

Statistics is unique among analytical techniques in that it gives us a measure of the empirical relationship between variables as well as – and here is the crucial element – the degree of certainty we can have about these measures. In other words, statistics tells us its best guess and *how confident we can be in that guess*. Such capabilities are very attractive and offer a smooth road to making increasingly confident conclusions. However, they can be a siren song. There is a big difference between being able to estimate a model (statistics alone) and build a useful one (the edifice of the scientific method). The advancement of Political Science, of our general knowledge, is contingent on those who can do both.

An honest, open-minded, demanding but humble scientist will say, 'Of course we are wrong. We are always wrong. We just want to be less wrong.' She will concede that it is nearly impossible to control and measure all the things in the complex and dynamic world to make conclusive claims about how the world works. That doesn't mean we shouldn't try to do so nor seek to improve in doing so.

Anyway, for a book on statistics, it sure has taken us a long time to get to it. Turn to the next chapter and let's get started.

End of Chapter Summary

- Scientific study places a heavy demand on objectivity, reducing bias in our research.
- Scientific knowledge grows by the repeated overthrow of theories with the help of hard facts in an attempt to decode the (political) world by seeking to make inferences on the basis of empirical information and probabilistic regularities about the world.
- The scientific study of politics shares the same goals – albeit by different means – as the hard scientist, but Political Science isn't necessarily the same as the statistical study of politics.
- Conceptualization and operationalization of our variables remain among the hardest problems for empirical study.
- Rendering observations into 'quantitative' data continues to challenge the study – and statistical analysis – of political phenomena.
- Political Science as well as our general knowledge is contingent on those who can both estimate a model (statistics alone) and build a useful one (the edifice of the scientific method).
- An honest, open-minded, demanding, but humble scientist will always say that we are wrong – but we're working on it.

Glossary

- This chapter integrates the key elements and terms of the Scientific Method with the study of Political Science. You can review the terms from Chapters 1–4.

Questions

1. Using a scientific approach to study political phenomena can help us answer many questions but it is unable to tell us whether our topic is important. How are we supposed to know?
2. In Political Science, there is a lot of focus on generalizing to a class of events or making inferences from our research rather than just explaining who will win the next election. Why is this the aim and why is that important (you might have to think back to Chapter 1)?
3. Name three things – in politics – that seem easy to 'quantify' – that is, they are relatively easy to define and measure. Now, name three that you think would be some of the hardest. Why are they difficult to quantify?
4. What does it mean, 'Politics are loaded (or value-laden)'? Why is this a potential problem for the scientific study of politics?

5. It seems strange that so many people are studying politics and still there is plenty on which to do research. Why are there still many questions to answer in Political Science?
6. In order for Political Science to outgrow the 'soft' science critique (i.e., 'it is not a "hard" science like Physics, Astronomy, or Biology'), ever more complex and sophisticated statistical methods will not be sufficient. Progress can only be built on research that engages theory and keenly considered concepts. Posed as a question, why will the advancement of Political Science emerge from our use of and progress with theories and concepts – rather than further development in statistics?

Annotated References and Further Reading

Almond, Gabriel A., and Stephen J. Genco. 1977. 'Clouds, clocks, and the study of politics' *World Politics* 29(4): 489–522.
The authors make one of the first comprehensive critiques of the social sciences' embrace of 'hard science' ontology and methodologies. A larger, philosophical read on the topic.

Farr, James, John Dryzek, Stephen Leonard (eds) 1995. *Political Science in History*. Cambridge: Cambridge University Press.
This is a broad survey of the origins, development, and subsequent division of the discipline of Political Science and its attendant sub-fields.

Gerring, John. 2004. 'What is a case study and what is it good for?' *American Political Science Review* 98(2): 341–354.
It's all there in the title. Gerring makes a compelling case for the use and utility of case studies in Political Science, particularly its contribution to the development of theory.

Gide, André. 1959. *Ainsi Soit-Il, Ou Les Jeux Sont Faits [So Be It: Or The Chips Are Down]*. Chatto & Windus: London. (Translated by Justin O'Brien.)
In the original French: 'Croyez ceux qui cherchent la vérité, doutez de ceux qui la trouvent;…'

Holland, P.W. 1986. 'Statistics and causal inference' *Journal of the American Statistical Association* 81(396): 945–960.
Holland takes a cross-disciplinary journal to assess the use of statistical methods to capture causal relationships. Although an earlier piece, many of the same critiques are there.

Mencken, Henry Louis. 1956. *Minority Report*. Knopf: New York.
Rogowski, Ronald. 1995. 'The role of theory and anomaly in social-scientific inference' *American Political Science Review* 89(2): 467–470.
This is a short review of King, Keohane, and Verba's *Designing Social Inquiry* (1995) with a keen eye toward the nevertheless crucial role of small-n and case studies.

Stein, M. 1998. 'Major factors in the emergence of Political Science as a discipline in Western democracies: A comparative analysis of the United States, Britain, France, and Germany' *Regime and Discipline: Democracy and the Development of Political Science.* **pp. 169–195. Ann Arbor: University of Michigan Press.**

Stein's contribution takes a less American-centred (although the Americans are in there) look at the development of Political Science as a discipline.

Signposts to Research and Empirical Examples

Almond, Gabriel. 1996. 'Political science: The history of the discipline,' in R.E. Goodin and H. Klingemann (eds) *The New Handbook of Political Science.* Oxford: Oxford University Press.

Hawking, Stephen. 1990. *A Brief History of Time: From the Big Bang to Black Holes.* New York: Bantam.

Inglehart, Ronald. 1997. *Modernization and Postmodernization. Cultural, Economic, and Political Change in 43 Societies.* Princeton: Princeton University Press.

Popper, Karl. 1957. *The Poverty of Historicism.* Routledge.

Putnam, Robert. 1993. *Making Democracy Work: Civic Traditions in Modern Italy.* Princeton: Princeton University Press.

Putnam, Robert. 2000. *Bowling Alone: The Collapse and Revival of American Community.* New York: Simon & Schuster.

Sen, Amartya. 1995. *Inequality Re-examined.* Cambridge: Harvard University Press.

For a great example of text and document analysis in European countries, see the comparative Manifesto Project: https://manifesto-project.wzb.eu/

The Perestroika Debate: https://archive.org/details/OnTheIrrelevanceOfApsaAndApsrToTheStudyOfPoliticalScience

General Entropy measures
www.un.org/en/development/desa/policy/wess/wess_dev_issues/dsp_policy_02.pdf

PART I
DESCRIPTIVE STATISTICS

6
UNIVARIATE DESCRIPTIVE STATISTICS

> **LEARNING OUTCOMES**
>
> In this chapter, you will be able to
>
> - Understand and use univariate descriptive statistics to summarize and describe variables of interest.
> - Distinguish variables by their level of measurement.
> - Select the most appropriate measure of central tendency and dispersion to analyse variable of interest using level of measurement.
> - Select and critically engage graphs to assess and improve data description.
> - Identify potential challenges to variable description.
> - Recognize the importance of data and variable description in statistical analysis

Introduction

The power of statistics comes from the abilities of description, inference, and control. Statistical analysis is comprised of two elements: Descriptive Statistics and Inferential Statistics. In this first section, we will look at the wide range of abilities the Descriptive Statistics offers us, not only to describe, but also to control. We take our first steps toward explicit statistical language, terms, and uses. Within the concept of measurement, we discuss the levels of measurement for variables and from these, confront measures of distribution, central tendency, and dispersion with emphasis on their relatedness.

The power of description in statistics sometimes gets overshadowed by the more sophisticated and fancier inferential statistics. This is unfortunate. The ability to describe something well is both challenging and useful. Remember, we use statistics to summarize variables, to summarize their relationships, to summarize what we can say about what we are studying. In summarizing, you have to choose what is important and find a way to achieve an effective summary. The ability to accurately describe something is a remarkably useful capacity of statistics.

We will look at how Descriptive Statistics:

- Summarize variables and tell us how good that summary is
- Summarize the relationships between variables
- Help us understand controlled comparisons (3 variables!)
- Provide the basis for the graphical summary of variables.

Doing Statistics

Description is essential in order to get to get a sense of our data as well as the first step in converting data into information. And description is not easy. For example, one would be 100% correct to say that everything in the universe is either a potato or not a potato. This, however, is of limited utility to nearly all questions in Political Science.

Statistical description is also different than the process of conceptualization. We aren't searching for the best *definition* of democracy, war, sovereignty, or legitimacy. We are looking to summarize a group of observations into a representative moment. If I describe someone as good-looking, smart, and funny, this can be helpful even if just to know that they are not ugly, stupid, and humourless. This description may be important and relevant if you are looking for someone to date. If, however, you are interested in finding a brain surgeon (for surgery, not dating), maybe these are not the most salient attributes or qualities for which to search.

Univariate Descriptive Statistics

The title of this chapter, and this section, is a fancy name for a simple concept. 'Univariate' means one variable and 'descriptive' refers to the summary of a variable for consumption and analysis. There is no generalization or inference.

Descriptive Statistics answer the questions:

- How can I best summarize a large number of observations?
- How good is this summary?

While the first question has direct, practical utility, the second is also important. At the heart of statistics is the acknowledgement that we will be wrong no matter what we do. We can, however, identify the extent of wrongness. In some cases, we can account for this problem by simply acknowledging that it exists. Other times we will be responsible to acknowledge this limitation and how it affects the results. In either case, measuring the quality of our summary is evidence of how statistical analysis incorporates, and takes seriously, uncertainty.

Descriptive Statistics summarize variables so improve our understanding of their nature and character. The process of doing so is often referred to as 'getting to know our data'.

Let's go over and introduce ourselves.

Data, Datasets, and Variables

To understand how statistics work their dark magic, let's quickly (re)introduce ourselves to data and variables (recall Chapter 3). Below you can see a table of data – organized into variables – on the 25 most populous countries, organized alphabetically.

Table 6.1 Dataset of 25 Most Populated Countries

Country	Main Religion	FH: Global Freedom Score	WGI: Voice & Accountability
Bangladesh	Islam	Partly Free	−0.72
Brazil	Christianity	Free	0.34
China	Unaffiliated Religions	Not Free	−1.61
Dem. Rep. of the Congo	Christianity	Not Free	−1.37
Egypt	Islam	Not Free	−1.43
Ethiopia	Christianity	Not Free	−1.30
France	Christianity	Free	1.14
Germany	Christianity	Free	1.34
India	Hinduism	Partly Free	0.29
Indonesia	Islam	Partly Free	0.16
Iran	Islam	Not Free	−1.37
Italy	Christianity	Free	0.97
Japan	Unaffiliated Religions	Free	0.96
Mexico	Christianity	Partly Free	0.02
Myanmar	Buddhism	Not Free	−0.84
Nigeria	Christianity	Partly Free	−0.41
Philippines	Christianity	Partly Free	0.03
Russian Federation	Christianity	Not Free	−1.10
South Africa	Christianity	Free	0.67
Thailand	Buddhism	Not Free	−0.83
Turkey	Islam	Not Free	−0.81
United Kingdom	Christianity	Free	1.26
Tanzania	Christianity	Partly Free	−0.50
United States of America	Christianity	Free	0.97
Viet Nam	Folk Religions	Not Free	−1.38

In this table, there are a number of things that we already know.

- **Datum:** a single piece of data.
    - 'Hinduism' in the *Main Religion* variable, for India, is a datum.
    - 'Not Free' in the *Global Freedom Score* variable, for Thailand, is a datum.
    - '0.03' in the Voice and Accountability variable, for the Philippines, is a datum.
    - Etc....
- **Data:** A collection of codified observations on a topic we are interested in.
    - The data for Voice and Accountability come from the World Governance Indicators series produced by the World Bank.
    - The data for the Global Freedom Scores come from the Freedom in the World series produced by Freedom House.
    - The data for the Main Religion come from the Our World in Data series produced by Pew-Templeton Global Religious Futures Project, Pew Research Center.
- **Variable:** the choice of indicator that draws data together conceptually and operationally.
    - *Voice and Accountability* is the name of the variable from the World Bank World Governance Indicators series that reflects perceptions of the extent to which a country's citizens are able to participate in selecting their government, as well as freedom of expression, freedom of association, and a free media.
    - *Global Freedom Score* variable is the name of the variable from Freedom House's Freedom in the Worlds series that reflect the combined average of their Political Rights and Civil Liberties. (Strangely) rating between 0 and 2.5 are 'Free'; between 3.0 and 5.0 are 'Partly Free', and between 5.5 and 7.0 are 'Not Free'.
    - *Main Religion* is the name of the variable from the 'Our World in Data' series produced by Pew-Templeton Global Religious Futures Project, Pew Research Center that identifies the largest religion in every country.
- **Case:** The unit of analysis – the subject of your study; in this case, countries.
    - Specifically, the 25 most populous countries.
- **Dataset:** A collection of variables for the included observations creates a set of data, a.k.a. a dataset.
    - Most commonly, datasets have cases as the first column (the start of each row) and variables are arranged as additional columns. Reading across each row, each case has a value for each variable. In this case, each case (i.e., *country*) has a value for the variables: *Main Religion*, *Global Freedom Score*, and *Voice and Accountability*.

This is the source material for statistics, a dataset. I propose we start with describing each variable. Specifically:

- In the 25 most populous countries in the world, what is the most common religion?

- In the 25 most populous countries in the world, how free are they? (I know, vague, but we'll get into the Freedom House measurements in just a bit.)
- In the 25 most populous countries in the world, how responsive are the governments?
- And finally, how good are each of these summary measures at describing these countries?

These are all good and potentially interesting questions. It is certainly a good place to start. But, there's just one more thing we need to know in order to provide the most accurate summary of these variables: their level of measurement.

Levels of Measurement

Even a casual glance at this dataset suggests that the variables *Main Religion* and *Voice and Accountability* don't look the same. Yes, they both contain data in that they are codified observations but one is much more mathematically tractable than the other. But the variable *Global Freedom Scores* is different still. They have some order (Not Free → Partly Free → Free), although not enough number-ness to be punched into a calculator. The difference is the metric of the variable or their **level of measurement**. This is necessary to know as it shapes all of our subsequent analytical choices.

The *Voice and Accountability* variable (World Bank: World Governance Indicators) is the most math-y looking one. This variable is an **interval**-level variable. For interval-level variables, the distance between measures – the intervals – have meaning, e.g., years between wars; 3% increase in GDP per capita; a decrease in income. While the interval between the numbers is meaningful, the placement of zero is not. In a sense, interval-level variables are the 'easy ones' with which to do statistics.

> ### RATIO-LEVEL VARIABLES
>
> The placement or location of zero can be important. There is another 'higher' scale variable: 'ratio-level'. These variables are fully mathematically tractable and conditional on a true zero point (for example, for the variable 'time', zero '0' is pretty meaningful). For our research in Political Science, there are instances in which this distinction is crucial; however, not many.

The *Global Freedom Scores* are not so math-y but do have order. This order is crucial and such variables are called **ordinal**-level variables. Ordinal variables categorize observations 'in order' but the 'jump' from one category to the next is not necessarily 'the same' mathematically. That is, while orderly, the intervals between the categories are not uniform.

Both of these characteristics are key. One, we retain the order of interval-level variables (moving in one direction is the opposite of moving in the other) but lose the uniform meaningfulness between each category/number. That is, while orderly, moving from 'Not Free' to 'Partly Free' isn't necessarily the same-sized conceptual 'jump' from 'Partly Free' to 'Free'. Simply, the relative value of moving from one category to another cannot be assumed to be the same.

Finally, the variable *Main Religion* represents the categories or classifications of the religion with the largest share of followers in each country that are both exhaustive and mutually exclusive – but lack order. These are **nominal**-level variables. Nominal variables simply divide data into categories, with no assumption about the order or relationships between groups. For nominal variables, every observation has a category – but the overall order of the categories is unimportant.

Ok, so, remember when I suggested that you commit to your long-term memory that 'Theories are not right or wrong. Theories are weak or strong?' Good, next to that, embed the knowledge that the differences between interval, ordinal, and nominal variables are essential. In stronger words: the *Levels of Measurement* distinction informs all of our choices of statistical techniques.

Starting now.

Measures of Central Tendency and Dispersion

If we want to describe a variable, we need a summary and something that tells us how good that summary is. Measures of central tendency summarize the variable with a single value and measures of dispersion tell us how good this summary is for this variable.

- **Measures of central tendency** give us the most representative value of a variable.
- **Measures of dispersion** tell us how representative the measure of central tendency is by providing the amount of variation around that value.

As we will see, this is far from banal. Summarizing variables with measures of central tendency provides an overview of our data, our cases, and even the basis for comparison between groups or over time. This is nice, but summarizing a variable necessarily loses some information by compacting the spectrum of data into a single measure. That is why the corresponding measures of dispersion are crucial for both our understanding as well as our comparisons by indicating how *representative* the summary is.

Dispersion – sometimes weirdly called 'spread' – is a measure of variance. **Variance** is a concept that plays a major role in statistics. Essentially, variance describes how close or far the observations are to our summary statistic (here, the measure of central tendency). It tells us how good our summaries are and in turn providing a level of confidence we can have in our results. As we will see, it is a very powerful and useful indicator.

As mentioned above, the choice of both central tendency and dispersion depends on the level of measurement of the variable.

Nominal: Univariate Descriptive Statistics

Recall that nominal-level variables categorize data without implying order. Because of this, there is no clear best way to summarize nominal-level variables as they are slightly anti-establishment ('No order! Anarchy'). Thus, in order to identify the measure that is the most representative, we quite literally choose the category that is the most oft-occurring. This is the **mode**. This is the 'most typical category' or simply, the category with the most observations.

Let's say that we are looking at a group of Erasmus students and we asked them where they were born (see Table 6.2a).

Table 6.2a Nominal-level Variable

Born in ...	Number of observations
The Netherlands	22
France	19
Italy	9
Spain	14
Germany	15
Total	*79*

This variable is a nominal-level variable as the categories include all of the responses but there is no overt order. That is, it is not necessary for the Netherlands to be first and Germany to be last. For nominal-level variables, the best summary – the measure of central tendency – is the mode, 'most typical category' or the most oft-occurring one.

In the table, we can see that of our 79 Erasmus respondents, the most common location (although not necessarily the majority location) in which people were born is the Netherlands ($n=22$). Thus, the mode of the variable 'where were you born' is 'the Netherlands' with 22 observations, more than any other country. Or imagined differently, if we had to guess the answer to where each of these Erasmus students were born, simply guessing 'the Netherlands' would be correct most often.

Clearly, this summary provides *some* information but does seem to leave substantial nuance at the door. However, how good this summary is cannot be determined by the summary itself. We need more information. There are two common ways to generate the additional necessary information about the descriptive quality of the mode.

The first way is to calculate relative frequencies. **Relative frequencies** reveal the proportional frequency of each category relative to the total of all categories. That is, it simplifies the distribution of all of the categories in terms of a percent of the total. In Table 6.2b, we can produce relative frequencies by dividing their actual frequency (here, 'number of observations') by the total. This produces a frequency relative to both the other categories and the total. We express these relative frequencies as percentages.

Table 6.2b Nominal-level Variable

Born in ...	Number of observations	Divide by total	Convert to percentage	Relative frequency
The Netherlands	22	=22/79	=0.279	→ 27.9%
France	19	=19/79	=0.241	→ 24.1%
Italy	9	=9/79	=0.114	→ 11.4%
Spain	14	=14/79	=0.177	→ 17.7%
Germany	15	=15/79	=0.190	→ 19.0%
Total	*79*	*79/79*	*1.000*	*100%*

In contrast to the 'raw data' of the number of observations, we can quickly and easily compare the relative outcomes by ranking the relative frequencies (by percentages). That is, for our nominal-level variable 'where were you born', the Netherlands has a relative frequency of 27.9% followed by France (24.1%), Germany (19.0%), Spain (17.7%), and, finally, Italy (11.4%). However, while commonly used, relative frequencies are less a means of assessing the *dispersion* about the mode but do offer a clearer, more common, standardized distribution (as a percentage of the total).

An actual measure of dispersion for nominal-level variables is the **variation ratio**. The variation ratio tells us how much variation there is around our measure of central tendency (the mode). Inasmuch as the variation ratio is 'small', we can have greater confidence in the measures of central tendency. As the variation ratio increases, our confidence in our summary measure of central tendency decreases.

The formula for the variation ratio is:

$$VR = \frac{\Sigma(F_{NON-MODAL})}{N}$$

This tells us how many observations fall in categories *other* than the modal category. So, if we follow the formula and sum ('Σ') all of the non-modal observations (19+9+14+15=57) and divide by the total number (79), we get a variation ratio of 0.72.

While that was fun and exciting to do, what does it tell us? That is, what does the variation ratio tell us about the *representativeness* of our modal category (i.e., the Netherlands) for the birth locations for these Erasmus students? 0.72 is not, on its own, obvious as to what it implies about the dispersion of observations around the mode. Perhaps to give it some context, let's compare the calculated variation ratio of 0.72 to another set of data in which the mode is the same but the variation ratio is different.

In Table 6.2c, we are looking at another group of Erasmus students. For this 79 Erasmus students, they responded as such.

Table 6.2c Nominal-level Variable

Born in ...	Number of observations
The Netherlands	40
France	14
Italy	3
Spain	10
Germany	12
Total	*79*

Once again, the most common location in which people were born is the Netherlands ($n = 40$). Remember, even if the list of countries was in a different order, such as alphabetically, this would not affect which was the mode. While the mode in this table is the same as in the previous table, we can already sense that because just more than half of the respondents were born in the Netherlands in this sample – versus only just over a quarter of them in the previous example (27.9%) – there's an important difference between these datasets.

Remember, a smaller measure of dispersion indicates a more representative measure of central tendency. So, while these datasets have the same mode, the crucial difference is demonstrated to us when we calculate the variation ratio. Again, we sum ('Σ') all of the non-modal observations (14 + 3 + 10 + 12 = 39) and divide by the total number (79) and arrive at a variation ratio of 0.49.

Ah! In the first dataset on where Erasmus students were born, the most common answer was the Netherlands ($n = 22$) – with a variation ratio of 0.72. In the second dataset on where Erasmus students were born, the most common answer was the Netherlands ($n = 40$) – with a variation ratio of 0.49.

The smaller variation ratio – or any smaller dispersion measure – indicates that the modal category – the Netherlands – is *more likely to be a good representative* as the number of other (i.e., non-modal) answers is lower. Coming from the other direction of this explanation, because the ratio of variation from the modal to non-modal category is smaller (closer to zero), there are fewer non-modal answers (i.e., countries other than the Netherlands). If fewer non-modal answers were given, there were more modal answers making the mode a better summary of the nominal-level variable.

Thus, returning to the description of the original variable of where these Erasmus students were born (Table 6.2a), the measure of central tendency, the mode, is 'the Netherlands' and the measure of dispersion, a variation ratio of 0.72, tells us that the modal category ('the Netherlands), as a summary, is weak or not a very representative summary.

> **NOMINAL-LEVEL VARIABLES**
>
> *Central Tendency:* **Mode**
> *Dispersion:* **Relative Frequencies** or **Variation Ratio**

Ordinal: Univariate Descriptive Statistics

The measure of central tendency for ordinal-level data is the median. The **median** indicates the exact midpoint of the variable, dividing the variable in half.

In Political Science, a common survey response used in the study of political behaviour is a psychometric response scale. This set of responses = Strongly Agree, Agree, etc.… – is an example of a *Likert scale* common in public opinion data collection (e.g., surveys and polls).

Agree strongly	Agree	Neither agree nor disagree	Disagree	Disagree strongly
1	2	3	4	5

Figure 6.1 Example of Likert Scale

Using such a scale, we can ask about whether immigrants should be allowed to come to the country, whether gay people should have the same rights as others, whether the government should take measures to reduce the differences in income levels, or whether the European Union should continue.

In the scale, the responses are clearly different from one another but also in an order. However, while the order is obvious, the interval between moving from 'strongly agree' to 'agree' isn't necessarily the same as moving between 'neither agree nor disagree' and 'disagree'. Mathematically, yes (1 to 2 is 1 unit; 3 to 4 is 1 unit) but conceptually, no. In this way, this response scale is a good example of an ordinal-level variable.

In a (fake) survey, we are interested in 'social trust' characterized by its horizontal nature aimed at fellow citizens. We ask 100 people, 'Would you say that most people in your country can be trusted?' These are the responses (Table 6.3a).

Table 6.3a Ordinal-level Variable

Would you say that most people in your country can be trusted?	N
Strongly Agree	42
Agree	25
Neither Agree nor Disagree	14
Disagree	10
Strongly Disagree	9
Total	*100*

In order to generate the median, you would literally order all of the responses: 42 Strongly Agrees, then 25 Agrees, then 14 Neither Agree nor Disagrees, then 10 Disagrees, and finally, 9 Strongly Disagrees. If the total number of observations is odd, you simply take the observation that puts an equal number of observations on both sides. If the total number of observations is even, as we have here, you take the two observations (in our case, observations 50 and 51) that puts the same number of observations on both sides.

In our example above, observations 50 and 51 are, in the line of ordered answers, both Agree and Agree (see Figure 6.2).

Strongly Agree - Strongly Agree - Strongly Agree - Strongly Agree - Strongly Agree - Strongly Agree - Strongly Agree - Strongly Agree - Strongly Agree - Strongly Agree - Strongly Agree -Strongly Agree - Agree - Agree - Agree - Agree - Agree - Agree - Agree - Agree *{THE MIDDLE}* Agree - Agree - Agree - Agree - Agree - Agree - Agree - Agree - Agree - Agree - Agree - Agree - Agree - Agree - Agree - Agree - Agree - Neither Agree nor Disagree - Neither Agree nor Disagree - Neither Agree nor Disagree - Neither Agree nor Disagree - Neither Agree nor Disagree - Neither Agree nor Disagree - Neither Agree nor Disagree - Neither Agree nor Disagree - Neither Agree nor Disagree - Neither Agree nor Disagree - Neither Agree nor Disagree - Neither Agree nor Disagree - Neither Agree nor Disagree - **Disagree - Disagree - Disagree - Disagree - Disagree - Disagree - Disagree - Disagree - Disagree - Disagree** - *Strongly Disagree - Strongly Disagree - Strongly Disagree - Strongly Disagree - Strongly Disagree - Strongly Disagree - Strongly Disagree - Strongly Disagree - Strongly Disagree*

Figure 6.2 100 Ordinal Likert Responses in Order

Thus, the measure of central tendency – the median – for this variable is 'Agree'. Agree is in the middle of the distribution of this variable. This makes intuitive sense if we look at the dataset as most of the answers are Strongly Agree and Agree, and there are fewer for the other response categories.

Table 6.3b Ordinal-level Variables

Would you say that most people in your country can be trusted?	N [Country: BBQ]	N [Country: Music]
Strongly Agree	4	2
Agree	3	2
Neither Agree nor Disagree	1	3
Disagree	1	2
Strongly Disagree	1	2
Total	***10***	***11***

Let's take a further simplified example to make the calculation of the median easier to see. Using the same survey question about social trust, we asked 10 people in the country of BBQ and 11 people in the country of Music.

- Ordering the responses in BBQ looks like this: SA, SA, SA, SA, A, A, A, NAD, D, SD
- Ordering the responses in Music looks like this: SA, SA, A, A, NAD, NAD, NAD, D, D, SD, SD

For the country of BBQ, because the total number of observations is even (10), there is not an observation that puts an equal number of observations on either side. The median – the one in the middle – is therefore responses 5 and 6. Fortunately, both observation 5 and 6 are Agree. Therefore, the median for social trust in the country of BBQ is Agree.

Note: Every blue moon or so, these two are different. Because it is so rare, there really isn't a solution other than to report it, which will be interesting to the reader ('That's highly unusual!') and also have the neato effect of splitting the dataset 50/50 neatly between categories. So, it's a win in any case.

The median – the one in the middle – for the country of Music is response 6. Response 6 puts an equal number of observations on either side (on one side are observations 1 (SA), 2 (SA), 3 (A), 4 (A), 5 (NAD), and on the other are observations 7 (NAD), 8 (D), 9 (D), 10 (SD), 11 (SD)). Response 6 is Neither Agree nor Disagree, therefore, the median for social trust in the country of Music is Neither Agree nor Disagree.

How representative are these ordinal-level measures of central tendency? How good are these medians as summaries for these ordinal-level variables?

The measure of dispersion for ordinal-level variables is the **range**. The range is (boringly) just that. The highest category with observations to the lowest category with observations. There is also the Inter-Quartile Range that effectively chops off any outlying observations. However, this used in specific cases.

In our three examples above (N = 100; N = 10; N = 11), the range is Strongly Agree to Strongly Disagree. In some disciplines, researchers will use the actual response values (Strongly Agree is 1, Agree is 2, Neither is 3, Disagree is 4, and Strongly Disagree is 5) to report the range. Thus, 1 – 5. In Political Science, there is no agreed-upon reporting standard.

This is a bit of a let-down, I know. It is admittedly not the most inspiring measure of dispersion but it can be useful. Let's take an extreme example.

Table 6.3c Ordinal-level Variable

Would you say that most people in your country can be trusted?	N
Strongly Agree	68
Agree	26
Neither Agree nor Disagree	6
Disagree	0
Strongly Disagree	0
Total	*100*

In this case, the median of social trust is Strongly Agree (I'll let you work it out) and the range is Strongly Agree to Neither Agree nor Disagree. What is clear from the measure of central tendency is that the data are highly skewed toward Strongly Agree (if the median is in this category, more than half are in it). This lopsidedness is underscored by the range that only includes the top three categories.

In other words, if we hadn't seen the table, the summary of 'the median of social trust is Strongly Agree and the range is Strong Agree to Neither Agree nor Disagree' tells us a lot about how these data are distributed. So, again, not stupendous but not too bad either.

Thus, returning to the description of the original variable of 'Would you say that most people in your country can be trusted?' (Table 6.3a), the measure of central tendency, the median, is 'Agree' and the measure of dispersion, the range of 'Strongly Disagree' to 'Strongly Agree', tells us that the modal category ('Agree'), as a summary, is moderate or only a modest representative summary.

> ORDINAL-LEVEL VARIABLES
>
> *Central Tendency:* **Median**
> *Dispersion:* **Range**

Interval: Univariate Descriptive Statistics

For interval-level variables, the measure of central tendency is the **mean** (a.k.a. the (arithmetic) average). It looks like this:

$$\bar{x} = \frac{\sum x}{n}$$

The mean is represented as $\bar{x}$, pronounced 'x bar' and refers to the mean of our sample (of data). The difference between the *sample mean* (and *sample* 'other things') will become apparent and we move into inferential statistics. However, to calculate the sample mean, simply add all of the data (Σ) and divide by the total number of observations in our sample (n).

For interval-level variables, the measure of dispersion is the **standard deviation**. It is the average amount the observations ($x_1, x_2, x_3, \ldots x_n$) deviate from the mean ($\bar{x}$).

It looks like this:

$$s_x = \sqrt{\frac{\sum (x - \bar{x})^2}{n-1}}$$

Technically, this is the formula for the *sample standard deviation* as we use it to estimate dispersion for our samples (taken from our total population of things in which we are interested). It looks scary but it's really not.

The formula helps us find the *average distance of all the observations from the mean*. Looking at the equation, let's follow the logic to do so:

- We subtract each observation (x) from the mean ($\bar{x}$). This gives us each observation's distance from the mean. Why? Well, if you wanted the average distance of *all* the data, collecting *all* the distances is a smart place to start.
- Then, we square that (^{2}) to make the all the differences positive.
- Then, we add all of them together (Σ).
- Then divide them by the total number of observations in our sample minus 1. This gives us the essentially the mean of the squared distances.
- Then, take the square root of this number ($\sqrt{}$). We do this to 'undo' the squaring used to make all the distances positive.

> ### BESSEL'S CORRECTION
>
> The use of n–1 is an attempt to reduce the bias of our sample standard deviation. It is called the *Bessel's correction* after its originator, Friedrich Bessel, famous for his use of the parallax method to judge interstellar distances. While using n–1 has been demonstrated to reduce bias in the variance component (everything under the square root), the use of the square root itself is still biased, although only partially.

Voilà! This gives us the average distance from the mean of all the observations. Which, if you think about it, is a pretty good measure of dispersion.

Recall that a big dispersion tells us that the observations are, on average, *far* from the measure of central tendency. This implies that our measure of central tendency is not very representative. The opposite also holds. A small dispersion tells us that the observations are, on average, close to our measure of central tendency and therefore more representative.

And let's be clear. It does not make sense for you to do this formula by hand. Statistical software, even spreadsheet software, can do this in a few clicks. It does, however, make sense to understand what it tells us (and even some of the intuition of its design) but the actual 'number crunching' is not necessary to use the mean and standard deviation effectively (and this is true for everything else that follows in this book).

As an example of interval univariate descriptive statistics for interval-level variables, let's consider national-level election turnout for European Parliamentary (EP) elections from the European Parliament itself. Let's say we want to know the average national-level turnout for the European Parliamentary elections across the member states over the history of the European Union.

In our interval-level variable of EP turnout in the table below (Table 6.4 is not a dataset as the data are not organized for analysis), we can calculate the mean – 51.2% – and standard deviation 19.9.

What does this tell us? Frankly not a whole lot. In the history of European Parliamentary elections, European member states average 51.2% turnout. And the standard deviation is 19.9, which is quite large, implying that 51.2 is not a great summary of EP electoral turnout.

Wait – how do you know that 19.9 is not great? We will get into the specifics of how we know this in the next section, but two pieces of information might help here.

One, if we look at the data in the table below, we can find turnout observations that are far from the mean of 51.2. *Note:* we will nearly always find observations that are far from the mean. Here, however, there are *a lot* of observations that are *very* far from the mean.

- Many of the early members have 70%, 80%, and 90% level turnout (e.g., Belgium, Italy, and Luxembourg).
- There are a lot that have 40%, 50%, and 60% level turnout (e.g., France, the Netherlands, and Denmark).
- But, at the same time, there are a lot with 30% and even 20% turnout (the UK, Finland, and unfortunately many (at the time, new) Eastern European members).

These data are widely dispersed – and we know what a large measure of dispersion tells us, the measure of central tendency is not doing a great job of summarizing the data.

Two, the standard deviation – 19.9 – is a lot of the range of the data. That is, the data range from 13.05% (Slovakia 2014) to 92.09% (Belgium 1984). 19.9 is a big chunk of that (approximately a quarter). We'll come back to this point in the next section.

In any case, look at you! Doing statistics! That's not so bad, is it?

INTERVAL-LEVEL VARIABLES

Central Tendency: **Mean**
Dispersion: **Standard Deviation**

Table 6.4 European Parliamentary Turnout by Country

Turnout by country (%)
Final results

Country	1979	1981	1984	1987	1989	1994	1995	1996	1999	2004	2007	2009	2013	2014	2019
Belgium	91.36		92.09		90.73	90.66			91.05	90.81		90.39		89.64	88.47
Denmark	47.82		52.38		46.17	52.92			50.46	47.89		59.54		56.32	66.08
Germany	65.73		56.76		62.28	60.02			45.19	43.00		43.27		48.10	61.38
Ireland	63.61		47.56		68.28	43.98			50.21	58.58		58.64		52.44	49.70
France	60.71		56.72		48.80	52.71			46.76	42.76		40.63		42.43	50.12
Italy	85.65		82.47		81.07	73.60			69.76	71.72		66.47		57.22	54.50
Luxembourg	88.91		88.79		87.39	88.55			87.27	91.35		90.76		85.55	84.24
Netherlands	58.12		50.88		47.48	35.69			30.02	39.26		36.75		37.32	41.93
United Kingdom	32.35		32.57		36.37	36.43			24.00	38.52		34.70		35.60	37.18
Greece		81.48	80.59		80.03	73.18			70.25	63.22		52.54		59.97	58.69
Spain				68.52	54.71	59.14			63.05	45.14		44.87		43.81	60.73
Portugal				72.42	51.10	35.54			39.93	38.60		36.77		33.67	30.75
Sweden							41.63		38.84	37.65		45.53		51.07	55.27
Austria								67.73	49.40	42.43		45.97		45.39	59.80

Turnout by country (%)
Final results

Finland	57.60	30.14	39.43		39.10	40.80
Czechia			28.30	38.60	18.20	28.72
Estonia			26.83	28.22	36.52	37.60
Cyprus			72.50	43.90	43.97	44.99
Lithuania			48.38	59.40	47.35	53.48
Latvia			41.34	20.98	30.24	33.53
Hungary			38.50	53.70	28.97	43.36
Malta			82.39	36.31	74.80	72.70
Poland			20.87	78.79	23.83	45.68
Slovenia			28.35	24.53	24.55	28.89
Slovakia			16.97	28.37	13.05	22.74
Bulgaria				19.64	35.84	32.64
Romania				29.22 38.99	32.44	51.20
Croatia				29.47 27.67	20.84 25.24	29.85
Total EU	**61.99**	**58.98**	**58.41**	**56.67**	**49.51**	**45.47**	**42.97**	**42.61**	**50.66**

A Passing Note on Measures of Central Tendency and Dispersion

It is commonly considered that interval-level data are the 'highest-order' data. They are attractive for being mathematically easy to manage and get all the best statistical techniques. Ordinal-level variables have some street credibility because they still have explicit order, which can make things like hypothesis testing easier (remember: hypotheses must be directional) but they struggle with 'meaningful' intervals. Nominal-level variables are kind of looked down on. I get it, I suppose. Statistically, there isn't much to do with them as the lack of both meaningful intervals and order makes them like herding cats.

Why am I telling you this? Because this preference plays out in many ways, statistically speaking. One example is that each level of measurement can use the measures of central tendency and dispersion from the ones 'beneath' them. In Table 6.5 you can see that while nominal-level variables can only use mode and variation ratio, ordinal-level variables can use median and range as well as mode and variation ratio. Interval-level variables, as you probably suspected, can use all of them.

Table 6.5 Measures of Central Tendency and Dispersion

	Measure of Central Tendency	Measure of Dispersion
Nominal	**Mode**	**Relative Frequencies** or **Variation Ratio**
Ordinal	Mode	Variation Ratio
	Median	**Range**
Interval	Mode	Variation Ratio
	Median	Range
	Mean	**Standard Deviation**

When does this make sense? Let's use a very common variable similar to, if a bit larger than, the Likert scales from above (Strongly Agree, Agree, etc....): left–right ideological self-placement.

	In politics people sometimes talk of 'left' and 'right'. Where would you place yourself on this scale, 0 means the left and 10 means the right?									
Left										**Right**
0	01	02	03	04	05	06	07	08	09	10

Figure 6.3 Left–Right Ideological Self-placement

Such questions are nearly ubiquitous in large public opinion surveys across the world. We can see that the order is important from extreme Left (0) to extreme Right (10). The challenge to the level of measurement is that moving from 4 to 5 may be more or less *mathematically* the same as moving from 9 to 10 – both are just a 1-unit increase; but what that 1-unit shift signifies or 'means' are not conceptually similar. That is, moving from 4, a lukewarm, centre-left position, to 5, essentially ideologically neutral, is unlikely to be congruent to moving from 9, an already extreme position, to 10, the *most* extreme position. These changes are not only different from one another but also likely driven by different processes.

So, there is a lot of evidence to treat this as an ordinal-level variable. Yet, in the use, the left–right ideological self-placement variable often gets treated as an interval-level variable. Note that some textbooks refer to nominal-level variables as 'discrete' variables and ordinal- and interval-level variables as 'continuous' variables. There are advantages and disadvantages of doing so. Without entering this debate, just be aware of this, but this left–right ideological self-identification is an example of why they might.

In any case, how best to summarize these data?

Let's use a real-world example: From the European Social Survey 2018, we can generate ordinal- and interval-level measures of central tendency and dispersion for our variable of interest: left–right ideological self-placement. In 19 countries, we have 30,850 European respondents (observations):

- As an ordinal-level variable, we calculate the median and the range:
  o The median is 5 and the range is Extreme left (0) to Extreme right (10) or simply, 0–10.
  o Since the median is 'the one in the middle', this tells us that 50% of the observations include 0 (extreme left) to some of the 5s (ideologically neutral) and 50% of the observations include some of the 5s (ideologically neutral) to 10 (extreme right).
- As an interval-level variable, we calculate the mean and standard deviation:
  o The mean is 5.1 and the standard deviation is 2.2.
  o This tells us that the average ideological position is 5.1 (more or less ideologically neutral) and that this is a good – not great – summary for the average left–right ideological self-placement in 19 European countries in 2018.

Which one is a better summary? It is hard to say. The first set of measures are not overly helpful in imagining what the distribution of this variable might look like. At the same time, they are the technically more correct summary statistics. The second set is more precise but at the cost of treating the data like they are more than they actually are (In order? Yes. Math-y? -ish).

> ### YOU MEAN MEDIAN
>
> The late comedian George Carlin (1937–2008) used to joke, 'Think of how stupid the average person is – and realize half of them are stupider than that.'
> But George wasn't quite right, was he?
> What he meant to say is: 'Think of how stupid the median person is – and realize half of them are stupider than that.'

I want to warn you, and you may have already experienced this, that many people have surprisingly strong feelings about statistics. When I say, 'statistics', I mean when they saw a poll on the news, or having failed a stats course twice, or actually knowing what they are talking about (*Note:* rare). However, and inevitably, you will come across someone who has not just one but this specific jab: 'Statistics are so stupid and don't really tell you anything useful. Did you hear about the statistician who drowned crossing a river that had, by his calculation, an average depth of ½ of a meter?' ('Yuk, yuk, yuk; har, har, har; Oh, man, that's funny – and true! Get a load of this guy!') My response usually is something like, 'A person familiar with basic statistics would not have made a decision based on such limited information and would have demanded a further description of the average depth in the form of a measure of dispersion to evaluate the potential inadequacy of the singular descriptive measure of central tendency.'

I do want to point out that saying this, like criticizing George Carlin, is not the most effective way to ingratiate yourself with people. But it's not wrong.

In any case, descriptive statistics can be a very powerful tool when used well.

Graphing

Measures of Central Tendency and Dispersion are a way of 'getting to know the data' by introducing you to their basic characteristics. Another way is graphing.

There is no definitive means to graph univariate data and below is not the extent of types and sophistication. However, some graphs are more appropriate to specific levels of measurement.

Nominal: Univariate Graphing

For nominal-level variables, the best graphs are bar or pie charts. There is a slight preference for pie charts as they offer a more intuitive visual cue to each category's size.

For continuity, let's use our nominal-level variable from above: in which countries the Erasmus students were born (Table 6.2a). Graphing this as a pie chart, we arrive at Figure 6.4:

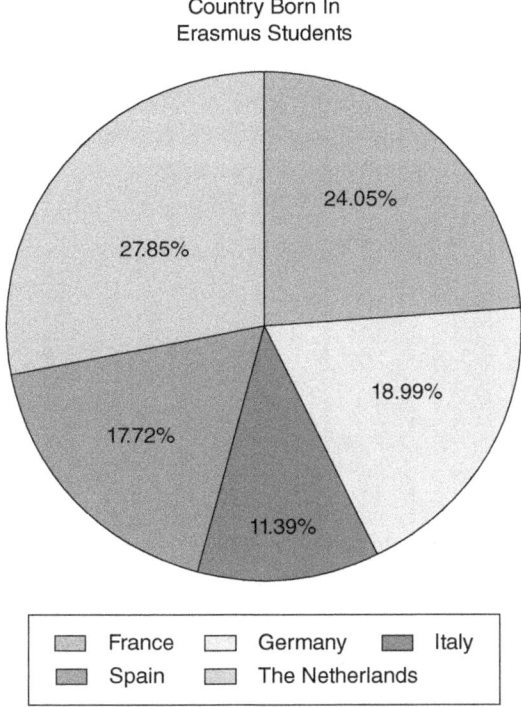

Figure 6.4 Univariate Nominal Graphing

Frankly, this is satisfying and explicitly reflects the relative frequencies. We saw this with the variation ratio of 0.72 in which 'the Netherlands' is the mode but Germany (15), France (19) and Spain (14) all offer close competition. Thinking this way, the graph makes this easier to visualize the variation ratio of those categories/countries not 'the Netherlands'.

Ordinal: Univariate Graphing

For ordinal-level variables, bar charts are often the most accessible and allow for an initial glance at the role of order that distinguishes ordinal- from nominal-level variables. Using our ordinal-level variable from above, we can produce a bar chart to 'see' Social Trust.

Recall, we found a median of 'Agree' and a range of 'Strongly Agree' to 'Strongly Disagree' for Social Trust. One could argue that there is a slight tendency for people to agree with trusting others. Interestingly, if we use the measures of central tendency and dispersion from nominal-level variables (which we can do, see Table 6.3a), this becomes even more apparent. The mode – the most oft-occurring one – is 'Strongly Agree' (which is normatively nice) with a variation ratio of (25+14+10+9=58)/100=0.58. This provides supporting evidence to our intuition that there is generally more social trust.

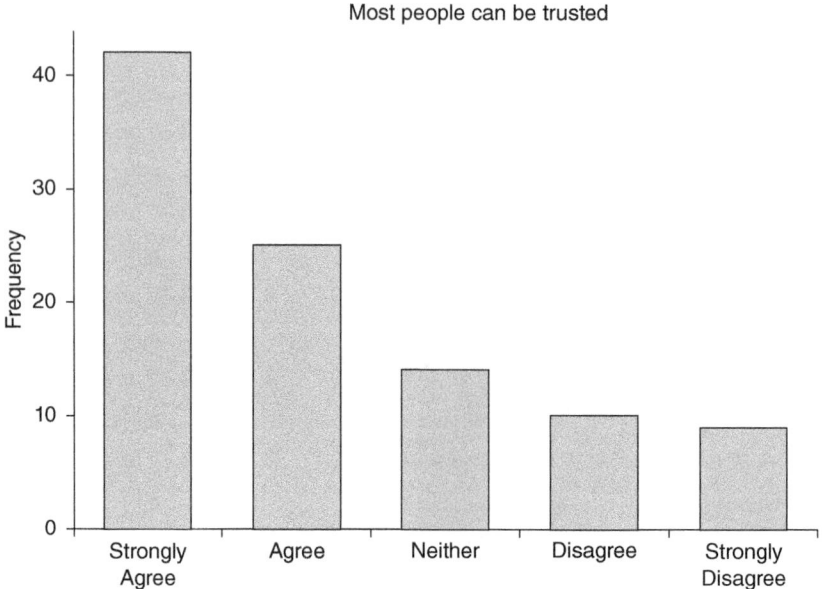

Figure 6.5 Univariate Ordinal Graphing

Interval: Univariate Graphing

Finally, for interval-level variables, the most common are histograms which differ from bar charts in that the columns are of equal intervals (like interval-level data). Histograms also offer a visual clue for dispersion or variation about the mean. Using EU Parliamentary electoral turnout, we can produce a histogram.

Recall that the mean for EU Parliamentary electoral turnout is 51.2% with a standard deviation of 19.9. One thing that is revealed is, as we sensed earlier, there are a few observations – particularly at the upper end – that don't behave like the others. This is not wrong or even particularly problematic. We are simply looking at how the data are distributed across the range of possible outcomes.

Recall our ideological self-placement variable from the European Social Survey above (Figure 6.3). Here, graphing this can help us choose between treating individuals' ideological self-placement as an ordinal- or interval-level variable. In one sense, we know that the intervals between each category are potentially problematic as they are directly incomparable and while mathematically the same – 1 unit change – not the same conceptually (recall: the lukewarm to neutral shift compared to the extreme to *extremely* extreme position). At the same time, the data do seem well-behaved and distributed nicely. It is a subjective choice; however, common usage is a good guide.

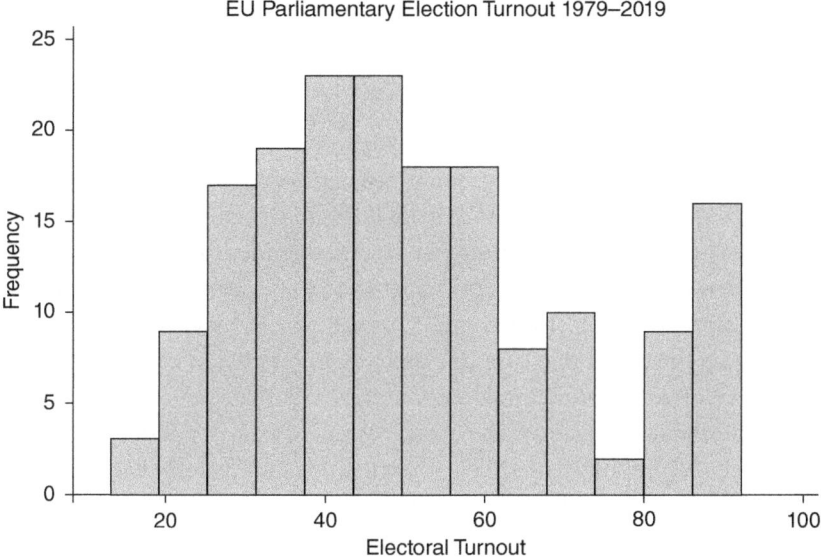

Figure 6.6 Univariate Interval Graphing

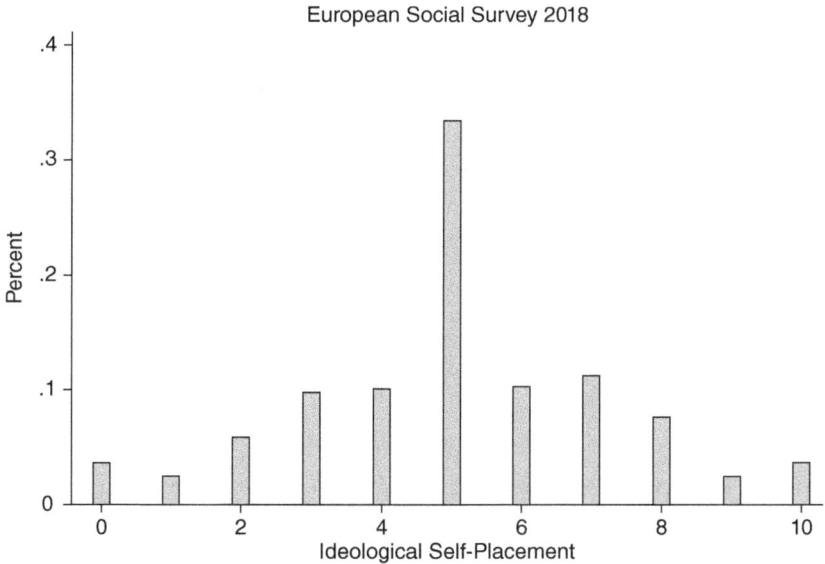

Figure 6.7 Univariate Interval Graphing: Ideology

One reason in favour of graphing is that univariate descriptive statistics can be helpful in understanding our data but struggle to reveal distributional peculiarities.

Problems

We want our data to be well-behaved. What does this mean?

In general, when we take a sample of something in which we are interested, the data tend to reveal a pattern. Using the measures of central tendency and dispersion are in fact reflections of this general orderliness. A challenge to that order is an outlier. **Outliers** are observations in the data (most often one observation – but sometimes more than one) that deviate from the rest of the data. They behave differently. In doing so, their eccentric behaviour can weaken the descriptive summarization process.

For our nominal-level example above on Erasmus students, adding one student from Japan makes 'the Netherlands' – as the best summary – slightly less effective. For our ordinal example in which 68 responded 'Strongly Agree' (Table 6.3c), 1 'Strongly Disagree' wouldn't affect the median by much but would change the range from 'Strongly Agree to Neither' to 'Strongly Agree to Strongly Disagree' which is clearly a less effective indicator of the nature of median as a summary for those data. For the EU Parliamentary election turnout interval-level data, if one country simply boycotted the election resulting in a 0.0% turnout, the mean would change from 51.2 to 50.9 and the standard deviation would change from 19.9 to 20.3. Again, not huge, but that's a noticeable impact for one election.

For all data, a single outlier can simply be addressed. In some cases, it can even be ignored. The course of action depends on how problematic the answers to the following questions are:

- Does the outlier fundamentally change the larger pattern?
- How far is the outlier from the others?
- Does the outlier represent a case that offers some reason to expect its 'wild behaviour'?
- Is there more than one outlier?

Unfortunately, there is no 'best practice' for outliers. Each case must be assessed on the answers to the above questions. However, don't be alarmed. Outliers can be an opportunity in disguise – forcing us to consider our analysis, the outlying case, as well as all the other cases. Perhaps it will lead us to an insight otherwise obscured.

Another problem is skew. **Skew** is the shift of data in one direction or another. Data are often skewed by the nature of the underlying variable or the presence of several or significant outliers.

This is easiest to see with interval-level data (see Figure 6.8). In a distribution of data that has no skew, all of the measures of central tendency will be more or less aligned. Data with a negative skew will stretch these measures out so that the mode is above both the median and mean. The opposite – positive skew – results in the mode being below median and mean.

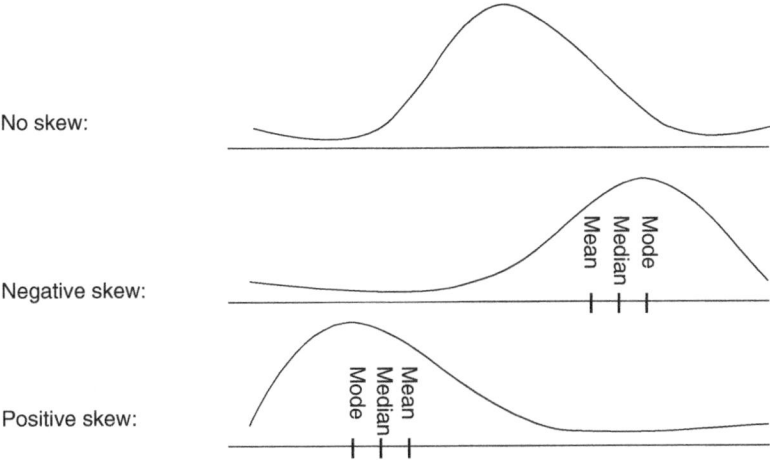

Figure 6.8 Skew

Thus, such deviations – such bad behaviour – are important to notice although rarely fatal flaws. But outliers and skew challenge the use of statistics. Statistical techniques do not automatically resolve issues that reside in the data. It is up to us to be aware of such problems. This is also 'getting to know our data'.

A Final Word

Description is difficult. Good description is more difficult. Our goal with Univariate Descriptive Statistics is to summarize the variables in which we are interested and understand how good that summary is. In some cases, distinguishing a potato from a non-potato can be sufficient. In International Relations, we might want to simply know whether countries in our sample are democracies or not. In other cases, we will want to exploit the mathematical basis of statistical techniques to squeeze as much detail out of our data. For example, in the study of Political Economy, we may want to know – with as much precision as we can – the impact of globalization on the change in economic performance of several countries. And other investigations will be somewhere in between. The good news is that both Univariate Descriptive Statistics and graphing start to help us do so.

End of Chapter Summary

- Univariate Descriptive Statistics summarize data and tell us how good that summary is. Measures of central tendency are the way we summarize data.

Measures of dispersion tell us how representative the measure of central tendency is by providing the amount of variation around that value.
- In order to know which measure of central tendency and dispersion to use, we need to know the level of measurement of our variable in which we are interested.
- There are three levels of measurement: Nominal, Ordinal, and Interval. They distinguish variables from one another and determine what types of statistical techniques can be used.
    - To describe nominal-level variables, we use the mode and variation ratio.
    - To describe ordinal-level variables, we use the median and range.
    - To describe interval-level variables, we use the mean and standard variation.
- Each level of measurement can use the measures of central tendency and dispersion from the ones 'beneath' them. Although this is uncommon, it can – in some cases – be useful.
- Description of our data is important. In order to get to know our data, we often will need to investigate what our data and variables look like using several methods including Univariate Descriptive Statistics and graphing.
- Good description is not always easy.
- The concept of dispersion – the spread or variance of data – is a useful tool in understanding how the data are behaving.
- Common challenges to univariate description are the presence of outliers.
- It is now impossible for you to say, 'I cannot do statistics.' You are doing them. Tell your friends.

Glossary

- **Datum**: a single piece of data.
- **Data:** A collection of codified observations on a topic we are interested in.
- **Variable:** the choice of indicator that draws data together conceptually and operationally.
- **Case:** The unit of analysis – the subject of your study; in this case, countries.
- **Dataset:** A collection of variables for the included observations creates a set of data.
- The **level of measurement** is a description of the type of data that comprise a variable which shapes the subsequent statistics techniques that can be used. **Nominal**-level variables are unordered values or categories. **Ordinal**-level variables are values or categories that, while having a clear order, do not lend themselves easily to statistical analysis as the intervals between each category are not the same mathematically. **Interval**-level variables have values and intervals that are mathematically tractable.
- **Measures of central tendency** summarize variables with a representative value.
- **Measures of dispersion** describe the distribution of values around the measure of central tendency in turn telling us how representative that measure is.
- **Variance** describes how close or far the observations are to our summary statistic.

- The **mode** is a measure of central tendency used for nominal-level variables. It is the category with the most observations.
- **Relative frequencies** are the proportional frequency of each category relative to the total.
- The **variation ratio** is a measure of dispersion used for nominal-level variables. It describes the variation around the mode.
- The **median** is a measure of central tendency used for ordinal-level variables. It is the observation in the middle such that 50% of the data fall on both sides.
- The **range** is a measure of dispersion used for ordinal-level variables. It describes extent of values for the variable: i.e., the highest to the lowest values.
- The **mean** is a measure of central tendency used for interval-level variables. It is the sum of all the values divided by the number of observations.
- The **standard deviation** is a measure of dispersion used for interval-level variables. It describes the variation around the mean by measuring the average distance of all the data from the mean.
- **Outliers** are observations in the data that deviate from the rest of the data.
- **Skew** is a shift in the distribution of data in one direction or the other away from convergence.

Questions

1. Let's look at Table 6.1 at the start of chapter. Identify each variable's level of measurement and the appropriate measure of central tendency and dispersion.
2. Still looking at Table 6.1, describe in words how the measures of central tendency and dispersion would change for *Main Religion* if all Italians were to go completely *Pastafarian*?
3. The process of summarizing is a tricky one. Using different measures of central tendency and dispersion accommodates the different levels of measurement of different variables. But the aim is the same, to present some form of intuition about a large – sometimes – unwieldly amount of data. What are some of the advantages of summarizing? What are some of the disadvantages?
4. In motorcycle riding, there is a concept called 'target fixation'. It means that a rider can become overly attentive to an object such as another motorcycle in front of them or a bridge abutment. This effect can be so strong – even for professional riders – that the rider will follow another motorcycle into a crash or run into the abutment – despite being able to easily avoid doing so. The outlier problem can be like this. While we prefer well-behaved patterns in our data, often there are outliers. However, even in big datasets with few outliers, explain how 'target fixation' and our attention to outliers are potentially similar phenomena?
5. Recall the processes of conceptualization and operationalization. Appropriateness in our choice of indicator is crucial. While statistical techniques are much easier to perform – with more precise results – on interval-level data, not all variables can be

measured at this level (think: 'Main Religion' or 'Country born in'). Explain how recognizing the appropriate *level of measurement* informs and improves our use of descriptive statistics.
6. Explain how *measures of dispersion* confers an indication of the representativeness of *measures of central tendency*?

Annotated References and Further Reading

Tufte, Edward R. (2001). *The Visual Display of Quantitative Information* 2nd edn. Cheshire, CT: Graphics Press. ISBN 0-9613921-4-2
A classic of data presentations that takes graphing to the next level.

Signposts to the Accompanying Digital Resources

Data used in this chapter

- **Percentage of national internet availability**: International Telecommunications Union
  - www.itu.int/en/ITU-D/Statistics/Pages/stat/default.aspx
- **Global Freedom Scores**: Freedom House
  - https://freedomhouse.org/countries/freedom-world/scores
- **Internet Freedom Scores:** Freedom House
  - https://freedomhouse.org/countries/freedom-net/scores
- **Democracy or Not:** Quality of Governance
  - Teorell, Jan, Aksel Sundström, Sören Holmberg, Bo Rothstein, Natalia Alvarado Pachon, and Cem Mert Dalli. 2021. The Quality of Government Standard Dataset, version Jan21. University of Gothenburg: The Quality of Government Institute, www.qog.pol.gu.se
- **Cabinet Composition** and **Electoral Systems:** *Comparative Political Data Set*
  - www.cpds-data.org/

Data:

- **Country (population)** United Nations Department of Economic and Social Affairs: Population Dynamics- World Population Prospects [*Note:* 2019].
  - https://population.un.org/wpp/
- **Largest religion**: https://ourworldindata.org/grapher/main-religion-of-the-country-inPew-Templeton Global Religious Futures Project, Pew Research Center (2017) [*Note:* 2010].

- o   www.globalreligiousfutures.org/
- o   Visually www.visualcapitalist.com/mapped-major-religions-of-the-world/
- **Global Freedom Scores** are a sum of measure for political rights and civil liberties: Freedom House: [*Note:* 2019].
    - o   https://freedomhouse.org/countries/freedom-world/scores
- **Voice and Accountability**: a measure reflecting the ability of citizens to participate in selecting their government, as well as freedom of expression, freedom of association, and a free media: World Governance Indicators: World Bank: [*Note:* 2019].
    - o   https://info.worldbank.org/governance/wgi/
- **European Parliamentary Turnout**: European Parliament website.
    - o   www.europarl.europa.eu/election-results-2019/en/turnout/
- **Left–right ideological self-placement**: range: 0 (Left) – 10 (Right): European Social Survey (2018).
    - o   ESS 1–9, European Social Survey Cumulative File, Study Description. Bergen: NSD – Norwegian Centre for Research Data for ESS ERIC. https://doi.org/10.21338/NSD-ESS-CUMULATIVE. Includes: Austria, Belgium, Bulgaria, Switzerland, Cyprus, Czech Republic, Germany, Estonia, Finland, France, the UK, Hungary, Ireland, Italy, the Netherlands, Norway, Poland, Serbia, Slovenia.

7
MEASURES OF ASSOCIATION I: NOMINAL- AND ORDINAL-LEVEL VARIABLES

> **LEARNING OUTCOMES**
>
> In this chapter, you will be able to
>
> - Construct and use a cross-tabulation table for nominal- and ordinal-level variables.
> - Identify and apply the correct Measurement of Association for bivariate relationships between nominal- and ordinal-level variables.
> - Correctly interpret the measures of association Lambda and Gamma.
> - Recognize the need and implications for controlled comparisons.
> - Appreciate the importance of associational description in statistical analysis.

Introduction

This chapter explores the often overlooked or under-examined nature of the relationship for nominal and ordinal-level variables. We explore the utility of cross-tabulation as well as the common Measures of Association: Lambda and Gamma. Specific attention is given to the relative ability of different measures to provide similar if not the same information and thus the capabilities and limitations to these approaches. The strengths and weakness (marked by the presence and absence of these techniques in various sub-fields) of these approaches are given special attention.

Bivariate Descriptive Statistics: Nominal- and Ordinal-level Variables

As part of the use of statistics to aid scientific research, Descriptive Statistics takes a bold step in the direction of Principle Number 2 of the Scientific Method: 'The scientific method attempts to identify, isolate, and explain the relationship under investigation.'

It is very often a relationship between variables that lies at the heart of scientific study. And while univariate description gives us a sense of our data and chosen variables, it is how these variables interact that most intrigues us (recall X -> Y). We need therefore to develop not only our sense of how we 'see' variables' mutual movements, their coordination, their relatedness, but how we measure it. To do this, we use Measures of Association.

Measures of Association assess the existence, strength, and, on occasion, direction of a relationship between variables. This is crucial as we want to be able to say more than two variables seem to move together. The appropriate Measure of Association is determined by variables' levels of measurement.

Cross-Tabulation

As mentioned above, interval-level variables tend to get the lion's share of attention, especially from the perspective of statistical techniques. But this is not exclusively the case. Sometimes nominal- and ordinal-level variables are preferred.

One huge advantage of working with nominal- and ordinal-level variables is that they are compact. And if we wanted to look at how they move together, we use cross-tabulation. **Cross-tabulation** shows the joint distribution of nominal- and ordinal-level variables. It is sometimes called a contingency table but most often 'cross-tab'. The basic concept of cross-tab is obvious. We simply put one variable across the top – the independent variable – and another down the side of a table – the dependent variable – and populate each cell with observations that satisfy the category of each row and column.

Let's take a straightforward example.

In Table 7.1, we can see data on whether a country is a democracy (or not) and the percentage of the population that has access to the internet. I have split the percentage of internet access into 'less than 50%' and 'more than 50%'. Using a random sample of 63 countries, we can see their **joint distribution**: that is, the distribution of responses as a function of the other distribution of responses. You can quickly see how this improves our ability to see how one variable 'moves' or is coordinated with another. That is, we see how a country being a democracy is distributed across aggregate internet access in that country.

Table 7.1 Democracy and Internet Access

		Internet access		
		<50%	>50%	*TOTAL*
Democracy	Yes	13	20	*33*
	No	8	22	*30*
	TOTAL	*21*	*42*	*63*

If we are interested in relationships between these two variables – as in our example here, a potential relationship between countries being a democracy or not and the level of internet access – this seems like a promising place to start. Why?

Three reasons, really.

1. We can start to see *if* a relationship may exist.
2. We can calculate the *magnitude* or *strength* of the joint distribution, based on their level of measurement.
3. For some relationships, cross-tabs can indicate a *direction*: i.e., whether the relationship is a positive or negative relationship.

In Table 7.1, at first glance at the cross-tab, for both democracies and non-democracies, the majority of cases have greater than 50% access to the internet. It seems initially clear that in democracies, the disparity of internet access is greater. That is, while for democracies, 22 (at >50%) is substantially larger than 8 (<50%) and for non-democracies, the difference is less so: 20 (>50%) to 13 (<50%). Additionally, the difference between the number of democracies and non-democracies with internet access over 50% is only 2. There is a lot of information in this cross-tab about the joint distribution of these two variables that we can already see!

Now that we have an easy and available means to visualize the joint distribution of two nominal- or ordinal-level variables, we can now seek to describe how they are related. Ultimately, measures of association tell us how well two variables are related in such a way that knowing one variable helps us know the other. That is, if two variables are highly associated, we know a lot about *both* variables by knowing about just one of them. If they are not highly associated, we know less about the other variable by knowing about the other one.

Measures of Association: Nominal- and Ordinal-level Variables

The Measures of Association used for Nominal- and Ordinal-level variables depends on the level of measurement of the two variables you are interested in (in this case, nominal-level or ordinal-level). The most common measures of association used to assess the relationship between nominal- and ordinal-level variables are Gamma and Lambda. I call these two the 'Forgotten Friends' as, although they are the most common and informative, they are less frequently used – even when appropriate.

Table 7.2 Measures of Association

	Nominal	Ordinal
Nominal	2 × 2: Yule's Q **[Gamma]** $N \times N$: **Lambda**	
Ordinal	**Lambda**	**Gamma**

Yule's Q (Gamma)

Let's revisit our cross-tab of Democracy and the Internet (Table 7.1). Both variables in this cross-tab are nominal-level variables, so category order is not important. Not only that but the cross-tab itself is a specific form, this is a 2 × 2 (pronounced: 'two-by-two') table. Again, the standard is to put the *dependent variable* down the left side (as the rows) and the *independent variable* across the top (as the columns).

> ### 1, 2, MANY
>
> A variable with two categories is called a dichotomous variable. A variable with three categories is called a trichotomous variable. More categories are referred to as polychotomous. This feels similar to the counting system of the Piranha of the Amazon, in which there are only words for '1', '2', and 'many'.

For a 2 × 2 nominal × nominal cross-tab, we use a special case of the measure of association Goodman and Kruskal's *Gamma*, called **Yule's Q**. This makes no difference to the output.

- Yule's Q ranges from –1.0 to 1.0. For our interpretation, 0 = no relationship between the variables and, as we approach 1 (or –1), we get closer to 'perfect association'.
- In the case of a 2 × 2 cross-tab, Yule's Q estimates the magnitude – but not the direction – of the relationship (because nominal variables don't have order).

Before we calculate Yule's Q (Gamma), let's revisit the joint distribution of the two variables in the cross-tab.

As we noted previously, the joint distribution of these variables suggests that there may be some relationship – i.e., these variables move together in a conspicuous way – between democracy and aggregate-level access to the internet.

$$\text{Yule's } Q = \frac{bc - ad}{bc + ad}$$

$$\text{if } \begin{array}{cc} a & b \\ c & d \end{array}$$

Therefore, to calculate Yule's Q (Gamma), we assign the a, b, c, and d to the appropriate cells and calculate the measure.

Table 7.3 Yule's Q (Gamma) for 2 × 2 Cross-Tab

		Internet access		
		<50%	>50%	TOTAL
Democracy	No	13 (a)	20 (b)	**33**
	Yes	8 (c)	22 (d)	**30**
	TOTAL	**21**	**42**	**63**

$$Yule's\ Q = \frac{(20)(8)-(13)(22)}{(20)(8)+(13)(22)} = -0.283$$

Yule's Q (Gamma) is a **proportion reduction of error** (PRE) measure, which means that knowing one variable reduces our error in predicting the outcome in the other. Therefore, we interpret Yule's Q (Gamma) = −0.283 as 'Aggregate access to the internet improves our prediction of whether a country is a democracy or not by 28.3%' or more accurately, 'We reduce our error in predicting the democratic status of a country by 28.3% by knowing the aggregate access to the internet.'

An Aside: Magnitude, Conceptually

Let's build our intuition about magnitude by using a set of fabricated 2 × 2 tables of democracy and internet access.

Table 7.4a Measure of Association – Yule's Q (Gamma) = 0

		Internet access		
		<50%	>50%	TOTAL
Democracy	No	25	25	**50**
	Yes	25	25	**50**
	TOTAL	**50**	**50**	**100**

Table 7.4b Measure of Association – Yule's Q (Gamma) = 0

		Internet access		
		<50%	>50%	TOTAL
Democracy	No	33	33	**66**
	Yes	17	17	**34**
	TOTAL	**50**	**50**	**100**

In Tables 7.4a and 7.4b Yule's Q (Gamma) is equal to 0. This means knowing the distribution of internet access in no way helps us know about the distribution of democratic countries. That is, the percentage of country-level internet access (here in the form of less than 50% or more than 50%) gives us no clue as to whether a country may be a democracy or not. Their association is zero.

Tables 7.5a and 7.5b illustrate the opposite.

Table 7.5a   Measure of Association – Yule's Q (Gamma) = 1

		Internet access		
		<50%	>50%	TOTAL
Democracy	No	0	50	50
	Yes	50	0	50
	TOTAL	*50*	*50*	*100*

Table 7.5b   Measure of Association – Yule's Q (Gamma) = 0.98

		Internet access		
		<50%	>50%	TOTAL
Democracy	No	1	49	50
	Yes	49	1	50
	TOTAL	*50*	*50*	*100*

In Table 7.5a, if we know the percentage of a country's level of internet access, we know whether that country is a democracy or not (namely: if more than 50% internet access, the country is a democracy. If less than 50% internet access, the country is not a democracy).

In Table 7.5b, while not as *perfect* perfect as Yule's Q (Gamma)=1, the relationship is very strong (0.98). We would have a very good expectation about whether a country is a democracy by knowing the percentage of internet access in that country. In other words, for both of these, knowing the percentage of internet access is a very good guide to the status of democracy in that country as they are very strongly associated.

Table 7.6   Measure of Association – Yule's Q (Gamma) = 0.58

		Internet access		
		<50%	>50%	TOTAL
Democracy	No	17	33	50
	Yes	33	17	50
	TOTAL	*50*	*50*	*100*

Finally, and a bit more realistically, somewhere between 'not knowing anything' (Tables 7.4a and 7.4b) and 'knowing everything' (Table 7.5a; and 'nearly everything' Table 7.5b). In this table (Table 7.6) we can see a tendency for countries with more than 50% internet access to more often be democracies, as they are moderately associated. Not always, but the data tend that way, more often than not.

The use of Yule's Q (Gamma) as a measure of association for two nominal-level variables in a 2 × 2 cross-tab is relatively straightforward. And the use of 2 × 2 tables is common in Political Science: e.g., yes/no; vote/not; war/no war; win/lose; passed/failed. The analysis of nominal bivariate relationships provides evidence of whether there is a relationship and its strength.

To tackle larger nominal-level variables and nominal-level variables' relationships with ordinal-level variables, we have to adjust our measurement of association to lambda.

Lambda

For larger cross-tabs of two nominal-level variables (n × n), we use the measure of association: Goodman and Kruskal's **Lambda**. We also use Lambda as the measure of association for nominal-level by ordinal-level variables (of any size; n × n).

- Lambda ranges from 0 to 1.0. For our interpretation, 0 = no relationship between the variables and as we approach 1, we get closer to 'perfect association'.
- Lambda estimates the magnitude – but not the direction – of the relationship.
    - Why no direction? Nominal variables are included but (still) don't have direction.
    - Note that some research has suggested that Lambda can be a bit conservative and therefore under-estimate the magnitude.

Like Yule's Q (Gamma), Lambda is also a PRE – proportional reduction of error – measure. It tells us how much we would reduce the number of errors we would make by knowing the joint distribution of the two variables rather than merely guessing the modal (or median) category.

Like many things in science, we are measuring how much we are *less* wrong.

$$Lambda\ (\lambda) = \frac{E_1 - E_2}{E_1}$$

Taking the X as the independent variable and Y as the dependent variable, we read this formula as such:

$$Lambda\ (\lambda) = \frac{[error\ of\ assuming\ mode\ of\ Y] - [error\ of\ assuming\ mode\ of\ Y\ in\ X]}{[error\ of\ assuming\ mode\ of\ Y]}$$

The more you look at it, the more it becomes clear that this is just a fancy way to say what we just said about reducing our errors: 'We are measuring how much we *reduce* being wrong.' Follow along:

- Lambda is (E_1): assuming that what we know about Y is captured by the mode (recall Univariate Descriptive Statistics) minus (E_2): what we know about Y *given what we know about X's relationship to Y* (all divided by E_1 to standardize it, that is, make it between 0 and 1).

Note: Lambda is also an asymmetric measure meaning that the result depends on which variable is the independent variable and which is the dependent variable. This is not a high hurdle as it simply reminds us to adhere to the standard of putting the dependent variable down the left side and the independent variable across the top. This will increasingly be the case.

When we walk through the example below, this 'less wrong' approach of reduction of error calculation is apparent as we move across the table. So, although Lambda can be used with two nominal-level variables in a cross-tab larger than 2 × 2, we will take a step that bridges an exclusively nominal-level example and an exclusively ordinal-level example by looking at a nominal- by ordinal-level cross-tab.

I propose to continue our example from above about democracy and the internet and expand one nominal-level variable into an ordinal-level variable. We can simply re-operationalize the percentage of national-level internet access from 'less than 50%' and 'more than 50%' to thirds; namely, 0–33.3%; 33.4–66.7%; 66.8–100%.

Table 7.7 Lambda Example – Nominal/Ordinal Variables

		Internet access			
		Low 1/3%	Middle 1/3%	High 1/3%	Total
Democracy	No	9	10	14	**33**
	Yes	6	7	17	**30**
	Total	*15*	*17*	*31*	*63*

Now, we have a nominal-level variable – 'Democracy or Not' – and an ordinal-level variable: 'Internet Access' in thirds [0–33.3%; 33.4–66.7%; 66.8–100%].

First, let's examine the cross-tab. Like our first impression of the 2 × 2 cross-tab, it appears there may be a relationship between a country's level of internet access and whether or not that country is a democracy. The least and medium amounts of internet access – '0–33.3% and 33.4–66.7% of internet access' – are common among non-democracies whereas '66.8%-100% of internet access' is more common in democracies.

Let's see what Lambda has to say about this relationship.

$$Lambda\ (\lambda) = \frac{E_1 - E_2}{E_1}$$

We first need E_1, the error of assuming mode of Y. Simply, if we assumed that the mode of the dependent variable ('Y': Democracy or Not) was always right, how often would we be wrong?

In our sample of countries, given that there are 30 democratic countries and 33 non-democratic countries, the mode of democracy is 'not a democracy'. If we were to just assume that this was the correct answer all the time – that countries are 'not a democracy' – we would be right 33 times, but wrong 30 times. Thus, the 'error of assuming the mode of Y' is 30.

Then we need E_2, the error in assuming modes of Y in X. This simply asks us to consider whether knowing the independent variable ('X') reduces the number of errors we would make in guessing the outcome of Y. To do so, we take the total, 63, and subtract the modal category for each one.

Table 7.8 Lambda – Modes of Y in X

Internet access	Mode	Number of observations
Low 1/3%	Not a democracy	9
Middle 1/3%	Not a democracy	10
High 1/3%	Democracy	17

Adding these, 9 + 10 + 17, we get 36. If we assumed the 'modes of Y in X,' we would be correct 36 times. But we want to know the errors we would make in doing so. Therefore, 63 – 36 = 27. These 27 are the errors we would make if we knew the joint distribution of the percentage of internet access and the state of democracy in a country.

FROM THE OTHER DIRECTION

Note: Another way to arrive at $E_2 = 27$ is to sum the *non*-modals within the dependent variable (i.e., the 6 in '0–33.3%' and 'Democracy', the 7 in '33.4 – 66.7%' and 'Democracy', and the 14 in '66.8%–100%' and 'Not a democracy'). 6 + 7 + 14 = 27. This is the sum of the non-modals (the errors we would make even if we knew the joint distribution).

Therefore, we can input the number of errors that we would make both knowing the joint distribution and not knowing the joint distribution. We would hope to reduce the number of errors. And it makes sense that if knowing one variable greatly reduces the errors in predicting the outcome of the other variable, they would be highly associated.

$$\text{Lambda}\ (\lambda) = \frac{30-27}{30} = 0.100$$

Here, we do not find this to be the case. This is interpreted as 'We are 10.0% better at determining whether a country is a democracy or not when we know the level of aggregate level of internet access than by simply choosing the modal category of democracy.' That doesn't sound sizeable and, honestly, it's not a lot.

Substantially, it would appear that knowing about the level of internet access of a country tells us very little about its democratic status. With the previous breakdown of 'less than 50%' and 'more than 50%', the relationship seemed a bit more coherent. Here, however, the expanded operationalization of internet access into three ordinal categories has muddied the water. Thus, while Lambda has given us a means to quantify the association between these two variables, it has also provided further nuance to the nature of the relationship.

Gamma, We Meet Again

Finally, for an ordinal × ordinal association, the measure of association is **Gamma**. Good news: we've already done Gamma (Yule's Q is a special case). Neutral news: calculating Gamma for ordinal-level variables is slightly more involved than a 2 × 2 cross-tab.

Goodman and Kruskal's Gamma:

- Is a Proportional Reduction of Error (PRE) statistic
- Ranges from –1 to 1
    - Estimates both magnitude *and direction*. Why? Because both variables are ordinal-level.

For our ongoing investigation into democracy and the internet, we can expand the measure of democracy from two categories (democracy or not) to an ordinal three. Freedom House provides a measure of democracy that articulates three categories: 'Not Free', 'Partly Free', and 'Free'. This offers us the opportunity to examine this relationship with greater precision.

Table 7.9 Gamma Example – Ordinal Variables

		Internet access			
		Low 1/3%	Middle 1/3%	High 1/3%	TOTAL
Democracy	Not Free	7	8	11	**26**
	Partly Free	8	7	7	**22**
	Free	0	2	13	**15**
	TOTAL	**15**	**15**	**33**	**63**

Before we calculate Gamma, let's take a longer look at the cross-tab above (Table 7.8). We are excited to find out whether greater operational precision provides more insight into the relationship between internet access and democracy. Looking at the table, 'partly free' democracies seem uniformly distributed across internet access, 'not free' and 'partly free' democracies are very similar. They are similar in that both have modal categories in the high 1/3%. Thus, moving from 'Low 1/3%' to 'High 1/3%' internet access, there is not a uniform shift from 'Not Free' to 'Free' for democracy that we might expect.

While we might be hoping for a clearer association, gamma may provide some guidance about this relationship.

To calculate Gamma, we need to calculate the following formula.

$$Gamma(\gamma) = \frac{n_c - n_d}{n_c + n_d}$$

We will need the concordant pairs (n_c) and the discordant pairs (n_d). Concordance refers to two variables 'moving together', specifically, they move 'in the same direction', for example, when one goes up, the other does as well. Discordance instead refers to two variables that move 'against one another', for example, when one goes up, the other goes down.

To calculate the concordant pairs, begin in the upper left-hand cell ('Low 1/3%' and 'not free': 7). Block out the rest of the row (8 and 11) and the rest of the column (8 and 0) and add the values in the cells below and to the right.

- This would be 7, 7, 2, and 13 = 29. Multiply this number (29) by the value in the upper left-hand cell (7) = 203.

Repeat, moving one cell to the right. Again, only add those cells below and to the right.

- That would be 8, blocking out the remainder of the row (11) and column (7 and 2), multiplied by the sum of the remaining cells, (7 + 13 = 20). 8 × 20 = 160.

Once you have finished a row, drop to the next one.

- On the next row down, we would choose 8 ('Low 1/3%' and 'Partly Free' Democracy), blocking out the remainder of the row (7 and 7) and column (0), multiplied by the sum of the remaining cells, (2 + 13 = 15). 8 × 15 = 120.
- Moving one cell to the right, we would choose 7, blocking out the remainder of the row (7) and column (2), multiplied by the sum of the remaining cells, (13). 7 × 13 = 91.

Dropping to the next row, we have no more cells below and to the right. We have computed the concordant pairs.

Concordant pairs (n_c) = ((29)(7 + 7 + 2 + 13)) + ((8)(7 + 13)) + ((8)(2 + 13)) + ((7)(13)) = 574

To calculate the discordant pairs, we do the same procedure but start from the top-right cell and work our way to the left. That is, starting with the percentage of internet access 'High 1/3%' and Democracy 'not free' (11), we block out the remainder of the row (7 and 8) and the column (7 and 13) and add the remaining cells, below and to the left.

- Here, that would be 8, 7, 0, and 2 = 17. Multiply this number (17) by the value in the upper right-hand cell (11) = 187.

Repeat, moving one cell to the left. Again, only add those cells below and to the left.

- That would be 8, blocking out the remainder of the row (7) and column (7 and 2), multiplied by the sum of the remaining cells, (8 + 0 = 8). 8 × 8 = 64.

Once you have finished a row, drop to the next one.

- On the next row down, we would choose 7 ('High 1/3%' and 'Partly Free' Democracy), blocking out the remainder of the row (8 and 7) and column (13), multiplied by the sum of the remaining cells, (0 + 2 = 2). 7 × 2 = 14.
- Moving one cell to the right, we would choose 7, blocking out the remainder of the row (8) and column (2), multiplied by the sum of the remaining cells, (0). 7 × 0 = 0.

Dropping to the next row, we have no more cells below and to the left. We have computed the discordant pairs.

Discordant pairs (n_d) = ((11)(8 + 7 + 0 + 2)) + ((8)(8 + 0)) + ((7)(0 + 2)) + ((7)(0)) = 265

$$Gamma\ (\gamma) = \frac{574 - 265}{574 + 265} = 0.368$$

Magnitude: Gamma is suggesting a moderate relationship between these variables. The interpretation is 'Knowing the level of internet access in a country, we reduce our errors in predicting their level of democracy 36.8%' OR 'Our prediction of the state of democracy in a country is 36.8% better by knowing its level of internet access.'

Direction: For Gamma, a 'positive' relationship is one that runs from the top left to the bottom right.

Table 7.10a Gamma Example – Positive Direction

		Internet access			
		Low 1/3%	Middle 1/3%	High 1/3%	TOTAL
Democracy	Not Free	7	8	11	26
	Partly Free	8	7	7	22
	Free	0	2	13	15
	TOTAL	15	15	33	63

A 'negative' relationship runs from the bottom left to the top right.

Table 7.10b Gamma Example – Negative Direction

		Internet access			
		Low 1/3%	Middle 1/3%	High 1/3%	TOTAL
Democracy	Not Free	7	8	11	**26**
	Partly Free	8	7	7	**22**
	Free	0	2	13	**15**
	TOTAL	**15**	**15**	**33**	**63**

That is, if we calculate a positive Gamma, as we have here (0.368), the relationship between these two ordinal-level variables runs from the top left to the bottom right and relates the variables in this direction. Thus, as internet increases, so does democracy.

Interpretation of Gamma: Let's Science for a Minute

For our analysis of the relationship between democracy and the internet, we have shown three analyses of several different measures of association between different measures of democracy and the internet.

- Between two nominal-level indicators, we found a Yule's Q (Gamma) of –0.283.
- Between one nominal-level indicator and one ordinal-level indicator, we found a Lambda of 0.100.
- Between two ordinal-level indicators, we found a Gamma of 0.368.

The evidence is not overwhelming. But neither is it ignorable. Each of these Measures of Association have provided us with information on the relationship at the levels we have asked. Maybe now is a good time to discuss how such *statistical* analyses can inform *scientific* study. And how scientific study is necessary to make these outputs both useful and informative. Given the three measures of associations we have produced above, we may feel ready to say something about the relationship between democracy and the internet. Let's check in with where this might work, and where we, as scientists using statistical analyses, are aware of the limitations of using statistics.

Association as the Nature of a Relationship

Here is a simple example. There are 50 people in the next room (that you cannot see) and I tell you that the modal hair colour is brown. If I ask you to guess each person's hair colour one-by-one (you can't see them) and pay you 5€ for every correct guess, you would be wise to say, 'brown' every time. Why? Because you would be right the most amount of time (it is the modal – the most typical – colour). However, if I told you that the modal hair colour is blond for men and brown for women, and repeat the process of asking the hair colour for each person – still unseen but now identified by their gender – you would say, 'blond' for every man and 'brown' for every woman. Why? You would get more money as you would be reducing the number of times you would be wrong.

Again, one can think of Measures of Association as the amount that knowing one variable helps us anticipate another. And technically, that is what PRE means: how much can we reduce the errors we would make in guessing what one variable would be (knowing only the modal or median category). These Measures of Association provide some insight as to the changes that take place across one of the variables in the context of the other one. That is, the level of association is *how much one variable tells us about the other*. With a high association, knowing one variable tells a lot about where we can expect to find the other variable. With a low association, we know less about where the other variable will be.

In the examples above, there is weak to moderate evidence that free democracies tend to have more internet access than other types of democracies, but not in a 'That's a fact!' kind of way. As we saw comparing two ordinal-level variables, this relationship may be more complicated (I'm looking at you, 'not free' democracies). At the same time, Measures of Association not only provide a summary of the variables in which we are interested but can also provide the basis for thinking about observations not in our sample. For example, let's consider the analysis here as the basis for our expectations of a country outside our sample.

- If the Democratic Republic of Congo has a Global Freedom score of 'not free', what – given the Gamma of 0.368 that we calculated for 'Global Freedom' and 1/3rds internet access – might we anticipate its level of internet access to be?
    o It is not unreasonable to expect the internet access in the Democratic Republic of Congo to be low.
    o In fact, the International Telecommunications Union reports the level of internet access in Congo as 8.7% (in 2017).

- However, be careful! Tanzania has a Freedom House 'Global Freedom' score of 'partly free' and – according to the International Telecommunications Union – only 16% (in 2017) internet access.
    o Given the gamma of 0.368 between 'Global Freedom' and internet access, we might be tempted to associate Tanzania's Global Freedom score of 'partly free' with the 'middle third' of internet access; yet, the Gamma reveals what *tends* to be related, not what *will* be related.

This is a reminder that Measures of Association are just that. A guide to thinking about the associative nature of the relationship rather than a definitive statement about the relationship. In other words, while these relationships tend implicate more internet access with more democracy, 'tend to move together' is not the same as 'do move together'.

For us as scientists, knowing that nature of this relationship – its magnitude and direction (Gamma) – can be helpful in directing our thinking about cases outside the sample.

The good news is that as we progress through our study of statistics, we will also improve our ability to know when our sample analysis can tell us a lot (or not) about observations outside that sample.

The Eternal Reliance on Conceptualization and Operationalization

At the same time, you are a scientist. Let's get feedback from other experts!

You apply to an academic conference, get accepted, and present your results. After your presentation, the hands shoot up. Here are some of the questions they will undoubtedly ask. Many want to confront the first 2 × 2 matrix in which we find the joint distribution of whether a country is a democracy or not and whether that country has 50% access to the internet.

- Why 50%? Who said 50% is the right number?
    - What happens when we use 40% and 60% or 25% and 75%?
    - Which one is most appropriate and why?
- Conceptualization and operationalization of *democracy*
    - With nominal-level indicators, can countries be meaningfully bifurcated into 'democracy' or 'not democracy'?
    - Are the Freedom House measures of civil society – Not Free, Partly Free, Free – the most appropriate indicators of a demcoracitc form of government?
- Conceptualization and operationalization of *'internet access'*
    - What does 50% of internet access tell us about the role of the internet in different countries?
    - Moving to ordinal-level indicators, can countries be meaningfully trifurcated into thirds of internet access?
    - Is access the best way to think about the role of the internet?

As a scientist, you must recognize these potential challenges. We must ask ourselves, aside from the statistical calculations that we have made,

- Are we providing clear – and consistent – conceptualization as well as operational measures of what it is we intend to study?
- Does increasing the level of measurement of what we want to study – as we have done here, from nominal to ordinal – reduce the challenges to our analysis?
- What is the interplay between what we choose to analyse and what we find?

Once again, we come to see how subjective the objective analysis of data can be and how important transparency is. To be clear, none of these questions raised at the academic conference mean that we are *wrong* wrong. Simply, they point directly at the challenges of identifying a relationship given the availability of data, the concepts we use, the measures we have, and how we are able to find associations among them. This is a clear example of how statistics can serve scientific study inasmuch as the choices that we make are clear, transparent, well-reasoned, and defensible. Hard to believe this little table (Table 7.2 reproduced here) would create all this information!

	Nominal	Ordinal
Nominal	2 × 2: Yule's Q [**Gamma**]	
	$N \times N$: **Lambda**	
Ordinal	**Lambda**	**Gamma**

Controlled Comparisons

Statistics can serve the scientific method by identifying and isolating the relationship in which we are interested. This is the relationship one expects to find: Independent Variable (X) → Dependent Variable (Y). This is called a **zero-order relationship**: the relationship between two variables and nothing else. The Measures of Association presented in this chapter are estimates of zero-order relationships. And as we have seen, these can be informative if we remain demanding, sceptical, and transparent.

However, it is unlikely to surprise you that simple relationships like this are rarely found in nature, and less so in the social sciences. It is diminishingly unlikely to find a two-variable relationship that is not impacted by anything else.

What we need to do is establish how much of the change in the dependent variable (Y) is due to changes in independent variable (X) and how much is due to something else such as another independent variable (e.g., Z). **Controlled comparisons** are a means to begin to examine the relationship between X and Y by introducing another potential explanatory variable, Z.

Controlled Comparison Example

Continuing with our democracy and internet access example above, we introduce an economic performance variable. There is no one established single economic indicator of performance so we can choose one of the most common: the unemployment rate. The rate of unemployment is not a direct measure of a country's economic performance but does reflect whether capacities and resources are being efficiently used. That is, when economic activity is moving slowly, unemployment reflects this by increasing.

To standardize the use of the unemployment rate across these countries, we will use the change in unemployment rates from 2018 to 2020 taken from the World Bank. If a country's rate of unemployment has remained steady (or slightly increased), we will assume that the country is performing moderately well economically. If, however, the unemployment rate is increasing more substantively, we expect the economy to be slowing down and potentially having an effect on the relationship between democracy and the internet.

- Can you think of some reasons why increasing unemployment may weaken – or potentially, strengthen – the strong relationship we have seen between democracy and internet access?
    o Recall: the *reasons* why they move together is a theory, what we expect to *observe* is a hypothesis.

Below I present Table 7.9 (from above) as two separate tables of the countries with low unemployment (less than 1% change) – Table 7.11a – and higher unemployment (more than 1% change) – Table 7.11b.

Table 7.11a Democracy, Internet Access, and Unemployment (<1% change)

		Internet access			
		Low 1/3%	Middle 1/3%	High 1/3%	TOTAL
Democracy	Not Free	7	6	3	16
	Partly Free	6	3	3	12
	Free	0	0	6	6
	TOTAL	*13*	*9*	*12*	*34*

Table 7.11b Democracy, Internet Freedom, and Unemployment

		Internet access			
		Low 1/3%	Middle 1/3%	High 1/3%	TOTAL
Democracy	Not Free	0	2	8	10
	Partly Free	2	4	4	10
	Free	0	2	7	9
	TOTAL	*2*	*8*	*19*	*29*

Given both of the main variables are still ordinal, and we have divided the large group into two smaller groups of low change in unemployment (less than 1% increase over 2 years) and moderate change in unemployment (more than 1% increase over 2 years), we can still use Lambda as our measurement of association.

Looking, as we should, at Tables 7.11a and 7.11b, we can see that separating this group of countries by unemployment – as a measure of economic performance – has created a potential divergence in the relationship between democracy and the internet. In Table 7.11a, in which unemployment has changed less than 1% between 2018–20, the pattern of democracies having more internet access seems stronger and more aligned, moving from top left to bottom right. Whereas in Table 7.11b, in which unemployment has changed more than 1% between 2018–20, all types of democracies are weighted toward greater internet access.

Rather than re-calculate Lambda, I provide them here:

- In Table 7.11a: Lambda = 0.506.
- In Table 7.11b: Lambda = –0.056.

What have we observed? Two really important things!

One, in this controlled comparison, our impression from examining the cross-tabs is confirmed. Introducing an economic element into this relationship seems to have created a divergent set of relationships. For countries in which unemployment has changed less than 1% between 2018–20, the relationship between democracy and internet access has increased in magnitude (0.506, and retained a similar direction) in comparison with the original Lambda (0.368). This is supported by the drop of Lambda in countries in which unemployment has risen more than 1% between 2018–20 (–0.056). Taken together, these suggest that the relationship between democracy and internet access should include an economic dimension to better differentiate the nature of this relationship.

Two, the strong differentiation between countries with changes in unemployment forces us to confront the theoretical basis for this controlled comparison. In the specific terms of this analysis, countries in which unemployment has changed less than 1% between 2018–20, the relationship between democracy and internet is quite strong. At the same time, in countries in which unemployment has changed more than 1% between 2018–20, the relationship between democracy and internet is weighted heavily toward higher internet access regardless of the level of democracy.

How can we explain this? Or maybe asked differently, is change in unemployment sufficient to do so? That is, is 'change in unemployment' the most correct and accurate measure that differentiates the nature of the relationship between democracy and internet access? Or does the concept and operationalization of 'economic performance' require greater investigation to find perhaps a different, more appropriate, economic measure?

In our example here, the first point underscores the importance of economic performance while the second urges us to consider both the theory (why) and measure (what) of economic performance. Once again, as we advance in our statistical techniques, we gain additional insights for relationships, yet we rarely receive a complete picture.

A Parting Note for Controlled Comparisons

Introducing other variables to identify, isolate and ultimately explain the relationships in which we are interested is a fundamental step in scientific study. Statistics, and in this specific case, the controlled comparisons of nominal and ordinal relationships, begin to show you how this is done. However, while controlled comparisons can be very useful in examining many nominal and ordinal relationships, they begin to become unwieldly trying to handle more than three variables. Additionally, controlled comparisons are not simply controlling for other effects, they are in fact simplified versions of more complicated relationships that we will cover in later chapters. Let it suffice to say that controlled comparisons – while somewhat limited – are a way to expand our thinking and understanding about the relationship in which we are interested and can help highlight some important elements. However, to discover more, we will have to increase our statistical sophistication.

Other Associational Measures

Just to be clear, there are other measures of association between nominal- and ordinal-level variables. We have discussed Gamma and Lambda as they are useful, straightforward, and common in Political Science.

Table 7.12 Other Measures of Association

	Nominal	Ordinal
Nominal	2 × 2: Phi (φ)	
	N × N: Cramer's V	
Ordinal	Cramer's V	Kendall's Tau b and Tau c, Somer's d, Spearman's rho

However, for 2 × 2 cross-tabs, N × N cross-tabs, and nominal × ordinal cross-tabs, one could additionally use Phi (φ) or Cramer's V. While not uncommon in the social sciences, fundamentally, Phi and Cramer's V require more inputs (and thus calculations) without providing a comparable improvement in estimating the association in which we are interested. In terms of estimating relationships, we are only able to say that associations are weak, moderate, or strong.

For ordinal × ordinal relationships, Kendall's Tau A, B, and C and Somers' D are all alternatives to Lambda but also derivatives of Lambda in the same way that most acid jazz is a derivative of Miles Davis's original riffs (*Hint:* they are all derivatives of Miles Davis's riffs). Spearman's Rho is an exception in that it approaches ordinal-level variables as difference in ranking (as in comparing the order of two separate lists). While useful in some cases, it is specific to a small group of particular relationships rather than the broader application of Lambda. While these other measures of association arrive at their summary in various ways, most derive from the same underlying principles of improving our predictive power from relatively naïve guessing to more informed prediction. That is, using these measures compliment, even augment, the more common use of Gamma and Lambda.

Nominal- and Ordinal-level Variable Graphing

Nominal- and ordinal-level bivariate relationships do not lend themselves well to graphing. The most common way to represent such relationships is by 'stacking' or grouping variables within bar charts (from the previous chapter) or newer versions such as mosaic plots. However, the most effective visual summary for nominal- and ordinal-level bivariate relationships is one in which the joint distribution of both variables is quickly understandable and efficiently summarized. This, in addition to being a good rule of thumb for graphs in general, describes the cross-tab. I would encourage you to embrace the cross-tab and use it to summarize for nominal- and ordinal-level bivariate relationships.

End of Chapter Summary

- Measures of Association quantify a relationship between variables.
- Measures of Association for nominal- and ordinal-level variables include Gamma and Lambda.
- Knowing the association between nominal- and ordinal-level variables allows us to better describe, compare, and understand those relationships.
- Both Gamma and Lambda must contend with the sometimes indiscriminate nature of nominal-level variables and the occasional murky order of ordinal-level variables. However, used correctly, they allow us to make claims about the nature, magnitude, and, in some cases, direction of nominal- and ordinal-level relationships.
- The best visual summary for bivariate nominal- and ordinal-level relationships is cross-tabulation.

Glossary

- **Measures of Association** assess the existence, strength, and, on occasion, direction of a relationship between variables.
- **Cross-tabulation** is an explicit means to show the joint distribution of nominal- and ordinal-level variables. A.k.a. 'cross-tab'.
- **Joint distribution**: The distribution of responses as a function of the other distribution of responses. You can already see how this is helpful in understanding how one variable 'moves' or is coordinated with another.
- **Yule's Q** is the specific 2 × 2 form of Goodman and Kruskal's gamma.
- Goodman and Kruskal's **Lambda** is a proportional reduction of error (PRE) measure of association for nominal-level by ordinal-level variables (of any size; N × N).
- Goodman and Kruskal's **Gamma** is a proportional reduction of error (PRE) measure of association for ordinal-level variables.
- A **proportion reduction of error (PRE)** measure indicates the reduction of errors in predicting the outcome of one variable by its relationship with another.

- The **magnitude** of a relationship is how closely the two variables are associated. A high magnitude of association implies that two variables move together in a conspicuous and predictable way. A low magnitude of association implies that two variables do not move together in a meaningful or obvious way.
- The **direction** of a relationship provided by gamma for ordinal-level variables tells us the nature of the relationship – whether the variables increase (and decrease) together – a positive relationship – or move in opposite directions (as one increases, the other decreases – a negative relationship).
- A **zero-order relationship** describes the relationship between two variables and nothing else.
- **Controlled comparisons** are a means to begin to establish how much of the change in the dependent variable (Y) is due to changes in independent variable (X) and how much is due to something else such as another independent variable (e.g., Z).

Questions

1. Which Measure of Association would best test the relationship between the following variables? Explain your choice.

    a. Esping-Andersen (1990, Table 11) trifurcates countries into three welfare state typologies: Liberal, Conservative, and Social Democratic based on three dimensions: decommodification, social stratification, and private–public mix. You want to compare this typology to the impact of the 2007/8 financial-turned-economic crisis (specifically, low impact, medium impact, or high impact).

    b. We want to test whether college-educated Brazilians (less than university/ university degree) voted more often in the most recent parliamentary election (yes/no).

    c. You want to see if oil-producing countries (yes/no) go to war more frequently (never, rarely, often).

2. Let's confront the change we made in the democracy variable in this chapter. We moved from the nominal, dichotomous variable (democracy or not) to an ordinal, trichotomous variable ('not free', 'partly free', 'free'). We also changed the data source: from Quality of Governance to Freedom House. Looking at Table 7.7, 30 countries are 'democracies'; yet, in the following table – Table 7.8 – only 15 are 'free' democracies with an additional 22 'partly free' democracies (for a total of 37). Comment on how this change potentially impacts our understanding of the relationship with internet access.3. Let's also confront the change we might have made in the internet access variable. Freedom House also publishes an 'Internet Freedom' variable. Instead of Table 7.8, we could have chosen to present the cross-tab of Freedom House Global Freedom Scores and Freedom House Internet Freedom Scores. Here is that cross-tab:

Table 7.13 Freedom House Party

		Internet freedom			
		Not Free	Partly Free	Free	TOTAL
Democracy	Not Free	20	1	0	**21**
	Partly Free	6	18	3	**27**
	Free	0	3	12	**15**
	TOTAL	**26**	**22**	**15**	**63**

Perhaps unsurprisingly, Gamma = 0.972. This is impressive. However, Freedom House is measuring 'internet freedom', not 'internet access'. What are some of the problems of choosing Freedom House' measure versus using the 1/3rds that used previously?

3. We were interested in studying how the electoral system of a country is related to the cabinet composition. From the Comparative Political Data Set, we can test this by examining European countries' electoral systems (i.e., Proportional Representation or Single-Member Districts) and cabinet compositions as measured by the Schmidt index (1992). A cross-tab of the most recent round (2016) looks like this:

Table 7.14 Cabinet Composition and Electoral Systems (2016)

		Electoral system			
		Single-member, simple plurality systems	Modified proportional representation	Proportional representation (PR)	TOTAL
Cabinet composition (Schmidt index)	Hegemony of right/centre parties	3	3	10	**16**
	Dominance of right/centre parties	0	0	5	**5**
	Balance of power	0	0	7	**7**
	Dominance of left parties	0	1	3	**4**
	Hegemony of left parties	0	1	2	**3**
	TOTAL	**3**	**5**	**27**	**35**

This ordinal- by ordinal-level variable cross-tab produces a Gamma of 0.40. Fully interpret by characterizing the magnitude or strength of the relationship. Does this relationship have a direction? If so, how would you interpret this? If not, why not? How do the results speak to our initial question?

4. Let's reconsider the relationship of cabinet composition and electoral systems by controlling for whether the countries in the sample come from Western or Eastern Europe. Using a Controlled Comparison, we arrive at the following two tables.

Table 7.15a Cabinet Composition and Electoral Systems (Western Europe 2016)

		Electoral system			
		Single-member, simple plurality systems	Modified proportional representation	Proportional representation (PR)	TOTAL
Cabinet composition (Schmidt index)	Hegemony of right/centre parties	3	2	8	*13*
	Dominance of right/centre parties	0	0	2	*2*
	Balance of power	0	0	5	*5*
	Dominance of left parties	0	0	2	*2*
	Hegemony of left parties	0	1	2	*3*
	TOTAL	*3*	*3*	*19*	*25*

Table 7.15b Cabinet Composition and Electoral Systems (Eastern Europe 2016)

		Electoral system			
		Single-member, simple plurality systems	Modified proportional representation	Proportional representation (PR)	TOTAL
Cabinet composition (Schmidt index)	Hegemony of right/centre parties	0	1	2	*3*
	Dominance of right/centre parties	0	0	3	*3*
	Balance of power	0	0	2	*2*
	Dominance of left parties	0	1	1	*2*
	Hegemony of left parties	0	0	0	*0*
	TOTAL	*0*	*2*	*8*	*10*

The data in the Table 7.15a produce a Gamma of 0.55.

The data in the Table 7.15b produce a Gamma of –0.08.

How do we update the interpretation of our initial results?

5. Measures of Association offer a means to say more than two variables seem to move together. These statistics allow comparison with something else – or something previous. How does this support the scientific study of politics?

Annotated References and Further Reading

Diamond, Jared and James A. Robinson. 2010. *Natural Experiments of History.* **Cambridge: Harvard University Press.**
Although they make an explicit case for historians to be ready to provide meaningful measure to claims about change, it applies just as readily to Political and Social Scientists.

Esping-Andersen, Gøsta. 1990. *The Three Worlds of Welfare Capitalism.* **Cambridge, UK: Polity Press.**
The book on the welfare state. Even if you are not interested in welfare states, this study speaks to nearly every field in Political Science.

Schmidt, Manfred G. 1992. Regierungen: Parteipolitische Zusammensetzung. In *Lexikon der Politik, Band 3: Die westlichen Länder,* **ed. Manfred G. Schmidt, 393–400. München: C.H. Beck.**
The origins of the Schmidt Index for Cabinet Composition.

Signposts to the Accompanying Digital Resources

Data used in this chapter

- **Percentage of national internet availability**: International Telecommunications Union.
    - www.itu.int/en/ITU-D/Statistics/Pages/stat/default.aspx
- **Global Freedom Scores**: Freedom House.
    - https://freedomhouse.org/countries/freedom-world/scores
- **Internet Freedom Scores:** Freedom House.
    - https://freedomhouse.org/countries/freedom-net/scores
- **Democracy or Not:** Quality of Governance.
    - Teorell, Jan, Aksel Sundström, Sören Holmberg, Bo Rothstein, Natalia Alvarado Pachon and Cem Mert Dalli. 2021. The Quality of Government Standard Dataset, version Jan21. University of Gothenburg: The Quality of Government Institute, www.qog.pol.gu.se
- **Cabinet Composition** and **Electoral Systems:** *Comparative Political Data Set.*
    - www.cpds-data.org/

8

MEASURES OF ASSOCIATION II: MEANS COMPARISON AND CORRELATION

> **LEARNING OUTCOMES**
>
> In this chapter, you will be able to
>
> - Identify the appropriate Measure of Association for relationships between interval-level variables and other types of variables.
> - Conduct and correctly interpret a Means Comparison for interval-level and nominal-/ordinal-level variables.
> - Correctly interpret a scatterplot.
> - Interpret and use Pearson's Product Moment Correlation Coefficient to summarize and describe the relationship between two interval-level variables.

Introduction

This chapter introduces bivariate Measures of Association between an interval-level variable and nominal-, ordinal-, and interval-level variables. We have encountered both Gamma and Lambda to satisfy our need for measuring association among nominal- and ordinal-level variables and now feel ready to take on the 'highest' level of measurement variables, interval-level. Because of interval-level variables' enviable mathematical properties, our choice of measurement will be dictated by the other variable's level of measurement.

Specifically,

- For nominal- and ordinal-level variables, we will use Means Comparisons.
- For interval-/interval- relationships, we will engage the more sophisticated and well-known statistical technique of correlation.

Descriptive Statistics' Measures of Association is outlined in the Table 8.1 below.

Table 8.1 Descriptive Statistics: Measures of Association

	Nominal	Ordinal	Interval
Nominal	2 ×2: Yule's Q [Gamma] N × N: **Lambda**		
Ordinal	**Lambda**	**Gamma**	
Interval	**Means Comparison**	**Means Comparison**	*Pearson's Product Moment* Correlation Coefficient

There are two main descriptive techniques used to assess bivariate relationships that involve interval-level variables: Means Comparisons and Pearson's Product Moment Correlation Coefficient. While Means Comparisons are conceptually fairly straightforward, the interval-/interval- relationship of correlation will require you to have eaten some leafy greens, nuts with high oil content, and/or small fish recently.

Let's begin.

Means Comparison

Examining a relationship between an interval-level variable and a nominal- or ordinal-level variable poses a problem. We can't use a cross-tab for interval-level variables for two reasons.

One, in contrast to the usually few categories of nominal- and ordinal-level variables, interval-level variables very often have lots of values. As such, a cross-tab would be an unwieldy means to visually compare the joint distribution given the necessary number of columns (or rows) to account for all the values. Two, nominal- or ordinal-level variables don't have the math qualities of interval-level variables limiting the nature of the comparison.

Consider the democracy and internet access example from the previous chapter. In the very first 2 × 2 cross-tab, we compared whether a country was a democracy or not against the percentage of national internet access. We bifurcated the percentage of 'internet access' into 'less than 50%' and 'more than 50%'. This made for a nice 2 × 2 cross-tab – and a nice example for Yule's Q – but the percentage of national internet access is actually an interval-level variable. By turning it into 'less than 50%' and 'more than 50%', we threw away a lot of information so it would fit into the 2 × 2 cross-tab.

Well, what if we could get that information back? What if we treated the percentage of national internet access as the interval-level variable that it is? This would be nice, but how would we compare it with the categories of nominal- or ordinal- level variables? We would need to 'shrink' the interval-level variable – here, the percentage of national internet access – into each category of the nominal-level variable: a percentage for the category for 'democracy' and a percentage for the category 'not a democracy'.

Wait, we know how to 'shrink' interval-level variables! The best way to summarize interval-level variables is to calculate a mean. We can calculate a mean for each category of the nominal- or ordinal-level variable. This would allow us to compare the means of each category. This is called a **means comparison**, which compares – as the name implies – the means of interval-level variables across the categories of the nominal-level variable.

So, for our example, we simply calculate the mean of national internet access for each category of the nominal-level variable (here: 'Democracy'/'Not a Democracy'). Doing so summarizes the interval-level variable across each of the nominal-level categories.

Table 8.2 Means Comparison – A Template

		Interval-level variable
Nominal-/Ordinal-level variable	Category A	Mean for Category A
	Category B	Mean for Category B
	Category C	Mean for Category C
	etc....	etc....

This would make the comparison more manageable and potentially more informative. I note that in doing so, we would also be measuring the same variable for *internet access*, that is, we wouldn't lose information by reducing internet access to nominal- and ordinal-level variables and thus maintain conceptual and operational consistency. The questions from the academic conference are starting to melt away!

Take a look. Note, I've added the number of observations so that we can see how the two sub-groups add up to the total number of observations (here, countries).

Table 8.3 Means Comparison: Nominal-level and Interval-level variables

	Internet access	Number of observations
Democracy	64.7%	30
Not a Democracy	56.1%	33
Overall Mean	**60.2%**	**63**

In Table 8.3, the mean level of national-level internet access is 60.2% for all of the countries. At the same time, countries that are classified as 'democracies' have a mean of 64.7% national-level internet access and countries that are classified as 'non-democracies', 56.1%.

At first glance, it appears that democracies, on average, have a higher level of national internet access. This is probably not very surprising but the means comparison of Table 8.3 provides some preliminary evidence of that difference.

Utility of Means Comparisons

Recall, we decided to recapture more information about internet access than by simply dividing the countries into more or less than 50% access. How does our Means

Comparison here compare to the cross-tab using the 50% division for internet access that we made previously?

The Yule's Q (Gamma) for this relationship was 0.283 and the joint distribution showed that countries with 50% or more internet access tended to be democracies while countries with 50% or less internet access tended to be non-democracies (see Table 8.4, which is Table 7.1 reproduced below). This is consistent with the Means Comparison in which we find that democracies, on average, have a higher level of national internet access. However, each provides a different perspective for this conclusion on the nature of the relationship.

Table 8.4 Democracy and Internet Access (same as Table 7.1)

		Internet access		
		<50%	>50%	TOTAL
Democracy	No	13	20	**33**
	Yes	8	22	**30**
	TOTAL	**21**	**42**	**63**

The good news is that we can also use Means Comparison for ordinal-level variables. Let's look at the Means Comparison between the interval-level variable percentage of national internet access and the ordinal-level variable Freedom House's Global Freedom score. Recall, this ordinal-level variable ranks countries as 'Not free', 'Partly free', and 'Free' (see Table 8.5).

Table 8.5 Means Comparison: Ordinal-level variable and an Interval-level variable

		Internet access	Number of observations
Democracy	Not Free	56.5%	26
	Partly Free	48.4%	22
	Free	83.8%	15
	Mean	**60.2%**	**63**

An unexpected – and potentially interesting – pattern emerges!

While 'free' democracies have the highest mean level of national internet access (83.8%) and 'not free' countries have a mean of 56.5% consistent with our previous analyses, 'partly free' countries have 48.4%.

Ok, wait, what is going on? Everything was going so nicely. So, why the discrepancy? I thought this would be straightforward. Statistics are supposed to make everything easy and obvious.

(*Narrator*: 'Mmmm, not exactly.')

Honestly, I don't know what is happening. It appears that we stumbled onto evidence that – based on Freedom House's ordinal, trichotomous measure of democracy – 'partly free' countries have the lowest levels of internet access.

Frankly, this is great. We may be on to something.

We already know that widespread access to the internet can be used to foster freedom and democracy in myriad ways (Dahlgren, 2000; Shirky, 2011; Zhang et al., 2010) but widespread access has also been associated with effective repression in authoritarian regimes as well (Hindmann, 2008; Hoffman, 2004; Morozov, 2011). That is, seeing higher levels of internet access in the most – and least – democratic countries may not be so anomalous. To our scientific minds, what needs explaining is 'partly free'.

While we won't search for an explanation here, what should be becoming obvious as we progress through the statistical techniques of Descriptive Statistics is that different techniques of examining variables and their relationships require some clear-headed understanding of how these measures are produced and what each actually tell us about those relationships. To understand – as well as to criticize – the use of statistics, we need to have peeked behind these curtains.

No, statistics are not always clear.

No, statistics are not always consistent.

Statistics do not necessarily make things obvious and easy.

They are an efficient and agreed-upon way to convert data into information by providing a means to summarize data and variables in which we are interested, which can often be helpful. Yet, statistics cannot make the final leap from information to knowledge for you. The discrepancy above is not uncommon and underscores the importance of taking a statistics course to understand this. This also underscores – again – that the indicator you choose to operationalize your concepts will shape what you will find.

Interval- by Interval-level Variables: Scatterplot

Up to this point, cross-tabs have been very useful in dealing with aiding our visualization of the joint distributions of two variables in which we are interested. In the previous section, however, introducing interval-level variables challenged the utility of cross-tabs in displaying the joint distributions of an interval-level variable and a nominal-/ordinal-level variable in a way that would fit on one page.

And while Means Comparisons enabled us to exploit the mathematical nature of interval-level variables to compare their means between different categories of nominal- and ordinal-level variables, with two interval-level variables, we are going to need a better way to both visualize and summarize the relationship in which we are interested. The relationship of two interval-level variables is better represented visually with a scatterplot.

A **scatterplot** is a graph that displays the joint distribution of two interval-level variables as a set of points on a Cartesian coordinate system. We put all the observations on a graph according to their values set by theory with the independent variable on the x-axis and the dependent variable on the y-axis. In this way, a scatterplot allows us to view the entirety of the relationship between two interval-level variables.

Let's continue with our example of democracy and access to the internet. We can finally return our 'access to the internet' variable to its full, interval-level character as a measure of the percentage of the population that has access to the internet. For measuring democracy with an interval-level variable, we can use a variable called, Voice and Accountability, that measures the extent of democratic freedoms.

Measuring Democracy and Internet Access

- The democracy variable 'Voice and Accountability' comes from the World Bank's *World Governance Indicators*. 'Voice and Accountability' reflects perceptions of the extent to which a country's citizens are able to participate in selecting their government, as well as freedom of expression, freedom of association, and a free media. Voice and Accountability ranges from approximately −2.00 to 2.00.
- As before, the percentage of internet access comes from the International Telecommunications Union (ITU) and ranges between 0% and 100%.

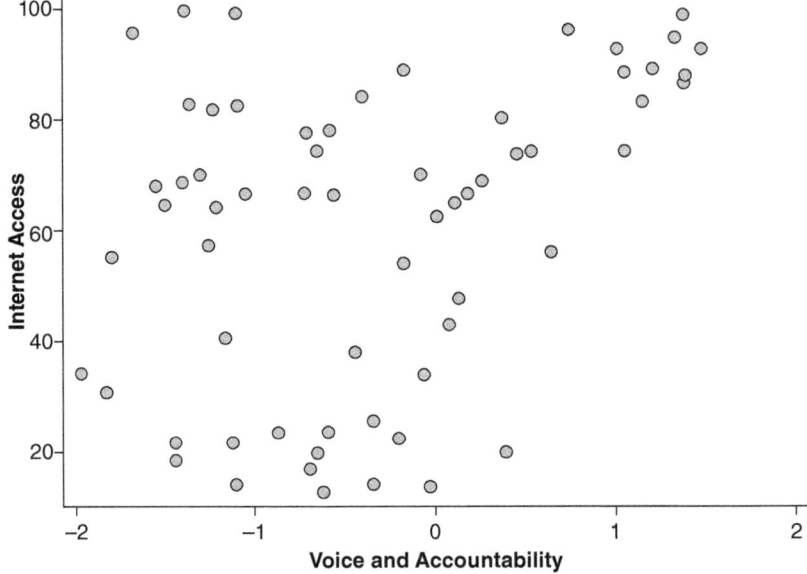

Figure 8.1a Scatterplot of Internet Access and Voice and Accountability

The findings thus far suggest that democracy (or not) may have more to tell us about internet access. Let's adjust our analysis and place 'access to the internet' on the vertical y-axis (as the dependent variable, Y) and 'Voice and Accountability' on the horizontal x-axis (as the independent variable X). The scatterplot of 'Voice and Accountability' and 'percentage of the population with internet access' includes all of the observations.

The position of each dot represents each country's simultaneous value of the 'percentage of internet access' and 'Voice and Accountability'.

For example, in Figure 8.1b, the dot representing Kyrgyzstan has a Voice and Accountability score of −0.44 and a percent of internet access of 38.2%. Whereas Italy,

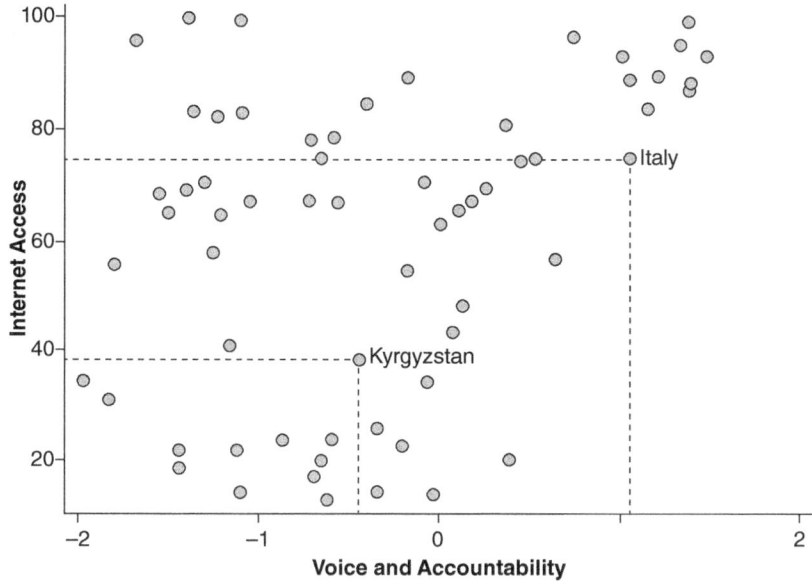

Figure 8.1b Scatterplot of Internet Access and Voice and Accountability

has a Voice and Accountability score of 1.05 and a percent of internet access of 74.4%. Each observation is placed similarly.

Ok, this seems reasonable. The scatterplot shows the joint distribution of an interval-level independent and an interval-level dependent variable and is more visually convenient than a cross-tab. But how in the world are we going to describe this relationship? How do we summarize a bunch of dots?

Correlation. Correlation is the answer to the question of how we summarize this bunch of dots. And in Figure 8.1b above, 'percent internet access' and 'voice and accountability' have a correlation of r = 0.35.

Quick Start: Correlation

Probably the most used and well-known Measure of Association is correlation. The most common correlation, formally known as **Pearson's Product Moment Correlation Coefficient**, is often – if confusingly – denoted 'r' (from ρ – 'rho') although pronounced 'r' as in the letter.

Pearson's correlation coefficient has a number of enviable characteristics and abilities. Unlike Gamma and Lambda, correlation is not a PRE statistic. Instead, **correlation** is a direct measure of the strength and direction of the extent to which two interval-level variables are linearly related.

It tells us two things.

1. *The magnitude – or strength – of the relationship:* The correlation coefficient tells us the degree to which two interval-level variables are related. The coefficient ranges between –1 and 1. At zero, there is no relationship (or, specifically, no *linear* relationship) and the further away the coefficient is from zero, the stronger the relationship all the way to 1 or –1, at which point we would say there is a 'perfect positive/negative relationship'.
2. *The direction of the relationship:* The positive or negative sign on the correlation coefficient is meaningful and indicates whether the variables move together in a positive or negative way. A **positive correlation** means that as one variable increases, so does the other. A positive correlation *also* means that as one variable decreases, so does the other. Conversely, a **negative correlation** means that as one variable decreases, the other one increases. And vice versa.

Correlation, like other Measures of Association, tells us to what extent two interval-level variables move in a coordinated way. It is useful because we can exploit what it tells us about the relationship between two variables. If two variables move in a coordinated way ('are highly correlated'), we can know a lot about one variable simply by knowing the other. If they don't move together in a coordinated way ('are not highly correlated'), knowing one doesn't help us know much about the other.

STRENGTH OF CORRELATION

Table 8.6 Descriptive Strength of Correlation

Perfect positive/negative correlation [*Note:* Not found in nature. If so, run.]	1.0
Very strong positive/negative correlation	0.75–0.99
Substantial positive/negative correlation	0.50–0.74
Moderate positive/negative correlation	0.30–0.49
Low positive/negative correlation	0.10–0.29
Negligible	0.00–0.09

Highlighting the fact there is no one agreed-upon interpretation, these are mine. There are other suggested interpretations of 'r' however, they are similar (although discipline specific!).

So, what does the correlation of r=0.35 for 'percent internet access' and 'Voice and Accountability' tell us. What can we learn about this relationship? A r=0.35 correlation tells that, for the countries in this dataset, our measures of internet access and democracy are moderately and positively correlated (see Box: Strength of Correlation). That is:

- *The magnitude – or strength – of the relationship:* The correlation moderately suggests that greater country-level access to the internet moves with greater voice and

accountability, (as an important facet of democracy). However, this relationship is not overwhelmingly strong and we are likely to have overlooked or excluded other important factors.
- *The direction of the relationship:* Positive indicates that as this measure of democratic performance increases, so does the percentage of internet access. And they decrease together.

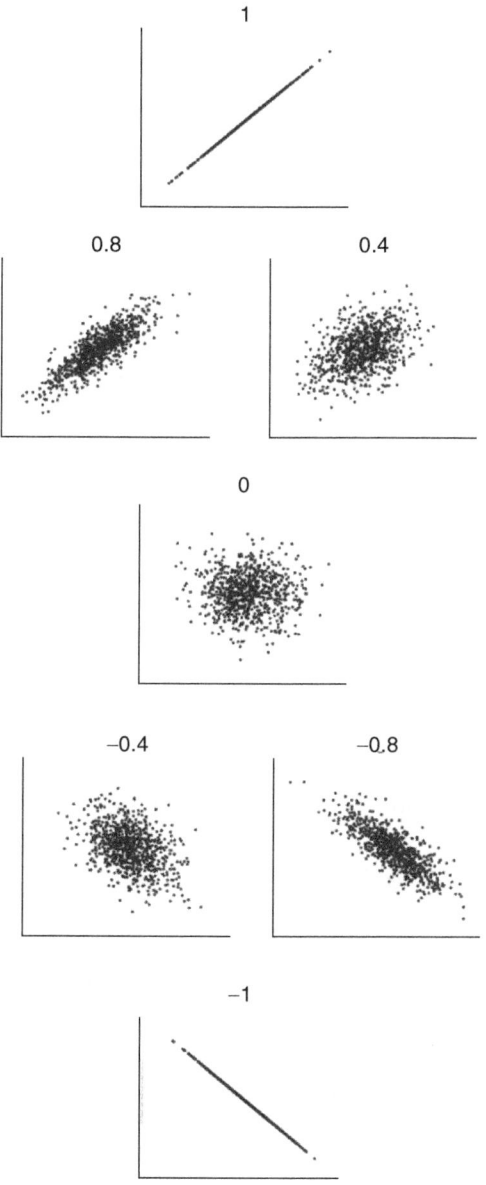

Figure 8.2 Correlation Coefficients: Magnitude and Direction

Therefore, from our example above (Figure 8.1a), knowing the level of democracy – measured by 'Voice and Accountability' – tells us a little bit about country-level percentage of internet access we can expect in a country. We would generally expect that for countries with greater 'Voice and Accountability', the percentage of internet access would also rise. However, as you can see from the scatterplot, a correlation of 0.35 indicates a fairly 'loose' – versus a 'tighter' – linear coordination between these two variables.

User's Manual: Correlation

Correlation and Linearity

Correlation tells us the extent to which two interval-level variables are *linearly* related to each other.

Why a line?

Well, linearity is the simplest and most commonly used functional form (to describe a relationship among variables). It is easy to use, makes intuitive sense, and is a surprisingly common manner in which many things are related.

Wait – using our example, are you saying that democracy and internet access should be related exactly on a line? Is that reasonable? Are other relationships like this? I mean, look at their scatterplot – this is clearly not the case.

You are correct.

Also, there is no line.

Instead, a line is used as a *summary* of the relationship between access to the internet and democracy (i.e., the independent variable, X, and the dependent variable, Y). Summaries, as you no doubt remember from previous chapters, can be good or bad (recall: measures of central tendency and dispersion). Linearity does not mean that X and Y are related only on a line, but that the relationship between X and Y can be *summarized* as a line.

It is not reasonable to expect a line – or frankly any functional form, such as a 'U' or other curve – to perfectly summarize the relationship between variables. What would be weird is if all the observations were on the line. There will always be 'imperfection' or deviations from this line.

Why are there always deviations?

1. We seek to summarize not provide a comprehensive report.
2. There are other reasons why one variable might change other than the influence of the other variable. That is, correlation is as a linear summary of these two variables and does not account for all other potential explanations that exist but are not included in this bivariate analysis.
3. There is always randomness, which, as we will shortly see, is better handled by other statistical techniques.

Another way of thinking about correlation as a measure of association that summarizes the relationship between two interval-level variables as a line is to think of correlation as an inverse measure of the blossom around a line. As you can see in Figure 8.2, the lower the correlation, the bigger the blossom; the higher the correlation, the smaller the blossom.

If the blossom of observations is large and the line does not do a good job of summarizing the relationship, we will find a low or unsatisfying correlation (*ahem*, r = 0.35). If, however, the blossom of observations is less dispersed and the line does a good job of summarizing the relationship, we will find a higher correlation. And, as other Measures of Association, higher association allows us to know more about one variable by knowing the other.

> ### LINEARITY
>
> Note: This assumption of linearity is an attribute of correlation. None of the previous Measures of Association makes a linear assumption. However, this assumption can limit correlation's ability to adequately describe the relationship (see Figure 8.3). In other words, two variables can be related and move in consistent, non-linear ways.
>
>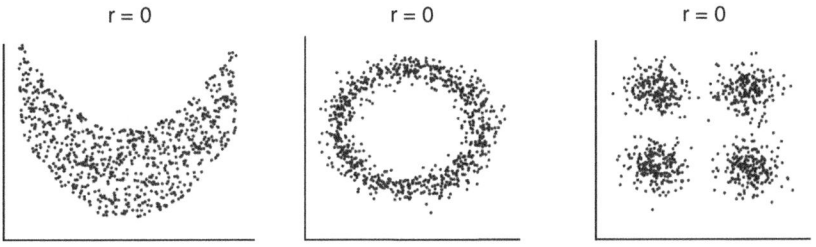
>
> **Figure 8.3** Non-linear, Zero Correlation Joint Distributions

Calculating Correlation

Correlation is a way to understand how interval-level variables move together. Those that deviate a lot from the order we expect are less coordinated with one another and those that do not deviate very much, are more coordinated with one another. And 'deviate' – as used here – is simply how far each observation differs (in terms of distance) from what we expect them to be.

In technical terms, correlation is a proxy measure of covariation. *Covariation* is how two variables change in relation to one another. High covariation means that big changes in one variable mean big changes in the other variable, and small changes in one variable mean small changes in the other variable. Low covariation reveals less of this coordinated movement.

Covariance is achieved by taking the sum of the products of the differences from the means of each variable:

$$Cov(x,y) = \frac{\Sigma(x_i - \bar{x}) * (y_i - \bar{y})}{N}$$

Correlation is merely a constrained measure – or scaled form – of covariance. By constraining the covariance, correlation provides not only direction but also a relative measure of strength. It does so by constraining the ratio of covariance between two variables with square root of those variables' variance (i.e., standard deviations). That is, we define the range from –1 to 1 by dividing the covariance with the product of the two standard deviations to normalize – or standardize – it.

As a formula,

$$r = \frac{Cov(x.y)}{\sigma_x * \sigma_y}$$

where σ_x is the standard deviation of x and σ_y is the standard deviation of y.

There are, however, several more approachable equations for calculating the correlation coefficient, most of which are mathematical transformations of one another. I propose that if you feel compelled to calculate correlation by hand, go old school and use the *original* original correlation equation from Karl Pearson himself in 1896.

$$r = \frac{n(\Sigma xy) - (\Sigma x)(\Sigma y)}{\sqrt{[n\Sigma x^2 - (\Sigma x)^2][n\Sigma y^2 - (\Sigma y)^2]}}$$

We should sharpen our teeth and develop our intuition about correlation. Here are some examples.

In the Field: Correlation and Scatterplot Examples

To better understand and explore the nature and information of correlation, let's expand the variety of variables for the 63 cases – from our democracy and internet sample – in search of other variables that might be associated with countries' quality of democracy ('Voice and Accountability').

Taken from the *Quality of Government* database, we can examine the relationship between several new variables and the 'Voice and Accountability' variable. Recall that 'Voice and Accountability' reflects the extent to which citizens of a country are able to participate in the selection and control of governments. It ranges from –2 to 2.

In Table 8.7, we can see the descriptions of five new variables – perception of corruption, life expectancy, renewable energy consumption, militarization, and press freedom – and their correlation coefficient with 'Voice and Accountability'.

Table 8.7 Correlation with Voice and Accountability

	Variable description	Correlation coefficient
Corruption Perceptions Index	Aggregated perceptions of members of the business community and country experts of the level of corruption in the public sector. Range: 0 [highly corrupt] to 100 [very clean]. Source: Transparency International	$r = 0.68$
Life expectancy at birth	Number of years a new-born infant would live if prevailing patterns of mortality at the time of its birth were to stay the same throughout its life. Range: 0–Methuselah. Source: *World Development Indicators* (*WDI*) – World Bank	$r = 0.43$
Renewable energy consumption	Share of renewable energy in total final energy consumption. Range 0–100. Source: *World Development Indicators* (*WDI*) – World Bank	$r = -0.02$
Global Militarization Index	Relative weight and importance of a country's military apparatus in relation to its society as a whole. Range: 0–1,000. Source: Bonn International Center for Conversion	$r = -0.40$
Press Freedom Index	Amount of freedom journalists and the media have in each country and the efforts made by governments to see that press freedom is respected. Range: 0 (total press freedom) to 100 (no press freedom). Source: Reporters Sans Frontières	$r = -0.88$

What does correlation tell us about these relationships? If we rely on the Table 8.6, the most straightforward interpretations would be the following:

- V&A and the Corruptions Perceptions Index are substantially and positively correlated
- V&A and 'Life Expectancy' are moderately and positively correlated
- V&A and renewable energy consumption are negligibly correlated
- V&A and the Global Militarization Index are moderately and negatively correlated
- V&A and the Press Freedom Index are very strongly and negatively correlated.

Alright, alright, alright. But what does it *mean*?

Before we expand and finalize our interpretations of these relationships, let's take a look at these relationships as scatterplots.

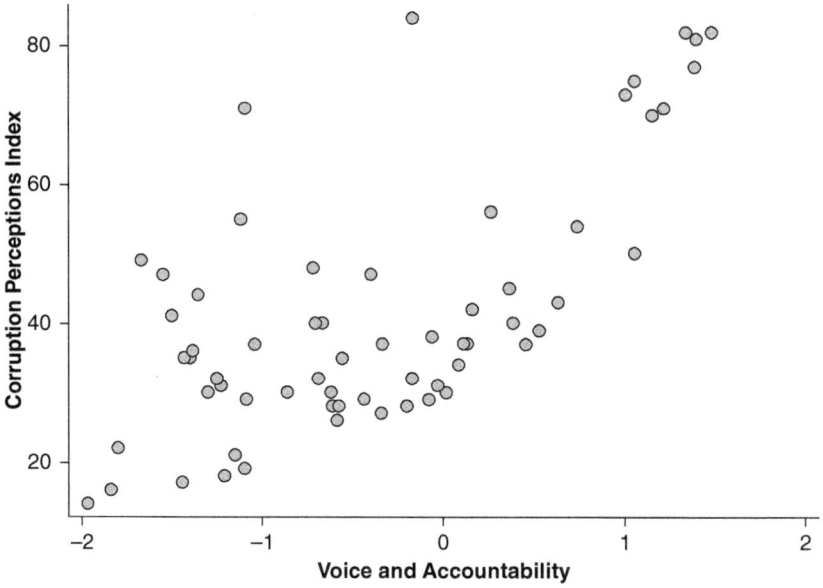

Figure 8.4a Scatterplot of Voice and Accountability and Corruption Perceptions Index

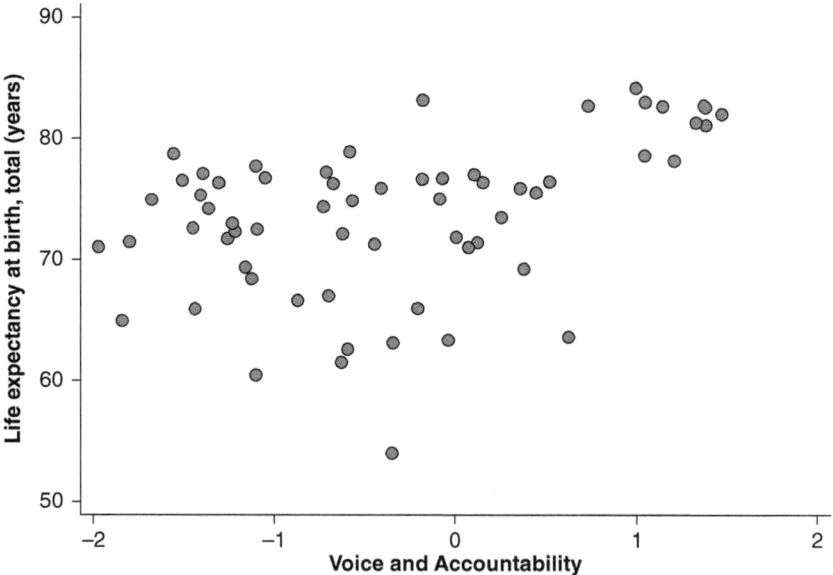

Figure 8.4b Scatterplot of Voice and Accountability and Life Expectancy

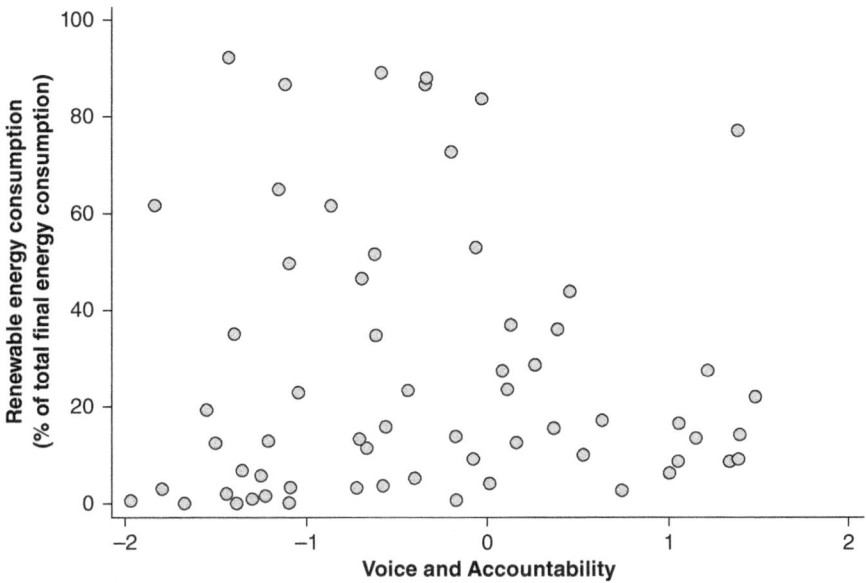

Figure 8.4c Scatterplot of Voice and Accountability and Renewable Energy Consumption

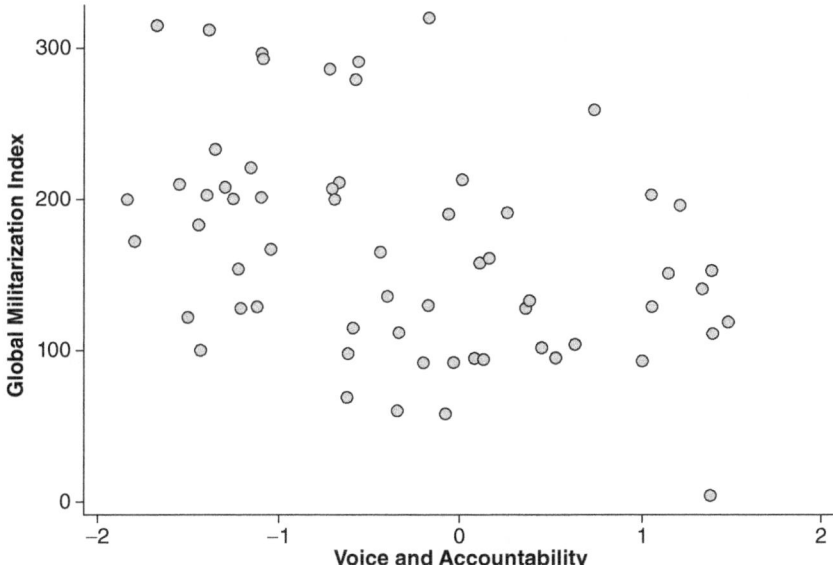

Figure 8.4d Scatterplot of Voice and Accountability and the Global Militarization Index

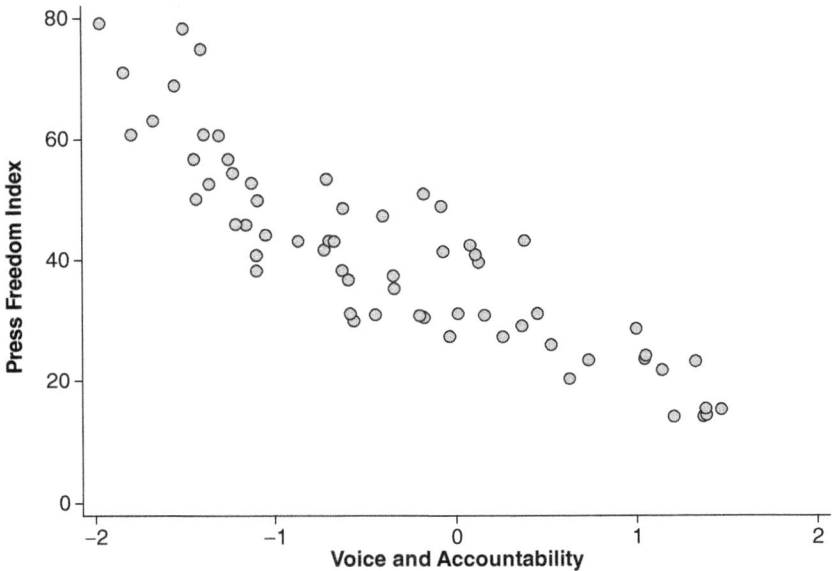

Figure 8.4e Scatterplot of Voice and Accountability and the Press Freedom Index

Again, correlation tells us about the magnitude and direction of a relationship between two interval-level variables. We have already described these relationship above. So, looking at the scatterplots is a way to poke and prod our curiosity.

- Is anything else going on?
- Are the relationships 'loose' or 'tight'?
- Do the correlations seem to accurately convey the nature of the relationship?

Here, the substantive, positive correlation between V&A and the Corruptions Perceptions Index (CPI) is a satisfying correlation in which the variables move together in relatively tight coordination (r=0.68). As the V&A measure of citizens' selection and control of governments increases, so does the CPI from low scores of corruption to high scores [note: the CPI is conceptually 'reversed' such that low scores mean more corruption and high scores mean less corruption]. There are probably any number of ways that we could begin to theorize about this substantial and positive relationship.

The moderate positive correlation between V&A and life expectancy is less obvious (r = 0.43). While the correlation is not overwhelming, there does appear to be a loose coordination between the quality of responsive government and the longevity of that country's populace. A curious relationship that is likely to require further investigation to make sense of it.

Very nice.

Perhaps frustrating to see is the negligible – nearly random – correlation between V&A and renewable energy consumption (r=–0.02). One might be tempted to align heightened levels of citizen control of government with an increased impetus for difficult collective battles such as climate change. Here, however, evidence is scant.

We might comfort ourselves with the moderate and negative correlation between V&A and the Global Militarization Index (r=–0.40). Increased citizen control over the government moves in loose coordination with the decrease of the importance of the military in society.

Finally, the very strong negative correlation between V&A and the Press Freedom Index (r = –0.88) at first glance seems odd. Shouldn't citizen control of government and press freedom move together (i.e., positive)? Recall that while a higher score for V&A is a normatively higher score (more control), the Press Freedom Index – like the CPI above – is reversed (0 (total press freedom) and 100 (no press freedom)). Thus, as Press Freedom increases ('gets worse'), V&A goes down, a negative relationship. The high (negative) correlation is intuitive and satisfying, showing that these variables move in a highly coordinated way. This is also a reminder that examining the scatterplot is a good way of avoiding confusion.

To investigate relationships between two interval-level variables we can use correlation and scatterplots. Commonly, correlation provides the grounds for continuing an investigation – or not. That is, without sufficient correlation, it is unlikely that we will find a more substantial relationship, even with more sophisticated techniques. However, that same lack of correlation – or discovery of an *unexpected* correlation – can as well be provocative (based on what we expect).

Troubleshooting: Challenges to Correlation

Correlation is a great way to summarize the relationship between two interval-level variables. However, and endemic to the enterprise of summarizing relationships among variables, there can be challenges to the ability of correlation to provide us with a reliable and comprehensive summary.

Outside of any problems within the relationship of the two interval-level variables we are investigating, there are several sources of potential problems in the calculation of 'r'.

1. *Symmetry:* Correlation is symmetrical. Calculating 'r' for X and Y is same as calculating 'r' for Y and X (in fancy: *Corr* (x,y) = *Corr* (y,x)). Put in a more useful way, correlation gives a generic measure of the *strength and direction* of the relationship: how well two variables move together. It does not relate the nature of the relationship for *these specific variables*.
2. *The number of observations:* Correlation – all measures of association, in fact – very often offers a better summary with a large number of observations than with fewer observations (and as we will see, larger samples, in particular). The reason is simple. A large number of observations – a large sample – of both variables is more likely

to better represent the data associated with the concepts in which we are interested and, therefore, better represent their relationship.
3. *Outliers:* As we discussed above, outliers are observations that act uniquely or out of synchronicity with the other observations. One or two outliers in a relationship is not necessarily problematic; although significant individual outliers can also have a disproportionate effect on the calculation of 'r'. However, a number of observations that diverge from the larger relationship suggest problematic coordination between the two variables – most likely in the form of the effect of other – more substantive – variables.
4. *Truncated range:* If one or both of the variables lack observations within a range of their values, correlation can be left scratching its head. A lack of observations offers little on which to base the calculation in this part of the range allowing for other parts of the range – the ones with observations – to disproportionately determine 'r'.
5. *Shape of the distributions:* We will engage more fully with the idea and use of distributions in the coming chapters. Here, we can think of this as similar to the previous challenge, truncated range. If the observations for a variable – or both – are skewed to one side or the other, we are left with an unevenness that doesn't *necessarily* disrupt the calculation of 'r'. But could.
6. *Non-linearity:* If a line is a poor summary for the joint distribution of two interval-level variables, correlation is a poor candidate to summarize that relationship (see above: Correlation and Linearity).

There is no one solution to any of these problems and there are no ironclad solutions for each and every one of these problems. At the same time, these problems can exist and not create trouble. Like most things, an excess of any one problem should cause us to be cautious in our use, reliance on, and reporting of correlation.

As we have done above, an intelligent and prudent idea when using correlation is to also look at the scatterplot. Very often we can *visually* identify challenges to the utility of correlation to summarize the interval-level relationship in which we are interested. For example, scatterplots can help us better identify and understand the challenges listed above.

1. *Symmetry:* Scatterplots help us 'see' the nature of the magnitude vs the steepness of the line (see Figure 8.5). All of these relationships are very strong but we can see that they imply different types of relationships between the variables.
2. *The number of observations:* The scatterplot is mostly empty or spotty.
3. *Outliers:* There is an observation or observations far from others on the scatterplot.
4. *Truncated range:* Sections of the variables lack observations on the scatterplot.
5. *Shape of the distributions:* Harder to see, but observations might 'clump' on the scatterplot.
6. *Non-linearity:* The implicit shape of the relationship on the scatterplot is not a line (see Figure 8.3).

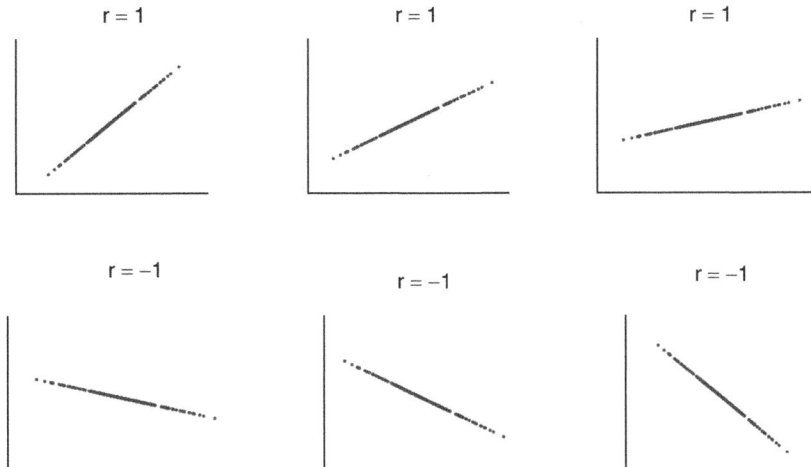

Figure 8.5 Scatterplots of r = 1 and r = −1

Correlation is Not (Necessarily) Causation

Once again, with feeling, for those in the back.

One can easily see that two variables cannot be casually related without being correlated ('correlation' standing in for what you now understand to be one form of many Measures of Association). No correlation, no causation. That you can put good money on.

However, in the case in which we do have correlation, I remind the reader of the scientific method as we discussed in Chapter 1. Causation is a theoretical concept while correlation is a statistical concept. Theory is the *how* and correlation is the *if*. Correlation provides the *necessary but not sufficient* state for a causal relationship.

Let's take up this question in the relationship between democratic political institutions and democratic political culture. There has been a long-standing debate as to the primacy or the causal order of democratic institutions and democratic political culture. Do democratic institutions cultivate democratic political culture or does democratic political culture generate democratic institutions?

Many on the democratic political culture side argued that institutions were a function of broader culture – people's values and attitudes (Almond and Verba, 1963; Norris, 1999; Putnam, 1993). Others argued that institutions set the rules and people's (political) values and attitudes were thusly shaped (Easton, 1975; Muller and Seligson, 1994; Rohrschneider, 1999).

While this may seem forever ago, the fall of the Berlin Wall and the collapse of Soviet Communism in Eastern Europe starting in 1989 was the most comprehensive testing ground for this debate. To the political culture adherents, there were nascent democratic movements – Solidarity in Poland, Charter 77 in Czechoslovakia, the dismantling of the barbed wire borders with Austria and reburial of Imre Nagy in the early summer of 1989 in Hungary – that took place before the removal of Soviet domination of national politics, seeding support for democratic institutions. At the same time, widespread support for democratic *values* seemed to follow the establishment of democratic institutions. The question thus raged – do the democratic values and attitudes of citizens generate democratic institutions or do democratic institutions create the space for citizens to learn and practice democracy?

This question is still without a clear answer. And here's an example of this from today.

Using data from the 2018 European Social Survey, we can create an (admittedly limited) measure of democratic political culture for some European countries by aggregating measures of citizens' 'trust in government', 'satisfaction with democracy', 'social trust', both 'internal and external efficacy', 'equality', and 'tolerance'. We can correlate this measure of democratic political culture with a measure of democratic institutional performance, here, the World Bank 2018 World Governance Indicator 'Voice and Accountability', which we have used before.

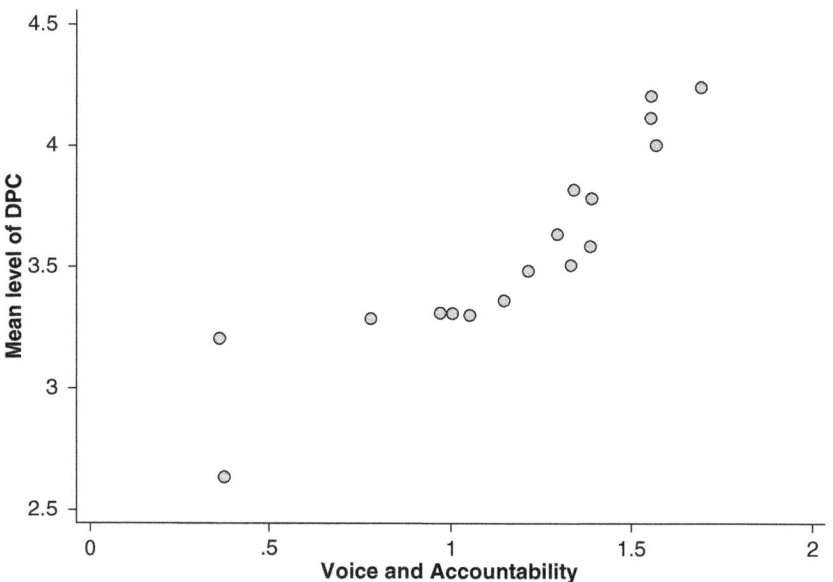

Figure 8.6 Democratic Political Culture and Democratic Political Institutional Performance

A Measure of Democratic Political Culture

Here, democratic political culture is an interval-level variable. It is the sum of the following questions, each standardized to range between 0 and 1. Thus, added together produce a variable that ranges from 0 to 6 with a mean of 3.54 and a standard deviation of 0.79.

- Satisfaction with Democracy (stfdem): How satisfied with the way democracy works in country; range: 0–10
- Trust in (National) Parliament (trstprl): Trust in country's parliament; range: 0–10
- Social or Horizontal Trust (piltrst): Most people can be trusted or you can't be too careful; range: 0–10
- Popular Influence (psppipla): Political system allows people to have influence on politics; range: 1–5
- Equality (ipeqopt): Important that people are treated equally and have equal opportunities; range: 1–6
- Tolerance (ipudrst): Important to understand different people; range: 1–6.

Voice and Accountability has a range of −2 to 2, a mean of 1.17, and a standard deviation of 0.36.

We can see that for these 18 European countries (Bulgaria, Hungary, Poland, Czech Republic, Slovenia, Cyprus, France, Estonia, United Kingdom, Belgium, Ireland, Austria, Germany, Netherlands, Finland, Switzerland. Norway, Italy), democratic political institutions and democratic political culture (DPC, in the graph above) appear to move together in systematic and observable ways with a correlation of r=0.90. According to Figure 8.6, this 'r' is very strong and positive. That is, knowing the level of Voice and Accountability tells us a great deal of where to expect the level of democratic political culture to be.

And vice versa.

So, which is it? Which causes the other?

This is not a question that a scatterplot and a correlation can resolve. We have simply learned that these two variables move together in highly predictable ways (consistent with a large if contentious literature). And, although the correlation is very high, we must remember that this is a relationship between one variable that we constructed and a second variable that measures democratic institutional performance in a specific way.

Correlation is not (necessarily) causation.

I do want to point out again that even with such a high correlation, the countries are not, in fact, a line. As we discussed previously, there are many reasons why this is so – even in a relationship of such high correlation.

- Correlation summarizes the relationship as a line (*although there is no line*).
- There are undoubtedly many other variables that are important to the changes in and distributions of both these variables.
- And. There. Is. Always. Randomness.

This brings us to the conclusion of correlation and nearly to the end of Descriptive Statistics.

Nearly.

I want to point out that some of the shortcomings of correlation have solutions. Both 'other variables' and 'randomness' can be addressed. However, in order to do so, we will need to ascend to the upper tiers of the Descriptive Statistics food chain to the apex animals – the orca whales and polar bears – killers with no natural predators. We have exhausted the introductory Measures of Association and now it is time to take an initial look at some serious statistical firepower.

Next up, (bivariate) regression analysis.

End of Chapter Summary

- Means comparisons allow us to examine relationships between interval-level variables and nominal-/ordinal-level variables.
- Once again for those in the cheap seats, the process of conceptualizing and operationalizing our variables will profoundly shape what we will find.
- Scatterplots show the joint distribution of two interval-level variables.
- Correlation tells us the strength of the linear association of a relationship between two interval-level variables by showing us how tightly or loosely – or randomly – scattered the points around the line. The incline or decline of the line tells us about the direction of the relationship.
- Using correlation and scatterplots together can strengthen our understanding of the relationship in which we are interested.
- Correlation is not (necessarily) causation.

	Nominal	**Ordinal**	**Interval**
Nominal	2 ×2: Yule's Q [Gamma]		
	N × N: **Lambda**		
Ordinal	**Lambda**	Gamma	
Interval	**Means Comparison**	**Means Comparison**	*Pearson's Product Moment* **Correlation** *Coefficient*

Glossary

- A **means comparison** compares the means of interval-level variable across the categories of the nominal-level or ordinal-level variable.
- A **scatterplot** is a graph that displays the joint distribution of two interval-level variables as a set of points on a Cartesian coordinate system.
- **Correlation** measures the extent to which two interval-level variables are *linearly* related to each other, indicating both strength and direction.
- The most used and well-known correlation is **Pearson's Product Moment Correlation Coefficient**. This is denoted by an 'r' and often simply referred to as 'correlation'.

- A **positive correlation** means that the two interval-level variables increase and decrease together.
- A **negative correlation** means that the two interval-level variables move in opposite directions (i.e., as one increases, the other decreases).

Empirical Examples/Signposts to Research

Almond, G.A., Verba, S., 1963. *The Civic Culture: Political Attitudes and Democracy in Five Nations*. Princeton University Press, Princeton, N.J.

Anscombe, F.J. 1973. 'Graphs in statistical analysis' *The American Statistician* 27(1): 17–21, https://doi.org/10.1080/00031305.1973.10478966

Dahlgren P. 2000. 'The internet and the democratization of civic culture' *Political Communication* 31/3: 329–84.

Easton, D., 1975. 'A re-assessment of the concept of political support' *British Journal of Political Science* 5, 435–57.

Hindman, Matthew. 2008. *The Myth of Digital Democracy*. Princeton University Press.

Hoffman, Bert. 2004. *The Politics of the Internet in Third World Development: Challenges in Contrasting Regimes with Case Studies of Costa Rica and Cuba*. Routledge.

Morozov, Eygeny. 2011. *Net Delusion: The Dark Side of Internet Freedom*. Public Affairs.

Muller, E.N., Seligson, M.A. 1994. 'Civic culture and the democracy: Question of causal relationships' *American Political Science Review* 88, 635–52.

Norris, P. 1999. *Critical Citizens: Global Support for Democratic Government: Global Support for Democratic Government*. Oxford University Press, USA.

Putnam, R.D. 1993. *Making Democracy Work: Civic Traditions in Modern Italy*. Princeton University Press.

Rohrschneider, R., 1999. *Learning Democracy: Democratic and Economic Values in Unified Germany*. Oxford University Press, Oxford and New York.

Shirky, C. 2011. 'The political power of social media: Technology, the public sphere, and political change' *Foreign Affairs* 90(1): 28–41.

Zhang, W., T.J. Johnson, T. Seltzer, and S.L. Bichard. 2010. 'The Revolution will be Networked: The Influence of Social Networking Sites on Political Attitudes and Behavior' *Social Science Computer Review* 28(1): 75–92.

Questions

1. When we were examining European Parliamentary election turnout by country (Table 6.4), we summarized the interval-level variable, percent turnout, in order to summarize these data. One thing that we noted is the apparent difference in turnout between the newer members in the East and the older members in the West.
    a. As percent turnout is an interval-level variable and East/West is a nominal-level variable, let's look at a means comparison.

Table 8.8 Means Comparison: EP Election Turnout

	EP election turnout	Number of observations [country/years]
Western Europe	57.5%	132
Eastern Europe	32.0%	43
Overall mean	51.2%	175

First, there are not 132 countries in Western Europe (or 43 in Eastern Europe). The 16 (11) countries have each participated in several elections. Second, of all, as a *description of these data*, it appears that there may be a higher level of turnout in the West (57.5% > 32.0%).

Perhaps, the East Europeans were excited by the prospect of being able to vote in the EP elections and quickly became disappointed. And West Europeans may have also been a little disappointed after Eastern Europe joined the EU by feeling their votes didn't count as much. Thus, the first full election of the expanded EU in 2004 brought on a post-expansion funk, thus explaining what seems to be the disparity in voting levels between East and West.

One way to start to uncover this it to compare the means of pre-2004 West and East (pre-funk era) with the means of post-2004 East and West (post-funk era). Why 2004? In 2004, the countries of Cyprus, the Czech Republic, Estonia, Hungary, Latvia, Lithuania, Malta, Poland, Slovakia, and Slovenia all joined the European Union, the largest expansion in its history.

We can do this by integrating the controlled comparisons of the previous chapter with the means comparisons of this chapter. **Controlled Means Comparisons** takes this one step further and subdivides the total group by a third variable to see if the original relationship is affected by this separation. That is, controlled means comparisons allow us to identify the potential influence of a third variable on bivariate relationships between interval-level variables and nominal-/ordinal-level variables. Thus:

Table 8.9 Controlled Means Comparison: EP Election Turnout

	2004 and previous (pre-funk)		After 2004 (post-funk)	
	EP election turnout	Number of observations [country/years]	EP election turnout	Number of observations [country/years]
Western Europe	59.4%	81	54.4%	51
Eastern Europe	31.2%	8	32.2%	35
Overall mean	56.9%	89	45.4%	86

Comment on two specific things that this Means Comparison and Controlled Means Comparison potentially has shown us about the East/West difference in European Parliamentary turnout. (*Hint:* 'no change' is also a result.)

2. Copy this axis five times on a piece of paper.

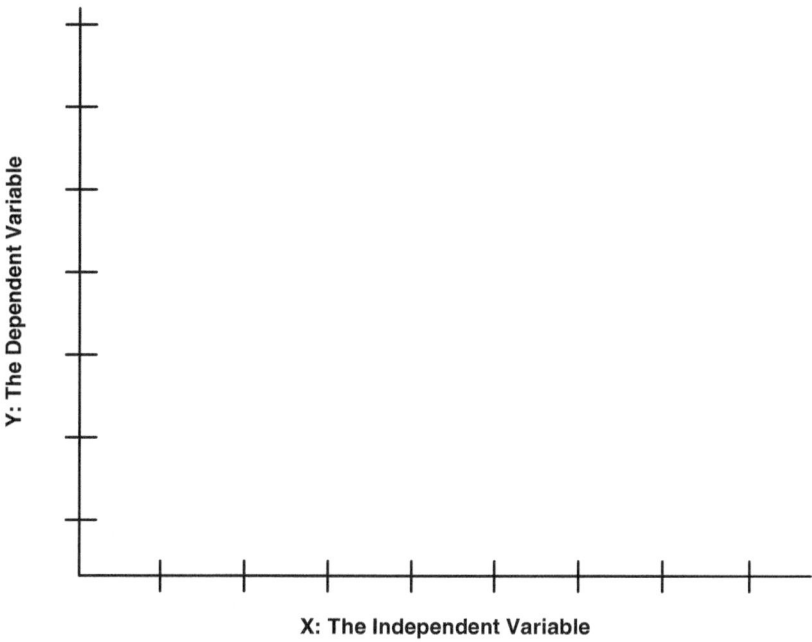

Figure 8.7 A Set of Axes

Draw a set of 10 dots for each set of axes that represent:

a. r = −1.0
b. r = 0.95
c. r = 0.0
d. r = −0.70
e. r = 0.25

3. Figure 8.8 is a scatterplot of the relationship between the percentage of daily smokers and total amount of arable/agricultural land by country for a random sample of countries with less than 10,000 hectares (*N*=21). The correlation is a moderate and positive r=0.38.

a. What does correlation tell us about this relationship?
b. What does correlation not tell us about this relationship?

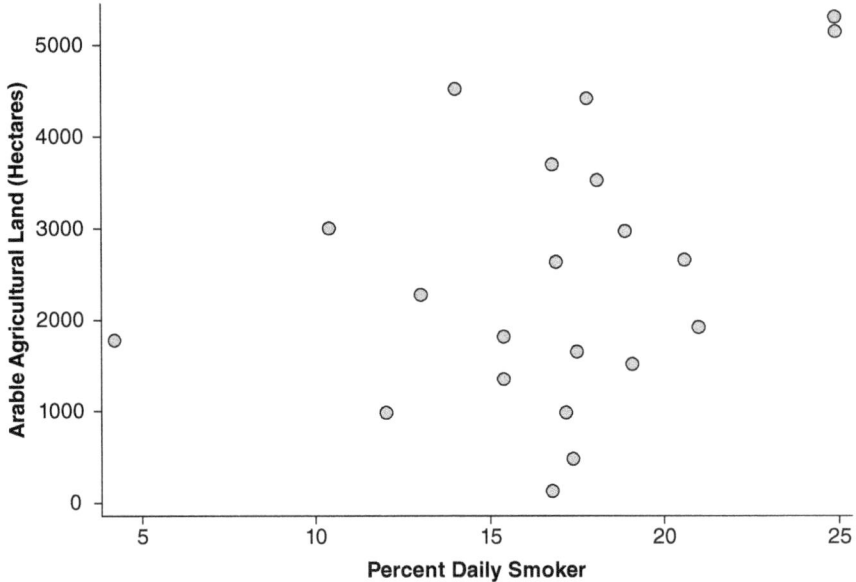

Figure 8.8 Percent Daily Smokers and Arable Agricultural Land (by Country)

4. A research study reports a Pearson's correlation of r=−0.64 between the individuals' party preference (Green Party, Centre Left Party, Centre Right Party, Extreme Far Right Party) and the amount they donate annually to Amnesty International. Which of the following statements is *most correct*:
   a. Party preference and donations to Amnesty International are negatively correlated.
   b. Party preference and donations to Amnesty International are substantially and negatively correlated.
   c. Pearson's correlation coefficient is inappropriate to establish an association between these variables as individuals' party preferences is not an interval-level variable.
   d. People who prefer far right parties do not donate to Amnesty International.
5. Play this 20 times and report your score: http://guessthecorrelation.com/
6. Why can we *not* use correlation in the following scenarios?
   a. We suspect that gender is very highly correlated with the decision to vote in national elections.
   b. Using the ideological spectrum, we expect extreme left – as well as extreme right – partisans to have higher levels of political interest than those in the centre. We can use correlation to estimate the strength between ideology and level of political interest.
   c. You want to compare the percentage of the population that voted in southern European states versus the percentage voting in northern European states.

d. You want to correlate the relationship between the amount of time candidates spend campaigning and the percentage of votes they receive and the number of years the candidate has been in office.
e. You want to test whether the percentage of military spending in national budgets is correlated with whether that country has instigated conflicts abroad.

Annotated References and Further Reading

See Tyler Vigen's collection of spurious correlations: www.tylervigen.com/spurious-correlations

Pearson, Karl. 1896. 'Mathematical contributions to the theory of evolution. III. Regression, heredity, and panmixia' *Philosophical Transaction of the Royal Society of London. Series A, Containing Papers of Mathematical or Physical Characteristics.* **187: 254–318. www.jstor.org/stable/90707**
The original paper for correlation. Essentially, 'I invented correlation!'

Wilkinson, Richard and Kate Pickett. 2010. *The Spirit Level. Why Equality is Better for Everyone.* **London: Penguin.**
Excellent display of highly consistent correlational evidence that, while not causal, makes a strong case for the negative role of high social inequalities in the West.

Signposts to the Accompanying Digital Resources

Data used in this chapter

- **Percentage of national internet availability:** International Telecommunications Union.
  - www.itu.int/en/ITU-D/Statistics/Pages/stat/default.aspx
- **Global Freedom Scores:** Freedom House.
  - https://freedomhouse.org/countries/freedom-world/scores
- **Voice and Accountability:** World Bank: World Governance Indicators.
  - https://databank.worldbank.org/source/worldwide-governance-indicators
- **Corruption Perception Index; Life expectancy at birth; Renewable Energy Consumption; Global Militarization Index; Press Freedom Index:** Quality of Governance Dataset.
  - Teorell, Jan, Aksel Sundström, Sören Holmberg, Bo Rothstein, Natalia Alvarado Pachon and Cem Mert Dalli. 2021. The Quality of Government Standard Dataset, version Jan21. University of Gothenburg: The Quality of Government Institute, www.qog.pol.gu.se

- **Democratic Political Culture:** European Social Survey (2018).
    - ESS 1–9, European Social Survey Cumulative File, Study Description. Bergen: NSD – Norwegian Centre for Research Data for ESS ERIC. https://doi.org/10.21338/NSD-ESS-CUMULATIVE
- **Agricultural land;** AGRLANDAREA – Total: OECD (2021), Agricultural land (indicator) https://doi.org/10.1787/9d1ffd68-en: Organisation for Economic Co-operation and Development.
- **Percent Daily Smokers:** SMOKER – Total: OECD (2021), Daily smokers (indicator). https://doi.org/10.1787/1ff488c2-en: Organisation for Economic Co-operation and Development.
    - https://data.oecd.org/

9
MEASURES OF ASSOCIATION III: (BIVARIATE) REGRESSION

> ### LEARNING OUTCOMES
>
> In this chapter, you will be able to
>
> - Use bivariate regression to describe the relationship between two interval-level variables.
> - Identify and interpret the elements of regression analysis, including the regression coefficient and intercept.
> - Explain what the Coefficient of Determination is and what it does.
> - Begin to fully model a relationship between two interval-level variables.

This is the final chapter in the Descriptive Statistics section. In it, we are introduced to (bivariate) regression analysis as a sophisticated statistical tool. Regression also allows us to draw together the descriptive power of statistical analysis into the process of modelling in order to more fully address the questions in which we are interested.

By the way, I put bivariate in brackets/parentheses in this chapter as we are interested in the power of regression to describe the relationship between two interval-level variables. (Bivariate) regression is not the only form of regression and the good news is that, for the most part, the mechanics, calculations, and assumption of other forms of regression – which we will come to in later chapters – are the same as (bivariate) regression.

Quick Start: (Bivariate) Regression

Regression analysis – or simply, regression – provides a variable-specific description of the linear relationship between a dependent and independent variable. It is a variable-specific way to look at and summarize the relationship between variables. Unlike the generic association of correlation, in which the independent and dependent variables can be reversed without changing the resulting measure, regression produces bespoke or tailored results for each relationship.

To do so, and differently from other Measures of Association, regression is not a number but rather an equation. In order to adequately explain the specific relationship between two specific, interval-level variables, regression is composed of a number of components that result in the **regression equation**.

Given a dependent variable, Y, and an independent variable, X, the regression equation is:

$$Y_i = \alpha + \beta (X_i) + \varepsilon$$

The results of estimating the regression equation will include a regression coefficient (β) and an intercept (α). There is also an error term (ε).

- β, or beta, is the **regression coefficient** – also called the 'slope' – which estimates the average change in Y associated with a unit change in X. That is, the regression coefficient tells us the specific unit change in the dependent variable brought about by a specific unit change in the independent variable. We also learn, like correlation, whether the relationship is negative or positive.
- α, or alpha, is the **intercept** – sometimes called the 'constant' – and denotes the point where the regression line 'intercepts' the Y-axis (i.e., when X = 0). The value of alpha depends on whether zero is a meaningful value of the independent variable X or not.
- ε, the **error term,** is part of the regression equations that handles the random elements. It represents the presence of error, thus accounting for the unavoidable randomness – the 'off-line' observations we keep seeing in scatterplots. This is not calculated.

REGRESSION EQUATIONS: POPULATION OR SAMPLE

Technically, $Y_i = \alpha + \beta (X_i) + \varepsilon$ is the *population regression equation*. The more commonly used *sample regression equation* is: $Y_i = \hat{\alpha} + \hat{\beta}(X_i) + \hat{\varepsilon}_i$. The hats on α, β, and ε in the sample regression model refer to the fact that these are estimates of the actual population parameters (that we will never know). For introductory simplicity, we investigate the distinction between these two forms of regression in Inferential Statistics and Multiple Regression sections.

Takeaway: hats mean 'best guess'!

User's Manual: (Bivariate) Regression

Let's take a closer look at the regression equation: $Y_i = \alpha + \beta (X_i) + \varepsilon$. We will focus on the regression coefficient (β) and the error term (ε) as, for the most part, the intercept alpha (α) is a necessary but only marginally informative component of the linear estimation procedure.

Regression Coefficient: Slope

In the regression equation, β – the regression coefficient – represents the 'slope' of the regression line.

The concept of 'slope' comes from algebra in which we consider the steepness of the line as an indicator of the strength of relationship. Algebraically, slope is the change of Y that corresponds to a change in X. Simply, slope is the change of Y divided by the change in X. As my algebra teacher used to say, 'rise over run'.

Regression exploits this specificity in the relationship between X – the independent variable (IV) – and Y – the dependent variable (DV). The regression coefficient simply imposes the change of X to 1-unit. Thus, the regression coefficient – β – is the change in the value of Y given a 1-unit change in X. In this way, and unlike correlation, the regression coefficient gives us an exact linear relationship between *this* DV and *this* IV.

How is this useful?

In both Figure 9.1a and Figure 9.1b, we see positive relationships between X and Y. As X goes up, Y, goes up. As X goes down, Y goes down.

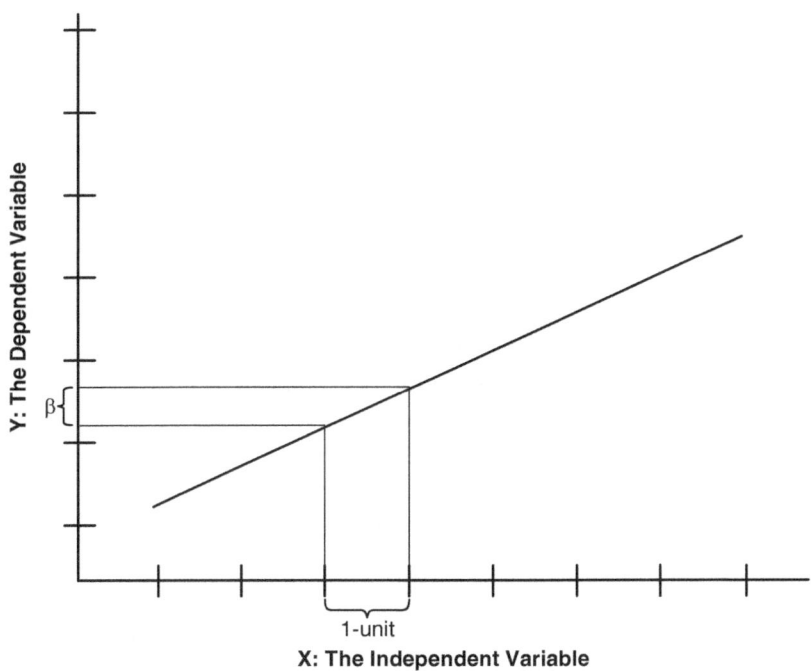

Figure 9.1a Smaller Regression Coefficient

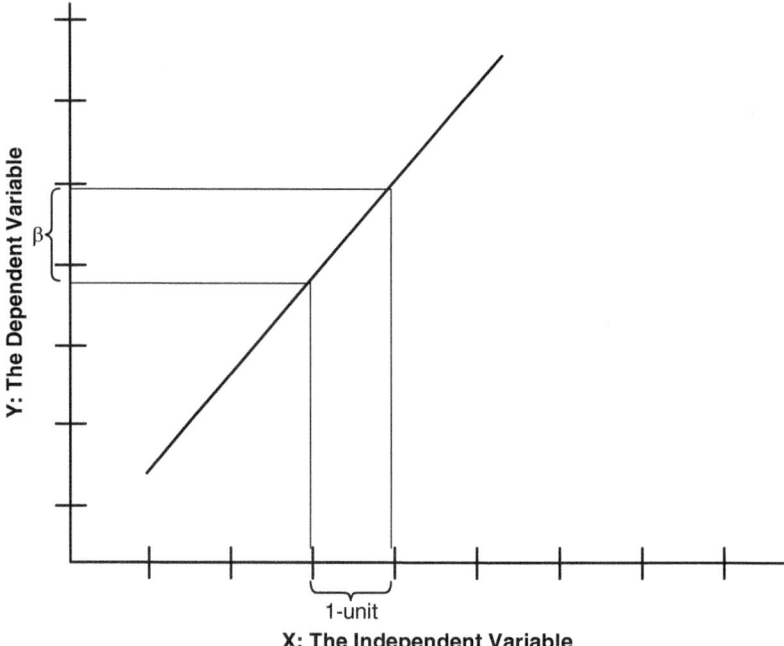

Figure 9.1b Larger Regression Coefficient

We see that in Figure 9.1a the regression line is a positive, mildly inclining line and a positive but steeply inclining line in Figure 9.1b. Assuming that the Xs and Ys are the same in both graphs, we can also see that a 1-unit change in X in Figure 9.1a produces a smaller β than the 1-unit change in X in Figure 9.1b. Reflecting this difference in 'steepness', the regression coefficient (β) in the regression equation for Figure 9.1a will be smaller than the regression coefficient (β) in the regression equation for Figure 9.1b.

As in algebra, the steepness of the line – the slope – is an indicator of the strength – as well as the direction – of the relationship between X and Y. And just as these graphs show modest and strong relationships between the two variables, you guessed it, a line with a flat slope (β = 0) represents no linear relationship between the two variables.

The regression coefficient is the *average* change in Y given a 1-unit change in X. This means that no matter which 1-unit change in X we refer to, whether at the low values of X or the higher values of X, the change in Y – the regression coefficient, β – remains the same. The regression coefficient relates the *average* state of the relationship between X and Y.

Producing the regression coefficient can be done by hand. Depending on your level of mathematical masochism, you can chose from any number of ways to calculate β.

Here are two algebraic variations:

$$\beta = \frac{(N \sum XY) - (\sum X)(\sum Y)}{\left(N \sum X^2\right) - (\sum X)^2} \qquad \beta = \frac{\sum\left[(x_i - \bar{x}) \times (y_i - \bar{y})\right]}{\sum (x_i - \bar{x})^2}$$

While this could be a lot of fun, I recommend using a statistical software package.

> ## REGRESSION BY HAND
>
>
>
> **Image 9.1** Photo K. Johnson
>
> *Source*: NASA; restored by Adam Cuerden
>
> If regression by hand makes your head swim, know that it can be done. Even when you need to do a lot of it.
>
> Katherine Johnson (26 August 1918 – 24 February 2020) was an African American mathematician who led a team to calculate – by hand – the mechanical data necessary for NASA orbital programs, including the manned Apollo missions. Regressions were a substantial portion of these calculations.
>
> This was made into a film: *Hidden Figures* [2016].

Together, the regression coefficient, along with an intercept – alpha (α, sometimes written 'β_0') – form the regression equation. This equation represents a linear solution for a descriptive summary of the (bivariate) relationship. For (bivariate) regression, the regression equation and regression line are the same thing, in different forms (the mathematical regression equation is equivalent to the graphical representation, the regression line).

You have undoubtedly noticed that there is one more component of the regression equation.

The Error Term: Systematic and Random Components of the Regression Equation

While the regression coefficient (β) and the intercept alpha (α) form the basis for the regression equation, the error term – ε – handles the random elements. Strictly, in sample regression, this is called the 'residual' ('μ'). The error term is a crucial inclusion in the regression equation as it represents the randomness of the 'real world'. This randomness can be our fault, such as measurement error, imprecise instruments, sampling error, or the regression equation may have a different form. Or truly random error derived from the complexity of social, economic, and political realities for which we fail to – or are unable to – account.

Excluding the error term assumes a deterministic relationship such as the conversion from Celsius (X) to Fahrenheit (Y). In this *deterministic* relationship, there is no randomness. We need merely insert a value for Celsius to get a reciprocal value in Fahrenheit.

$$F = 32 + \frac{9}{5}(C)$$

However, as we well know, relationships in Political Science – whether we are measuring people's attitudes or feelings, the performance of a political institutions, or bias in the news – are neither so insulated nor so exact. Such relationships are instead *probabilistic*, allowing variability in the values of Y for each value of X. Although we try to control for as much as we can, the error term is included to capture the rest, in a sense, resolving the distances we see between the observations and the regression equation.

What does the error term include?

Frankly, outside of what we explicitly control for (by including an independent variable), everything else in the world. That is, the main body of the regression equation '$\alpha+\beta x$' is the **systematic component**, the part of the regression equation that we specifically articulate by including the variables we think are important and estimating parameters. The **random component** – the error term 'ε' – is the sum of the unaccounted-for, random (or 'stochastic') influences.

$$y = \{\alpha + \beta x\} + \{\varepsilon\}$$

STOCHASTIC

By now, it is unlikely that you need any more phrases for you to make friends and impress others. You have probably used with great success: 'Wouldn't you agree that the difficulty of operationalization is problematized by weak conceptualization?' Or perhaps you have even developed your own, such as: 'Clearly, the epistemological basis of case studies is dubious at best.' But, if you still needed something quick and punchy, 'stochastic' in place of 'random' will work in a pinch (e.g., 'OMG, that was *so* stochastic!').

The error term is 'what's left over that we didn't explain' or how far our regression line is from each and every observation. And its inclusion is consistent with the metaphysical position that real-life situations are impossible to fully and completely model or measure (they are *probabilistic*). Some heavy philosophical lifting!

For now, we introduce the neat trick that all the effects in the world (galaxy/universe) on our dependent variable sum to zero. That is, the influence of everything in the world cancels out. And I suspect you will have one of three responses to the discovery that the error term is literally 'everything else in the world' and sums to zero.

- One, I just need to pass this class, 'error term is assumed to be zero', check.
- Two, alright, 'I can buy that. I mean, the key independent variable is explicitly included in the regression and that seems reasonable.'

- Or three, 'Mmm, I don't know about that. That seems like it could be a problematic assumption.'

If you are 1 or 2, I applaud your practicality. Just keep reading.

If you are a 3, I've got some good news for you. It's called the field of *Econometrics*. But we won't be taking that up here as I only have 165,000 words available to me.

Clearly the error term is a whole thing – and we will return to it.

How to Find the 'Best' Regression Line

Together, the regression coefficient (β) and the intercept alpha (α) constitute the regression equation and form the basis for the regression line.

But, how do we find the best solution, the best line, for our relationship?

Let's look at the scatterplot for democratic political culture and democratic political institutional performance from the previous chapter (Figure 8.6, reproduced here), if we held a piece of string both taut and vertically across the graph, the string (as a line) would not seem to be an intuitively good summary of that relationship (Figure 9.2a). Neither would holding the string horizontally (Figure 9.2b). However, diagonally from the bottom left to the top right seems a more appropriate or better line for this relationship (Figure 9.2c).

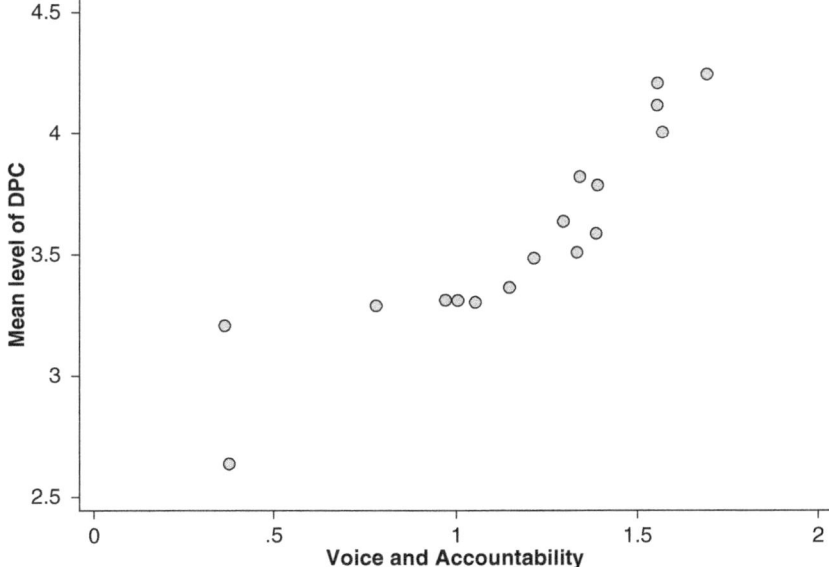

Figure 8.6 Democratic Political Culture and Democratic Political Institutional Performance

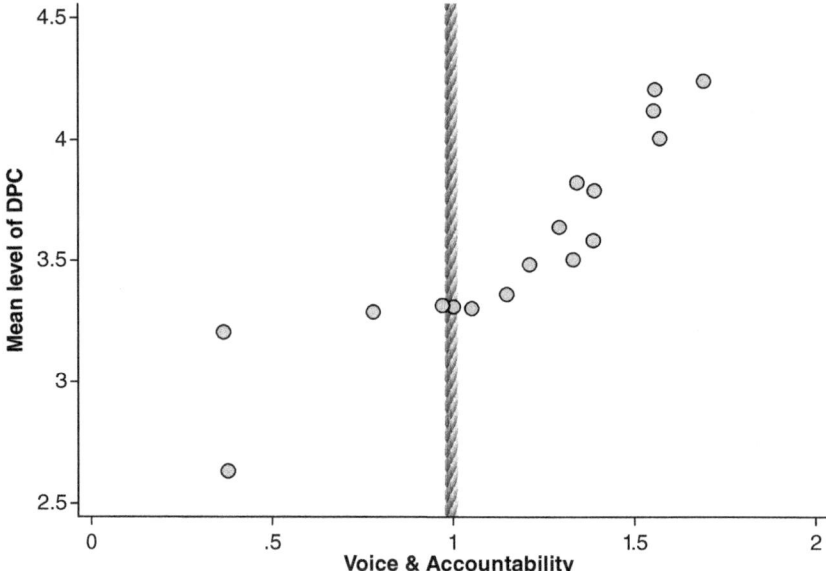

Figure 9.2a Finding the Best Line – String Method

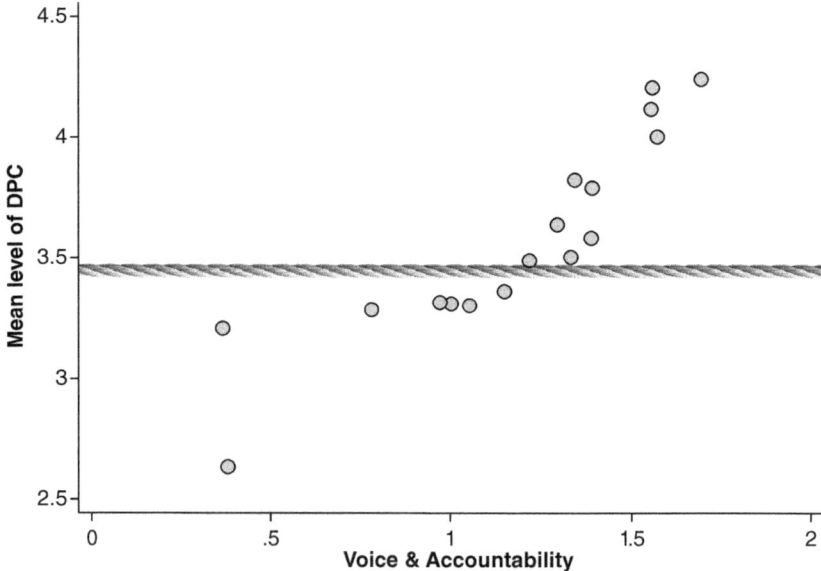

Figure 9.2b Finding the Best Line – String Method

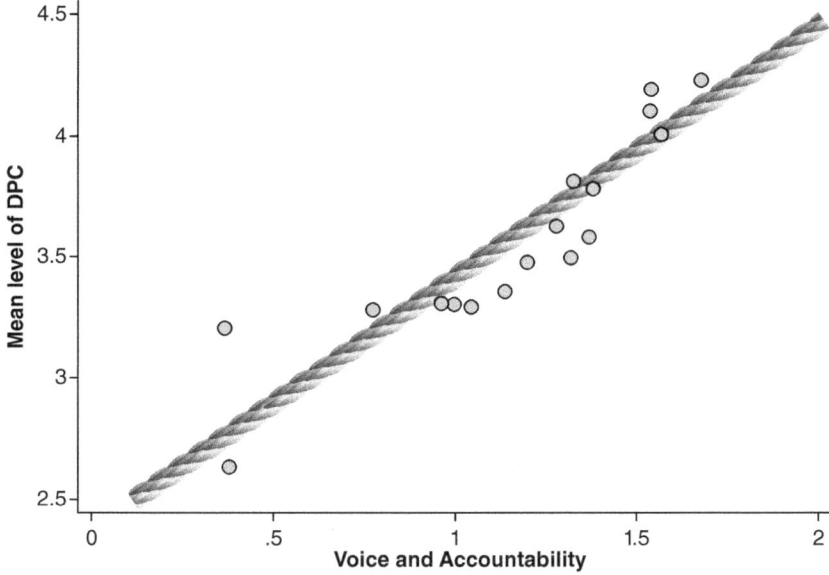

Figure 9.2c Finding the Best Line – String Method

Which line is 'best' for describing this relationship? Figure 9.2c seems to be getting close. And, intuitively, one thing stands out: we want all the observations to be simultaneously as 'close to the line' as they can.

Obviously, we can't draw a line in which all of the observations are on it (as we have seen over and over again, some observations are always off the line). However, as we just tried, we can find a line that gets as close as it can to each one at the same time. Perhaps one might try to find a line that makes all of the observations' distances simultaneously as small as possible.

And, in fact, this is essentially correlation.

Regression is based on the same idea but uses different distances. The estimation of the regression equation essentially advances the 'smallest distance' idea one step further by engaging the specificity of the relationship between these two variables.

Similar to correlation, the estimation of the regression equation takes distance as very important: 'closeness good, distance bad'. But rather than a generic comparison, regression exploits the specific attributes of the relationship between these two specific variables. Regression therefore minimizes the distance between the observations on the dependent variables and the predicted values of the dependent variable, *given what we would expect from its relationship to the independent variable*. That is, regression analysis seeks to simultaneously minimize the distance between each observation and a line of potential predictions of what those observations would be if our independent variable predicted perfectly.

More technically, finding the 'best' regression line is based on the *prediction error*. Prediction error is the distance between the actual value of the dependent variable we have in hand (i.e., Y in the dataset) and the estimated value of the dependent variable $\hat{Y}$ from the regression equation. $\hat{Y}$ (pronounced, 'Y-hat', and hats mean 'best guess') is what the regression equation predicts for each X_i given the parameter estimates β and α. You can think of $\hat{Y}_i$ – our best guess – as a doppelgänger of Y_i

Anyway, because we are guessing, we will be wrong by a little bit (and occasionally a lot). That is, $\hat{Y}_i$ will be not exactly Y_i. Formally, we write this as: $Y_i = \hat{Y}_i + \hat{\varepsilon}_i$ where $\hat{Y}_i$ is our best guess and $\hat{\varepsilon}_i$ represents the amount that we are wrong. This might be easier to see solving for the error term: $\hat{\varepsilon}_i = Y_i - \hat{Y}_i$

IOW, $\hat{\varepsilon}_i$ is the amount we are wrong for each value of Y_i

Quick note to dispel any confusion, this error is variously referred to as 'error', 'distance', or 'difference' (and not very consistently across sources). For us here, it simply refers to the difference between the observed value and our best guess of that value.

So, in trying to find the 'best line', regression tries to make these errors/distances/differences as small as possible for every observation at the same time. The estimation technique is taking the lowest sum of the squared errors of all the data points from our line. Technically, this estimation technique is called the *sum of squared errors* – which is exactly what it is. The total amount ('the sum') that we would be wrong ('errors'), squared (see Box: Why Squared Differences?).

Thinking about it this way, it makes a lot of sense to want to minimize our total amount of being wrong. Not only does this sound like an effective motivational phrase ('Today I will minimize my total amount of being wrong!'), it's simple: the lowest sum (of errors) gets to be the line.

WHY SQUARED DIFFERENCES?

One, squaring errors/distances/differences makes them positive so when you sum them, they won't all cancel each other out. Two, squaring errors/distances/differences more heavily weighs outliers. That is, squaring 'weights' bigger errors (more distant observations) than smaller errors (closer observations). This makes distance more 'costly' to the line trying to summarize the relationship.

As an example, using the bivariate scatterplot and regression equation for CPI and V&A (Figure 9.3), we can see two examples of prediction error. These errors are the distances that are crucial to calculating the regression equation (*ahem*, $\hat{\varepsilon}_i = Y_i - \hat{Y}_i$). To find the 'best line', regression uses not only these two errors, but *every* distance from *every* point to the regression line. Hence, seeking to minimize the (squared) errors we make is a good basis on which to summarize the relationship.

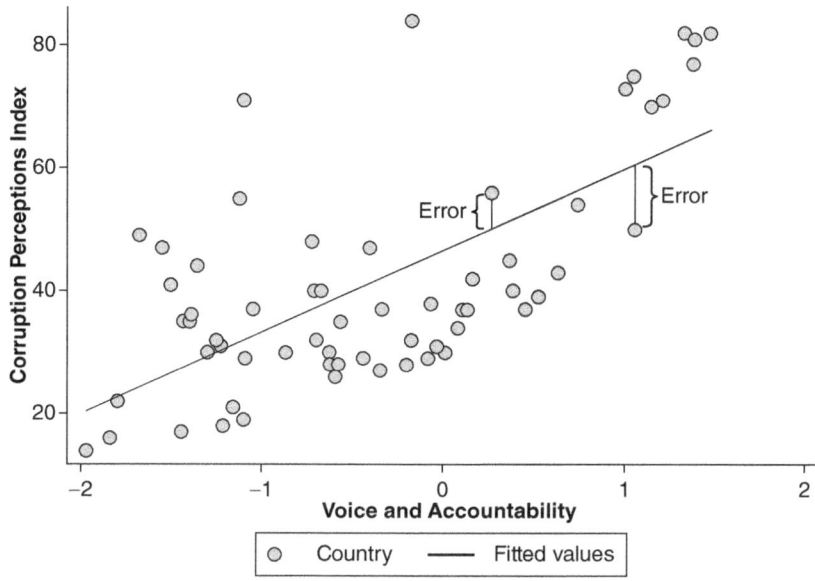

Figure 9.3 Voice and Accountability and Corruption Perception Index

One more thing.

The most common estimating procedure for finding the 'best regression line' – and the one described above – is called Ordinary Least Squares (OLS) regression. Given the right circumstances (mostly the data meeting a set of assumptions), OLS outperforms other linear estimators earning it the acronym B.L.U.E.: the Best, Linear, Unbiased, Estimator. BLUE is a super-nerdy way to say that OLS finds the regression equation – i.e., estimating the regression coefficient (β) and the intercept alpha (α) – very close to the real values of that relationship (that we can never know). The approach is so widely used that the 'regression line' is sometimes referred to as the 'least squares line'.

Neato.

In the Field: (Bivariate) Regression

Let's bring this all together and look at (bivariate) regression in its simplest form.

Recall the correlation and scatterplots in the previous chapter. Some are reproduced below (Figures 8.4b, 8.4d, and 8.4e). Let's see how **(bivariate) regression** informs us about these relationships.

For each relationship, let's take Voice and Accountability as the independent variable (i.e., that representative democratic institutions can explain quite a lot). Below, we have the correlations, scatterplots, and regression equations – the regression coefficient (β) and the intercept alpha (α) – generated by a statistical software program.

Table 9.1 Example of Regression Equations

Independent variable	Regression equation	Correlation coefficient
Life expectancy at birth	$y = 74.54 + 2.88(x) + \varepsilon$	$r = 0.43$
Global Militarization Index	$y = 157.92 - 29.97(x) + \varepsilon$	$r = -0.40$
Press Freedom Index	$y = 35.86 - 14.91(x) + \varepsilon$	$r = -0.88$

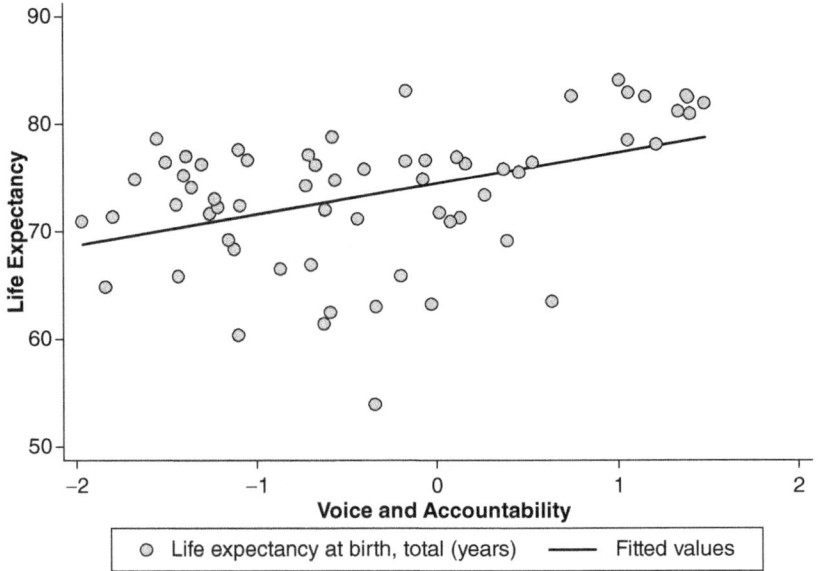

Figure 9.4a Scatterplot of Voice and Accountability and Life Expectancy

With Life Expectancy as the dependent variable (DV) and Voice and Accountability as the independent variable (IV), the regression equation is:

$$y = 74.54 + 2.88\,(x) + \varepsilon$$

The regression coefficient, β, is 2.88 and the intercept, α, is 74.54. The interpretation is: 'On average, for every 1-unit change in Voice and Accountability, there will be a 2.88-unit increase in the Life Expectancy.' (Notice both the β *and* direction are reported.) 'Given that zero is a meaningful value in the range of the Voice and Accountability, when the Voice and Accountability is 0, the Life Expectancy is 74.54' (which we can see when Voice and Accountability=0).

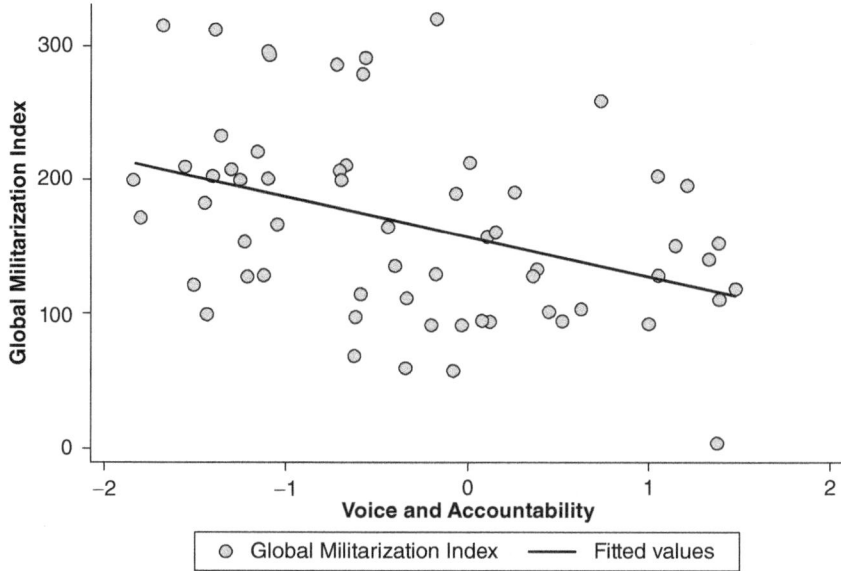

Figure 9.4b Scatterplot of Voice and Accountability and Global Militarization Index

With Global Militarization Index as the dependent variable (DV) and Voice and Accountability as the independent variable (IV), the regression equation is:

$y = 157.92 - 29.97\ (x) + \varepsilon$

The regression coefficient, β, is −29.97 and the intercept, α, is 157.92. The interpretation is: 'On average, for every 1-unit change in Voice and Accountability, there will be a 29.97-unit decrease in the Global Militarization Index. Given that zero is a meaningful value in the range of the Voice and Accountability, when the Voice and Accountability is 0, the Global Militarization Index is 157.92.'

Using the Press Freedom Index as the dependent variable (DV) and Voice and Accountability as the independent variable (IV), the regression equation is:

$y = 35.86 - 14.91\ (x) + \varepsilon$

The regression coefficient, β, is 14.91 and the intercept, α, is 35.86. The interpretation is: 'On average, for every 1-unit change in Voice and Accountability, there will be a 14.91-unit decrease in the Press Freedom Index. Given that zero is a meaningful value in the range of the Voice and Accountability, when the Voice and Accountability is 0, the Press Freedom Index is 35.86.'

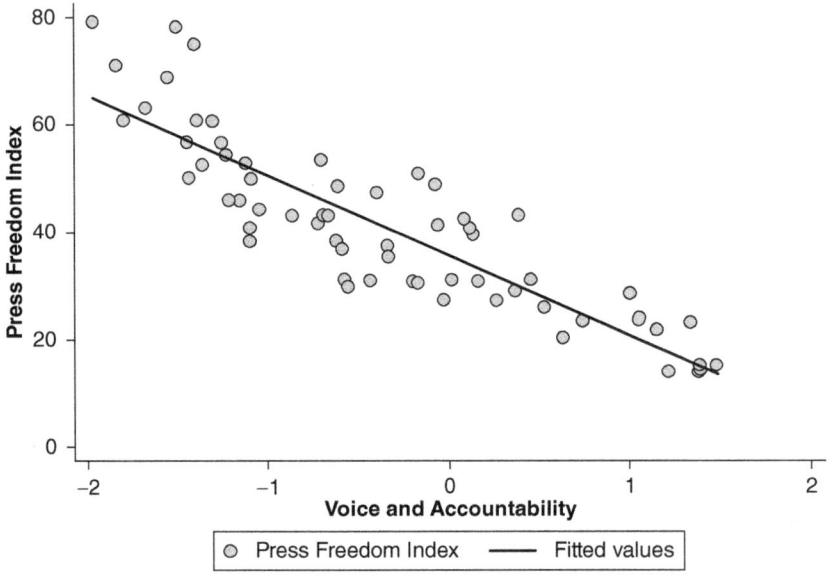

Figure 9.4c Scatterplot of Voice and Accountability and the Press Freedom Index

In each example of (bivariate) regression above, we have learned:

- Whether the relationship is positive or negative.
- Depending on the significance of a zero value for the independent variable, we learn the intercept (IV = 0).
- And most importantly, the specific amount of change in the dependent variable that each of these independent variables produce (i.e., the regression coefficient).

Coefficient of Determination: R^2

If you can believe this, there is a final element of regression analysis not found in the actual regression equation. It is produced as a by-product of the estimating process and determines how much of the variance in the dependent variable is explained by variance in the independent variable. Commonly reported as how much – or how well – your independent variable 'explains' your dependent variable.

This element is called the **coefficient of determination** or 'R^2', pronounced 'R-squared'. It represents the proportion of common variation between the two variables. It ranges from 0 to 1, for which 0 means that changes in your independent variable offer no explanation for the changes observed in the dependent variable, and 1 means that changes in your independent variable perfectly explain the changes observed in the dependent variable.

Like Gamma and Lambda, 'R^2' is a PRE – proportional reduction of error – statistic telling us how much better are we predicting the dependent variable by knowing the independent variable than predicting the dependent variable while not knowing the independent variable.

The coefficient of determination falls under the larger umbrella of measures that provide model fit. **Model fit**, also known as 'goodness of fit', refers to the model's appropriateness. 'R^2' is a measure of how well the regression equation has performed based on what we have chosen to include. In a sense, 'R^2' merges information about the strength of the relationship (from correlation) with the quality of explanation between these specific variables (from regression). It is interpreted as: 'variation in the independent variable explains ['R^2']% of variation in the dependent variable'. However, making things slightly less clear, a higher value does not necessarily mean that our regression is 'better' in each and every case. Yet, in general, the coefficient of determination can be useful in comparing different regressions.

Table 9.2 Coefficient of Determination: Example

Independent variable	Regression equation	Correlation coefficient	R^2: Coefficient of Determination
Life expectancy at birth	$y = 74.54 + 2.88 (x) + \varepsilon$	$r = 0.43$	$R^2 = 0.169$
Global Militarization Index	$y = 157.92 - 29.97 (x) + \varepsilon$	$r = -0.40$	$R^2 = 0.142$
Press Freedom Index	$y = 35.86 - 14.91 (x) + \varepsilon$	$r = -0.88$	$R^2 = 0.772$

These R^2s are interpreted as:

- Variation in Voice and Accountability explains 16.9% of variation in Life Expectancy.
- Variation in Voice and Accountability explains 14.2% of variation in the Global Militarization Index.
- Variation Voice and Accountability in explains 77.2% of variation in the Press Freedom Index.

It must be pointed out that, for example, 'variation in the Voice and Accountability explains 77.2% of variation in the Press Freedom Index' does not mean that there is only 22.8% [100%–77.2%] left of the Press Freedom Index to explain.

What the coefficient of determination reveals about the nature of this relationship is how well the regression is specified. *Specified* means the selection of included variables. Therefore, in the case of Voice and Accountability, the R^2 of 77.2% means that *this* independent variable coordinates well with this dependent variable (Press Freedom Index). Specifically, as a measure of 'fit', R^2 tells us how well the specification of the regression equation – the model - *fits* the dependent variable.

Remember, in (bivariate) regression, we are controlling for only one independent variable. There are very likely other explanations that we have excluded so our one variable can often initially seem overly important. (Or not very important, as in the case of Voice and Accountability and Renewable energy consumption and the R^2 of 1.6%.)

Notably, these R^2s correspond to the blossom of the observations around the regression lines in Figures 9.5a, 9.5b, and 9.5c. This is not an accident. Representing the proportion of common variation between the two variables, R^2 reflects the quality of the regression line as a summary of the relationship. Visually, we can see this in the 'tightness' of dots (the joint distribution of observations) around the regression lines. As R^2 increases, so does the 'tightness' or coordination of the relationship. Which of course makes sense as R^2 is 'r' – the correlation coefficient – squared.

But, wait, there's more!

Farther In the Field: (Bivariate) Regression as Modelling

(Bivariate) regression – and regression in general – is the full package. And we have definitely moved from the descriptive summarizing of data as variables to a much more sophisticated analysis of relationships between variables.

So, how does it work? How does it all fit together? This has been a long walk, there better be a good view at the end.

There is.

Ultimately, the previous chapters here have brought us to the first big plateau of our study of statistics. (Bivariate) regression analysis is the culminating analytical technique of Descriptive Statistics. To demonstrate this, we are going to walk through the process of Modelling – from research question to interpretation – for two variables of interest. **Modelling** is a process to fully examine a relationship in which we are interested. We accumulate information provided by various statistical techniques to gather a comprehensive understanding of the nature of the relationship.

THE MODELLING PROCESS

- *Step One:* A Research Question
- *Step Two:* Identify Variables
- *Step Three:* Pearson's Product Moment Correlation Coefficient
- *Step Four:* The Regression Equation
- *Step Five:* Model Fit
- *Step Six:* Interpretation

Let's model the relationship of the two interval-level variables Voice and Accountability (V&A) and the Corruption Perceptions Index (CPI) using an array of scientific and statistical techniques that we have learned up to this point, including (bivariate) regression analysis. From the Box: The Modelling Process, we can follow the six steps.

Step One asks for us to determine the research question. As correlation is agnostic on the order of V&A and the CPI, we can choose how we want to think about this relationship.

We could propose either of the following:

- *RQ1:* To what extent does the level of corruption affect the capacity for citizens to influence and exercise control over their government?
- *RQ2:* To what extent does the capacity for citizens to influence and exercise control over their government shape the level of corruption in their country?

The literature surrounding this question is robust with a core consensus that 'poor performance' of state institutions corresponds to higher levels of perceived corruption. Which way that influence flows has many contenders on both sides. Here, we will take the position that democratic institutions that are not responsive to citizens shield elites, already disinclined to change the rules, from accountability creating incentives for corruption to take place (IOW, RQ2).

Step Two asks us to identify the variables

- *Dependent Variable (DV):* Corruptions Perceptions Index (CPI):
    - Aggregated perceptions of business people and country experts of the level of corruption in the public sector.
    - Range: 0 (highly corrupt) to 100 (very clean).
    - Mean: 42.1; Standard Deviation: 18.5; N = 63
    - Source: Transparency International.
- *Independent Variable (IV):* Voice and Accountability (V&A):
    - A measure reflecting the ability of citizens to participate in selecting their government, as well as freedom of expression, freedom of association, and a free media.
    - Range: −2 (very low) to 2 (very high).
    - Mean: −0.34; Standard Deviation: 0.96; N = 63
    - Source: *World Governance Indicators (World Bank).*

Note: we use our knowledge of univariate descriptive statistics to describe these interval-level variables (see mean and standard deviation above).

Step Three: The correlation is r = 0.68. We can add a scatterplot to visualize this correlation (see Figure 9.5).

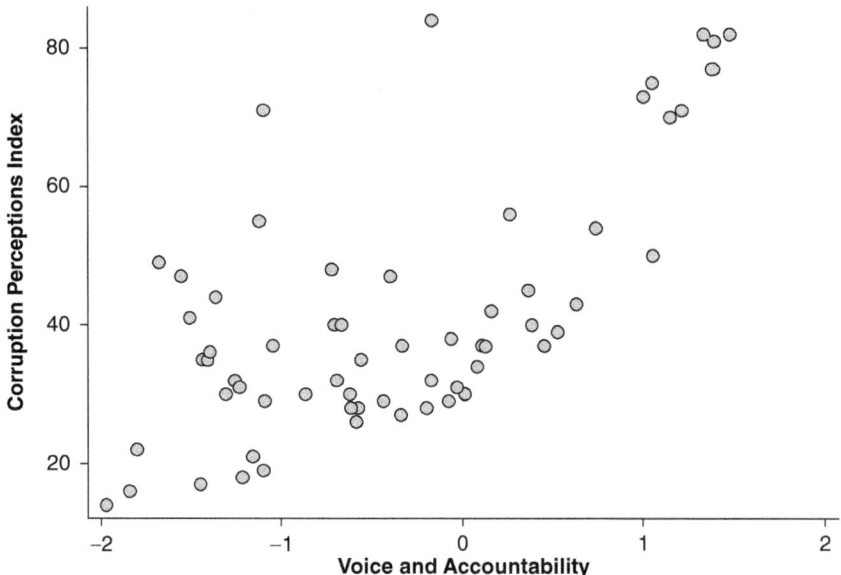

Figure 9.5 Scatterplot of Voice and Accountability and Corruption Perceptions Index

Step Four asks for us to calculate the regression equation. Using statistical software, we calculate the regression equation with CPI as the DV and V&A as the IV. The result is:

$$y = 46.58 + 13.27\ (x) + \varepsilon$$

The regression coefficient, β, is 13.27 and the intercept, α, is 46.58. As regression is variable-specific, sometimes you may see the Y and X replaced with the actual DV and IV:

$$CPI = 46.58 + 13.27\ (V\&A) + \varepsilon$$

THE *OTHER* RESEARCH QUESTION

By the way, for those of you still harbouring a grudge that we didn't go with RQ1, the regression equation would look like this:

$$Y = -1.83 + 0.04\ (X) + \varepsilon$$

or

$$V\&A = -1.83 + 0.04\ (CPI) + \varepsilon$$

This doesn't look like what we produced with RQ2. That is correct. Regression takes the order of the DV and IV very seriously and will punish you for getting it wrong.

> The regression coefficient, β, is 0.04 and the intercept, α, is −1.83. This means that for every 1-unit change in the IV, there is a positive 0.04-unit change in DV. As regression is variable-specific, this translates into: 'On average, for every 1-unit change in CPI, there will be a 0.04-unit increase in the V&A.' Given that zero is a meaningful value of the CPI, we can interpret the intercept (α) as, 'When the CPI is zero, the V&A is −1.83.'

With the regression equation, we can also create a Prediction Equation. A prediction equation (sometimes: 'prediction model') estimates what Y would be given the parameter estimates β and α of the regression equation. And, as we assume that the sum of errors is zero (i.e., everything in the world cancels out), and like the penultimate step in a magic trick, the error term disappears into thin air. Poof.

Thus, we arrive at:

$$\hat{Y}_i = 46.58 + 13.27 \, (X_i)$$

In this prediction equation, $\hat{Y}$ is not expected to be one of the numbers in the dataset but merely the expectation of what we might find. It will very unlikely be one of the numbers in the dataset we are using (1) because the regression equation is a summary of the relationship (we are guessing where we *think* it will be) and (2) because we assumed there was no error in our prediction. [*Sotto voce*: $\hat{Y}$ will be on the line because it is a literal function of the regression equation.]

PREDICTION EQUATION

Technically, the entire prediction equation is a guess. While we will take this up more in the Inferential Statistics section, β and α are also (sample-specific) estimates of the actual (population) parameters (that we will never know). As such, for prediction, we indicate this by adding hats to both: $\hat{\beta}$ and $\hat{\alpha}$ (hats = best guesses!).

Hence, the prediction equation is more correctly written as: $\hat{Y}_i = \hat{\alpha} + \hat{\beta}(X_i)$. Interestingly, this can also be written as an expectation equation: $E(Y | X_i) = \hat{Y}_i = \hat{\alpha} + \hat{\beta}(X_i)$. In this equation, $\hat{Y}_i$ is the expected value we estimate using the prediction equation for X_i.

I propose, for the moment, to leave it so that we can wrestle with the implications.

Right, so what?

Now we can use the prediction equation to estimate values of the dependent variable based on the parameter estimates β and α and our choice of the value of the independent variable. We simply plug in a value for our IV and see what the equation predicts the DV will be. That is, in our example, we can predict where we expect a country's CPI to be depending on the value of V&A.

Given that the range of V&A is −2 to 2, let's plug in −1.

$\hat{Y}_i = 46.58 + 13.27 \, (-1)$
$\hat{Y}_i = 33.31$

If a country's Voice and Accountability is −1, Corruption Perception Index is expected to be 33.31. Looking at the scatterplot just above, we can see that this aligns quite nicely with the joint distribution of both variables.

> ### PREDICTION: THE AVERAGE SOLUTION
>
> At V&A = −1, there are not any countries with 33.31 CPI.
> Yes. True.
> However, regression is an analysis of the entire relationship. Recall that the regression coefficient represents the *average* of the entire relationship between X and Y. That is, *on average*, we would expect to find countries behaving as the regression equation implies. As a means to summarize a relationship, regression – like all forms of summarizing – cannot account for all the variation at all points of the relationships in which we are interested.

One of the super awesome things you can do by hand in bivariate regression analysis is draw the regression line. Given that we have already calculated one point (V&A = −1; CPI = 33.31), we need only another point to draw a line. Using our prediction equation $[\hat{Y}_i = 46.58 + 13.27 \, (X_i)]$, if V&A = 1; CPI = 59.85.

Plotting these two points on the scatterplot, we could draw a line through both. This is the actual regression line. That is, with the Corruption Perceptions Index as the dependent variable (DV) and Voice and Accountability as the independent variable (IV), the regression equation is $y = 46.58 + 13.27 \, (x) + \varepsilon$ which is represented by the line in Figure 9.6.

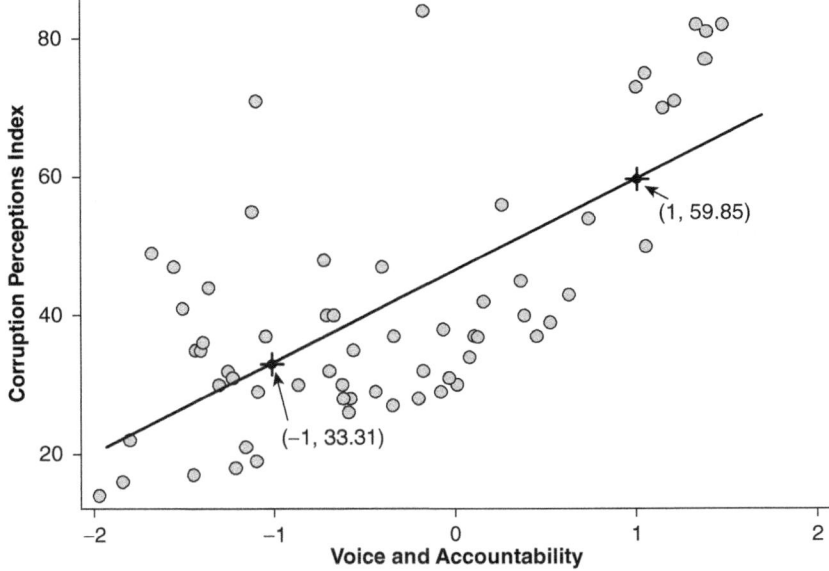

Figure 9.6 Plotting the Regression Line (by Hand!)

What fun! Invite your friend(s)!

Step Five: What is the coefficient of determination? R^2 tells us how much of the variance in the dependent variable is explained by variance in the independent variable. Our statistical software returns $R^2 = 0.468$.

Let's, however, do as sceptical scientists do. We prefer the adjusted R^2 which accounts for the number of independent variables included in the regression. Here we have one independent variable, so the adjusted-R^2 is only slightly discounted (for having the temerity to try to explain the DV with a single IV), adj-$R^2 = 0.459$. This is interpreted as 45.9% of the variation in the Corruption Perception Index can be explained by variation in Voice and Accountability. This nuance comes up again in Multiple Regression and we will not investigate it further there.

Step Six: Possibly the hardest step in the modelling process, interpretation. What does this all mean? As a full interpretation of the bivariate relationship we have investigated, one could offer:

> *Interpretation:* To provide a provisional answer to our research question, 'To what extent does the capacity for citizens to influence and exercise control over their government shape the level of corruption in their country?', we use two variables available for 63 countries. The dependent variable is the level of corruption for which we use the Corruptions Perceptions Index. The independent variable is the ability of citizens to shape their own government for which we use the Voice and Accountability measure. These interval-level variables have a substantial positive correlation of $r=0.68$. The regression equation $y = 46.58 + 13.27 (x) = \varepsilon$ tells us that, on average, for every 1-unit change in V&A, there will be a 13.27-unit increase in the CPI. Given that zero is a value in the range of V&A, when V&A is 0, the CPI is 46.58. The adj-$R^2=0.459$ tells us that 45.9% of the variation in the CPI can be explained by variation in V&A.

As a summary of the statistical results, this is a lot of information about the relationship between the functioning of democratic institutions and corruption. Someone working on this topic, familiar with the related academic research, would be able to continue to contextualize these results so that we could understand how the results specifically advance what we didn't know about this relationship.

- Does this comport with other work in this area?
- Are the results consistent with what we know?
- Are they consistent with what we expected?
- What problems remain?

Clearly these are important questions that can be found only outside the statistical analysis. A reminder that statistics serve our scientific endeavours and do not solely constitute them. However, the six steps of the modelling process help us amass the information necessary start to understand the relationship in which we are interested as well as to plot the next steps in our investigation.

Troubleshooting: Five Assumptions

(Bivariate) regression functions well when certain criteria are met. These criteria are assumptions about the variables, the functional form of the regression model, and the error term.

There are five **assumptions**. Or four, or six, or seven. Don't be alarmed when you search the internet for the assumptions of the linear regression model and it says, 'The Four Assumptions of...' or 'The Six Assumptions of...'. This is the same information packaged differently. It depends on how you slice it. I like five.

1. *Linearity:* The dependent variable is a linear function of the model as specified (i.e., which variables are included). The estimation procedure of the regression coefficient and intercept assume that this is the case. If not, our estimates will be inefficient (i.e., not very informative).
2. *Multicollinearity:* As we will see, (bivariate) regression will become multiple regression allowing us to account for other variables. The problem is, if two of these independent variables are highly correlated, they 'explain' much of the same information. The estimation procedure will not be able to assign 'ownership' of their separate and independent effects on the dependent variable.

You may be surprised to discover that the last three assumptions refer to the error term. One of the potential problems with assuming that the error term is zero and well-behaved is that sometimes it is – and sometimes it is not. This can create a number of problems.

The assumptions about the error term are written thusly:

$\mu_i \sim N(0, \delta^2)$

This says that the stochastic component is normally distributed, has a mean of zero, and has constant variance. This can be broken down differently but it's all here.

3. *Multivariate Normality:* This assumption has two parts and means that errors have uniform variance and are uncorrelated.
   a. *Uniform Variance:* We expect the error terms to be the same across all of the values of the IV. This is called *homoscedasticity* [$Var[\varepsilon_i | x_i] = \sigma^2$.] or less creatively, 'constant variance'. The opposite of homoscedasticity is heteroscedasticity in which the variance is not constant and makes the estimates of the regression components become less reliable as they are solving some parts of the equation better than others.
   b. *Autocorrelation:* We assume that the values of residuals are independent and not correlated with each other. Simply, errors affecting errors violates the assumption that they are random.

Non-normality of errors means that there is substantial unexplained variance in the dependent variable. Most likely, we have not specified our regression equation well (i.e., included the best independent variable(s)). Or, in a more entrepreneurial way, if the errors are behaving poorly, you have extra information that allows you to improve your prediction of the dependent variable and must find a better way to incorporate that information into the model itself.

4. *The Exogeneity Assumption:* The errors in the regression should have an expected mean of zero: $E(\mu_i) = 0$. When the mean is not zero, it implies systematic error, meaning our model is inadequate because it is not correct on average. A violation of exogeneity is endogeneity – which invalidates the OLS parameter estimates of our regression equation.
5. *Independence of observations:* Simply, the independent variable is uncorrelated with the error term. The independent variables are assumed to be error-free (sometimes 'fixed in repeated samples') and not contaminated by (usually, measurement) error. If they were correlated, we could use the independent variable to predict the error term providing clear evidence that, once again, the error term is not random.

Remember, the error term captures the effects of randomness, measurement error, and things for which we have not accounted – or even omitted. Ideally, random chance and nothing else should determine the values of the error term. If the errors behave erratically, there is very likely something wrong or missing in our regression equation which will in turn influence (or 'bias') our estimates of the regression components.

Pro-tip: Bias is bad.

To the extent that these criteria are reasonably satisfied, the regression analysis should provide us with a reasonably good model of the relationship in which we are interested. To the extent that they do not, well, that's why this section is called, 'Troubleshooting'. In any case, despite their scary names, the solutions to these can often be relatively straightforward. We will revisit these assumptions when we get to Multiple Regression.

A Parting Comment

Conceptually, (bivariate) regression is a simplified model of reality. It is a more statistically complex model of reality than Measures of Association – but a model still. It has a great deal to offer and serves as the basis for much of what comes later.

The introduction of **(bivariate) linear regression** in the Descriptive Statistics section has necessarily forced us to exclude some key details about regression and its larger function. We will cover that material in the coming sections of Inferential Statistics and beyond. However, (bivariate) regression does provide two key insights as we move into the next stage of statistical techniques.

One, in our scientific approach to studying the relationship in which we are interested, we aim to isolate this relationship – which implies the existence of other potential explanatory (i.e., independent) variables. That is, while we are interested in investigating X → Y, we are not so naïve to think that, for example, the level of corruption in a country can be entirely understood by knowing that country's quality of democracy. There are several other potential explanations. Linear regression is one statistical tool that we can use to address this problem and is introduced here so that you can get a clear look at – and start to understand – key moving parts before we take on the more challenging task of controlling for several other variables. But take heart, what you have learned in this chapter is as difficult as it gets.

Two, we have learned to describe the data that we have, which are very often not the data we want. We would like to be able to test every observation on the relationship in which we are interested but must often settle for a sample of it. The next section will show us how to overcome this limitation and use many of the descriptive statistics we have learned – as well as some newer techniques – to make claims not only about the data that we have – but also the data we want.

Together, Descriptive Statistics and Inferential Statistics make a powerful team. We will be moving from the statistical description of data, variables, and relationships to the power of inference. This is the next level of your statistical training: Inferential Statistics. What is important – and specific to a chapter on regression – is that the results only hold for the data for which you estimate the regression equation, but they should also correspond to the larger literature.

By the way, at this point, in terms of statistics, you are well beyond others' casual and even moderately informed statistical knowledge. Keep going.

End of Chapter Summary

- (Bivariate) regression quantifies the strength and direction of the relationship between two interval-level variables differently than correlation. It provides specific information about the relationship between these specific two variables including how they move together, how good – or 'fit' – the equation is, and even allows us to do some rudimentary prediction.
- (Bivariate) regression is a natural fit for scientific research as it forces us to be clear about the order of our variables, their performance, and their relationship.
- (Bivariate) regression provides greater statistical evidence for causation.
- Once again for those in the cheap seats, the process of conceptualizing and operationalizing our variables will profoundly shape what we will find.
- Modelling is a process that integrates statistics techniques and scientific thinking.
- Updating Table 8.1, see Table 9.3.

Table 9.3 Descriptive Statistics: Measures of Association (and Bivariate Regression)

	Nominal	Ordinal	Interval
Nominal	2 x 2: Yule's Q [Gamma] N xx N: Lambda		
Ordinal	Lambda	Gamma	
Interval	Means comparison	Means comparison	Pearson's Product Moment Correlation Coefficient (Bivariate) regression

Glossary

- **Regression analysis** a description of the linear relationship between a dependent and independent variable that is variable-specific.
- The **regression equation**, given a dependent variable, Y, and an independent variable X, is: $Y_i = \alpha + \beta (X_i) + \varepsilon$.
- **(Bivariate) linear regression** is a specific form of regression in which we examine the relationship between two interval-level variables.
- **Regression coefficient** (β – beta) is a component of the regression equation that relates the average change in Y associated with a unit change in X. It also describes the relationship as negative or positive. It is sometimes called the 'slope' of the line.
- **Intercept** (α – alpha) is a component of the regression equation that indicates the point where the regression line 'intercepts' the Y-axis (i.e., when X = 0).
- **Error term** (ε) is a component of the regression equation that represents the presence of error of trying to match the regression analysis to the real world.
- **Systematic components** of the regression equation capture a deterministic relationship in which there is no randomness. It is the part that we try to explain: $\{\alpha + \beta x\}$.
- **Random components** of the regression equation refer to the error term $\{\varepsilon\}$ in which the impact of everything else in the world sums to zero.
- The **coefficient of determination** (R^2) represents the proportion of common variation between the two variables.
- **Model fit** is the appropriateness of the included independent variables as a solution for the variation in the dependent variable. A.k.a. Goodness of Fit.
- **Modelling** is the process through which we fully examine the relationship in which we are interested. The steps move from scientific design, to the use of statistical techniques, to interpretation.
- The **assumptions or criteria of regression analysis** are necessary so that the estimation of the regression components provides reliable (i.e., unbiased and efficient) estimates of the real parameters. *When met, these assumptions strengthen our confidence in the results of the regression.*

Questions

1. Correlation, as we learned in the previous chapter, describes the relationship between two interval-level variables. What then is the new information we get from regression?
2. Although R^2 is just correlation times correlation ($R^2 = r \times r$), it provides us with a specific set of information. What is that information and how does it help us understand the relationship?
3. Recall that Reporters Without Border's Press Freedom Index is strongly correlated with the World Bank's World Governance Indicator 'Voice and Accountability': r = −0.88.
   - The regression equation is $y = 35.86 - 14.91(x) + \varepsilon$
   - Fully model this relationship in six steps.

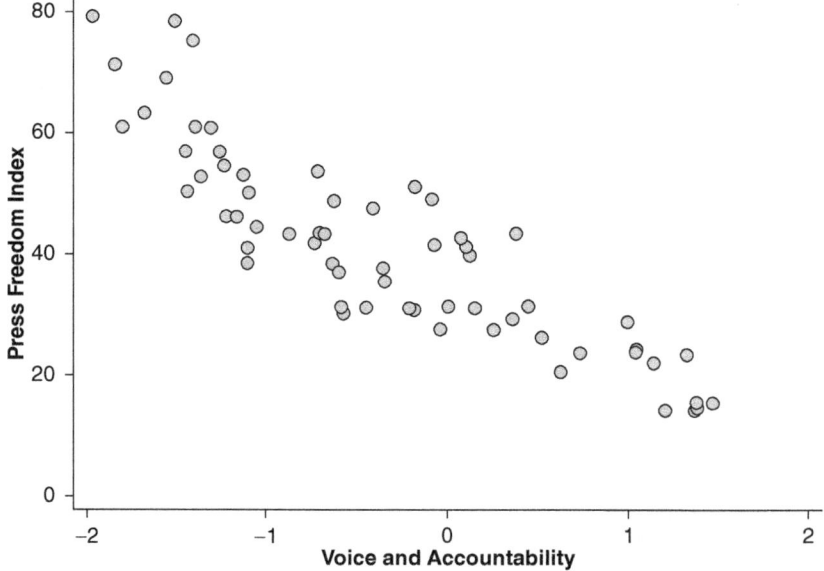

Figure 9.7 Voice and Accountability and the Press Freedom Index

4. What is the role of statistics in modelling?
5. Explain the difference between the systematic and random parts of the regression equation.
6. The assumptions for regression are necessary in order for the results of regression analysis to be reliable. If the assumptions are not met, for example, are we always unable to interpret the results?
7. Model fit is a term that refer to the performance of the regression model. What does this imply?

Annotated References and Further Reading

Wonnacott, Thomas H. and Ronald J. Wonnacott. 1990. *Introductory Statistics.* **New York: Wiley. 5th ed.**

If you want to see the most confident, most rigorous introduction to regression, this book will relentlessly give it to you. Not for the faint of heart.

Signposts to the Accompanying Digital Resources

Sources for the data used in this chapter can be found at the end of Chapter 8.

PART II
INFERENTIAL STATISTICS

10

AN INTRODUCTION TO INFERENCE

> ### LEARNING OUTCOMES
>
> In this chapter, you will be able to
>
> - Understand the logic of **inference** that underpins the use of Inferential Statistics.
> - Define and identify the relationship between samples and populations and the importance to making statistical inferences.
> - Distinguish statistical significance from substantive significance and explain the necessary difference between them.
> - Explain the importance of randomization not only to understanding the role of samples but also to the use of inference in statistics.
> - Recognize and use the basic concepts in probability theory.

Introduction

We are stepping into new territory. Some of the underpinnings of Inferential Statistics are mathematical in nature, others theoretical. Together, they allow us to harness the powers of Descriptive Statistics to make substantive empirical claims about the relationships in which we are interested. In this chapter, we are introduced to a number of new terms and techniques involved in making this inferential leap.

Inferential Statistics involves making informed guesses about population values – or parameters – from a sample by estimating the probability that the result we observe in the sample could be due to chance. Using a random sample, we estimate the probability – using sampling distributions – that a resulting sample statistic could be due to chance. If the resulting statistic – a description, relationship, or pattern – is unlikely due to chance, we infer that it exists in the population. As the process of sampling is inherently imperfect and uncertain, we are additionally explicit about our confidence in our sample estimate of the population parameter. Thus, **Inferential Statistics** is making informed guesses based on our analysis of a sample to the population from which that sample was drawn with some (reported) level of confidence.

The Logic of Inference

Recall from the first chapters Principle Number 3 of the Scientific Method: 'The scientific method seeks to derive and make appropriate inferences from the results of our research.' Scientists are interested in what our research questions can tell us about phenomena just beyond our question. We seek to generalize – to explain a class of event – from the objective analysis of what we can observe. The ability to generalize from observation to a class of events includes the crucial use of theory – the aggregate process of building general knowledge – as well as inference – the ability to speak beyond the evidence at hand. It is the latter in which statistics demonstrates its power.

The **logic of inference** is that evidence, or results, from our sample are so unlikely to be a function of chance that they must represent a real relationship in the population from which that sample was drawn. In other words, if we have a sample representative of the population we are interested in studying, the statistical analysis we conduct on that sample – describing data, measuring associations, correlations and the components of regression equations – can be substantive enough to move from 'Well, that just happens sometimes' to 'Oh, this really seems like it might be something'.

> ### INFERENCE AND GENERALIZATION, TAKE 2
>
> We have encountered the word 'inference' before in our discussion of generalization. For example, we included descriptive and causal inferences as elements of generalizing from our observations to a larger class of events (recall the German Bundestag election example).
>
> The concepts of generalization and inference are closely related. Again, generalization refers to developing the broader applicability of theory associated with the Scientific Method by trying to understand – and even explain – the world with the little part we actually observe. Inference, on the other hand, is a specific and technical term in statistics. As we will discover, statistical inference is the process of using observed data to determine patterns in the population from which our data were drawn. Rather than seeking to generalize about why these things are related, inference tells us whether we can expect the observed patterns to exist in the population based on our analysis of a (representative) sample of that population.

Inferential statistics relies on two elements that we discuss in this chapter. One, the ability to make inferential claims rests on the characteristics of the sample. A sample is a diminished version of the population ('a copy of a copy of a copy'). To improve its representation of the population, we insist on the sample being both random and sufficient. That is, the quality – the representativeness – of the sample is directly related to it being a random sample of the population and sufficiently large.

Two, the random sample assumption allows us to estimate the probability that a sample result could be due to chance. We do this by comparing how confident we are in our results – think measures of dispersion and variance – with probability distributions. In this way, the probability assumption allows us to make qualified inferences about unobserved phenomena and report how confident we are.

Inferential Statistics sounds like it has a lot of moving parts. Frankly, it does. However, at each stage of the inferential process, as long as the assumptions are met, we can move quite easily from one stage to the next. Again, inference allows us to make probabilistic guesses about the population in which we are interested based on our analysis of a sample of that population. The calibre of those guesses is improved by characteristics of the sample and the conditions of probability. In other words, inferential statistics has the ability to tell us how confident we can be in making claims about a population based on a sample of that population.

> ### INFERENCE AND IMPLICATION
> This is your chance to get it right forever: A speaker implies, a listener infers.

The logic of inference also clearly delineates Inferential Statistics from Descriptive Statistics. In Descriptive Statistics we try to determine the **substantive significance** in the sample: a description, relationship, or pattern in the data such as 'how big is the measure of association' or 'how correlated are these variables'? Inferential Statistics tells us whether the substantive significance of the result (description, relationship, or pattern in the data) can be inferred to the population. This is, whether we can conclude that the result is 'real' and not just chance. Such inferential claims are the basis of **statistical significance**.

These are two related but distinct concepts that will reveal their distinctiveness as we pass through this section. Keep an eye out for mentions of this difference as we progress.

Samples and Population

In Chapters 2 and 3, we were introduced to the terms sample and population. A **population** is the entire set of your unit of analysis that you wish to draw conclusions about. A **sample** is a subset of units in the population of interest. When we collect and analyse data, we are often collecting some – rather than all – of the data in which we are interested. As such, when we arrive at the results of our statistical techniques, we are ultimately describing the data that we have and, as a consequence, not the data that we want. The results we seek are the actual, really real parameters of the population not the descriptions of the sample of that population. And, if we had all the data, we could find them. But we don't, so we can't.

What we *can* do is take good samples and use the results of the samples as good and reliable guesses about what the population parameters actually are.

> ### SAMPLING FRAME
>
> There is a third concept related to samples and populations. **Sampling frame** – the sub-population from which the sample is actually drawn (given the practical constraints of trying to even collect data). The sampling frame can be important in designing a study. For example, we might be interested in how Portuguese citizens engage with national parties' online presence, such as their official website. We could use an online survey but then think, 'Wait, not everyone has equal access – thus equal chance – of being a part of the study.' In this case, our intended sample – Portuguese citizens – is limited by the sampling frame – those who have access to the internet. For our study, however, we are less concerned as those who don't have access to the internet are not particularly useful to our study (i.e., Portuguese who do not have access to the internet are unlikely to visit parties' official websites).
>
> Can you imagine another situation in which the sampling frame create a problem for achieving a representative sample?

In fact the word 'statistic' is related to the relationship between sample and population. A **parameter** is a descriptive characteristic of a population whereas **statistic** refers to the estimate of a parameter from sample data.

We have seen this before. In Chapter 6, we talked about the measures of central tendency and dispersion for interval-level variables: the mean ($\bar{x}$) and standard deviation (s_x). These are technically referred to as 'the sample mean' and 'sample standard deviation' These are estimates of the 'population mean' (μ, pronounced 'myu') and 'population standard deviation' (σ, pronounced 'sigma'). These latter population parameters are useful for our intuitive understanding of samples and populations, however, we do not try to calculate – or *gasp* dare try to know – them.

In Political Science research, it is often impossible to collect data on your entire population (see Table 10.1). Therefore, when collecting data, it is necessary to take a sample of the entire population. The quality of that sample is positively associated with the quality of the estimations (guesses) we can make about the actual population parameters.

Table 10.1 Examples of Populations and Samples

Population [-what we want to know-]	Sample [-what we can use to estimate or guess-]
Level of EU support among European voters	We use the European Election Studies series that samples citizens' opinions about the EU every 5 years from each EU country.
Success of environmental legislation	We compile an account of national legislation that advances environmental efforts from the past 5 years.
Effectiveness of crisis management in sub-Saharan Africa	Evaluate the role of the European Union to develop and implement crisis management techniques in Sudan, Mali, and the Democratic Republic of Congo.
Ideological tenor of political posts on Twitter	Using machine learning, we scrape Twitter for 1 week prior to a national election in a country and sort the results by 'support for the Left' or 'support for the Right'.

Population [-*what we want to know*-]	Sample [-*what we can use to estimate or guess*-]
Impact of political consumerism in America	We collect information on the most visible political consumerist activities over the past year in California and New York.
Closing of the gender gap in local Japanese politics	Compare the number of female and male representatives in the political offices of each prefecture now and from 10 years ago.
National court decisions on LGBTQ rights	An account of (highest) national courts that addresses LGBTQ issues (negatively or positively) from the past 10 years.
Changing nature of authoritarianism in Latin America	We search for similarities and differences in the rise of personalist dictators (e.g., Manuel Noriega (Panama); Alberto Fujimori (Peru)) and 'bureaucratic authoritarianism' (e.g., Salvador Allende (Chile)).
Covid-19 and national sovereignty in Europe	We compare the success of responses to Covid-19 in four European countries with different institutional and cultural attributes.
The impact of multilateral institutions in mediating ethnic conflict in Southeast Asia	We evaluate the success of United Nations' efforts to address refugees, displaced persons and migrant labour in Thailand, Myanmar, and Malaysia.

While not every one of these examples in Table 10.1 is quantitative – not that there's anything wrong with that – let's consider the population of 'EU Support among European voters'.

At a practical level, while fielding a large survey every 5 years in almost 30 countries is a significant task, it is much less difficult, costly, and time-consuming than asking every single European citizen their level of support for the EU. We can instead rely on representative samples of each country's population to provide us sufficient evidence to make a good guess at what that level of support actually is (in the entire population). That is, given both the practical constraints of asking everyone and our statistical capabilities, we are comfortable with a really strong guess for a fraction of the cost and effort than knowing the actual population parameter (here, level of support for the EU). Or put slightly more confrontationally, using inferential statistics, we don't need to ask everyone what they think to get a very good sense of what everyone is likely thinking.

Simply, the samples that we inevitably will analyse will allow us to make inferences about population parameters. We want to know whether a result from the sample – a description, summary, relationship, or pattern – can be inferred to the population. Is the pattern in your data strong enough to conclude that the apparent relationship is potentially 'real' and not just chance?

Using samples incurs uncertainty in doing so but we can improve our ability to make these inferential claims in many ways.

Randomization

Randomization is key to samples being representative of the population from which they are drawn. In order to exploit statistical inference – inferring from a sample to a (statistical) universe by estimating the probability that a sample result could be due to chance – we must have random samples. Essentially, that the selection (or for experiments, the assignment) of observations are not related to any of the variables included in the analysis. **Randomization** is the selection of units of analysis on the basis of chance and not design.

While a key element in Research Design, the nature of randomness is important to the overall discussion of inferential statistics.

Randomization for Inference

How does randomization in the selection of a sample allow us to assume that the sample is valid? Again, the processes for random selection can vary but they share the assumption that randomizing the sampling process produces a very high quality approximation – the most representative sample – of the population. How does randomization achieve this?

Maybe the best example is one literally close to home, cooking.

When your dad asks you to stir the pot of chili on the stove, he is asking you to randomize the chili. When you toss a salad, you are randomizing. When you mix your favourite recipe for salsa, you are randomizing the salsa.

Why?

Because we want the samples (bowls and spoons of chili, plates and forks of salad, and chips of salsa) to have the closest approximation to the populations, that is, the exact proportional mix of flavours that constitute the taste of chili, salad, and salsa.

AN EXAMPLE OF SAMPLING: DIFFERENT TYPES OF SAMPLES FOR SURVEYS

As a technique to gather data, sampling is a practical issue. Like the ideal 'law of supply and demand' in Economics, we need to find the optimal level between the advantage of samples being cost-effective and low effort with the disadvantage of samples giving us data that is incomplete and potentially inaccurate and thus misleading.

This is a problem with which survey companies and networks of academics that gather data on citizens of different countries deal all the time. How do they collect survey data from national populations?

In Europe, there are several that do (to name some of the most prominent, cross-national ones):

- European Election Studies Survey series
- European Social Survey series
- European Values Surveys series
- Eurobarometer
- Survey of Health, Ageing and Retirement in Europe (SHARE).

In large-N analyses like using large, cross-national surveys of European citizens, we tend to assume random selection of observations. But can we? The answer is yes, because all use one form of the following *probability samples* in which the probability of being chosen is known.

1. *Simple random sample:* Each unit has an equal chance of being selected.
    a. This is the equivalent of putting every person's name in a hat and selecting 2,500 of them per country. In the past, randomly dialling phone numbers was commonly done.
2. *Systematic sample:* Units are selected from a list in predetermined intervals with a random starting point.
    a. Imagine we put everyone's name in alphabetical order and took every 7th person. The only 'difficulty' is selecting how the 'list' is organized (i.e., by some arbitrary characteristic of the population?).
3. *Stratified sample:* Populations are grouped by some variable or variables and then units are selected depending on their characteristics on this variable.
    a. *Proportionate stratified sample:* A common approach to get the correct proportion of people in each group (based on their population in the country). For example, one might stratify the sample by education to make sure you get enough low-educated respondents (who are often working with less availability to stop and respond).
    b. *Disproportionate sample:* Another common approach for under-represented groups from which you may not get enough respondents otherwise. For example in the US, efforts are made to purposely (over-)sample key minority groups such as African-Americans and Native Americans.
4. *Cluster samples:* Choosing a cluster of the population and then sample the correct number within that cluster. For example: (1) Randomly selecting a region within a country, then a province, and then a census block (e.g., EU Population and Housing Census). (2) Then sample some subset of that block. (3) Repeat with a dozen or two dozen census blocks.
    a. A cost-efficient way to collect representative samples as clustering makes valuable person-to-person surveys more convenient. For example, a simple random survey would require several interviewers to go to several different places to interview 2 or 3 people.

Ideally, we sample randomly. When it is a practical impossibility, it is possible to *assign* randomly – here in a form of sophisticated probability sampling – to produce a random, representative sample. It is this linchpin that, as we will see, allows probabilities to do their work.

You don't prepare salsa for a party by placing a can of crushed tomatoes in one bowl, a diced green chili in a small adjacent bowl, one quarter of a finely chopped shallot in yet another bowl, a grated garlic clove, 25 g of chopped cilantro, and the juice of a quarter of a lime in smaller and smaller bowls (plus a twist of pepper and a shake of salt) and then ask everyone to take separate scoops proportional to the bowls in order to enjoy your salsa. You mix them together in these proportions to achieve two things: the taste of the salsa that you want with this proportion of ingredients and for that proportional distribution of flavour to end up on the sample your friends take of the salsa.

If we wanted to, we could think of the population of your salsa as everything in the bowl. The sample is a chip being dipped into the salsa.

Let's engage this thought experiment a bit more.

Do you think that the size of the sample – the scoop of my chip – would affect the experience of the salsa? That is, if you took a large scoop, do you think your larger sample would be a better approximation of the population? If you took a smaller scoop, do you think your smaller sample would be a worse approximation of the population? That answer is, nearly always, yes to both. To better know the population, we need a sufficiently sized sample. Thus, data should be not only representative but also sufficient, in that there is enough of it. In nearly all cases, more data are better than less data on your topic of interest. A larger sample is likely to be a better sample and a smaller one worse.

> ## 'I KNOW A GUY'
>
> Invariably, for any relationship we discover empirically, there will be someone who says, 'yeah, well, I know a guy…'. For example, we could be discussing the moderate correlation between education level and income and someone will say, 'Yeah, but I know this guy who dropped out of high school and is now a millionaire.' Good for that guy. However, this is an example of *exceptio probat regulam in casibus non exceptis* ('the exception that proves the rule').
>
> As a general rule in statistics: anecdotes are not evidence.

Let's expand on the salsa thought experiment even further.

What conclusions could you draw from your salsa sample? Would you feel, having sampled this salsa at this party, that you could comment on the quality of *this* salsa overall? Would you feel, having sampled this salsa at this party, that you could comment on the quality of *all salsas*? Would you feel, having sampled this salsa at this party, that you could comment on the *concept of salsa*? One could respond, yes, possibly, and potentially. A sufficient, random sample allows us to make qualified claims about the population from which it drawn (i.e., inference) although we may be limited in our ability to speak to potentially different populations (i.e., generalization). At the same time, this salsa is part of the salsa universe – salsas are salsas because they share some conceptual and measurable similarities – and represents a manifestation of the concept of salsa.

Wild.

Now, replace salsa with democracy (in the thought experiment, not in real life. That would not work). Not all democracies are the same although they share many of the same elements that distinguish a regime as democratic. If we studied a random sample of democracies for their ability to withstand sharp economic decline, would you instinctively feel that you could comment on the nature of the sampled democracies to withstand sharp economic decline? Would you instinctively feel that you could comment on the nature of all democracies to withstand sharp economic decline? Would you instinctively feel that you could comment on the concept of democracy? Again, yes, possibly, and potentially.

A sufficient, random sample allows us to make qualified claims about the population from which it is drawn although it may limit our ability to speak to potentially different populations. At the same time, our sample of democracies is part of the 'democracy' universe and represents a manifestation of the concept of democracy.

Randomization More Formally

More formally, we link samples to populations in the following way. The expected value of our variable for that sample is equal to the actual value for the population:

$$E\left(\hat{\theta}\right) = \theta$$

That is, the sample value is an estimate of the population value – the one which we wish we had. Randomization is improved by not systematically excluding any group and offering an equal opportunity to be selected – both functions of the sampling procedures of the research design.

What brings the expectation that our sample value is close to the population value are the characteristics of the sample: random and sufficiently large.

Randomization and Sample Size

Any single sample may not yield the actual population value. However, if we take larger and larger samples, the sample value is more and more likely be the actual population value. Simply, sample value is more likely to estimate population value as sample size increases. This is referred to as probability's **law of large numbers**.

If we draw observations at random from any population, as number of observations increases, our sample statistics closes in on the population parameter. From our thought experiment above, the more chips with salsa you eat, the better you can claim to know that salsa. This is exactly the same effect in statistics in which, when we increase our sample size, the sample mean ($\bar{x}$), for example, starts to approach the population mean (μ), which we can never really know.

You already know this. Sample size is something you use all the time. In Figure 10.1, which review do you think is the most accurate as to the actual quality of the product?

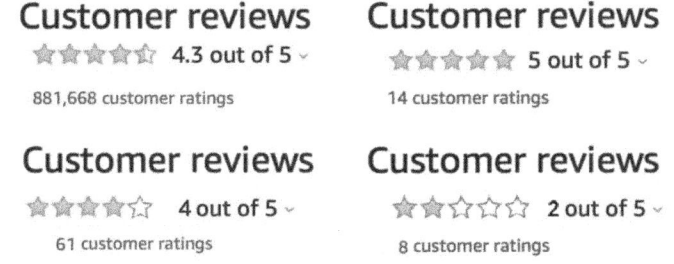

Figure 10.1 The Importance of Sample Size

A Brief Note on Randomization

As we have seen, as a practical matter, using samples is necessary as it is often impossible to collect data on the entire population. Rather than be limited by this, statistics has developed the concept and techniques of inference which involves making informed guesses from a sample to a population (sometimes called the 'statistical universe').

Sampling is an important component for determining the characteristics of a population in which we are interested. Randomized samples of sufficient size allow us to make inferences or confident guesses about what the populations parameter – the really, real value – from the analysis of that sample. However, the process of sampling – minimizing or eliminating sources of bias in our measures or selection – more properly belongs in the discussion on Research Design.

The inferential power of statistics allows us to make claims about a population based on a sample of that population. More precisely, the inferential power of statistics allows us to make claims about a specific population based on a sample of that specific population. Generalization is the process of understanding how what we have found is relevant not only in the population from which we sampled, but also to similar populations. Generalization is a theory-building exercise of explaining a class of events – determining how much we can explain with our theory. Recall Figure 1.1.

As we will see in the following chapters, inferential statistics informs the scientific process of generalization by allowing us to test hypotheses and thus determine the fate of theories. These same theories – weak or strong – can be used to generalize what we have observed to what we have not observed, seeking the outer bound of our explanatory power.

Thus, no randomization, no inference, no generalization. Or more succinctly (and positively): Randomization for Generalization!

Probability Theory

This short section is an introduction to some basic concepts of probability that will be useful and informative as we progress through the discussion of inferential statistics, distributions, statistical significance, and hypothesis testing.

Probability is a formal model of uncertainty. Simply, probability assigns a numerical measure of the chance, or likelihood, that a particular event will occur. In many activities, we are well aware of the potential outcomes – e.g., for a soccer game, a coin toss, an election – and, if we don't already know about the likelihood of the outcomes, can often make rough guesses about the chance of each outcome.

In more advanced forms, we simply make those guesses explicit based on assumptions about how these events have previously concluded. Inasmuch as our assignment of the probabilities aligns with the evidence (and the data are reasonably well-behaved), we can use probabilities to improve our expectation of the outcome.

This should sound very familiar and potentially useful. *Hint:* 'Making reliable guesses about population parameters based on results from samples drawn from that population.'

Core Concepts of Probability

At the simplest level, we can talk about discrete probability distributions which account for outcomes or events that take place in a well-defined and, importantly, limited sample space. In the simplest form, called the **classical method**, the assignment of probabilities for each outcome or event are equally likely (in fancy, *equiprobable*). Thus, the probability of an outcome or event is simply: 1/n where 'n' is the number of possible events or outcomes.

An example of this is rolling a die or flipping a coin, or any similar process that generates well-defined outcomes such as a statistical or random experiment.

We arrive at this 'classical' distribution of probabilities via two rules.

- *One:* A sample space (sometimes called 'probability space') – in which all possible events or outcomes are located – exists. In this sample space, the probability of any event 'E_i' is $0 \leq P(E_i) \leq 1$, where '0' means this event will not occur and '1' means this event is the only outcome.
- *Two:* Adding all the probabilities of all outcomes equals 1: $P(E_1) + P(E_2) + \ldots + P(E_n) = 1$; in other words, the probabilities of each event in the sample space sum to 1.

A simple example of this is the roll of a die. There are six possible outcomes: rolling a 3 or 2 or 6 or 4 or 1 or 5. They have – according to point ONE above, some probability of taking place. In the case of the die, each is equally likely (or 'equiprobable') with a 1/6 likelihood of doing so. Further, drawing from point TWO, summing these equals 1: 1/6 + 1/6 + 1/6 + 1/6 + 1/6 + 1/6 = 1.

Unfortunately, while attractive, consistent, and mathematically well-behaved, the classical method – and its well-defined outcomes and equiprobable probabilities – are not common outside of highly controlled processes or experiments.

The **relative frequency method** assigns probabilities based on data available to estimate the likelihood of outcomes.

To see the difference between these two methods, let's use a Political Science example.

Some European countries have constitutional rules that allow presidents, prime ministers, or cabinets to call early elections. They do not use this power frequently, but it is occasionally used for potentially strategic reasons.

Here is the data from the past 40 years in Europe for how early those early elections were called before the regularly scheduled election (by months). *Note:* 'Number of early elections called' has an $n=30$ (countries), a mean of 14.2 (months), and a standard deviation of 11.5 (months).

Table 10.2 Early Election Calling in Europe

Months early	Number of early elections called
0–6	10
7–12	6
13–18	6
19–24	3
25–30	1
31–36	2
37–42	2
43–48	0
	N=30

Given these observations on early election calling in Europe over the past 40 years (in Table 10.2), we are interested in the likelihood that there will be early elections called within one year before the regularly scheduled election (i.e., ≤12 months).

There are two outcome categories that assign this probability:

$(E : \leq 12 \text{ months}) = \{(0 - 6); (7 - 12)\}$

(0–6) months has occurred 10 out of the 30 early elections called and (7–12) has occurred 6 out of 30 times:

$P(E : \leq 12 \text{ months}) = \{(10/30) + (6/30)\} = 0.53$

Thus, there is a 53% chance that, if an early election is called, it will be called within one year before the regularly scheduled election.

This is technically referred to as the **union** of events. In our example here, (0–6) and (7–12) contain all outcomes we are interested in (the outcome can be in either range). The notation for this is: $E_i \cup E_k$ or in our example: $(0 - 6) \cup (7 - 12)$.

Using these data on early election calling, we can also ask another question.

What is the likelihood that the early election will be called *later* than one year before the regularly scheduled election (i.e., > 12 months)? Using the approach above, we can sum the remaining probabilities:

$(E: > 12 \text{ months}) = \{(13 - 18); (19 - 24); (25 - 30); (31 - 36); (37 - 42)\}$

$P(E: > 12 \text{ months}) = \{(6/30) + (3/30) + (1/30) + (2/30) + (2/30)\} = 0.47$

The chance that an early election will be called more than a year before the regularly scheduled election is 47%.

WATCH THE INTERSECTION

One could also determine the probabilities of an intersection of events. Rather than focusing on a single event/outcome, an **intersection** – also called the *joint probability* – contains the outcomes which belong to *both* E_i and E_k. The notation for this is $E_i \cap E_k$. In the notation of probability theory, the intersection is calculated: $P(E_i \cap E_k) = P(E_i)$ B $P(E_k)$, which is simply the probability of E_i occurring multiplied by the probability of E_k occurring.

Why this is interesting is that in the notation of probability theory, the *union* actually relies on the intersection. The formula is $P(E_i \cup E_k) = P(E_i) + P(E_k) - P(E_i \cap E_k)$. In our example, there is no intersection of (0–6) and (7–12) – no outcomes common to both – making $P(E_i \cap E_k) = 0$. This is why we can remove the intersection and simply sum the probabilities:

$$P(E_i \cup E_k) = P(E_i) + P(E_k) - P(E_i \cap E_k); \text{ where } P(E_i \cap E_k) = 0$$

Becomes

$$P(E_i \cup E_k) = P(E_i) + P(E_k) - 0$$

or simply,

$$P(E_i \cup E_k) = P(E_i) + P(E_k)$$

I point out that we could save ourselves some time and effort by calculating the complement of the previous answer. The **complement** of an event is all the other outcomes that are not part of the event:

$$P(E_c) = 1 - P(E)$$

Therefore, in this case, seeing that we had already calculated all the events less than or equal to 12 months: $P(E: \leq 12 \text{ months}) = \{(10/30) + (6/30)\} = 0.53$, the remaining probabilities represent the likelihood of the complement:

$$P(E: > 12 \text{ months}) = 1 - P(E: \leq 12 \text{ months})$$

$$0.47 = 1 - 0.53$$

That is, knowing that the total sum of all the outcome probabilities has to equal 1, we can exploit the mutual exclusivity of an event and its complement. **Mutual exclusivity** simply means that when one event occurs, the other cannot.

Conditional Probability

One further development in probability theory that you may be familiar with is the concept of conditional probability. **Conditional probability** is when the probability of an event is influenced by whether or not a related event has occurred.

The conditional probability of E_i given E_k is written $P(E_i \mid E_k)$ – pronounced, 'The probability of E_i given E_k.' The calculation of the conditional probability is:

$$P(E_i \mid E_k) = P(E_i \cap E_k) \mid P(E_k)$$

Conditional probabilities are as important as they are intimidating (that is to say, to some extent). Let's explore them using an example from Chapter 7 (Table 7.7, renamed Table 10.3):

Table 10.3 Lambda Example – Nominal/Ordinal Variables

		Internet access			
		Low 1/3	Middle 1/3	High 1/3	Total
Democracy	No	9	10	14	*33*
	Yes	6	7	17	*30*
	Total	*15*	*17*	*31*	*63*

In Table 10.3, we can see the distribution of democratic and non-democratic countries and their aggregate level of internet access.

Let's ask the question, what is the probability that a country is a democracy given that they have the Middle 1/3 of internet access? Or more formally as a conditional probability:

$$P(Dem \mid Middle\ 1/3) = P(Dem \cap Middle\ 1/3) \mathbin{/} P(Middle\ 1/3)$$

Before we start, in Table 10.3, we don't have probabilities, we have observations in each cell. To make things easier, we can convert these observations to probabilities by simply dividing each cell by the (grand) total (i.e., n=63).

If we do this, we get an equivalent table (see Table 10.4). These are the probabilities of each observation in each cell based on the relative frequency method. That is, for example, the probability we observe a democracy with Middle 1/3 of internet access is 7/63 or 0.11.

Table 10.4 Probabilities for Democracy and Internet Access

		Internet access			
		Low 1/3	Middle 1/3	High 1/3	TOTAL
Democracy	No	0.14	0.16	0.22	*0.52*
	Yes	0.10	0.11	0.27	*0.48*
	TOTAL	0.24	0.27	0.49	*1.00*

But recall, that's not what we are asking. We are asking what is the probability that a country is a democracy given Middle 1/3 of internet access.

To solve for this conditional probability, what is P (Dem ∩ Middle 1/3)? Wait! We've seen this before – this is the joint probability – or intersection – which contains the outcomes which belong to both E_i and E_k. Thus, for democracy and Middle 1/3 internet access, this is 0.11.

But hang on, almost there.

What is P (Middle 1/3)? It is the marginal probability of Middle 1/3 internet or 0.27. That is, what is the probability that a country has Middle 1/3 internet access at all. Again, 0.27. Thus,

P (Dem | Middle 1/3) = 0.11 / 0.27
P (Dem | Middle 1/3) = 0.41

To interpret this, we used the conditional language implied by the conditional probability: 'Given that a country has Middle *1/3* internet access, there is a 41% chance that country will be a democracy.' Considered differently, conditionality isolates the column of Middle *1/3* so that, of all the countries in that column (i.e., Middle *1/3* internet access), 41% of them are democracies (i.e., 7 out of 17).

But be careful!

The order of conditional probabilities is important. We can see this by simply reversing the question: What is the probability that a country has Middle 1/3 internet access if it is a democracy?

P (Middle 1/3 | Dem) = P (Dem ∩ Middle 1/3) / P (Dem)

Again, what is P (Dem ∩ Middle 1/3)? It is the joint probability – or intersection – of democracy and Middle *1/3* internet access, or 0.11.

What is P (Dem)? It is the marginal probability of a country being a democracy – or 0.48. Thus,

P (Middle 1/3 | Dem) = 0.11/0.48
P (Middle 1/3 | Dem) = 0.23

Once again interpreted in the language of conditionality: 'Given that a country is a democracy, there is a 23% chance that country will have Middle *1/3* internet access.' As above, this conditionality isolates the row of democracies, and among these, 23% of those have Middle *1/3* internet access (i.e., 7 out of 30).

> ### CONDITIONAL PROBABILITIES: ORDER OF EVENTS MATTERS
>
> Yuo olny need the frsit and lsat ltters of a wrod to prcoess it. The leettr oerdr bteween deos not maetter. Hoevwer, as we hvae seen abvoe, chingnag the oerdr of envets maettres for conitdinaol proibitlaibes.

Just to be clear, you can solve the table of observations (Table 10.3) in the same way. Rather than the probabilities for each outcome (as we calculated), you can use the observations in the same cells.

P (Dem $\cap$ Middle 1/3 is 7; P (Middle 1/3) is 17; therefore,

P (DemMiddle1/3)=7/17

P (Dem | Middle 1/3)=0.41

$P(Dem)$ is 30. Therefore,

P (Middle 1/3 | Dem)=7/30

P (Middle 1/3 | Dem) = 0.23

These are the same as what we calculated above. We converted the observations in Table 10.3 to probabilities in Table 10.4 because we wanted to maintain consistency when talking about probabilities and using probabilities in our formulas.

Probability and Independence

Why is conditional probability useful in the context of inferential statistics? A lot of what we are searching for in statistics is a relationship between variables in which we are interested. Can we find evidence that these two (or more) variables move together in ways that are very unlikely to be just happenstance?

To the extent that they are related, they are dependent. That is, when things we observe do move together in coordinated ways, we think of them as being dependent on one another. Simply, knowing one variable tells us a lot about what we can expect from the other variable. Remember, in Descriptive Statistics, we calculated measures of association, correlation, and even regression that tell us just this.

However, the dependence of two (or more) variables can also be determined by how independent they are. The dependence of a relationship is inversely related to how independent it is, which in the case of quantitative social science, can sometimes be easier to measure. If two (or more) variables don't move together in any coordinated way, knowing one variable doesn't give us a clue about what we can expect from the other variable. They are both casually and formally referred to as 'independent from one another'.

In the context of probability theory, when an event occurs and does not affect the probability of another event, we call these **independent events**.

In the formal notation of conditional probabilities, events are independent if:

$P(E_i | E_k) = P(E_i)$ or $P(E_k | E_i) = P(E_k)$

In words, the likelihood that E_i will occur given E_k is the same as the likelihood of E_i occurring. The occurrence of E_k does not make E_i more or less likely to occur.

And events are dependent if:

$P(E_i \mid E_k) \neq P(E_i)$ or $P(E_k \mid E_i) \neq P(E_k)$

We can use the conditional language implied by the conditional probability: The likelihood that E_i will occur given E_k is contingent on the likelihood of E_i occurring. Or simply, the occurrence of E_k makes E_i more or less likely to occur.

A Final Word: The Ring of Fire

Don't be dismayed by the topics in this chapter. You have come a long way. So far, among many other things, we have engaged in detailed discussions of the scientific method, conceptualization and operationalization, theory, hypotheses, and Descriptive Statistics. You know a great deal about the use and application of statistics. This is the final incline to surmount. The biggest difference between Inferential Statistics and these previous discussions is that (1) this is the focus of this book so it gets the most attention – meaning pages – and (2) there are a number of things that have to be in place so that we can reach the summit.

While describing what we see in our sample is a necessary step, what we really want to know is whether the relationship or pattern in the sample can be inferred to apply to the population. We use probability theory (and other things) to determine the extent to which our sample estimates of population parameters are any good. That is, is the pattern in your data strong enough to conclude that the apparent relationship is 'real' and not just chance?

As we will see, we make inferences about population parameters in two ways. One, we estimate population parameters using information from sample and two, we test hypotheses about the value of parameters. These processes inform our use of theory – by providing evidence, or not – in turn allowing us to make larger claims about the nature of the relationship under investigation (generalization).

More broadly, to communicate what you have found, to speak the language common to many empirical researchers and scientists, and to demonstrate to others what your work shows, you need to continue your journey. You must pass through the ring of fire to emerge, forged in training, on the other side.

Let's continue.

End of Chapter Summary

- The key to being able to make proper inferences in statistical analysis is good sampling.
- The keys to good sampling are randomization and sufficient sample size.
- The fundamentals of probability theory allow us to make qualified inferential claims about the patterns we observe in our data.
- The pattern we observe in the sample is the substantive significance of a relationship.

- Whether we can infer the substantive relationship observed in the sample to the population from which the sample was drawn is statistical significance.
- Statistical significance is based on the notion of whether what we have observed in the sample is likely to have been a function of chance or not.
- Inferential Statistics draws together strengths, insights, and techniques to convert our ability to describe what is in our sample to making statistical inferences about the parameters of the population from which that sample was drawn.
- Inferential Statistics is a part of the larger process of scientific investigation by generating, testing, and advancing theoretical knowledge.

Glossary

- **Inference** is the general process by which one uses observed data to learn about the social system and it outputs.
- **Inferential Statistics** involves making informed guesses about population values – or parameters – from a sample by estimating the probability that the result could be due to chance.
- The **logic of (statistical) inference** is that the results from our sample are so unlikely to be a function of chance that they must represent a real relationship in the population from which that sample was drawn.
- **Substantive significance** is the size or magnitude of a description, relationship, or pattern in the data.
- **Statistical significance** is whether we can conclude that the result from our analysis of the sample data is 'real' and not just chance.
- A **population** is the entire set of your unit of analysis that you wish to draw conclusions about.
- A **sample** is a subset of units in the population of interest.
- **Sampling frame** is the sub-population from which sample is practically drawn.
- A **parameter** is a descriptive characteristic of a population.
- A **statistic** refers to the estimate of a parameter from sample data.
- **Randomization** is the selection of units of analysis on the basis of chance and not design.
- The **law of large numbers** states that if we draw observations at random from any population, as number of observations increases, our sample statistics closes in on the population parameter.
- **Probability** is a formal model of uncertainty that assigns a numerical measure of the chance, or likelihood, that a particular event will occur.
- The **classical method** assigns equiprobability for each outcome or event (1/n where 'n' is the number of possible events or outcomes).
- The **relative frequency method** assigns probabilities based on data available to estimate the likelihood of outcomes.
- A **union** of events contains all outcomes in which we are interested. The notation is: $E_i \cup E_k$ and the formula is: $P(E_i \cup E_k) = P(E_i) + P(E_k) - P(E_i \cap E_k)$.

- An **intersection** – a.k.a. the joint probability – contains the outcomes which belong to both E_i and E_k. The notation is $E_i \cap E_k$. The formula is: $P(E_i \cap E_k) = P(E_i) \text{ B } P(E_k)$.
- The **complement** of an event is all the other outcomes that are not part of the event: $P(E_c) = 1 - P(E)$.
- **Mutual exclusivity** simply means that when one event occurs, the other cannot.
- **Conditional probability** is when the probability of an event is influenced by whether or not a related event has occurred. If E_i given E_j: $P(E_i | E_k)$. The formula is: $P(E_i | E_k) = P(E_i \cap E_k) / P(E_k)$.
- **Independent events** are when an event occurs and does not affect the probability of another event.

Questions

1. In Table 10.1 'Examples of Populations and Samples', pick three and explain why they are samples and not the entire population of what we are interested in explaining.
2. Explain the difference between substantive significance and statistical significance.
3. Contrast inference and inferential statistics.
4. Explain how statistical inference differs from generalization.
5. What is the relationship of samples and sampling to inference? What is the relationship of randomization to inference? What is the relationship of probability to inference?
6. What does statistical significance tell us about causation?

Signposts to the Accompanying Digital Resources

European Election Studies: http://europeanelectionstudies.net/
European Social Survey: www.europeansocialsurvey.org/
European Values Survey: https://europeanvaluesstudy.eu/
Eurobarometer: www.europarl.europa.eu/at-your-service/en/be-heard/eurobarometer
SHARE: www.share-project.org/home0.html

11
INFERENCE FOR NOMINAL- AND ORDINAL-LEVEL VARIABLES

> **LEARNING OUTCOMES**
>
> In this chapter, you will be able to
>
> - Understand how to determine whether an association in a sample is a product of chance by comparing sample-specific statistics with existing probability distributions.
> - Explain the step-by-step procedure of Classical Hypothesis Testing and its importance to statistical significance.
> - Interpret the χ^2 test for independence to determine the statistical significance of a result for nominal- and ordinal-level variables.
> - Use χ^2 test for independence to provide evidence toward inferential claims.

Introduction

Nominal- and ordinal-level variables do not lend themselves easily to mathematical management and handling. For both, we cannot assume equidistance between each category – and in the case of nominal-level variables, neither can we assume any order of those categories. However, as we saw producing descriptive measures of central tendency and dispersion as well as measures of association, we are only slightly constrained.

Here, we are interested in not only whether two nominal- or ordinal-level variables are associated in a sample but also whether this relationship can be inferred to the population from which it was drawn. Stepping clearly from Descriptive Statistics into Inferential Statistics, we do this by determining the probability that the relationship we observe is a function of chance or a potentially 'real' empirical relationship between the variables. For nominal- and ordinal-level variables, this test of significance is χ^2 (pronounced 'chi-squared' with a hard 'k' sound, not the 'ch' sound because of the entire country and history of Greece).

To do so, we use Classical Hypothesis Testing. This is a step-by-step process in which we set up a contest between null and alternative hypotheses, compare sample-specific statistics with existing probability distributions, and determine whether we can infer our result to the population or not. This process confers evidence of 'statistical significance' to our result from which we can make inferential claims (with a level of confidence).

Classical Hypothesis Testing

When discussing hypotheses in Chapter 2, we were introduced to the idea that we don't directly test our research hypotheses. Instead, we construct the exact opposite of our research hypothesis – called the 'null hypothesis' – and we test that. The null hypothesis states that nothing is happening, that your variables are independent, there is no relationship. Hypothesis testing is therefore a test to see if our result – evidence from the data in the sample – is so unlikely to have occurred, it must be a real result, and thereby we reject the null hypothesis of no relationship.

Therefore, this logic leads us to:

- If we cannot reject the null hypothesis, whatever result we have found in the data in the sample is not sufficiently different from chance. And, thus, not statistically significant.
- If we do reject the null hypothesis, we are left with the alternative, our research hypothesis. And we have therefore found a statistically significant result in our data in the sample.

Ok, but how do we know when we reject or not? **Classical hypothesis testing** provides the step-by-step procedure through which we determine statistical significance. The step-by-step procedure details the utility of classical hypothesis testing for all inferential statistics and, as such, is often referred to as **significance testing**. And fortunately, the procedure requires very little math and relies primarily on simply asking the right questions.

CLASSICAL HYPOTHESIS TESTING – OR SIGNIFICANCE TESTING

1. Null hypothesis
2. Alternative hypothesis
3. Test statistic
4. Critical or rejection region
5. Interpretation and conclusion.

Steps One and Two: The Null and Alternative Hypotheses

Your research hypothesis – sometimes generically called the **alternative hypothesis** – is a general, non-normative, directional statement of the expected relationship derived from theory (often written as: H_1 or H_a). The **null hypothesis** is the condition that the expected relationship in your hypothesis does not exist (H_0). The null hypothesis may seem to be an odd creation. However, it is necessary as we do not directly test the hypothesis in which we are interested. Instead, we either 'reject' or 'fail to reject' the null hypothesis.

For example, perhaps we are interested in whether partisans – those with strong, psychological, identifications with specific parties – were more likely to vote, not just for their candidates, but in general, than those who did not express strong support for any specific party.

We might construct our research and null hypotheses like this:

- H_0: There is no relationship between an individual's partisanship and whether that individual votes.
- H_a: There is a positive relationship between an individual's partisanship and whether that individual votes.

The classical hypothesis testing procedure will allow us to determine whether we can fail to reject the null hypothesis (H_0: no relationship) or that the null hypothesis can be rejected (implying support for our hypothesis, H_a).

Step Three: Test Statistic

A **test statistic** is a value calculated from our sample data. The test statistic is a value of how much our result - calculated from our sample data - deviates from chance. The test statistic is sample-specific and represents the extent to which the two variables deviate from an expected relationship of independence (i.e., no relationship). We compare the test statistic to a standard distribution that has *a priori* established the hurdle for statistical significance.

Step Four: Critical or Rejection Region

This hurdle is called the **critical value**. The critical value defines the **critical or rejection region** which determines whether we reject or fail to reject the null hypothesis. This represents the hurdle our test statistics must clear to be considered 'statistically signfcant'. We do not need to create or produce a critical value as they already exist. The critical values are determined by the degrees of freedom (from the sample) and the level of confidene that we want to have in our results. Our level of confidence is represented by alpha (α), sometimes called the 'significance level'. Together, we can identify the critical value necessary to define the critical or rejection regions against which we test our test statistic.

Step Five: Interpretation

At the simplest level, hypothesis testing is comparing the test statistic – specific to our sample – versus the critical value – that already exists and defines the rejection region.

If the test statistic falls in the critical or rejection region, we reject the null hypothesis (H_0). This means that we can 'accept' the alternative hypothesis H_a, although technically, we don't. If, however, the test statistic does not fall in the critical region (or 'fails to reach the rejection region'), we 'fail to reject' the null hypothesis of no relationship (H_0). That is, we are unable to discard the null hypothesis of no relationship, rendering the alternative hypothesis moot.

Admittedly, generating the test statistic and finding the critical value is not effortless but the actual hypothesis test or comparison is the straightforward if/then:

- If Test Statistic > Critical Value, **Reject the null hypothesis.**
- If Test Statistic < Critical Value, **Fail to reject the null hypothesis.**

For example, a test statistic of 7.1 and a critical value of 4.8:

- = Reject the null hypothesis.

A test statistic of 3.6 and a critical value of 5.9:

- = Fail to reject the null hypothesis.

Classical Hypothesis Testing, Conceptually

Imagine that you walk into a pub and sit down at the bar scattered with other patrons. Someone sitting near you asks you if you want to play a game. She says, 'Let's flip a coin. If it comes up heads, I win, and you have to buy me a beer. And if it comes up tails, you win, and I have to buy you a beer.'

You think about this for a minute and, remembering that you have already finished your statistics assignment for this week, accept. Under one condition! That condition is the coin must be fair.

To establish that the coin is indeed fair, you need some data on the coin.

Before the game begins, you propose to flip the coin 20 times. You know that the probability of getting a head or a tail on a single flip is ½. So, in 20 flips, the coin should produce exactly 10 heads and 10 tails.

It very certainly could. However, this is a bit strict.

While 10 heads (and 10 tails) is a likely outcome in this scenario, we also know that it is possible, and not terribly unlikely, that you might flip 11 heads (and 9 tails) or even 12 heads (and 8 tails) with a fair coin. We know this from experience. (If you don't have this experience, take a minute and flip a coin 20 times. I can wait.) This is not so uncommon or outrageous. That is, if you flip a coin 20 times, many times it will be 10 heads and 10 tails – or something pretty close to that.

At the same time, you are unlikely to get 1 head and 19 tails, right?

So, that's the question. What is the cut-off? I mean, 19 heads is clearly too many and 10 is seemingly just right.

In order for you to decide whether this coin is fair or not, what is the number of heads, outside of which, you say, 'Sorry, amiga, maybe your coin isn't fair. I don't want to play your titillating but suspicious game?'

For now, let's say you feel generous and agree that the coin is fair if the number of heads in 20 flips is less than 15. Simply, you flip the coin 20 times and get 11, 12, 13, 14 heads and you will still consider the coin to be fair. And just to be safe in this strange game, we can also choose between 5–15 as too few heads (i.e. too many tails) might also be a tip off that the coin isn't fair.

So, you and your new acquaintance flip the coin 20 times and record the outcomes. If the results – the number of heads – comes back with 15 or more heads (or 5 or less heads), you can decide that the coin is not fair. However, if there are 14 or less heads (or between 6 and 14), you accept the results and agree that the coin is fair.

This is hypothesis testing. This is not 'hypothesis testing at its essence' or 'this is similar to hypothesis testing'. This is actual hypothesis testing.

It has all five of the steps.

- The null hypothesis is that the coin is fair.
- The alternative hypothesis is that the coin is not fair.
- The test statistic is the number of heads in our sample of 20 flips.
- The '5 or less' and '15 or more' criteria are critical values for the rejection region(s).
- Your interpretation depends on the value that you get from a sample of flipping the coin 20 times, the test statistic.
   o If the number of heads in your sample is equal to or greater than 15 (or equal to or less than 5), your test statistic falls outside the critical value and into the rejection region. You conclude that you must reject the null hypothesis that the coin is fair.
   o If, on the other hand, the number of heads is less than 15 (and greater than 5), your test statistic fails to reach the rejection region. You conclude that you must fail to reject the null hypothesis that the coin is fair (meaning, in a cumbersome manner, that you accept the null hypothesis of a fair coin).

The concepts of classical hypothesis testing and statistical significance are concepts we already think about and use. Perhaps in this way it is somewhat easier to see, and appreciate, as a way of forcing us to formalize our thinking about what is likely and what is not likely.

But, wait! Before you start the game, know one last thing!

We could be wrong.

Hypothesis testing is based on likelihood and probability. While highly improbable, it is not impossible that your new acquaintance is honest, the coin is fair, and on this day, at this pub, the coin flipped 16 heads. While (very) unlikely, the role of chance is one inescapable consequence of hypothesis testing. Yet again, since such a result is highly unlikely, we are very much more likely to draw a correct conclusion based on our hypothesis test.

Statistical Significance, Conceptually

Classical hypothesis testing, as a means to determine the statistical significance, can initially seem a bit complicated. Yes, there are five steps and some of the terminology is new. Yet, it is important that the intuition is clear. Let's take a moment to consider the design of hypothesis testing as a means to determine statistical significance.

Using classical hypothesis testing, comparing the performance of our sample to established hurdles, is the process through which we determine statistical significance. If what we find in our sample is not sufficiently robust, we cannot conclude that what we are observing is a function of chance. If, however, the result allows us to conclude that we have a high level of confidence that our result is very highly unlikely, we can say that what we have observed in the sample is **statistically significant** and exists in the population from which it was drawn (at the level of confidence we have selected: alpha). That is, statistical significance is our test statistic falling in the rejection region (where we can reject the null hypothesis of nothing happening).

Oops!: Type I and II Errors

In the example above, and more generally, hypothesis testing is based on probabilities and assumptions such as a random and representative sample of data. However unlikely as it is, it is still possible to reach an incorrect conclusion. Rare but mistaken conclusions are called Type I and Type II errors.

Why Type I and Type II Errors? This is statistics, we have to give our mistakes – even potential ones – names.

- **Type I error** is an incorrect null rejection error. You reject a null hypothesis (H_0) of no relationship that is in fact true. This is the odds of saying there is a relationship when in fact there is none. Colloquially known as a 'false positive'.
- **Type II error** is the failure to reject a false null hypothesis (H_0) that is in fact false. This is the odds of saying there is no relationship when in fact there is one. A.k.a. a 'false negative'.

Wait, what?

Recall the coin flip game. A Type I error is a false positive – our statistical test tells us that there is a relationship when in fact there isn't one. This is rejecting the coin as fair even though this was an honest person with a fair coin that happen to produce 16 heads out of 20 flips on this day in that pub. A Type II error is a false negative – we accept that the coin is fair even though it is not (see Table 11.1).

H_0: The coin is fair

Table 11.1   Type I and II Errors

	Fails to reject H$_0$	**Rejects H$_0$**
In fact, the coin is fair	*No error*	*Type I*
In fact, the coin is *not* fair	*Type II*	*No error*

One way to minimize making a Type I error is to choose a high level of confidence (alpha) which is functionally our acceptable level for getting a Type I error. The smaller the alpha, the smaller the chance we make a Type 1 error. High confidence is a stringent criteria and that is a good position for a scientist to be in. One way to minimize making a Type II error is increasing the sample size or generating more data. With sufficient sample size, we reduce the likelihood of missing a potentially significant result – as results from larger samples converge toward population parameters and values. Perhaps we should have asked to flip the coin 100 times to be more confident in our test.

Did you know that 'sequire' in Italian means 'to follow'? You could probably guess that – assuming you don't already know that – as it shares the same root as segue – as in 'to segue to the next section' – with the Vulgar Latin *sequire or Latin sequor*.

χ^2: Chi-squared: A Test for Independence

The χ^2 test for independence allows us to make inferential claims about the performance of single variables and relationships among nominal- and ordinal-level data. χ^2 allows us to determine whether the dependence between two variables in a sample is sufficiently strong to infer that it also exists in the population. As a test for independence, χ^2 does this by answering the question: 'Is the observed relationship between two variables in my sample highly unlikely to occur by chance and thus exist in the population?'

We merge classical hypothesis testing – again, 'significance testing' – with this test for independence by calculating a χ^2 test statistic from our sample and comparing that χ^2 test statistic to the critical value of a χ^2 distribution. The χ^2 distribution is appropriate to nominal- and ordinal-level data.

To calculate the χ^2 test statistic from our sample, we use the following formula:

$$\chi^2 = \Sigma \frac{\left(observed - expected\right)^2}{expected}$$

This formula creates a χ^2 test statistic that summarizes the relationship between what we observe in the data (i.e., the observed cell frequencies in the cross-tab) with what we would expect from these data (i.e., the expected cell frequencies derived from the marginal frequencies of the cross-tab) if in fact the variables were independent (i.e. unrelated). That is, using the data in our sample, we generate a sample-specific value: the χ^2 test statistic.

In order to determine whether what we have observed can be inferred to the population from which the sample was drawn, we compare our sample-specific χ^2 test statistic with a critical value from the χ^2 distribution. We determine the critical value with two elements: the **degrees of freedom** and a **level of confidence**.

The degrees of freedom – often written 'df' – refer to the number of columns and rows in the cross-tab. We calculate the degrees of freedom in the following way:

df = (# of columns – 1) B (# of rows – 1)

Our level of confidence is represented by **alpha (α)**. Alpha – often called a 'significance level' – is used to identify the critical values of sampling distributions.

Nearly all levels of confidence are 95%; 99%; or 99.9% confident. Alphas are written as the complements to this, respectively: .05; .01; or .001.

- $\alpha = 0.05 = 95\%$ confidence
- $\alpha = 0.01 = 99\%$ confidence
- $\alpha = 0.001 = 99.9\%$ confidence.

100%

By the way, $\alpha = 0.05$ as a percentage is written $\alpha = 5\%$. 5% + ? = 100%.
95%.
This is why it represents 95% confidence. This is the same for the other common significance levels: $\alpha = 0.01$ is 1% and thus 99% confidence (1% + 99% = 100%); $\alpha = 0.001$ is 0.1% and thus 99.9% confidence (0.1% + 99.9% = 100%).

In this way, like two pieces of a puzzle, the significance level reports the 'missing' confidence.

Yes, there are other levels of confidence that we can use. In fact, we can use any level of confidence between 0 and any number that asymptotically approaches 1 (as close as you can get to 1 without actually getting to 1). However, standard practice is to use one of these three (see Box: R.A. Fisher).

Let's consider a picture of alpha in the χ^2 distribution.

In Figure 11.1, we can see the probability density function of the χ^2 distribution. The x-axis – across the bottom – is the critical values of χ^2 whereas the y-axis represents the probabilities associated with each value. One can also see the alpha hiding in the shaded tail of the distribution.

INFERENCE FOR NOMINAL- AND ORDINAL-LEVEL VARIABLES | 247

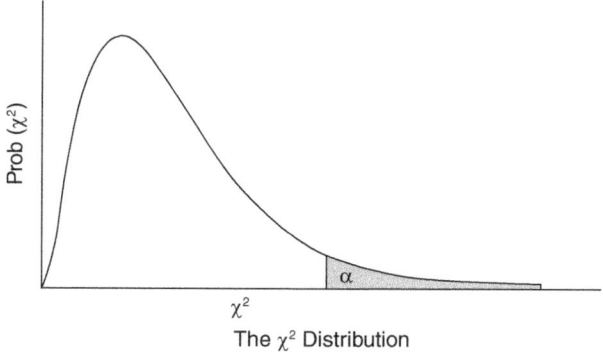

Figure 11.1 The χ^2 Distribution

> ### PROBABILITY DENSITY FUNCTION
>
> A probability density function (PDF) produces a distribution that represents the full range of possible values for a continuous random variable or statistic. As we saw in the previous chapter, based on probability theory, the area under the curve is 1 (all the probabilities of all outcomes summed) and height represents the likelihood of each value of the variable or statistic.

Look at Figures 11.2a – 11.2c. Alpha is the shaded area under the tail. For example, for Figure 11.2a in which we have $\alpha = 0.05$, the unshaded area under the curve is 95% – as in where we would expect 95% of the outcomes to be.

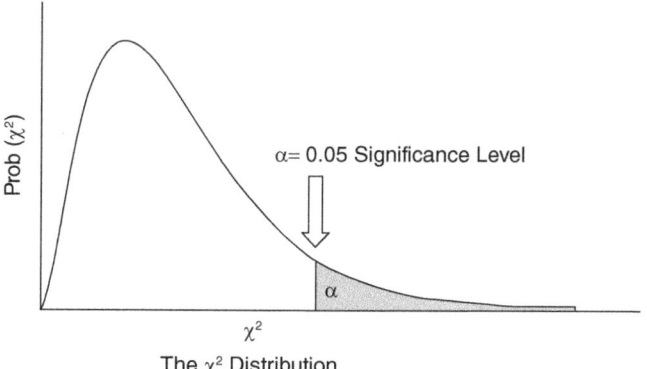

Figure 11.2a 95% Confidence

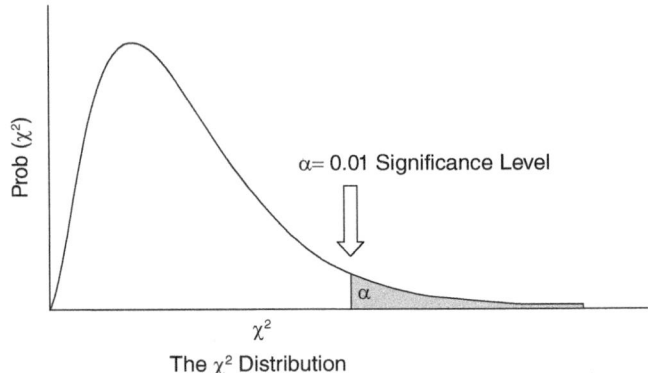

Figure 11.2b 99% Confidence

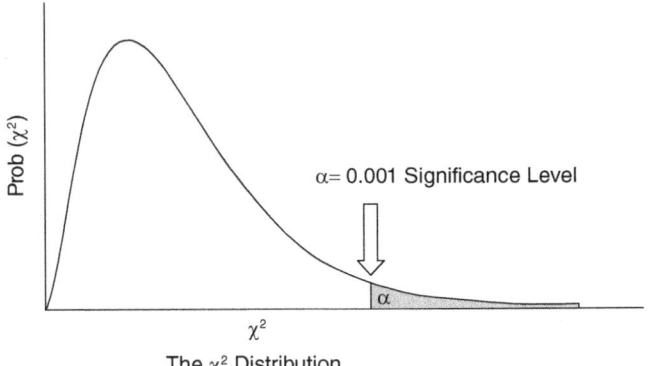

Figure 11.2c 99.9% Confidence

As we move to higher levels of confidence, 99% or 99.9%, the alphas get (correspondingly) smaller. As we demand more confidence in our results, the critical value gets larger and larger which makes the rejection region more and more difficult to reach. This makes intuitive sense as the more confident we want to be in the ability to infer our result to the population, the higher and more difficult the hurdle to do so must be.

So, what is that critical value for $\alpha = 0.05$ or $\alpha = 0.01$ or $\alpha = 0.001$?

Good question. But remember, the critical value doesn't only depend on alpha. It also depends on the degrees of freedom (df). While the χ^2 distribution in Figure 11.1 allows us to visualize the relationship between χ^2 our choice of alpha and the χ^2 critical value, the actual χ^2 critical value comes from the χ^2 distribution table.

In Table 11.2, we can see how the two necessary elements of alpha and *df* direct us to the correct χ^2 critical value. The numbers in these cells are the χ^2 critical values along the x-axis that are determined by your choice of significance and the degrees of freedom in your data.

Table 11.2 The χ^2 Distribution Table

Degrees of freedom	Alpha: Significance level				
	0.10	0.05	0.025	0.01	0.001
	Critical values of χ^2				
1	2.71	3.84	5.02	6.64	10.83
2	4.61	5.99	7.38	9.21	13.82
3	6.25	7.82	9.35	11.35	16.27
4	7.78	9.49	11.14	13.28	18.47
5	9.24	11.07	12.83	15.09	20.52
6	10.65	12.59	14.45	16.81	22.46
7	12.02	14.07	16.01	18.48	24.32
8	13.36	15.51	17.54	20.09	26.13
9	14.68	16.92	19.02	21.67	27.88
10	15.99	18.31	20.48	23.21	29.59
11	17.28	19.68	21.92	24.73	31.26
12	18.55	21.03	23.34	26.22	32.91
13	19.81	22.36	24.74	27.69	34.53
14	21.06	23.69	26.12	29.14	36.12
15	22.31	25.00	27.49	30.58	37.70
16	23.54	26.30	28.85	32.00	39.25
17	24.77	27.59	30.19	33.41	40.79
18	25.99	28.87	31.53	34.81	42.31
19	27.20	30.14	32.85	36.19	43.82
20	28.41	31.41	34.17	37.57	45.32

So, for example, if we want to be 99% confident (alpha = 0.01) with 4 degrees of freedom, the χ^2 critical value would be, looking down the alpha = 0.01 column and across the df = 4 row, 13.28. If we wanted to be more confident, e.g., 99.9% confident (alpha = 0.001), we see the χ^2 critical value would be, looking down the alpha=0.001 column and across the df = 4 row, 18.47. A much higher critical value for much higher confidence! And that makes sense. If we want to be more confident that our result can be inferred from the sample to the population, we must clear a higher hurdle.

Also notice that, as mentioned above, 95%, 99%, and 99.9% represent only the most common levels of confidence we can have. We can also see that 90% confidence (alpha = 0.10) and 97.5% confidence (alpha = 0.025). But again, it seems a little strange to speak of 97.5% confidence.

'Are you sure?'

'Yeah, I'm 97.5% sure!'

> ### R.A. FISHER
>
> Ronald A. Fisher is a candidate for the 'father of modern statistics'. His book, *Statistical Methods for Research Workers*, published in 1925, had the great fortune of being timely, widely read, and well-written. His work built on previous giant steps in statistical methodology accelerated by Karl Pearson (who you may recall from Gamma and Lambda fame).
>
> Unfortunately for Fisher's book, he was not allowed to reproduce tables from the then-standard *Tables for Statisticians and Biometricians* published in 1914 by none other than Karl Pearson himself. *Tables* was the reference book at the time, composed of statistical theorems, proofs, and, importantly, tables of probabilities to the third digit and degrees of freedom to the hundreds. Many of the tables ran to dozens of pages each.
>
> Stuck in this conundrum, Fisher, in an inspired stroke of simplification, created the tables that he needed using only a handful of probabilities such as: 90%, 95%, 98%, and 99%. He argued that these were just the most common and intuitive. For example, he correctly pointed out that '20 to 1' or '100 to 1' odds – that is, 95% and 99% confidence, respectively – were simply more intuitively accessible than '19 to 1' or '102 to 1' odds.
>
> So, instead of tables spanning pages and pages with minute changes over every three-digit probability, Fisher inadvertently created a standardized table that was compact, easy to use, and for as far as most users cared, more than sufficient.
>
> I note that for χ^2, he included df up to 30 and the probabilities of 0.99; 0.98; 0.95; 0.90; 0.80; 0.70; 0.50; 0.30; 0.20; 0.10; 0.05; 0.02; 0.01.
>
> Although, perhaps Pearson had the last laugh. He created χ^2.

Let's take χ^2 out for a test drive.

χ^2 Example: Political Gender Parity

Democracy, as a form of government, is rooted in the idea of equality. Each person, without discrimination, should be able to exert the same amount of influence on choosing and thus directing government. So, let's ask, does democracy do this? Does democracy allow, for example, women to have the same access to political power as men?

At the outset, we would expect to find a positive relationship between these variables such that, as we observe increasingly democratic governments, we would expect to see a concomitant rise in the political power of women.

Using the most recent data from the V-Democracy dataset, we look at an ordinal-level variable that measures the extent to which rights and freedoms of individuals are protected equally across all social groups and resources are distributed equally across all social groups. The variable we will use is called the Egalitarian Democracy Index and as it relates a measure of egalitarianism to democracy, the index also considers the level of electoral democracy of the country. The ordinal categories include: Autocratic (0), Electoral Authoritarian (1), Minimally Democratic (2), and Democratic (3).

To estimate whether the nature of political institutions is beneficial to women, we use a measure that assesses how political power is distributed according to gender. The ordinal responses include: 'Men have a near-monopoly on political power' (0); 'Men have a dominant hold on political power. Women have only marginal influence' (1); 'Men have much more political power but women have some areas of influence' (2); 'Men have somewhat more political power than women' (3); and 'Men and women have roughly equal political power' (4).

> ### GENDER DISEQUILIBRIUM
>
> I'll say it. Where is the category for 'women have more power than men'?
>
> Why is there not a category that indicates societies in which the preponderance of political power rests with women? Why is gender parity the limit? Perhaps, there is no category for the unfortunate reason that there may be no observations – for example, there are no national legislatures with a female majority in the world.
>
> However, in the same dataset (V-Democracy), there is a variable that measures the political power distributed by sexual orientation (v2pepwrort). While this variable has a questionable design – clumping heterosexuals and LGBTQ+ who are not open about their sexuality together as 'heterosexuals', against LGBTQ+ who are open about their sexuality – it also contains an additional response category: 'LGBTs enjoy somewhat more political power than heterosexuals by virtue of greater wealth, education, and high level of organization and mobilization.'
>
> Why is this not an option for women? We could easily imagine: 'Women enjoy somewhat more political power than men by virtue of greater intelligence, education, and high level of organization and mobilization skills.' La Liberté guidant le peuple!

We can see the joint distribution of the Principle of Egalitarian Democracy and the Political Power of Women as a cross-tab (Table 11.3a). The pattern in the cross-tab is promising, given our research question. Autocratic countries tend to be countries in which males dominate politics. Similarly, gender parity and quasi-equality is more common in democracies or quasi-democracies.

Table 11.3a Egalitarian Democracy and the Political Power of Women

		Principle of egalitarian democracy				
		Autocratic	Electoral authoritarian	Minimally democratic	Democratic	Total
Political power distributed by gender	Male monopoly	1	1	0	0	**2**
	Men dominant, women marginal	4	11	12	0	**27**
	Men more, women some	0	8	17	5	**30**
	Men more than women	0	0	3	9	**12**
	Gender parity	0	1	1	3	**5**
	Total	*5*	*21*	*33*	*17*	*76*

As both of these variables are ordinal-level variables, we will need to use the correct Measure of Association. Recall the formula for Gamma:

$$\text{Gamma}(\gamma) = \frac{n_c - n_d}{n_c + n_d}$$

We will need the concordant pairs (n_c) and the discordant pairs (n_d). Although we will not review the calculation here (Chapter 7), we arrive at:

$$\text{Gamma}(\gamma) = \frac{1271 - 175}{1271 + 175}$$

$$\text{Gamma}(\gamma) = 0.76$$

First of all, as expected, the relationship is positive – the relationship runs from the top left cell to the bottom right cell – and rather substantial. We can interpret this result as, in this sample, 'Knowing the nature of government in a country, we reduce our errors in predicting the level of political gender parity by 76%.' Or 'Our prediction of the level of political gender parity in a country is 76% better by knowing the nature of government.' In terms of **substantive significance**, this means knowing the type of government tells us a great deal about political gender parity in that country.

With these data, this is a fairly compelling answer to our research question of whether democracy allows women to have the same access to political power as men. However, perhaps this is just in our sample and what we have observed is just chance.

Can we infer this substantive relationship we have identified in our sample data ($\gamma = 0.76$) to the population? That is, is this result statistically significant, and thus 'real'?

To find out, we can do a χ^2 test of independence.

Steps One and Two: The Null and Alternative Hypotheses

- The Research or Alternative Hypothesis (H_a): Variables are dependent; they are related
  o 'The greater the extent of democracy, the greater political gender parity.'
- The Null Hypothesis (H_0): Variables are independent; there is no relation
  o 'The greater the extent of democracy has no effect on political gender parity.'

Step Three: Test Statistic

- Again, the χ^2 test statistic comes from our sample using the formula above. The observed values are the values in the cross-tab (Table 11.3a). As before, we calculate the expected values based on the marginal frequencies (the row and column totals):

- Male Monopoly/Autocratic: (2*5)/76=0.1
- Male Monopoly/Electoral Autocratic: (2*21)/76=0.6
- Male Monopoly/Minimally Democratic: (2*33)/76=0.9
- Male Monopoly/Democratic: (2*17)/76=0.4
- Men Dominant/Autocratic: (5*27)/76=1.8
- [...]
- Gender Parity/Minimally Democratic: (5*33)/76=2.2
- Gender Parity/Minimally Democratic: (5*17)/76=1.1

We can use these values to populate the cells of the cross-tab with the expected values we produced (see Table 11.3b).

Table 11.3b Expected Values of Egalitarian Democracy and Gender Power

		Principle of egalitarian democracy				
		Autocratic	Electoral authoritarian	Minimally democratic	Democratic	Total
Political power distributed by gender	Male monopoly	0.1	0.6	0.9	0.4	2
	Men dominant, women marginal	1.8	7.5	11.7	6.0	27
	Men more, women some	2.0	8.3	13.0	6.7	30
	Men more than women	0.8	3.3	5.2	2.7	12
	Gender parity	0.3	1.4	2.2	1.1	5
	Total	5	21	33	17	76

To calculate the χ^2 test statistic, we input the observed (from Table 11.3a) and expected values (from Table 11.3b) into the χ^2 formula. Recall the formula:

$$\chi^2 = \Sigma \frac{(observed - expected)^2}{expected}$$

$$\chi^2 = \frac{(1-0.1)^2}{0.1} + \frac{(1-0.6)^2}{0.6} + [...] + \frac{(1-2.2)^2}{2.2} + \frac{(3-1.1)^2}{1.1}$$

$$\chi^2 = 45.7$$

The χ^2 test statistic for our sample is 45.7.

Step Four: Critical or Rejection Region

In order to determine whether our test statistic is sufficient to reject the null hypothesis, the critical value of χ^2 requires two pieces of information: the level of significance and the degrees of freedom.

Let's begin with 95% confidence ($\alpha=0.05$) and the degrees of freedom are determined by the formula:

df = (5 of columns – 1) B (5 of rows – 1)

df = (4 – 1) B (5 – 1)

df = 12

Consulting the χ^2 Distribution Table (Table 11.2), we can see that our χ^2 critical value [$\alpha = 0.05$; $df = 12$] is 21.03. With a selected value for alpha and the degrees of freedom, this can be represented in Figure 11.3:

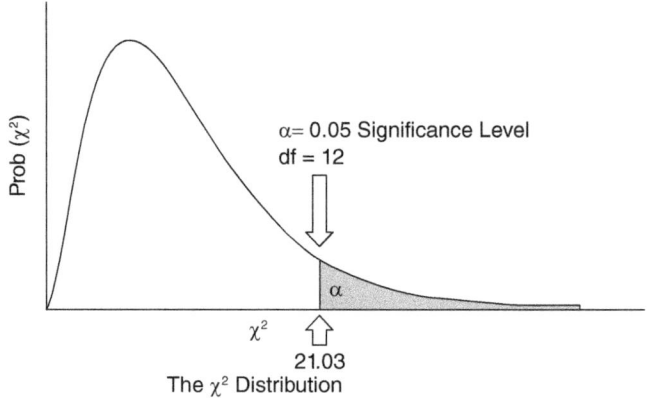

Figure 11.3 The Critical Region for a χ^2 Critical Value of 21.03 [$\alpha=0.05$; $df=12$]

Crucially, beyond 21.03 is the critical or rejection region (the shaded region in Figure 11.3).

Step Five: Interpretation

Summarizing the previous steps:

χ^2 Test Statistic = 45.7

χ^2 Critical Value ($\alpha = 0.05$; $df = 12$): 21.03

Interpretation: We *reject* the null hypothesis of no relationship.

With a χ^2 test statistic of 45.7 for our sample and a χ^2 critical value ($\alpha=0.05$; $df=1$) of 21.03, we can determine whether $\gamma = 0.76$ in the sample data can be inferred to the population from which the sample was drawn.

45.7 is larger than 21.03 and falls in the rejection region. Following the rules of hypothesis testing, we reject the null hypothesis (H_0) that the variables are independent and conclude that this relationship in fact exists in the population from which it was drawn.

A full interpretation would read: 'At the 95% confidence level, we conclude that there is a relationship between the nature of a government – how autocratic or democratic it is – and political gender parity. We reject the null hypothesis of no relationship and conclude that the observed relationship ($\gamma = 0.76$) exists in the population from which it was drawn.'

But wait! There's more!

95% confidence is impressive! And well done, democracy; although clearly there is some improvement to be made (see Box: Gender Disequilibrium).

However, we have a χ^2 test statistic of 45.7.

Can we be more confident in our result?

Let's look at the χ^2 critical value for 99% confidence ($\alpha=0.01$). Consulting the χ^2 Distribution Table (Table 11.2), we can see that our χ^2 critical value ($\alpha=0.01$; $df=12$) is 26.33. Our test statistic is higher than this allowing us to reject the null hypothesis of no relation at 99% confidence!

That is really exciting – but… shall we?

Yes, we shall.

The χ^2 critical value for 99.9% confidence ($\alpha=0.001$; $df=12$) is 32.91. Our test statistic is 45.7. That is to say, we can reject the null hypothesis of no relation at 99.9% confidence!

We can therefore update our interpretation to: 'At the 99.9% confidence level, we conclude that there is a relationship between the nature of a government – how autocratic or democratic it is – and political gender parity. We reject the null hypothesis of no relationship and conclude that the observed relationship ($\gamma = 0.76$) exists in the population from which it was drawn.'

Very nicely done.

OTHER MEASURES OF ASSOCIATION FROM χ^2

In Descriptive Statistics, we briefly mentioned other Measures of Association that we didn't examine such as Cramer's V and Phi (φ). Many are based on, and include in their formulas, χ^2.

A Final Word

This chapter has introduced you to the *how* and *why* of statistical significance using nominal- and ordinal-level variables. We have worked through examples of how we determine statistical significance using chi-squared (χ^2) and classical hypothesis testing. And, having seen it in action, we can appreciate the *purpose* of statistical significance. Namely, we determine the statistical significance of our analysis of the sample data because it allows us to make confident claims about population parameters.

We now have the ability to ask – and answer – 4 big questions with statistics.

1. Is there a relationship between the Independent Variable and Dependent Variable?
2. How strong is the relationship?
3. What is direction of relationship?
4. Is the relationship statistically significant?

Descriptive Statistics allows us to answer the first three. To answer the fourth, classical hypothesis testing creates a high hurdle for us to clear in order to make inferential claims about what we have found. A savvy understanding of statistics is revealed by not confusing substantive significance (1, 2, and 3) with statistical significance (4).

The classical hypothesis testing procedure may seem overly oblique. In fact, the scientific method sounds oblique. Theories are just simplified guesses about how the world might work that we often try to make fail using hypothesis that we don't test directly but rather test their opposite of which we decide to reject or not.

Yet, this process put the onus on the data. If we discover that nominal- or ordinal-level variables are associated in a sample, we can also determine the level of confidence and probability that the relationship we observe in the sample is one that is likely to exist in the population from which it is drawn. We allow the data the opportunity to demonstrate whether any substantive finding can also be an inferential finding as well.

End of Chapter Summary

- Nominal- and ordinal-level variables have their own measures of association that account for their less-mathy nature. However, we can still determine whether relationships among these variables exist only in the sample or can be inferred to exist in the population from which that sample was drawn.
- Classical hypothesis testing is a step-by-step procedure that allows us to make inferential claims of statistical significance by comparing a sample-specific test statistic to an already existing critical value that defines a rejection region.
- We do not test our research hypothesis. Instead, we reject or fail to reject the null hypothesis of no relationship.
- Rejecting the null hypothesis confers statistical significance on the result and promotes the research or alternative hypothesis.
- Failing to reject the null hypothesis annihilates any result we find in the sample data.
- Our decision to reject or fail to reject the null hypothesis is based on probability. While we can have a high level of confidence, we can still be wrong. We can incorrectly reject the null (Type I error) – saying there is a relationship when there is none – or incorrectly fail to reject the null hypothesis (Type II error) – saying there is no relationship when in fact there is one.
- A test statistic is a number generated from a specific set of data.

- The critical value defines the critical or rejection region in significance testing. The critical value is determined by a selected level of confidence and the sample-specific degrees of freedom. The more confident we want to be in the ability to infer our result to the population, the higher the critical value.
- 'Chance' in the context of significance testing refers to the noise in a sample. This can include natural variation in the sample as a *sample*; data collection problems such as a problematic sampling frame, measure, or instrument; reverberations of something else going on in the sample; anything that suggests differences but doesn't amass to represent a possible relationship in the population. Sample noise is totally normal (hence, the critical value).
- By comparing what we observe to what we expect, χ^2 answers the question: 'Is the observed relationship between two variables in my sample highly unlikely to occur by chance and thus exist in the population?'

Glossary

- **Classical hypothesis testing** is a step-by-step procedure to determine statistical significance. It is also commonly referred to as **significance testing**.
- **Alternative hypothesis** or research hypothesis (H_1 or H_a) is a general, non-normative, directional statement of the expected relationship derived from theory.
- The **null hypothesis** (H_0) is the condition in which there is no relationship or dependence among your variables.
- A **test statistic** is calculated from our sample data and indicates the extent our result deviates from what is expected.
- **Alpha** (α) is the level of significance.
- A **critical value** defines the **critical region** in the sampling distribution with which we decide to reject or fail to reject the test statistic.
- **Reject the null hypothesis** indicates that there is sufficient evidence to conclude that observed relationships in the sample can be inferred to the population from which that sample was drawn.
- **Fail to reject the null hypothesis** indicates that there is insufficient evidence to conclude that observed relationships in the sample can be inferred to the population from which that sample was drawn.
- **Substantive significance** is the magnitude and sometimes direction of a relationship described in a sample.
- **Statistical significance** is ability to make inferences from sample to population with our results.
- **Type I error** is an incorrect null rejection error. **Type II error** is the failure to reject a false null hypothesis that is in fact false.
- χ^2 is a test for independence that allows for inferential claims about the performance of relationships among nominal- and ordinal-level data.

- **Degrees of freedom** are a measure crucial to the selection of critical values that relate the number of observations or dimensions of the variables under investigation.
- **Confidence** is the extent a result is statistically significant or not. Its complement is alpha.

Questions

1. Using our conceptual discussion of statistical significance, what would happen to your critical regions if you had flipped the coin 100 or 500 times to determine whether the coin was fair? Do you think increasing the sample size of your fairness hypothesis test would improve your ability to reach an accurate conclusion?
2. Why do we 'seek to reject the null hypothesis'? Perhaps recall that statistical significance is ability to make inferences from sample to population based on the idea that we have found something *unlikely* to be a function of chance.
3. If you are a cautious scientist and want to make *sure* sure that your results are real (or more importantly, that you weren't presenting results that have no support), which error would you prefer to make, a Type I error or Type 2 error? Why?
4. Why might the following be an unsafe conclusion? In the χ^2 examples in this chapter, we found a weak $\lambda = 0.074$ which was not statistically significant and in the second example, we found a very strong $\gamma = 0.76$ which was statistically significant at $\alpha = 0.001$. It was clear from the substantive significance which ones would be statistically significant.
5. Why is the 'critical region' also called the 'rejection region'? How does this inform Classical Hypothesis Testing?
6. To determine statistical significance, χ^2 compares the distribution of expected values versus the distribution of observed values. Again, recalling that statistical significance is based on the idea that we have found something *unlikely* to be a function of chance, why does this approach make sense? For example, if $\chi^2 = 0$, the distribution of expected values would be the exact same as the distribution of observed values. As χ^2 grows larger, what – in the language of statistical significance – is χ^2 trying to tell us?

Annotated References and Further Reading

Fisher, Ronald A. 1925. *Statistical Methods for Research Workers*. 1st edn. Edinburgh: Oliver & Boyd.
Aside from the term 'Research Workers' needing to make a comeback, this is the source code for the statistics we are still doing.

Pearson, Karl. 1914. *Tables for Statisticians and Biometricians*. 1st edn. Cambridge: Cambridge University Press.
This is available on our website. While more compact and recent tables exist, the data in *Tables* are in fact the same and thus a way, if one wanted, to go 'old school'.

Signposts to the Accompanying Digital Resources

Data used in this chapter

- **Egalitarian democracy index** (v2x_egaldem): The egalitarian principle of democracy holds that material and immaterial inequalities inhibit the exercise of formal rights and liberties, and diminish the ability of citizens from all social groups to participate. Egalitarian democracy is achieved when (1) rights and freedoms of individuals are protected equally across all social groups; and (2) resources are distributed equally across all social groups. To make it a measure of egalitarian *democracy*, the index also takes the level of electoral democracy into account. Varieties of Democracy (V-DEM).
- **Distribution of political power** (v2pepwrgen): 'Men have a near-monopoly on political power' (0); 'Men have a dominant hold on political power. Women have only marginal influence' (1); 'Men have much more political power but women have some areas of influence' (2); 'Men have somewhat more political power than women' (3); 'Men and women have roughly equal political power' (4). Varieties of Democracy (V-DEM).
    - Coppedge, Michael, John Gerring, Staffan I. Lindberg, Svend-Erik Skaaning, Jan Teorell, with David Altman, Michael Bernhard, M. Steven Fish, Adam Glynn, Allen Hicken, Carl Henrik Knutsen, Kelly McMann, Pamela Paxton, Daniel Pemstein, Jeffrey Staton, Brigitte Zimmerman, Frida Andersson, Valeriya Mechkova, and Farhad Miri. 2016. 'V-Dem Codebook v6.' Varieties of Democracy (V-DEM) Project. www.v-dem.net/en/data/data/

12
THE CENTRAL LIMIT THEOREM

> **LEARNING OUTCOMES**
>
> In this chapter, you will be able to
>
> - Identify and characterize a Normal Distribution.
> - Explain the role of the Central Limit Theorem in linking Standard Normal sampling distributions to expected probabilities.
> - Use the Standard Normal Z-distribution and z-scores to generate expected probabilities of outcomes.
> - Determine expected probabilities for various sets of outcomes.
> - Demonstrate a deeper understanding and appreciation of statistical significance and its role in our ability to make inferential claims.

Introduction

As mentioned previously, interval-level variables receive the most attention in statistics. The reason for this is obvious. Interval-level variables represent the highest-order level of measurement in terms of our ability to manage and handle them (not necessarily the best measure overall but certainly the most math-y).

In this chapter, we will use the math-iness of interval-level variables to weave together the theoretical basis for Inferential Statistics with the actual underpinning mathematics. To do so, we will return to probability. Specifically, we are going to look directly at the whirring engine of Inferential Statistics. We will answer the question: 'How exactly do we assign confidence to the inferential claims of our results?'

Perhaps the answer is not immediately obvious and requires a few steps, but the logic is straightforward. We will introduce ourselves to the Normal distribution and a specific form called Standard Normal. This Standard Normal is commonly called a Z-distribution and we will see how this standardization is done by using it ourselves. We will then make some strong assumptions about this distribution – in the form of the Central Limit Theorem – and link it to the expected probabilities of outcomes. Once we understand expected outcomes, we can talk about confidence.

At first this can seem a bit daunting but, passing through each step, we build the ability to make inferential claims of statistical significance. Inferential Statistics – that is, taking something that we know and trying to make reasonable guesses about something we do not know – is a function of probability. Here, we undertake a deeper investigation of how and why that is.

Sampling Distributions

A **sampling distribution** is a summary of the probabilities of outcomes, also called a probability density function or probability density curve. Remember this from the previous chapter?

If we wanted to create a distribution of the outcomes for a coin flip, we would end up with two columns – one for each outcome: heads/tails – each with a 50% chance of being the outcome. That is the probability density function of flipping a coin. The same with rolling a die. You would have 6 columns of the same height – one for 1, one for 2, one for 3, one for 4, one for 5, and one for 6 – each with a 16.7% chance of being the outcome.

As the nature of the outcomes change, so does the shape of distribution of probabilities.

Take for instance rolling two dice. While the chance for each die remains the same as before – a 16.7% chance of being the result, the combinations of two dice converge toward rolling a combined total of 7.

Why? Think of it this way (and see Figure 12.1), what is the lowest combination you can roll? A 2 – each die is 1. How many other combinations are there for 2? 0 is the answer, you need both die to be 1. Same for 12. There is only one combination: 6 and 6. However, for 7, you can roll 1, 6; 2, 5; 3, 4; 4, 3; 5, 2; 6, 1. There are six combinations. I'll let you figure out the other combinations but it is easiest to get a 7, then 6 and 8, then 5 and 9, then 4 and 10, then 3 and 11, and then 2 and 12. If you plot these outcomes on a set of axes, with probability on the y-axis and the outcomes across the bottom, the distribution of probabilities looks a little like a mound. This mound illustrates why you are more likely to observe a 7 as an outcome than 11. And 8 more likely than 5. Etc....

> ### ROLL THE BONES
>
> There are six combinations for two dice rolling a 7:
>
> - 5 combinations for 6 and 8
> - 4 combinations for 5 and 9
> - 3 combinations for 4 and 10
> - 2 combinations for 3 and 11
> - 1 combination for 2 and 12.

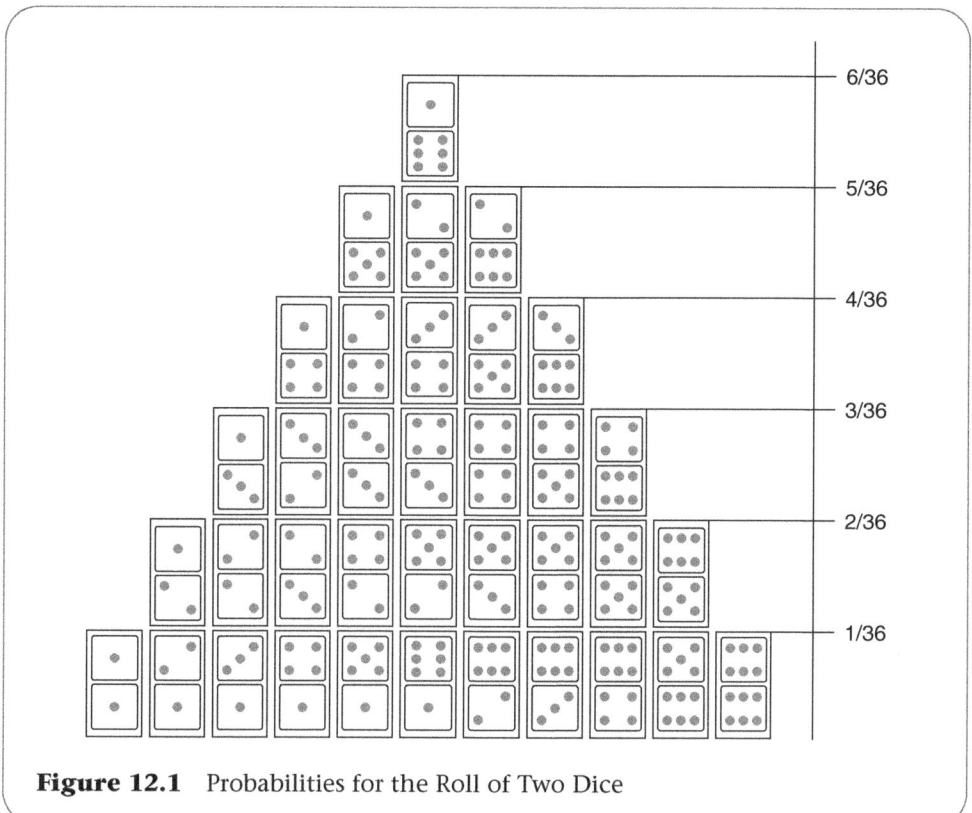

Figure 12.1 Probabilities for the Roll of Two Dice

For **random variables**, variables in which the outcomes can be infinite (or very high), the columns for each of the outcomes get skinnier and skinnier until they literally disappear. The tops of these former columns create a curve. This curve becomes the probability density function, the distribution of the probability of outcomes. As we will see, their characteristics enable us to connect what we know – sample statistics – to what we want to know – population parameters.

Now, there is no one sampling distribution and we have already been introduced to one, recall χ^2. And there are others such as the exponential, Poisson, binomial distributions. However, there is one sampling distribution that lies at the heart of statistics – and you probably already know its name: the **Normal distribution**.

The Normal Distribution

Normal distributions are actually a family of distributions that have the same general shape. They are a bell-shaped curve – as most scores are concentrated in the middle and fewer in its tails – and their tails asymptotically approach zero. A Normal distribution refers to the probabilities associated with interval-level variables. As such, the shape is specified by a mean and standard deviation (see Figure 12.2a).

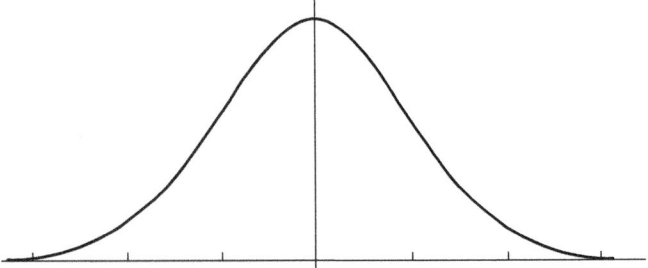

Figure 12.2a The Normal Distribution

> ### ALMOST ZERO
>
> Asymptotically means they never touch the axis. While also a nice thought experiment, this represents the notion that while any value is technically possible, the farther from the mean an outcome is, the less likely it will occur. That is, many things are possible but not necessarily probable.

The Normal distribution has three neat properties that are extremely useful.

1. It is symmetric. The mean is the median is the mode. The curve is the same on both sides of the mean/median/mode centre line.
2. The total area under the curve is 1. As a probability distribution, this makes sense as it represents all the probabilities added together.
3. The areas under the curve have fixed proportions. Between the mean and, for example a standard deviation, there is a fixed proportion of observations.

These three properties refer to all Normal distributions and only Normal Distributions. Further, together, they converge on the 68-95-99.7% Rule.

The 68-95-99.7% Rule

The left half of the curve – from the mean all the way to negative infinity – is 50%. The chance of an observed value falling in that part of the curve is 50%. And, because the Normal distribution is symmetric, the total area under the curve equals 1, and has fixed proportions, the right side equals 50%, too.

- What is true of the left side is true of the right side is an example of *symmetry*.
- 50% + 50% = 100% reflects *total area = 1*.
- 50% between the mean and the end of the tail is a *fixed proportion*.

It is this last point that is worth a further look and brings us to the 68-95-99.7% Rule. This rule is not hard and fast and can be better thought of as a rule of thumb (Figure 12.2b).

- Approximately 68% of the observations fall within 1 standard deviation of the mean.
- Approximately 95% of the observations fall within 2 standard deviations of the mean.
- Approximately 99.7% of the observations fall within 3 standard deviations of the mean.

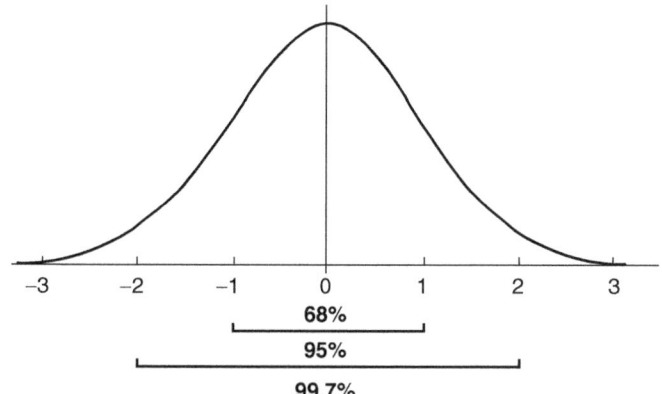

Figure 12.2b The Normal Distribution and the 68-95-99.7% Rule

So, for a Normal distribution, almost all values lie within 3 standard deviations of the mean. Remember that the rule applies to all Normal distributions and only to Normal distributions.

68-95-99.7% Example

Using the Gini Index as a measure of national-level income inequality (World Bank), in a random sample of 48 countries, we find the distribution of income inequality is approximately normally distributed with a mean of 37.8 and a standard deviation of 8.0.

From the 68-95-99.7% rule, it follows that:

- Approximately 68% of the observations are between 37.8−8.0 and 37.8+8.0: 29.8 and 45.8
- Approximately 95% of the observations are between 37.8−2*8.0 and 37.8+2*8.0: 21.8 and 53.8
- Approximately 99.7% of the observations are between 37.8−3*8.0 and 37.8+3*8.0: 13.8 and 61.8.

What's more, since the Normal distribution is symmetrical with fixed proportions, because 68% of the observations fall within 1 standard deviation of the mean, the proportion of observations between the mean and one standard deviation – in either direction – is half of 68%. I personally find this amazing that 34% – more than one third of the observations – fall between the mean and one standard deviation in one direction. Remarkably, this is true for the other proportions as well (see Figure 12.2c).

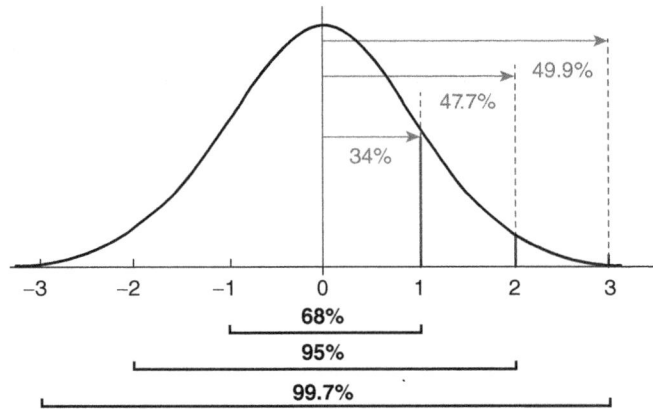

Figure 12.2c The Normal Distribution, Symmetry, and Fixed Proportions

So, This is the famous Normal Distribution

Yeah. Why is it important again? Frankly, for practical and theoretical reasons.

Practically, it is easy for statisticians to work with as it is well-behaved and mathematically tractable. Again, the three properties that make it wonderful are symmetry, total area under the curve is 1, and fixed proportions. The Normal distribution holds for large, random samples and thus can be used to find significance levels in many hypothesis tests and confidence intervals. As such, many classical statistical tests are based on the assumption that the data follow a normal distribution (although not our beloved χ^2).

Theoretically, the Normal distribution is important because of the Central Limit Theorem.

The Central Limit Theorem

The **Central Limit Theorem** (CLT) states that as sample size increases, the sampling distribution of sample means approaches Normal with a mean the same as the mean of the population and a standard deviation equal to the standard deviation of the population divided by the square root of n (the sample size). This is true even if the population distribution is not distributed normally.

Ok, there's a lot to break down in there. Let's take it one step at a time.

Let's start from the core mechanism (and pretty big assumption). The CLT states that if we take repeated samples of the same size from a population, and then we assemble the *means* of all those samples, our distribution of those *means* will look like a Normal distribution. Stated differently, the CLT refers to a distribution of means that come from infinite samples taken from a population. This distribution of sample means is a 'sampling distribution'.

Assuming we have a random sample, as our sample size increases, the more our distribution will approximate Normal.

What is sufficiently large? About 30 observations.

And, finally, as our distribution approaches Normal, the mean of the sampling distribution will become equal to the mean in the population. And the **standard error** of the sampling distribution can be estimated by the standard deviation of the population divided by the square root of n – the number of observations in the sample. One way to think about this is that the standard deviation is the dispersion of observations around the mean and the standard error is merely the dispersion of means around the mean of the means in a sampling distribution. In this sense, standard deviation and standard error are doing essentially the same thing, except standard error takes into account sample size.

> ### PRESTIDIGITATION
>
> The Central Limit Theorem is not wrong. And it is not mere handwaving or sleight of hand. It is, however, an assumption. And this assumption does a lot of heavy lifting in modern statistics.

This has a number of implications but one important one is the ability to use and exploit the characteristics of a Normal distribution. That is, the CLT justifies the use of the Normal distribution in a wide range of statistical applications. This means that we can continue to use the Normal assumption associated with many statistical tests even if the variables we are investigating are not normally distributed in the population.

For example, we already know that income is not Normally distributed, it is very heavily positively skewed (toward poverty, by the way). But, the CLT says that no matter what the distribution of the population looks like, the sampling distribution will be distributed Normally (that is, the distribution of means from the infinite samples), as long as your sample size is big enough.

Setting our income example aside, it should be pointed out that Normally distributed populations are in fact very common. Even populations which are not strictly Normal are very often bell-curved or camel-hump-shaped. Some may be flatter or slightly misshapen because of skew or outliers but many will not only resemble a Normal curve but also act like one. Therefore, in large random samples, we can use the sample mean and standard deviation to be our best guess for the true population parameters.

In this way, the CLT allows us to make informed inferences from our sample (known) about the true population parameters (always unknown).

Standard Normal and Z-Scores

A more practical way to exploit the properties of the Normal distribution is to standardize a distribution. In a special case of the Normal distribution, called the Standard Normal, the mean is set at zero, and the 'standard unit' – which is a standardized standard deviation – is 1. We call this standard unit, a Z-score. As such, this Standard Normal Probability distribution is commonly called the **Z-distribution**.

You've probably never heard of – or would have imagined – the existence of z-scores and a Z-distribution. So, the question naturally arises, why would we even think to do this?

Standardizing interval-level variables to the Z-distribution converts all interval-level variable distributions into a single, standardized distribution. This allows us to do two very useful things. One, compare different interval-level variables with one another and two, determine the expected probability of different outcomes.

How?

Z-scores convert observations into standard units which represent the distance from the mean in standard deviations. Simply, the z-scores represent how many standard deviations an observation falls from the standardized mean (good ol' zero, '0'). Merged with what we know about Normal distributions, this gives us a lot of power to make (very) informed guesses.

The formula for a z-score is exactly what you think it is:

$$z = \frac{(x_i - \mu)}{\sigma}$$

in which x_i is an observation, μ is the mean of the population, and σ is the standard deviation of the population.

And perhaps now you can see why the CLT is so important as we can never know the population parameters μ and σ. But, we do know $\bar{x}$ – the sample mean – and s – the sample standard deviation. And, under a few conditions, these can be used as really good estimates of the population parameters we don't know.

Therefore:

$$z = \frac{(x_i - \bar{x})}{s}$$

And, here we can see, we find the distance between the observation (x_i) and the mean ($\bar{x}$) and divide that difference by the (sample) standard deviation. Doing this for all the observations gives us a standard unit – a z-score – that represents the distance between an observation and the mean in the metric of standard deviations. To make the obvious example of an observation that is exactly 1 standard deviation from the mean, we would divide a standard deviation difference (observation minus the mean) by the standard deviation thus arriving at 1. The resultant 1 z-score would mean that the observation was 1 standard deviation away, which it is. While a neat trick, this holds for all other observations as well.

STANDARDIZATION

What is **standardization** anyway? Standardizing allows us to compare across different measures but also within the same measure. You are no doubt familiar with the concept of the Gross Domestic Product (GDP). GDP is a measure of the added market value of all the goods and services produced by a group over a specific measure of time. That group usually being a country (although GDP for regions is not uncommon) and the time being either a quarter or full year.

Here are the GDPs for three countries in 2020:

Table 12.1a GDP 2020

Ukraine	155,582,008,717
New Zealand	210,886,315,369
Cyprus	23,804,340,377

Clearly, in Table 12.1a, New Zealand is the GDP powerhouse with Cyprus grossly producing very little. However, this is an unfair comparison as Cyprus (approx. 1.2 million) has a much smaller population than both New Zealand (approx. 5.1 million) and very sizeable Ukraine (approx. 44.1 million). So, in order to compare these, we standardize them by population size so that we can get a sense of the productive by number of persons. This is a more comparable number although many differences remain in levels of technology, size of work force, types of industries, and economic development.

Doing so, as we see in Table 12.1b below, we find that Cyprus is actually doing middling, between a strong New Zealand and weaker Ukrainian economy.

Table 12.1b GDP per capita 2020

Ukraine	3,727
New Zealand	41,478
Cyprus	26,624

In this way, standardization can be useful in making better comparisons, in turn improving our ability to make informed comparisons.

Let's Get Normal: Standardization and Z-scores

Table 12.2 is one of many Z-distribution tables. There are different ones not because the values are different but there are several ways to think about the area under the curve.

If we review the properties associated with a Normal distribution, including the Standard Normal Z-distribution, as each of these properties will help us use the z-scores, often in concert.

- They are symmetric: the mean is the median is the mode.
- The total area under the curve is 1.
- The areas under the curve have fixed proportions.

So, for example, in Table 12.2, we will use a table that gives us the area between a z-score and the mean (the shaded area). Since the distribution is symmetrical and the area under the curve has fixed proportions, a positive z-score and a negative z-score will have the same area.

Table 12.2 A Z-Distribution Table

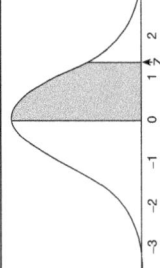

STANDARD NORMAL TABLE (Z)

Entries in the table give the area under the curve between the mean and z standard deviations above the mean. For example, for z = 1.25 the area under the curve between the mean (0) and z is 0.3944.

Z	0.00	0.01	0.02	0.03	0.04	0.05	0.06	0.07	0.08	0.09
0.0	0.0000	0.0040	0.0080	0.0120	0.0160	0.0190	0.0239	0.0279	0.0319	0.0359
0.1	0.0398	0.0438	0.0478	0.0517	0.0557	0.0596	0.0636	0.0675	0.0714	0.0753
0.2	0.0793	0.0832	0.0871	0.0910	0.0948	0.0987	0.1026	0.1064	0.1103	0.1141
0.3	0.1179	0.1217	0.1255	0.1293	0.1331	0.1368	0.1406	0.1443	0.1480	0.1517
0.4	0.1554	0.1591	0.1628	0.1664	0.1700	0.1736	0.1772	0.1808	0.1844	0.1879
0.5	0.1915	0.1950	0.1985	0.2019	0.2054	0.2088	0.2123	0.2157	0.2190	0.2224
0.6	0.2257	0.2291	0.2324	0.2357	0.2389	0.2422	0.2454	0.2486	0.2517	0.2549
0.7	0.2580	0.2611	0.2642	0.2673	0.2704	0.2734	0.2764	0.2794	0.2823	0.2852
0.8	0.2881	0.2910	0.2939	0.2969	0.2995	0.3023	0.3051	0.3078	0.3106	0.3133
0.9	0.3159	0.3186	0.3212	0.3238	0.3264	0.3289	0.3315	0.3340	0.3365	0.3389
1.0	0.3413	0.3438	0.3461	0.3485	0.3508	0.3513	0.3554	0.3577	0.3529	0.3621
1.1	0.3643	0.3665	0.3686	0.3708	0.3729	0.3749	0.3770	0.3790	0.3810	0.3830
1.2	0.3849	0.3869	0.3888	0.3907	0.3925	0.3944	0.3962	0.3980	0.3997	0.4015
1.3	0.4032	0.4049	0.4066	0.4082	0.4099	0.4115	0.4131	0.4147	0.4162	0.4177
1.4	0.4192	0.4207	0.4222	0.4236	0.4251	0.4265	0.4279	0.4292	0.4306	0.4319

z	0.00	0.01	0.02	0.03	0.04	0.05	0.06	0.07	0.08	0.09
1.5	0.4332	0.4345	0.4357	0.4370	0.4382	0.4394	0.4406	0.4418	0.4429	0.4441
1.6	0.4452	0.4463	0.4474	0.4484	0.4495	0.4505	0.4515	0.4525	0.4535	0.4545
1.7	0.4554	0.4564	0.4573	0.4582	0.4591	0.4599	0.4608	0.4616	0.4625	0.4633
1.8	0.4641	0.4649	0.4656	0.4664	0.4671	0.4678	0.4686	0.4693	0.4699	0.4706
1.9	0.4713	0.4719	0.4726	0.4732	0.4738	0.4744	0.4750	0.4756	0.4761	0.4767
2.0	0.4772	0.4778	0.4783	0.4788	0.4793	0.4798	0.4803	0.4808	0.4812	0.4817
2.1	0.4821	0.4826	0.4830	0.4834	0.4838	0.4842	0.4846	0.4850	0.4854	0.4857
2.2	0.4861	0.4864	0.4868	0.4871	0.4875	0.4878	0.4881	0.4884	0.4887	0.4890
2.3	0.4893	0.4896	0.4898	0.4901	0.4904	0.4906	0.4909	0.4911	0.4913	0.4916
2.4	0.4918	0.4920	0.4922	0.4925	0.4927	0.4929	0.4931	0.4932	0.4934	0.4936
2.5	0.4938	0.4940	0.4941	0.4943	0.4945	0.4946	0.4948	0.4949	0.4951	0.4952
2.6	0.4953	0.4955	0.4956	0.4957	0.4959	0.4960	0.4961	0.4962	0.4963	0.4964
2.7	0.4965	0.4966	0.4967	0.4968	0.4969	0.4970	0.4971	0.4972	0.4973	0.4974
2.8	0.4974	0.4975	0.4976	0.4977	0.4977	0.4978	0.4979	0.4979	0.4980	0.4981
2.9	0.4981	0.4982	0.4982	0.4983	0.4984	0.4984	0.4985	0.4985	0.4986	0.4986
3.0	0.4987	0.4987	0.4987	0.4988	0.4988	0.4989	0.4989	0.4989	0.4990	0.4990
3.1	0.4990	0.4991	0.4991	0.4991	0.4992	0.4992	0.4992	0.4992	0.4993	0.4993
3.2	0.4993	0.4993	0.4994	0.4994	0.4994	0.4994	0.4994	0.4995	0.4995	0.4995
3.3	0.4995	0.4995	0.4995	0.4996	0.4996	0.4996	0.4996	0.4996	0.4996	0.4997
3.4	0.4997	0.4997	0.4997	0.4997	0.4997	0.4997	0.4997	0.4997	0.4997	0.4998

As an introduction to using Table 12.2, let's use what we already know.

In a Z-distribution, z-scores convert observations into distances from the mean, measured in standard deviations. Thus, as before, any observation 1 standard deviation from the mean is 1 z-score. From Figure 12.2c above, in a Normal distribution, there should be 34% of the observations between the mean and 1 standard deviation. We can see the area under the curve for this in Figure 12.2a.

If we look at Table 12.2, we can see that going down the left column to 1.0 and over to the 0.00 column (1.0+0.00=1.00), we find 0.3413 or 34.13%. This is what we expected to find. 34% of the observations will fall between the mean and 1 z-score.

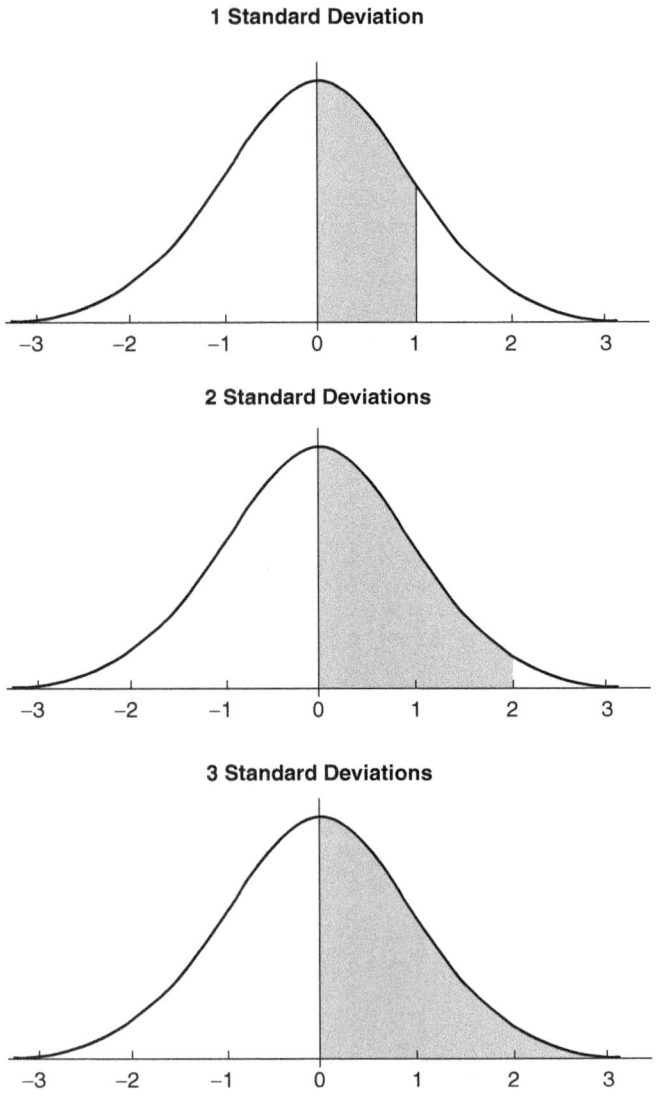

Figure 12.3 Standard Deviations from the Mean in Standard Normal

For 2 standard deviations, Figure 12.2c from above tells us there will be 47.7% of the observations. As above, 2 standardized standard deviation is 2 z-scores. In Table 12.2, we can see that going down the left column to 2.0 and over to the 0.00 column (2.0+0.00=2.00), we find 0.4772 or 47.72%.

You can try 3 standard deviations on your own.

Fine. This is easy for observations that fall exactly on 1 or 2 or 3 standard deviations. But most don't, so then what?

This is the sweet magic of z-scores. Z-scores, using the formula above, one can convert *any* observation into distances from the mean, measured in standard deviations.

This means:

- If your observation has a z-score of 1, it is 1 standard deviation above the mean.
- If your observation has a z-score of 1.7, it is 1.7 standard deviations above the mean.
- If your observation has a z-score of −2.1, it is 2.1 standard deviations below the mean.
- … *[please continue as long as you like]*.

We use the formula above to convert observations into z-scores which tell you where your observation is on this Standard Normal curve – called the Z-distribution. And using the properties of the Normal curve, we can know quite a lot about that observation and its distance from the mean.

Like what exactly?

Using Z-scores

As mentioned above, all this standardizing allows us to do two very useful things:

1. *Compare different interval-level variables with one another.* If we can standardize variables, they become directly comparable. This can be, for example, quite useful when you have different measures for the same concept.
2. *Determine the expected probability of different outcomes.* Recall, the properties of the Normal distribution allowed us to determine the percentage of observations that fall to the right of the mean, or outside 2 standard deviations, or between the mean and one standard deviation. Similarly, using the area under the curve as the expected probability, we can also determine the probability of various outcomes – or even the likelihood of the occurrence of a single event.

Let's take a look at each.

Comparing Interval-level Variables

We are interested in studying corruption. You identify two measures you are interested in using. One is the Corruptions Perceptions Index (CPI) from Transparency International and the other is the Political Corruption Index (PCI) from V-Democracy. We might expect that measurements of corruption would be pretty consistent with one another. However, each have their own methodologies which might reveal some interesting differences.

The CPI is measured on a 0 to 100 scale in which 0 is complete corruption and 100 is no corruption. The PCI, however, is measured on a 0 to 1 scale in which 0 is no corruption and 1 is complete corruption. Note: to make these conceptually comparable, I reverse coded the CPI so that 0 is no corruption and 100 is complete corruption because, sorry Transparency International, that's more intuitive.

Using data on 63 countries, we can see that these measures of corruption are very similar for our sample. In Figure 12.4, we see the correlation of the CPI and PCI. Unsurprisingly, these have a very high correlation of r = 0.896.

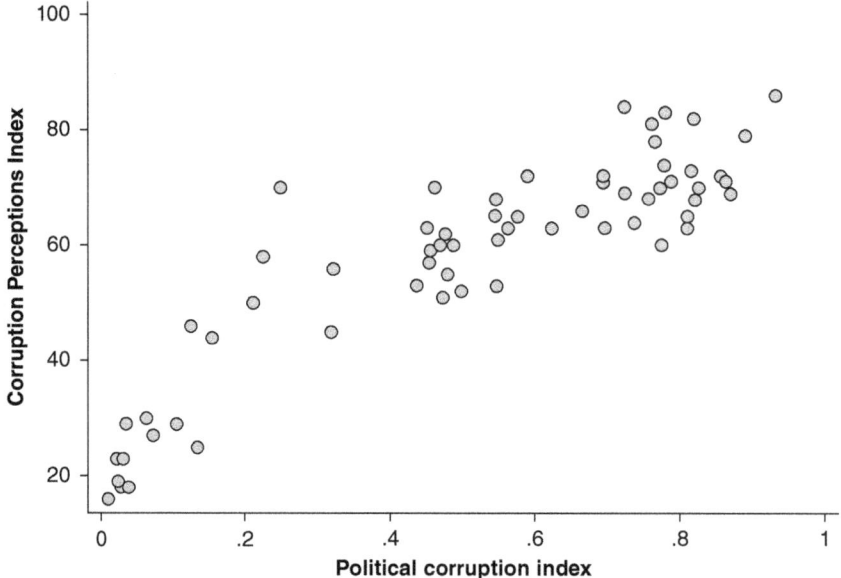

Figure 12.4 Corruptions Perception Index and Political Corruption Index

We also find that:

- CPI: mean: 57.9 with a standard deviation of 18.5
- PCI: mean: 0.512 with a standard deviation of 0.286.

We are curious how each measure compares with each other. As each measure has their own methodology, how does this affect the scoring of countries?

Using z-scores, we can standardize both and compare observations directly. We would expect countries (our observations) to fall in more or less the same location on the Standard Normal distribution when the measures are capturing the same thing. And we would expect for the countries to differ when these measures are not capturing the same thing.

Chosen more or less randomly, let's look at two countries, Argentina and Turkey.

The CPI for Argentina is 61 and the PCI is 0.549. If we standardize these, we can compare where they fall on the Normal distribution to see whether they are similar or not.

$$z_{ARG} = \frac{(x_i - \bar{x})}{s}$$

Corruptions Perceptions Index Z-score

$$z_{CPI} = \frac{(61 - 57.9)}{18.5}$$

$$Z_{CPI} = 0.17$$

Political Corruption Index Z-score

$$z_{PCI} = \frac{(0.549 - 0.512)}{0.286}$$

$$Z_{PCI} = 0.13$$

If we standardize the value for Argentina's CPI score, we get a z-score of 0.17. If we standardize the value for Argentina's PCI score, we get a z-score of 0.13. The difference is 4/100ths. In fact, if we computed the areas under the curve, we can see that 0.13 (down the left column to 0.1 and over to 0.03 = 0.13), 5.17% of the observations fall between the mean and 0.13 z-score. For 0.17, (down the left column to 0.1 and over to 0.07 = 0.17), 6.75% of the observations fall between the mean and 0.17 z-score. These are very close to one another. For Argentina, the z-scores tell us that the CPI and PCI represent very similar measures.

The CPI for Turkey is 60 and the PCI is 0.776. Let's calculate their z-scores for each.

$$z_{TUR} = \frac{(x_i - \bar{x})}{s}$$

Corruptions Perceptions Index Z-score

$$z_{CPI} = \frac{(60 - 57.9)}{18.5}$$

$$Z_{CPI} = 0.11$$

Political Corruption Index Z-score

$$z_{PCI} = \frac{(0.776 - 0.512)}{0.286}$$

$$Z_{PCI} = 0.92$$

Unlike the CPI and PCI for Argentina, Turkey's scores are quite different. The standardized z-score for Turkey's CPI score is 0.11, while the standardized z-score for its PCI score is 0.92. Computing the areas under the curve, we can see that 0.11 (down the left column to 0.1 and over to 0.01 = 0.11), 4.38% of the observations fall between the mean and 0.11 z-score. For 0.92 (down the left column to 0.9 and over to 0.02 = 0.92), 32.12% of the observations fall between the mean and 0.92 z-score. These are considerably different locations on the Z-Distribution.

Substantively, these standardized z-scores demonstrate that Turkey's CPI of 60 and PCI of 0.776 represent very different locations on their respective distributions. In other words, the CPI and PCI rate Turkey quite differently. This difference is worth understanding so that the nature of corruption, as captured by the PCI and CPI, offers evidence of the difference in what is being measured.

Determine the Expected Probability of Different Outcomes

Above we have used areas under the curve as a means to compare between z-scores. That was not the best use of that area. Let's re-utilize the area under the curve as a window into expected probabilities.

Recall from above that Argentina has a CPI score of 0.17 which means 6.75% of the observations fall between the mean and 0.17 z-score. It also means that Argentina's CPI score is higher than 56.75% of the observations.

How did I get 56.75%? A 0.17 z-score represent 6.75% above the mean and the full other side of the mean is 50%, thus, 50%+6.75%=56.75%. See Figure 12.5a.

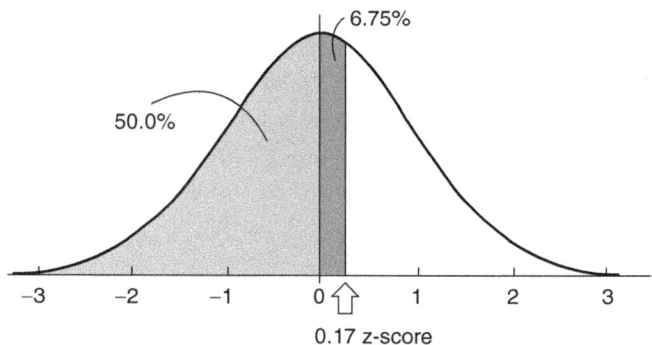

Figure 12.5a Expected Probabilities: Area Under the Curve

Try this.

How many observations are higher than Argentina's? 100% − 56.75% = 43.25%. Or even, 50% − 6.75% = 43.25% because we know everything below − to the left of − the mean is 50%. Both of these calculations provide us the remaining part of the curve above a 0.17 z-score (i.e., the remaining white area under the curve in Figure 12.5a).

Using the same approach, this also means that if we wanted to know the percentage of observations less than Turkey's PCI of 0.92 z-score, we would add 32.12% to 50% = 82.12% (see Figure 12.5b). What percentage of the observations are higher than Turkey's score? 100% = 82.12% = 17.88% (i.e., again, the remaining white area under the curve in Figure 12.5b).

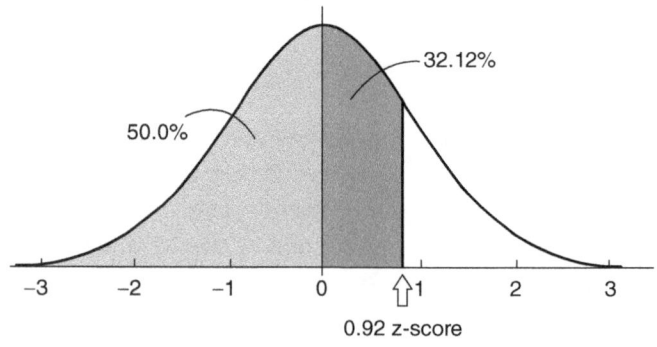

Figure 12.5b Expected Probabilities: Area Under the Curve

How does this help us understand expected probabilities?

In the example of Turkey, we could say that the probability of randomly choosing a country with a PCI score higher than Turkey's score is 17.88%. Similarly, the probability of randomly choosing a country with a CPI score lower than Argentina is 56.75%. That is, we are starting to understand how the Z-distribution, as a specific Standard Normal curve, helps us anticipate or expect where observations will fall. And how likely those observations will be.

This can be used in more complex ways.

Between standard deviations – on either side of the mean – we have some expectations about the likelihood of observations: namely, 68% of the observations will fall between −1 and 1 standard deviation, 95% will fall between −2 and 2 standard deviations, 99.7% will fall between −3 and 3 standard deviations.

As we have just seen above, there is no reason we need to be constrained to these boundaries.

In examining different measures of corruption above, we found the distance between the mean and 0.13 z-score, 0.17 z-score, 0.11 z-score, and 0.92 z-score as well as the distance above 0.17 z-score and 0.92 z-score just by doing some addition and subtraction.

In this way, this simple standardizing technique of converting interval-level variables into z-scores gives us enormous power over expected probabilities.

$$z = \frac{(x_i - \bar{x})}{s}$$

Let's improve on our use of the data from our 'rule of thumb' 68-95-99.7% example above. In a random sample of 48 countries, national-level income inequality has a mean of 37.8 and a standard deviation of 8.0.

What is the probability of randomly selecting (or observing) a country with income inequality between a Gini Index of 27.5 and the mean (37.8)?

First, we standardize 27.5 to a z-score.

$$z_{27.5} = \frac{(27.5 - 37.8)}{8.0}$$

$$z_{27.5} = -1.29$$

Second, from Table 12.2, we know that the z-scores represent the area between a z-score and the mean even if that z-score is negative as the curve is symmetrical. So, −1.29 z-score is associated with 0.4015 (see Figure 12.5c). Therefore, the probability of randomly selecting (or observing) a country with a Gini Index of income inequality between 27.5 and the mean of 37.8 is 40.15%.

What is the probability of randomly selecting (or observing) a country with income inequality less than a Gini Index of 35?

$$z_{35} = \frac{(35 - 37.8)}{8.0}$$

$$z_{35} = -0.35$$

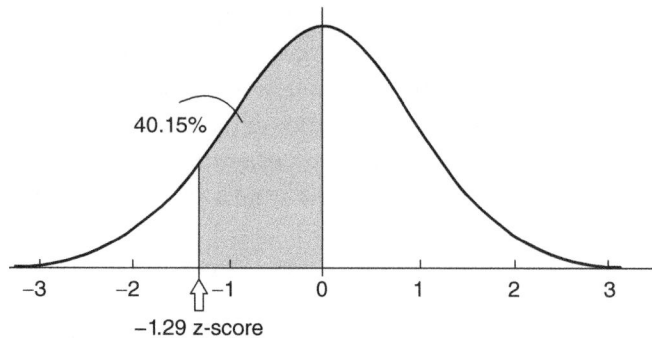

Figure 12.5c Expected Probabilities: Area Under the Curve

From Table 12.2, −0.35 z-score is associated with 0.1368. This means that 13.68% of observations fall between −0.35 z-score and the mean (see Figure 12.5d). But the question is about less than a Gini Index of 35 (z-score −0.35). As the percent of observations that fall to the left of the mean is 50% and we know that between −0.35 z-score is 13.68% of the observations, those that fall below −0.35 z-score is 50% − 13.68% = 36.32%. Thus, the probability of randomly selecting (or observing) a country with income inequality less than a Gini Index of 35 is 36.32%.

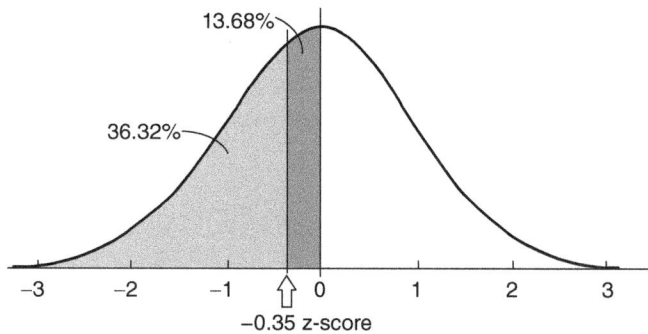

Figure 12.5d Expected Probabilities: Area Under the Curve

What is the probability of randomly selecting (or observing) a country with income inequality more than 30?

$$z_{30} = \frac{(30 - 37.8)}{8.0}$$

$$z_{30} = -0.98$$

From Table 12.2, −0.98 z-score is associated with 0.3365. So, randomly observing a country with income inequality higher than a Gini Index of 30 is the distance from 30 to the mean plus the while right side of the curve, which we know is 50 (see Figure 12.5e).

Therefore, there is a 50%+33.65%=83.65% probability of randomly selecting (or observing) a country with a Gini Index of income inequality more than 30.

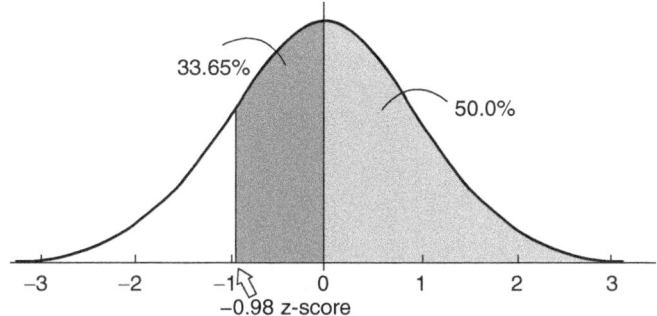

Figure 12.5e Expected Probabilities: Area Under the Curve

What is the probability of randomly selecting (or observing) a country with a Gini Index of income inequality between 40 and 45?

$$z = \frac{(x_i - \bar{x})}{s}$$

$$z_{40} = \frac{(40 - 37.8)}{8.0} \qquad z_{45} = \frac{(45 - 37.8)}{8.0}$$

$$z_{40} = 0.28 \qquad z_{45} = 0.90$$

This is a bit tricker. But, to find the area between these two, we first take the area under the curve of the larger z-score, 0.90 z-score, and subtract from it the area under the curve for the smaller z-score – 0.28 z-score – and the mean (see Figure 12.5f). Thus, 31.59% – 11.03% = 20.56%. The probability of randomly selecting (or observing) a country with a Gini Index of income inequality between 40 and 45 is 20.56%.

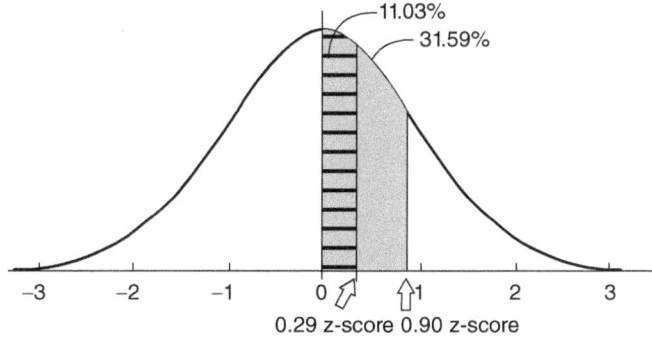

Figure 12.5f Expected Probabilities: Area Under the Curve

What is the probability of randomly selecting (or observing) a country with income inequality between 20 and 35? We already know the z-score for 35 from above, 35 has a −0.35 z-score – associated with 0.1368.

And, based on the above calculation, 20 has a z-score of −2.23 associated with 0.4871.

$$z_{20} = \frac{(20 - 37.8)}{8.0}$$

$$z_{20} = -2.23$$

Like the previous example, to find the area between these two, we first take the areas under the curve of the (absolute) larger z-score, −2.23 z-score, and subtract from it, the area under the curve of the (absolute) smaller z-score − −0.35 z-score. Thus: 48.71% − 13.68% = 35.03% (see Figure 12.5g). Therefore, the probability of randomly selecting (or observing) a country with a Gini Index of income inequality between 20 and 35 is 35.03%.

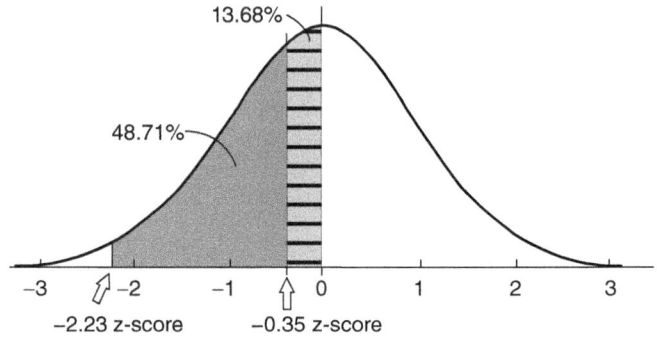

Figure 12.5g Expected Probabilities: Area Under the Curve

Finally, what is the probability of randomly selecting (or observing) a country with income inequality between 25 and 40? We know from above that the z-score for 40 is 0.28 z-score associated with 0.1103 area under the curve.

$$z_{25} = \frac{(25 - 37.8)}{8.0}$$

$$z_{25} = -1.60$$

The z-score for 25 is −1.60 z-score associated with 0.4452 area under the curve. The area between them, on opposite sides of the mean is simply to add them together: 11.03% + 44.52% = 55.55% (see Figure 12.5h). Therefore, the probability of randomly selecting (or observing) a country with a Gini Index of income inequality between 25 and 40 is 55.55%.

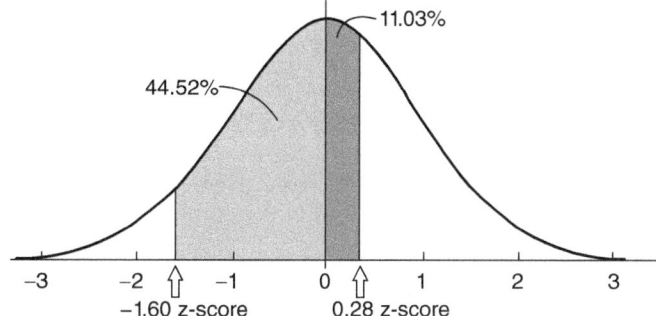

Figure 12.5h Expected Probabilities: Area Under the Curve

These exercises demonstrate how expected probabilities are represented by the area under the curve. Expected probabilities allow us to anticipate how likely outcomes are.

You may have to find it between the mean and a positive z-score, all below a positive z-score, all above a positive z-score, between the mean and a negative z-score, all below a negative z-score, all above a negative z-score, between two positive z-scores, between two negative z-scores, and between a negative z-score and a positive z-score.

And that's ok, because you just did.

But why?

Why do we want a whole chapter on Normal distributions, the Central Limit Theorem, and z-scores?

We don't just want it, we need it.

Remember when we talked about alphas (α) and levels of confidence? That $\alpha=0.05$ is 95% confidence level; $\alpha=0.01$ is 99% confidence level; and $\alpha=0.001$ is 99.9% confidence level. And remember when we talked about critical values and rejection regions as part of the process of hypothesis testing? Bringing these concepts together, we can exploit the Z-distribution to conduct a wide range of tests of statistical significance for interval-level variables as estimates of population parameters.

That is, we can reverse engineer this whole chapter to serve as the basis for statistical significance in a wide range of tests.

Say what?

As a standardized distribution curve for all interval-level variables, the Z-distribution tells us how likely different outcomes are expected to occur. If we consider the three levels of confidence that are most common – 95%, 99%, and 99.9% – we can find a standard score – a z-score – that represents each of these for all interval-level variables (because, *again* again, of the standardization to a Z-distribution).

In other words:

- If we want to be 95% confident ($\alpha=0.05$) in our results, we can find the z-score that is associated with 95% of expected outcomes, outside of which would be equal to or above 95% confidence.

- If we want to be 99% confident ($\alpha=0.01$) in our results, we can find the z-score that is associated with 99% of expected outcomes, outside of which would be equal to or above 99% confidence.
- And, of course, if we want to be 99.9% confident ($\alpha=0.001$) in our results, we can find the z-score that is associated with 99.9% of expected outcomes, outside of which would be equal to or above 99.9% confidence.

How do we do this?

Well, you are now very familiar with the three properties of the standardized Z-distribution that make it very useful and easy to use. Thinking in reverse of what we did above, simply imagine that we want to find the z-score that includes 95% of the expected outcomes that centre on the mean. The symmetry and fixed proportions of the Z-distribution tells us that the z-score will be the positive and negative of the same number.

Me: Yes, you in the back.

You: The 68-95-99.7% Rule says that 95% of the observations fall between 2 standard deviations which, in z-scores, is between –2 z-score and 2 z-score.

Me: I'll need you to be a bit more precise.

You: [*slowly closing flip phone*] How precise?

Me: More. Precise.

Remember that the 68-95-99.7% Rule is more like a rule of thumb or a party trick. It is a rough guide and can impress the uninitiated. However, that is no longer you.

If we want to know at what point 95% of outcomes are expected to fall, we need to find the z-score associated with 47.5% [95%/2] on either side of the mean. Looking at Table 12.2, 0.4750 is associated with the 1.96 z-score. Thus, 95% of expected outcomes will fall between –1.96 and 1.96 z-scores. Outside of this z-score would be exceptional to 95% confidence. This exceptional and remaining 5% is split between the two tails with 2.5% (0.0250) in each tail (see Figure 12.6a).

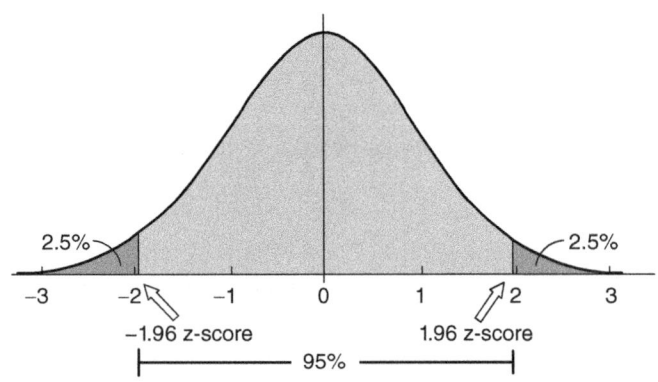

Figure 12.6a The Z-score of 95% Confidence Level

For 99% confidence, we would need to find the z-score associated with 49.5% [99%/2] on either side of the mean. Looking at Table 12.2, 0.4949 is associated with 2.57 z-score and 0.4951 is associated with 2.58. Therefore, we can assume that 0.4950 is associated with a 2.575 z-score. Thus, 99% of expected outcomes will fall between −2.575 and 2.575 z-scores. Outside of this z-score would be exceptional to 99% confidence. With the exceptional 1% remaining, there is 0.5% (0.005) in each tail (see Figure 12.6b).

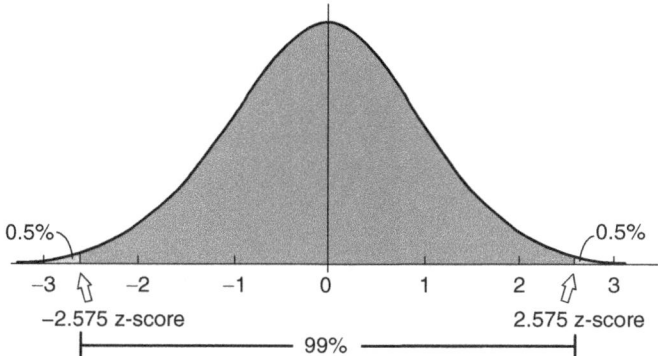

Figure 12.6b The Z-score of 99% Confidence Level

For 99.9% confidence, we would need to find the z-score associated with 49.95% [99.9%/2] on either side of the mean. Looking at Table 12.2, 0.4995 is associated with every z-score between 3.27 and 3.32. Therefore, we can assume that a z-score of 3.29 something is sufficiently close (turns out it is 3.291). Outside of this z-score would be exceptional to 99.9% confidence. With the exceptional 0.1% remaining, there is 0.05% (0.0005) in each tail (see Figure 12.6c).

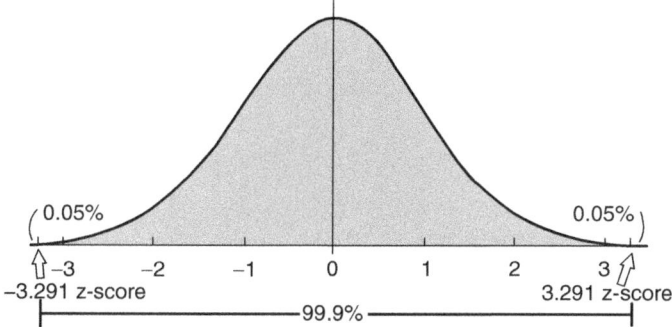

Figure 12.6c The Z-score of 99.9% Confidence Level

Therefore, in this way, we now know the critical values defining the rejections regions for 3 common levels of confidence – 95%, 99%, and 99.9% – for all interval-level variables.

- The 1.96 z-score creates a critical value for 95% confidence
- The 2.575 z-score creates a critical value for 99% confidence
- The 3.291 z-score creates a critical value for 99.9% confidence.

And this, like the χ^2 critical values, makes sense. The more confident we want to be in our statistical significance, the greater the critical value. Outside of which is the rejection region, in which we can reject the null hypothesis of no relation.

A Final Word on Standard Distributions and Statistical Significance

Perhaps I could have just told you these values and moved on to the next chapter. It would have certainly been easier.

First of all, no. That wouldn't have been any fun as we wouldn't have learned about measures of corruption or the probability of finding countries with various levels of income inequality.

Second, and more importantly, I want to lift the hood and let you see the running motor of statistics. It is not scary or even tremendously complicated. That isn't to say it is easy but it is not logically complicated. Once you can see how it fits together, it makes sense. That is, passing from sampling distributions, to Normal distributions, to the Central Limit Theorem, to the Standard Normal distribution or Z-distribution, to z-scores, and finally to expected probabilities makes sense. It is not dark magic, secret recipes, or shadowy creatures lurking in a mist. Each step progresses from the previous in order that we can exploit their utility to advance our ability to make inferential claims of statistical significance.

And that is what this is about. The fundament of statistical significance, the basis for Inferential Statistics, rests heavily on these various aspects of probability. We take what we know and try to make reasonable guesses about something we do not know or cannot examine directly. We use the characteristics of large and random samples, exploit the known behaviours of probability, and employ the assumptions of the Central Limit Theorem. Drawn together, this allows us to make probabilistic claims about population parameters from our sample estimates with varying levels of confidence.

This is Inferential Statistics.

End of Chapter Summary

- Distributions of outcomes for interval-level variables can very often be summarized by a bell-shaped curve or density function. These curves constitute a family of curves known collectively as Normal distributions.
- For inferential statistics, we use a special form of a Normal distribution called Standard Normal or Z-distribution.
- The Normal distribution has three useful properties: They are symmetric; the total area under the curve is 1; and has fixed proportions.
- 68-95-99.7% Rule is a rough description of the distribution of observations in a Normal curve.

- Even if the population distribution is not distributed normally, the Central Limit Theorem states that as sample size increases, the sampling distribution of sample means approaches Normal with a mean the same as the mean of the population and a standard deviation equal to the standard deviation of the population divided by the square root of the sample size.
- Z-scores are the distances standardized to standard deviations between observations and the mean.
- We can use z-scores in two ways. One, to compare different interval-level variables with one another and two, determine the expected probability of different outcomes.
- In probability density functions, like the Z-distribution, the area under the curve describes the expected probability of outcomes.
- The 1.96 z-score creates a critical value for 95% confidence; the 2.575 z-score creates a critical value for 99% confidence; and the 3.2951 z-score creates a critical value for 99.9% confidence.
- We use the characteristics of large and random samples, exploit the known behaviours of probability, and make the assumptions of the Central Limit Theorem to make probabilistic claims about our sample estimates of population parameters with varying levels of confidence.

Glossary

- **Sampling distributions** are a summary of the probabilities of outcomes for random variables. These are sometimes more formally called probability density functions.
- For **random variables**, outcomes can be infinite or a very high number of outcomes.
- The **Normal distribution** is a camel-humped shaped probability density function in which the tails asymptotically approach zero. Its specific shape is defined by a mean and standard deviation.
- The **Central Limit Theorem** states that if we were to take an infinite number of samples of size n from a population of N subjects, the means of these samples would be normally distributed.
- The **standard error** of the sampling distribution is the measure of the distribution of means and can be estimated by the standard deviation of the population divided by the square root of n, the number of observations in the sample.
- The **Z-distribution** is a standardized Normal distribution for interval-level variables in which the mean is zero and the units of dispersion are standardized standard deviations called z-scores.
- **Z-scores** represent how many standard deviations an observation falls from the standardized mean in a Z-distribution, which is zero.
- **Standardization** is the process of making different measures comparable by establishing a similar metric.

Questions

1. Below are five more countries and their measures of corruption. Standardize each (to z-scores) and compare each country's two different measures of corruption. Which countries have similar scores? Which have dissimilar ones? Why do you think the latter differences exist (or, more broadly, do you see a pattern between the countries in which the scores are similar and dissimilar)?

Table 12.3 Corruption Indices

Country	Corruptions Perception Index	Political Corruption Index
France	30	0.063
Belarus	56	0.321
Nigeria	73	0.815
United Kingdom	18	0.039
United States	25	0.135

2. The variable 'Conflict Intensity' from the Quality of Government dataset. It ranges from 1 – no conflict – to 10 – widespread violent conflict and is approximately Normally distributed with a mean of 5.4 and a standard deviation of 2.1 (n = 54). Using what we know about the Z-distribution, what are the probabilities of randomly observing a country with conflict intensity less than 5.4? Greater than 7? Less than 5? Between 5.4 and 6? Between 4 and 7?
3. The variable 'Ethnic Fragmentation' – also from the Quality of Government dataset – ranges from 0 in which a country is perfectly homogeneous to 1 in which a country is highly fragmented. It is Normally distributed with a mean of 0.460 and a standard deviation of 0.254 (n = 61). Using what we know about the Z-distribution, what are the probabilities of randomly observing a country with ethnic fragmentation greater than 0.460? Less than 0.400? Greater than 0.500? Between 0.460 and 0.750? Between 0.400 and 0.750?
4. We are somewhat fortunate in that, for the most part, observations of events or things in which we are interested tend to aggregate into a Normal or quasi-Normal distribution. This is not always true, as we talked about before, as income, for example, tends to be positively skewed (more at the bottom, less at the top). Explain again how the Central Limit Theorem resolves this.
5. Can you articulate how using a Z-distribution and z-scores standardize variables so that they can be directly compared?
6. Once again, as in the discussion of probability in the previous chapter, we are confronted with the strong application of assumptions. Both the Central Limit Theorem and Normal distribution, for example, make a number of strong assumptions. Why are assumptions necessary? It also feels like we don't give them a lot of attention. Do you see this as a problem and if so, why?

Signposts to the Accompanying Digital Resources

Data used in this chapter

- **Political Corruption Index:** The corruption index includes measures of six distinct types of corruption that cover both different areas and levels of the polity realm, distinguishing between executive, legislative, and judicial corruption. Varieties of Democracy (V-DEM).
- **Corruption Perception Index:** The CPI focuses on corruption in the public sector and defines corruption as the abuse of public office for private gain. The surveys used in compiling the CPI tend to ask questions in line with the misuse of public power for private benefit, with a focus, for example, on bribe-taking by public officials in public procurement. Varieties of Democracy (V-DEM).
    - Coppedge, Michael, John Gerring, Staffan I. Lindberg, Svend-Erik Skaaning, Jan Teorell, with David Altman, Michael Bernhard, M. Steven Fish, Adam Glynn, Allen Hicken, Carl Henrik Knutsen, Kelly McMann, Pamela Paxton, Daniel Pemstein, Jeffrey Staton, Brigitte Zimmerman, Frida Andersson, Valeriya Mechkova, and Farhad Miri. 2016. 'V-Dem Codebook v6.' Varieties of Democracy (V-Dem) Project. www.v-dem.net/en/data/data/
- **GDP (current US$):** NY.GDP.MKTP.CD. World Bank.
- **Population, total:** SP.POP.TOTL. World Bank.
- **GDP per capita (current US$):** NY.GDP.PCAP.PP.CD. World Bank.
    - World Bank national accounts data, and OECD National Accounts data files. https://data.worldbank.org/
- **Ethnic Fractionalization:** This variable reflects the probability that two randomly selected people from a given country will belong to different groups. 0–1: 0 (perfectly homogeneous) to 1 (highly fragmented). Quality of Governance.
- **Conflict Intensity:** How serious are social, ethnic, and religious conflicts? 1–10. 1. There are no violent incidents based on social, ethnic, or religious differences. … 10. There is civil war or a widespread violent conflict based on social, ethnic, or religious differences. Quality of Governance.
    - Teorell, Jan, Aksel Sundström, Sören Holmberg, Bo Rothstein, Natalia Alvarado Pachon, and Cem Mert Dalli. 2021. The Quality of Government Standard Dataset, version Jan21. University of Gothenburg: The Quality of Government Institute, www.qog.pol.gu.se

13

INFERENCE FOR INTERVAL-LEVEL VARIABLES

> **LEARNING OUTCOMES**
>
> In this chapter, you will be able to
>
> - Understand the two ways of making inferences about population parameters: point estimation and hypothesis testing.
> - Calculate and use margins of errors to link point estimates from a sample to population parameters.
> - Generate and interpret confidence intervals.
> - Use Student's t for point estimates, including a difference of means test.
> - Be able to identify and use varying estimates of statistical significance for interval-level variables.

Introduction

In the previous chapter, we used the probability attributes of Normal distributions – specifically the Standard Normal Z-distribution – and the theoretical justification of the Central Limit Theorem to advance our claims of inference. Stated more plainly, probability and the Central Limit Theorem allow us to use estimates from good, random samples to get a good sense of what the population parameter might be. Small differences that we sometimes find between samples – whether samples from the same population or over time – are not necessarily evidence of change or substantial difference but rather more often a function of the sampling procedure itself.

Thus, different samples – good, random samples – and the correct statistical techniques can lead us to very similar estimates of the population parameter despite any apparent differences.

We ultimately make inferences about population parameters in two ways:

- **(Point) Estimation:** Estimate the population value using information from sample.
- **Hypothesis Testing:** Test hypothesis about value of parameters.

We can use the same properties and justifications (or assumptions) from above to make point estimates. Essentially, we use our sample to approximate what the population parameter may be and build an interval around that point. This interval gives a range of plausible values of varying level of probability. And, of course, we report our level of confidence in the result.

And, we have done hypothesis testing before with χ^2 and will update this for interval-level variables.

Point Estimates, Margins of Error, and Confidence Intervals

A **point estimate** is simply our best guess of the population parameter based on our sample.

What can we guess? Well, just about anything. Nearly any population parameter can be estimated from sample data; for example, the mean, a standard deviation, a correlation coefficient, and as we will see in the next section, regression coefficients. In other words, the logic of inference for point estimates extends to most parameters. However, at the outset, our discussion will focus on the mean in that the sample mean is a point estimate of the population mean.

A **confidence interval** is a range of values around a point estimate that contributes to the probability that the interval contains the population parameter between the upper and lower limits of the interval. Or simply, confidence intervals tell us a range in which we can expect to find the population parameter, with some associated level of confidence.

Confidence intervals have two parts: the sample statistic (or point estimate) and an interval called the margin of error. The margin of error is the interval centred on the sample statistic (or point estimate). It is a function of both a level of confidence and the variation of the sampling distribution of the estimate. Recall that the measure of dispersion that we use for sampling distributions is the **standard error**. Therefore, the margin of error is simply the standard error of the estimate.

Together, a confidence interval is formed as 'estimate +/− margin of error' and looks like this:

$$C.I. = Sample\ Statistic \pm (z - score_{confidence\ level})\ (s.e.)$$

$$\text{in which s.e.} = \frac{s_x}{\sqrt{n}}$$

In which s_x is the sample standard deviation and n is the number of observations.

Wait a minute! Z-scores?!?

Yeah, can you believe that? Z-scores will determine the level of confidence. In doing so, they set the critical value that defines the rejection region.

Recall from the previous chapter that we discovered that:

- The 1.96 z-score creates a critical value for 95% confidence.
- The 2.575 z-score creates a critical value for 99% confidence.
- The 3.291 z-score creates a critical value for 99.9% confidence.

We can use each of these z-scores to plug into the formula for confidence intervals to produce an interval – or margin of error – around our sample statistic or point estimation for differing levels of confidence.

$C.I._{95\%}$ = Sample Statistic ± (1.96) (s.e.)

$C.I._{99\%}$ = Sample Statistic ± (2.575) (s.e.)

$C.I._{99.9\%}$ = Sample Statistic ± (3.291) (s.e.)

Example: Confidence Intervals

Let's try to estimate a population mean (μ) using the confidence interval approach. In the *Quality of Governance* dataset, we can find the variable 'Ethnic Fractionalization'. Ethnic Fractionalization ranges from zero (0) – meaning it is perfectly unlikely to randomly select two people from the same country that are from different ethnic groups – to one (1) in which two randomly selected people in the same country are from different ethnic groups. In the case of 0, the country is completely homogenous. In the case of 1, the country is ethnically diverse.

'Ethnic Fractionalization' has 61 observations with a (sample) mean of 0.46 and a (sample) standard deviation of 0.25. It ranges from 0.004 to 0.930. In our sample, based on 61 observations, the mean level of ethnic fractionalization is 0.46. This is our best guess of the actual population parameter although the population mean (μ) is unlikely to be exactly 0.46. But it is likely to be nearby.

Let's produce a confidence interval of 95% confidence.

$C.I._{95\%}$ = Sample Statistic ± (1.96) (s.e.)

in which s.e. = $\dfrac{s_x}{\sqrt{n}}$

Therefore, using the data available from our sample:

$C.I._{95\%} = 0.46 \pm (1.96)\left(\dfrac{0.25}{\sqrt{61}}\right)$

$C.I._{95\%}$ = 0.46 ± (1.96) (0.032)

$C.I._{95\%}$ = 0.46 ± (0.063)

$C.I._{95\%}$ = 0.397 and 0.523

What is the margin of error in this calculation? It is 0.063. 0.063 creates the intervals on either side of our sample statistic. We interpret the result as, 'There is a 95% chance that the confidence interval 0.397 and 0.523 contains the true population mean.'

Wait, that doesn't sound right. It sounds like a graduate student in statistics trying to put you down when you say that you are taking a statistics course in Political Science.

Although it is tempting and seemingly more intuitive to interpret a 95% confidence interval as: 'We are 95% confident that the unknown population parameter lies within our intervals around our estimate', that is not correct as it is not technically what a confidence interval produces. The (full) correct interpretation is: 'In repeated samples of the same size from our population, for each sample, we estimate the upper and lower bounds of the confidence interval for that probability. About 95% of these confidence intervals would contain the true probability of the population parameter.'

So, while we really want to say the other one, you can in fact correctly say, 'There is a 95% chance that *the confidence interval* you calculated contains the true population parameter.' This is the best of both worlds as it is both easy to remember and correct.

> ### 95% CONFIDENCE INTERVAL IN THE WILD
>
> 'Unemployment is rising – or is that statistical noise?' – Ben Goldacre in The Guardian; Friday 19 August 2011. Link: www.theguardian.com/commentisfree/2011/aug/19/bad-science-unemployment-statistical-noise
>
> And kudos to Ben for this interpretation: 'What does this mean? Strictly (it still makes my head hurt), this means that if you repeatedly took samples of 100, then on 95% of those attempts, the true proportion in the jar would lie somewhere between the upper and lower limits of the 95% confidence intervals of your samples. That's all we can say.'
>
> And, yes, I know the article is old, but it is a very clear explanation. Earth, Wind and Fire's 'September' is also 'old' (it was released in 1978). But I have yet to encounter anyone who won't get up and shake it when this song comes on. Try it.

Changing Intervals

All of this is very cool, but can we improve our confidence interval? For example, what if our sample size was larger?

Before we even put numbers into the calculation, what do you think? If we have a larger sample, is our sample statistic likely to be more representative of the population or less representative of the population (think: salsa)?

Let's find out.

Imagine that the descriptive statistics of Ethnic Fractionalization remain the same except that our sample size is increased to 100. To be clear, these data do not exist in the Quality of Governance dataset as this is an exercise to demonstrate the impact of a larger sample size on the confidence interval.

Therefore:

$$C.I._{95\%} = 0.46 \pm (1.96)\left(\frac{0.25}{\sqrt{100}}\right)$$

$C.I._{95\%} = 0.46 \pm (1.96)(0.025)$

$C.I._{95\%} = 0.46 \pm (0.049)$

$C.I._{95\%} = 0.435$ and 0.509

What does a larger sample size do to our estimate of the population mean of Ethnic Fractionalization (μ)?

We find that a larger sample size narrows the confidence interval *ceteris paribus* (Latin: 'all things being equal'). That is, 'There is a 95% chance that the confidence interval 0.435 and 0.509 contains the true population mean.' Thus, a larger sample size means you can be more certain about your estimate of mean. That is both intuitive and good news!

What else might have an effect on our estimates of population parameters using confidence intervals? What if the standard deviation was smaller or larger? Again, the data in the Quality of Governance dataset cannot be changed for our convenience; however, for this example, we can propose a thought experiment in which the standard deviation is different in order to develop a sense of how confidence intervals function. Therefore, what if Ethnic Fractionalization has a smaller standard deviation of 0.15?

Now, knowing what you already know from the first half of this book, a smaller measure of dispersion suggests that the measure of central tendency is a better summary of the variable (see Chapter 6). Therefore, we would then expect that our sample statistic as an estimate of the population parameter would be better.

Let's find out.

$$C.I._{95\%} = 0.46 \pm (1.96)\left(\frac{0.15}{\sqrt{61}}\right)$$

$C.I._{95\%} = 0.46 \pm (1.96)(0.019)$

$C.I._{95\%} = 0.46 \pm (0.038)$

$C.I._{95\%} = 0.422$ and 0.498

I don't mean to be rude but that is a vast improvement over sample size (as well as our original confidence interval). Again, the smaller measure of dispersion confers more support for the measure of central tendency – in this case, how good a summary the sample mean is – in turn doing a great deal of work in improving our guestimation of the population mean of Ethnic Fractionalization (μ).

Finally, what if we want to increase our level of confidence in our estimation of the population parameter (μ)?

To find out, we can raise the confidence interval, in this case, from 95% confidence to 99% confidence. Therefore,

$$C.I._{99\%} = 0.46 \pm (2.575)\left(\frac{0.25}{\sqrt{61}}\right)$$

$C.I._{99\%} = 0.46 \pm (2.575)(0.032)$

$C.I._{99\%} = 0.46 \pm (0.082)$

$C.I._{99\%} = 0.378$ and 0.542

First of all, where did 2.575 come from? We know from the previous chapter that 2.575 z-score represents 99% of expected outcomes outside of which would be exceptional to 99% (also above). And therefore, thusly interpreted as: 'There is a 99% chance that the confidence interval 0.378 and 0.542 contains the true population mean.'

Wait, the confidence interval got larger? Yes, the more confident we want to be, the larger the margin of error and thus the larger the intervals of the confidence interval. If we want to make confidence intervals tighter, we can increase the number of observations or hope for a smaller measure of dispersion. However, increasing confidence levels increases the associated z-scores in turn making the margins of error, and thus the confidence interval itself, larger.

Probability Confidence Intervals: Binomial Probability Distribution

This chapter focuses on interval-level variables. However, we needed to understand confidence intervals and z-scores before we could move toward the common use of the binomial probability distribution on non-interval-level variables.

Imagine we ask a sample of citizens from a particular country who they intend to vote for Prime Minister in the upcoming election, Candidate M or Candidate L. In our sample of 1,000 citizens, the results are 459 will vote for Candidate M and 541 will vote for Candidate L. How can we use this?

Binomial probability distributions allow us to make inferences about proportions in a population. They assume four crucial properties:

- There is a fixed number of trials (or observations).
- Two outcomes are possible on each trial/observation (*hint:* binomial): Success or Failure.
- The probability of success, denoted by π, does not vary across each trial/observation.
- The trials (or observations) are independent of one another.

Unfortunately, outside an experimental setting, these rarely occur. Particularly the first one.

ROULETTE

The easiest way to remember the four crucial properties of the binomial probability distribution is to think of the casino game roulette.

1. The wheel spins and the ball is tossed identically for a fixed number of times.
2. Ignoring the green zero and the numbers, there are two outcomes, red and black.
3. No changes are made to the little wheel or the toss of the ball.
4. Getting a black (or red) in one turn has no effect on getting a black (or red) on the next.

One reason confidence intervals are commonly used for interval-level data (continuous random variables: variables that can have a nearly infinite number of results) is that the probability of obtaining a specific value is extremely small. Thus, the *interval* of confidence intervals is more appealing. By contrast, for non-interval-level variables (discrete random variables: a finite number of values within a range), the sampling statistic and intervals don't make intuitive sense. From our example above, what is the mean of citizens' vote intention? It doesn't make any sense.

But we can think of the citizens' vote intention as a (binomial) probability, either citizens will vote for Candidate M or Candidate L. Thus, the probability that a person in our sample of 1,000 citizens will vote for Candidate M is 459/1000 or 0.459 and the probability that a person in that same sample will vote for Candidate L is 541/1000 or 0.541. We can use this information to produce a confidence interval for one or the other outcome which is what we would expect to see in the population.

The formula to produce this is similar to the confidence interval above and is called the binomial confidence interval:

$$B.C.I. = \pi \pm \left(z - score_{Confidence\ Level}\right)\sqrt{\frac{\pi(1-\pi)}{n}}$$

For Candidate M with 45.9% of the vote intentions, what can we expect this proportion to be in the population from which this sample was drawn?

$$B.C.I. = 0.459 \pm (1.96)\sqrt{\frac{0.459(1-0.459)}{1,000}}$$

$$B.C.I. = 0.459 \pm (1.96)\sqrt{\frac{0.459(0.541)}{1,000}}$$

$$B.C.I. = 0.459 \pm (1.96)(0.016)$$

$$B.C.I. = 0.459 \pm 0.031$$

When asked by the handsome newscaster who we project as the current leader in the campaign, what do we say? We might report: 'There is a 95% chance that the interval 0.428 and 0.490 contains the true population mean. In this two-person contest, Candidate M needs more than 50% to win. Our analysis suggests Candidate M needs to start shaking more hands and kissing more babies! Back to you in the studio, Derek.'

Example 1: Binomial Confidence Interval

What is even more interesting is that a discrete random variable need not even be binomial in nature for us to use this approach.

Take for example, the question from the 2017–2020 World Values Survey, 'Taking all things together, would you say you are "not at all happy", "not very happy", "rather happy", or "very happy"?' If we limit the responses to European countries, this 'happiness' variable ranges from 1 to 4, has a (sample) mean of 3.04, a (sample) standard deviation of 0.691, and 9,403 observations (see Table 13.1).

Table 13.1 Feeling of Happiness – World Values Survey in Europe

Response category	Frequency	Percent
Not at all happy	257	2.73%
Not very happy	1,283	13.64%
Quite happy	5,667	60.27%
Very happy	2,196	23.35%
Total	**9,403**	**100%**

Researchers studying happiness ask, given that 2,196 or 23.35% of the sample report being 'very happy' in Europe, what can we expect this value to be in the population? That is, what is our expectation of the population's response to this question about happiness, based on this sample?

We can construct a 95% confidence interval to find out. We can consider 'very happy' or 23.35% to be one outcome and the others combined as the other. Thus,

$$B.C.I. = \pi \pm \left(z - score_{Confidence\ Level}\right) \sqrt{\frac{\pi(1-\pi)}{n}}$$

$$B.C.I. = 0.2335 \pm (1.96) \sqrt{\frac{0.2335(1-0.2335)}{9.403}}$$

$$B.C.I. = 0.2335 \pm (1.96)\,(0.004)$$

$$B.C.I. = 0.2335 \pm 0.0086$$

Thus, what is the probability that Europeans in general would report being 'very happy'? From the World Values Survey sample, we would report: 'There is a 95% chance that the interval 22.5% and 24.2% contains the true population mean.'

Intermission

Except that we don't use z-scores for confidence intervals in the real world. Z-scores are an antiseptic, over-stylized version of reality. Instead, we use the t-test.

Excuse me?

As we will see, an all-purpose test improves our univariate inferential statistics – point estimates and confidence intervals – by adjusting the distribution to reflect the size of our sample. I present the t-test.

The t-test is a system upgrade for inferential statistics that takes us to the white-hot leading edge of modern statistics. What we will further discover is that in addition to updating our critical values (and thus rejection regions), it is not the probability of falling *within* the interval that is really that interesting but rather the probability of falling *outside* the critical value.

The t-test

The 't-test' includes the t-distribution, t-scores/t-statistics, and t-values and is a substantial upgrade to our use of Inferential Statistics. A **t-distribution** is essentially a z-distribution that adjusts to the number of observations in the sample. If the sample size is low, the t-distribution 'flattens out' making the critical values that define the rejection regions (i.e., the tails) farther and farther out. However, as the sample size increases, the t-distribution becomes practically indistinguishable from the Standard Normal z-distribution.

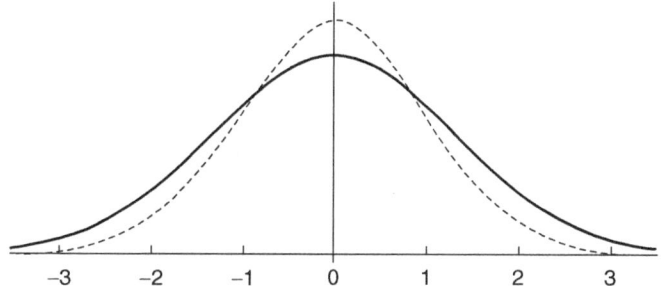

Figure 13.1a Standard Normal and Student's t-Distribution: Low N

In Figure 13.1a, we can see that when the number of observations is low, the t-distribution (solid line) is both 'flatter' and 'fatter' compared to a Normal distribution (dotted line). When our sample size is small, not only are fewer observations crowding around the centre but also the dispersion from the middle is also greater. This essentially widens the boundary to account for random errors that occurs because of small samples where things often are a lot messier.

But we already know this. As sample sizes increase, we tend to get better summaries of the data with less variance. And when sample sizes are small, our summaries tend to be poorer with greater variance or distribution of probabilities.

The t-distribution therefore formalizes this notion in our calculations.

So What?

Why is this important? Recall that a 1.96 z-score on a Standard Normal distribution is equivalent to 95% confidence. 95% confidence leaves 5% with half (2.5%) in each tail on either side of the distribution. In Figure 13.1b, this 2.5% is represented by the small dark grey section under the black Standard Normal distribution. However, in the case of a low number of observations, we can also see that a **t-score** of 1.96 in a t-distribution leaves a great deal more in the tail (the light grey part) than the z-score. That means we have more than 2.5% in the tail (i.e., we are not yet 95% confident).

Again, we already know this. Fewer observations make us less confident about our sample statistics; thus, the probability that an observation may fall farther from the others is greater as we just don't know with a smaller sample size. And if there is greater probability for observations to fall in the tail, a 1.96 **t-value** – as the value defining the critical or rejection region – does not bring us to the point at which 2.5% remains in each z-score tail. That is, in the case of a small sample, the t-value for 95% confidence will need to be farther out, and thus larger. This is also consistent with other distributions that take the sample size seriously (recall χ^2).

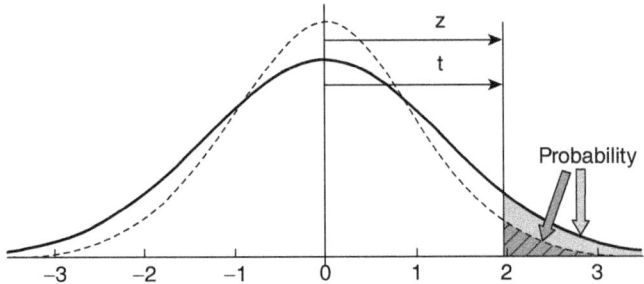

Figure 13.1b Student's t-Distribution

With supreme utility, as the number of observations increases, as our sample size grows, the t-distribution comes to resemble the Standard Normal distribution. That is, the light grey t-distribution in Figures 13.1a and 13.1b approaches the familiar shape of the black Standard Normal z-distribution. As such, t-values draw closer and closer to z-scores.

STUDENT'S t: GUINNESS IS GOOD FOR STATISTICS

Image 13.1
W.S. Gosset photo

One of the first large businesses to incorporate the work of 'research workers' and scientists of different stripes was beer producer Guinness. They saw the sampling techniques as a leap forward in quality testing. One of those scientists was a biochemist named William Sealy Gosset.

Gosset would test samples of ingredients, such as barley, as well as the finished product. Unlike his predecessors and Guinness's competitors, Gossett developed a statistical formula that allowed him to make claims about the population – the ingredients and beer as a whole – based on substantially smaller samples. To advance this concept but mask his identity (as to not break Guinness's rule not to publish potential 'trade secrets' under employees' real names), he published this 't-test' under the nom de plume, 'Student'. Thus, because of both progress and beer, we have 'Student's t' as the basis for our all-purpose t-test.

A t-value is specified by degrees of freedom and a confidence level, and defines the critical or rejection region. The degrees of freedom are the number of observations minus 1 (*n*-1) and essentially adjust z-scores for smaller samples and take into account the use of the sample standard deviation.

And recall our three most common levels of confidence:

- α = 0.05 for 95% confidence
- α = 0.01 for 99% confidence
- α = 0.001 for 99.9% confidence.

Table 13.2 demonstrates not only the divergence of t-values as the number of observations – captured by degrees of freedom – gets smaller but also the convergence of the t-values to the z-scores of Standard Normal. For example, at the very bottom of the table, we can see for 95% confidence, the t-value for degrees of freedom = 1,000 is 1.962. Just below we can see that this is very close to the z-score, 1.96. The same for 99% and 99.9%, with t-values of 2.576 and 3.291, respectively. However, at the top of the table, where the degrees of freedom (as a measure of the number of observations) is low, the t-values are different. (*Hint*: Larger because of Figure 13.1b.)

For 10 observations at 95% confidence, the t-value is 2.228. This is clearly higher than 1.96 z-score for 95% confidence. For 10 observations at 99% and 99.9% confidence, we find 3.169 and 4.587 t-values, respectively. Again, as expected, both are higher than the z-scores for the same confidence levels.

We are motivated to use the t-distribution in two circumstances. One, if we use the sample standard deviation to estimate the population standard deviation. And two, if the distribution is approximately normal but the number of observations is low. However, this motivation is more or less moot. For one, we nearly always use the sample standard deviation to estimate the population standard deviation. And two, if the t-distribution accounts for a low number of observations but also resembles Standard Normal when observations are high, it is, in fact, an all-purpose distribution. In other words, we can use it all the time as it replaces the need to use the z-distribution at all.

Confidence Intervals Revisited

Recall that a confidence interval has two parts: the sample statistic and the margin of error. The margin of error is calculated using the standard error and a critical value that represents our level of confidence. Because the t-distribution accounts for the number of observations – based on the degrees of freedom – it provides a level of confidence based on properly adjusted critical values, The formula for confidence intervals is the same as before simply replacing the z-score with a t-value.

$$C.I. = Sample\ Statistic \pm (t-value_{confidence\ level})(s.e.)$$

in which $s.e. = \dfrac{s_x}{\sqrt{n}}$

Let's update the confidence interval that we produced above in which we estimated the population mean (μ) of the variable 'Ethnic Fractionalization'. 'Ethnic Fractionalization' has 61 observations with a (sample) mean of 0.46 and a (sample) standard deviation of 0.25.

Table 13.2 t-Distribution Table – Area Under the Curve

tTable	t.50	t.75	t.80	t.85	t.90	t.95	t.975	t.99	t.995	t.999	t.9995
cum. prob one-tail	0.50	0.25	0.20	0.15	0.10	0.05	0.025	0.01	0.005	0.001	0.00051
two-tails	1.00	0.50	0.40	0.30	0.20	0.10	0.05	0.02	0.01	0.002	0.001
df											
1	0.000	1.000	1.376	1.963	3.078	6.314	12.71	31.82	63.66	318.31	636.62
2	0.000	0.816	1.061	1.386	1.886	2.920	4.303	6.965	9.925	22.327	31.599
3	0.000	0.765	0.978	1.250	1.638	2.353	3.182	4.541	5.841	10.215	12.924
4	0.000	0.741	0.941	1.190	1.533	2.132	2.776	3.747	4.604	7.173	8.610
5	0.000	0.727	0.920	1.156	1.476	2.015	2.571	3.365	4.032	5.893	6.869
6	0.000	0.718	0.906	1.134	1.440	1.943	2.447	3.143	3.707	5.208	5.959
7	0.000	0.711	0.896	1.119	1.415	1.895	2.365	2.998	3.499	4.785	5.408
8	0.000	0.706	0.889	1.108	1.397	1.860	2.306	2.896	3.355	4.501	5.041
9	0.000	0.703	0.883	1.100	1.383	1.833	2.262	2.821	3.250	4.297	4.781
10	0.000	0.700	0.879	1.093	1.372	1.812	2.228	2.764	3.169	4.144	4.587
11	0.000	0.697	0.876	1.088	1.363	1.796	2.201	2.718	3.106	4.025	4.437
12	0.000	0.695	0.873	1.083	1.356	1.782	2.179	2.681	3.055	3.930	4.318
13	0.000	0.694	0.870	1.079	1.350	1.771	2.160	2.650	3.012	3.852	4.221
14	0.000	0.692	0.868	1.076	1.345	1.761	2.145	2.624	2.977	3.787	4.140
15	0.000	0.691	0.866	1.074	1.341	1.753	2.131	2.602	2.947	3.733	4.073
16	0.000	0.690	0.865	1.071	1.337	1.746	2.120	2.583	2.921	3.686	4.015
17	0.000	0.689	0.863	1.069	1.333	1.740	2.110	2.567	2.898	3.646	3.965
18	0.000	0.688	0.862	1.067	1.330	1.734	2.101	2.552	2.878	3.610	3.922

	0%	50%	60%	70%	80%	90%	95%	98%	99%	99.8%	99.9%
19	0.000	0.688	0.861	1.066	1.328	1.729	2.093	2.539	2.861	3.579	3.883
20	0.000	0.687	0.860	1.064	1.325	1.725	2.086	2.528	2.845	3.552	3.850
21	0.000	0.686	0.859	1.063	1.323	1.721	2.080	2.518	2.831	3.527	3.819
22	0.000	0.686	0.858	1.061	1.321	1.717	2.074	2.508	2.819	3.505	3.792
23	0.000	0.685	0.858	1.060	1.319	1.714	2.069	2.500	2.807	3.485	3.768
24	0.000	0.685	0.857	1.059	1.318	1.711	2.064	2.492	2.797	3.467	3.745
25	0.000	0.684	0.856	1.058	1.316	1.708	2.060	2.485	2.787	3.450	3.725
26	0.000	0.684	0.856	1.058	1.315	1.706	2.056	2.479	2.779	3.435	3.707
27	0.000	0.684	0.855	1.057	1.314	1.703	2.052	2.473	2.771	3.421	3.690
28	0.000	0.683	0.855	1.056	1.313	1.701	2.048	2.467	2.763	3.408	3.674
29	0.000	0.683	0.854	1.055	1.311	1.699	2.045	2.462	2.756	3.396	3.659
30	0.000	0.683	0.854	1.055	1.310	1.697	2.042	2.457	2.750	3.385	3.646
40	0.000	0.681	0.851	1.050	1.303	1.684	2.021	2.423	2.704	3.307	3.551
60	0.000	0.679	0.848	1.045	1.296	1.671	2.000	2.390	2.660	3.232	3.460
80	0.000	0.678	0.846	1.043	1.292	1.664	1.990	2.374	2.639	3.195	3.416
100	0.000	0.677	0.845	1.042	1.290	1.660	1.984	2.364	2.626	3.174	3.390
1000	0.000	0.675	0.842	1.037	1.282	1.646	1.962	2.330	2.581	3.098	3.300
Z	0.000	0.674	0.842	1.036	1.282	1.645	1.960	2.326	2.576	3.090	3.291
	0%	50%	60%	70%	80%	90%	95%	98%	99%	99.8%	99.9%

Confidence Level

In the previous example, we assumed that the sample distribution approximated Standard Normal and used z-scores. Now, noting that we have only 61 observations, our sample mean of 0.46 may not be as good an estimate as we previously calculated.

Using z-scores, we found that 'There is a 95% chance that the confidence interval 0.397 and 0.523 contains the true population mean.'

$$C.I._{95\%} = 0.397 \text{ and } 0.523$$

We can update our estimate of the population mean using a t-value. With 61 observations (and therefore 60 degrees of freedom) and 95% confidence level, looking at Table 13.2, we find a t-value of 2.000. Therefore, recalculating our confidence interval:

$$C.I._{95\%} = 0.46 \pm (2.000)\left(\frac{0.25}{\sqrt{61}}\right)$$

$$C.I._{95\%} = 0.46 \pm (2.000)(0.032)$$

$$C.I._{95\%} = 0.46 \pm 0.064$$

$$C.I._{95\%} = 0.396 \text{ and } 0.524$$

Not an overwhelming change, but the margin of error did widen slightly. We can interpret this as, 'There is a 95% chance that the confidence interval 0.396 and 0.524 contains the true population mean.'

In order to make the point more clearly, let's take a hypothetical example to demonstrate how the t-values can make a more substantive difference. Perhaps we had 25 rather than 61 observations. Remember, the number of observations impacts two elements of the confidence interval, the number of observations in the denominator of the standard error and the t-value. Looking at Table 13.2, the t-score for 95% and degrees of freedom (25−1)=24 is 2.064.

The new calculation of the confidence interval would be:

$$C.I._{95\%} = 0.46 \pm (2.064)\left(\frac{0.25}{\sqrt{25}}\right)$$

$$C.I._{95\%} = 0.46 \pm (2.064)(0.05)$$

$$C.I._{95\%} = 0.46 \pm 0.103$$

$$C.I._{95\%} = 0.357 \text{ and } 0.563$$

In the case of a smaller number of observations, we can see that the margin of error of the confidence error becomes substantially larger. We can interpret this as, 'There is a 95% chance that the confidence interval 0.357 and 0.563 contains the true population mean.' Again, the effect comes from not only a smaller denominator for the standard error but also from the slightly larger t-value as the t-distribution 'flattens' out.

The t-test as Hypothesis Testing

In addition to improving our point estimates by improving the validity of confidence intervals, the Student's t can also be used in hypothesis testing. Similar to χ^2, we can use Student's t in a variety of ways. Most commonly, we can determine whether a sample statistic, such as a sample mean, is equal to a specific number, or whether an observed difference between groups is statistically significant. Both have myriad applications and are commonly used across all fields in Political Science.

Hypothesis testing, as we did in Chapter 11, has five steps.

- ONE: Null hypothesis H_0
- TWO: Alternative hypothesis H_a or H_1
- THREE: Test statistics
- FOUR: Critical or rejection region
- FIVE: Interpretation and conclusion.

Student's t updates both the test statistics that we generate from a specific set of data (the 't-score,' also called the 't-statistic') as well as the critical value that defines the critical or rejection region in significance testing (the t-value).

> ### t-TERMINOLOGY
>
> The terms related to the t-distribution are sometimes used inconsistently, or at least loosely. Even in preparing this textbook, my review of other textbooks found a wide set of discrepancies. Obviously, this can be confusing. Here, we will be internally consistent and use the t-terms in what seems to be the most common ways. Therefore: the 't-test statistic' is the test statistic generated from the sample data, often called simply 't-statistic' or, more generally, 't-score'. The critical value defining the critical or rejection region is called the 't-value'.

Testing the Specific Value of a Sample Statistic

What if I asked you to guess the mean level of online governance that governments around the world have? That is, what do you think the 'level of e-governance' in the world is, on average?

From the Quality of Governance dataset, there is a measure called the E-Government Index. It is a combination of three related measures – the Online Service Index, Telecommunication Infrastructure Index, and the Human Capital Index – that attempts to capture the scope and quality of governments' online services. It ranges from zero – no online capacities – to 1.0 – full online capabilities. Thus, based on this measure, you might think of the Australian (0.905), South Korean (0.901), or UK (0.900) governments as leaders or the Sudan (0.239), Malawi (0.271), or Cambodian (0.375) governments as stragglers.

You mention this casually in a conversation and the other person says, 'I'll bet the mean level is pretty average. I mean, even though most of everything is done online in places that have Silicon valleys or their equivalents, most of the rest of the world is way behind. The average level in the world is probably, on the 0 to 1 scale, probably half, like 0.5 or something.'

Framed in the language of statistics, is the global average – the (population) mean – of the level of E-governance 0.500? Our sample of 63 observations from the Quality of Governance dataset tells us that the mean is 0.617 with a standard deviation of 0.188. Let's set up a hypothesis test to find out if 0.500 is in fact a good guess based on what we know from our sample.

ONE: Null hypothesis: H_0: $\mu = 0.500$

TWO: Alternative hypothesis H_a: $\mu \neq 0.500$

Intuitively, we need to be presented with sufficient evidence in our data to reject the hypothesis of your friend that 0.500 is the population mean. Thus, our alternative hypothesis test is that 0.500 is *not* the population mean (our data tell us it is 0.617 or close to it, but that's only our best guess).

THREE: Test statistic

The test statistic for Students' t is called the **t-test statistic** or simply **t-statistic** (also sometimes called 't-score'). In the context of our hypothesis testing here, we will use the more descriptive 't-statistic'. The formula is:

$$t - statistic = \frac{\bar{x} - x}{\left(\frac{s}{\sqrt{n}}\right)}$$

The difference of the mean and the observed value divided by the standard error (the standard deviation divided by the square root of the number of observations).

Therefore, for our E-Governance example:

$$t - statistic = \frac{0.500 - 0.617}{\left(\frac{0.188}{\sqrt{63}}\right)}$$

$$t - statistic = \frac{0.117}{(0.024)}$$

$$t - statistic = 4.875$$

4.875 is our t-statistic generated from our sample data.

FOUR: Critical or rejection region

Just like χ^2, the critical value that defines the rejection region comes from our choice of confidence level and the sample size. Here, the t-value at 95% confidence and 62 degrees of freedom (63–1) is 2.000.

FIVE: Interpretation and conclusion

Does our t-statistic, generated from our sample data, fall outside the critical t-value into the rejection region? Is 4.875 larger than 2.000?

Yes, it falls in the rejection region. Therefore, with 95% confidence, we reject the null hypothesis that µ=0.500. In other words, based on our sample data, your friend's guess of 0.500 can be rejected as being the population mean with 95% confidence.

Let's bolt this finding to the ground.

- What if we wanted to be more confident? The t-value defining 99% confidence (with 62 df): 2.660. Is 4.875 larger than 2.660? Yes, it falls in the rejection region. We can reject the null hypothesis that µ=0.500 with 99% confidence.
- More! The t-value defining 99.9% confidence (with 62 df): 3.460. Is 4.875 larger than 3.460? Yes, and it thus falls in the rejection region. We can again reject the null hypothesis that µ=0.500 with 99.9% confidence.

The t-distribution accounts for smaller sample sizes, making the critical values wider than the z-scores of a Standard Normal distribution. Our very high level of confidence also pushes those critical t-values even wider. Yet, accounting for the small number of observations and being extremely demanding in terms of confidence, we are still able to reject the null hypothesis that the mean level of governments that function online is 0.500.

Impressive.

Difference of Means t-test

There is a very useful adaptation to testing whether our sample statistic is equal to a specific number. Specifically, the **difference of means t-test** determines whether the difference between two means is zero (or not). The difference of means t-test can be used to show whether two different groups have a different mean of the same variable – or whether a single variable, separated by another variable, produces significantly different means. Think of this as a more powerful form of a Means Comparison from Descriptive Statistics.

The first is called an independent difference of means t-test. We can use this to compare the mean levels of variables across two – presumably independent – groups. The latter is called a dependent difference of means t-test. In this test, we have data collected twice (or more) – commonly, *before* and *after* an event or (experimental) treatment. Because we are sampling the same group, we can effectively control for a great deal of between-group variation and therefore attribute at least part of the within-group variation to the treatment.

$$t-statistic_{\text{Diff of Means}} = \frac{(\bar{x}_1 - \bar{x}_2)}{s.e._{\text{Diff}}}$$

$$s.e._{Diff} = \sqrt{\left(\frac{s_1}{\sqrt{n_1}}\right)^2 + \left(\frac{s_2}{\sqrt{n_2}}\right)^2}$$

$$df = n_1 + n_2 - 2$$

In both the independent and dependent difference of means t-tests, the underlying logic is the same.

- The numerator calculates the observed difference between the means. We want to know if this number is zero or not. That is, if there is no difference between the means, the difference will be zero (or very, very close to it). If, however, there is a difference, the difference will be statistically different than zero.
- The denominator is the **standard error of the difference** which is a weighted average of the two sub-samples' standard errors.
- We calculate our degrees of freedom as we would for each (n_1–1) and (n_2–1), or $n_1 + n_2 = 2$.

Difference of Means t-test Example

There has long been a contest between the older, Western member states of the European Union and the newer, Eastern member states as to which region is more supportive of the European Union. Let's see if we can shed some light on this discussion.

Using the European Social Survey from 2018, there is a question that asks EU respondents whether they think European unification has gone too far (0) or could go further (10). We can group the respondents by their countries into Western EU members – Austria, Belgium, Cyprus, Germany, Finland, France, Ireland, Italy, and the Netherlands – and Eastern EU members – Bulgaria, the Czech Republic, Estonia, Hungary, Poland, and Slovenia.

- For Eastern respondents (N=9,821), the mean is 5.09 with a standard deviation of 2.72.
- For Western respondents (N=16,892), the mean is 5.26 with a standard deviation of 2.66.

At first glance, it would seem that the Western respondents are slightly higher in support of continuing European unification than their Eastern counterparts. However, as we well know, these samples are rough estimates of the actual population mean levels of support for (or opposition to) continuing unification. So, keeping in mind that our samples are good guesses of the actual level, let's see whether they represent meaningfully different responses across West and East.

To do so, we can set up the hypothesis test that will walk us through the decision-making process. First, is the difference between the mean support for EU unification zero or not? Or in the language of hypothesis testing:

One: H_0: The difference between the means is zero ($\mu_1 - \mu_2 = 0$).
Two: H_a: The difference is not zero ($\mu_1 - \mu_2 \neq 0$).
We will estimate the population means (μ_i) with our sample means ($\bar{x}_i$).
Three: Test statistic.
We can generate the difference of means test statistic t-statistic using the formula:

$$t-statistic_{Diff\ of\ Means} = \frac{(\bar{x}_1 - \bar{x}_2)}{\sqrt{\left(\frac{s_1}{\sqrt{n_1}}\right)^2 + \left(\frac{s_2}{\sqrt{n_2}}\right)^2}}$$

Therefore,

$$t-statistic_{Diff\ of\ Means} = \frac{(5.09 - 5.26)}{\sqrt{\left(\frac{2.72}{\sqrt{9,821}}\right)^2 + \left(\frac{2.66}{\sqrt{16,892}}\right)^2}}$$

[vigorously clicking calculator]

$$t-statistic_{Diff\ of\ Means} = -4.97$$

−4.97 is our difference of means t-statistic generated from our sample data.

Four: Critical or Rejection Region

The rejection region is defined by the critical value which is based on our chosen level of confidence and the degrees of freedom ($n_1 + n_2 - 2$). Here, the t-value defining 95% confidence and 26,713 degrees of freedom (9,821+16,892 − 2) is, looking back to Table 13.2, 1.962.

Five: Interpretation and conclusion

Is our t-statistic of −4.97 greater than the critical t-value of 1.962? Yes, it is. Wait, negative 5.02 is greater than positive 1.962? Yes, recall that 1.962 determines the rejection region on both tails of the t-distribution – that is, 1.962 to the right of the mean and −1.962 to the left of the mean. Therefore, −4.97 falls into the rejection region (on the left side of the distribution).

Thus, we can, at 95% confidence, reject the null hypothesis that the difference between the means is zero ($\mu_1 - \mu_2 = 0$). In other words, at 95% confidence, there is a statistically significant difference between the citizens of Western and Eastern Europe on the question of whether EU unification has gone far enough in which Western Europeans more strongly support more unification than Eastern Europeans.

Can we be more confident?

- The t-value defining 99% confidence (with 26,713 df): 2.576. Is −4.97 greater than 2.576? Yes, falling in the rejection region. Therefore, we can reject the null hypothesis that the difference between the means is zero ($\mu_1 - \mu_2 = 0$) with 99% confidence.

- The t-value defining 99.9% confidence (with 26,713 df): 3.291. Is −4.97 greater than 3.291? Yes, falling in the rejection region. Therefore, we can reject the null hypothesis that the difference between the means is zero ($\mu_1 - \mu_2 = 0$) with 99.9% confidence.

This was an independent difference of means t-test. A further question would be whether East Europeans' support has in fact dropped over the last decade. This would be a dependent difference of means t-test. If we look back to the European Social Survey of 2008, we can again examine the question of whether they think European unification has gone too far (0) or could go further (10).

Difference of Means t-test Example 2

From above, we know that the mean level for European unification for Eastern respondents ($N = 9,821$) is 5.09 with a standard deviation of 2.72. The East European countries included in the ESS 2008 include Bulgaria, Croatia, the Czech Republic, Estonia, Hungary, Latvia, Poland, Romania, Slovakia, and Slovenia. We find that the mean level for European unification for Eastern respondents ($N = 15,365$) is 5.84 with a standard deviation of 2.74.

Our first impression is that East Europeans in 2008 were substantially more supportive or EU unification (recall: European unification has gone too far (0) or could go further (10)). But there's only one way to find out.

One: H_0: The difference between the means is zero ($\mu_1 - \mu_2 = 0$)
Two: H_a: The difference is not zero ($\mu_1 - \mu_2 \neq 0$)
As before, we will estimate the population means (μ_i) with our sample means ($\bar{x}_i$).
Three: Test statistic
We can generate the difference of means test statistic t-statistic using the formula:

$$t\text{-}statistic_{Diff\ of\ Means} = \frac{(\bar{x}_1 - \bar{x}_2)}{\sqrt{\left(\frac{s_1}{\sqrt{n_1}}\right)^2 + \left(\frac{s_2}{\sqrt{n_2}}\right)^2}}$$

Therefore,

$$t\text{-}statistic_{Diff\ of\ Means} = \frac{(5.09 - 5.84)}{\sqrt{\left(\frac{2.72}{\sqrt{9,821}}\right)^2 + \left(\frac{2.74}{\sqrt{15,365}}\right)^2}}$$

$$t\text{-}statistic_{Diff\ of\ Means} = -21.3$$

−21.3 is our difference of means t-statistic generated from our sample data.
Four: Critical or rejection region
The rejection region is defined by the t-value which is based on our chosen level of confidence and the degrees of freedom ($n_1 + n_2 - 2$). Here, the t-value defining 95% confidence and 25,184 degrees of freedom (9,821+15,365 − 2) is, again looking back to Table 13.2, 1.962.

Five: Interpretation and conclusion

Is our t-statistic of −21.3 greater than the critical t-value of 1.962? Again, recall that the distribution is symmetrical about the mean. So, we are looking at which is 'absolutely' greater (as in the absolute value).

Therefore, yes, our t-statistic is greater than the critical t-value and thus falls into the rejection region. Therefore, at 95% confidence, we can reject the null hypothesis that the difference between the means is zero ($\mu_1 - \mu_2 = 0$). In other words, at 95% confidence, there is a statistically significant difference between East Europeans' support for European unification in 2008 than in 2018.

We must always ask whether we can be more confident.

- The t-value defining 99% confidence (with 25,184 df): 2.576. Is −21.3 larger than 2.576? Yes (again, in absolute terms), it falls in the rejection region. Therefore, we can reject the null hypothesis that the difference between the means is zero ($\mu_1 - \mu_2 = 0$) with 99% confidence.
- The t-value defining 99.9% confidence (with 25,184 df): 3.291. Is −21.3 larger than 3.291? Yes, (again, in absolute terms) it falls in the rejection region. Therefore, we can reject the null hypothesis that the difference between the means is zero ($\mu_1 - \mu_2 = 0$) with 99.9% confidence.

One- and Two-tailed Tests

For those paying careful attention, you may have noticed that in Table 13.2, it says 'two tails'. What does that mean? Recall the shape of our t-distribution. It is shaped so there is a hump in the middle and two tails extending out. A **two-tailed test** is based on the idea of a confidence interval. That is, the test is designed so that the t-statistic can be either positive or negative but must still reach the critical value to be statistically significant. That is, there is no *a priori* direction assumed. A **one-tailed test** is for directional hypothesis testing in which the direction of the difference is known or anticipated. That is, one group is expected to have a higher or lower level of something before the testing.

Technically, if we know the expected direction of the difference, for example, we highly suspect Western Europeans to have higher levels of support for EU unification than Eastern Europeans, then we would use a one-tailed test. However, there is one catch in doing so. One-tailed tests make it *easier* to reach statistical significance by lowering the critical value. And, in the eyes of many researchers, are simply not demanding enough.

Why is that?

In either a Standard Normal or t-distribution, if we are interested in 95% confidence, the remaining 5% must be split between the two tails, 2.5% in each. We also know that to achieve 95% confidence in a z-distribution or t-distribution (with a high number of observations), the critical value is 1.96. In Figure 13.2, we can see both the 1.96 critical value and the 2.5% in each tail (the red section).

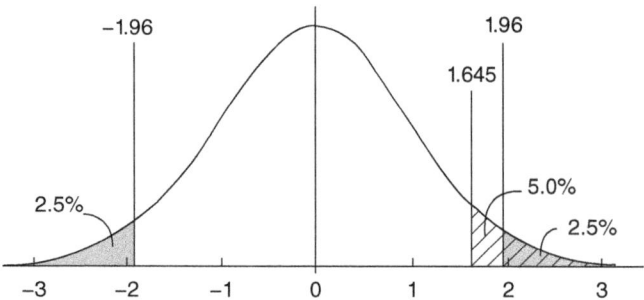

Figure 13.2 One-tailed t-test – 95% confidence

However, for a directional – or one-tailed t-test – the remaining 5% will be in one tail. In that case, with 5% under the curve in one tail, the critical value will have to be adjusted downward. We can find this critical value using Table 13.2 by deducing that 5% in each tail (a two-tailed t-test) would be 90% confidence. Looking at the table, we can see the t-value defining 90% confidence is 1.645.

For a one-tailed test to be 95%, you would need to clear a critical value of 1.645, for a two-tailed test, 1.96. Which value is more demanding? Clearly, 1.96 is more difficult to achieve and thus serves as a 'higher' hurdle. In this way, most researchers are slow to use one-tailed tests as they 'lower' the stringency of the t-test.

A Final Word on the All-Purpose t-test

First of all, sorry for making you do all the z-score stuff but it makes an ideal introduction to finding probabilities on a distribution. Once you get the idea, the t-test and its adjustment for sample size is less intimidating and even welcome.

As you can also see, t-tests come in many useful forms. It can be used to see if a sample statistic such as a mean is equal to a specific number, if two different variables have the same mean, or if a single variable, separated by another variable, produces significantly different means. One thing to make clear, in this chapter we have focused on estimating population means. These are not the only population parameters for which we can create confidence intervals. We will encounter additional uses soon.

Why is Student's t so important? Student's t accounts for sample size thus making it an adaptable and improved version of the Standard Normal distribution. We already know that sample size is important. Bigger samples tend toward population parameters and smaller samples struggle to provide confident estimates. That is, in doing so, we are improving the quality of our estimates and the confidence in those estimates will be higher.

End of Chapter Summary

- We ultimately make inferences about population parameters in two ways: estimation and hypothesis testing.

- Point estimation produces a best guess from the sample and constructs a margin of error on either side called a confidence interval *or* estimate of what the sample tells us is the population parameter and builds an interval around that point that gives a range of plausible values of varying level of probability.
- A confidence interval is a range of values around a point estimate that expresses the probability that the interval contains the population parameter between the upper and lower limits of the interval.
- The margin of error creates an interval centred on the sample statistic or point estimate based on a level of confidence and the variation of the sampling distribution of the mean.
- The standard error is the measure of dispersion that we use for sampling distribution.
- Binomial probability distributions allow us to make inferences about proportions in a population.
- We use Student's t in all of its forms to update our analysis to accommodate the size of our sample.
- We accommodate for the size of our sample as we know that larger samples tend toward better estimates of population parameters while smaller samples give us less confidence in our estimates.
- Although one-tailed t-tests exist, it is preferred to use the statistically more demanding two-tailed t-test.
- A difference of means t-test allows us to determine whether our sample statistic is equal to a specific number or whether the difference between two numbers is meaningfully not zero.
- We must try to determine the highest level of confidence for our finding.

Glossary

- We make inferences about population parameters from our sample in two ways: **estimation** and **hypothesis testing.**
- One form of **(point) estimation** is constructing a **confidence interval** around our sample estimate of a population parameter.
- A **confidence interval** is range of values consisting of a margin of error – based on sample size and our level of confidence – on either side of a sample estimate in which we expect to find the population parameter with the chosen level of confidence.
- **Hypothesis testing** can include testing whether a specific value from our sample – a statistic – is equivalent to a potential parameter or other value (usually zero).
- The **standard error** is the measure of dispersion that we use for sampling distributions, the standard error of the mean.
- A **t-distribution** is a Standard Normal distribution that adjusts according to the number of observations in the sample.

- The (critical) **t-value** defines the critical or rejection region by cleaving the t-distribution into probabilities according to the degrees of freedom and a chosen confidence level.
- A **(t-test) t-statistic** – or **t-score** – is the test statistic generated from our sample for hypothesis testing.
- A **difference of means t-test** determines whether the difference between the means is zero (or not).
- The denominator in the calculation for a difference of means t-test is a weighted average of the two sub-samples' standard errors, known as the **standard error of the difference**.
- A **two-tailed t-test** is a non-directional test based on the symmetry of the t-distribution about the mean. A **one-tailed test** treats direction – negative or positive – as crucial and converts the t-distribution by placing all of the chosen level of confidence on one side or the other.

Questions

1. In our example of vote intention, calculate and interpret a 99% binomial confidence interval. How does this fit with what we found previously?
2. For the example on happiness, what gives this particular sample such confidence even at the 95% confidence level? Perhaps sample size, but perhaps also 'very happy' makes up nearly a quarter of the responses. If that is the case, produce a 95% confidence interval for 'quite happy' – which is almost 2/3rds of the responses – and look at the margin of error. Avoiding the maths of it, why might the modal category have narrower confidence interval than other categories?
3. In our ethnic fragmentation study, with 61 observations (and therefore 60 degrees of freedom) and 95% confidence level, looking at Table 14.2, we find a t-statistic of 2.000. Therefore, recalculating our confidence interval: $C.I. = 0.46 \pm (2.000)\left(\dfrac{0.25}{\sqrt{61}}\right)$. Predict whether the CI would get wider or narrower if we wanted 99.9% confidence? Calculate to check.
4. Let's revisit the example on support for European unification. We found that East Europeans were both more supportive in 2008 than 2018 (with 99.9% confidence) but less supportive than their Western counterparts in 2018 (with 99.9% confidence). Perhaps West Europeans felt the same – that is more supportive in 2008 than they do in 2018. Conduct a difference of means test to find out. What is the highest level of confidence that we can have?
    - In 2018, the mean support was 5.251 with a standard deviation of 2.652 for Western respondents ($N=16,210$).
    - In 2008, the mean support was 5.032 with a standard deviation of 2.500 for Western respondents ($N=21,622$).
5. Of course, to be fully informed, we must ask if West Europeans had stronger support than East Europeans in 2008. Conduct a difference of means test to find out. What is the highest level of confidence that we can have?

- For West Europeans in 2008, the mean support was 5.032 with a standard deviation of 2.500 for Western respondents ($N=21,622$).
- For East Europeans in 2008, the mean support was 5.837 with a standard deviation of 2.731 for Eastern respondents ($N=16,494$).

6. Student's t makes evaluating our sample estimates of population parameters more strenuous. That is, it is more difficult to achieve statistical significance. Yes, it accounts for the size of the sample, but how does this make the test of statistical significance more strenuous?

Signposts to the Accompanying Digital Resources

Data used in this chapter

- **Ethnic fractionalization (fe_etfra)**: Restricting attention to groups that had at least 1 percent of country population in the 1990s, Fearon identifies 822 ethnic and 'ethnoreligious' groups in 160 countries. This variable reflects the probability that two randomly selected people from a given country will belong to different such groups. The variable thus ranges from 0 (perfectly homogeneous) to 1 (highly fragmented). Quality of Governance.
- **E-Government Index** (egov_egov) The E-Government Development Index (EGDI) is a weighted average of scores on the three most important dimensions of e-government, namely: scope and quality of online services (Online Service Index, OSI), status of the development of telecommunication infrastructure (Telecommunication Infrastructure Index, TII), and inherent human capital (Human Capital Index, HCI). Quality of Governance.
    - Teorell, Jan, Aksel Sundström, Sören Holmberg, Bo Rothstein, Natalia Alvarado Pachon & Cem Mert Dalli. 2021. The Quality of Government Standard Dataset, version Jan21. University of Gothenburg: The Quality of Government Institute. www.qog.pol.gu.se
- **Feeling of happiness (Q46):** Taking all things together, would you say you are: 1 Very happy, 2 Rather happy, 3 Not very happy, 4 Not at all happy. World Values Survey.
    - EVS/WVS (2021). European Values Study and World Values Survey: Joint EVS/WVS 2017–2021 Dataset (Joint EVS/WVS). GESIS Data Archive, Cologne. ZA7505. Dataset Version 2.0.0, https://doi.org/10.4232/1.13737
- **European Unification** (Euftf): Now thinking about the European Union, some say European unification should go further. Others say it has already gone too far. What number on the scale best describes your position? 0 Unification has already gone too far – 10 Unification should go further. European Social Survey (2018).
    - ESS 1–9, European Social Survey Cumulative File, Study Description. Bergen: NSD – Norwegian Centre for Research Data for ESS ERIC. https://doi.org/10.21338/NSD-ESS-CUMULATIVE

PART III
MULTIPLE REGRESSION

THE END

14
MULTIPLE REGRESSION

> **LEARNING OUTCOMES**
>
> In this chapter, you will be able to
>
> - Use multiple regression to test the relationship between a dependent variable and a set of independent variables.
> - Explain how multiple regression provides three key powers of statistics: description, inference, and control.
> - Recognize and interpret three key elements of multiple regression: regression coefficients, inferential additions, and model fit.
> - Use the Modelling Process to develop, analyse, and ultimately interpret a multiple regression model.
> - Appreciate the appeal of multiple regression to address the larger questions of uncertainty and inference in the study of Political Science.

Introduction

This chapter introduces the fundamental form, estimation, and interpretation of multiple regression. This includes the design, key components, and interpretation of a multiple regression model. Of all the parts in this book, this chapter will be the one that serves you best. This is the *grand plateau* of your statistical ascent. We have traversed the plains of description. We have mined the caverns of inference. Now, we claim dominion over multiple regression.

Multiple Regression: Description, Inference, and Control

Thus far we have seen the power of statistics to describe relationships and impart inference on observed relationships. What we lack at this point is the ability to make substantive and inferential claims about the *exclusivity* of the relationship in which we are interested. That is, what is the relationship between X – our independent variable – and Y – our dependent variable, controlling for other explanations.

Multiple regression is a statistical technique that allows us to simultaneously test the impact of several independent variables on a dependent variable. In doing so, it unites three key analytical abilities:

1. *Description:* Multiple regression provides a clear understanding of the substantive and comparative relationship between the independent variables and the dependent variable.
2. *Inference:* Multiple regression gives us the statistical significance of each included independent variable, thus identifying relationships that can be inferred to exist in the population from which the sample data was drawn.
3. *Control:* Multiple regression allows us to make stronger claims about the relationships between independent variables and the dependent variable by controlling for the impact of several independent variables simultaneously. In this way, multiple regression advances our statistical abilities by approximating experimental control with statistical control.

Together, these three analytical abilities (the 'Illustrious Triumvirate') – description, inference, and control – give us substantial power to more accurately describe relationships in which we are interested by including a closer approximation of complex social and political worlds. This power also allows us greater inferential claims.

Quick Start: Multiple Regression

Recall bivariate regression. Bivariate regression is an equation that gives a variable-specific description of the linear relationship between a dependent and independent variable. It takes the following form in which we have a dependent variable (Y), an independent variable (X), a regression coefficient (β), an intercept (α), and an error term (ε).

$$Y = \alpha + \beta(X) + \varepsilon$$

The regression coefficient (β) estimates the average change in Y associated with a unit change in X; the intercept (α) is the value of Y when X=0; and the error term (ε) contains the random or unaccounted-for elements (assumed to be zero). Multiple regression has the same elements of bivariate regression and simply expands to include other potentially (or theoretically) relevant variables.

Thus:

$$Y = \alpha + \beta_1(X_1) + \beta_2(X_2) + \ldots + \beta_n(X_n) + \varepsilon$$

Which variables should we include? Ideally, the variables that have been demonstrated – or are theorized – to be relevant to variation in the dependent variable derive from the literature review, a step in the scientific study of our question. Multiple regression will calculate most any variables that you put in; however, the appropriateness or importance of those independent variables comes from our knowledge about the question we are investigating. This happens in the research process before we estimate the above equation.

Assuming that we have included the most appropriate variables, multiple regression allows each independent variable to have an effect on the dependent variable while controlling for the other variables' impact. This allows multiple regression to calculate and assign the *partial* effect of each independent variable on the dependent variable.

This is huge. This is control.

In doing so, we can observe the effect that our independent variable of interest has on the dependent variable controlling for other potential explanations. Fortunately for us, in technical terms, very little changes from the logic of bivariate regression and we get a great deal more information.

SPURIOUSNESS

Another motivation for controlling for other potential explanations of our variable of interest is the possible discovery that X is in fact not related to Y. This is called a spurious relationship. In a spurious relationship, both X and Y might appear to move together (and even do so in an intuitive way) but we come to discover that they are in fact being driven by a common variable (e.g., Z). This might look like Figure 14.1:

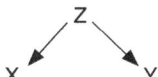

Figure 14.1 Spurious Relationship

A spurious relationship reveals itself when the relationship between X and Y weakens substantially or disappears when we introduce Z. A simple example is that we observe a relationship between individuals' education levels (X) and their propensity to vote in national elections (Y). We might consider theorizing about that relationship such that education captures content knowledge, critical thinking, or information processing skills that may in some way be related to the act of voting. Investigating this relationship, we come to discover that education and vote propensity move together because they are both related to that individual's income level (Z). That is, income is what correlates with education level and voting and the relationship we observed between education and voting is in fact spurious (i.e., explained by something else).

User's Manual: The Elements of Multiple Regression

There are three key elements in multiple regression that are relevant to its performance. The first two relate directly to the regression coefficients (β) which articulate the linear relationship between the independent and dependent variables. This includes the substantive interpretation of the regression coefficients themselves and the determination of the statistical significance of the regression coefficients. The third and final element refers to overall performance of the regression model.

Element 1: Regression Coefficients (β)

In bivariate regression, the regression coefficients – or betas (β) – are called 'zero-order correlation coefficients'. The value of the regression coefficient represents the substantive and variable-specific relationship between the independent and dependent variable. For multiple regression, betas are called 'first-order correlation coefficients' – or you may also hear someone call them **partials**. In the setting of multiple regression, these regression coefficients represent each independent variable's *partial* contribution to the total explained variance of the dependent variable.

What we are ultimately interested in is the extent to which the independent variable and dependent variable move together. In a bivariate relationship, the independent variable we have included gets the lion's share of the explanatory credit. This is because in bivariate regression, we are not controlling for other potential explanations as to why the dependent variable my change or vary. The only explanation for any changes is the independent variable we have included.

However, as we well know, the world is complex. In this crowded room, it becomes more difficult to be the *only* reason the dependent variables changes. Therefore, adding other possible explanations – other independent variables – allows the regression to assign only the changes in the dependent variable that can be uniquely assigned to each of the independent variables.

The multiple regression coefficients – the betas – still mean the same thing. They provide the average change in Y associated with a unit change in X. The crucial difference is that we can and should follow this with, '…controlling for the effects of the other variables'. We correctly interpret the regression coefficients of multiple regression as, 'For every 1-unit change in X, we can expect a *beta*-unit change in Y, while holding all other variables constant.' It is precisely this last phrase which launches us from largely descriptive bivariate regression to the multiple regression of the Illustrious Triumvirate.

'Holding all other variables constant' isolates the independent-dependent variable relationship in which we are interested and improves our ability to identify the substantive nature of the relationship – having controlled for the competing impacts of the other potential explanations (namely, the other included independent variables). In doing so, we draw closer to the potentially 'real' value of the relationship – the population parameter – in which we are interested.

STANDARDIZED REGRESSION COEFFICIENTS

One nuance of multiple regression is that each independent variable's regression coefficient (β) represents a specific and unique mathematical relationship with the dependent variable. Betas give us variable-specific information about how the dependent variable changes with the independent variable in the metric of each variable. As such, this makes comparing the betas directly somewhat challenging.

A practice that has ebbed and flowed out of popularity is **standardized regression coefficients**. Standardization, as we have seen above in several forms, allows us to compare variables on different scales by standardizing their distance from the mean. For multiple regression, we can standardize all the betas in a multiple regression to have 'unit variance' – essentially the same process as producing z-scores – and this would allow us to make elementary comparisons of relative strength.

The interpretation of standardized regression coefficients is: 'For one standard deviation change in the independent variable, we see a "standardized beta" change in the dependent variable, holding all other variables constant.' For some practitioners, this provides the relative importance of independent variables. This is a common but disputed procedure.

An aside: Correlation and regression are often discussed together because correlation is a special case of regression. Correlation – Pearson's 'r' – is simply the standardized regression coefficient between two variables.

Element 2: Inferential Additions

The regression coefficients allow us to make claims about the substantive impact of various independent variables – controlling for the effects of other independent variables. Multiple regression also reports the t-scores (or test statistics) and p-values for each of the regression coefficients. In this way, for each independent variable, we can determine if the relationship observed in the analysis can be inferred to exist in the population from which the sample was drawn.

That is, not only does multiple regression assess the partial explanation of each independent variable on the dependent variable ('statistical control'), but it also produces a t-score and p-value for each of the regression coefficients so that we can determine whether the relationship in the analysis can be inferred to exist in the population from which the sample was drawn.

Multiple regression will calculate and produce t-scores for determining statistical significance for each regression coefficient.

The t-score is calculated as:

$$\text{t-score}_\beta = \frac{\beta}{\text{s.e.}_\beta}$$

in which degrees of freedom = n − k

(n = number of observations)

(k = number of independent variables)

Why does the regression coefficient have a standard error instead of a standard deviation? Remember that the standard error of the regression coefficient is a measure of the amount of variability that would be present among different betas estimated from samples drawn from the same populations (IOW, CLT). Therefore, a standard error is a measure of how robust our estimate is. In terms of statistical significance, it is a key element of determining how likely our estimated parameter – the regression coefficient itself – is the relationship we would expect to find.

More importantly, we can use the t-score to determine the statistical significance of the regression coefficient in precisely the same manner as we have done previously with χ^2, z-scores, and t-scores.

Recall the steps of hypothesis testing for statistical significance (and Student's t, in particular):

- *ONE:* Null hypothesis H_0.
- *TWO:* Alternative hypothesis H_a or H_1.
- *THREE:* Test statistics.
- *FOUR:* Critical or rejection region.
- *FIVE:* Interpretation and conclusion.

Therefore, the test of statistical significance for each regression coefficient in a multiple regression would look like this:

- *ONE:* The null hypothesis H_0: $\beta_n=0$.
- *TWO:* The alternative hypothesis H_a: $\beta_n \neq 0$ (the regression coefficient that was estimated by multiple regression represents a 'real' relationship).
- *THREE:* Test statistics: the t-score test statistic is equal to the beta divided by its standard error.
- *FOUR:* Critical or rejection region is defined by a level of confidence and degrees of freedom (df=n-k).
- *FIVE:* Interpretation: Determining whether the t-test statistics falls in the rejection region or not.

Recall that our *level of confidence* is represented by alpha (α). If we take one of the three levels of confidence: 95%; 99%; or 99.9%, alphas are written as the complements to this: .05; .01; or .001, respectively.

In other words,

- $\alpha=0.05$ for 95% confidence
- $\alpha=0.01$ for 99% confidence
- $\alpha=0.001$ for 99.9% confidence.

For the regression coefficients in multiple regression, all statistical software programs will return a p-value rather than an alpha. A **p-value** is the precise level of significance for each independent variable's regression coefficient; i.e., the probability contained in the region of the curve beyond your test statistic.

Very often the statistical software will report something like this:

Table 14.1 Statistical Software Output Example

Regression coefficient	Standard error	t-score	p-value
2.881	0.7811	3.69	0.00012

The p-value is the exact probability that the estimated value could have occurred by chance, sometimes more accurately called the *'achieved* significance'. In precisely this way, it provides the exact level of confidence one can have that the relationship in the sample exists in the population from which it was drawn (using 1−'p-value'). Thus, given the p-value in the above example, we can be, precisely, 99.99988% confident (i.e., 1−0.00012).

Remember though, we only need to go beyond 0.05 or 0.01 or 0.001 to reject the null. Therefore, we report p-values in a standardized form that is reminiscent of alphas (above). Therefore, in our example above (p=0.00012), we could report 95% confidence in our estimated parameter using the notation: 'p<0.05'. Why? Because p=0.00012 is smaller than p=0.05. To indicate this, we use the 'less than' symbol: 'p<0.05'. Of course, we could also report 99% confidence ('p<0.01') and even 99.9% confidence ('p<0.001') as p=0. 00012 is smaller than both 0.01 and 0.001. As we seek to report the highest level of confidence, would you rather say that you are 95% confident in the results or 99.9% confident?

Thus, we have 99.9% confidence in the result. And that's a lot.

In Table 14.2, you can see that p-values, alphas, and confidence relate in obvious ways.

Table 14.2 Statistical Significance Reporting

Reported p-value	Alpha	Confidence
p < 0.05	α = 0.05	95%
p < 0.01	α = 0.01	99%
p < 0.001	α = 0.001	99.9%

SUBSTANTIVE AND STATISTICAL SIGNIFICANCE IN MULTIPLE REGRESSION

Be careful. It is common and frankly tempting to conclude that big regression coefficients are automatically statistically significant or a high level of statistical significance means greater substantive effects of an independent variable on the dependent variable. While this is not necessarily inaccurate – in that independent variables can have big regression coefficients or high levels of statistical significance – they represent different properties of the regression coefficients.

Big regression coefficients and high levels of statistical significance seem to signal that 'something is going on'. However, remember two things.

(Continued)

> One, each regression coefficient is the mathematical relationship between that independent variable and the dependent variable. Given the range of different variables, what may seem to be big substantive effects may simply be a function of different scales of different variables. This does not automatically mean that the coefficient is statistically significant.
>
> Two, statistical significance is determined by the probability that what we are observing is unlikely to be a product of chance and therefore exists – at some level of confidence – in the population from which the sample data was drawn. Although this is a function of the relationship between the regression coefficient and its standard error, it is not a function of the size of the regression coefficient alone. Thus, a high degree of statistical significance does not automatically translate into substantive significance – i.e., the effect is stronger or bigger than variables with less statistical significance. A high level of statistical significance tells us about the probability our sample estimate exists in the population and nothing more.

Element 3: Model Fit

Thus far, each element has focused on the individual performance of the included independent variables. But what of overall performance? How can we determine that our multiple regression is, in effect, working well?

This evaluation process is often called 'model fit' or 'goodness of fit'. Measures of **model fit** tell us how well our model – this specific assemblage of independent variables – perform in explaining the variation in the dependent variable. There are several of these, two of which we will look at now, and a few more that we will take up in future chapters.

One we have already seen before. Recall from bivariate regression, the coefficient of determination (R^2) reports the proportion of common variation between the independent and dependent variables. It has a range from 0 – no common variation – to 1 – complete coordination. In multiple regression, R^2 now tells us the common variation of all the independent variables (X's) with the dependent variable (Y). Rather than identifying each independent variable's contribution, it is a measure of the collection or assembly of the included independent variables.

Most statistical software programs will, in addition to reporting the coefficient of determination (R^2), report an 'adjusted-R^2'. The **adjusted-R^2** accounts for both the number of independent variables ('k') as well as the number of observations ('n'). In doing so, it reports a lower level of common variation. Perhaps this seems like a strange penalty. However, the adjusted-R^2 discounts the 'kitchen sink' approach in which we just throw everything into the regression we possibly can with hope of raising the level of common variation, often called over-specification. The more variables we include, the more discount we incur. This serves as a governor to any impulse to just dump independent variables into the model. As such, adjusted-R^2 is preferred to R^2 as a measure for model fit.

Its rollercoaster equation is:

$$Adjusted - R^2 = 1 - (1 - R^2)\left(\frac{n-1}{n-k-1}\right)$$

We want a parsimonious model. We want our multiple regression analysis to be sleek and efficient. While multiple regression allows us to include a number of independent variables, we are seeking an equilibrium between applying too little control versus crowding the model with too many unnecessary elements. If we don't control for all the elements necessary to isolate a relationship, we run the risk of our assessment being biased toward or away from the one in which we are interested. Technically, if we omit important variables in our analysis, the remaining variables 'soak up' some of the explanatory power of the variable we left out. As such, these results would misrepresent the nature of the relationship. In other words, we would not have a lot of confidence in our guess about that relationship. On the other hand, we can't simply throw everything in to our analysis (again, the kitchen sink approach). While statistics are efficient handlers of large amounts of data, every additional included variable imposes on the estimating procedure.

NESTED MODELS AND ADJUSTED R^2

In addition to overall model fit, adjusted-R^2 allows the comparison of nested models. Nested models are separate regression models than contain the set of another model. Or conversely, each regression model is a subset of the previous one.

For example, a set of nested models of individual=level political participation might look like this (see Table 14.3):

Table 14.3 Example: Adjusted-R^2

Model 1: Political Participation = Age + Education	Adjusted-R^2=0.117
Model 2: Political Participation = Age + Education + Income	Adjusted-R^2=0.210
Model 3: Political Participation = Age + Education + Income + Civic Skills	Adjusted-R^2=0.340

Because Model 1 is nested in both Models 2 and 3, we could compare the relative improvement of the performance of the model – by including 'income' and then 'income and civic skills' – by comparing the adjusted-R^2s. That is, the adjusted-R^2 of Model 1 tells us that 'age' and 'education' explain about 11.7% of the variation in the political participation. Adding 'income' to Model 1 not only improves the overall explanatory power – despite having added more variables – to 21.0% but we can approximate that 9.3% [21.0% – 11.7%=9.3%] of that is the introduction of 'income'. Similarly for Model 3, we can compare Model 3 to both Models 1 and 2, explaining not only greater overall model performance but the addition of additional variables.

The second model fit measure is the F-test. The **F-test** is a test of whether the model is legitimate by testing the joint probability that all the regression coefficients are simultaneously zero ('0'). That is, $H_0: \beta_1=\beta_2=\beta_3=\ldots \beta_n=0$. Whereas t-tests evaluate the statistical significance of individual regression coefficients, the F-test can tell us whether this collection or assembly of independent variables works at all by testing their joint performance. One can easily imagine that if all the regression coefficients performed so poorly (close to zero substantive effect), this suggests that the choice of independent variables is not optimal. Like other tests, the F-test has its own distribution that we will not engage. However, the F-test reports the likelihood that your chosen and included independent variables work to jointly explain variation in the dependent variable – or not.

In the Field: Modelling with Multiple Regression

In the Descriptive Statistics section, we looked at bivariate regression, and as a specific example, the relationship between 'Voice and Accountability' (V&A) and the Corruption Perceptions Index (CPI). We modelled this relationship with our 6-step Modelling Process. With multiple regression we can follow the same modelling process with the added ability to simultaneously control for the influence of other independent variables and determine the statistical significance of each one.

The Modelling Process

- *Step One:* A research question
- *Step Two:* Identify variables
- *Step Three:* Pearson's Product Moment Correlation Coefficient
- *Step Four:* The regression equation
- *Step Five*: Model fit
- *Step Six:* Interpretation.

Based on our research choices and analytical design, with the CPI as the dependent variable and V&A as the independent variable, we arrived at the following model:

$y = 46.58+13.27\ (x) + \varepsilon$

Or

$CPI = 46.58+13.27(V\&A)+\varepsilon$

We can summarize this relationship from the interpretation in *Step Six*:

> To provide a provisional answer our research question, 'To what extent does the capacity for citizens to influence and exercise control over their government move with the level of corruption in their country?', we use two variables available for 63 countries. The dependent variable is the level of corruption for which we

use the Corruptions Perceptions Index. The independent variable is the ability of citizens to shape their own government for which we use the Voice and Accountability measure. These interval-level variables have a substantial, positive correlation of r=0.68. The regression equation y = 46.58+13.27 (x) + ε tells us that, on average, for every 1-unit change in V&A, there will be a 13.27-unit increase in the CPI. Given that zero is a value in the range of V&A, when V&A is 0, the CPI is 46.58. The adj-R^2=0.459 tells us that 45.9% of the variation in the CPI can be explained by variation in V&A.

As we noted then, while an impressive initial analysis, it is plausible to suggest that the CPI may respond to the influence of variables other than merely democratic institutional performance as measured by V&A. With multiple regression we can determine to what extent it does. Let's expand on this example using the 6-step Modelling Process.

Step One asks for a research question. Let's stay with our interest in the bivariate relationship: 'To what extent does the capacity for citizens to influence and exercise control over their government shape the level of corruption in their country?'

Step Two asks us to identify the variables. We already have Voice and Accountability as a measure of democratic performance. What additional variables might influence the level of corruption in a country?

The answer to this question is neither banal nor obvious. One way to identify key independent variables is to see what work has been done, what consensuses and disagreements exist in the literature (see a fuller discussion in Chapter 5). In addition, and perhaps more conceptually, we can consider what is likely to confound the relationship that we have already observed between corruption and Voice and Accountability. For example, one might consider that the Human Development Index – as a measure of the quality of life in a country – might 'confound' some of the explanatory power of Voice and Accountability as a higher quality of life – even if also loosely related to the performance of political institutions – may be more believably linked to the inability of corrupt practices to take root in a society.

In any case, using both methods, we identify a wide variety of potential variables: a measure of a country's overall social development (Human Development Index); a measure of the country's attractiveness, thus the number of people staying or leaving the country (Human Flight and Brain Drain); the level of media freedom (Press Freedom Index); and a macro-economic indicator (unemployment rate). In this exercise, we will use only interval-level variables. Multiple regression can handle ordinal- and nominal-level variables as well; however, we will take this up in greater detail in a subsequent chapter.

Most IR students are familiar with using countries as the unit of analysis, so here we return to the random sample of 63 countries from the Quality of Governance dataset used previously.

- Dependent Variable (DV)
  - Corruptions Perceptions Index (CPI):
    - Aggregated perceptions of business people and country experts of the level on corruption in the public sector.

- Range: 0 (highly corrupt) to 100 (very clean).
- Mean: 42.1; Standard Deviation: 18.5; N=63
- Source: Transparency International
- Independent Variables (IVs)
  - Voice and Accountability (V&A):
    - A measure reflecting the ability of citizens to participate in selecting their government, as well as freedom of expression and association.
    - Range: −2 (very low) to 2 (very high).
    - Mean: −0.34; Standard Deviation: 0.96; N=63
    - Source: World Governance Indicators (World Bank)
  - Human Development Index (HDI):
    - A measure of average achievement in key dimensions of human development: a long and healthy life, being knowledgeable, and have a decent standard of living.
    - Range: 0.0 (low) to 1.0 (high).
    - Mean: 0.74; Standard Deviation: 0.14; N=63
    - Source: UNESCO Institute for Statistics
  - Human Flight and Brain Drain (HF/DB):
    - A measure to capture migration per capita, human capital, and the emigration of the educated population.
    - Range: 0 (low) to 10 (high).
    - Mean: 5.27; Standard Deviation: 1.97; N=63
    - Source: The Fund for Peace
  - Press Freedom Index (PFI):
    - A measure of the amount of freedom journalists and the media have and the efforts made by governments to see that press freedom is respected.
    - Range: 0 (total press freedom) and 100 (no press freedom).
    - Mean: 40.94; Standard Deviation: 16.18; N=63
    - Source: Reporters Sans Frontières
  - Unemployment Rate (UNEMP):
    - Percent of the labour force without work but available and seeking employment.
    - Range: 0.0 (no unemployment) to 100 (all unemployed).
    - Mean: 6.86; Standard Deviation: 5.13 N=63
    - Source: World Development Indicators (World Bank)

Step Three: The correlation between each of the independent variables and the dependent variable is less informative than in an investigation of the bivariate relationship. However, it can give us an importance sense of the relationships in the data (see Table 14.4).

Table 14.4 Step Three: Correlation

	V&A	HDI	HF/BD	PFI	UNEMP
CPI	r=0.68	r=0.72	r=−0.75	r=−0.52	r=−0.17

Based on the interpretations from Table 14.4, V&A and HDI have a *substantial positive* correlation with CPI. HF/DB has a *very strong negative* correlation with HDI. PFI has a *substantial negative* correlation with CPI. And UNEMP has a *low negative* correlation with CPI. Although we are about to apply multiple regression to these variables, looking at these bivariate correlations is helpful in a crucial way.

As we have seen in the previous paragraph, it is important to get a sense that the data are acting the way we would expect. Recall that a high value for CPI means a less corrupt country. Thus, as V&A – the ability of citizens to meaningfully participate in politics – and HDI – broader social development – increase, their positive relationship means that we expect to see countries move from more corrupt (a low CPI score) to a less corrupt country (a high CPI score). As Brain Drain – the loss of educated citizenry to emigration – increases; Press Freedom becomes worse (from low score of total press freedom to a high score of no press freedom); and unemployment rises, their negative relationship leads us to expect to see countries move from less corrupt (a high CPI score) to a more corrupt country (a low CPI score).

We need to make sure that we understand what the directions of the relationship really mean. For many practitioners, such unintuitively coded variables can be 'reverse coded' meaning that we can reverse the numbers so that higher numbers are more intuitively linked to preferred outcomes rather than 'negative' outcomes. Checking on this now can potentially save you a lot of time later as it gives you a working intuition of these data and how they relate to one another. Thus, taking a moment to examine the relationships among the data is always a prudent and intelligent choice.

Step Four asks for the regression equation. The multiple regression model for CPI would look like this:

$$Y_i = \alpha + \beta_1(V\&A) + \beta_2(HDI) + \beta_3(HF/BD) + \beta_4(PFI) + \beta_5(UNEMP) + \varepsilon$$

Using a statistical software package to produce the results of a multiple regression analysis with CPI as the dependent variable and V&A, HDI, HF/BD, PFI, and UNEMP as the independent variables, the result is Table 14.5a. While there is a lot of information here, we can use this output to create the regression equation.

Let's break it down.

Looking at the table across the lower half in Table 14.5a, we can see CPI at the top of the far-left column and the independent variables lined up below. The column labelled 'coefficient' is just that, the regression coefficient – β – for each independent variable (in Table 14.5b).

Therefore, inserting these values in the regression model, we arrive at:

$$Y_i = 53.46 + 11.2\,(V\&A) + 11.4\,(HDI) - 4.02(HF/BD) + 0.20(PFI) - 0.46(UNEMP) + \varepsilon$$

These regression coefficients represent the variable-specific relationship between each independent variable and the CPI (the dependent variable). This is the substantive significance of this set of independent variables on CPI. However, not all of these are statistically significant.

Table 14.5a Multiple Regression Output: CPI

Corruptions Perceptions Index	Unstandardized regression coefficient	Standard error	t	p>|t|
Voice and Accountability	11.204	3.383	3.31	0.002
Human Development Index	11.400	24.382	0.47	0.642
Human Flight and Brain Drain	−4.019	1.637	−2.45	0.017
Press Freedom Index	0.203	0.185	1.10	0.278
Unemployment Rate	−0.460	0.266	−1.73	0.090
Constant	53.464	25.178	2.12	0.038
Number of observations	63			
$F_{(5,57)}$	26.93			
Prob.> F	0.0000			
R^2	0.7026			
Adjusted-R^2	0.6765			

Table 14.5b Multiple Regression Output: Regression Coefficients

Corruptions Perceptions Index	Unstandardized regression coefficient	Standard error	t	p>|t|
Voice and Accountability	11.204	3.383	3.31	0.002
Human Development Index	11.400	24.382	0.47	0.642
Human Flight and Brain Drain	−4.019	1.637	−2.45	0.017
Press Freedom Index	0.203	0.185	1.10	0.278
Unemployment Rate	−0.460	0.266	−1.73	0.090
Constant	53.464	25.178	2.12	0.038
Number of observations	63			
$F_{(5,57)}$	26.93			
Prob.> F	0.0000			
R^2	0.7026			
Adjusted-R^2	0.6765			

Recall that to produce a t-score (our test statistic for statistical significance), we divide the beta by its standard error. In Table 14.5c, we can see that doing so, dividing 'Coefficient' by the 'Std. err.' produces the t-test statistic ('t', highlighted in the box below).

Table 14.5c Multiple Regression Output: t-test Statistics

Corruptions Perceptions Index	Unstandardized regression coefficient	Standard error	t	p>|t|
Voice and Accountability	11.204	3.383	3.31	0.002
Human Development Index	11.400	24.382	0.47	0.642
Human Flight and Brain Drain	−4.019	1.637	−2.45	0.017
Press Freedom Index	0.203	0.185	1.10	0.278
Unemployment Rate	−0.460	0.266	−1.73	0.090
Constant	53.464	25.178	2.12	0.038
Number of observations	63			
F(5,57)	26.93			
Prob.> F	0.0000			
R^2	0.7026			
Adjusted-R^2	0.6765			

We compare the t-test statistic – generated from these data – to the critical t-value determined by the sample size (by way of degrees of freedom). Remember, this is why we use the t-distribution as it accommodates smaller sample sizes and comes to resemble the Standard Normal z-distribution as the sample size grows large.

Wait. I thought we used degrees of freedom but also chose a level of confidence to determine the critical or rejection region? Yes, we used to select a level of confidence – and corresponding alpha – as part of determining the t-value that defines critical or rejection region (see Table 14.2 above). However, in multiple regression, we are instead given p-values. The p-values tell us exactly how confident we can be in our regression coefficient estimate. For our multiple regression model of CPI, we can see that while we have estimates for the regression coefficients for every independent variable, not all of them are statistically significant (see Table 14.5d).

Let's start at the top (in the grey box). V&A has a regression coefficient β_1=11.20. This estimate has a t-test statistic of 3.31 with a probability of 0.002. This means that we can be p<0.05 confident. We can also be p<0.01 confident but we cannot be p<0.001 confident that this estimated beta can be found in the population from which this sample was drawn. That is, the p-value for the V&A regression coefficient is 0.002, which falls in the rejection region for 99% confidence (defined by the t-value for α=0.01) but does not fall in the rejection region of 99.9% confidence (defined by the t-value for α=0.001). Or put another way, again referring back to Table 14.2, we can be 99.8% confident and in terms of statistical reporting, we can only report the level of confidence we exceed, here, 99% confidence but not 99.9% confidence. Thus, for every 1-unit increase in V&A, the CPI would increase 11.2 units (α<0.01), controlling for all other variables.

Table 14.5d Multiple Regression Output: p-values

Corruptions Perceptions Index	Unstandardized regression coefficient	Standard error	t	p>|t|
Voice and Accountability	11.204	3.383	3.31	0.002
Human Development Index	11.400	24.382	0.47	0.642
Human Flight and Brain Drain	−4.019	1.637	−2.45	0.017
Press Freedom Index	0.203	0.185	1.10	0.278
Unemployment Rate	−0.460	0.266	−1.73	0.090
Constant	53.464	25.178	2.12	0.038
Number of observations	63			
F(5,57)	26.93			
Prob.> F	0.0000			
R^2	0.7026			
Adjusted-R^2	0.6765			

- For HDI, we have low expectations. Look at the t-test statistic, 0.47. We know that the lowest critical value is 1.96 (the Standard Normal critical value for 95%) and the t-distribution critical value when the sample size is high. This is nowhere close. Thus, not surprisingly, we find the p-value is 0.642 meaning we can have 35.8% confidence.
- For HF/BD, we find that the regression coefficient of −4.02 is statistically significant at p<0.05. Why? The p-value is 0.017 which falls in the rejection region for 95% confidence (defined by the t-value for $\alpha=0.05$) but does not fall in the rejection region of 99% confidence (defined by the t-value for $\alpha=0.01$). Thus, when HF/BD increases by 1-unit, CPI would decrease by 4.02 units ($\alpha<0.05$), controlling for all other variables.

Finally, both PFI and UNEMP are found to be statistically insignificant. Both variables' p-values – 0.278 and 0.090 – are greater than the lowest level of confidence (95%, defined by the t-value for $\alpha=0.05$). What does this mean? Well, that's a big part of bringing the Illustrious Triumvirate together. We have been able to describe the relationship we are interested in, controlling for other potential explanations, and identify the relationships that we can infer to the population from which the data were drawn.

Therefore, in our analysis of what drives the CPI, the multiple regression analysis has identified V&A and HF/BD as statistically significant which means that the regression coefficients estimated by multiple regression can be inferred to the population at the associated levels of confidence. In the case of those that failed to reach statistical significance – HDI, PFI, UNEMP – the regression coefficients cannot be inferred to the population. This implies that we cannot reject the notion that these relationships are not meaningfully different from zero.

STATISTICAL INSIGNIFICANCE

One question that invariably arises is: 'If independent variables are found to be statistically insignificant, should I take them out of the regression model?'

There are competing sides of this debate. However, the majority would encourage us to keep statistically insignificant variables in if they are theoretically expected to be included. One reason is simply that removing them may bias the other regression coefficient estimates. That is, while they may not be significant, multiple regression can appropriately assign what little effect each included variable has. Even if you are interested in prediction as the only goal (i.e., inference is not your concern) in which the beta may be more important than the p-value – it doesn't make a lot of sense to bias the remaining betas.

Keep in mind that independent variables can become insignificant for many reasons. Small or limited datasets, measurement issues, or a dynamic state of your topic. This is an important question that leads us to significant challenges in multiple regression such as omitted variable bias and multicollinearity.

We take this up further in the following chapters.

Finally, like bivariate regression, we can create a Prediction Equation. As in bivariate regression, we simply remove the error term. This allows us to predict the value of CPI given the various regression coefficients of the included independent variables and intercept (α).

$$\hat{Y}_i = 53.46 + 11.2 \ (V\&A) + 11.4 \ (HDI) - 4.02(HF/BD) + 0.20(PFI) - 0.46(UNEMP)$$

Remember that $\hat{Y}$ is not expected to be one of the numbers in the dataset but merely the expectation of what we might find. Thus, we could put in the mean value for each IV and predict the level of CPI for such a country.

$$\hat{Y}_i = 53.46 + 11.2 \ (-0.34) + 11.4 \ (0.74) - 4.02(5.27) + 0.20(40.94) - 0.46(6.86)$$

$$CPI = 41.94$$

At the mean level of each independent variable (assuming such a boring country existed), the expected value for the CPI is 41.94. However, unlike bivariate regression, we cannot draw the regression line.

Why not?

Well, the number of independent variables included in the regression model are the dimensions of the solution. That is, in bivariate regression we have 1 independent variable. The solution is a 1-dimensional solution, a line. If we have 2 independent variables, the solution is 2-dimensional, a plane. If we have 3 independent variables, the solution is a 3-dimensional shape. *Ad infinitum*.... Therefore, in our multiple regression model, we have 5 independent variables and thus the solution is a 5-dimensional shape, which is hard to draw.

Step Five asks us for measures of Model Fit. In Table 14.5e, at the bottom, we can see two of such measures (in the grey box). First is the R^2, or, more precisely, in a multiple regression, the adjusted-R^2. The adjusted-R^2 tells us that 67.65% of the variation in the dependent variables can be explained by the combination of these five independent variables. Second, the null hypothesis of the F-test tells us whether the included independent variables are simultaneously equal to zero, suggesting a very bad combination of independent variables. Here, we can see that the F-test statistic of 26.93 is statistically significant ('Prob> F=0.0000') above $p<0.001$. That is, the probability of observing 26.93 on the F-distribution is very unlikely and the test statistic falls in the rejection region allowing us to reject the null hypothesis of the joint values of all the regression coefficients are zero.

Table 14.5e Multiple Regression: Model Fit

Corruptions Perceptions Index	Unstandardized regression coefficient	Standard error	t	p>|t|
Voice and Accountability	11.204	3.383	3.31	0.002
Human Development Index	11.400	24.382	0.47	0.642
Human Flight and Brain Drain	−4.019	1.637	−2.45	0.017
Press Freedom Index	0.203	0.185	1.10	0.278
Unemployment Rate	−0.460	0.266	−1.73	0.090
Constant	53.464	25.178	2.12	0.038

Number of observations	63
F(5,57)	26.93
Prob.> F	0.0000
R^2	0.7026
Adjusted-R^2	0.6765

Step Six asks us to comprehensively interpret the results. What do we include and how do we report it?

Our analysis has attempted to answer the following question: 'To what extent does the capacity for citizens to influence and exercise control over their government shape the level of corruption in their country?' Using data on 63 countries, we have regressed Voice and Accountability (V&A), the Human Development Index (HDI), Human Flight and Brain Drain (HF/BD), the Press Freedom Index (PFI), and the unemployment rate (UNEMP) on the Corruption Perceptions Index (CPI). The adjusted-R^2 tells us that 67.7%

of the variation in the CPI can be explained by the independent variables in our model. Although not all the independent variables reached statistical significance, the F-test tells us that the model is sufficient (p<0.001). V&A and HF/BD are statistically significant at p<0.01 and p<0.05, respectively. Specifically, for every 1-unit increase in V&A, the CPI would increase 11.2 units (α<0.01), controlling for all other variables. As HF/BD increased by 1-unit, CPI would decrease by 4.02 units (α<0.05), controlling for all other variables.

If we wanted to increase transparency of our results, we could also create a table summarizing the key elements (see Table 14.6). One common reporting flamboyance is the use of asterisks or 'stars' to indicate the level of confidence. Very often they will use one star ('*') to signify p<0.05 or 95% confidence; two stars ('**') to signify p<0.01 or 99% confidence; and three stars ('***') to signify p<0.001 or 99.9% confidence. Every now and then, particularly if the number of observations is low, you may find one star ('*') to signify p<0.10 or 90% confidence (and an adjustment to the other stars to accommodate this). It is good practice to always check quickly.

Table 14.6 Multiple Regression Analysis of the Corruption Perceptions Index

Corruptions Perceptions Index	Unstandardized regression coefficients (se)		
Voice and Accountability	**11.20** (3.38)**	Number of observations	63
Human Development Index	11.40 (24.38)	F-test (5,57)	26.93***
Human Flight and Brain Drain	**−4.02* (1.64)**	Adjusted-R-squared	0.6765
Press Freedom Index	0.20 (0.19)		
Unemployment Rate	−0.46 (0.27)		
Constant	**53.46* (25.18)**	*p<0.05; **p<0.01; ***p<0.001	

There is no one 'most correct' way to report the output of a multiple regression analysis. However, at a minimum, we need to report the substantive impact of the statistically significant variables (including beta and level of confidence), making sure that we state that we are controlling for the impact of the other included variables. We also report the measures of model fit. Not always, but *relative strength* (using standardized betas) can be interesting although we do not include them here.

A Reflection on Multiple Regression

For the empirical study of Political Science, and the social sciences more generally, the most difficult problems are:

1. *Uncertainty:* the challenge of clearly demonstrating a relationship between our variables of interest

2. *Inference:* demonstrating what we have observed is not merely chance but likely to be a 'real' relationship.

The cumulative power of multiple regression provides the ability to address both of these problems by estimating the substantive and statistical significance of the relationship between a dependent variable and a set of independent variables. The ability of multiple regression to assign *partial* explanatory power to each independent variable by controlling for the effects of the other independent variables strengthens our claims to approach the real substantive nature of each relationship. At the same time, the ability to estimate the probability of each relationship being a function of chance or not strengthens our ability to make inferential claims about the results of the analysis. Together, this improves our ability to rigorously test theory and advance the collective theoretical knowledge.

To be clear, multiple regression is no analytical panacea. Its sophistication comes with some non-trivial problems and challenges. Many of these problems are common and relatively easy to address. Other challenges will require a deeper consideration on how to proceed. We troubleshoot multiple regression in Chapter 16.

However, before we do so, we will be introduced to additions to multiple regression in the following chapter. We examine the use of dummy variables, interactions, and multi-item indices, which will allow us to include and evaluate a wider range of potential variables. In particular, this includes the intuition and practical aspects of including non-interval variables. This will reinforce the use and interpretation of a standard multiple regression model developed above.

End of Chapter Summary

- Multiple regression simultaneously tests several variables in order to control for the impact of all included independent variables on the dependent variable.
- Multiple regression gives us three key analytical abilities: Description, Inference, and Control (the 'Illustrious Triumvirate').
- The independent variables included in a multiple regression model to explain the dependent variable should be selected on the basis of clear reason or theory.
- Isolating the substantive nature of the relationship is crucial in moving our estimate toward its true state.
- 'Holding all other variables constant' is the power of controlling for other possible explanations of variation in the dependent variable.
- Statistical significance is important to our understanding and testing of theory but less relevant to prediction.
- Model fit is basically an assessment of how much 'predictive value' we get from this or that set of independent variables.
- Multiple regression provides the ability to address both uncertainty and inference by estimating the substantive and statistical significance of relationship between a dependent variable and a set of independent variables.

Glossary

- **Multiple regression** is the technique to test several independent variables simultaneously, thus controlling for the impact of each independent variable on the variation of the dependent variable.
- **Partials** or 'first-order correlation coefficients' are each independent variable's *partial* contribution to the total explained variance of the dependent variable.
- **Standardized regression coefficients** allow us to make rudimentary comparisons of relative strength by standardizing each regression coefficient to have unit variance.
- The **p-value** is calculated probability that – in the case of multiple regression – the estimated regression coefficient is a function of chance.
- Measures of **model fit** tell us how well our model – this specific assemblage of independent variables – performs in explaining the variation in the dependent variable.
- The **adjusted-R^2** reports the explained variance in the dependent variable by the set of independent variables and 'adjusts' for both the number of independent variables as well as the number of observations.
- The **F-test** is a measure of model fit that tests whether the joint probability that all the regression coefficients are simultaneously zero ('0').

Questions

Let's work through the Modelling Process for multiple regression. I will start us off with *Steps One* and *Two* and you can complete *Steps Three, Four, Five,* and *Six* as Questions 1, 2, 3, and 4.

Given the state of the literature, Brexit, and what may be described as democratic backsliding in both Poland and Hungary, we are interested in the relationship between EU unification and citizens' orientations to democracy as a system of government.

Thus, a research question for *Step One* might be: 'To what extent do citizens' preferences for democracy shape their views about EU unification?'

Step Two asks us to identify the variables. Using the European Election Study 2019, let's take a look at European citizens' support for the ongoing EU project. Using survey data from all 27 EU member states and the United Kingdom, we can propose a straightforward model of support with four key independent variables capturing citizens' personal ideological position, their pro-/anti-market stance, pro-/anti-democracy stance, and pro-/anti-immigration stance.

- Dependent Variable (DV):
    o European Unification (EU Unification):
        ❑ Some say European unification should be pushed further. Others say it already has gone too far. What is your opinion? (Q23)

- Range: 0 to 10, where 0 means unification 'has already gone too far' and 10 means it 'should be pushed further'
- Mean: 5.38; Standard Deviation: 3.09; N=20,230
- Independent Variables (IVs):
    - Ideological Self-Placement (Left–Right Ideology):
        - In political matters people talk of 'the left' and 'the right'. What is your position? (Q11)
        - Range: 0 means 'left' and 10 means 'right'
        - Mean: 5.22; Standard Deviation: 2.59; N=20,230
    - Role of the Market (Support for the Market):
        - What do you think of state regulation and control of the economy? (Q14_1)
        - Range: 0 means 'You fully favour state intervention in the economy' and 10 means 'You fully oppose state intervention in the economy'
        - Mean: 5.01; Standard Deviation: 2.60; N=20,230
    - Democracy (Support for Democracy):
        - How important is it for you to live in a country that is governed democratically? (Q16)
        - Range: 0 means 'Not at all important' and 10 means 'Absolutely important'
        - Mean: 8.60; Standard Deviation: 2.09; N=20,230
    - Immigration (Immigration Position):
        - What do you think of immigration? (Q14_5)
        - Range: 0 means 'Fully in favour of a restrictive policy on immigration' and 10 means 'Fully opposed to a restrictive policy on immigration'
        - Mean: 4.40; Standard Deviation: 3.27; N=20,230

1. *Step Three:* Below are the correlations for all the variables (see Table 14.7). Describe these correlations and provide an intuition of how they relate to one another.

Table 14.7 Step Three: Correlation

	Left–Right	Market	Democracy	Immigration
EU unification	−0.04	0.01	0.17	0.21

2. *Step Four* asks for the regression equation. Use the regression output in Table 14.8 to complete the regression equation, report the substantive and statistical significance of each independent variable. Then, produce the prediction equation and, using the mean values from above, calculate the prediction for someone with 'average' values on each of the included variables.

Table 14.8 Multiple Regression Output – European Unification

EU unification	Unstandardized regression coefficient	Standard error	t	p>|t|
Left–Right Ideology	−0.006	0.008	−0.72	0.471
Support for Markets	0.005	0.008	0.57	0.572
Support for Democracy	0.268	0.010	26.21	0.000
Immigration Position	0.201	0.007	31.00	0.000
Constant	2.263	0.111	20.46	0.000
Number of observations	20,230			
$F_{(4, 20225)}$	424.17			
Prob.> F	0.0000			
R^2	0.0774			
Adjusted-R^2	0.0772			

3. *Step Five* asks us for measures of Model Fit. Continuing with Table 14.8, fully report the measures of model fit.
4. *Step Six* asks for a comprehensive interpretation. Please include one paragraph – a table is not necessary.
5. To what extent does multiple regression – as a sophisticated statistical technique – address the two central problems in the study of Political Science or the social sciences more broadly?
6. Why do you think only interval-level variables can be included in multiple regression analysis? Is this a problem?
7. In the Box: 'Nested Models and the Coefficient of Determination (R^2)', calculate the overall explanatory improvement for Model 3 over Models 1 and 2. Also calculate the explanatory power of adding civic skills (comparing Model 3 to Model 2). Explain fully what this tells us.

Annotated References and Further Reading

It would be nearly impossible to include a 'best of' list of articles that include multiple regression. Multiple regression is the standard and widely used. It would be like trying to make a list of people that wear shoes.

Loveless, Matthew and Robert Rohrschneider, 2011. 'Public perceptions of the EU as a system of governance' *Living Reviews in European Governance* **6(11). http://europeangovernance-livingreviews.org/Articles/lreg-2011-2 https://doi.org/10.12942/lreg-2011-2**
This is a summary of the determinants of EU support for questions 1–4 above.

Signposts to the Accompanying Digital Resources

Datasets used in this chapter

- *Quality of Governance:* Teorell, Jan, Aksel Sundström, Sören Holmberg, Bo Rothstein, Natalia Alvarado Pachon, and Cem Mert Dalli. 2021. The Quality of Government Standard Dataset, version Jan21. University of Gothenburg: The Quality of Government Institute, www.qog.pol.gu.se
- *European Election Study 2019:* Schmitt, Hermann, Hobolt, Sara B., van der Brug, Wouter, and Popa, Sebastian Adrian (2020). European Parliament Election Study 2019, Voter Study. GESIS Data Archive, Cologne. ZA7581 Data file Version 1.0.0, https://doi.org/10.4232/1.13473

15
EXTENSIONS TO MULTIPLE REGRESSION

> **LEARNING OUTCOMES**
>
> In this chapter, you will be able to
>
> - Include both nominal- and ordinal-level variables as independent variables in a multiple regression model in the form of dummy variables.
> - Understand the importance of the reference category for interpreting dummy variables.
> - Develop and include indices as independent variables in multiple regression that capture multi-dimensional measures or variables that are difficult to measure directly.
> - Use interaction terms to capture the contingency of two independent variables' relationship on the dependent variable.

Introduction

Multiple regression has a lot of power. It allows us to confront and even address many of the challenges central to theoretical and methodological analyses in Political Science. However, you may have also noticed that in the last chapter all of the independent variables used to explain the dependent variable were interval-level variables. The reason is simply that regression, as an analytical technique, performs mathematical transformations of the data in order to determine their substantive and statistical significance. Interval-level variables, in which the intervals are important and uniform, lend themselves most easily to this type of data wrangling.

However, recall our example on corruption in the previous chapter. There may be non-interval-level variables that may be important to understanding why a country is corrupt or not. Perhaps, international membership (or not) of organizations such as the EU, WTO, G7, or Mercosur, help maintain and enforce a higher standard of transparency and thus less corruption. Yet, membership (or not) is not an interval-level variable.

Or recall the model of EU support in the Questions in the previous chapter. What if we wanted to control for a respondent's marital status or their social class? These are not interval-level variables: marital status is a nominal-level variable, and social class is an ordinal-level variable. Or perhaps we simply want to know whether the respondent was from Western Europe or Eastern Europe?

Figure 15.1 is the scatterplot for support for EU unification and the location of the respondent (0 = France; 1 = Poland). It would be hard to argue that a line best summarizes the nature of this relationship. This seems deeply problematic. How do we include nominal- and ordinal-level variables in multiple regression?

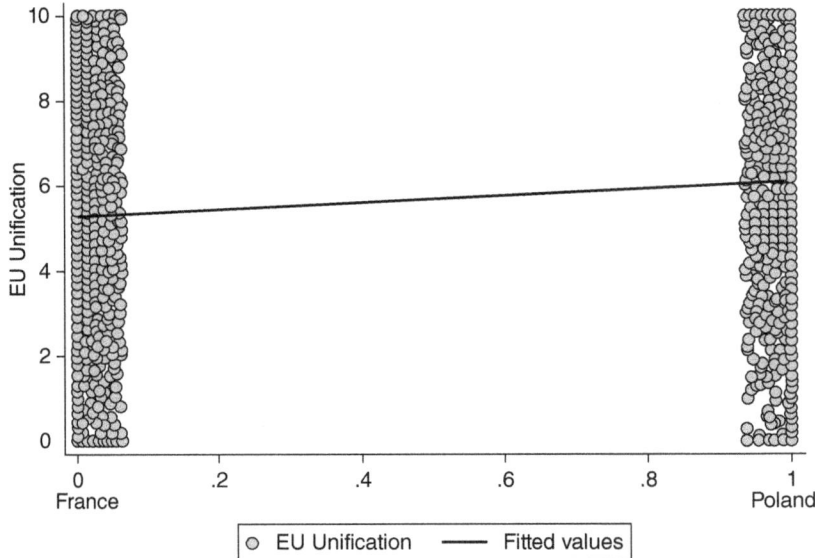

Figure 15.1 Support for EU Unification: Western and Eastern Europeans

We use dummy variables. Dummy variables allow us to include both nominal- and ordinal-level variables as independent variables in multiple regression. In addition, we will explore two types of multi-item indices that can merge existing variables to measure underlying or unmeasured concepts in which we may be interested. Finally, we will also explore the use of interactions to model the impact of two independent variables that may explain variation in the dependent variable both independently – as well as by interacting with one another.

Why do we have all these aftermarket accessories for the all-powerful multiple regression? Multiple regression is the chassis of statistical analysis. A chassis is the core or frame that maintains an object's integrity of both form and function. You can imagine, for example, the frame of a car. Features and colours can be added and changed, but the core frame constitutes the necessary essence of 'a car'. Thus, multiple regression is the core operating function that can accommodate a wide range of updates and extensions. As we will see, there are few places multiple regression cannot take us.

This chapter aims to expand your ability to account for a wide range of potential independent, explanatory variables. Fortunately for us, the underlying performance of multiple regression is unchanged.

Dichotomous Dummy Variables

Recall interval-level variables have nice mathematical properties such as order and meaningful intervals between categories that make them amenable to statistical analysis. In contrast to this, nominal-level variables are a series of categories that lack any natural order. And ordinal-level variables are categories that, while they have a reasonable order, the intervals between each category are neither conceptually nor mathematically the same.

Thus, the question becomes, how do we include variables that lack mathematical properties into the estimating procedure of multiple regression that assumes a linear relationship between the independent and dependent variables?

The answer is, aside from the least impressive moniker in statistics, dummy variables. **Dummy variables** allow us to include nominal- and ordinal-level variables in a multiple regression analysis by getting multiple regression to perform a difference of means t-test for each category against a reference category.

A dummy variable is a recoded nominal- or ordinal-level variable that 'tricks' the least squares estimation procedure of multiple regression to estimate a difference in the means between each category and a **base** or **reference category**. Specifically, we use '0' as the absence and '1' as the presence of one category of the variable. (*Note:* It is important to use '0' as the base category as '0' is mathematically meaningful.) In this way, we can include nominal- and ordinal- level variables in our multiple regression models.

The base or reference category is crucial and refers to the value of the variable against which the regression tests. For dichotomous variables that have two categories: member/non-member; democracy/non-democracy; government party/opposition party; etc.... one category is the base/reference and one is the dummy. The choice of which is the base category is important for a proper test of theory and an intuitive understanding of the results.

Let's imagine that you have a multiple regression model such as the following in which x_2 is a dummy variable that has two values: '0' (the absence of a value) and '1' (the presence of a value):

$$y = \alpha + \beta_1 x_1 + \beta_2 x_2 + \varepsilon$$

Recall that the intercept is the value of the dependent variable when the independent variable(s) are zero. So, the dummy variable technique simply adjusts the intercept (α) by adding or subtracting the value of β_2. This is why it is crucial to use '0' as the reference category and '1' as the dummy category. The dummy variable effectively creates two regression models contained within the original above.

First, if the dummy variable is '0', β_2 becomes '0' and disappears. In turn, the intercept and β_1 represent the value of the dependent variable.

$$\hat{y}_{x_2=0} = \alpha + \beta_1 x_1 + \beta_2(0) \quad \text{or} \quad \hat{y}_{x_2=0} = \alpha + \beta_1 x_1$$

However, if the dummy variable is '1', β_2 gets added to the intercept. Thus, when our dummy variable equals '1', the intercept is changed by the regression coefficient of the dummy variable, β_2.

$$\hat{y}_{x_2=1} = \alpha + \beta_1 x_1 + \beta_2(1) \quad \text{or} \quad \hat{y}_{x_2=1} = (\alpha + \beta_2) + \beta_1 x_1$$

Why is this important? What is it telling us?

If a dummy variable is significant it means that there is a statistically significant difference in means of the dependent variable for each of the two groups. And that difference is β_2. In other words, it is a 'difference of means test' between one group (the base or reference category) and another group (dummy variable).

Dichotomous Dummy Variable Example

One of the questions we examined previously in Chapter 13 was support for EU unification. We used a difference of means t-test to determine whether the difference in the level of support between the older Western EU members and the newer Eastern members was substantively and statistically significant. We found that Western respondents, with a mean response of 5.26 (std. dev.: 2.66 and $N = 16,892$), had a statistically higher level of support than their Eastern counterparts, with a mean response of 5.09 (std. dev.: 2.72 and $N = 9,821$) with 99.9% confidence.

Recall that the dependent variable we used is the question of whether European unification should go further or has gone too far (range: 0 Unification already gone too – 10 Unification should go further). For the difference of means t-test in Chapter 13, we simply compared respondents from Western Europe to respondents from Eastern Europe. Keeping with this division and aiming to adhere to the coding specification of dummy variables, we could assign Western respondents '0' and Eastern respondents '1' and call it 'Eastern Europe dummy'.

DUMMY VARIABLES AND THE DIFFERENCE OF MEANS T-TEST

How does the difference of means t-test relate to dummy variables? A multiple regression with one independent dummy variable is essentially a bivariate regression that conducts a t-test. So, using the same ESS data as our example, our statistical software gives us the following output:

Table 15.1 One Independent Dummy Variable Regression

EU unification	Unstandardized regression coefficient	Standard error	t	p>|t|
East dummy variable	−0.171	0.034	−5.02	0.000
Constant	5.257	0.021	255.09	0.000
Number of observations	26,713			
F(1,26711)	25.24			
Prob.> F	0.0000			
R^2	0.0009			
Adjusted-R^2	0.0009			

While the 'Eastern Europe dummy' doesn't explain much of the support for EU unification (the adjusted-R^2 tells us 0.09% of the variation in support for EU unification is explained by the West/East dummy variable), the coefficient of −0.17 is exactly the difference between the means: 5.09 − 5.26 = −0.17. In fact, this is represented in the regression output. Our regression looks like this:

$$y = 5.26 - 0.17 \, (W/E) + \varepsilon$$

And creates two regression models, one for West '0' and one for East '1':

$$\hat{y}_{W/E=0} = 5.26 - 0.17(0) \quad \text{or} \quad \hat{y}_{W/E=0} = 5.26$$
$$\hat{y}_{W/E=1} = 5.26 - 0.17(1) \quad \text{or} \quad \hat{y}_{W/E=1} = 5.09$$

Further, the t-value for the dummy variable (−5.02) is nearly exactly the same as our difference of means t-statistic generated from our sample data (− 4.97, a likely function of our rounding). That is, this regression model has conducted a difference of means t-test on EU support by the two groups of Western and Eastern respondents.

One of the most consistent predictors of EU support is respondents' positions on immigration. Those opposed to more immigration tend to dislike the EU and those with more open immigration positions tend to support the EU. Let's examine the relationship between immigration positions and EU support to demonstrate how a dummy variable changes what we learn about this relationship.

Respondents are asked to respond to the following statement: 'Immigrants make this country a worse or better place to live' with the response categories: '0' a worse place to live – '10' a better place to live. Therefore, the model of immigration on EU support – with our West/East dummy variable – would look like this:

$$EU \ support = \alpha + \beta_1(Immigration \ position) + \beta_2(West/East) + \varepsilon$$

Inserting this into a statistical software package, we get the following:

Table 15.2 EU Support and Immigration Position

EU unification	Unstandardized regression coefficient	Standard error	t	p>|t|
Immigration position	0.453	0.007	68.71	0.000
East dummy variable	0.199	0.032	6.19	0.000
Constant	2.934	0.039	75.61	0.000
Number of observations	26,034			
F(2, 26031)	2376.56			
Prob.> F	0.0000			
R^2	0.1544			
Adjusted-R^2	0.1543			

Therefore:

$$EU\ support = 2.93 + 0.45(Immigration\ position) + 0.20(West/East) + \varepsilon$$

For each 1-unit increase in immigration position (in the direction of anti- to pro-immigration), EU support goes up 0.45 points (at 99.9% confidence or $p < 0.001$). Also from the dummy variable, East Europeans are 0.20 points on average more supportive of the EU ($p < 0.001$) controlling for respondents' positions on immigration.

For those paying close attention, one thing might seem weird. We found that the mean level of EU support is lower in Eastern Europe using both the difference of mean t-test and the one independent dummy variable regression (which is the same). So, why has this now reversed? There are a number of potential reasons. One, in the single variable model, all of the available explanation was assigned to the dummy variable. Clearly positions on immigration vary between East and West as well as impacting on support for EU unification, hence, the change in the dummy coefficient reflects multiple regression search for the best *average* solution for support for the EU as a function of *both* immigration positions and West/East. Two, respondents' immigration positions and their location are likely related. Thus, this regression reflects some of that relationship (i.e., the effect of immigration position on West/East differences). Finally, while we see dramatic improvement of our model to explain EU unification: including immigration position improves our ability to explain variation in EU support as we can see in Table 15.2 that the adjusted-R^2 is nearly 15.4% versus the West/East dummy alone at 0.09% in Table 15.1; we are far from a fully-specified model. Just as our single variable model – with only the West/East dummy – soaked up all the available explanatory power that it could, this two variable model is doing the same. Yet, what explains EU support is far from completely represented in this model. We lack the necessary independent variables so that multiple regression can most efficiently, accurately, and appropriately assign their explanatory power. When we omit the most theoretically important variables, the results are not optimized (i.e., they are imperfect estimates of the population parameters). This is a common problem that we will take up in Chapter 16.

For our regression output here, we acknowledge that this is an under-specified model with some limitations; however, it has instructional value for dummy variables. So, as shown above, the dummy variable changes the intercept, the mean level of EU unification:

For West ('0'):

$$\hat{y}_{x_2=0} = 2.93 + 0.45(IP) + 0.20(0)$$

$$\hat{y}_{x_2=0} = 2.93 + 0.45(IP)$$

For East ('1'):

$$\hat{y}_{x_2=1} = 2.93 + 0.45(IP) + 0.20(1)$$

$$\hat{y}_{x_2=1} = (2.93 + 0.20) + 0.45(IP)$$

$$\hat{y}_{x_2=1} = 3.13 + 0.45(IP)$$

In the case of the West ('0'), the intercept is 2.93. For the East ('1'), it is 3.13. These represent the mean value of the dependent variable – EU support – when we control for the impact of the other independent variable, position on immigration.

Graphically the regressions created by the dummy variable look like Figure 15.2, in which there are functionally two solutions: one for Western European and one for Eastern Europeans.

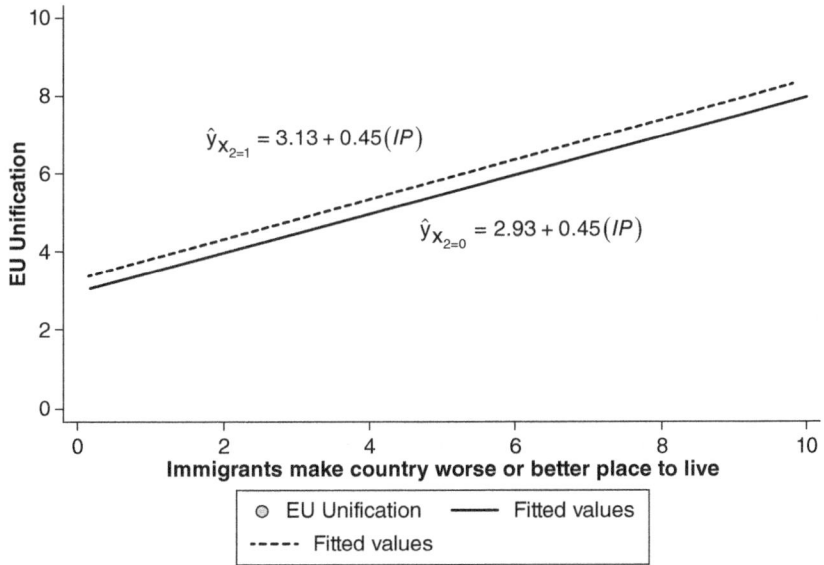

Figure 15.2 East and West Dummy: Support for EU Unification

A concise way to report this result is simply: 'There is a statistically significant difference of 0.20 (p < 0.001) between East and West Europeans' views on EU unification, holding immigration position constant.'

Fine, but what does a statistically significant dummy variable *mean*?

Well, that can be easy or difficult to say. A dramatic approach is to inhale sharply and exclaim, 'Well, in the context of EU support, there is something about being East European!' (pointing your index finger towards the ceiling to drive this home). Or, theatrically, stare into a flickering fireplace and slowly intone, 'The East/West division in Europe remains relevant.' More practically, one could search for an existing theoretical reason for Western and Eastern Europeans to have (statistically significant) different levels of support. Or, one could reflect on the findings and propose a potential explanation for observing East Europeans to be more supportive of EU unification than Western Europeans, controlling for positions on immigration. Or, perhaps, the real reason eludes us and we should continue our investigation.

We will return to this in Chapter 18.

Polychotomous Nominal-level Dummy Variables

This works great for variables that have two categories, like in our example above, West or East. However, nominal- and ordinal-level variables can have more than two responses. Both can have two or three or four or more response categories.

For nominal-level variables, we simply use the same dummy variable as difference of means t-test approach. The only challenge is choosing the reference category. Let's look at an example.

We might be suspicious that our West/East division above is not sufficiently fine-grained as Europe has more than this singular geographical division. Perhaps we can expand the division to Western, Eastern, and Mediterranean countries. To compare these, instead of one nominal-level variable, we will have to choose a reference category and make two dummy variables.

Why only two for three categories? Recall, the base category is estimated by the regression model when the other categories drop out.

Therefore:

- East [East = 1; West and Med = 0]
- Med [Med = 1; West and East = 0]

This implies that West would be West = 1; East and Med = 0. And, regression will do this for us. As above, the dummy-variable approach creates a series of regressions within the one model.

$$y = \alpha + \beta_1(East) + \beta_2(Med) + \varepsilon$$

If the region is East = 1, the resultant equation is:

$$y_{East} = \alpha + \beta_1(1) + \beta_2(0)$$

$$y_{East} = \alpha + \beta_1$$

If the region is Med = 1, the resultant equation is:

$$y_{Med} = \alpha + \beta_1(0) + \beta_2(1)$$

$$y_{Med} = \alpha + \beta_2$$

If the region is West = 1, the resultant equation is:

$$y_{West} = \alpha + \beta_1(0) + \beta_2(0)$$

$$y_{Wst} = \alpha$$

Thus, we are essentially testing whether 'East' ($\alpha + \beta_1$) and 'Med' ($\alpha + \beta_2$) are substantively and statistically different from 'West' (α) as the base category.

If we estimate exactly this choice of included dummy variables with the variable on immigration position, our statistical software produces the following:

Table 15.3 Polychotomous Nominal-level Variable Dummy Variables

EU unification	Unstandardized regression coefficient	Standard error	t	p>|t|
Immigration position	0.419	0.007	62.18	0.000
East dummy variable	0.267	0.035	7.57	0.000
Mediterranean dummy variable	0.597	0.046	13.07	0.000
Constant	2.913	0.042	68.92	0.000
Number of observations	25, 544			
F(3, 25540)	1329.12			
Prob.> F	0.0000			
R^2	0.1350			
Adjusted-R^2	0.1349			

We find that not only is 'immigration position' still substantively and statistically significant (p < 0.001), both 'East' and 'Med' dummy variables as well. This means that respondents in these regions have statistically higher support than 'West' respondents ($\alpha = 2.91$):

- In the 'East' 0.27, points higher (p < 0.001): $y_{East} = \alpha + \beta_1$: 2.91 + 0.27 = 3.18
- In the 'Med', 0.60 points higher (p < 0.001): $y_{Med} = \alpha + \beta_2$: 2.91 + 0.60 = 3.51

Choosing a Different Reference Category

To be clear, you can choose 'East' or 'Med' to be the reference category and the results will be substantively and statistically the same. The regression coefficients will differ given the combination, but the differences will be the same size, the same level of statistical significance, and produce the identical model performance output.

In the first table we find that both 'West' and 'East' respondents are substantively and statistically significant ($p < 0.001$) lower than 'Med' respondents ($\alpha = 3.51$):

- 'West' is 0.60 points lower ($p < 0.001$): $y_{West} = \alpha + \beta_1$: $3.51 - 0.60 = 2.91$
- 'East' is 0.33 points lower ($p < 0.001$): $y_{East} = \alpha + \beta_2$: $3.51 - 0.33 = 3.18$

Table 15.4a Changing the Reference Category

EU unification	Unstandardized regression coefficient	Standard error	t	p>|t|
Immigration position	0.419	0.007	62.18	0.000
East dummy variable	−0.331	0.049	−6.79	0.000
West dummy variable	−0.597	0.046	−13.07	0.000
Constant	3.510	0.051	68.38	0.000
Number of observations	25, 544			
F(3, 25540)	1329.12			
Prob.> F	0.0000			
R^2	0.1350			
Adjusted-R^2	0.1349			

Table 15.4b Changing the Reference Category

EU unification	Unstandardized regression coefficient	Standard error	t	p>|t|
Immigration position	0.419	0.007	62.18	0.000
West dummy variable	−0.267	0.049	−7.57	0.000
Mediterranean dummy variable	0.331	0.049	6.79	0.000
Constant	3.180	0.040	80.50	0.000
Number of observations	25, 544			
F(3, 25540)	1329.12			
Prob.> F	0.0000			
R^2	0.1350			
Adjusted-R^2	0.1349			

Lastly, in the second table we find that 'West' respondents are lower and 'Med' respondents are higher than 'East' respondents ($\alpha = 3.18$) and both statistically significant ($p < 0.001$):

- 'West' is 0.27 points lower ($p < 0.001$): $y_{West} = \alpha + \beta_1$: $3.18 - 0.27 = 2.91$
- 'Med' is 0.33 points higher ($p < 0.001$): $y_{Med} = \alpha + \beta_2$: $3.18 + 0.33 = 3.51$

In each regression model, the combination of dummy variables results in statistically significant differences between 'West' respondents (2.91), 'East' respondents (3.18), and 'Med' respondents (3.51).

Ordinal Dummy Variables

For ordinal-level variables, the choice of the base category is an important decision. One approach is to use an extreme category. For example, one could choose the 'lowest' (or 'highest') category so that we can see how much further away each 'higher' (or 'lower') category is from 'the base'. That is, in response to a question about the level of support for a new legislation, one could respond: 'none', 'a little', 'some', 'a lot'. It makes intuitive sense to set 'none' (or 'a lot') as the base or reference category. Another approach, particularly for Likert scales asking whether the respondent 'Strongly Disagrees – Disagrees – Neither – Agrees – Strongly Agrees' with some statement, is to use the middle category ('Neither') to capture moving in either direction.

While there is no hard and fast rule, the choice depends primarily on your research question and what you intend to demonstrate. At the same time, we should make sure that the chosen reference category has a sufficient number of observations. If it has a low number, this will inflate the standard error and, because it is the category against which all of the others are compared, will make the tests less accurate. Why? remember that as measures of dispersion grow (i.e., the standard error gets bigger), we have less confidence in the quality of the summary measure. And lower confidence produces lower quality tests.

In practice, we can add an ordinal-level variable to multiple regression much like the polychotomous nominal-level variables above. Take, for example, an independent variable commonly associated with EU support: political interest.

The question asks the respondent to report their level of interest in politics: 'not at all interested', 'hardly interested', 'quite interested', or 'very interested'. While we have the order of an interval-level variable, we do not have the clear mathematical uniformity between each category of an interval-level variable. Therefore, setting the base category to 'not at all interested', we include the ascending categories just like the previous polychotomous nominal-level variable.

This produces:

$$y = \alpha + \beta_1(ImmPos) + \beta_2(Hardly) + \beta_2(Quite) + \beta_2(Very) + \varepsilon$$

We ask our statistical software to estimate the multiple regression model and we arrive at the following (see Table 15.5).

Table 15.5 Ordinal-level Dummy Variables

EU unification	Unstandardized regression coefficient	Standard error	t	p>|t|
Immigration position	0.401	0.006	67.20	0.000
PI: Hardly interested	0.042	0.040	1.04	0.299
PI: Quite interested	0.152	0.041	3.68	0.000
PI: Very interested	0.230	0.053	4.33	0.000
Constant	3.032	0.042	72.75	0.000
Number of observations	32,363			
F(4, 32358)	1215.99			
Prob.> F	0.0000			
R^2	0.1307			
Adjusted-R^2	0.1306			

Setting aside the consistent substantive and statistical performance of 'immigration position' ($\beta = 0.40$; $p < 0.001$), we find that 'hardly interested' is not statistically significant and thus the regression coefficient is effectively indistinguishable from zero ($\beta = 0.04$; $p < 0.299$). This implies that there is no difference for EU support between respondents who report 'not at all interested' in politics and those who report 'hardly interested'.

However, there is a substantive and statistically significant difference between those who report being 'quite interested' and 'very interested' in politics versus the reference category 'not at all interested'. Those who report being 'quite interested' are 0.15 points ($p < 0.001$) more supportive of EU unification than those who report being 'not at all interested'. And those who are 'very interested' are 0.23 points ($p < 0.001$) more supportive of EU unification than those who report being 'not at all interested' (see Figure 15.3a).

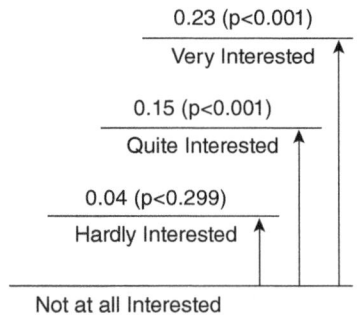

Figure 15.3a Reference Category of Dummy Variables with Ordinal Variables

Dummy Variable Limitations

Both the nominal- and ordinal-level dummy variable approaches resolve the challenge of including non-interval-level variables in multiple regression. However, they are not perfect. The choice of the base or reference category is crucial and sometimes a problem.

For ordinal-level variables, while we might observe a greater and greater substantive and statistical difference between ascending categories and the base (Figure 15.3a), we mostly learn about the first two categories and less about the differences between the other categories (Figure 15.3b).

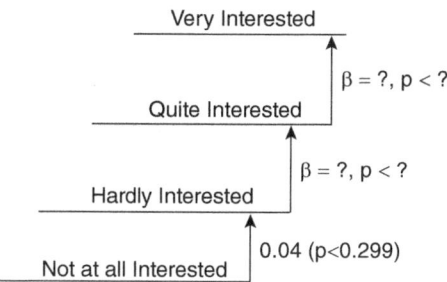

Figure 15.3b Difference between each Category in Ordinal Variables

For the polychotomous nominal-level variables, the largest challenge is that there may not be a clear or intuitive base category. Or perhaps we are interested in the differences between several of the categories. Neither can be completely resolved by the dummy variable approach and this presents us with an analytical challenge that is not easily overcome.

We saw this in Table 15.5. Although 'hardly interested' is not statistically different from 'not at all interested', both 'quite interested' and 'very interested' are. And, the statistically significant differences between the reference category 'not at all interested' are large for 'quite interested' – and larger for 'very interested'. Which is what we would expect as 'very interested' is at the other end of the ordinal response range. Yet, the dummy variable approach struggles to address the crucial *order* of ordinal-level variables. That is, for ordinal-level variables, it might be more helpful to know about the differences between each *adjacent* category than the difference between each category and an unmoved, reference category (again, Figure 15.3b). A potential solution is to run a series of regressions in which the reference category is changed and make note of the substantive and statistical significance of the next higher category. However, this is a cumbersome and inelegant solution.

At the same time, the limits to using dummy variables are not fatal flaws. Dummy variables work well in many situations of including nominal- and ordinal-level variables to multiple regression; the ability to include a wider range of explanations alerts us to potentially important relationships.

Alternatives for Ordinal-level Variables

In some cases, the order of ordinal-level variables is too important to disregard. Take the example we were working on. Rather than finding out only whether 'hardly interested' is statistically different than 'not at all interested' (recall that it is not: $\beta = 0.04$ ($p < 0.299$)) or using the inelegant solution of running a series of regressions, we can do one of two things.

We might try to identify if there is a 'jump' between two categories that is the most interesting to our research. That is, rather than only testing the 'jump' from 'not at all interested' to 'hardly interested', perhaps the jump from 'quite interested' to 'very interested' is more helpful for our research question and what we really want to know. In this case, we can simply make 'quite interested' the reference category of a dummy variable and run the regression (see Table 15.6a).

Table 15.6a Ordinal-level Dummy Variable with Different Reference Category

EU unification	Unstandardized regression coefficient	Standard error	t	p>|t|
Immigration position	0.401	0.006	67.20	0.000
PI: Not at all interested	−0.152	0.041	−3.68	0.000
PI: Hardly interested	−0.110	0.034	3.27	0.001
PI: Very interested	0.078	0.048	1.65	0.100
Constant	3.184	0.040	79.89	0.000
Number of observations	32,363			
F(4, 32358)	1215.99			
Prob.> F	0.0000			
R^2	0.1307			
Adjusted-R^2	0.1306			

We find that while 'quite interested' is statistically significantly different from both 'not at all interested' $\beta = -0.15$ ($p < 0.001$) and 'hardly interested' $\beta = -0.11$ ($p < 0.001$), it is not different from 'very interested' $\beta = 0.08$ ($p < 0.100$). Depending on our research question, this may serve us well.

An alternative approach is to include the ordinal-level variable as an interval-level one. This is – and is not – controversial. Clearly, everything that we have talked about in this book suggests that this is potentially a bad idea and possibly violates the original statistical liturgical text. However, some argue that ordinal-level variables that have more than 5 or 6 categories 'behave' more or less like interval-level variables and are, thus, minimally problematic. That is, the problems of this mistreatment are less than the benefits of determining the relationship between an ordinal-level independent variable and an interval-level variable.

In this case, using political interest from our example above, we would get the following:

Table 15.6b Ordinal-level Variable Treated as Interval-level Variable

EU unification	Unstandardized regression coefficient	Standard error	t	p>|t|
Immigration position	0.401	0.006	67.25	0.000
Political interest	0.082	0.016	5.26	0.000
Constant	2.928	0.045	64.92	0.000
Number of observations	32,363			
$F_{(2, 32360)}$	2431.41			
Prob.> F	0.0000			
R^2	0.1306			
Adjusted-R^2	0.1306			

We find that for every 1-unit increase in political interest (from 'not at all interested' to 'hardly interested' to 'quite interested' to 'very interested'), support for EU unification increases by 0.08 (p < 0.001). Again, this doesn't square perfectly with the previous findings but it is broadly in line.

But, wait. There is a third solution.

We could combine the two 'negative' categories ('not at all interested' and 'hardly interested') and the two 'positive' categories ('quite interested' and 'very interested') and include this new variable with two categories: 'low interest' and 'high interest'. Then, you simply include this as a dummy variable [0: little interest; 1 interest]. This is not uncommon, but you are potentially throwing away information by collapsing categories. There is less variation as there are fewer categories. Thus, while possible, this strategy may be more costly in terms of our ability to accurately identify the nature of the relationship in which we are interested (see Table 15.6c).

Table 15.6c Ordinal-level Variable Re-shaped to a Lower Level Variable

EU unification	Unstandardized regression coefficient	Standard error	t	p>|t|
Immigration position	0.401	0.006	67.51	0.000
PI: Positive categories	0143	0.029	5.02	0.000
Constant	3.056	0.033	92.56	0.000
Number of observations	32,363			
$F_{(2, 32360)}$	2431.41			
Prob.> F	0.0000			
R^2	0.1306			
Adjusted-R^2	0.1305			

We find that respondents who are 'quite interested' or 'very interested' [1: interest] are 0.14 more supportive of EU unification than respondents who are 'not at all interested' or 'hardly interested' [0 little interest], (p < 0.001). Again, the value of this result depends on the nature of your research question.

Multiple Regression Accessories

Explicit Indexes: Multi-item Indicators

Another problem that arises before we use regression is that an indicator may not sufficiently operationalize the intended conceptual definition of a variable of interest. We might therefore include them as a single indicator. The most common and explicit form of this is an **additive index**.

A good example of an additive index is political participation. Let's measure someone's level of activity in non-traditional forms of political participation, forms of political engagement beyond, for example, voting or contacting politicians. The European Values Survey asks respondents about signing a petition, attending a demonstration, joining a boycott, or joining a strike. For each activity, the respondent is asked to say whether they 'would never participate', 'would participate', or 'had participated'.

Now, if someone had participated in all four, we would want to assign them a higher score (for non-traditional political participation) than someone who responded 'would never participate' in all four activities. If we were to assign a score of 0 to 'would never participate', a 1 to 'would participate', and a 2 to 'had participated' and simply add each respondent's four scores for each activity, we would achieve the following scoring. The person who 'had participated' in all four would have a score of 2 (petition) + 2 (demonstration) + 2 (boycott) + 2 (strike) = 8. The person who 'would never participate' in all four would have a score of 0 (petition) + 0 (demonstration) + 0 (boycott) + 0 (strike) = 0. All others would fall between. In this way, additive variables are useful in that they can solve problems in which no single indicator is a clear best measure.

There are two things to keep in mind.

First, different (additive) combinations can give similar profiles. In the political participation example above, if someone had participated in two activities (2 + 2) and would not in the other two (0 + 0), they would have the same 'profile' (additive variable total: 4) as someone who reported 'would participate' in all four (1 + 1 + 1 + 1 = 4). How problematic conflating these two different profiles is depends on the goal of the research.

Second, fortunately, we can have a measure of confidence in the choice of included variables by using **Cronbach's alpha**. If you want to scare yourself out of your socks, go look at the Wikipedia page. However, Cronbach's alpha essentially tells you how inter-related the different variables you include in your additive measure are. It is a measure of the reliability of your additive variable. Ideally, we would like our Cronbach's alpha to be, on a scale from 0.0 to 1.0, 0.8 or higher.

Implicit Indices: Latent Variables

There are other ways to include multi-item measures derived from the common conceptual challenge of a difficult or ambiguous definition. Some things in which we are interested are not easily 'one thing' and resist easy conceptualization. For example, we might be interested in studying political efficacy, that is, the extent to which individuals conceive of and act in their own political benefit or, simply, their belief in affecting political outcomes.

While 'how people feel about their ability to affect politics' is an actual question in some large surveys, this question feels insufficient. We might then consider using more than one measure to identify the nominally singular concept. That is, we might attempt to triangulate the underlying concept. Operationalizing 'political efficacy' could include a measure of 'how people feel about their ability to affect politics' but also include measures of their own self-confidence, their level of attention to political matters, and even a reverse measure of their level of political apathy. We could merge these different but related dimensions of efficacy onto a single indicator using factor analysis.

Factor analysis is a form of latent variable analysis. If we are unable to directly capture what we want, we can measure aspects or elements of the concept. In a similar way that a regression line is the best summary of the common variance for two variables, imagine that the regression line itself became a variable that represented the highest correlation between the two (or more) variables. This new factor we constructed is a variable that we did not measure, but now can use.

Factor analysis is both useful – and controversial. By creating a new dimension along which the greatest amount of any number of factors commonly load, it reduces a complex system of correlations into fewer dimensions. The neat trick is that this new 'factor' exists only as a function of the commonalities among the variables chosen. Proponents of this approach assert that although the factor is a directly unobservable variable, it does exist as the commonality among a number of observed variables that captures a crucial – if latent – concept.

More interestingly, there are very often not one but several potential factors. Inasmuch as there as several variables, there are several possible ways to combine them to maximize the amount of combined variation they can explain.

FACTOR VOCABULARY

Factor analysis broadly refers to a number of statistical techniques that share the basic design (see for example, Principal Components Analysis). Although the computations become a great deal more involved, the basic principle of expressing two or more variables by a single factor is consistent among them. While this not only allows us to reduce the number of variables (and potentially problems, such as multicollinearity), the manufactured factor can also be used as a standalone variable – to explain or be explained.

(Continued)

> The language of factor analysis is intimidating, with new concepts such as eigenvalues – indicators of importance or strength in linear transformations – scree – residuals that reveal the outer limit of meaningful factors – and varimax rotation – a reshuffling of the coordinates of data within the coordinate system to achieve a random (or in the language of factor analysis, orthogonal) and hopefully improved factor alignment. While specific to factor analysis, don't let the vocabulary discourage you from engaging this technique as it can be quite useful when used correctly.

Newer forms of latent variable analysis, such as **Item Response Theory** (IRT) graded response model, can also combine variables into a single scale capturing their commonality. Innovatively, the IRT approach is optimal for estimating the latent factor when the variables are nominal- or ordinal-level variables. IRT models also deal well with missing data, allowing researchers to preserve the always precious degrees of freedom.

Interaction Terms

In multiple regression, the included independent variables are considered additive, that is, the model is the arithmetic sum of independent influences. However, as we have frequently noted, reality is very clearly a complex blend of political, social, and economic worlds. That is, it is a very strong assumption that reality is simply the sum of independent things happening. It is not unlikely that independent variables can interact and do so in a manner that influences the dependent variable. When we suspect this may be the case, we can use an **interaction term** to capture the separate effects of different independent variables, as well as their interactive effect on the dependent variable.

Including interaction terms also changes the nature of the 'general' regression solution, that is, the relationship between each independent variable and the dependent variable. With an interaction term, the solution becomes 'conditional'. Conditional solutions represent changes in the impact of one independent variable (on the dependent variable) by a change in the values of another independent variable. More technically, in a standard model, our 'partials' – or regression coefficients – for X_1 and X_2 are considered independent contributions to explaining Y. However, with interactions, an independent variable's total impact depends on the values of the other independent variable with which it interacts.

The simplest form is the interaction between two independent variables: for example, X_1 and X_2, this creating an interaction term: X_1X_2, in which the two independent variables are multiplied with each other. For the regression model itself, all three terms – X_1, X_2, and X_1X_2 – are included.

$$\hat{Y} = \alpha + \beta_1(X_1) + \beta_2(X_2) + \beta_3(X_1)(X_2) + \varepsilon$$

Thus, the total impact for each independent variable will be its own 'partial' or regression coefficient (for each X_1 and X_2) called the main effect and the regression coefficient of the interaction for X_1X_2 ('the interaction effect').

When should we use interaction terms?

The most defensible position is that there is a clear theoretical reason to do so. That is, its inclusion has been previously demonstrated and empirically supported. Alternatively, we propose to include an interaction to remedy a theoretical or analytical problem. Omitting an interaction forces the regression model to 'explain' the missing interactive effect and this can significantly bias the included regression coefficients.

Given the complexity of using interaction terms, some researchers hesitate to use them. Others, however, see the potential benefits and, despite the complexity, incorporate interaction terms into their analysis to identify and capture potential complexities in the relationship in which they are interested.

Interaction Terms: Dummy Variable Example

Let's start with the simplest form of interaction term, the interaction of an interval-level variable and a dichotomous nominal-level variable (a 'dummy variable'). Let's use the example in the first part of the chapter, support for EU unification, which had one interval-level variable – position on immigration – and one dummy variable – Western or Eastern Europe.

$$EU\ support = \alpha + \beta_1\ (Immigration\ position) + \beta_2\ (West/East) + \varepsilon$$

Perhaps there is evidence or a theory that the impact of how people feel about immigration is different in the West than in the East. One might suggest that as Eastern European countries serve as the border to the near abroad – the Asian continent and Middle East – citizens of those countries have different perspectives on immigration than those in the more distant Western countries. We therefore expect their support for the EU to be different because of this different perspective.

We can introduce an interaction term to account for the expectation of a differential effect of immigration from West and East Europeans, arriving at the following model (*Note:* 'Immigration Position' is now 'IP'):

$$EU\ support = \alpha + \beta_1\ (IP) + \beta_2\ (West/East) + \beta_3\ (IP)(West/East) + \varepsilon$$

How does the interaction term identify the potential differential impact of immigration position on EU support between a respondent from Western or Eastern Europe? It does so by determining the contingency of a respondent's location to the impact of 'immigration position' on 'EU support'. That is, we not only determine whether there is a statistically significant difference between West and East respondents (the difference of means t-test from above), but also whether the regression coefficient on 'immigration position' is substantively changed. If the regression coefficient – the β – is changed, the relationship of 'immigration positive' to 'EU support' is also changed.

In the context of the example on EU support, when the dummy variable – West/East – is '0' (West), the equation looks like this:

$$EU\ support = \alpha + \beta_1\ (IP) + \beta_2\ (0) + \beta_3\ (IP)(0) + \varepsilon$$
$$EU\ support = \alpha + \beta_1\ (IP) + \varepsilon$$

The impact of 'immigration position' on 'EU support' is β_1. However, when the dummy variable – West/East – is '1' (East), the equation looks like this:

$$EU\ support = \alpha + \beta_1\ (IP) + \beta_2\ (1) + \beta_3\ (IP)(1) + \varepsilon$$
$$EU\ support = (\alpha + \beta_2) + (\beta_1 + \beta_3)(IP) + \varepsilon$$

The interaction term changes not only the intercept (here, $\alpha + \beta_2$), but also the value of the regression coefficient of 'immigration position' on 'EU support' is $(\beta_1 + \beta_3)$! This is a conditional solution.

Statistical software gives us the estimates for this multiple regression model.

Table 15.7 EU Support and a Dummy Variable Interaction Term

EU unification	Unstandardized regression coefficient	Standard error	t	p>|t|
Immigration position	0.473	0.008	57.67	0.000
East dummy variable	0.459	0.071	6.47	0.000
ImmPos*East dummy	−0.057	0.014	−4.10	0.001
Constant	2.831	0.046	61.32	0.000
Number of observations	26,034			
F(3, 26030)	1590.95			
Prob.> F	0.0000			
R²	0.1549			
Adjusted-R²	0.1549			

Using this output, the full multiple regression model becomes:

$$EU\ support = 2.83 + 0.47(IP) + 0.46(West/East) - 0.06(IP)(W/E)$$

In which the main effects of 'Immigration Position' and 'West/West are 0.47 0.46, respectively. The interaction effect is −0.06.

For Western respondents (West/East = 0), the equation looks like this:

$$EU\ support = 2.83 + 0.47(IP) + 0.46(0) - 0.06(IP)(0)$$
$$EU\ support = 2.83 + 0.47(IP)$$

For Eastern respondents (West/East = 1), the equation looks like this:

$EU\ support = 2.83 + 0.47(IP) + 0.46(1) - 0.06(IP)(1)$

$EU\ support = 3.29 + 0.41(IP)$

I want to point out that there are not two multiple regression models. There is only one. However, using interaction terms with dummies effectively creates separate solutions, one for the reference group ('0') and one for the other group ('1'). We can visualize this difference plotting the relationship between 'immigration position' and 'EU support' for Western and Eastern respondents – see Figure 15.4.

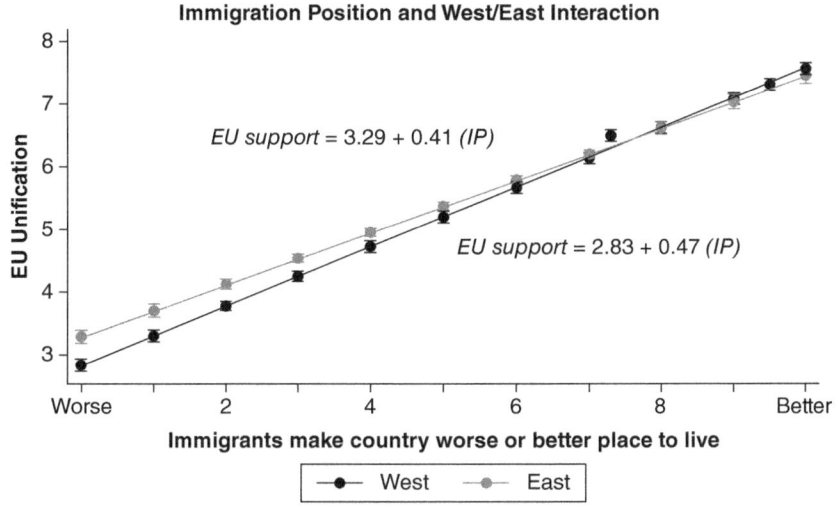

Figure 15.4 EU Support, Immigration Position, and West/East Interaction Term

So, what does this tells us that a multiple regression model without an interaction doesn't? Unlike the example above in which we saw two parallel lines separated by a constant difference between the two groups defined by the dummy variable (i.e., '0' West and '1' East], here – given the additional change to the regression coefficient – we identify the change in the nature of the relationship between the independent and dependent variable. That is, impact of 'immigration position' on 'EU support' is both positive and statistically significant for all respondents (0.47; $p < 0.001$). However, the effect is stronger in the West. We know this as the solution of the multiple regression model for Western respondents (when the dummy variable is '0') produces the regression coefficient of 0.47. Crucially, on the other hand, for Eastern respondents, because of the inclusion of the interaction term, this coefficient is lowered by 0.06, a difference that is statistically significant (t-score: −4.10; $p < 0.001$). This results in a regression coefficient for 'immigration position' for Eastern respondents of 0.041. Thus, as we can see in Figure 15.4, the slopes reflect this as the 'West' (black) slope is steeper than the 'East' (grey) slope.

What does this imply for the idea that citizens of Eastern European countries have different perspectives on immigration than Western countries? While important in both regions, the findings suggest that as Western respondents' positions on immigration move toward being more accommodative, they become more impactful on their views about EU unification than Eastern respondents.

Interaction Terms: Interval-level Variables Example

The solution to an interaction term with one interval-level variable and one dummy variable is relatively straightforward. We are comparing one solution – when the dummy variable is '0' – to another – when the dummy variable is '1'. The complexity increases somewhat when we interact two interval-level variables as the values can be, hypothetically, anything. Thus, trying to determine the impact of the interaction term has more to do with how we interpret the results than the computational part.

Let's continue with our example on support for EU unification. One of the clearest determinants for continuing the EU project is individuals' socio-economic location. We can use a cross-nationally standardized measure of income (by deciles) to measure this and interact it with respondents' positions on immigration. We might suspect that respondents in low socio-economic locations with prohibitive views on immigration will have even less support for EU unification than those in low socio-economic locations or those who hold prohibitive views on immigration alone. Similarly, we might suspect that those in high socio-economic locations with accommodative views on immigration will be even more supportive of EU unification than those in high socio-economic locations or those with accommodative views on immigration alone.

Setting aside the interaction with the dummy variable West/East for the moment, we can include an interaction between the variables 'immigration position' ('IP') and 'individual socio-economic status' ('SES').

The multiple regression model becomes:

$$EU\ support = \alpha + \beta_1(IP) + \beta_2(SES) + \beta_3(IP)(SES) + \varepsilon$$

The complexity of this type of interaction terms rests on contingent solution of the two variables included in the interaction term. For example, to know the impact of 'immigration position' on 'EU support', in addition to the partial of immigration position, β_1, we must also know the value of 'individual SES for each immigration position, β_3.

Unlike the dummy variable interaction term above, we cannot simply add these regression coefficients as they are not the same units. That is, the value of β_1 is the impact of immigration position while the value of β_3 includes the impact of immigration position given the value of their SES.

$$EU\ support = \beta_1(IP) + \beta_3(IP)(SES)$$

In Table 15.8, we can see the statistical output for the interval-by-interval interaction.

Table 15.8 EU Unification: Interval-level Variables Interaction Term

EU unification	Unstandardized regression coefficient	Standard error	t	p>|t|
Immigration position	0.349	0.014	25.30	0.000
SES: Income	0.014	0.013	1.03	0.303
*ImmPos*Income*	0.008	0.002	3.20	0.001
Constant	3.105	0.075	41.48	0.000
Number of observations	26,410			
F(3, 26406)	1258.78			
Prob.> F	0.0000			
R^2	0.1251			
Adjusted-R^2	0.1250			

The model solution looks as follows.

EU support = 3.11 + 0.349(*IP*) + 0.014 (*SES*) + 0.008 (*IP*)(*SES*)

Unlike our solution with the dummy variable, the new interaction term creates a solution in which the total effect of each independent variable is contingent on the main effects of the independent variables as well as the interaction effect. As with the dummy variable interaction, the effects change both the intercept and the slopes.

The total effect of SES on EU support is:

EU support = 3.11 + 0.014(*SES*) + 0.008 (*IP*)(*SES*)

The total effect of immigration position on EU support is:

EU support = 2.91 + 0.349(*IP*) + 0.008 (*IP*)(*SES*)

That is, there is no way to summarize the effect of SES without knowing the respondent's position on immigration. And vice versa. This makes it a challenge to interpret the results and there is no one superior way.

However, a non-tabular means to present the findings is to represent these results graphically. Given that both the main effects for both independent variables and the interaction term are statistically significant, we can see that in fact income appears to further differentiate the effect of respondents' immigration positions (see Figure 15.5).

In this solution, we can see that those respondents with accommodative immigration positions are more supportive of EU unification than those with prohibitive immigration positions. This effect is magnified by the respondent's SES in that poorer respondents have less EU support at the same immigration positions as richer respondents and this effect grows as the respondents' immigration position becomes more accommodative.

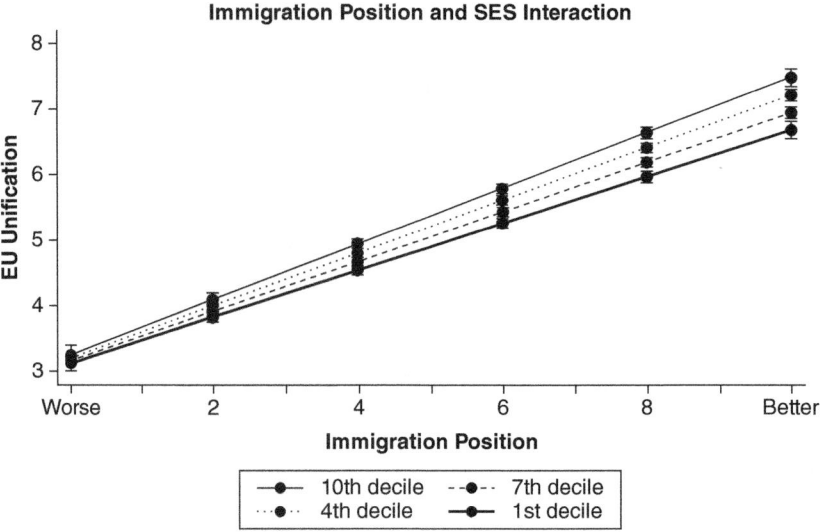

Figure 15.5 EU Support, Immigration Position, and Income Interaction

> ### CENTRING
>
> You can see in Table 15.8 the interaction term is 'IP_SES'. For interaction terms of two interval-level variables, one can 'centre' both variables. Centring is simply subtracting the mean of the observed values from each variable. This makes the new mean for each variable zero. Again, it is not necessary, although proponents argue there are two reasons for doing so.
>
> One, it can yield lower correlations between the interaction term and the main variables. Two, it can accommodate the additional information by choosing the zero (the 'centred value') to represent a substantively interesting value. This can aid the interpretation without changing the substantive significance of the variables in the model. In other words, centring also allows us to estimate the model at the mean values of many of the variables while having no impact on the substantive interpretation of the model.

For the purpose of interpretation, adding an interaction term can change – and depending on the substantive performance of the interaction, drastically so – the statistical significances of the main effects and interaction term. When we include an interaction, given what we suspect or what theory demands, we are primarily concerned whether it is has an impact on the results of the estimated model, that is, its substantive and statistical significance. What do I do about regression results that have various statistical significances?

A common result is that the interaction term becomes statistically significant and one or both of the main effects become statistically insignificant (as SES in Table 15.8). In this case, this does not mean that the main effect(s) are irrelevant. It means that on average that insignificant main effect is not important, but it does have significant effects at other values (i.e., in relation to the other main effect). This means that main effects do not have to be statistically significant for interaction to be important. Graphing helps.

Interaction Terms: Problems

There are two potential analytical problems with the use of interactions. The first is that estimation of the regression model becomes sensitive to the sample it is estimating. Interactive models ask more from the data than additive models and, particularly in cases of small or insufficient sample sizes, trivial changes in the variables can lead to non-trivial changes in the estimators. However, post-estimation analysis can be of some help to determine the robustness of the estimated parameters.

Second, interactions work well with interval-level data and nominal-level data – particularly dichotomous dummy variables – but struggle to accommodate ordinal-level variables. As we have seen before, while the order of ordinal-level variables can be useful to our analysis, the non-uniform interval between adjacent categories undermines their 'mathematical' precision. As with all theoretically important independent variables, the substantive results of excluding interaction terms can be significant, ultimately misleading the researcher in interpretation.

Final Thoughts

This chapter has introduced the manner in which multiple regression can accommodate non-interval-level independent variables to advance our ability to include and either assess or control for a wide variety of potential variables. For Political Science, this is crucial. Much of what we are interested in cannot be measured on mathematically convenient scales or unlimited continua. That we can include a wide range of variously measured independent variables speaks to the power (and attractiveness) of multiple regression. As such, we increase our ability to 'hold all other variables constant'. The ability to include a wide variety of independent variables – nominal-, ordinal-, and interval-level variables – strengthens our ability to isolate and identify the substantive relationship in which we are interested.

End of Chapter Summary

- Multiple regression can accommodate both nominal- and ordinal-level variables.
- Dummy variables 'trick' regression into performing a difference of means t-test on two groups, defined by the absence of something '0' and the presence of something '1'.
- The number of dummy variables that you include in the regression is the number of categories minus 1. For example, a dichotomous nominal-level variable has two categories and thus one dummy variable is included. This is so the regression

model in which all dummy variables are equal to zero solves for the reference category.
- We can also include variables that are hard to conceptualize and difficult to measure by combining several related measures.
- An additive variable allows us to combine (read: add) related variables as a means to capture multi-faceted or multi-dimensional variables.
- Factor analysis reduces the number of variables by creating a common, unobserved factor that refers to an underlying structure in the data that reveals a latent variable.
- An interaction term empirically captures an effect on the dependent variable in which the value of one independent variable depends on the value of another independent variable.
- If a dummy is significant it means that the presence of that variable ('1') means there is a statistically significant difference between the two groups for the mean of the dependent variable.

Glossary

- **Dummy variables** are dichotomous variables that allow us to include nominal- and ordinal-level variables in a multiple regression analysis. They essentially make multiple regression to perform a difference of means t-test for each category against a reference category.
- The **base** or **reference category** is the category of response against which all dummy variables are compared.
- An **additive index** is the combination of separate variables into a single one by adding them together.
- **Cronbach's alpha** is a score of how inter-related the different variables in your additive variable are (on a scale from 0.0 to 1.0).
- **Factor analysis** reduces the complexity (or problem) of inter-relatedness among independent variables by creating an unobserved dimension along which the greatest amount of any number of factors commonly load.
- **Item Response Theory** (IRT) graded response model combines variables into a single scale capturing their commonality, including, unlike factor analysis, nominal- or ordinal-level variables.
- An **interaction term** captures the separate effects of different independent variables, as well as their interactive effect on the dependent variable.

Questions

1. In a multiple regression with only one independent dummy variable, the output is the same as a difference of means t-test. Why do the regression coefficient and t-value of the dummy variable change when other independent variables are added?
2. Write a regression model in the form of: $y = \alpha + \beta_1 x_1 + \ldots + \beta_n x_n + \varepsilon$ with

a. A dependent variable of 'Percentage of Seats Won'
   b. Two independent variables: 'Party System Polarization' and 'Effective Number of Competitive Parties' and
   c. A series of dummy variables to capture 'Party Family': Social Democratic; Liberal; Conservative; Ethnic; Green; or Populist. Identify the reference group.
3. Solve the above regression model for each party family. That is, what will the regression model look like when each of the dummy variables – including the reference category – is '1' and the others are '0'?
4. Often in research, we have to rely on the respondents to tell us what they did. For example, if we want to know if people were exposed to a particular event or were paying attention during an important period, we can ask them about their media-use habits. For example, if they watched something on the television – or if they listened to radio or read a newspaper – about news/politics/current affairs on an average weekday. Let's assume that our current research question is not interested in the differences *between* these media but rather how much the respondent uses media *in general*. Perhaps we can consider making a single variable called the 'Media Consumption' variable, from these three. The response categories for television, radio, and newspaper are (per day): (1) less than ½ an hour, (2) ½ an hour to 1 hour, (3) between 1 and 1½ hours, (4) 1½ hours to 2 hours, (5) between 2 and 2½ hours, (6) 2½ hours to 3 hours, and (7) more than 3 hours. If 'Media Consumption' has a very high Cronbach's alpha (e.g., >0.90), discuss the advantages and disadvantages of using this new additive variable as an independent variable to explain EU support.
5. Following the section 'Interaction Terms: Dummy Variable Example', what if we considered gender rather than West/East. We might suspect that immigration positions are different between men and women and interact these positions with a simple gender variable. The output appears in Table 15.9. Produce the regressions for both men and women. That is, what are the resulting regressions when gender is '1: Male', and gender is '0: Female'? And how would you interpret these results?

Table 15.9 EU Unification, Immigration Positions, and Gender

EU unification	Unstandardized regression coefficient	Standard error	t	p>|t|
Immigration position	0.394	0.008	48.00	0.000
Male dummy variable	−0.104	0.064	−1.63	0.104
*ImmPos*Male*	0.026	0.012	2.22	0.026
Constant	3.145	0.045	69.82	0.000
Number of observations	32,409			
F(3,32405)	1617.28			
Prob.> F	0.0000			
R^2	0.1302			
Adjusted-R^2	0.1301			

Annotated References and Further Reading

Brambor, T., Clark, W., and Golder, M. 2006. 'Understanding interaction models: Improving empirical analyses' *Political Analysis* **14(1), 63–82. https://doi.org/10.1093/pan/mpi014**

This is 'the' article on using interactions. Has not been improved on since.

Gould, Stephen Jay. 1997. 'The Real Error of Cyril Burt: Factor Analysis and the Reification of Intelligence' in *The Mismeasure of Man.* **2nd edn. New York and London: W.W. Norton & Company.**

If you want to know more about factor analysis, including the dramatic story of its origin, see Chapter 6: pp. 264–350.

Hardy, M.A. 1993. *Regression with Dummy Variables.* **SAGE Publications, Inc. https://dx.doi.org/10.4135/9781412985628**

It is a nerdy Green Book from Sage but there is no equivalent in discussing the range and extent of using dummy variables.

Niemi, R., Craig, S., and Mattei, F. 1991. 'Measuring internal political efficacy in the 1988 National Election Study' *American Political Science Review* **85(4), 1407–1413. https://doi.org/10.2307/1963953**

Factor analysis applied to the study of political efficacy.

Signposts to the Accompanying Digital Resources

Data used in this chapter

- **European Unification** (Euftf): Now thinking about the European Union, some say European unification should go further. Others say it has already gone too far. What number on the scale best describes your position? '0' Unification has already gone too far – '10' Unification should go further. ESS (2018).
- **Immigration Position** (imwbcnt): Immigrants make country worse or better place to live: '0' Worse place to live – '10' Better place to live. ESS (2018).
- **Media Use:** How much did you watch television (vpol), listen to radio (rdopol), or read the newspaper (nwsppol) about news/politics/current affairs on average weekday. ESS (2018).
- **Regions**: ESS (2018).
    - *WEST/EAST:* WEST: Austria, Belgium, Germany, Finland, Ireland, the Netherlands, Denmark, UK, Spain, Portugal, France, Cyprus, and Sweden. EAST: Bulgaria, Czech Republic, Estonia, Hungary, Poland, Latvia, Romania, Slovenia, Croatia, and Slovakia
    - *WEST/EAST/MED:* WEST: Austria, Belgium, Germany, Finland, Ireland, the Netherlands, Denmark, UK, and Sweden. EAST: Bulgaria, Czech Republic,

Estonia, Hungary, Poland, Latvia, Romania, and Slovakia. MEDITERRANEAN: Slovenia, Croatia, Spain, Portugal, France, and Cyprus
- **Gender** (gndr): recoded to '0' female, '1' male. ESS (2018).
- **Income** (hinctnta): Household's total net income, all sources: 1 (1st decile), 2 (2nd decile) ... 9 (9th decile), and 10 (10th decile). ESS (2018).
    o European Social Survey 1–9, European Social Survey Cumulative File, Study Description. Bergen: NSD – Norwegian Centre for Research Data for ESS ERIC. https://doi.org/10.21338/NSD-ESS-CUMULATIVE

16

ISSUES WITH MULTIPLE REGRESSION

> **LEARNING OUTCOMES**
>
> In this chapter, you will be able to
>
> - Enumerate the key assumptions of multiple regression and explain their importance.
> - Identify common problems with multiple regression such as multicollinearity, auto-regression, measurement error, and omitted variable bias.
> - Apply fixes in the case of an assumption violation.
> - Use these assumptions and their implications as a means to improve model specification, fit, and performance.

Introduction

Recall from Chapter 9 that we briefly introduced the five key assumptions of bivariate regression. They hold for multiple regression and include assumptions about the variables, the functional form of the regression model, and the error term. Violations of these assumptions can produce misleading estimates of the coefficients, their standard errors, or the overall model. Thus, it is important for us to understand why these specific assumptions are made, what violates them, and how we might remedy such a situation.

Once we are satisfied that we have included the appropriate independent variables and have run our model, we can perform a diagnostic check-up on our regression. This can seem to be a complicated business. However, for the most part, most of the crucial checks are relatively easy to perform. This diagnostic check-up is crucial for all multiple regression models although, it would be wise to pay particular attention to the performance of our regression model when we have a small number of observations. If we have learned anything in this book, big samples are strongly preferred as they improve our ability to describe our data, control for other competing effects, and make stronger inferential claims.

Think of the importance of assumptions to multiple regression as the importance of normal maintenance to driving a car. To optimize our driving experience as well as our safety, we should make sure that the wheels are inflated properly, all the fluids – oil, brake, transmission, windscreen – are topped off, there is gas in the tank, all the exterior lights work, and there is nothing unusual such as the car drifting to one side or the other. In the same way that we maintain elements of our car to keep it in working condition, making sure that the assumptions of multiple regression are met gives us confidence in its performance and results.

As we engage the assumptions for multiple regression, keep in mind that they are necessary in order for us to maximize the quality of the estimating process. More than anything, we want the regression coefficients – as estimates of the true population parameters – to be both unbiased and efficient. Unbiased means that the mean of its sampling distribution is close to the true 'β' in the population and efficient means they have the smallest variation. All of the violations, as we will see below, are challenges to being able to maximize these qualities of the estimating process.

The bad news of this chapter is that violations to these five assumptions are not uncommon. The good news of this chapter is that there are, many times, uncomplicated fixes so that we can quickly right what is wrong and get back to taking care of business.

Regression Troubleshooting and Diagnostic Checks

In the following sections, we will review the five assumptions of multiple regression, discuss why we need them, determine if they have been violated, and review any potential means to correct them. The first two assumptions refer to problems often found in the systematic part of the regression equation [$\alpha + \beta x$], while the last three assumptions refer to problems in the random (or 'stochastic') part (ε).

$$y = \{\alpha + \beta x\} + \{\varepsilon\}$$

Assumption Number One: Underlying Linearity

The dependent variable is a linear function of a specific set of independent variables plus an error term.

Why Do We Need this Assumption and What Happens if it Isn't Satisfied?

Linearity is an assumption about model specification, that is, the choice of which variables to include and *how* to include them. More precisely, the estimating procedure of multiple regression assumes linearity as the expected or 'true' nature of the relationships between each independent variable and the dependent variable.

Mathematically, the OLS estimation procedure of the regression coefficients (and intercept) assumes that each independent variable is linearly related to the dependent variable. Assuming that two variables are related in a way they are not creates a problem not only for the estimation of that specific coefficient but also for the entire model. That is, not only will the non-linear relationship be inappropriately estimated, this will also impact the performance of the model as a whole. All of the estimates will be inefficient and thus not be very informative. Our model will be an untrustworthy guide for discerning reality.

It is neither very common nor very uncommon for relationships between two variables to be non-linear. The problem is that it introduces inefficiency to the estimating procedure. This makes sense. If we try to summarize a non-linear relationship with a line, we fail to minimize the errors we make in predicting the relationship, we provide a poor summary of the relationship, and we very likely solve different parts for the relationship differently. Imagine describing a slithering snake by only referencing a pencil.

How Can We Correct This?

The assumption of linearity is that a line is the best means to summarize that relationship. The simplest and most effective way to identify this is to look at a scatterplot of each independent variable and the dependent variable.

In Figure 16.1a, we have plotted a scatterplot of individuals' self-placement on an ideological continuum from far-left (0) to far-right (10). On the y-axis, we include a variable that asks how close the same respondent feels to any particular party (the data are for the countries of the Czech Republic and Germany).

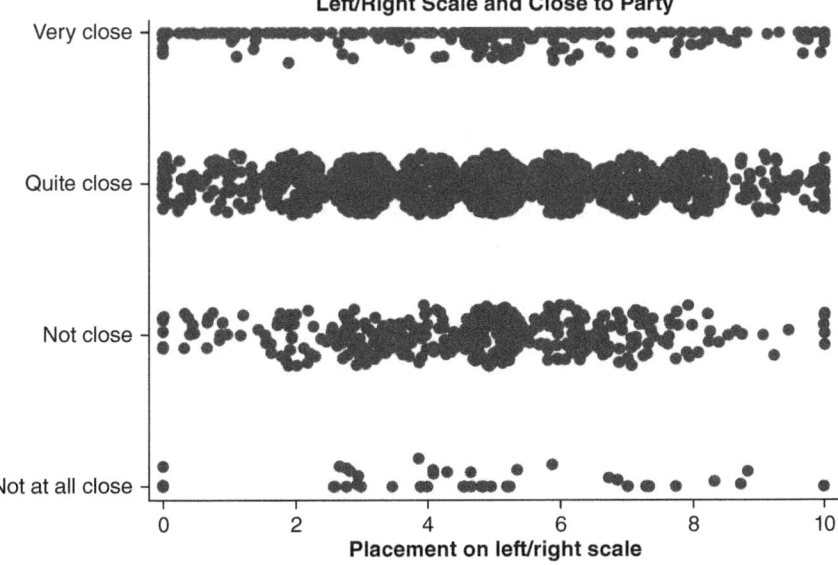

Figure 16.1a Left/Right Scale and Feel Close to Party

The distribution of observations appears to fall most heavily in the centre and upper left and right corners. This makes intuitive sense as those in the middle are less likely to feel the strong attachment to a particular party that those at the left or right extremes would feel. Taking more extreme stances requires a greater commitment and perhaps (party) loyalty than those with more moderate ideological locations. This, however, creates the obvious problem that a line would fail to represent the relationship adequately, much less ideally.

In Figure 16.1b, we have modelled the relationship so that a possible summary of the relationship can be curvilinear and thus more closely represent the underlying pattern and thus nature of the relationship.

How do we do this?

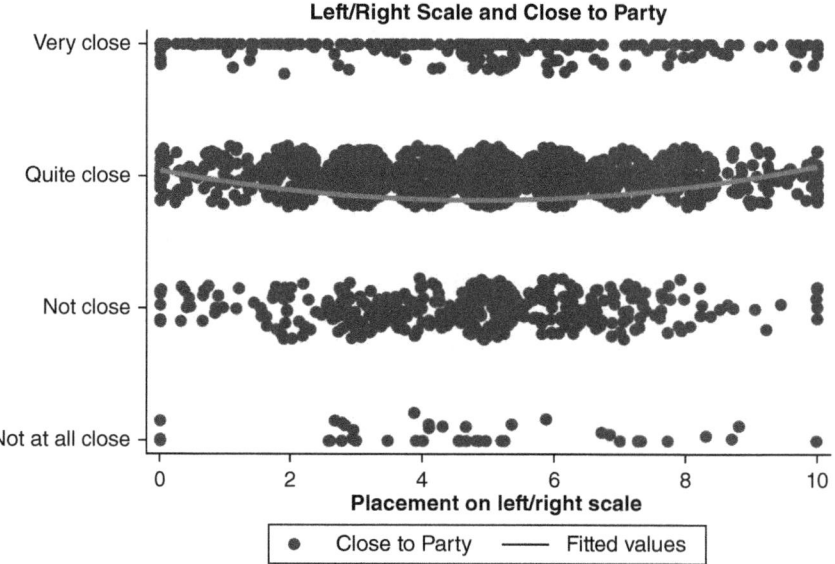

Figure 16.1b Non-linear Solution to Left/Right Scale and Feel Close to Party

We can transform the mathematical summary of the relationship between the independent and dependent variables. That is, non-linearity can be potentially resolved by applying a summary shape other than a line. Other forms can be used to summarize the relationship between two random variables: quadratic (X^2), cubic (X^3), even polynomial (X^k) regression elements.

We could transform our fully linear model with our non-linear term X_1:

$$\hat{Y} = \alpha + \beta_1(X_1) + \ldots + \beta_n(X_n) + \varepsilon$$

A quadratic term:

$$\hat{Y} = \alpha + \beta_1\left(X_1^2\right) + \ldots + \beta_n(X_n) + \varepsilon$$

A cubic term:

$$\hat{Y} = \alpha + \beta_1(X_1^3) + \ldots + \beta_n(X_n) + \varepsilon$$

Or other polynomial term (including fractions):

$$\hat{Y} = \alpha + \beta_1(X_1^k) + \ldots + \beta_n(X_n) + \varepsilon$$

If we discover the relationship to be more or less 'U-shaped' (for example, as we do in Figure 16.1b), we might choose a quadratic term (X^2) as the best mathematical summary of the relationship. Other relationships may require different solutions.

Which of these solutions is the best or most correct solution? There is no exact method of determining the best solution shape. However, one approach is to try the most likely forms, run a bivariate regression of the new term and the dependent variable, and compare each model's adjusted-R^2. The non-linear term that produces the highest R^2 is likely to be the best fitting term to, in turn, include in the multiple regression. Note: this is 'a method' not 'The Method'. However, if a solution shape summarizes the relationship between that independent variable and the dependent variable well (largest R^2), this is not the worst indicator of the best non-linear solution.

Another approach is to transform the data themselves. That is, there are situations in which adjusting the nature of the data themselves resolves the non-linearity, although this will impact the subsequent interpretation. Another reason to do such a transformation is that it is called for by theory. In either case, the most common of these is to apply a log-linear transformation to the data. This applies primarily to independent variables as transformations of dependent variables can require a great deal more attention (as we will see in the next Chapter).

In the simplest case, such a transformation makes the data 'act' as if they were linear. For data that resemble an exponential curve – one that gets steeper and steeper as they increase – **log-linear transformations** essentially shift such highly skewed data toward a more symmetrical distribution (one resembling a Normal distribution). In doing so, curves are often smoothed to a more or less linear shape.

Take, for example, the Alliance Treaty Obligation and Provisions (ATOP) project that summarizes data on military alliances since 1815 in the entire world. If we look at the simplest indicator, the number of alliances each country may have, we arrive at the graph in the left panel of Figure 16.2. The vast majority of countries have very few military alliances whereas fewer countries have a significantly greater number of such alliances. These data are clearly not normally distributed, creating potential problems for our standard deviations to accurately convey the dispersion of data around the mean as well as any subsequent t-tests for statistical significance.

However, with a log-linear transformation of the data themselves, seen in the right panel of Figure 16.2, the data take on the preferred and mathematically convenient Normal-ish distribution. This improves our ability to describe, test, and report any subsequent results that include these data.

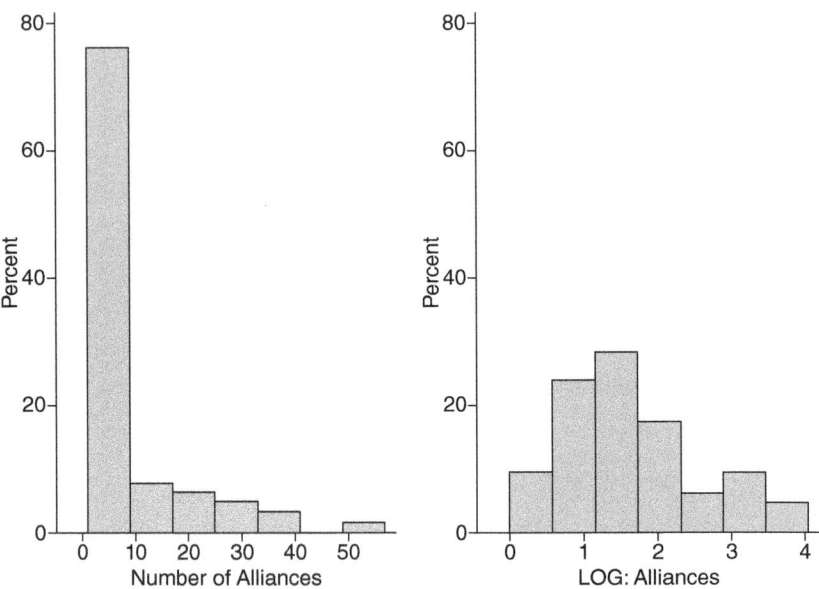

Figure 16.2 Log-Linear Transformation: Histogram

In the case of a log-linear transformation to the data, the interpretation of the relationship between the log-linear adjusted independent variable and the dependent variables becomes 'a 1-unit increase in the independent variable would lead to a '$\beta'/100$ change in the dependent variable holding all other variables constant'. This does not change the interpretation of the other included independent variables or model fit.

Note, a log-linear transformation is not, however, a technique that we should use to, for example, try to eliminate outliers or to make the data 'nicer' or more 'well-behaved'. We must try to do our best to deal with all the data as best we can and deal with these peculiarities not by sweeping them under a statistical rug but by engaging with their challenge.

Assumption Number Two: Uncorrelated Independent Variables

In a regression model, there should be no strong (linear) relationship between independent variables. This can be tricky. In a multiple regression setting, we are looking for independent variables related to the dependent variable. However, many of these independent variables can be related to each other. Inasmuch as they are not, our regression model is more efficient and produces better estimates of the population parameters we so desire to capture.

Why Do We Need this Assumption and What Happens if it Isn't Satisfied?

In multiple regression, as long as we do not violate the degrees of freedom of having more variables than observations, we can include any number of independent variables. While including many variables may seem attractive, we must keep in mind that we are looking at a number of processes that are very likely to be related in some way. More specifically, it is often the case that the independent variables are not only correlated with the dependent variable, but also with each other. We are, after all, examining many related processes. This introduces the likelihood of multicollinearity.

Multicollinearity is high or near perfect correlation between independent variables. A rule of thumb for 'high or near perfect correlation' is roughly $r>0.80$. The problem with high correlation between independent variables in multiple regression is that it is difficult for the estimating procedure – OLS – to distinguish the effect of one independent variable on the dependent variable from another independent variable's effect.

The potential for independent variables being related is common. If we are looking at what drives ethnic conflict and we include measures of government performance and economic indicators, we know that politically high-performing countries are very often economically high-performing countries and *vice versa*. In this case, and more generally, variation of the two independent variables can be classified into three types: variation unique to the first variable, variation unique to the second variable, and variation common to both.

In Figure 16.3a we can see the effects of these three types, including the variation common to both (indicated by the arrow).

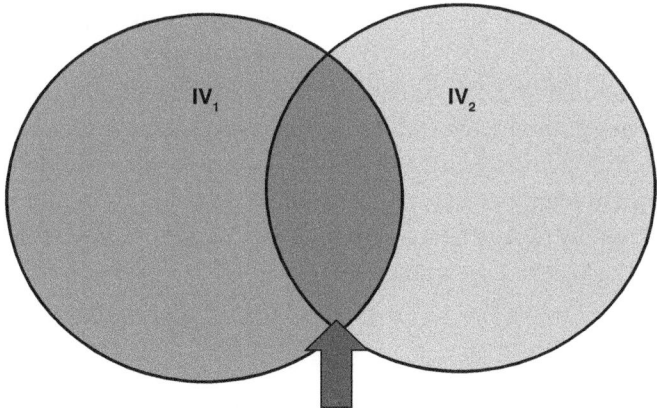

Figure 16.3a Two Independent Variables: Low Correlation

In measuring the effect of the first variable, only the variation unique to it can be used, variation shared by the second variable cannot be used because there is no way of knowing whether the dependent variable variation was due to variation in the first or in the second variable (see Figure 16.3b). In other words, OLS uses *only* the unique to the first regressor in calculating the estimate of the coefficient of the first regressor. Same for the second variable. The common variation is effectively ignored (it is technically unassignable).

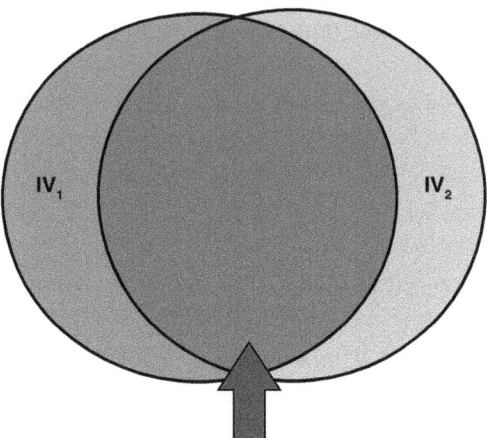

Figure 16.3b   Two Independent Variables: High Correlation

Ergo, if these two independent variables are highly correlated, there is little independent variation from which to generate a reliable parameter estimate for each independent variable. This means that OLS has little information to make effective estimates for each independent variable. Any estimate based on little information is likely to have a high variance and thus cannot be held with much confidence (like having a small sample size).

Technically, the inability to 'assign' common variation between each independent variable and dependent variable inflates the standard errors. This creates two specific problems. One, this creates greater uncertainty in our parameter estimations and two, an inflated standard error increases the probability of ignoring a significant factor (a.k.a. Type II Error). Together, we are left with imprecise parameter estimates that diminish our ability to conduct effective hypothesis testing.

How Can We Correct This?

The most direct way to detect multicollinearity is simply to produce correlations between your chosen independent variables. Again, as these correlations approach 0.80, the likelihood of a problem increases. However, multicollinearity can also be a problem between several variables acting together. A more stringent test of multicollinearity is a **Variance Inflation Factor** (VIF) test. A VIF test essentially estimates how much the variance of each independent variable is inflated due to multicollinearity. Although there is no hard rule, VIFs higher than 10 (in some cases, only 5) are considered a problematically high correlation between independent variables.

If we have multicollinearity, what do we do?

Well, it depends.

One, if two independent variables are highly correlated, the simplest solution is to drop one of them from the model. That is, given what high correlation means (knowing the value of one tells you a great deal about where to expect to find the other), you don't need both. The choice to do so, of course, rests on the theory that imposes upon your model. But if the two independent variables are potentially *conceptually* redundant, excluding one may solve this problem with a minimum of fuss.

Two, data reduction. Combine the two highly correlated independent variables into a single variable. If they are so inter-related, they might be capturing mostly the same thing. Therefore, one might choose to combine the two highly correlated, independent variables. This can be done as an additive variable or by using factor analysis (as we saw in the previous chapter).

Three, for the 'can't be bothered' people out there, do nothing. This can be an appealing option in several scenarios. If, for example, the two correlated independent variables are statistically significant. Given that multicollinearity makes it more difficult to achieve statistical significance (larger standard errors mean large denominators for t-scores), this suggests that they are substantial parts of the model. This is particularly true if the two correlated variables are theorized to be included. Dropping an independent variable that (theoretically) should be in the model can cause omitted variable bias which, in turn, distorts the estimate of the coefficient estimates of the other independent variables in less consistent and predictable ways. For other 'less important' variables in the model, it may simply matter less. An example is the common use of a wide array of socio-economic or socio-demographic variables that are likely correlated (*think*: income and education) but not central to the theory being tested. Such variables, as controls, are likely less problematic to the performance of other, more relevant, parts of the model.

Being aware of multicollinearity has its payoffs. Reducing the number of independent variables can potentially produce a leaner, better performing, model (and fewer discounts on the adjusted-R^2). At the same time, the inclusion of the 'right' variables can provide more accurate estimates and subsequently t-tests (i.e., substantive and statistical significances).

ROBUSTNESS TESTING

Common to many uses of statistics, particularly multiple regression, are robustness checks (sometimes called sensitivity tests). There is no one check. Rather, this refers to the researcher pushing and pulling on the estimating procedure and results to demonstrate that what is being promoted as 'the findings' are in fact the results of a transparent and durable process. Such deep dives into the performance of the model are often the domain of statisticians and the field of Econometrics.

(Continued)

> For our purposes, these checks can take several forms of re-estimating the model to demonstrate that minor changes to the model do not drastically change the direction and magnitudes of the estimated regression coefficients. The regression coefficients should stay more or less the same and are, in the context of the topic, plausible. Robustness checks can be re-estimating the model, for example, with a variable added or removed; with a variable using a different measurement (changing the operational form); or for a series of sub-samples. More advanced methods include a detailed analysis of the error term. In any case, the goal of robustness checks is to demonstrate that the results are not fragile, that is, not subject to this model specification and/or these data, but rather the findings are, in fact, 'robust'.

Intermission

Although Assumption Number Three uses the description, 'the error term is well-behaved', 'well-behaved' really applies to Numbers Three, Four, and Five, as any problem with the error term is the 'high fever' of assumption violations. In other words, the error term not being 'well-behaved' indicates any number of – not critical, but serious – problems. We will need to raise our level of attention and attune to the next challenges at a deeper/higher level to be able to address the challenges to the assumptions of our multiple regression model.

Assumption Number Three: The Error Term is Well-Behaved

The error terms have uniform variance and are uncorrelated. Uniform variance is a strong indication that our regression model is dealing with the variance of the dependent variable quite well. That is, what isn't explained by the included independent variables (i.e., what the error term captures) contains no (or very few) surprises. Correlation between error terms is not a hugely common problem but can happen, especially in data that look at the same process over time.

Why Do We Need this Assumption and What Happens if it Isn't Satisfied?

Recall that the error term 'ε' – is the sum of the unaccounted-for, random (or 'stochastic') influences.

$$y = \{\alpha + \beta x\} + \{\varepsilon\}$$

The error term (ε) captures the effects of randomness, **measurement error**, and omitted variables. 'Captures' may be the wrong word, 'reflects' may be more correct. To the extent that the error term is well-behaved – that is, calm, undistinguished, a bit boring, perhaps – we can consider this is a sign that our multiple regression model is more or less properly specified. 'Properly specified' means that the model includes – and excludes – what it should include – and exclude. However, for many of the complex models on such topics as voting, party competition, or the likelihood of conflict, the level and complexity of model specification can be quite high. That is, the assumption that the error term is well-behaved can sometimes be rather optimistic.

What does well-behaved mean in technical terms? It means that the error term is normally distributed, has a mean of zero, and has constant variance. This is written:

$$\mu_i \sim N(0, \delta^2)$$

Not well-behaved means that any unaccounted-for process or coordination going on in – or with – the error term can potentially influence the estimates of the entire model. And by 'influence the estimates', we mean distort their ability to approximate the actual, desired population parameters. As the population parameters are the things we want, violations to these assumptions move us away from them.

Here, the third assumption – **Multivariate Normality** – has two parts. One in which the error term has uniform variance and one in which it is uncorrelated with another error term.

To the first part, uniform variance is simply the expectation that the variation of the error terms across all values of the independent variables in relation to the dependent variable are constant (or 'uniform'). Recall that multiple regression prefers to minimize squared errors (or distances). Inasmuch as these distances are more or less the same across the entire range of the relationship between the independent and dependent variable, the estimate of the population parameter – the regression coefficient – is a satisfying estimate of the entire relationship. This is called constant variance or, more creatively, **homoscedasticity**.

When the assumption of a uniform variance of error terms is violated, we are confronted with **heteroscedasticity**. Heteroscedasticity is the non-constant variance across the relationship between the independent and dependent variables. In practical terms, this indicates that the model is solving some parts of the relationship between an independent variable and the dependent variable better than others. In the case of heteroscedasticity, the estimate of the relationship – the regression coefficient – becomes an inadequate guide to the nature of the relationship. The implication of heteroscedasticity is that you have information you are not using by failing to include a variable that may be important (this also comes up again in the next assumption).

The second part of the third assumption refers to the assumption that the values of error terms are independent or random and not correlated with each other. This is often called **autocorrelation** as the error terms are correlated with themselves (i.e., from the Greek: 'auto' meaning 'self'). The crucial disadvantage of autocorrelation is that you have less information than you think you do as the model appears to perform better than it actually is.

This is not commonly a problem unless you are working with data over time, such as time series or panel data which look at similar processes at different time periods. This is also why autocorrelation is often called by its alternative moniker: **serial correlation**.

Using cross-temporal or over-time data increases the chances that an error term at one point in time likely correlated with an error term in a previous time period. That is, a good predictor for today is yesterday and thus, by including both 'today' and 'yesterday' – common in over-time analysis – it may appear that you are explaining more than you really are (more highly technically called, non-spherical disturbances). However, there are examples of data at a single time point that can exhibit autocorrelation. **Spatial autocorrelation** is a case in which a change in one unit of analysis affects other units of analysis. For example, one country experiences a large shock such as political violence or sudden economic crisis that – due to proximity or close ties to neighbouring countries – also impacts the political or economic stability in an adjacent country.

The consequences of either violation are not biased estimates but inefficient ones. Inefficiency is the goblin that makes estimates less informative. Why? Because inefficiency refers to the distribution of values around the estimate, the standard error. As we know, as the variance increases, the precision of – and thus our confidence in – the estimate decreases.

In either case, non-uniform variance or autocorrelation, the non-normality of errors means that there is unexplained variance in the dependent variable. Both violations to Assumption Three underscore the role of understanding whether there is information that is underused or overlooked – or that we think we know more than we do. In this way, such violations help us adjust our approach to eliciting information by figuring out better ways to incorporate information into the model itself. That is, this comes down to model specification meaning our choice of which variables to include and exclude.

How Can We Correct This?

The evidence for violations to Assumption Three are not obvious. We will need to dig a bit deeper. To test for heteroscedasticity, we can look at a scatterplot of the residuals versus the predicted (or fitted) values of each independent variable. In Figure 16.4a, we can see the distribution of errors are constant across the range of **fitted values** (i.e., the predicted values of the dependent variable given the independent variables in the model). This illustrates the constant or uniform variance we hope to find.

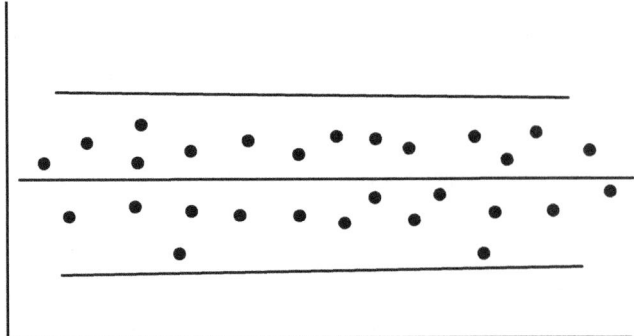

Figure 16.4a Homoscedasticity

Whereas in Figure 16.4b, this is not the case. As the fitted values between the independent and dependent variable increase, the variation increases as well. That is, the variance is not constant.

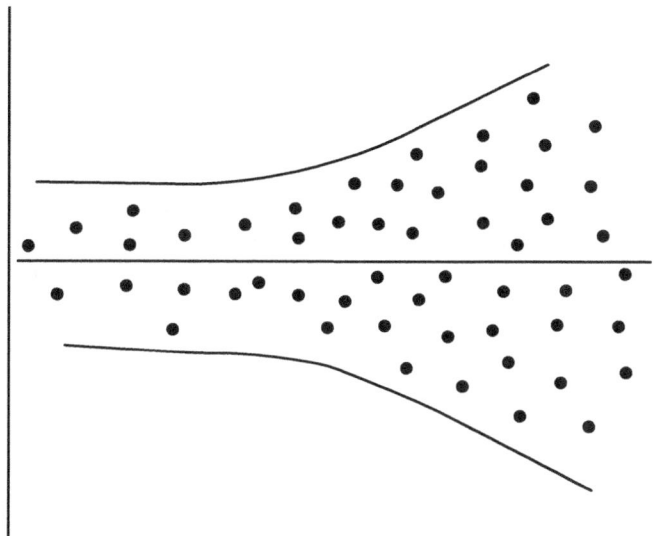

Figure 16.4b Heteroscedasticity

Another resolution to this problem is to use a multiple regression model that arrives at the best estimates via novel means. In the situation in which we have identified heteroscedasticity, we can use an approach that accounts for substantive correlation between the residuals in a regression model. The Generalized Least Squares (GLS) generates a linear unbiased estimator by minimizing a sum of squared residuals that are weighted inversely to the expectation of residual size. That is, rather than using the estimating procedure of Ordinary Least Squares (OLS), the GLS estimating procedure helps us minimize the impact of heteroscedasticity in the model. Importantly, like OLS, the resultant GLS estimators are considered BLUE (Best Linear Unbiased Estimator) in this case.

Autocorrelation means that the model is 'wrong' or more correctly, 'not as correct as it could be'. The model is mis-specified in that, usually, something is missing. One can also diagnose autocorrelation by plotting the residuals using a correlogram (ACF plot) and using the Durbin–Watson test. The Durbin–Watson test is a first-order test to eliminate the alternative explanation of potential autocorrelation, namely, sampling error. Therefore, the solution to autocorrelation is most often identifying and including the crucial missing variable(s). Another potential methodological fix is to incorporate the autocorrelation into the model itself and using greatly more complicated analytic approaches such as Autoregressive Integrated Moving Averages (ARIMA) models.

Assumption Number Four: Mean of Error Term is Zero

While above, we concerned ourselves with the variance and coordination of the error term, Assumption Four pertains to its mean. The expected value of the error term is zero: $E(\varepsilon) = 0$. This is the **exogeneity assumption**.

Why Do We Need this Assumption and What Happens if it Isn't Satisfied?

Again, the error term (ε) captures the effects of randomness, measurement error, and omitted variables. The systematic part of the multiple regression model includes the independent variables crucial to explaining the observed changes in the dependent variable. While we know that our model – as a simplification of reality – will certainly have errors, we expect these effects – unaccounted for in the model – to cancel one another out. As such, we very often do not include independent variables that have either very small observable effects on the dependent variable or no meaningful connection to the dependent variable. Given the small to negligible effects, it is assumed simply that at some point they resolve to a mean of zero.

If the error term mean is not zero, a very common reason is having overlooked or failed to include an independent variable that should be included. This is called **omitted variable bias**. If we fail to include relevant variables in the model that are meaningfully correlated with the dependent variable, the estimates of the included variables are biased away from their 'true' value. Their effects will be overestimated by being forced to 'explain' what should have been explained by the omitted variable (recall our example in Chapter 15 on EU support and the West/East dummy variable, see Table 15.2).

Perhaps we seek to explain why voters choose extreme parties over mainstream parties. Our model might include individual ideology, partisanship, and socio-economic variables such as income, education, and gender. However, recent research has pointed toward including individuals' views on immigration as well. Failing to include such views forces the independent variables already in the model to 'soak up' the potential explanatory power of the respondents' views on immigration. Thus, the estimates produced by the regression model will be biased toward the included variables.

The bad news is that when the mean of the error term is not zero, it implies a problem in the systematic part of the model. Our model is inadequate because it is not correct on average. The good news, however, is that omitted variable bias is a common issue in statistical analysis. While it signals that we have not correctly specified the model, this can be remedied somewhat straightforwardly.

ENDOGENEITY

Note that a violation of exogeneity is **endogeneity**. This term can refer to the problem of omitted variable bias but is more often indicative of a larger host of theoretical and methodological problems. In this sense, endogeneity is the problem in which the causal order of variables is difficult to untangle or ambiguous.

Endogeneity might include the inversion of previous theoretical thinking. For example, early research into political campaigning showed that when an incumbent politician was spending more time campaigning, they were more likely to lose. Such results were initially confusing as one would expect the extra effort in campaigning to pay off in the form of stronger electoral support (i.e., more votes). If we reverse the causal arrow, we arrive at a more satisfying answer hidden by the problem of endogeneity. Incumbent politicians' seats are historically safer than challengers' attempts to get them. However, when these incumbent politicians feel a real, legitimate threat to their seat, they often spend more time campaigning to mobilize supporters in order to fend off the challenger. That is, incumbent politicians can afford not to campaign only when their seat is safe. As an example of endogeneity, campaigning wasn't causally related to winning or losing, the prospect of losing was causally related to campaigning (and campaign spending in particular).

How Can We Correct This?

We have some guides to optimal model specification. One is the literature. What have others demonstrated to be important to understanding changes in our dependent variable? What do the theories that apply to my research question propose to include? Two, we have measures of model fit – such as R^2 and the F-test – that we can use to compare between differently specified versions of the model. That is, we can identify potentially important variables and include them as to maximize their explanatory power. Finally, is the exogeneity assumption itself: the expected value of the disturbance is zero: $E(\varepsilon) = 0$. Although we are unable to calculate all of the necessary elements to provide a direct test, most statistical software packages will offer a means to test the exogeneity assumption. Technically, using the logic of hypothesis testing, exogeneity is the null hypothesis and a test will determine whether there is sufficient reason to reject that assumption.

Model specification, like most scientific endeavours, is not an exact science. Including the 'most appropriate' independent variables to fully specify a model and avoid omitted variable bias may take some trial and error. To achieve an optimal model specification, we have to maintain a tension between these two impetuses. One is tempted, given the ability of multiple regression to control for the competing impacts of different independent variables, to throw everything in. As we previously noted, this is sometimes called the 'kitchen sink approach' in which we throw everything at the problem. But including irrelevant or spurious variables not only puts unnecessary strain on the estimating procedure (using our perfectly good degrees of freedom for nothing) it is also an inelegant and inefficient solution. We violate the scientific norm of parsimony. While we do not want to leave out key variables in order to obtain the most accurate estimate, there is no need to overreact to omitted variable bias.

Assumption Number Five: Fixed in Repeated Samples

The independent variables are uncorrelated with the error term. This state of being 'error-free' is sometimes called, 'fixed in repeated samples' or the 'error-in-variables' problem.

Why Do We Need this Assumption and What Happens if it Isn't Satisfied?

Our observations on the independent variables should measure what we say they do. To the extent that they do not, we introduce more noise in the form of measurement error into our model. That noise ends up in the error term. Recall, again, the error term (ε) captures the effects of randomness, measurement error, and omitted variables. And we should be particularly concerned if this extra noise is moving with the observations on the independent variable. If they do move together in a conspicuous manner, we are assigning explanatory power to the independent variables that is not theirs to have.

We assume to have measured our independent variables without error. That is, in collecting or processing the data, the variable remains a reliable indicator of the concept in which we are interested and intend to analyse. However, error can be introduced in any number of ways. The data collection process can influence poor instruments or questions to capture the data. It can be input or recorded incorrectly. Or simply, the data themselves are suspect. A common example of measurement error is using surveys. It is considered standard that respondents will – on average – under-report their age and over-report their income.

Why is this a problem? Well, other than having poorly measured variables, it makes the error term suspicious. This is easier to see if we approach the problem from the other side. If an independent variable and the error term *were* correlated, we could use the independent variable to predict the error term thus providing clear evidence that the error term is not, in fact, random.

Simply, if variation in the dependent variable arises from an independent variable that is not completely independent of the error term, the dependent variable is being explained by variation in the independent variable and something else.

Note that errors in measuring the dependent variable do not cause a similar set of problems as these errors are completely absorbed by the error term. However, in a worst-case scenario, a more problem-inducing form is when both the dependent and independent variables are affected by an unobserved or unaccounted-for variable(s). This is fairly difficult to identify unless the effect is large enough and thus often left unobserved.

How Can We Correct This?

As a basic test for this problem, one can plot the error terms against each independent variable and look for any non-random pattern. Perhaps the pattern moves off in a peculiar direction, one could consider including a quadratic coefficient to capture the curvilinear form. This would indicate the possibility of an error-in-variables problem. One could also use a Hausman test that essentially compares the performance of the potentially mismeasured independent variable against an alternative in the form of an instrumental variable (discussed below). Inasmuch as these estimators differ, there is an increased likelihood of correlation between the independent variable and error term. This alerts us to the potential problem of error-in-variables.

One approach is to use instrumental variables. **Instrumental variable estimation** is, in a sense, substituting one variable for another. To achieve optimal instrumentality, any replacement variable must be uncorrelated with the error term and at the same time correlated (preferably, very much so) with the problematic independent variable. This choice can be guided theoretically, seeking to substitute a similar concept or practical, such that the instrumental variable is most effective in satisfying the two necessary criteria regardless of its relationship to the substituted variable. In either case, the instrumental variable is substituted in place of the problematic independent variable producing a consistent and asymptotically unbiased estimator.

There are more complicated applications of instrumental variables that include replacing an independent variable with the predicted values of a dependent variable from another regression model (whether simultaneously generated or not). In either case, done well, an instrumental variable estimation can produce consistent estimators although there is unavoidable inflation in the variation between the instrumental variable and dependent variable (inversely proportional to their correlation). This is not a *problem* problem but – to the extent that the correlation between the instrumental variable and dependent variable is unsatisfying – there may be technical reasons to prefer the original independent variable despite its limitations (specifically, a biased estimator). One of the main limitations to this approach is simply finding a variable that meets the challenging assumptions and also performs reasonably well. That is, instrumental variable estimation can provide a solution but is not always the superior approach.

PROXY VARIABLES

The instrumental-variables approach is a process through which we seek to substitute one variable with another that meets specific performance criteria. There are a variety of ways to do this but very often we simply replace the problematic variable with another. The use of 'proxies' – or **proxy variables** – in Social Science is not to be confused for the instrumental

(Continued)

variable approach. The instrumental variable approach seeks to substitute a problematic variable with one that is both highly correlated with the original variable and uncorrelated with the error term. Very often this is done to maximize exogeneity (i.e., avoid endogeneity or potential circular causality) as well as to avoid violating the above assumptions. By contrast, **proxies** are intended to capture concepts that evade easy operationalization or are very often directly unobservable rather than replacements of other variables. This is common among assigning socio-psychological attributes to individuals or anthropomorphizing inanimate objects such as states or political parties.

For example, we might be researching the lack of or uneven partisan re-alignment in Europe and be interested in individuals' levels of 'political sophistication'. Political sophistication asserts that individuals are more highly educated and politically savvy and thus less likely to rely on parties to provide information or guidance to political phenomena. However, there is no political sophistication variable to include in our analysis. We might, therefore, proxy a respondent's level of 'political sophistication' by their level of interest in politics. We can reason that the more attentive one is to politics, the more likely they are to have well-rehearsed and consistent political orientations to political phenomena, i.e., attributes of political sophisticates. Or perhaps we proxy countries' 'willingness to go to war' by the 'percent increases in military budgets', reasoning that funnelling money into the military is a form of preparation. Or that parties are taking strategic action in their electoral marketplace to offset new challengers by measuring their 'change in issue salience' for various issues.

Other examples include proxying for a respondent's social class by asking whether they shower before or after work (namely, white collar workers shower before, blue collar workers, when they arrive home). Or determining the intellectual *milieu* of one's upbringing by asking respondents to comment on how many books they remember seeing in their house growing up (as a clear determinant of future education success, Evans, et al. 2010).

In any case, the use of proxies can be an effective means to tap concepts we need (or want) but struggle to capture directly.

Final Thoughts

The five assumptions promote good modelling practices and aid our quest for the correctly specified multiple regression model. These assumptions train our attention on the most common and immediate set of problems, which has an additional value beyond merely rectifying problems within the model itself. Namely, we are starting to get a sense of how models should work. That is, we have already reviewed some of the useful indicators of model fit such as R^2 and the F-test. These help us to make changes to the specification of our model – to play with the model – with the intention of improving its performance by finding a balance between fit and parsimony.

Technically, if these assumptions are satisfied, the **Gauss–Markov theorem** asserts that OLS is the best estimator – by having the lowest sampling variance – among the class of linear estimators for linear regression. In this sense, our attention to these assumptions strengthens our use of multiple regression to accurately estimate the processes in which we are interested. In doing so, the assumptions here further develop our intuitive sense of how a multiple regression should perform. We can more accurately recognize the problems of omitting crucial variables, inefficiently including too many, simultaneous causality, measurement error, or even the wrong functional form of the model. This search for the 'true model' – in which our model embodies the intended theoretical model – rests on our ability to incrementally improve our **model specification**. The goal is 'good fit'.

End of Chapter Summary

- Assumption Number One is underlying linearity.
- Assumption Number Two is uncorrelated independent variables.
- Assumption Number Three is that the error term is well-behaved.
- Assumption Number Four is that the mean of error term is zero.
- Assumption Number Five is 'fixed in repeated samples'.
- The tension between trying to achieve high-quality model fit and the availability of data (and suitability of variables) is normal.
- Fixes to some of the common problems not only allow us to use key assumptions but very often improve the specification, fit, and performance of our multiple regression model.
- Violations of the five assumptions can produce misleading estimates of the coefficients, their standard errors, or the overall model.
- The problems most difficult to identify and solve involve the error term. We often will need the help of a statistical software program to find them.

Glossary

- **Log-linear transformations** transform skewed data toward a more symmetrical distribution.
- **Measurement error** can include instrument bias or expectation/confirmation bias.
- **Multicollinearity** is high or near perfect correlation between independent variables.
- **Variance inflation factor** (VIF) estimates how much the variance of each independent variable is inflated due to multicollinearity.
- **Multivariate normality** – has two parts: one in which the error term has uniform variance and one in which it is uncorrelated with another error term.
- **Homoscedasticity** assumes constant variance for the error terms. [Var[$\varepsilon_i \mid x_i$] = σ^2]
- **Heteroscedasticity** is non-constant variance across the relationship between the independent and dependent variables.
- **Autocorrelation** is when the error terms are correlated with themselves.

- **Serial correlation** is an over-time correlation between error terms.
- **Spatial autocorrelation** is autocorrelation between error terms driven by a simultaneous event over different (geographical) spaces.
- A **fitted value** is the model's prediction of the mean outcome value of the dependent variable controlling for all the independent variables.
- The **exogeneity assumption** is that the expected value of the error term is zero: $E(\varepsilon) = 0$.
- **Omitted variable bias** distorts the estimates of the included variables away from their 'true' value when we fail to include relevant variables in the model that are meaningfully correlated with the dependent variable.
- **Endogeneity** refers to the problem in which the causal order of variables is difficult to untangle or ambiguous.
- **Instrumental variable estimation** addresses the problem in which an independent variable is correlated with the error term by substituting a variable that is uncorrelated with the error term and highly correlated with the problematic independent variable.
- **Proxy variables** or **proxies** are intended to capture concepts that evade easy operationalization or are directly unobservable.
- The **Gauss–Markov theorem** says that as long as the five assumptions are met, OLS is the best estimating procedure for multiple regression.
- **Model specification** refers to the variables that are included in our model and represent the process of optimizing our model so that it reflects the intended theoretical model.

Questions

1. You are interested in studying national-level income inequality. To understand why it differs across Europe, you decide to analyse cross-national differences in the Gini Index of income inequality by including five independent variables in a multiple regression model. You have data from a random sample of European countries ($N = 37$) and include GDP per capita, total population, percent rural population, the unemployment rate, and GDP per hour worked (from the Quality of Government dataset). See Table 16.1. Unfortunately, you discover that GDP per capita and GDP *per hour worked* are correlated at $r = 0.922$. Discuss your next steps of how to deal with this problem. *Note*: GDP per capita is divided by 10,000 and Total Population is divided by 1,000,000.

Table 16.1 Income Inequality in Europe

Income inequality [Gini Index]	Unstandardized regression coefficient	Standard error	t	p>|t|
GDP per capita	0.021	0.012	1.75	0.090
Total population	0.001	0.000	3.42	0.002
Rural population	−0.001	0.001	−1.30	0.203

Income inequality [Gini Index]	Unstandardized regression coefficient	Standard error	t	p>|t|
Unemployment rate	0.007	0.002	4.28	0.000
GDP per hour worked	−0.003	0.001	−3.21	0.003
Constant	0.364	0.037	9.72	0.000
Number of observations	37			
F(5,31)	10.84			
Prob.> F	0.0000			
R^2	0.6362			
Adjusted-R^2	0.5776			

2. If the concept of GDP *per hour worked* is important in the literature as a means to understanding why income inequality varies cross-nationally, what are some strategies to retain this concept in the model? And what would you need to avoid in order not to create more problems?
3. Finally, just to be sure you also check the distribution of the error terms for your income inequality regression. In Figure 16.5, we can see the distribution of the error terms. It is not clear whether this is heteroscedasticity or not, so we run the test and find that we must reject the null hypothesis that the error terms are constant (p<0.001). Now what should we do?

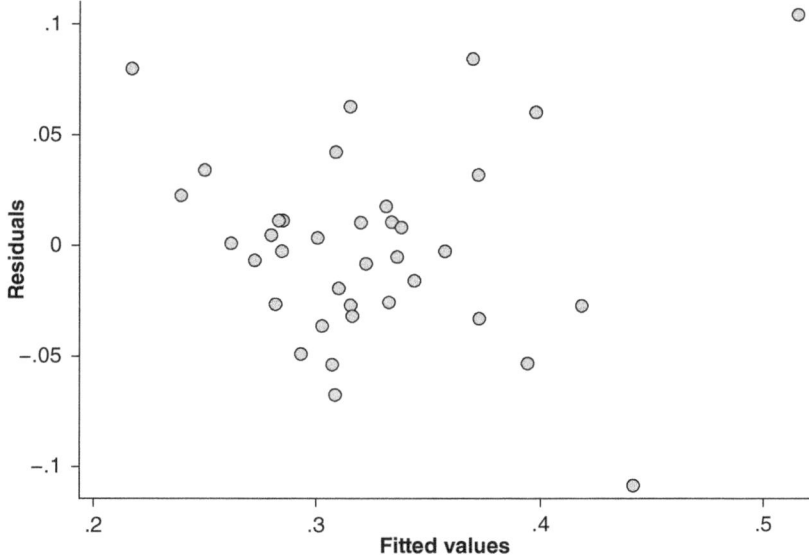

Figure 16.5 Scatterplot of the Error Terms and the Fitted Values

4. Dropping an independent variable that should be in the model (theoretically) can cause omitted variable bias (OVB). OVB biases or distorts the estimate of the coefficient estimates of the *other* independent variables. Why?
5. One thing that is clear from these assumptions is that the error term is quite important. Three of the assumptions (assumptions 3, 4, and 5) are about its performance. This seems counter-intuitive as we have a lot of independent variables. Explain: why is the error term the 'high fever' of assumption violations?

Annotated References and Further Reading

Aitken, Alexander. C. 1936. 'On least-squares and linear combinations of observations' *Proceedings of the Royal Society of Edinburgh* **55: 42–8.**
The Generalized Least Squares (GLS) solution has been with us for a long time.

Hausman, Jerry A. 1978. 'Specification tests in econometrics' *Econometrica: Journal of the Econometric Society* **pp. 1251–1271.**
This is one of the original and most-cited articles on robustness checks.

Lewis-Beck, M.S., Bryman, A., and Futing Liao, T. 2004. *The SAGE Encyclopaedia of Social Science Research Methods. Vol 1.* **Thousand Oaks, CA: Sage Publications, Inc. https://doi.org/10.4135/9781412950589**
This is a nice summary of when and how to use proxy variables.

Evans, M.D.R., Jonathan Kelley, Joanna Sikora, Donald J. Treiman. 2010. 'Family scholarly culture and educational success: Books and schooling in 27 nations' *Research in Social Stratification and Mobility* **28(2): 171-197. doi.org/10.1016/j.rssm.2010.01.002**
Children's educational achievement improved by parents simply having books in their home.

Signposts to the Accompanying Digital Resources

Data used in this chapter

- **Number of Alliances** from the Alliance Treaty Obligations and Provisions Project.
    o www.atopdata.org/. Leeds et al. (2002)

17
BINARY LOGISTIC REGRESSION

> **LEARNING OUTCOMES**
>
> In this chapter, you will be able to
>
> - Understand how the estimation of categorical models with dichotomous dependent variables differs from the estimation of linear models.
> - Use multiple regression to analyse dependent variables that have only two outcomes.
> - Assess the model performance and fit as well as use odds ratios and predicted probabilities to interpret the results.
> - Develop interpretive strategies for the regression results that are consistent with research questions.

Introduction

We can make several types of adjustments for non-linearity in a linear regression model. In previous chapters, we have been able to address the problem of non-interval-level data in the independent variables in a number of ways. We can include dichotomous independent variables by using dummy variables, a nominal (non-dichotomous) independent variable as a set of dummy variables, and even handle non-linearity by transforming the functional form of problematic independent variables. These capabilities are remarkably useful for including a wide variety of independent variables in our analysis thus expanding our ability to control, describe, and infer with multiple regression.

What if, however, the dependent variable is not an interval-level variable? This is a pretty serious and relevant question as there are a lot of things that we would like to explain that are not measured – or measurable – at the interval-level:

- Did the two countries go to war: Yes or No?
- Was the legislation successfully passed in to law: Yes or No?

- Is the country a democracy or not: Democracy or Not a Democracy?
- How likely is the governing coalition to form: Unlikely, Somewhat likely, Very likely?
- How much can you trust the citizens of your country: None, A bit, Some, A lot?
- Which MP candidate won the election: Candidate A, Candidate B, or Candidate C?
- Which Ministry received the largest budget increase in the following fiscal year: Finance, Health, or Employment?
- Has the economy 'Gotten better', 'Gotten worse', or 'Stayed the same' over the last 12 months?
- Any question with Likert response categories: Strongly disagree, Disagree, Neither, Agree, Strongly agree.
- ...

Just as multiple regression was a step up to a new plateau of statistics, dealing with categorial and limited dependent variables is also a new plateau. The analysis of dependent variables that are not interval-level are a subset of a larger group of regression models commonly called **categorical and limited dependent variables**.

In this chapter, we are going to explore how multiple regression can accommodate a change in the level of measurement of the dependent variable. Specifically, we are going to focus on dependent variables that have two outcomes – dichotomous dependent variables – so that we can understand the estimation process, the results, and how to interpret these slightly more complicated models. Once we understand how multiple regression is adjusted for this type of dependent variable, we will have a solid understanding of the approaches to other non-interval-level dependent variables.

Why is a dependent variable with two outcomes a problem? Consider an example in which we classify a country as democratic or not (1=Democratic, 0=Not

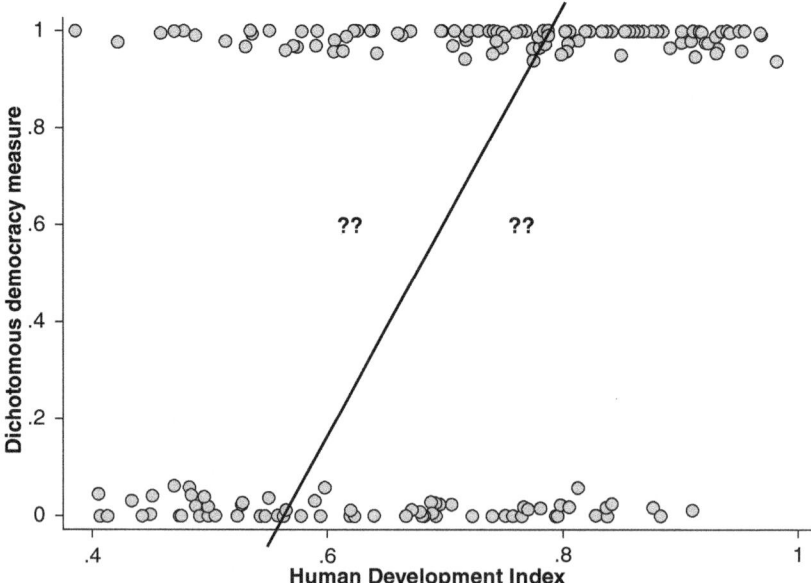

Figure 17.1 Democracy or Not: Human Development Index

Democratic). Using the Quality of Government dataset, we can use a variable that classifies 194 countries and regions as democratic or not. We can look at the distribution of democracies and non-democracies by the level of the Human Development Index (HDI). In Figure 17.1, we can see the joint distribution of these data, including a scatterplot and regression line.

While the random variable HDI can take on values from 0 to 1, the state of democracy is either 'democracy' (1) or 'non-democracy' (0). There are no values between democracy and non-democracy. Thus, it is clear that a regression line is a poor summary of the relationship between whether a country is a democracy or not and the HDI. If in fact we were given a linear solution, what would the slope of the line even mean? The interpretation of a 1-unit change producing a β-change in the dependent variable would not give us anything to understand about this relationship as there are no 'mid-way' steps from 'not a democracy' to 'democracy' in this dichotomous variable.

As you can see, dealing with a dichotomous dependent variable – one with two outcome categories – creates a brand-new set of challenges. However, if our aim is to maximize the overlap of a solution (thus far we have been using a line) with the observations, there is hope! For a dichotomous dependent variable, the solution is called Binary Logistic Regression.

Quick Start: Binary Logistic Regression

The class of regression models with dichotomous, ordinal, or multinomial dependent variables is called log-linear models. Essentially, such models transform the probabilities of the outcomes using a natural log transformation of the odds of those outcomes. You may recall log-linear transformations discussed earlier in making highly skewed data look more 'Normal'. This is not unlike what Logistic Regression does.

Let's start with the simplest example (like Figure 17.1) in which we have two outcomes or two states of being. The logistic regression model is a probability model. We are interested in how well an independent variable (or set of them) predict the probability of one state or another of the dependent variable. (*Note*: because of this, we use the term 'binary' for the regression model rather than 'binomial' as binary refers to two mutually exclusive states of being whereas binomial refers to simply two terms.)

Therefore, we can understand the intuition of binary logistic regression in two steps.

- *ONE:* As a means to find a solution, binary logistic regression tries to predict when the dependent variable is '1' (i.e., not '0').
- *TWO:* The odds that something will happen are equal to the probability that it will happen divided by the probability that it won't. Thus, if p is the probability that $y=1$, the odds of it happening are $\frac{p}{1-p}$. As we have seen above, logistic regression simply adjusts this one step further, making the dependent variable the natural log of the odds of $y=1$ (versus $y=0$).

Therefore, binary logistic regression looks like this:

$$\ln\left[\frac{p}{1-p}\right] = \alpha + \beta_1 x_1 + \beta_2 x_2 + \ldots + \beta_n x_n$$

Exactly the same but with explicit probability substituted (if this helps):

$$\ln\left[\frac{Pr(y=1)}{1-Pr(y=1)}\right] = \alpha + \beta_1 x_1 + \beta_2 x_2 + \ldots + \beta_n x_n$$

NO ERROR?

You can correctly write a Binary Logistic Regression model with or without the error term. As we will see below, the Logit estimation does not model the individual values of the dependent variable but rather the mean of the dependent variable given the values of the independent variable(s). Thus, we don't necessarily need an error term at all. Technically, logistic regression makes the assumption that the expected value of the error term is zero although the variance of the errors is fixed at: $\pi^2/3$ (=3.29), called the Standard Logistic distribution. While this assumption is very strong for the reason that it cannot be tested directly (and it is pretty easy to show that it does not hold), it is necessary in order to identify the model. This means that using this 'standard logistic distribution' for the errors aids the use of the natural log of the odds so that we can have a linear relationship with the set of independent variables.

Fine, but why the natural log of the odds?

The natural log of the odds is technically called the link function. A link function is a fancy name for the adjustment to the model so that the set of independent variables are connected linearly with an expected value of the dependent variable (in this case, the mean). Log transformations are the use of logarithms, in which we can express numbers as exponentials of various bases. Base 10 to the third power – 10^3 – is 10*10*10 or 1,000. Such log transformations are common in different fields. And the base can change. It can be 2 or 12 or, as we will use here, the natural log, 'e', written $\log_e(x)$ or, from its Latin name *logarithmus naturali*, ln(x). Like π, 'e' is a transcendental number, approximately equal to 2.71828[…∞] and can be expressed in many equivalent ways.

In Table 17.1, each row is equivalent.

Table 17.1 Examples of the Natural Log 'e'

The natural log of 1 is 0	e^0 is 1	$\ln(1) = 0$
The natural log of 2 is 0.69315	$e^{0.69315}$ is 2	$\ln(2) = 0.69315$
The natural log of 50 is 3.91202	$e^{3.91202}$ is 50	$\ln(50) = 3.91202$
The natural log of 250 is 5.5214	$e^{5.5214}$ is 250	$\ln(250) = 5.5214$
The natural log of 2000 is 7.6009	$e^{7.6009}$ is 2000	$\ln(2000) = 7.6009$

Recall that linear regression estimates the change in the dependent variable for each unit change in the independent variable. **Logistic regression** (or **logit regression**) is a specific case of 'natural log transformations' that estimates the change in the logged odds of the dependent variable for each unit change in the independent variable.

Look at those two sentences again. There is only one crucial difference. For linear regression, the parameter estimate, β, represents the change in the dependent variable for a 1-unit change in the independent variable. For logistic regression, the parameter estimate, β, represents the change *in the logged odds* of the dependent variable for a 1-unit change in the independent variable. That's the trick – that's it. **Logits** are simply the natural log of the odds. So again, in logistic regression, the independent variable does not have a linear relationship with the dependent variable but rather a linear relationship with the natural logged odds of the dependent variable.

Ok, I realize that this may not immediately seem like a real improvement as our casual use of the natural logged odds to understand outcomes is probably not super common. However, while the underlying mathematics may appear to be an extreme sport, the intuition is straightforward.

What is initially reassuring about the Logistic regression model in the equation above is that it estimates the familiar elements of multiple regression models that we have used before including an intercept (α) and regression coefficients (β). And these are the elements that we will both pay attention to as well as interpret (below).

In any case, some assumptions are common to linear regression models, namely that that the data are independent and there is little or no multicollinearity. However, different from linear regression, logistic regression does not require a linear relationship between the dependent and independent variables but rather assumes independent variables are linearly related to the log-odds of the dependent variable. And, as we have seen above, binary logistic regression also makes strong and differing assumptions about the error term.

ALSO, PROBIT

Logistic regression is not the only estimating procedure to handle dependent variables that are not interval-level. A similar estimating procedure is called Probit. Logit and Probit are different on their distribution of errors and in calculating procedure. Probit uses a cumulative density function of a Normally distributed error term to model the inflection from one value of the dependent variable to the other. If the cumulative density function is a logistic function, this will be a Logit model. There are some differences between the procedures although each have different advantages in more advanced analyses. However, Logit is the most common, perhaps because it is easier to calculate and thus jumped out to an early and wider usage, although statistical software has no difficulty performing either now.

User's Manual: Logistic Regression
The Shape of the Solution

Linear solutions are nice and easy. For OLS, a regression coefficient is uniform over the range of the relationship between an independent variable and the dependent variable.

That is, β is β is β for that relationship, no matter which value of the independent variable we look at. Technically, the **marginal effect** is the ratio of the change in the dependent variable to the change in the independent variable. The marginal effect is the common name for the partial derivative in which this ratio holds even when the change in the independent variable is infinitely small. In a linear model, the partial derivative or marginal effect is the same at all values of the independent variable. Simply, it is the slope: β is β is β at all values of that relationship.

The **discrete change**, however, is the expected change from one value of the independent variable to another. That is, it is the change in the dependent variable as we move from one value of the independent variable to the next value. In a linear model, the discrete change is the same at all values of the independent variable (again, the regression coefficient: β). Thus, in linear models, the partial derivative – the marginal effect – and discrete change are exactly the same (β). This is why we can say that they provide a nice and easy solution.

For a regression with a dichotomous dependent variable, the solution is elegant but not nice and easy. Without engaging the substantial technical details underpinning the transformation of linear regression to Logit regression here, the intuition is fairly straightforward and we can use things we already know to guide us to a reasonable solution.

In Figure 17.2a, the y-axis hosts a dichotomous dependent variable 'Y'. It has the value of '0' and '1', the absence and presence of some quality or attribute (similar to Figure 17.1: 'not democracy' or 'democracy'). Across the x-axis at the bottom is an independent variable 'X'.

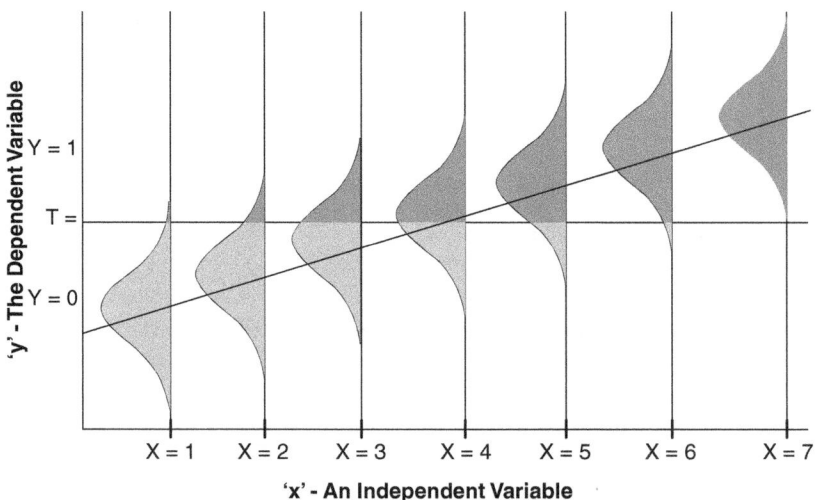

Figure 17.2a A Linear Solution to a Dichotomous Outcome?

In this example, as the independent variable 'X' gets larger the probability that 'Y' is '0' gets smaller, this is represented by the light grey part of the distribution.

Consistently, as the independent variable 'X' gets larger, the probability that 'Y' is '1' gets larger, represented by the dark grey part of the distribution. What is clear is that at some value, 'T', the dependent variable 'Y' is more likely to be '1' than '0'. This probability can be associated to the values of the independent variable 'X'.

That is, if we zoom in on Figure 17.2a, we can see in Figure 17.2b, the probability that Y=1 for the X value of 3 is the dark grey part of the distribution and the probability that Y=0 for the X value of 3 is the light grey part of the distribution. This can be done for each value of X. And as so, one can quickly realize that these probabilities (i.e., whether Y=1 or Y=0) will be specific to each value of X.

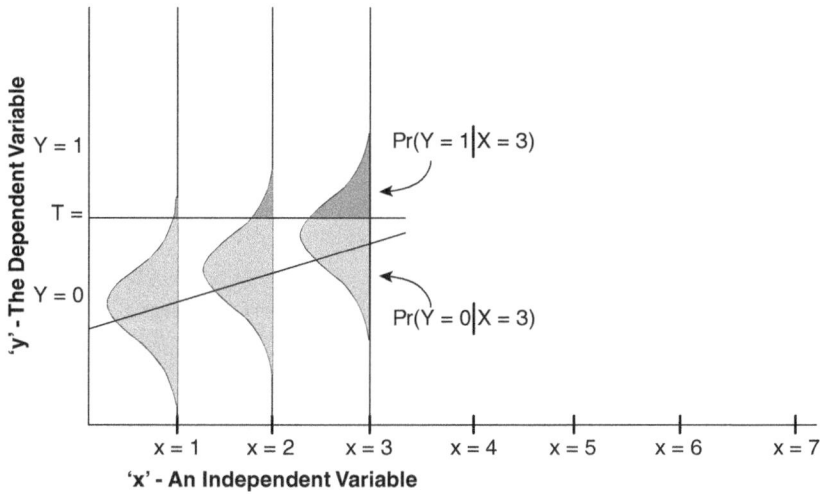

Figure 17.2b The Probabilities of a Dichotomous Variable

We can visualize this change in probability distribution for each value of the independent variable by considering the various forms of the probability distributions.

The probability distribution we are familiar with is the Standard Normal distribution. We like the Standard Normal distribution because we can exploit known properties to estimate the probability of an event. Restated, the density under curve is distributed to assign probabilities to various outcomes. As such, probability distributions can be thought of as a **probability density function** (PDF) precisely because the area under the curve – the density – describes the probability.

However, another way to represent probability density is to let it accumulate. So rather than have a rise and fall in the distribution, the probabilities are added thus creating a **cumulative density function** (CDF). Unlike PDFs, CDFs indicate the probability up to a particular value. In this case, the functional form changes to look more like an S-shaped curve than a line (see Figure 17.3a).

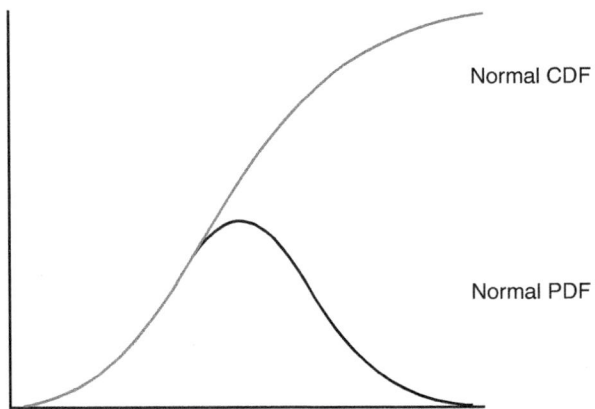

Figure 17.3a Normal Probability and Cumulative Density Functions

We can exploit the functional form of the CDF to attach probabilities to an independent variable – running across the bottom (x-axis) – that Y is one value of another (on the y-axis). Using our example at the start of the chapter (Figure 17.1), if we adjust our linear solution toward a CDF solution, we can see that when the HDI is low, the probability that a country is not a democracy (Y=0), many (but not all) observations are clustered around one 'tail' of the CDF. At the same time, when the HDI is high, the (accumulated) probability that a country is a democracy (Y=1) is also clustered around the other 'tail' of the CDF (see Figure 17.3b). Simply, when the HDI is low, the probability of being a 'non-democracy' is more likely and when the HDI is high, the probability of being a democracy is more likely.

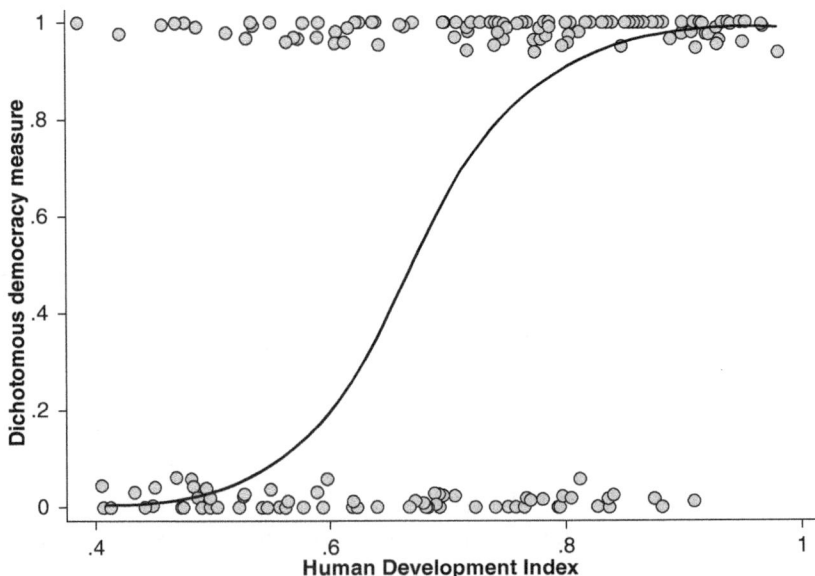

Figure 17.3b Cumulative Density Function: Democracy or Not and the HDI

The cumulative density function also reflects this change in probabilities by reflecting the inflection point in which the majority of cases move from 'non-democracy' to 'democracy'. That is, the probability of Y=0 becomes Y=1 quite quickly as the curve exponentially changes the steepness and thus rapidity of the change in the dependent variable from '0' to '1'. In other words, we can think of the CDF centred on 'T'.

Yes, there are some observations that are not comprehensively captured by this curve. That is, although we can see that the 'tails' of the curve end up being closer to where the majority of points are when Y is '0' or when Y is '1', there are some non-democracies at higher levels of the HDI and some democracies at lower levels of the HDI. Like linear regression, the curve is a summary of the relationship and not a comprehensive accounting. That is, we know that linear regression can be a good summary of a relationship or a poor one, reflected in the substantive and statistical performance of the model and the estimator itself (the regression coefficient). Similarly, the location of the curve in Logit regression can be adjusted to be more to the left or right (reflected in differing value of α) and the steepness of the curve can be increased or decreased (reflected in differing value of β) in order to improve its summary of this relationship. However, while we can increase its alignment with observations, it is not meant - or able - to capture every single one.

In any case, this is why we use the natural log of the odds. A CDF function can be used so that the independent variable can have a linear relationship with the natural logged odds of the dependent variable. Our only challenge then is to figure out which curve best fits the data and how in the world to interpret the results. Let's look at the procedure to produce the estimates. One thing, though: instead of using Ordinary Least Squares (OLS), we use Maximum Likelihood Estimation.

Maximum Likelihood Estimation

Maximum Likelihood Estimation (MLE) is based on the idea that our sample (of data) is more likely to have come from a 'real world' characterized by one particular set of parameter values than from a 'real world' characterized by any other set of parameter values. Searching over different possible population values, it selects the parameter estimates that are most likely to be 'true' for this observed sample. MLE rests on likelihood as a model for inference, rather than probability. One way to think about it is the maximizing of the following expression: L(parameters|data), which is read, 'Let's maximize the likelihood of having these parameters given these data.' Simply, the estimated $\hat{\beta}$ is simply the value of β that maximizes the probability of drawing our sample.

As we will see below, we can often see trace evidence of the MLE procedure in statistical output. To achieve the minimum log likelihood, the model is first estimated empty (with no independent variables). That is, MLE initially establishes our probability of correctly guessing the value of the dependent variable without any help from the independent variables. Then, and this simplifies the process somewhat, it introduces the independent variables to estimate how much better our guess would be knowing the value of each independent variable. This is called an iteration, running the estimation again to see if it can't improve – or maximize – our probability of correctly guessing the value of the dependent variable with this set of independent variables. Thus, iteration by iteration, the aim is zeroing in on the 'best' solution (the minimum log likelihood). When the iterations no longer produce any clear improvement (set by some very small threshold), it stops or, in statistical vocabulary, it converges. The results of this process are then presented as the model solution.

And this form of estimation is not unfamiliar to us. Recall the Proportional Reduction of Error (PRE) statistics from Descriptive Statistics. PRE statistics tell us how much we 'reduce our errors' in predicting a variable by knowing another variable than by knowing nothing at all (or a lesser set of variables). This is the essential procedure of MLE, to move us toward a solution that squeezes the greatest predictive power out of the independent variables we have included by maximizing the probability of the dependent variable equalling 1.

Recall that the OLS regression coefficient estimates are the value of β that minimize the sum of the squared residuals/differences/errors. When all five assumptions are more or less met, OLS is the MLE for multiple regression. That is, OLS is the Best Linear Unbiased Estimator ('BLUE') for an additive linear model. However, confronted with a dependent variable that is non-linear, OLS creates more problems than it solves. Trying to estimate a non-linear dependent variable with OLS will produce, as we already noted, heteroscedasticity (the variance of the errors is not constant) and violate multivariate normality (i.e., the errors are not normally distributed), creating a situation in which the estimation of the regression coefficients – as well as the testing of any hypotheses – become unavoidably erroneous.

Thus, MLE provides an alternative estimating procedure. MLE does not tell us how to specify our model or guide model fit but rather provides rules for producing estimates in the model. The estimates produced by MLE are consistent, efficient, and asymptotically Normal. Consistent refers to the probability that as the sample size increases, the difference between the MLE estimator and the true parameter increasingly diminishes. Efficiency simply means that the MLE estimator has the smallest variance among competing, consistent estimators. Again, from Measures of Dispersion, recall that small variance tells us how good our summary is, thus the MLE estimator is technically the best by being the most precise.

Finally, Normal is of course extremely important. One, it tells us that the MLE estimates are unbiased and two, this allows for a wide array of statistical tests. For our purposes here, when the distribution of our dependent variable is not Normal but takes a different distribution shape, we will need a way to account for this in the estimation of the model. MLE does just this.

Binary Logistic Regression Example

Let's take up the decision to participate politically. While there are an expanding number of types and forms of political participation – including online, consumerist, and more individually expressive forms (Theocharis and Van Deth, 2018) – let's explore individuals' participation in classic forms of political participation. Let's start with the not so simple act of voting (Dalton and Wattenberg, 1993). There are a number of datasets which ask respondents about their voting choices. In the European Social Survey 2018, there is just such a question. It asks respondents whether they voted or not in the most recent national parliamentary election. While there are other outcomes (e.g., the respondent is not legally allowed to vote), we are primarily interested in explaining the difference between those who chose to vote ('1') versus those who chose not to ('0').

The Model and Output

Let's begin with a simple model that includes potential explanatory variables 'age', 'left–right ideological location', and whether the respondent 'feels close to a particular political party' to predict whether the respondent voted or not.

As a logistic regression equation:

$$Vote_i = \alpha + \beta_1(Age_i) + \beta_2(Left/Right_i) + \beta_3(Close_i) + \varepsilon$$

Putting this model into a statistical software program, we arrive at the following output (see Table 17.2a).

Table 17.2a Logistic Regression Example: Voting in Last Parliamentary Election

Voting: Parliamentary election	Logit coefficient	Standard error	z	p>|z|
Age	0.022	0.001	23.35	0.000
Left–Right ideology	0.039	0.008	4.98	0.000
Close to party [Dummy: Yes]	1.421	0.035	40.17	0.000
Constant	−0.427	0.063	−6.80	0.000
Number of observations	27,771			
LR chi² (3)	2732.94			
Prob.> chi²	0.0000			
Pseudo R²	0.1013			
Log Likelihood	−12121.206			

Interpretation: Measures of Model Performance and Fit

As above with the multiple regression models, the output reports a number of different and important elements including the regression coefficients, their statistical significance, and measures of model fit. We take these up in reverse order.

Table 17.2b Logistic Regression Example: Model Fit

Voting: Parliamentary election	Logit coefficient	Standard error	z	p>|z|
Age	0.022	0.001	23.35	0.000
Left–Right ideology	0.039	0.008	4.98	0.000
Close to party [Dummy: Yes]	1.421	0.035	40.17	0.000
Constant	−0.427	0.063	−6.80	0.000
Number of observations	27,771			
LR chi² (3)	2732.94			
Prob.> chi²	0.0000			
Pseudo R²	0.1013			
Log Likelihood	−12121.206			

For categorical models, there are a wide array of measures although no one measure does the best job. However, for model fit and performance, we can focus on the **Likelihood Ratio chi² test** ('LR chi²'). This test essentially compares the estimated model to a 'constrained model' in which all of the regression coefficients are simultaneously equal to zero (i.e., $\beta_1=\beta_2=\beta_3=0$). This is similar to linear regression's F-test. In Table 17.2b, we can see that the test, 'LR chi²', has 3 degrees of freedom (because of the three included independent variables) and gives us a chi² test statistic, 2732.94. Given our experience with chi², this is a very high test statistic. This is confirmed by the reporting of the probability, just below 'LR chi²', in the form of a p-value (or conversely, a level of confidence that we can have in the substantiveness of the model). Here, it is clear we can be very confident that these regression coefficients are not simultaneously equal to zero (p<0.001). Note, the log likelihood is the sum of the likelihood residuals and has no direct interpretive meaning but can be used in the estimation of the likelihood ratio test under specific circumstances. While a **pseudo-R²** is provided, it doesn't tell us about explained variance. It can be a rudimentary guide to compare models with different specifications. In any case, as we see in Table 17.2b, it is not overwhelmingly substantial: 10.13%.

Additional measures of model performance that are not automatically provided but can be asked for include the Wald test. The **Wald test** is similar to a Likelihood Ratio test that compares nested models or more varied specification such as some, but not all, of the regression coefficients are equal to zero, another number, or even each other. Other useful metrics include Akaike's Information Criterion (AIC), which allows us to compare models across different samples or to compare non-nested models. The Bayesian Information Criterion (BIC) takes the Bayesian approach of indicating which model is more likely to have generated the observed data. Like the AIC, a smaller BIC is preferred.

Interpretation: Statistical Significance

Table 17.2c Logistic Regression Example: Statistical Significance

Voting: Parliamentary election	Logit coefficient	Standard error	z	p>|z|
Age	0.022	0.001	23.35	0.000
Left–Right ideology	0.039	0.008	4.98	0.000
Close to party [Dummy: Yes]	1.421	0.035	40.17	0.000
Constant	−0.427	0.063	−6.80	0.000
Number of observations	27,771			
LR chi² (3)	2732.94			
Prob.> chi²	0.0000			
Pseudo R²	0.1013			
Log likelihood	−12121.206			

In Table 17.2c, as we estimate the model with MLE (rather than OLS), we are presented with z-scores rather than t-scores. However, as we know, the t-distribution approaches Standard Normal (the z-distribution) when the number of observations increases. Here, the assumption is that the significance tests can be assessed using a z-distribution. In any case, we are familiar with the results.

- Age is statistically significant with a z-score test statistic of 23.35 ($p<0.001$) or 99.9% confidence level.
- Left/Right ideological location is statistically significant with a z-score test statistic of 4.98 ($p<0.001$) or 99.9% confidence level.
- 'Close to a party' is statistically significant with a z-score test statistic of 40.17 ($p<0.001$) or 99.9% confidence level.

Note that in the case where an independent variable is not statistically significant, the null hypothesis is that the regression coefficient is indistinguishable from zero. Therefore, we should keep this in mind as we go forward.

Interpretation: Regression Coefficients

Finally, in Table 17.2d, we need to interpret the Logit regression coefficients. The non-linear nature of the relationship between the independent variables and the dependent variable creates a challenge not only in the interpretation of coefficients themselves but how best to present the output. It is important to point out that there is no one best way to do any of this. That is, there is no single approach that can fully describe the relationship between the variable and the outcome probability. However, let's take a look at the two most common methods for interpreting Logit regression: Odds Ratios and Predicted Probabilities.

Table 17.2d Logistic Regression Example: Regression Coefficients

Voting: Parliamentary election	Logit coefficient	Standard error	z	p>|z|
Age	0.022	0.001	23.35	0.000
Left–Right ideology	0.039	0.008	4.98	0.000
Close to party [Dummy: Yes]	1.421	0.035	40.17	0.000
Constant	−0.427	0.063	−6.80	0.000

Number of observations	27,771
LR chi² (3)	2732.94
Prob.> chi²	0.0000
Pseudo R²	0.1013
Log likelihood	−12121.206

The challenge of interpretation is twofold. One, the effect of an independent variable in a linear model is uniform as it does not depend on the value of the independent variable. Two, and at the same time, the effect of an independent variable depends on the values of other independent variables in the model. Both of these cannot be said for Logit regressions. When the solution is non-linear, the marginal effect and the discrete change are not the same at all values of the independent variable. And, as we will see, the effect of one independent variable on the dependent variable will also depend on the values of the other independent variables in the model. Keep in mind that both Odds Ratios and Predicted Probabilities consider the Logit regression model a formula for the outcome y=1.

Odds Ratio

In logistic regression, the independent variable has a linear relationship to the *logged odds* of the dependent variable. Therefore, for a unit change in an independent variable, we expect the logit – the logged odds – to change by β, holding all other variables constant. Thus, the results of our model on voting in the most recent parliamentary election, in Table 17.2d, could be interpreted as:

- For each additional year of the respondent's age, we expect a 0.022 increase in the log-odds of having voted, holding all other independent variables constant.
- For each unit moving from Left to Right on the ideological scale, we expect a 0.039 increase in the log-odds of having voted, holding all other independent variables constant.
- If a respondent feels close to a party, we expect a 1.421 increase in the log-odds of having voted, holding all other independent variables constant.

This is not satisfying as trying to untangle logged odds transformations in our heads – or more importantly, our audience's heads – is not optimal.

The odds of something are how often something happens relative to how often it does not happen. We can un-transform the log-odds transformation of the relationship to produce the more intuitive odds ratio or factor change. An **odds ratio** in Logit regression gives us the multiplicative effect on the odds that y is equal to 1 over y is equal to 0. That is, how many times higher the odds of $y=1$ would be if the regression coefficient of our independent variable increases by one unit. This is sometimes called a factor change and allows us to interpret the results as: 'For every unit change in the independent variable, the odds are expected to change by a factor of e^β, holding all other variables constant.' If e^β is larger than 1, the odds are 'e^β times larger'. Conversely, if e^β is smaller than 1, the odds are 'e^β times smaller'. That is, the interpretation for odds less than 1 are the same but represent decreases in the likelihood of the dependent variable =1.

- For every additional year of age, the odds of having voted increase by a factor of 1.0223 (i.e., $e^{0.022}$), holding all other variables constant.
- For each unit moving from Left to Right on the ideological scale, the odds of having voted increase by a factor of 1.0400 (i.e., $e^{0.039}$), holding all other variables constant.
- Feeling close to a party, the odds of having voted increase by a factor of 4.141 (i.e., $e^{1.421}$), holding all other variables constant.

The factor increases of both age and Left/Right scale seem small (and they are). However, let's remember that these odds represent 1-unit changes in these independent variables. We can assess different sized changes in the independent variable by raising the odds ratio (e^β) by the number of intervals.

Therefore:

- For every additional *decade* of age, the odds of having voted are increased by a factor of 1.246 (i.e., $(e^{0.022})^{10}$), holding all other variables constant.
- On the Left (0) to Right (10) ideological scale, moving from far-left (0) to centre (5), the odds of having voted are increased by a factor of 1.215 (i.e., $(e^{0.039})^5$), holding all other variables constant.
- Feeling close to a party is a dichotomous dummy variable. Unlike interval-level variables such as age and (quasi-)ordinal-level variables such as Left/Right, a 1-unit change in a dummy variable is the maximum odds difference between the two groups, here not feeling close to a party and feeling close to a party. However, 414.1 is a substantial factor change.

If a respondent feels close to a party, they were more than four times more likely to have voted than those who did not feel close to a party. And even though the factor changes for both age and left/right ideological scale are statistically significant, their substantive effects are mild. To make a more realistic interpretation, we can choose to present the second set of factor changes. Recalling that 1 is the odds of something being the same, decade older respondents were about 25% more likely to have voted than their decade younger counterparts; self-identified ideological moderates (those in the centre) were 22% more likely to have voted than far-left ideological self-identifiers.

This also gives us another way to think of the complicated nature of logistic regression. Again odds at 1 signify no change. Factor changes or odds greater than 1 mean an increase in the probability – a greater likelihood – and factor changes or odds less than 1 mean a decrease in the probability – a lower likelihood. So, why natural logged odds? Because all decreases must be between 0 and 1 and increases can be any number above 1 which corresponds to ln(1)=0 (see Table 17.1). This is also a highly skewed distribution. However, recall that log-linear transformations can make such highly skewed data behave. Thus, by transforming the odds by the natural log, we are 'straightening' or linearizing a highly skewed distribution of odds around the threshold between the odds decreasing and increasing.

Predicted Probabilities

What is crucial to understand is that odds ratios describe the relationships in this model in a specific way. However, the constant factor change in the odds that we have found above do not correspond to a constant change in the probabilities for each value of the independent variable. Thus, the predicted probabilities approach has a great deal more flexibility in reporting the results and, in many cases, is more popular. However, with that flexibility comes a responsibility for understanding – and maintaining control over – each moving part.

Therefore, instead of saying that the odds of voting are 1.246 times or 25% more likely for a 40-year-old than a 30-year-old, controlling for left–right ideological location and feeling close to a party, we could say the probability of voting is 'this much' greater for a 40-year-old than a 30-year-old, controlling for left–right ideological location and feeling close to a party. 'This much' is filled in by using predicted probabilities. **Predicted probabilities** are summary probabilities that are the result of different values of the included independent variables. The regression coefficients can be used to calculate the probabilities by using the following formula

$$\pi = \frac{e^{a+\beta_1 X_1 + \ldots + \beta_n X_n}}{1 + e^{a+\beta_1 X_1 + \ldots + \beta_n X_n}}$$

Using our example, this looks like this:

$$\pi = \frac{e^{a+0.022(Age)+0.039(L/R)+1.421(Close)}}{1 + e^{a+0.022(Age)+0.039(L/R)+1.421(Close)}}$$

Predicted probabilities are commonly used in two ways. One, we can examine various values of the independent variable in which we are interested holding the other independent variables at a specific value, very often their mean.

LOGITS, ODDS, AND PROBABILITIES

One intuitive way to think about the relationship between Logit regression coefficients is that the coefficients actually have a pretty small range (see Table 17.3). This is a function of using the natural log.

Table 17.3   Logit Coefficients and Probability

Logit	Probability
8	1.000
6	0.998
4	0.982
2	0.881
0	0.500
−2	0.119
−4	0.018
−6	0.002
−8	0.000

Putting this all together, we can convert logit to odds to probabilities in the following way:

- Un-/de-log the coefficient (use e^{Logit}). This becomes the odds.
- Change to probability = odds / (1+odds).

The second, more sophisticated, approach exploits the fact that the impact of one independent variable is affected by the values of the other included independent variables. In this approach, we can summarize the marginal effects of key variables over a series of profiles, or **Ideal Types**, that we choose.

Reporting predicted probabilities is not easy. Even in the most basic form, we will have to produce a large table of probabilities across a range of values for each independent variable. Because of this, the most common reporting method for Logit regression output is producing a graphical summary of the key variables or the variables relevant to the hypothesis/hypotheses being tested. How these graphs are produced will depend on the statistical software program that you choose to use, but they can be reconciled by asking them to perform specific tasks.

One can think of the predicted-probabilities approach as an equalizer to change the sound of the music with the independent variables as the frequency ranges across the bottom (see Figure 17.4). For the first approach, we fix all of the variables at their mean (in Figure 17.4, at 0dB perhaps) and move one variable up and down to see how it

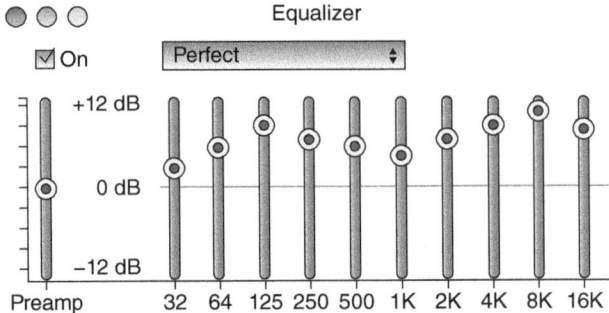

Figure 17.4 A Graphic Equalizer

changes the output. In this approach, we are usually interested in one variable. This is the simplest solution; we examine different values of the independent variable in which we are interested holding the other independent variables at, usually, their mean. This can be expanded, as we will see, into the Ideal Types approach in which we can adjust entire profiles of variables as one might adjust an equalizer to a specific type of music.

In our example of having voted or not in the most recent parliamentary election, let's set all the variables at their mean and see what effect age has on the probability of having voted. We hold the left–right scale at its mean, 5.110, and 'close to a party' at its mean, 0.523. We then produce the predicted probabilities for various ages. This is a discrete change approach which looks at the different probabilities between various values or various intervals – such as a standard error or other meaningful distance – of the independent variable. This approach works for both interval-level and dummy variables.

Here, using a statistical software program, we have produced the predicted probabilities for the ages 20, 25, 30, 35, 40, 45, 50, 55, and 60. As a table of predicted probabilities, this looks like Table 17.4a.

Table 17.4a Predicted Probabilities: Voted and Age

Age	Margin	Standard error	z	Prob.>|z|
20	0.723	0.007	111.41	0.000
25	0.744	0.005	136.91	0.000
30	0.765	0.005	169.54	0.000
35	0.784	0.004	210.00	0.000
40	0.802	0.003	256.44	0.000
45	0.819	0.003	301.77	0.000
50	0.835	0.003	334.71	0.000
55	0.849	0.002	348.35	0.000
60	0.863	0.003	346.13	0.000

We can see that the probability of having voted slowly increases as age increases from 72.3% probability of voting for 20-year-olds to 86.3% probability of voting for 60-year-olds. However, this table, as much as we like tables, might be better represented as a graph. Let's do this.

Figure 17.5a displays the same information in Table 17.4a graphically. The little wings of each predicated probability reflect the confidence intervals reported in Table 17.4a for each probability.

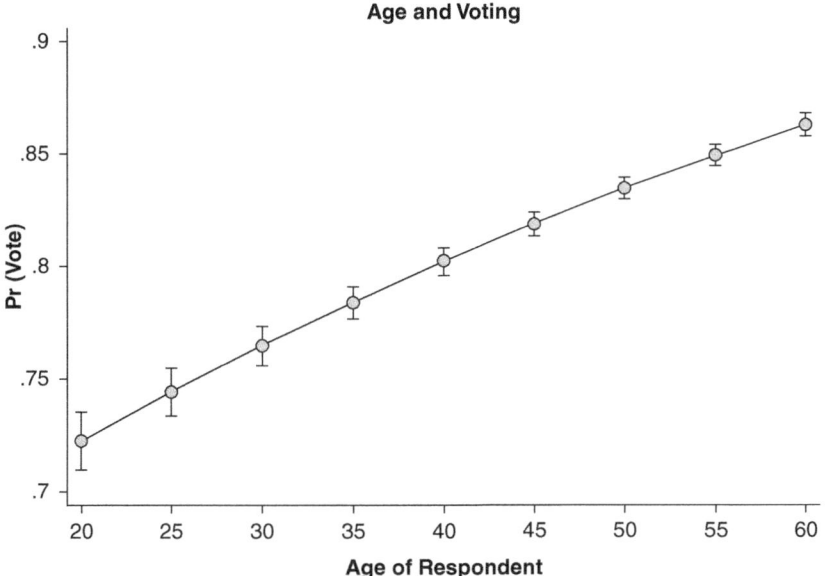

Figure 17.5a Predicted Probabilities: Voted and Age

> ### PREDICTIONS AND CONFIDENCE
>
> Notice the little wings for each point that look like Tie-Fighters from Star Wars. As we are predicting a probability, we have a distribution around how good our predicted probability is. The standard is 95% confidence interval around the predicted value. And, as always, the smaller the distribution, the better the prediction. As you can see in Table 17.5a, our prediction improves as we move from younger to older respondents, very likely the function of having more respondents at those older ages (and thus more data for better predictions).

At this point, you may remember that we held all the other variables at their means. Well, the mean of 'close to a party', 0.523, doesn't mean anything as the variable takes the value '0' 'not close to a party' and '1' 'close to a party'. We can't report being 52.3% close to a party. This is a first step toward creating an ideal type.

So, returning to our equalizer, let's move the 'close to a party' slider to either '0' or '1'. Or both. In Table 17.4b, we have the predicted probabilities across the same age range but also calculate these probabilities for those who do not feel close to a party and those who do, holding the left–right scale at its mean, 5.110.

Table 17.4b Predicted Probabilities: Voted, Age, and 'Close to Party'

Age	Close to party	Margin	Standard error	z	Prob.>|z|
20	No	0.553	0.007	69.71	0.000
20	Yes	0.837	0.005	150.74	0.000
25	No	0.580	0.007	83.72	0.000
25	Yes	0.852	0.005	179.04	0.000
30	No	0.607	0.006	101.05	0.000
30	Yes	0.865	0.004	212.25	0.000
35	No	0.633	0.005	121.52	0.000
35	Yes	0.878	0.004	249.71	0.000
40	No	0.658	0.005	143.43	0.000
40	Yes	0.889	0.003	290.34	0.000
45	No	0.682	0.004	162.81	0.000
45	Yes	0.899	0.003	331.55	0.000
50	No	0.706	0.004	175.04	0.000
50	Yes	0.909	0.003	370.19	0.000
55	No	0.728	0.004	178.46	0.000
55	Yes	0.918	0.002	403.48	0.000
60	No	0.749	0.004	175.44	0.000
60	Yes	0.923	00.002	430.15	0.000

Table 17.4b is becoming untenable to read and clearly report this output. Let's use a graphical presentation. In Figure 17.5b, we can see the output of Table 17.4b represented graphically.

This is a remarkable look at the effect of both age and 'close to a party'. We can see the same increase in probability in having voted with age. However, separating these probabilities by 'close to party' reveals that while those who 'do not feel close to a party' have a lower probability of having voted than those who do 'feel close to a party' overall, the slope is slightly steeper. This has two implications. One, 'feeling close to a party' significantly increases the probability of having voted as all age groups have predicted probabilities above 80%, unlike any of the age groups among those who 'do not feel close to a party'. And, as another observation, age may (potentially) have a stronger effect on this for those who 'do not feel close to party'.

At this point, as we are using the more sophisticated ideal types approach, it is up to the researcher to choose what to present. At this point, how we continue has more to do with the nature and direction of the research rather than any predetermined method. So, since I am in control here, I propose to embrace the sophistication and go one step further.

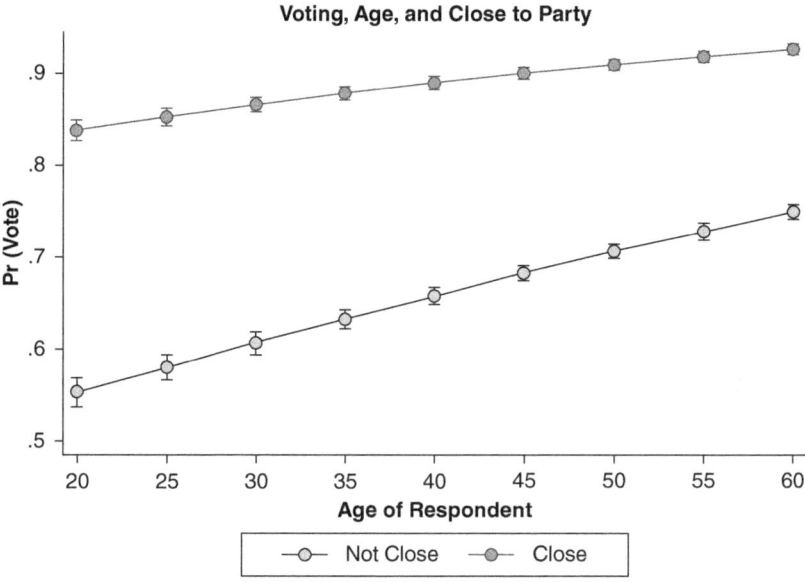

Figure 17.5b Predicted Probabilities: Voted, Age, and 'Close to Party'

We can change the age groups that we are looking at or focus on a subset. However, here I want to bring left–right into our understanding of having voted. I propose to look at the same effects from above (Figure 17.5b) and further disaggregate the predicted probabilities across different ideological locations. I have added the distinction between respondents who report being far-left (0), centre (5), and far-right (10). In lieu of including a long, complicated table, the distribution of predicted probabilities is in Figure 17.5c.

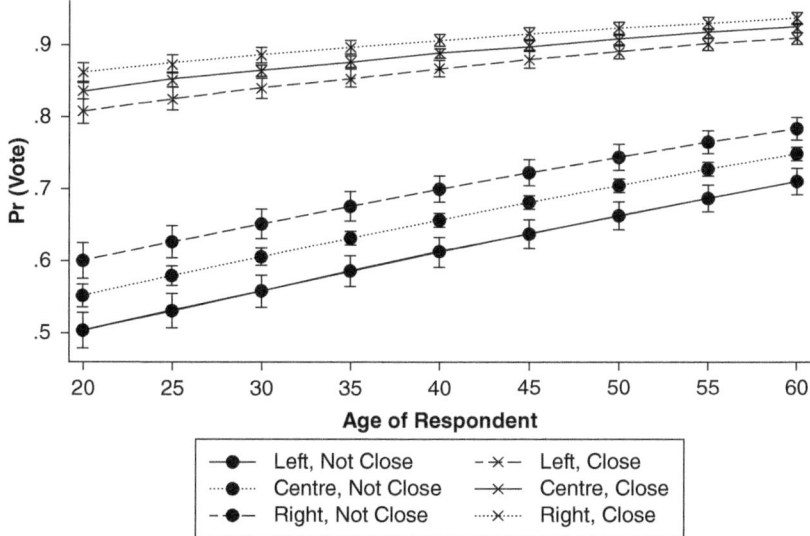

Figure 17.5c Predicted Probabilities: Voted, Age, 'Close to Party,' Ideology

We find the patterns of the previous results for age and 'close to party' endure. The probability of having voted increases with age and those who feel 'close to a party' have higher predicted probabilities of having voted. What we additionally learn by including left/right ideology is that far-right respondents have higher predicted probabilities than those in the centre. And those in the centre have higher predicted probabilities than those on the far-left. This distinctive effect is clear for those who 'do not feel close to a party' as the confidence intervals do not overlap egregiously. For those who feel 'close to a party', the distinctive difference in probabilities is less pronounced, particularly as age increases.

Thus, as ideal types, we might expect:

- A respondent who identifies as far-right, close to a party, and 60 years old to be about 90% likely to have voted in the most recent parliamentary election.
- A similarly far-right respondent, who is not close to a party, and aged 40, is about 70% likely to have voted in the most recent parliamentary election.
- A 20-year-old respondent who identifies as far-left but not close to a party is about 50% likely to have voted in the most recent parliamentary election.
- …

Clearly, the advantages of being able to unpack the effects on having voted are numerous. Again, our interpretative approach taken here is not the only or even the best. The interpretative approach most appropriate to your research will depend on what it is you are investigating.

A Reflection on Categorical Regression Models

Binary Logistic regression models – and as we will see with the other categorial regression models – hold open the door for us to step through, equipped with the ability to use the strengths of regression to investigate questions regardless of the level of the dependent variables. This is not a small achievement. However, as stated at the outset, with such power comes a great responsibility. We must be very careful to understand what the models are telling us. And we must take care in presenting the results. There are other forms of interpretation that we can use to interpret categorical regression models, such as relative risk ratio and proportional odds. None of the approaches is the optimal method in all cases. We must dig down into our research questions and deeply consider what it is we intend to demonstrate. We cannot make up into down or black into white, but our choice of interpretation will be the only guide for our audience so the onus of scientific objectivity and intellectual honesty are upon us.

End of Chapter Summary

- For dichotomous dependent variables, we use binary logistic regression. Or binary Probit.
- For an interval-level independent variable, the coefficient is the log-odds ratio associated with a unit change in that variable.

- Binary logistic regression models are estimated with the Maximum Likelihood Estimation procedure.
- In addition to regression coefficients, binary logistic regression produces interpretable measures of model fit and performance.
- The most common means of interpreting the regression coefficients of binary logistic regression are using odds ratios and predicted probabilities.
- Odds ratios are constant across all values of the independent variable and can be interpreted as factor changes.
- Predicted probabilities require a great deal of attention but allow highly specific presentations of the results, often in the form of Ideal Types.
- It is often much easier to present the results of a binary logistic regression using a graph.

Glossary

- **Categorical (and limited) dependent variables** are a class of regressions in which the dependent variables are *not* interval-level variables.
- **Logits** are the log of the odds.
- In **Logit regression,** the independent variable has a linear relationship with the logged odds of the dependent variable.
- The **marginal effect** is the ratio of the change in the dependent variable to the change in the independent variable.
- The **discrete change** is the change in value from each value of the independent variable.
- A **probability density function** (PDF) is a curve under which the area depicts the probability of particular values.
- A **cumulative density function** (CDF) is a curve under which the area describes the probabilities up to a value.
- **Maximum Likelihood Estimation** (MLE) selects estimates for population parameters for which the probability of the sample observations is the highest.
- **Likelihood Ratio chi² test** compares the estimated model to a model in which all of the regression coefficients are simultaneously equal to zero.
- A **pseudo-R²** is a guide to compare models with different specifications.
- The **Wald test** compares models in which regression coefficients are equal to zero, another number, or even each other.
- **Odds ratios** give us the odds that y is equal to 1 over y equal to 0.
- **Predicted probabilities** are summary probabilities given different assigned values to different independent variables.
- **Ideal Types** summarize the marginal effects of key variables into profiles in which we might be interested.

Questions

1. Give five examples of questions in Political Science that would require binary logistic regression (that we haven't confronted above). Remember, binary means that there are only two exclusive outcomes.
2. Why are predicted probabilities, and in particular Ideal Types, an effective method to interpret the results of a categorical regression model?
3. Create and interpret three additional Ideal Types for 'having voted in the most recent parliamentary election' (use Figure 17.5c).
4. In Figure 17.5a, the relationship between having voted in the most recent national election and age is not a line but a curve. Using the terms 'marginal effect' and 'discrete change', explain why this is so.
5. Both conceptually and technically, why does binary logistic regression determine only the probability of the dependent variable = 1?
6. In linear models, R^2 can be very helpful as it tells us the amount of explained variance of the dependent variable. Explain why, although the output for a binary logistic regression model includes pseudo-R^2, it is rarely used to show model fit.

Annotated References and Further Reading

Dalton, Russell and Martin Wattenberg. 1993. 'The not so simple act of voting' in A. Finifter (ed.) *The State of the Discipline*, 2nd edn. Washington, D.C.: American Political Science Association. pp. 193–218.

Apropos of the 'not so simple act of voting', we have used a decidedly abbreviated model of voting in this chapter for the sake of space. As Dalton and Wattenberg write, 'We review some of the recent major research advances in comparative political behavior, and specifically voting. It is not possible to provide a comprehensive review of the field in a few pages or even several.'

Long, Scott. 1997. *Regression Models for Categorical and Limited Dependent Variables*. Thousand Oaks, CA: Sage.

One of the original path-breaking books on the topic which is still an enormously accessible introduction to categorial and limited dependent variables.

Mood, Carina. 2010. 'Logistic regression: Why we cannot do what we think we can do, and what we can do about it' *European Sociological Review* 26(1): 67–82. https://doi.org/10.1093/esr/jcp006

As pointed out above, the interpretation of these categorical models can be difficult. This difficulty is the result of several imperfect solutions to the problem of estimating non-linear relationships. Mood's article points to real issues in the interpretation including omitted variable bias and the use of odds ratios to interpret results and compare among models. It is technical but correct.

Theocharis, Y., and Van Deth, J.W. 2018. 'The continuous expansion of citizen participation: A new taxonomy' European Political Science Review 10(1), 139–163.
This article proposes new varieties of political participation to accompany the long-standing traditional and non-traditional types.

Signposts to the Accompanying Digital Resources

Data used in this chapter

- **Dichotomous democracy measure** (bmr_dem), Range: 0 Not a democracy 1 Democracy. Quality of Governance.
- **Human Development Index** (undp_hdi), Range: 0.386 – 0.954. Quality of Governance.
    - Teorell, Jan, Aksel Sundström, Sören Holmberg, Bo Rothstein, Natalia Alvarado Pachon, and Cem Mert Dalli. 2021. The Quality of Government Standard Dataset, version Jan21. University of Gothenburg: The Quality of Government Institute, www.qog.pol.gu.se
- **Vote** (vote): Voted last national election: No '0'; Yes '1'. ESS (2018).
- **Close to Party** (clsprty): Feel closer to a particular party than other parties: No '0'; Yes '1'. ESS (2018).
- **Left/Right ideological location** (lrscale): Placement on left–right scale: 0 Left – 10 Right. ESS (2018).
- **Age** (agea): Age of respondent, calculated from birth year. ESS (2018).
    - European Social Survey 1–9, European Social Survey Cumulative File, Study Description. Bergen: NSD – Norwegian Centre for Research Data for ESS ERIC. https:// https://doi.org/10.21338/NSD-ESS-CUMULATIVE

18

CATEGORICAL AND LIMITED DEPENDENT VARIABLES

> ### LEARNING OUTCOMES
>
> In this chapter, you will be able to
>
> - Appreciate regression's potential applicability to a wide range of research questions.
> - Discern the essential elements of the estimating process and general results of more advanced techniques – even if you have not been formally introduced to them.
> - Recognize recent and ongoing developments in quantitative research to extend and exploit the abilities of multiple regression to advance our theoretical knowledge.
> - Envision the continuing development of statistical analysis as a means to improve our understanding of the world.

Introduction

If you can believe it, both the challenges and advantages to using multiple regression continue. In the previous chapters, we have looked at bivariate and multiple regression. We have looked at analysis that confronts independent variables that are not interval-level data by using dummy variables. We have been introduced to techniques – such as polynomial and log-linear transformations – that can adjust independent variables so as to be included in our regression model. We have accounted for relationships among independent variables that jointly affect the dependent variable that can be included by explicitly modelling interactions. We have also dealt with hard to capture variables by using indirect measures of latent concepts using factor analysis and to some extent instrumental variables. We have also been introduced to analytical techniques that allow for the dependent variable to be dichotomous (Binary Logistic Regression).

Here, we expand on this. The aim of this chapter is to demonstrate that nearly everything else that you will encounter in quantitative methods is an extension to – or variation on – the multiple regression that you have already learned. Some elements of the basic model are changed to accommodate 'realities' that look or behave differently; however, the core elements of what you have already learned are there.

We continue with the various categorical forms of the dependent variable. Building on our knowledge of the Binary Logistic Regression model to handle dichotomous nominal-level dependent variables, we move to dependent variables with ordered but few outcomes (ordinal-level variables: e.g., Disagree, neither disagree or agree, Agree) and multi-category, unordered outcomes ((poly)nominal-level: e.g., East, North, West, South). We will also delve into the world of limited dependent variables including the use of truncated or count data often found in Political Science.

Finally, we will look at advances in quantitative methods that are revitalizing and expanding the use of multiple regression for a wider field of research questions. We will examine the the ability of regression to incorporate context into our research by modelling different levels of influence. This empowers our statistical capabilities by accounting for previously unachievable control. In doing so, these extensions have recently revitalized and extended regression's capabilities to be an integral part of empirical, scientific research. What remains unchanged across each of these challenges is the regression model itself.

Categorical Dependent Variables Beyond Binary Logit

In many cases, and even probably most cases, Social Science researchers will treat ordinal-level variables like interval-level variables. We did two chapters ago by using the left/right ideological scale. This is neither a fatal flaw nor even necessarily problematic if the independent variable behaves more or less in a linear fashion and, in particular, is a control variable and not of central importance to the analysis. Please understand that just because these words exist in a textbook on statistics does not give you licence to do this wantonly. It depends on a lot of things, an being a dependent variable is one.

Ordered Logit: Ordinal-level Dependent Variable

In most cases, ordinal-level variables must be treated like ordinal-level variables. Especially when the variable is clearly ordinal and a dependent variable. In such cases, several assumptions of OLS linear regression are strained to their breaking point. Therefore, we will need to upgrade the binary or dichotomous Logit model to accommodate more than two outcomes. This model is commonly called the **Ordinal Regression Model** (ORM).

AKA

Acronyms are pronounced like words, for example: NATO, RADAR, FAQs, and YOLO
Initialisms are pronounced by individual letters: WTO, EU, USA, OLS, CLT, and MLE

The Model and Output

Functionally, the ORM is solved using Maximum Likelihood Estimation (MLE) to estimate the change in the probability that the outcome is one and not another outcome category. Recall from the previous chapter that there is some threshold in which the probability of being the other category is greater. This is more of less the same for the ORM; the only difference is that there are more thresholds (T'), or, their equivalents in the ORM, **cutpoints**.

See Figure 18.1.

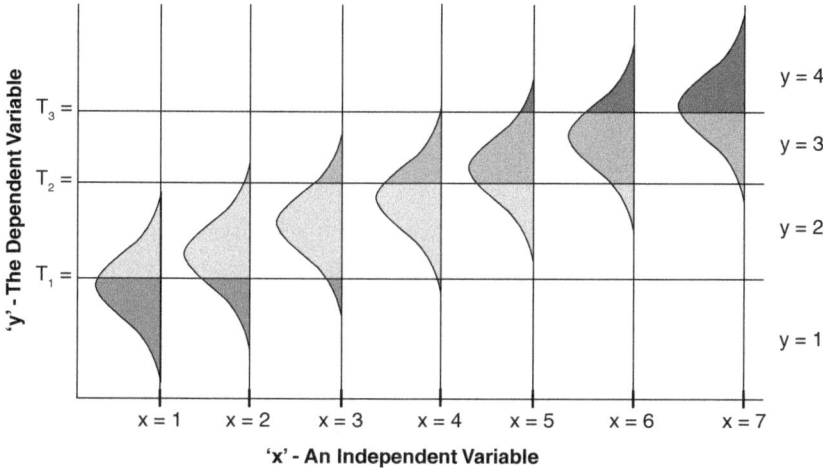

Figure 18.1 An Example Distribution of Ordinal-level Dependent Variable

In Figure 18.1, we have an example of an ordinal-level dependent variable distributed across an independent variable along the x-axis at the bottom. As we know for ordinal-level variables, the distances between adjacent categories are unknown, thus the thresholds – here T_1, T_2, and T_3 – are not necessarily fixed at regular intervals (as we would assume with interval-level variables). That is, when Y goes from '1' to '2' cannot be inferred to be the same distance as when Y goes from '2' to '3' or even '3' to '4'. However, unless we want to produce a unique set of predictors for every outcome category (similar to using binary logistic regression for each outcome versus the others), we need the proportional odds assumption.

The **proportional odds assumption** states that the relationship between each adjacent outcome is, in fact, uniform. In other words, that the thresholds are more or less equidistant. Thus, the odds ratios derived from the regression coefficient are assumed to describe category changes at all levels of the dependent variable (i.e., y=1 to y=2 is the same as y=3 to y=4). This assumption is also sometimes referred to as the parallel regression assumption. We know this is not always and exactly the case as this is one of the primary motivations to use ordered Logit rather than OLS linear regression. However, the proportional odds assumption is needed to produce interpretable results to avoid overwhelming complexity.

Let's take an example. Staying with our focus on political participation, we can assess how much interest someone has in politics. Staying with the European Social Survey, we can use the question, 'How interested are you in politics?' The response categories are as shown in Table 18.1.

Table 18.1 Political Interest – European Social Survey 2018

	Frequency	Percent
Not at all interested (1)	7,389	20.56
Hardly interested (2)	13,152	36.59
Quite interested (3)	11,499	31.99
Very interested (4)	3,901	10.85
Total	**35,941**	**100.00**

To keep matters simple, let's continue with the independent variables we are familiar with in our example on voting: age, left/right, and 'close to a party'. Therefore, we use ordinal logit in our statistical software package to estimate the following model.

$$\text{Political Interest}_i = \alpha + \beta_1(Age_i) + \beta_2(Left/Right_i) + \beta_3 Close_i + \varepsilon$$

Table 18.2 Ordinal Logit Regression: Political Interest

Political interest	Logit coefficient	Standard error	z	p>|z|
Age	0.011	0.001	18.18	0.000
Left–Right ideology	−0.021	0.005	−4.18	0.000
Close to party [Dummy: Yes]	1.118	0.022	50.02	0.000
Cut 1	−0.780	0.041		
Cut 2	1.126	0.041		
Cut 3	3.117	0.045		
Number of observations	30,118			
LR chi² (3)	3275.53			
Prob.> chi²	0.0000			
Pseudo R²	0.0423			
Log likelihood	−37087.592			

Interpretation

The results are in Table 18.2. To interpret the results, we can use both odds ratios and predicted probabilities as we have done previously. However, given the nature of the dependent variable, there are some qualifications to make. For odds ratios and of course predicted probabilities, as before, we can report them in a number of different ways. Here I present one only for simplicity and not for outright preference as the other forms are available and potentially more useful to different research questions.

The Likelihood Ratio chi^2 test returns a chi^2 test statistic of 3275.53 (p<0.001), giving us high confidence in the model as it is currently specified. For the regression coefficients, I use the factor change approach, in which every unit change in the independent variable produces a change in the odds by a factor of e^β, holding all other variables constant. Remember, and this is important here, that if e^β is larger than 1, the odds are 'e^β times larger' and if e^β is smaller than 1, the odds are 'e^β times smaller'.

For political interest:

- For every additional year of age, the odds of increasing one's level of political interest are increased by a factor of 1.0108 (i.e., $e^{0.0107}$), holding all other variables constant.
- For each unit moving from Left to Right on the ideological scale, the odds of increasing one's level of political interest actually *decrease* by a factor of 0.9797 (i.e., $e^{-0.0205}$), holding all other variables constant. Note, this decrease corresponds to the negative regression coefficient (in Table 18.2).
- Feeling close to a party, the odds of increasing one's level of political interest increase by a factor of 3.058 (i.e., $e^{1.1179}$), holding all other variables constant.

For odds ratios, we can use the multiplicative approach to interpret more useful results. Thus:

- For every additional *decade* of age, the odds of increasing one's level of political interest are increased by a factor of 1.113 (or $(e^{0.0107})^{10}$), holding all other variables constant.
- On the Left (0) to Right (10) ideological scale, moving from centre (5) to far-right (10), the odds of increasing one's level of political interest are decreased by a factor of 0.9026 (i.e., $(e^{-0.02055})^5$), holding all other variables constant.

The use of predicted probabilities is the same as before. One word of caution, though.

Although statistical software programs can produce predicted probabilities on all the outcome categories simultaneously, the results, particularly if we are interested in more than one or two independent variables, can be messy. A common technique is to choose an outcome category of the dependent variable about which we generate the predicted probabilities. Most commonly, this is the highest or lowest category (the ordinality of the data suggests that a focus on direction is not unwarranted). In some sense, this constrains the generalizability of our presentation of the results; however, we must consider what it is we have asked of the data and what we want our results to demonstrate.

In our example of Political Interest here, we can set the outcome category of interest as 'very interested'. Therefore, these parameters allow us to look at the probability for being 'very interested' across a range of values of the included independent variables:

$$\pi_{Very\ Interested} = \frac{e^{a+0.0107(Age)-0.0205(L/R)+1.1179(Close)}}{1+e^{a+0.0107(Age)-0.0205(L/R)+1.1179(Close)}}$$

As the choice of values for each of the independent variables is large and depends what we on we want to focus, perhaps the easiest presentation is to replicate the array of variables and their values in the final graph for having voted in the most recent parliamentary election (in Figure 17.5c). The results for predicting 'very interested' level of Political Interest are in Figure 18.2.

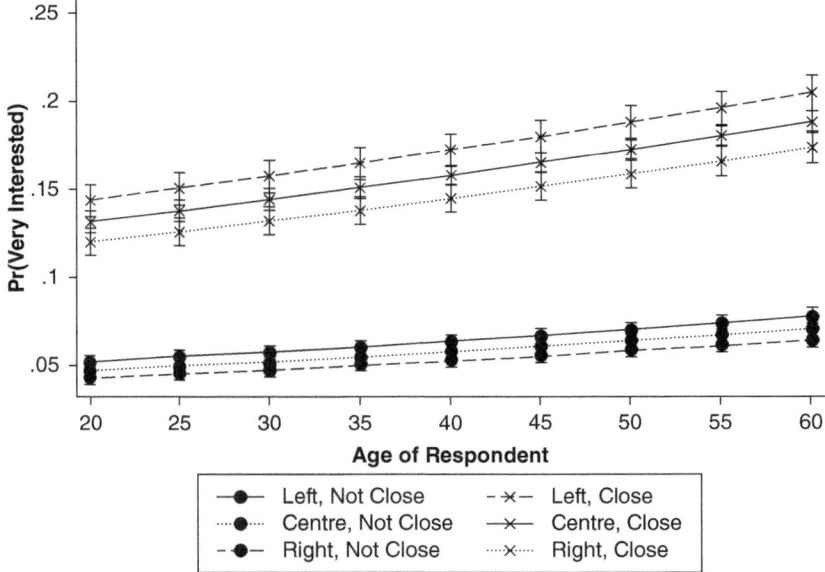

Figure 18.2 Predicted Probabilities for 'Very Interested': Age, 'Close to Party', Ideology

Again, 'feeling close to a party' separates the predicted probabilities quite substantially, with those with close attachments showing a greater probability for being 'very interested' in politics. Age, on the other hand only marginally increases the probability of being 'very interested' in politics. And ideological location seems to have a more significant effect on those who feel close a party, with those on the left more likely than moderates to be 'very interested' in politics, and moderates more likely than those on the right to be 'very interested' in politics.

Thus, as ideal types, we might expect:

- A respondent who identifies as far-left, close to a party, and near retirement age to be about 20% likely to be 'very interested' in politics.
- A similarly aged respondent on the right with little or no attachment to a party is only 6 or 7% likely to be 'very interested' in politics.
- Or even, a respondent who identifies as far-left, close to a party, but is 20 years old is about 15% likely to be 'very interested' in politics.
- …

Multinomial Logit: Polychotomous Nominal-level Dependent Variable

In the case of a nominal-level dependent variable with more than two outcome categories, we must retreat a bit. A multinomial dependent variable has more than two outcomes, but the order of the outcome is arbitrary, such as religion or country of birth. For example, we might use the cardinal directions – North, South, East, West – as the dependent variable. While we usually say them this way, there is no inherent argument why we can't say, North, East, West, South. This lack of underlying order obviously introduces some mathematical problems.

The Model and Output

The solution is a multinomial logit model. A **multinomial logit** model can be thought of as simultaneously estimating binary logits for each outcome category against a base or reference category. This is good in the sense that we already know a lot about binary logistic (see the previous chapter).

There is one potential problem. These various 'binary logits' are based on different samples. Although we can choose a common reference outcome category, we are comparing different outcome categories to this reference category. And each of the outcome categories have their own sub-sample of the sample. That is, if we choose 'north' as the reference category, the people who live in 'south', 'west', and 'east' are not the same people and thus different sub-samples. The potential problem is simply that these different pairings are wildly different in distribution or characteristics. Although, perhaps unsurprising at this point, we very often assume that they are not.

In keeping with our focus on political engagement, let's use a constructed variable from questions about political participation. Coming full circle back to the expanding number of types and forms of political participation (Theocharis and Van Deth, 2018), we can divide respondents' political participation into four categories. Given that the mean level of non-voting political participation is often very low, we put respondents into 1 of 4 exclusive categories.

- *Traditional Political Participation* (1): If, in the last 12 months, they contacted a politician or government official, worked in political party or action group, worked in another organization or association, or wore or displayed campaign badge/sticker, and nothing else.
- *Non-Traditional Political Participation* (2): If, in the last 12 months, they signed a petition or took part in lawful public demonstration, and nothing else.
- *Political Consumerism* (3): If, in the last 12 months, they boycotted certain products, and nothing else.
- *Digital Participation* (4): If, in the last 12 months, they posted or shared anything about politics online, and nothing else.

> ## TRANSFORMING DATA
>
> In the example of transforming the political participation data into four categories, we can create a series of new problems. First, scaling data down – in this case, from instances of different forms of participation to four strictly defined groups – we lose information by clumping separate categories into a single category. Additionally, as here, we can lose observations. Given the severity of our definition for the four categories, we lose individuals who engage in multiple forms of political participation – potentially a very interesting group!
>
> Second, and more broadly, transforming the data, we will need to evaluate the applicability of the new data to our research question. Very often, transforming data transforms the questions that you can answer. Here, in our example, we now have data that cannot address variations of individual political participation choices – recall our multiple forms of political participation individuals – but can answer questions specific to differences between these groups as we have defined them.

The resultant multinomial model looks like:

$$Types\ of\ Pol\ Part_i = \alpha + \beta_1(Age_i) + \beta_2(Left/Right_i) + \beta_3 Close_i + \varepsilon$$

Thus, we get a distribution of political participation that looks like (see Table 18.3):

Table 18.3 Four Types of Political Participation

	Frequency	Percent
Traditional	10,068	59.61
Non-Traditional)	4,221	24.99
Political Consumerism	1,571	9.30
Digital Political Participation	1,029	6.09
Total	*16,889*	*100.00*

Given that Traditional Political Participation is the largest (and most common form), it makes some sense to set it as the reference outcome category against which we compare the other forms of political participation. That is, we can investigate why people might choose the more provocative non-traditional, political consumerist, or digital forms of participation instead of the boring, traditional forms.

The estimation of this model is a simultaneous model of binary logits and the results reveal the structure shown in Table 18.4.

Table 18.4 Multinomial Logit Regression: Four Types of Political Participation

Traditional political participation	Logit coefficient	Standard error	z	p>|z|
Non-traditional participation				
Age	−0.011	0.001	−9.33	0.000
Left–Right ideology	−0.022	0.009	−2.54	0.011
Close to party [Dummy: Yes]	−0.286	0.040	−7.24	0.000
Constant	−0.099	0.072	−1.37	0.170
Political consumerism				
Age	0.007	0.002	4.34	0.000
Left–Right ideology	−0.007	0.013	−0.57	0.573
Close to party [Dummy: Yes]	−0.401	0.058	−6.89	0.000
Constant	−1.975	0.111	−17.88	0.000
Digital political participation				
Age	−0.333	0.002	−15.42	0.000
Left–Right ideology	0.061	0.017	3.73	0.000
Close to party [Dummy: Yes]	−0.445	0.071	−6.26	0.000
Constant	−0.881	0.127	−6.94	0.000
Number of observations	15,440			
LR chi² (3)	523.28			
Prob.> chi²	0.0000			
Pseudo R²	0.0163			
Log likelihood	−15750.574			

Interpretation

Like both binary and ordered Logit, interpreting multinomial Logit requires some attention. Let's remain focused on our interest, which is why people might choose other forms of political participation than contacting a politician or government official, working in a political party or action group, working in another organization or association, or wearing or displaying campaign badge/sticker.

The Likelihood Ratio chi² test returns a pseudo-chi² test statistic of 523.28 (p<0.001) which gives us confidence in the model in its current specification. The pseudo-R^2 is not very informative for multinomial logit models so we can afford to ignore it.

Our interpretation allows us a clear comparison. Like before, let's use the factor change approach to interpret the multinomial logistic regression coefficients. It is important to understand that the multinomial logit regression coefficient is the comparison from the category we are looking at to the reference category. Thus,

Non-traditional Political Participation

- For every additional year of age, the odds of Traditional forms of political participation to non-Traditional forms are decreased by a factor of 0.9900 (or $e^{-0.0105}$), holding all other variables constant.
    - For every additional *decade* of age, the odds of Traditional forms of political participation to non-Traditional forms are decreased by a factor of 0.9003 (or $(e^{-0.0105})^{10}$), holding all other variables constant.
- For each unit moving from Left to Right on the ideological scale, the odds of Traditional forms of political participation to non-Traditional forms are decreased by a factor of 0.9781 (or $e^{-0.0222}$), holding all other variables constant.
    - On the Left (0) to Right (10) ideological scale, moving from centre (5) to far-right (10), the odds of Traditional forms of political participation to Political Consumerism are decreased by a factor of 0.8949 (or $(e^{-0.0222})^5$), holding all other variables constant.
- Feeling close to a party, the odds of Traditional forms of political participation to non-Traditional forms are decreased by a factor of 0.7510 (or $e^{-0.2863}$), holding all other variables constant.

Digital Political Participation

- For every additional year of age, the odds of Traditional forms of political participation to Digital forms are decreased by a factor of 0.9673 (or $e^{-0.0333}$), holding all other variables constant.
    - For every additional *decade* of age, the odds of Traditional forms of political participation to Digital forms are decreased by a factor of 0.7168 (or $(e^{-0.0333})^{10}$), holding all other variables constant.
- For each unit moving from Left to Right on the ideological scale, the odds of Traditional forms of political participation to Digital forms are increased by a factor of 1.0632 (or $e^{0.0613}$), holding all other variables constant.
    - On the Left (0) to Right (10) ideological scale, moving from centre (5) to far-right (10), the odds of Traditional forms of political participation to Digital forms are decreased by a factor of 1.3587 (or $(e^{0.0613})^5$), holding all other variables constant.
- Feeling close to a party, the odds of Traditional forms of political participation to Digital forms are decreased by a factor of 0.6410 (or $e^{-0.4448}$), holding all other variables constant.

We can also use the predicted probability approach and, given the similar nature of multinomial logistic regression to binary logistic regression, the best method to present the results may be the use of graphs.

Like Binary Logit, we can set the values of the variables at a specific value, such as their means, or ask for the graph to display the predicted probabilities across a range of values of each independent variable. Like Ordered Logit, we need to choose the outcome category. Therefore, let's look at the impact of age and 'close to a party' on Digital political participation (see Figure 18.3).

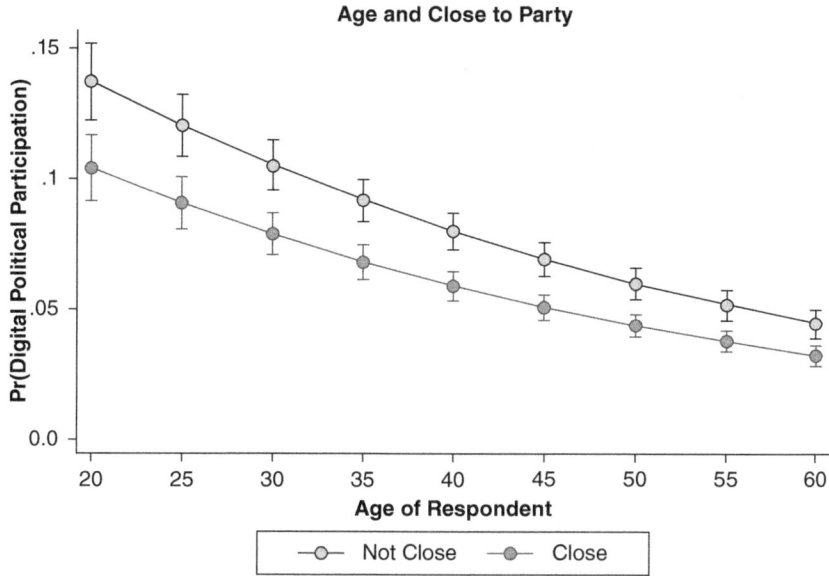

Figure 18.3 Digital Political Participation vs Traditional Political Participation

We could also choose to also disaggregate the probabilities by left/right ideological location. The predicted probabilities approach is quite flexible and can serve your specific research needs, i.e., bringing evidence to bear on your research question. In any case, we can see that the probability of moving toward digital political participation from traditional forms is higher for both young people and those who do not feel close to a party. Both results are interesting and, in the case of 'close to party', probably worth further investigation.

Again, we can develop some ideal types. Holding ideology at its mean, we can see that:

- A 20-year-old respondent who feels close to a party is about 10% more likely to choose digital political participation over traditional forms. A 60-year-old respondent who does not feel close to a party is less than 5% likely to do so.
- A 45-year-old respondent who feels close to a party is about 5% more likely to choose digital political participation over traditional forms.
- …

Once again, the specific interpretive strategy is up to the researcher. However, keep in mind that we often can present evidence relevant to the testing of our hypotheses without extraneous interpretations that may be interesting but ultimately just take up space.

Limited Dependent Variables: Data Constraints
Truncated or Censored Dependent Variables

There are events that produce variables that are limited descriptions of what we are interested in. They do not fully represent what is happening and thus what we want to measure. In one form, the data are **truncated** such that some cases are systematically excluded from observation. Beyond or below some boundary, the data are no longer observed.

As an example, researchers have consistently pointed out this problem in the study of ethnic conflict and minorities at risk (Hug, 2003). They argue that data used to analyse these questions are inherently undercounting potentially discriminated groups. Such minorities, e.g., ethnic/religious/linguistic sub-populations, can be increasing difficult to identify particularly if their total number are low. Thus, smaller groups who may also suffer discrimination or attacks are not included or are swept into a larger but inappropriate category.

Similarly for analyses on party competition or even voting. Very often researchers focus on the 'main' competitive parties and exclude the smaller ones. According to the website Ballotpedia, there are 209 state-level political parties in America (as of December 2021) including the Greens, Socialist, and Constitution parties; yet, we very rarely see analyses of more than the two dominant parties, Republicans and Democrats. This can also be observed for multi-party systems that have thresholds. Parties that compete but do not reach the threshold are often excluded from the analysis.

Thus, it is not unreasonable to suggest that excluding data from the analysis, for whatever reason, is likely to have an impact on the solution of any model analysing these data. That is, the regression estimation will solve the model for some of the data but not all of the potentially available and important data.

Alternatively, **censored** data have unknown values because the researcher has imposed a restriction on the data. These unknown values exist beyond some terminal value at either end of the distribution. An extremely common example is household or individual income. Respondents are often presented with value of equal increments until some arbitrarily chosen upper bound, e.g., >€200,000/year (nearly €17,000/month, can you imagine?). In this case, we have information about those respondents – we know their income is more than >€200,000/year – but how much more, 201,000 or 2,000,000?

In order to evaluate such data as dependent variables, a common approach is to use the **Tobit model**. We will not engage in the technical details of the Tobit model; suffice to say that it uses all of the information available and provides consistent estimates of the parameters.

Count Outcomes

As Gary King (1989) has pointed out, a great deal of International Relations (IR) is looking at events rather than processes. That is, very often IR scholars are summarizing discrete events instead of analysing continuous processes. That is, we count.

- How many alliances were broken since 1900?
- What were the number of international crises last year?
- What is the number of nations involved in a specific economic sanction?
- How many conflicts have become all out wars since the end of the Second World War?
- ...

But, this is not limited to IR. In Comparative Politics, we also ask the number of bills introduced by specific members of parliament per year? What was the number of riots and protests since the financial-turned-economic recession of late 2007? How many new parties have entered an electoral market?

The importance of recognizing this is that count data are often skewed quite heavily toward low numbers, particularly zero. **Count data** are non-negative integers that represent the number of occurrences of an event within a fixed period. A common feature of such data are a lot of zeros, non-Normal distribution, and curves that have one fat tail and one tiny tail.

In order to deal with such data, the **Poisson regression model** is the most basic model. The probability of a count is determined by a Poisson distribution, where the mean of the distribution is a function of the independent variables. This model has the defining characteristics that the conditional mean of the outcome is equal to the conditional variance. In practice the conditional variance often exceeds the conditional mean.

This model essentially treats events as rare. That is, the Poisson distribution has a parameter lambda, λ, the intensity parameter. This is the expected number of occurrences in a fixed period of time: $\lambda = E[x]$.

$$P(x) = \frac{\lambda^x e^{-\lambda}}{x!} \text{ in which } x = 0, 1, 2, 3, 4, \ldots$$

The shape of the Poisson distribution is an approximation of a binomial random variable in which the number of events is large, but the probability of a success is small. However, as λ gets large, the Poisson distribution resembles a Normal distribution. A critical assumption of a Poisson process is that events are independent, meaning that when an event occurs it does not affect the probability of the event occurring in the future. Variations on this include zero truncated models in which observations enter the sample only after the first count occurs. In this case, we can use a related model (and distribution) called the negative binomial model.

The Abundant Variety of Dependent Variables

We can take some comfort in the similarity of the categorical and limited dependent variable models to linear multiple regression. Yes, the underlying estimation, the interpretations, and assumptions can differ. However, that gives you the handle of the hammer. That you know and can recognize the necessity for different models and interpretation speaks to you as someone knowledgeable about statistics. You don't have to remember everything in this book, you can always look it up, but what was once foreign is now less mysterious. The flexibility of multiple regression to confront an abundant variety of challenges also speaks to the versatility of multiple regression, rather than to any limitation. Multiple regression has demonstrated remarkable tenacity and continues to confer the necessary description, control, and inference essential to Social Science research.

Both the intuition and formal structure of the regression model constitutes the basis for a wide range of analytical techniques. Two centuries of applied research have modified and improved the Econometric and statistical techniques used to estimate regression models. And nearly all improvements and modifications are built on chassis of regression. Now, we press forward with an example of how the multiple regression chassis has continued to serve and advance the changing state of research.

Multi-Level Modelling

One element of studying Political Science that has blossomed under the introduction of new statistical techniques is the incorporation of context into the modelling process. Specifically, we can embed units of analysis in larger groups – their context – that may have their own influence on the dependent variable. Data collected at the lowest level are referred to as **level-1 data**. Any data that contextualize level-1 data are called **level-2 data**. Depending on how many levels, this can go on. Take for instance national-level representative surveys. If we sample from 10 European countries, we will have 10 sets of surveys. So, for our example, the individual-level data are the level-1 data and the countries are the level-2 data.

We could choose to ignore country variation and analyze the surveys together, or cluster the surveys. This is called a **pooled analysis** and will produce a generalized result for these 10 countries. Assuming that we do this, our sample, this one-time slice of the population, is called **cross-sectional** data. In doing so, and certainly as we enter the analysis phase, we may be making some strong assumptions about the data, of which two stand out:

- *ONE:* The level-1 variables – in this example, the individual-level surveys – are constant or fixed across countries.
- *TWO:* The level-2 contexts – here, nations – do not matter.

We know, or at least strongly suspect, that neither of these are likely to be the case.

In our example, can the individual-level data be assumed to be fixed across the countries? If we consider some of the standard included variables in our survey such as socio-economic variables, is, for example, the level and quality of education uniform across all 10 countries? Does the level of income reflect similar socio-economic status or uniform purchasing power in these 10 different countries? Or even for attitudes in which we are interested, can we reasonably expect there to be little variation or intensity in the impact of political views such as tolerance for immigration, support for democracy, or social trust across 10 countries? That is, we expect these attitudes to vary within each country as well as between them. However, are some of these attitudes more salient or meaningfully different in some of those countries than others?

Secondly, do national contexts matter? Variation across units is referred to as **cross-unit heterogeneity**. A great deal of research has shown that national-level institutional differences – in politics and economics – as well as social or cultural differences can have a substantial effect on the populations of different countries. As a simple example the difference between majoritarian and multi-party systems (Anderson and Guillory, 1997) and constitutional laws governing early election calling (Morgan-Jones and Loveless, 2021) have been demonstrated to have a clear impact on citizens' levels of satisfaction with democracy. That is, citizens' satisfaction levels have been demonstrated to move with individual-level variables (level-1) as well as differences in country-level variables (level-2).

We know enough about statistics to know that ignoring any such cross-unit heterogeneity is not only theoretically problematic but also analytically so. If countries do differ, and we ignore it, where does all of this variation across countries for which we have not accounted go? It goes into the error term of the pooled regression model which is likely to absorb the between-country differences and thus behave poorly. Why? Because it is soaking up unaccounted-for explanatory power. As we have seen, poorly behaving error terms can play havoc with the performance of our model. In essence, not taking potential country differences seriously is likely to produce models that do not describe the relationships in which we are interested, and we are likely to have a low level of confidence in this pooled model.

The simplest approach is to give that country-level variation some place to go. The earliest, and easiest, response has been to simply add dummy variables for all (but one) of the level-2 variables in the analysis. This is still the choice of some Social Scientists. In our example, by adding in a dummy variable for the country, we 'soak up' any country-specific 'noise'. Including dummy variables for all but one – the reference country – we would discover whether there is a statistically significant difference in the means of the dependent variable between the dummy variable country and the reference country.

Let's assume that we do this and all of the countries' dummy variables are statistically significant. The 'effect' of each country has been absorbed into the dummy variable and captures some of the cross-national variation. Unfortunately, this difference can only be seen in the intercept and represents an average difference between the two countries over the whole model (recall that a dummy variable is simply a difference of means test).

So, the country dummy variable only tells us that the average value of the dependent variable for one country is statistically higher/lower than the reference country's value of the dependent variable.

Is this helpful? Satisfying? Sufficient?

Maybe not, as it leaves us in a bit of an analytical lurch. First of all, does that result mean anything? With 10 countries, we could be interested in whether one country simply has a higher/lower level of a dependent variable controlling for a number of individual-level variables, but that seems to be an overly narrow question with all the data we have. Second, what does the difference between the two countries mean? What explains this overall, statistically significant difference, other than, well, these countries are different on average? We don't know, we only know that there is a difference. Again, some researchers may not care, as some cross-national variation has been controlled for. Yet, it seems odd to just say, there's a difference and not want to know what it is.

> ### YES TO WHAT WE WANT! NO TO WHAT MUST GO!
>
> It is a difficult position to maintain that cross-national differences do not exist or that any differences are unimportant. One limitation to all forms of cross-national studies is capturing or at a minimum controlling for potentially important differences.
>
> Sometimes we are given explicit guidance in the form of existing theory and the works of others (often in the form of a literature review). Macro-economic variables such as inflation, unemployment, or GDP per capita are common controls as they represent economic performance differences between countries. Similarly, macro-political variables such as electoral laws, thresholds, and the effective number of parties are common controls that represent differing electoral markets that can shape vote choice or party strategies. However, some cross-national variation is harder to capture, even though we know it is there.
>
> One variable that often gets left out is political culture. For example, as we mentioned before, there are numerous potential explanations for the differences in strike activity across countries. In the UK, strikes are often announced well in advance and every effort is made to recompense both the employer and customers with alternative timings and availabilities. In other words, a strike in which workers end up simply re-scheduling their work. By contrast, in Italy, strikes are common, frequently announced at the last minute, and comprehensive in the sense that they make little effort to reduce the inconvenience to customers. However, in contrast to both Italy and the UK, in the US, striking is a significant event. Strikers often face immediate dismissal (and employment is often the only affordable avenue to healthcare), harassment, and coordinated (if often illegal) anti-strike campaigns by businesses.
>
> While there are institutional differences between these countries that partially explain these differences, political culture – the norms and beliefs of citizens – play an outsized role in conditioning individuals' choices to strike or not in each of these countries. In any cross-national investigation of non-traditional political participation – such as striking – identifying and including elements of political culture is both challenging and exciting. And in doing so may advance our understanding of why 'this happens here' and why 'this doesn't happen here'. This is precisely a case in which context – regardless of how hard it may be to capture empirically – can make a difference in our understanding.

> As we mentioned before, the UK and Italy share an affinity for the sciopero bianco ('white strike') or work-to-rule strike – in which workers adhere strictly to the conditions of their contracts. Such strikes can cause slowdowns and other problems, including safety issues. More importantly, they also demonstrate that the performance and completion of employees' jobs require individual efforts beyond the strict definition of their jobs (i.e., their participation is crucial to the success of the business). The Americans have picked up on this effective technique in what is currently being called, 'quiet quitting'.

Hierarchical Thinking, Hierarchical Modelling

Another approach has been to take context – and thus the differences – seriously and explicitly. This originates from the simple observation that data are very often hierarchical. The classic example is student performance. To determine the performance of students, we need to understand that there are impacts coming from a number of different levels. Students are in classes, in schools, in school systems, in regions/states, and then countries. Each of these levels has the potential to impact or provide partial explanation for individual student performance by, for example, class size, teacher quality, tax-base of the system, or regional/national educational legislation and priorities.

Questions in Political Science struggle with the same hierarchical embeddedness. That is, citizens live in households, neighbourhoods or quarters, cities or regions, these regions are in countries, and even these countries can be part of a larger organization – such as the EU – or geographical location. In this case, just like our students above, this hierarchical arrangement which delineates citizens' memberships in different groups can have their own internal influences on individuals' attitudes or behaviours in which we might be interested.

Developments to address the recognition of this hierarchical structure of influence are called **hierarchical linear modelling** (HLM), also known as **multi-level modelling**. The HLM approach is an improvement on the single-level, dummy-variable approach. It also is an improvement on the temptation to put macro-level variables in individual-level models. The core advancement is the inclusion of error terms for the different levels of variables to be included in the multiple regression model. In doing so, we eliminate the bleed of unmeasured variation into other parts – specifically, other levels – of the model.

What further substantially distinguishes the HLM approach is that the researcher is forced to articulate what explains the cross-unit heterogeneity. That is, in contrast to merely including a series of dummy variables (i.e., 'France'=1, 'Not France'=0; 'Germany'=1, 'Not Germany'=0, etc....), we are asked to include a variable specifying an explanation. Why does the value of the dependent variable differ across these countries? Is it something economic, political, social, cultural, historical, *inter alia*? We cannot simply shrug our shoulders and say, 'Well the average values of the dependent variable are statistically different. Maybe like snails (or Oktoberfest), it's just a French (or German) thing?'

> **THE N-RAY AFFAIR**
>
> In 1903, René Blondlot (1849–1930), a French physicist, discovered a novel form of radiation, which he termed the 'N-Ray'. Oddly, only French scientists were able to detect these new rays. Others, however, could not – especially the Americans (Robert W. Wood), British (Lord Kelvin, himself), and Germans (including Otto Lummer and Heinrich Rubens). Blondlot's excuse was that other scientists were not sensitive enough to see the novel N-Rays because the Germans drank too much beer and the Anglo-Saxons were dulled by the constant exposure to fog. In any case, the search for the très French N-Rays was thereafter abandoned.

If we think that it is related to economic performance differences, we can begin to identify measures that represent what can explain the cross-national/-unit difference. HLM incentivizes us to articulate why unemployment or inequality or GDP per capita. Similarly, we can propose specific political differences to explain various outcomes. Or cultural differences or social differences. Thus, instead of being left to the dummy variable approach of, 'well there is something going on', HLM forces researchers to develop clear and defensible ideas of why we observe discernible differences between countries/units.

In this way, HLM uses the ability of multiple regression to incorporate context into the estimation procedure to create the opportunity to specify the nature of cross-national/-unit differences. Admittedly this can vastly complicate the model specification process. However, as with all statistical techniques, a clear understanding of what it is we want to know can guide our choices.

A (Final) Reflection

> Don't try to understand. It's enough if you do not misunderstand. – S.N. Maharaj

Statistics and its central element, multiple regression, offers researchers a great deal. The various forms of multiple regression that allow us to analyse, include, and control a multitude of variables is a powerful tool of the scientific approach. Like a fast car or young horse, there is a lot of potential and payoff if used correctly (and safely). There is also a great deal of danger. That danger is not only to ourselves but to others in the scientific, academic, and broader community. It is not necessary to know everything in this book to do statistics well. It is, however, important to have a clear sense and understanding of what we can do – and cannot do – in our analysis of data to turn them into information, a result that can then be converted into knowledge. This path of analysis and design is fraught with perils seen and unseen. It is our preparation, attention, and rigorousness that distinguishes our analysis from the arbitary and irresponsible misuse of data. This chapter has intended to introduce you to a wide variety of applications of multiple regression. Engage them, be wary of them, be demanding and sceptical.

End of Chapter Summary

- The adaptive nature of multiple regression to various specifications and types of dependent variables underscores the importance and value of multiple regression to quantitative researchers.
- Pay careful attention to the nature of the data as it determines the choice of regression model.
- For ordinal-level dependent variables, we use ordered Logit regression.
- For polynomial nominal-level dependent variables, we use multinomial Logit regression.
- Truncation changes the sample, censoring does not. Both require a Tobit model.
- Count data differ from normally distributed random variables as they all have to start from the same value. This attribute especially affects data on uncommon events.
- Multi-level modelling specifies and manages cross-unit heterogeneity allowing for context to be explicitly included and controlled for.

Glossary

- The **Ordinal Regression Model** (ORM) estimates dependent variables with more than two outcomes.
- **Cutpoints** are when the probability of the impact of values of independent variables changes for outcome categories of the ordinal-level dependent variable.
- The **proportional odds assumption** allows the the odds of moving from the base category to the other categories to be the same between each category.
- A **multinomial logit** model handled a polychotomous nominal-level dependent variable by estimating binary logits for each outcome category against a base or reference category.
- **Truncated data** have data in which some observations are systematically excluded from observation.
- **Censored** data have observation but unknown values often beyond some terminal value at either end of the range of outcomes.
- The **Tobit model** is used to address both truncated and censored data.
- **Count data** are data that represent occurrences of an event within a fixed period.
- The **Poisson regression model** is used to resolve count-data problems.
- Data collected at the lowest level are referred to as **level-1 data**. Any data that contextualize or group level-1 data are **level-2 data**.
- A **pooled analysis** ignores cross-unit differences and generates a general solution.
- **Cross-sectional** data are a one-time sample of the population.
- Variation across units is referred to as **cross-unit heterogeneity**.
- **Hierarchical linear modelling** (HLM) or **multi-level modelling** estimates the impact of level-1 data in the context of level-2 (and potential more level) influences.

Questions

1. Create and interpret 3 Ideal Types for 'Very Interested' (use Figure 18.2).
2. Calculate the odds ratios for Political Consumerism (from Table 18.4).
3. What are three other events that would qualify as count data in Political Science?
4. Other than people in countries, give three examples of hierarchical data in Political Science.
5. Cross-sectional data are one of the most common types of data and often include a wide range of variables to associate and analyse. However, a key limitation is that cross-sectional data struggle to explain dynamic change. Explain how this limitation constrains cross-sectional from being used to provide sufficient evidence for causality.
6. In the paper, 'Opium for the Masses: How Foreign Media Can Stabilize Authoritarian Regimes' (2009, *Political Analysis* 17: 377–99), Holger Lutz Kern and Jens Hainmueller study the impact of West German television on public support for the East German communist regime during the Cold War. One big problem with studying media use – particularly at that time in a Communist country – was identifying the effect of media. However, they noticed the topographical oddity that allowed some cities to receive West German over-the-air television broadcasts and others not to (such, as they note, the Dresden district). They find that 'contrary to conventional wisdom, East Germans exposed to West German television were more satisfied with life in East Germany and more supportive of the East German regime' (2009: 377). Aside from the counter-intuitive finding, why is this a natural experiment and how does this affect the quality of their findings?

Annotated References and Further Reading

Anderson, Christopher J., and Christine A. Guillory. 1997. 'Political institutions and satisfaction with democracy: A cross-national analysis of consensus and majoritarian systems' *American Political Science Review* **91(1): 66–81. https://doi.org/10.2307/2952259**

Opening up a fantastic sub-field of research on satisfaction with democracy and institutional legitimacy, Anderson and Guillory show that electoral laws have a direct impact on the level of satisfaction citizens have about their own government by separating them into electoral winners and losers.

Hug, Simon. 2003. 'Selection bias in comparative research: The case of incomplete data sets' *Political Analysis* **11(3): 255–74. www.jstor.org/stable/25791732**

A discussion of the problems introduced by incomplete data, including truncated data, with a particular focus on selection bias.

Jones, Bradford S. 2008. 'Multilevel models' in J.M. Box-Steffensmeier, H.E. Brady, and D. Collier (eds) *The Oxford Handbook of Political Methodology*. https://doi.org/10.1093/oxfordhb/9780199286546.003.0026

This is a great chapter on hierarchical linear modelling.

King, Gary. 1989. 'Event count models for international relations: Generalizations and applications' *International Studies Quarterly* 33(2): 123–147. https://doi.org/10.2307/2600534

An excellent article on count data in International Relations that also introduced the Hurdle model.

Klotz, Irving M. 1980. 'The N-ray affair' *Scientific American* 242(5): 168–75. www.jstor.org/stable/24966330

The full article on the N-ray affair. Hilarious.

Morgan-Jones, Edward and Matthew Loveless. 2021. 'Early election calling and satisfaction with democracy' *Government and Opposition* 1–25. https://doi.org/10.1017/gov.2021.44

When early elections are called by individually identifiable representatives such as Prime Ministers or Presidents, citizens see it as opportunistic and react strongly and negatively. However, when parliaments do so, there is usually little negative response.

Snijders, T.A.B. and R.J. Bosker. 2012. *Multilevel Analysis: An Introduction to Basic and Advanced Multilevel Modeling*. London: Sage Publishers.

An indispensable text to start on any multi-level journey.

Theocharis, Y. and Van Deth, J.W. 2018. 'The continuous expansion of citizen participation: A new taxonomy' *European Political Science Review* 10(1): 139–163.

This article proposes new varieties of political participation to accompany the long-standing traditional and non-traditional types.

Signposts to the Accompanying Digital Resources

Data used in this chapter

- **GDELT**: The GDELT Event Database records over 300 categories of physical activities around the world, from riots and protests to peace appeals and diplomatic exchanges:
    - www.gdeltproject.org/
- Contacted politician or government official last 12 months (contplt), 0 No 1 Yes.
- Worked in political party or action group last 12 months (wrkprty), 0 No 1 Yes.
- Worked in another organization or association last 12 months (wrkorg), 0 No 1 Yes.

- Worn or displayed campaign badge/sticker last 12 months (badge), 0 No 1 Yes
- Signed petition last 12 months (sgnptit), 0 No 1 Yes.
- Taken part in lawful public demonstration last 12 months (pbldmn), 0 No 1 Yes.
- Boycotted certain products last 12 months (bctprd), 0 No 1 Yes.
- Posted or shared anything about politics online last 12 months (pstplonl), 0 No 1 Yes.
  - European Social Survey 1–9, European Social Survey Cumulative File, Study Description. Bergen: NSD – Norwegian Centre for Research Data for ESS ERIC. https://doi.org/10.21338/NSD-ESS-CUMULATIVE

PART IV
CURRENT DEBATES

19
BIG ALTERNATIVES

> **LEARNING OUTCOMES**
>
> In this chapter, you will be able to
>
> - Expand your knowledge of the ongoing debates within the field of statistical analysis.
> - Identify the potential advantages of the Bayesian approach to statistical inference.
> - Develop your intuition on how Big Data is advancing statistical analysis.
> - Recognize that no statistical approach is perfectly superior to the other with each bringing varying advantages and disadvantages to statistical analysis.

Introduction

This chapter is an introduction to two other 'players on the field' of quantitative analysis. For our study of statistics that we have undertaken in this textbook, despite all the work we have done, we are not alone. There is more than one way to approach data, samples, and inference. Two approaches – one old, one new – stand out. We will take a look at the popularity, advantages, and disadvantages of the Bayesian approach and the new field of Big Data, Data Science, and Machine Learning.

The older challenger is the Bayesian approach, which confronts the approach we have learned here head on. Practitioners of this approach point to problems with testing hypotheses, doing significance testing, and making inferences. Advocates of Bayesian techniques and methods offer potential solutions to some of these problems and means to avoid others. If that sounds pretty convincing, it can be. However, the Bayesian approach is not without its own limitations and isn't always a clearly dominant approach. We will engage the most common of these debates below.

The newer challenger is Big Data. Big Data, or more accurately Data Science, challenges what we call data, how we use statistics, and what we intend to achieve with our research. These differences are crucial to any research project and have re-awakened debates over long-dormant choices and assumptions other approaches such as ours have made. Ultimately, the Data Science approach produces results that are not only applicable to specific types of research but in many cases, the only manner to produce results.

In doing so, this newer form of data analysis brings a lot to the table. However, like any approach, it is no panacea in the use of quantitative methods.

While both approaches confront shortcomings in the common statistical techniques widely used and presented here, they both suffer weaknesses that limit their own ability to eclipse the approach we have learned here. At the same time, their challenges help us better understand and appreciate the strengths and weaknesses of the techniques presented in the chapters above.

Bayesian Statistics

Let's return to inferential statistics for a moment. The basis of inferential statistics is drawing conclusions about a population based on a (sufficient and random) sample of that population. Whatever methods we use, we are making an informed guess about what we would like to know but don't have, using what we do have and know. Because of this extrapolation, we are always uncertain about our guess.

How we manage and report this uncertainty can vary. In this textbook, we had made extensive use of hypothesis testing, significance levels, and levels of confidence. This is an empirical approach to inference. This common form of statistics, as we have learned here, is called the **frequentist approach**. Within this approach, we manage and report uncertainty by using probabilities. We consider probabilities a function of the repeated proportions of outcomes, that is, the accumulated probabilities of different outcomes over time.

Let's think about this in terms of statistical inference. If we want to reject (or fail to reject) a null hypothesis, we need to know, in repeated sampling of the same population, how many times our null would be 'true'. That is, if we frequently fail to find evidence to reject our null, it is less and less likely that we can do so. If, on the other hand, we find evidence to do so again and again, the frequency of such evidence strengthens our confidence in rejecting the null.

There are other ways to manage and report this uncertainty and this brings us to the Bayesian approach.

AN EXTRAORDINARILY BRIEF STORY OF BAYES' THEOREM

The origin of the theory resides in the story of a reverend by the name of Thomas Bayes (c.1702–1761), who developed the theorem and subsequently put it in a drawer to be 're-discovered' independently over the ages by more well-known mathematicians such as Pierre-Simon Laplace and Alan Turing. For example, Karl Pearson himself referred to it as the 'Bayes–Laplace theorem'. Although, to be clear, he and R.A. Fisher only used this moniker in the context of arguing – often ferociously – against it. Despite the theorem's rough and tumble emergence and increasingly widespread use in the present day, history has rightly identified Thomas Bayes as the original source of the theorem.

Bayesian Subjectivity

The argument for a Bayesian approach is the rather obvious notion that we can update what we think we know with evidence. The results of the Bayesian approach are therefore an improvement on what we knew. The problem – at least as its critics perceive it – is that it runs counter to the notional objectivity of science inquiry.

The Bayesian approach rests on an initial starting point – what are called prior probabilities as we will see below – that can be highly subjective. This subjectivity is at the heart of the problem and has animated most of the resistance to the Bayesian approach. As we have seen through the book, certainly in the first five chapters, the scientist appeals to objectivity through transparent and replicable choices about what to measure and how to measure it, how to summarize, describe, and draw inferences from results.

However, one does not need to stretch very far to argue that the choices that we make in the frequentist approach are subjective choices as well. Yet, in addition to the necessity of a researcher making decisions about the research strategy, the Bayesian approach further differs as a subjective approach to inference by originating probabilities from the researcher and the evidence available to her. In practice, this approach often looks very much like a frequentist approach as the 'available evidence' is usually the same and shared empirical literature. However, this is not always the case. There are new discoveries and unique events that lack a history or track record of empirical evidence, thus thwarting frequentist claims of extant probabilities. And small differences in these originating probabilities – either between frequentists and Bayesian or even among different Bayesians – can potentially produce differing outcomes with crucial substantive and statistical implications.

Implications for Hypothesis Testing

Originally, hypothesis testing consisted of a direct test of the null hypothesis. This Fisher hypothesis testing method, named after you-know-who, looks at how a test statistic moves away from its conditional expected value. The farther these are apart, the less plausible the null hypothesis. The point of Fisher hypothesis testing was that the null hypothesis was 'something to be nullified' rather than the immediate assumption of 'no relationship'. The more common form, and the one used in the Scientific Method, is the null and alternative hypothesis testing (recall: Neyman–Pearson hypothesis testing). In this process, significance is chosen *a priori*, a test statistic is generated from the data and compared to a known distribution under the assumption that the null is 'true'. Bayesians point to the very real issue that this is an artificial dichotomy between the null and alternative hypotheses and creates an illusion of theory confirmation.

The reasoning of the critique rests on the extension of a logical test to probabilistic application. Specifically, the use of *modus tollens* ('denying the consequent') – or if A then B, ~B then ~A – breaks down in the use of probabilistic reasoning. If the null hypothesis is true, then the data are highly likely to follow an expected pattern. If the data do not follow the expected pattern, the null hypothesis is therefore highly unlikely.

Taking a cue from an example provided in Gill (1999):

- If a person is an Italian, then it is highly unlikely she is a member of the Chamber of Deputies. The person is a member of the Chamber of Deputies, therefore, it is highly unlikely she is an Italian.

This implies that a hypothesis that may be true may be rejected because it has not predicted observable results that have not occurred. It is essentially untenable to state that results are atypical under a given assumption as it implies that the assumption is likely false. In probabilistic language: *almost* contradiction of the null hypothesis does not imply that the null hypothesis is *almost* false. In other words, if the probability of the consequence is low, it does not necessitate that the probability of the premise is also low.

Bayesians argue that this type of significance testing does not allow for the costs of possible wrong actions to be taken into account in any precise way. They offer instead an alternative to the Neyman–Pearson hypothesis testing. Inferences about unknown model parameters are expressed and summarized in probability statements in the form of confidence intervals. These confidence intervals, often called credible intervals, are argued to contain more and better information on the probability of the parameters and avoid common misinterpretation.

This is not hard to imagine.

Recall the correct interpretation for a frequentist confidence interval: 'In repeated samples of the same size from our population, for each sample, we estimate the upper and lower bounds of the confidence interval for that probability. About 95% of these confidence intervals would contain the true probability of the population parameter.' Not only does this imply the existence of (infinitely?) repeated samples that are difficult to verify but also says nothing about the current investigation. By contrast, Bayesian confidence intervals can be accurately and intuitively interpreted as the probability that the true value of the parameter lies in the interval is – in fact – 95%. That statement aligns more smoothly with what people think a confidence interval actual means.

Not the Central Limit Theorem, Too?!

The problem with hypothesis testing leads directly into another Bayesian critique of the frequentist approach; specifically, the theoretical construct around sampling and, in particular, the use of the Central Limit Theorem. Recall that the Central Limit Theorem (CLT) states that as sample size increases, the sampling distribution of sample means approaches Normal with a mean the same as the mean of the population and a standard deviation equal to the standard deviation of the population divided by the square root of the sample size (N). This is true even if the population distribution is not distributed normally. In this way, the CLT allows us to make powerful inferential claims based on our sample (known) about the true population parameters (always unknown).

But there is a pretty serious catch buried in this assumption.

Specifically, the CLT makes the presumption that if we were to take an infinite number of samples of size n from a population of N, the means of these infinite samples would be normally distributed. And, it is this 'sampling distribution of means' that will have a mean equal to the population mean and a standard error equal to the population standard deviation divided by the square root of the sample size. Thus, imagine taking a sample from a population, writing down the mean, putting it back, taking another same-sized sample, writing down the mean, putting it back, etc.... Imagine doing this a lot. For a while. What the CLT states is that the mean of this new list of means will be Normally distributed. Classical statistical inference (i.e., Neyman–Pearson) is based on these results. Thus, when you take a sample, you are really taking a sample from the 'sampling distribution of means'. That is, that you are sampling a theoretical collection of means and not cases from your actual sample.

The Central Limit Theorem is one of the most important theorems in the field of probability as well as statistical inference as it establishes the probability that our sample findings are within a certain distance from the true population parameters in which we are interested. This is justified theoretically as Normal distributions are widely used, well-behaved, mathematically tractable, and applicable to an array of statistical applications. Yet, we know this may not be the case with our sample. Defenders say, well, you have taken one of the many probable samples, thus allowing the CLT to hold.

But, have we really?

A Bayesian Solution?

Bayesians argue – not without merit – that frequentist results rest on assumptions of asymptotic properties and infinite samples and in doing so, cannot provide a probabilistic statement about the parameter in which we are interested. A Bayesian approach suggests taking the initial uncertainty about the population parameters in which we are interested and determining to what extent this uncertainty is changed by what we learn from the sample. Bayesian statistical inference, therefore, assigns probabilities to potential values of the population parameters *before the analysis* and updates with evidence from the sample data (using Bayes' Theorem). **Bayes' Theorem** merges the information given by the prior distribution with the information from the sample, giving us a posterior distribution for the population parameter.

Bayes' Theorem is concerned with conditional probability (see Chapter 10) and tells us the probability that a theory or hypothesis is true *if* some event has happened (i.e., the availability of related evidence).

Bayes' Theorem is written:

$$P(A|B) = \frac{P(B|A)P(A)}{P(B)}$$

We can see that the probability of A, given B is true, is equal to the sum of probability of B, given A is true, multiplied by the probability of A all divided by the probability of B.

Both the probabilities of A and B are, separately, the prior probabilities of observing outcome A and B, respectively. This notion of prior probability contains the information based on the available evidence, consensus in the literature, or, in a worst-case scenario of no existing information, the researcher's best subjective guess.

The probability of A, given B is true, is called the posterior probability, which reflects the Bayesian contribution to statistical inference, namely, the updated information that incorporates the sample's performance into the prior probabilities. That is, the Bayes' posterior probability merges any existing prior information about conditions related to an outcome with the performance of the sample to produce the probability of an outcome.

This merge is the key to understanding the theoretical and methodological advantage to the Bayesian approach. For example, if we know that democracies are more likely to produce substantial elite schisms as income inequality grows, the Bayesian approach merges this information into the estimation of the probability of governmental breakdown – via fissures of elite alignments – by accounting for the level in (or change in) national-level income inequality rather than the generic occurrence of elite schisms in democracies.

To a Bayesian, data are fixed evidence not varying samples. Bayesians treat the unobserved population parameters for which we are searching as probabilistic and the data in hand, our sample of observations, as known quantities. Thus, Bayesians want to know about the viability of their hypothesis given these data rather than some probability originating from the data themselves. In precisely this way, the Bayesian approach avoids the necessity of the strong assumptions (for example, associated with the CLT) and replaces assumptions with 'really existing' states of probability that can be merged and updated to reflect the state or conditions of the processes under investigation.

A (Very) Simple Bayesian Example

Let's imagine that we have four different potential populations which represent possible origins of our sample.

In a national referendum to expand the use of renewable energy:

- POP_1: 10% of the population voted 'yes'
- POP_2: 15% of the population voted 'yes'
- POP_3: 30% of the population voted 'yes'
- POP_4: 60% of the population voted 'yes'.

Choosing at random from one of the four populations, we sample one person who voted 'yes' in a national referendum to expand the use of renewable energy. We know nothing about the potential population from which they came. All we know is our sample.

What is the probability that our sample came from POP_1, POP_2, POP_3, or POP_4? We must first determine our prior probability, the information given by the prior distribution. The prior probability is that these four potential populations each had an initially equal chance to be the population from which the sample was drawn, therefore, 0.25

(i.e., 0.25 + 0.25 + 0.25 + 0.25 = 1). These represent the probability of each population being the likely origin of the sampled 'yes' voter.

Now, we need to determine how the data shape these priors. That is: P(Sample|POP_1), P(Sample|POP_2), P(Sample|POP_3), and P(Sample|POP_4). If the person who voted 'yes' came from POP_1 in which 10% of the population voted 'yes', the probability is 0.10. Therefore:

- P(Sample|POP_1) = 0.10
- P(Sample|POP_2) = 0.15
- P(Sample|POP_3) = 0.30
- P(Sample|POP_4) = 0.60.

At this point, we involve Bayes' theorem. Given that there are potential populations that represent the universe of possible populations (in this example), the Probability of Sample (P(B)) is actually a sum of the conditional probabilities weighed by the probability of the populations themselves.

$$P(POP_1|Sample) = \frac{0.10(0.25)}{0.10(0.25)+0.15(0.25)+0.30(0.25)+0.60(0.25)} = \frac{0.025}{0.2875}$$

P(POP_1|Sample) = 0.087

$$= \frac{0.15(0.25)}{0.10(0.25)+0.15(0.25)+0.30(0.25)+0.60(0.25)} = \frac{0.0375}{0.2875}$$

P(POP_2|Sample) = 0.130

$$P(POP_3|Sample) = \frac{0.30(0.25)}{0.10(0.25)+0.15(0.25)+0.30(0.25)+0.60(0.25)} = \frac{0.075}{0.2875}$$

P(POP_3|Sample) = 0.261

$$P(POP_4|Sample) = \frac{0.60(0.25)}{0.10(0.25)+0.15(0.25)+0.30(0.25)+0.60(0.25)} = \frac{0.15}{0.2875}$$

P(POP_4|Sample). = 0.522

These are the posterior probabilities that are updates to our expectations at the outset – our prior probabilities – given the sample data. Note that these four are the universe of potential populations: 0.087 + 0.130 + 0.261 + 0.522 = 1.000.

While it would appear that the sample is most likely to come from POP_4 (prob = 0.522), we would benefit from continuing to bring evidence to bear on the initial probabilities. In this over-simplified example, however, we can see the explicit function of the

Bayesian approach to determine the change in uncertainty given the sample. This also demonstrates the core difference in the approach to statistical inference.

Potential Limitations of the Bayesian Approach

There is no shortage of debate over which approach – the 'frequentist' or Bayesian – is superior. Perhaps the main difference lies in the results. Frequentists attach a level of confidence to estimates of population parameters based on whether the results are highly unlikely or not. If they are highly unlikely, frequentists 'reject the null' and award the alternative hypothesis the crown of statistical significance. Bayesians, however, try to answer the question, 'What is the probability of the hypothesis given the data?' In most cases, Bayesians estimate a ratio of probabilities of the two different hypotheses that quantifies the support for one hypothesis over another (FYI: this is called, cleverly, the Bayesian ratio or Bayesian factor).

These approaches are to a great extent compatible, meaning that, for the most part, they arrive at more or less the same conclusions – albeit from different directions. And this is one of the main critiques of the Bayesian approach. Given the complicated estimating procedure and reliance on the subjectivity of the prior probabilities, it makes some intuitive sense to get more or less the same answer with less work.

However, arriving at the same answer over-simplifies what Bayesian statistics offer. Rather than a point estimate with an associated level of significance, Bayesian produce a probability distribution which can make interpretation and communication of the results of the analysis easier. This is a debatable point. While the frequentist approach is the most commonly taught approach to probability and statistical analysis (as is here), there is some evidence that interpreting results still results in misconceptions about the nature of the findings.

Other critiques point out the unique and subjective role of the prior probabilities necessary to the generation of the prior probabilities. In the Bayesian universe, the prior probability embeds past knowledge of salient research and is then merged with the data under analysis to arrive at a more fully informed conclusion. Yet, the information needed and used to establish the prior can be limited or non-existent (as per our example) and, in such cases, the advertised advantages of the Bayesian approach shrink quickly. Subjectivity, rather than a potential advantage of the individual researcher, now acts instead as a possible constraint.

There is an extensive debate between the frequentist and Bayesian approaches that could fill more than a single chapter. From statistics lore, even if the chance of rain is low, a Bayesian is much more likely to carry an umbrella than a frequentist and be inconvenienced – but also drier in case of an unexpected storm. However, the differences in these approaches are non-trivial to specific users with specific intents of analysis or specific research questions. For the most part, however, this debate lies in the realm of academic controversy.

Big Data, Machine Learning, or Computational Social Science

In terms of data analysis, the field of Big Data seems to have developed a reputation for surpassing other statistical and analytical approaches. The availability of new sources and quantities of data not only require new methods to handle and analyse the data, but allow us to look at processes we have not had the opportunity to do before in ways we are only now beginning to appreciate. Undoubtedly this approach adds a great deal to our ability to capture, measure, and understand a wider range of economic, political, and social processes. However, Data Science struggles with a number of issues that has limited its initial promise and is not the one-size-fits-all solution for the challenges of quantitative research in political and social sciences.

Data Science is an approach to handling and analysing huge amounts of data. (*Note:* Data Science and **Machine Learning** are, for our discussion here, more or less synonymous.) In any case, there has been an exponential growth in data availability – including various forms of data on the internet but also the digitalization of institutional documents such as governmental records.

Large datasets provide thousands, millions, or more observations on thousands of variables and units of analysis. Because of this unprecedented size and structure of such data, Data Science approaches require specific software, powerful computers, and specific tools developed by corporations and governments – although often open source – to manage and analyse the data. For example, you may have heard of or worked with Google File System, which supports files so large that they have to be distributed across hundreds of computers. Together, this is captured under the recognizable name **Big Data**.

Here, instead of trying to present one or two techniques of Data Science in the narrow confines of this one chapter, let's confront Data Science, as it has many Social Scientists reconsidering the contours of research, what we can and cannot do.

So, What's All the Hubbub About?

There are clear advantages to being able to access and analyse massive datasets. Above all, having data at such a large scale provides an enormous number of potential relationships that may have avoided detection in smaller datasets. While this gives us many advantages to analysing smaller-sized datasets, four such advantages stand out.

One, statistical power is not a big concern as sample size asymptotically rises to meet population. Fundamental to statistical analysis is the notion that as our sample size grows, our estimates inevitably approach the 'true' population parameter. Although, there is some debate among researchers on the nature of statistical significance. For example, some argue that if a dataset represents all the data for a given set of variables, should we compute standard errors, t-scores, p-values, etc.… ultimately with an eye to estimate statistical significance? The answer is not obvious.

The common practice is to do so in order to avoid or minimize omitting potentially relevant explanatory variables, allowing included variables to soak up their explanatory power (or end up in the error term) as well as minimizing the potential error in which variables are measured. Both can impact the error term of a model and we know both *omitted variable bias* and *measurement error* are substantial problems for the performance of the statistical model.

Two, Big Data collection methods – such as web scrapes, the use of bots, trace data, *inter alia* – can improve both the nature and quality of data, both of which are clear benefits to research. For example, using the internet to collect data, not only can experiments enrol millions of users with the click of a button, experiments can also be mixed into the real lives of people as they go about work or leisure. The internet is always on. Further, if we want to know whether a treatment or event – e.g., a rapid change in the state of politics, economics, or society – impact people's choices or attitudes and opinions, the so-called 'pre-/post-'analysis, we can collect data that exist both before and after. This beats waiting for natural experiments to take place.

As another example of this, the advantage of Big Data can circumvent the commonly used and crucial instrument on media studies, namely, self-reported media use. Often, in order to study and understand how people are affected by media, we ask them what device they use, how much they use it, and what they watched. Big Data collection can include simply tracking individuals' media choices at a very high level of precision. This substantively improves the nature of the data – in this case, the measure of actual media choice and use – in which we are interested.

Third, using the traditional forms of data collection such as interviews or surveys, we consider the **reactivity of data.** Is the subject we are interested in studying affected in a way that changes what is being measured? This is commonly referred to as the 'interviewer effect'. For experiments, this is your knowledge of being watched as your participation is central to the experiment. For surveys, this could be an item on a questionnaire, the interviewer himself, the survey organization conducting the study, or the environment where the survey is taking place. For research on extreme political or social positions or hostile or intolerant views (e.g., racism), the interviewer effect can sharply dampen the sincerity – and thus validity – of responses. The data collection methods of Data Science can often avoid this reactivity of the subject by collecting information about individuals', groups', organizations' choices and content often without interacting with the subject at all.

Fourth and finally, the methods of collecting Big Data have also altered and increased the types of variables we can examine. The availability of data on social networks or even as a simple example, data on emails, offers researchers new variables to investigate. Not to mention the reams of archival institutional data that are being digitalized. Such new forms of data offer potential for new solutions and results.

Data Science (Machine Learning) Methods

Again, while it does not make sense to try to engage the actual techniques of Data Science in such a short space, the broad strokes give a sense as to how this analytical approach differs from the statistics we have just seen.

For Data Scientists, the first step is data acquisition. Where do the data come from? Are they open source, randomized experiments, gathered via an Application Programming Interface (API), crowdsourced, etc....? A crucial difference with traditional datasets is that Big Data do not come in the classic N×K rectangular shape – in which 'N' represents the observations and 'K' represents the variables – necessary for statistical analysis. As such, this requires the use and development of computer systems that are able to manage such datasets and make them interpretable and useable.

Data Science has introduced unique applications to data collection. As one example, **digital trace data** are large, digital datasets evidence of human choices. Trace data are the remnant or indirect data left by patterns of behaviour, mostly commonly left by journeys across the internet but not exclusively. These observable 'footprints in the sand' don't require participants to be able to answer well – or to answer at all. Accumulating and tracking these data provides potential insight into choices or preferences of the participant.

Another application unique to Data Science is **mass collaboration**. Mass collaboration is the approach of splitting big tasks into 'micro-tasks' and re-aggregating them. Sometimes called, 'citizen science' or 'crowdsourcing', mass collaborations are collections of human input to a complex problem. Crowdsourcing exploits the vast number of humans to make small observations (or share existing observations) that can be aggregated into a large dataset of observations. Alternatively, this approach can take advantage of the capabilities of (again, many) humans to make nuanced decisions, such as evaluating texts, images, audio samples, or symbols.

Second, a Data Scientist will focus on model building. How will they choose to interrogate these data? While significant differences exist and are regularly introduced, in order to identify patterns in the data, the majority of research uses Machine Learning methods. This is the introduction of algorithms and statistical models to analyse and draw inferences from patterns identified in data.

These methods generally fall into one of two categories: Unsupervised and Supervised Machine Learning. **Unsupervised Machine Learning** is a form of analysis that 'hunts' covariates using techniques such as data mining and principal components analysis. **Supervised Machine Learning** includes methods that primarily focus on prediction. Given a 'training dataset' with data on a target variable Y ('the dependent variable') and covariates X ('independent or explanatory variables'), the goal is to estimate a model for predicting the target Y as a function of X. For example, the creation of an exploration scenario to test different validation settings. This is sometimes called 'what if' analysis. This is similar to robustness testing done with a multiple regression model – albeit at scale – in order to determine the stability of the model estimates and validity of the results.

Data Science and Complementarity

Data Science also complements traditional forms of data collection. In forms such as text analysis, Data Science improves both the capture and organizing of data; in particular, the problem of character coding (UTF-8) and the use of less common languages.

Data Science has advanced the ability to alter the unit of analysis from word to phrase, manage punctuation, and exploit stemming (i.e., 'stem-', 'stemm-', or 'st-'), and improve the organization and storage by valence and topic.

For the use of nationally representative surveys of individuals, Data Science has improved the ability to achieve random sampling within the sampling frame as well as deliver surveys. Specific to Data Science, researchers can use Data Science to deepen surveys, aligning survey respondents and their data to provide more information on included questions. Using the predictive power advantage, Data Science can develop on surveys by improving imputation for missing data given what is available in other parts of the survey.

Finally, experiments have been effectively super-sized. Fully digital, randomized assignment and delivery or treatment has made experiments – once the gold standard of causal investigation – a cost-effective approach. Data Science allows a near costless up-scale of any experiment as well as moving experiments out of the lab into the field. At the leading edge of this, machine learning techniques can also be useful for developing better estimates of the counterfactuals through predictions. This essentially allows us to predict what the treatment group would look like without the treatment, a role that is usually – if imperfectly – played by the control group.

Problems with Data Science

In the social sciences, the scientific approach is chiefly concerned with decoding the world in order to understand it. Whether the analytical approach is quantitative or qualitative, the commonality remains an attempt to draw closer to a clearer comprehension of why the world is the way it is. A common goal across the social sciences has long been to make causal claims about a relationship in which we are interested. Researchers can differ on the means to demonstrate causal claims but theory is advanced by accumulating evidence as a means to increase the strength of causal claims. As such, the theoretical model determines what is included. In quantitative analysis, this theoretical 'causal model' has us searching for the right data, the right variables, the right model specification, the right estimation, the right controls, and the right interpretation. That is, effort is aimed at matching what we can measure with what we 'need' to measure in order to advance our causal claims.

Statistics (and Econometrics) focus on description, control, and inference. This includes summarizing data, estimating models, testing hypotheses, and yes, prediction. Ultimately, however, the main goal of Machine Learning and Data Science is to build statistical models that maximize predictive power. This is not a problem if that is what you want to do. However, prediction – in capital letter 'S' Science – is secondary to explanation and this has created a growing gap in the field of quantitative methods and statistical analysis.

Prediction and Explanation

> Prediction is very difficult, especially about the future. – Danish proverb

Data Science techniques revolve around prediction, that is, providing the most accurate predictions of a target variable (given the focus on prediction rather than explanation, it is not correct to call the target variable 'the dependent variable'). This shift toward the prioritization on prediction – at the direct cost of 'plausible' explanation – has negative implications for the scientific study of political phenomena. In the case of prioritizing on prediction, the right model is the one that explains the greatest amount of variance in the target variable. That is, what assemblage of variables – related or not to the target variable – make it change the most? Highly predictive statistical models or algorithms not only provide a guide to the change in the target variable but can also be confidently applied to the new dataset to predict new or future observations.

With the use of theory as the basis for designing a model relating an independent variable to the dependent variable, estimating the impact of an independent variable on the dependent variables (holding everything else constant) is the effort to estimate unbiased effects with carefully constructed standard errors in order to infer (theoretically determined) causal effects. Data Science, on the other hand, seeks to predict how a given outcome varies with a large number of potential predictors with or without the help of prior theory to establish which predictors are relevant. This approach is **data-driven** in that model selection is driven by the identification of meaningful predictive variables. This difference is apparent in the evaluation of model performance. For those seeking explanation, a causal model is assessed by its explanatory power: the substantive and statistical performance of the included variables, model specification, and model performance and fit. Predictive models are evaluated on their ability to predict the target variable in a new dataset.

A bit more technically, as a data-driven approach, Data Science gives less attention to statistical uncertainty and standard errors and more attention to model uncertainty. In technical terms, bias – trying to get the correct impact of the independent variable on the target variable – is allowed in order to reduce variance. This bias–variance trade-off is made in order to improve prediction. For example, some techniques exclude covariates (think multicollinearity but with an 'eliminate with extreme prejudice' protocol), thus allowing the included variable to reflect the impact of both it and the excluded variable, thus introducing omitted variable bias.

This is not to say there is no value in prediction. Machine Learning can deal with data that are too high-dimensional for standard estimation methods and pure prediction problems in which causal inference is not necessary. For example, the benefits of building a stormproof room in your house depends on the probability of a sufficiently severe storm. Or, the benefits of refurbishing a piece of machinery – versus buying a new one – depend on whether that piece of machinery will be in use long enough afterward. These are important questions on the nature of pure prediction, but ones that limit us to questions of pure association. Thus, while we can use Data Science to answer such questions without any particular need of theory, this leaves us less theory to manage and interpret empirical results.

Perhaps it is worth noting that while causal models can also be used to predict new and even out-of-sample outcomes, predictive models cannot be assessed for explanatory power as they are, by definition, models of association. In this case, perhaps we can live with the difficult constraint of theoretical plausibility as a means to adhere to the traditional aims of science: as a means to understand how the world (really) works. There are, as far as we know, any one of manifold potential realities, and prediction frees itself from any constraint by simply ignoring reality altogether.

Prediction models and causal models (focused on explanation) are different in the way mining and farming are different. That is, for prediction, we are only concerned with the substantive association between the variables. In the case of explanation, we demand, at a minimum, some reason to include a particular independent variable, some plausible causal relationship to the dependent variable. Simply, whether the main goal of our research is to explain or to predict has crucial implications for our choice of both data and the methods to analyse them.

This is not an idle debate. If we place a premium on prediction, we may be able to predict an outcome but we forfeit understanding how it became the outcome. Data analysis is no longer a search for reality but rather a formula to be tweaked into supercharged predicting performance. Choosing prediction over explanation challenges what it means to be a scientist, to be fascinated by the wonders of the world and the way it can surprise us. Prediction minimizes scientific surprises, spontaneity, and serendipity.

These Aren't the Data You Are Looking For

One constraint on even the largest sets of data is whether they are in fact, what we want to analyse. Converting data into variables by conceptualizing them and ultimately choosing a measure is common to all quantitative approaches. However, it has become clear that some of the data that can be hoovered up in great quantities do not always optimize the alignment of our intended concepts with the available measures.

One substantial problem with using trace data, for example, data that we leave lying around on the internet as we go blazing from one location to another, is that these data can be assembled to resemble profiles or narratives about our internet usage. However, like the revealed preferences approach, this is many times reverse engineering our understanding. That is, instead of capturing data on 'why' we made the choices we have made, we are capturing the 'if' of those choices. The story is bolted on later because we don't actually know. With the benefit of non-reactivity of the data comes the limitation that – unless we have been told – we do not have the data to tell us whether we are correct.

Data Science must also contend with the ebb and flow of user preferences such as 'drifting' across various platforms as well as algorithmic confounding, in which an algorithm, deep inside the digital platform, changes users' click behaviour in real time, thus confounding the data collection and any subsequent theorizing about the nature of decision-making. These are sometimes referred to as, with I hope a touch of irony, the 'unknown unknowns' of Data Science.

Nor are the data – despite its size – necessarily the most representative of what we want to know. For example, the ability to collect and analyse data from all of Twitter related to an upcoming national election, in response to a politician's polarizing statement, or during a frightening or significant event, is certainly impressive. Twitter, however, is a small facet of political discussions that can vastly over- and under-represent socio-demographic groups (as well as the slightly more congruent base of internet users).

Yet, even broad-based online studies on internet users can potentially skew a representative sample of a country's citizens. According to the International Telecommunications Union (ITU), in the EU, approximately 85% of people have regular access to the internet (approximately 80% in the US). Thus, roughly more than 1 out of 10 Europeans (and 1 out of 5 Americans) that very likely also represent specific socio-demographic and socio-economic clusters. And despite the availability of data from the internet, the ITU also points out that, in both the EU and the US, television is still the primary source for political information.

This may feel a bit weird to read. But I remind you that we – you and me – are objectively and numerically different from the majorities in our respective countries taking university-level courses, at all, and a statistics course, specifically. While our lives are very online, we are not the modal citizen. This is to remind ourselves that many of the Big Data processes under investigation can produce dazzling and unprecedented insights. These same insights may – despite the Big Data association – also be only narrowly applicable.

A Broad Conclusion (in a Small Space)

'Is it progress if a cannibal uses a knife and fork?' – S.J. Lec (1957: 59)

The focus on prediction has cast a new light on an old debate; namely, the contest between deterministic causality and probabilistic explanation. Prediction has introduced a third position in turn creating a fragile alliance between probabilistic explanation and deterministic causation to handle the challenge. Early in the book we defended a non-causal stance in lieu of a theoretical and probabilistic understanding of the world. However, both explanation and causation share orientations unified in seeking the 'real world' – if disagreeing on how close we can get to uncovering the mechanisms that govern reality. Classical statistical methods, as we have learned here, are an attempt to advance the ability to describe, control, and infer as a means to satisfy, at a minimum, the ability to make confident statements about what we observe and, at a maximum, to make claims about the explicit causality of those mechanisms.

We return to this debate briefly as some of the same critiques used in the probabilistic/deterministic debate are relevant to the focus on prediction that has grown substantially in the recent decade.

The notion of prediction itself is not problematic. Prediction, referring to the use of the Bayesian updating, although more specifically Data Science, methods, improves how we anticipate outcomes. From song selection on Spotify to Google Flights to shopping online, there is a lot of attention (read: money) given to these capabilities. Just as the incentives for determining causality in Social Science are not insubstantial, they are being eclipsed by the incentives for prediction.

That is, in contrast to the milquetoast contingency and probability of academic studies and reporting, presenting results in which the researcher has complete confidence is more convincing to groups that spend money, such as governments, NGOs, and other investors. This can lead to observable improvements in, for example, alleviating poverty in non-Western areas. For example, someone might assert to have 'proven' that poor learning in elementary schools is related to malnutrition or hunger rather than poor teachers or textbook scarcity. But note, this wasn't previously unknown. In fact, it had been demonstrated previously without 'causal techniques' for many years. However, the application of causal methods to 'prove' this opens pocketbooks (often held by those unaware of the fundamental theoretical role of causation in scientific work). The same is true for prediction, those in the position of wanting to know (and often willing to pay) are not concerned about what is in the model, it must simply perform. Fine. But there is an unclear boundary between when and where we can and should use prediction.

Secondly, both prediction and causality are ephemeral. Prediction's fleeting contributions are event-specific and bound by time. At least this is obvious. Yet, causality is similarly constrained in a manner unacknowledged by many of its adherents. Establishing a causal relationship may have a short-term thrill, payoff, or benefit. However, we are limited by the non-experimental nature of reality, and as such, causality is never absolute. Causality suffers from solution instability. That is, given the dynamic nature of social, economic, and political phenomena, for how long is this causal mechanism valid? How far can we export this causal relationship? When is it wrong? Or, taking causal claims seriously, if in fact we now know the actual (inside the black box) mechanics of the relationship, when do we shut down that area of research? If we now know why X -> Y, we don't need more research in that area. Clearly no one would advocate for this suggesting that, perhaps, we haven't quite explained everything so neatly. Perhaps the dog has finally caught the (causal) car and doesn't know what to do.

Third, both causality and prediction adjust our aim. One practical reason to be suspicious about embracing either an exclusively predictive or causal approach to studying Political Science is that the questions that we can 'fully answer' and the questions that we want or need to answer are not perfectly overlapping circles. The data necessary to perfectly specify a causal model are very often absent or incomplete or, simply, bad. In the case that it is available, the question is very often quite narrow with little broader application. And within the realm of social sciences, very few approaches simply want to know what will happen next – versus being able to explain why this and other similar outcomes occur.

The questions that persist in the discipline, that remain to some extent unsolved, are the most interesting ones that require substantially more than mere mathematical manipulation. Putting a premium on research that is causal or predictive – over 'messier' questions – jeopardizes a discipline with increasingly obscure and ultimately irrelevant efforts. In other words, for many of the central debates in Political Science, there simply may not be any means to statistically demonstrate causality – even if you thought that you could – beyond a highly circumscribed or tertiary facet of any debate. Nor does prediction do much for advancing theory – that is, our shared knowledge as to why things happen. Focusing on questions we can answer is not necessarily progress and often distracts us from the questions needing the greatest attention. The distinction between questions that we can answer and questions we should be answering is fundamental to whether we consider our discipline relevant to society.

What we fail to appreciate is that primarily focusing on prediction myopically reformulates our approach as model fit is not fully compatible with understanding how the world 'really' works. There was once a similar debate around the coefficient of determination (R^2). Some argued that because R^2 reports the percentage of variance of the dependent variable explained by the assemblage of independent variables in the models, it must be somehow possible to achieve 100%. This does make initial intuitive sense. If a measure ostensibly varies between 0% – no explanatory power – to 100% – full explanatory power, this upper value can be reached. Others argued, in the end successfully, that this upper bound of full explanation represents perfect explanation but that we can only approach this value asymptotically, that is, we can get closer and closer but never get there because we just cannot ever fully say, 100%, that we explained all of the variance in the dependent variable. And although 100% is unachievable, it continues to have value to the reporting of model fit as we can use it to compare differently specified models (which is pretty much how we use it today). The new powers and predilection for prediction in the social sciences may simply represent the latest iteration of this argument.

Finally, the question of data is the root of the divergence in methods. We can assume to always suffer some deficiency in the data, whether in quantity, accuracy, or quality. In response, there is one of two stances to take. One stance is to acknowledge that the data are a mess and respond by increasing the sophistication of the techniques with which we analyse them. The other approach is to build this knowledge into our interpretation. To some extent, Big Data has taken the first, the Bayesians have taken the second. And this divergence speaks to a larger debate, namely how data become information and information is then converted into knowledge. How we convert data into information is at the heart of all statistical, even empirical, analysis. Yet, how we convert this information into knowledge is by making this information relevant and useful. Any conspiracy theorist can contort data into information by 'connecting the dots'. However, a grounding in a coherent, verifiable, and responsive system of understanding the world is perhaps the least fallible means of changing information into knowledge. Thus, the focus on sophistication seems secondary to understanding what it is we have – in terms of information – and what that brings to bear on what we know.

End of Chapter Summary

- The Bayesian approach incorporates as much available information as possible into statistical analysis.
- Bayesian critiques of the frequentist approach point to substantial issues with hypothesis testing and the Central Limit Theorem that may need to be recognized and potentially resolved.
- Bayesian statistical techniques are computationally more demanding and often result in similar findings to those from frequentist techniques.
- In specific cases, particularly ones with a lack of long run probabilities or novel events, a Bayesian approach can be more effective.

- Big Data and Data Science are generic labels for the handling, management, and analysis of extremely large datasets.
- Machine Learning is a method of analysing large datasets that are both autonomous and self-updating.
- A shift toward the maximization of predictions – at the direct cost of 'plausible' explanation – has potentially negative implications for the scientific study of political phenomena.

Glossary

- The **frequentist approach** considers probabilities a function of iterated probabilities of different outcomes over time.
- **Bayes' Theorem** merges the information given by the prior distribution with the information from the sample giving us a posterior distribution for the population parameter. This posterior information is then used to update the prior.
- **Data Science** is the use and development of computer systems that are able to learn and adapt by using algorithms and statistical models to analyse and draw inferences from patterns in data.
- **Machine Learning** is the method of data analysis that automates model building so that the analysis can learn from the data.
- **Big Data** is the popular and generic term for the availability and analysis of large datasets.
- **Reactivity of data** refers to whether our collection of data affects the nature of that data.
- **Digital trace data** are remnant data left by the use of the internet.
- **Mass collaboration** breaks large questions into widely assigned micro-tasks and re-assembles the results to produce results that otherwise would overwhelm any one researcher.
- **Unsupervised and Supervised Machine Learning** refers to the use of largely autonomous algorithms to describe and analyse large datasets.
- **Data-driven** approaches are focused on predicting a target variable with any large number of potential predictors.

Questions

1. Use your favourite web browser to search, 'Applications of Bayes' Theorem' and briefly describe its use in three 'real-world' examples. They do not need to be examples in Political Science.
2. One use of the Bayesian approach is probing of existing techniques. Last chapter we talked a bit about hierarchical linear modelling or multi-level models. Look at the article below and summarize the author's reasoning for asserting that Bayes estimations are superior to MLE.

- Stegmueller, Daniel. 2013. 'How many countries for multilevel modeling? A comparison of frequentist and Bayesian approaches' *American Journal of Political Science* 57(3): 748–761. https://doi.org/10.1111/ajps.12001

3. In Benoit et al. (2016, see below for link), the authors use mass collaboration to produce core elements of their results. Was this the only way to do so and if not, what are the advantages and disadvantages of having so?
    - Benoit, K., Conway, D., Lauderdale, B., Laver, M., and Mikhaylov, S. 2016. 'Crowd-sourced text analysis: Reproducible and agile production of political data' *American Political Science Review* 110(2): 278–295. https://doi.org/10.1017/S0003055416000058

4. Using Mahdavi and Ishiyama's (2020) article as an example, describe the potential advantage of Data Science to get at novel questions.
    - Mahdavi, Paasha, and John Ishiyama. 2020. 'Dynamics of the inner elite in dictatorships: Evidence from North Korea' *Comparative Politics* 52(2): 221–40. www.jstor.org/stable/26867765.

Annotated References and Further Reading

Gill, Jeff. 1999. 'The insignificance of null hypothesis significance testing' *Political Research Quarterly* 52(3): 647–74. https://doi.org/10.1177/106591299905200309
A clear discussion of the limitations to classic statistical inference and an introduction to the Bayesian approach.

Hoekstra, R., Morey, R.D., Rouder, J.N., Wagenmakers, E.J. 2014. 'Robust misinterpretation of confidence intervals' *Psychon Bull Review* O21(5): 1157–1164. https://doi.org/10.3758/s13423-013-0572-3
Demonstrates the difficulty of interpreting frequentist results in the form of null hypothesis significance testing.

Iversen, Gudmund. 1984. *Bayesian Statistical Inference.* Volume 43 of *Quantitative Applications in the Social Sciences* Series. Newbury Park, CA: Sage.
A more formal but gentle introduction to the use of the Bayesian approach in the social sciences.

Jungherr, Andreas and Yannis Theocharis. 2017. 'The empiricist's challenge: Asking meaningful questions in political science in the age of big data' *Journal of Information Technology and Politics* 14(2): 97–109.
A provocative article on the use and misuse of Data Science in Political Science.

Lec, Stanisław Jerzy. 1957. *Unkempt Thoughts* [*Myśli Nieuczesane*]. Krakow: Krakow Literary Publications.
In the original Polish: 'Czy jeżeli ludożerca je widelcem i nożem to postęp?'

McGrayne, Sharon Bertsch. 2011. *The Theory that Would Not Die*. New Haven: Yale University Press.

A non-technical history of Bayes that draws together a surprising number of historical and current uses of Bayes in nearly all industries.

Shmueli, G. 2010. 'To explain or to predict?' *Statistical Science* 25(3): 289–310.

This article expands on some of the themes discussed above.

Varian, H. 2014. 'Big data: New tricks for econometrics' *Journal of Economic Perspective* 28: 3–28.

A technical discussion of the implications of Data Science for the social sciences, in particular, Economics.

Signposts to the Accompanying Digital Resources

Data used in this chapter

- **Percentage of national internet availability**: International Telecommunications Union.
    - www.itu.int/en/ITU-D/Statistics/Pages/stat/default.aspx

Check out the *Summer Institute in Computational Social Science* website for more and free information and seminars on Data Science (with a slight tendency toward Sociology)
    - https://sicss.io/

20
THE ETHICS OF DATA ANALYSIS

> **LEARNING OUTCOMES**
>
> In this chapter, you will be able to
>
> - Cite ethical guidelines appropriate to research in political and social sciences.
> - Understand the need, utility, and content of Informed Consent.
> - Identify common and novel sources of ethical challenges in Social Science research.
> - Recognize the increased importance of data security.

Introduction

Collecting, analysing, and presenting data in the social sciences comes with a great deal of responsibility. The goal of our analysis is to bring evidence to bear on questions that we think are important. In order to do so with the greatest impact, we are rewarded by making our choices – which data, which techniques, accurate conclusions – as appropriate to the challenges of analysis as possible. Making appropriate choices in our investigation is further buttressed by the Scientific Method's strong requirements of transparency and replication. Thus, Political Science, Sociology, Psychology, Economics, and other Social Science fields can incentivize researchers' ethical attitudes and behaviour by supporting individual and disciplinary adherence to such norms of appropriateness, transparency, and replication.

While the Scientific Method is neutral, scientists are not. The choices we make in our design, analysis, and delivery are subjective. As discussed in various places in previous chapters, our goal is to be as objective as we can with the aim of minimizing the inevitable impact of our own subjectivity. And the choices that we make, regardless of their appropriateness, do not automatically absolve us of our own influence which, in turn, can introduce opportunities for unethical behaviours and choices.

It is crucial to understand that Social Science research seeks to understand processes that are very often important, personal, and potentially frightening or dangerous to many people. Racism, protests, ethnic conflict, political animosity, authoritarianism, war, income/social/racial/gender inequality, oppression, riots are not dead caterpillars under glass awaiting dissection or distant stars patiently waiting for identification. The topics of our research, the questions we want answers to, can involve uncomfortable elements to respondents and researchers alike. Getting at these topics, analysing the data, presenting what we find, can challenge us to remain objective and ostensibly ethical.

This challenge reflects a broader debate concerning the ethical nature of allowing unethical behaviour in order to achieve a greater ethical outcome: the debate of the ends versus the means. The Scientific Method takes a **deontological approach** of focusing on the means of investigation as a nearly unimpeachable method to produce objective and ethical results. The validity and trustworthiness of such results are rendered so by maintaining a rigorous attachment to the defensibly objective and ethical collection, analytical, and presentation choices. On the other side is the **consequentialist approach** that the results that we need (i.e., to make a decision or act) require us to, for example, extract data, breach confidence, or misrepresent conclusions – act unethically. The results are rendered defensible by balancing the smaller negative impact of such research violations against the potential larger negative outcomes of failing to achieve the results.

Despite the potential negative outcomes of many of the topics in Political Science, for the most part, Political Scientists have chosen both individual and disciplinary rigorous adherence to the ethical norms of research. Much to the benefit of all. In practice, modern Social Science research is often discussed under a trifold rubric of ethical behaviour: beneficence, respect for persons, and justice. Here, I incorporate these key elements into a potentially more practical approach separating ethics into the different parts of a research project: data collection, data handling, and data presentation.

MORALS VERSUS ETHICS

Both morals and ethics are means to categorize things as right or wrong. Morals are individuals' personal guiding principles on what is right or wrong and even good and bad. Ethics are rules or norms set out or practiced by a group that guide allowable or correct attitudes and behaviours.

Morality is often a function of lifetime socialization with agents of family, friends, cohort, and institutions such as school and places of worship. Ethics originate in a group or institutional setting in which certain attitudes and behaviours are preferred. A common example of this is the moral/ethical conflict of a public defender asked to provide a defence for an action the lawyer finds personally morally indefensible. The moral belief of the individual lawyer complicates her ethical obligation of the legal requirement of providing a defence.

Individual morals and ethnical norms can align or be at odds with one another. Individual morals, to the extent that they are widely and exhaustively shared, can serve as the basis for ethics. However, in a diverse moral setting in which individuals bring together a wider set of morals, ethics can attempt to merge commonalities into a set of rules that all can abide.

The Ethics of Data Collection

The nature of collecting data can create a number of ethical issues. Paramount is the process in which another human submits themselves to the measure and/or manipulation by another person. Familiar to any advanced student of healthcare is the phrase 'First, do no harm' (*primum non nocere*) or non-maleficence. We are compelled to protect subjects of our study from known harm (or minimize the harm to which they are exposed) and maximize potential benefits. As indicated in the introduction, the deontological approach imposes this constraint regardless of potential benefits to society or future outcomes.

Beneficence and Informed Consent

The term used commonly to describe this is beneficence. **Beneficence** is protecting people from harm by making them aware that their participation is voluntary such that they, the subjects, are free to stop participating in the data collection process at any time. Beneficence also includes a disclosure of what the study is intended to achieve, that is, knowledge of what the data collected are designed to assess.

The crucial facet of beneficence is the recognition of the potential for harm. The **potential for harm** refers to any possibility for physical, psychological, emotional, or legal harm incumbent on participating in the study. The researcher should be upfront and comprehensive in acknowledging the potentially various ways the study may impact the participants. This is not limited to pain or injury but also strong emotional or psychological responses to questions or tasks. In addition, the stress of social embarrassment or stigma for participation or even the risk uncovering potentially illegal information or instances of extreme privacy. Very often, the researcher(s) can provide information about counselling services that are available if needed.

To ensure that both the subject(s) and the researcher(s) conducting the data collection have mutually communicated agreement, all subjects will provide an informed consent document to the researcher(s). **Informed consent** is a document that sets out who the researchers are, the source of the funding, the aims/purpose of the study, how subjects have been selected and recruited, their voluntary participation, the research procedures, the risks/discomfort anticipated, who will benefit from the study, how findings will be disseminated, the right to opt out at any time without concern of reprisal, how they can register any concerns or queries arising from the process (including contact details for the PI, including a national/EU level contact), and the steps taken to protect the privacy and confidentiality of the data. It is verified by the subject agreeing to have read and submitted the informed consent document which they must do before the study begins. Only if they agree, can they continue. This is not merely common but a requisite of collecting data from individuals in laboratory or field experiments, all forms of surveys, focus groups, ethnographies and participant observation, and nearly all other forms of data collection that involve individuals.

Note, I want to make clear that the researchers do not have to identify each and every element of the data collection process – for example, telling the potential respondents what the actual mechanism of data collection is, such as the nature or location of the treatment embedded in the data collection process. Nor do they have to give specific details about all aspects of the data collection. Assuming that nothing untoward or unethical is used, this is a satisfactory hedge to full disclosure.

Take, for example, the large, cross-national surveys such as the ones we have been using in this textbook: the European Social Survey, the European Elections Studies, and the Eurobarometer. Companies and organizations that field surveys and collect data have procedures established to ensure ethical practice. This includes the use of informed consent and sampling methods designed to avoid discriminatory in/exclusion while aligning the samples to the population distributions of socio-demographic profiles of the country. Respondents are not selected on an *ad hominem* basis and no one sub-population is singled out. All survey companies abide the ethical codes of the ICC/ESOMAR International Code of Marketing and Social Research Practice, ESOMAR/WAPOR Guide to Opinion Polls, and the ESOMAR Guidelines on Conducting Marketing and Opinion Research Using the Internet.

AN EXAMPLE OF INFORMED CONSENT

I am a researcher from Lamneth University. I am conducting a research study to learn more about your views toward important policy issues. This survey will ask you some questions for my research. It will take less than 10 minutes of your time.

It's your decision, and there are no consequences to saying no. I don't anticipate any major risks to participation, but you may feel uncomfortable answering some questions. If at any time during the survey you want to stop participating, you are free to end your participation by simply closing the survey on your computer or device. Your information will not be recorded.

Your responses may be used in publications or presentations. I will not possess nor share identifiable information about you.

Below you can find my contact information and the contact information of the research oversight board at Lamneth University, the Lamneth University Social Behavioural Research Institutional Review Board (SBR IRB), if you need to get in touch about this research at any point in the future.

For questions or concerns about the research study or procedures, or if you need to notify someone of a complaint, please contact the researcher:

Otto Manfrenjensenden, PhD

Lamneth University

Department of Political and Social Sciences

Email: O.Manfrenjensenden@ Lamneth.eu

Phone Number: +118 867-5309

If you have questions or concerns about your rights as a research participant, or if you would like to discuss the study with someone outside of the research team, contact the Lamneth University SBR IRB:Lamneth University SBR IRB: Telephone: +1 (800) 273-8255; Email: sbrirb@ Lamneth.eu

Website: www. Lamneth.eu/sbrirb/

Do you agree to participate in this study? Yes or No.

Your Signature: _____ Today's Date:_____

New Challenges to Beneficence

However, informed consent, while an effective hurdle intended to protect potential participants in the data collection process, some of the new data collection methods in Big Data have introduced a new ethical grey area centred on individuals' expectation of privacy. There have been a number of relatively recent studies that have created a novel conundrum on how we interpret 'informed consent' for participation.

One problem is the use of trace data and other crumbs left on the internet of individuals' use. Whose data are they? Are my cookie crumbles legally part of someone else's dataset about which I can say little, or simply, let me out? What if I don't want to make any data? What is my expectation of privacy when reading the news or looking at train tickets? These are questions that have been introduced into the discussion of beneficence as a function of the expanding use of Data Science data collection methods. Legally, ethically, and legislatively, these questions still have no universally clear answer.

Another problem is the involvement in experiments that are otherwise non-obvious to the participant but potentially harmful to the individual. One such example is Kramer et al. (2014). Researchers at Cornell University teamed with Facebook researchers to study emotional contagion, the name given to the synchronization and convergence of the emotional states of separate people. The researchers, under the cloak of self-awarded immunity from external ethical review by Facebook, filtered positive and negative content from individuals' news feeds. This experiment – while weakly demonstrating emotion contagion on the platform – enrolled more than 650,000 Facebook users without their knowledge. The study disrupted individuals' emotional expression, thus creating the potential for – even if entirely unintended – significant negative outcomes.

This controversy is not the only one, however; many of these types of issues originate from the overlap of academia – in which there are strict institutional protocols for maintaining ethical standards – and practitioners – where there are often fewer institutional constraints. This highlights how the power of Big Data collection methods to scale up an experiment online is not the same as providing free rein to enrol unsuspecting platform users into a study without their consent. Some defenders have pointed out that platform users have consented to the use of their data by signing the platform's Terms of Service document (in 2022, I timed myself). Facebook's Terms of Service would require more than 17 minutes to read the 4,132-word document. And this is one of the shorter Terms of Service which is why most of us – roughly 97% – don't in fact read them and just click right past it. Thus, reframed as an ethical question, are we comfortable that 'agree with our terms' is the same as 'informed consent'?

Overall, the ethical consideration of data collection on the internet has been slow to change or be updated. Even the norms of practice appear to be outpaced by the expanding innovation of data collection variations. The pace of legislative response in nearly all countries has been slow. The reasons are obvious but largely grounded in the observation that the rate of change of platform development is simply exponentially faster than the deliberative legislative process. However, this is not to say that there are not laws in place that seek to address these issues as we will see below.

The Ethics of Data Analysis

In our role as good stewards of research, once we have collected our data, we are obliged to (1) continue to safeguard the data and (2) make analytical choices transparent. These obligations are not merely 'best practices' for data handling but often also legal requirements. We must demonstrate both compliance with the relevant laws, adhere to professional norms, as well as respect the public interest.

Data Protection and Security

Safeguarding data serves both the subjects and the researchers. The primary focus is on the subject and in particular, guaranteeing their **right to privacy**, which includes both anonymity and confidentiality. Our respect for persons obliges us to treat subjects as autonomous agents. Not only are participants to be protected from harm during the data collection process but this also includes continuing protection for their personal data.

Respect for persons refers to handling and securing data that could potentially lead back to and harm participants. Each participant has a right to privacy whether they participate or not. One means to do this is through anonymity. **Anonymity** refers to data collection and analysis in which the identities of the participants are unknown. One way to guarantee an absolute level of anonymity is not collecting any data that could be used to potentially identify any participant. This includes such potential identifiers as names, addresses, demographic identifiers, phone numbers, IP addresses, physical attributes, or visual representations. Given the rise in telephone and online surveys, this has been increasing difficult to ensure as such data are inevitably carried by electronic exchange protocols.

Confidentiality, on the other hand, refers to data collection in which the researcher(s) know who the participants are but make personally identifiable data unavailable to others to thwart identification. Confidentiality differs from anonymity by the state of the researchers' knowledge. Thus, confidentiality is central to the right to privacy as participants' data should be protected not only in the collection phase but also in the use and storage phase.

At the practical level, some link between participant and their data is needed so that if they ask to be excluded from the study at a later point, this can be done. Such a link is often in the form of a third key that translates participant identity to participant data, often held separately and in isolation (in a literal locked drawer or password-protected file) accessible only by those approved and allowed before the start of the project. For example, you can give participants a random participation number. This number connects the actual participants to their data. Once you remove personally identifying information from the data collection instrument and replace it with the random number, this random number is associated with participants' information in a separate location.

Confidentiality also extends to other participants. If, in the case of the data collection design, participants interact with one another, such as a focus group, they are obliged by agreement not to reveal the other participants or their views.

Why are anonymity and confidentiality so important to potential subjects? One reason, as we have discussed previously, is that we are often trying to get at topics that subjects may be hesitant to acknowledge such as extreme political positions or hostile or intolerant views like racism, antisemitism, fascism, ultra-nationalism, homo-/transphobic, white supremacist without the ironclad guarantee that they could be later identified. In an environment in which participants could express their 'true' feelings and views, researchers have a more accurate set of data to study the origins, reinforcement mechanisms, and effects of such views.

The threats of the ability to attach an identification to such views are manifold. Participants could suffer not only embarrassment but also social sanctioning leading to psychological effects such as depression. More grave results could be economic repercussions such as losing their job or even liability for criminal or illegal behaviour (it is ostensibly illegal to express overtly fascist views in both Germany and Italy, for example).

AN EXAMPLE OF THE ANONYMIZATION PROCESS

Protecting participants' personal information is taken very seriously by all survey data collection groups. For example, the American National Election Survey (ANES) includes socio-demographic data on respondents but withholds location data in order to minimize the possibility of any one respondent being identified. In some US states and counties, there are locations in which sampling numbers are low and particular profiles – such as a middle-aged, Asian American female nurse in sparsely populated Helena, Montana – may make it easier to

(Continued)

determine the respondent and subsequently their responses/views. Therefore, location data are held separately.

To access or merge these data with the respondents, researchers have to submit a ANES Restricted Data Access Application to the ANES board with detailed information on the contact information of all the researchers who want access; which data are requested and why; the research plan; a disclosure protection plan in case there is an accidental disclosure; and a data protection plan with the availability of a computer that is 'air gapped' (isolated in a room with no connection to the internet or other computers).

This problem has been substantially enlarged with Big Data, with several recent examples of seemingly fully anonymized data being used to identify specific people.

Institutional Responsibility for Ethical Standards

Maintaining ethical standards in practice has been divided among two responsible parties. The first is the informed consent, including participants' safety and confidentiality, implemented by the researcher(s) responsible for the study. The second is the role of independent ethical oversight. To support this, most universities and research institutes have put in place well-developed data protection policies that outline the requirements of researchers at those facilities as well as requiring institutional ethical review boards.

Data Protection Policies

The protocols of a data protection policy will detail several aspects of data collection, analysis, and even presentation and will include the identification and capture of personal/sensitive data such as racial or ethnicity; political opinions; religious affiliation; physical or mental health information; trade union membership; sexual orientation; or genetic or biometric data. Such policies, which focus on the legality, fairness, and transparency of data processing including data collection, will include only what is necessary (this is referred to as 'data minimization'); data will be solely used for the stated or intended research purpose; storage limits and protection (from unauthorized access as well as loss); and, finally, data accuracy. To account for the large and growing amount of regulations, many universities will have comprehensive and separate managing, processing, protection, and storage codes set in place to adhere to legal obligations and guide researchers in accordance with the General Data Protection Regulation.

The **General Data Protection Regulation** (GDPR) is legislation at the European Union (EU) level that imposes possibly the strictest privacy and security law in the world on any organization in the EU that collects data on individuals, not just for research. In particular, Regulation 1725/2018 is a revised and updated framework of ethical norms, behaviours, and oversight in the protection of personal data in research at EU institutions and facilities. It harmonizes and simplifies the collection, handling, processing, analysis, and presentation of data collected on individuals. This includes the first ever 'right to be forgotten', data portability, and requirements in case of a data breach, protection of minors, and a dramatic increase in sanctions and penalties including substantial fines in the millions of Euros as well as jail.

The necessity of this regulation was in response to the exponential digitization, collection, and analysis of personal data in the EU. Particular attention has been given to how this impacts international research collaborations, particularly for researchers across different institutions, countries, and with countries in/outside the European Union which have lower data security and protection standards.

> ### DATA STORAGE IN THE EU
>
> All companies that store or use personal data must comply with one or more of the following legal requirements: Informed consent; contract obligation; vital or public interest; and legitimate interest. There are a number of large data storage archives for surveys and other types of data in Europe. These organizations follow and often exceed the GDPR guidelines. Two of the largest archives for Political Science data are the GESIS Data Archive for the Social Sciences at the Leibniz Institute for the Social Sciences: www.gesis.org or the Consortium of European Social Science Data Archive (CESSDA): www.cessda.net. These organizations are committed to the purpose of hosting and securing data as well as the most effective way to make the data available and at the same time secure the confidentiality of the participants.

Institutional Review Board

At the university-level, in the US, research projects that include collecting data from people must be submitted to an Institutional Review Board (IRB). In the EU, although not universally obligatory, this practice is widespread and growing more common with many universities adopting comparable **Ethics Committees** (EC). The primary objective is to protect participants from harm. These committees review proposals in order to assess the risks and benefits for participants, including the recruitment, informed consent procedures and content, and privacy protection.

In the US, the committee must have five members of varying intellectual backgrounds, including at least one scientist, one non-scientist, and one unrelated to the university in any way. Similarly, ECs are committees of diverse scholars that evaluate research proposals on the basis of their adherence to university data protection policies, ethical disciplinary norms, any relevant code of conduct. A research project must be successful for you to proceed (to start it or submit it for potential funding). It is not uncommon for a project to require some modifications or revisions and be revised and re-submitted. If a project is not successful, it will need to be withdrawn and significant effort invested to address the concerns articulated by the Board/Committee's recommendation.

Research Transparency

Finally, conducting scientific research obliges a forthright and transparent research design including our choices of what to do in the analysis of the data. Recall Principle Number 1: The scientific method requires a transparent and replicable description of the research design and analysis. The motive for transparency is one of the distinguishing characteristics of the scientific method as how a researcher chooses to investigate a question is subjective and these choices have a profound effect on the results.

In order to establish the ethical consideration of data analysis, it is incumbent on us to provide a clear and comprehensive reporting of our chosen methodology including variables, data, conceptual and operational choices, and analytical approach. Again, in academic publishing, presentations, discussions, and conferences, how we arrived at the results must be clear. The inevitable subjectivity of analytical choices is crucial to demonstrate how we arrived at these specific results. Whether we choose to use this variable or that one, summarize with this technique or that, recode a 4-category variable into a 2-category variable, treat an ordinal-level variable as an interval-level variable, ignore multicollinearity in the model, estimate the model using multinomial Logit or OLS, or any number of small and large choices we make, these impact the results. Our research is improved by a clear and comprehensive guide to how we arrived at our conclusions. This is why in academic articles (or other forms of public display) there is a long descriptive section on the methodological and analytical choices called the 'Methods Section' or 'Methodology'.

Transparency is a facet of data protection and security as it demonstrates the handling, manipulation, and analysis of the data in order to assuage any worries of inappropriate use or abuse of the data. As such, transparency has crucial implications for data presentation.

The Ethics of Data Presentation and Results

There is an apocryphal saying about the use of statistics: 'lies, damn lies, and statistics'. However, the saying should instead be 'lies, damn lies, and statisticians'. That is, a statistical software program will, if you don't make any coding mistakes, give you an answer to your statistical query. Or, calculating the descriptive and inferential formulas from previous chapters will produce a result. What is crucial to understand is that neither of these answers are correct. The answers will be correct only when you validate their veracity by using your training and expertise to decide use them as means to report your findings and results. It is you, the gatekeeper, with your choices of data, variables, model specification, estimating procedure, controls, and interpretation that bestow the accuracy and correctness of the result. This is the final element of ethical data analysis: data reporting and presentation.

> Measure a thousand times, cut once. – Turkish proverb

Data reporting and presentation refers to the presentation or publication of your research – including the methods and results – to an audience in order to demonstrate what your research shows. The importance of this cannot be overstated. The audience for your research will assume that, at every critical decision-making moment in your investigation, you have made the best effort not to mislead the audience or misrepresent the results. Only after following the law, abiding disciplinary norms, and addressing all ethical considerations in data collection and analysis, can you proceed to report what you have found.

The importance of accurately communicating our results is not merely making sure we haven't made any mistakes. That is, it is not only for our professional reputation, but also for the development of trust, respect, and accountability among collaborating research partners; the public stature of our discipline; our accountability to the public (as very often public funding supports our work, directly or indirectly); public support for the importance and saliency of high-quality, impactful research; and the public good by aligning research with broader social and even moral values. Our reporting must be honest, it must be credible, and it must be replicable. Individual or disciplinary failure to do so lowers trust in scientists and science.

Replicability

Transparency in our analysis is not only to lay bare the subjective choices we've made but also to allow others to replicate our results. As Gary King makes the point, technically, duplication is the process of 'running the same analyses on the same data to get to the same result' (1995, 451). Replication, on the other hand, is examining, or, technically, re-examining published work with either new data or differently analytical techniques to determine the validity of the finding. Conceptualizing replication this way, we are more likely referring to testing the robustness of the results. This definition, while valid, more closely resembles the process of testing theory with new data and/or methods; that is, creating a piece of original academic research rather than evaluating existing work.

What we intend here is duplication – using the same data and methods to reproduce existing research (to the extent these data are available and there are instructions (or code) provided by the author(s)) – but, to avoid unnecessary definitional knife fights, we use the more colloquial 'replication' to describe it. Therefore, we refer to the common definition of **replication** as reproducing the results given a transparent 'set of instructions' made available to others. Not only does this strengthen the reliability of the results, but also buttresses empirical claims and underscores the quality of the research.

The goal of replication is not to embarrass or intimidate scholars but rather buttress good findings by demonstrating their veracity. This has clear public benefit – the health of the discipline and its outputs – as well as the theoretical advantage of strengthening research to advance research. For example, while the number is not precise, a generous approximation is that just more than 30% of Economics papers published in the top journals cannot be reproduced (Vilhuber, 2020). Some of this is accounted for by existing and growing issues of data privacy, proprietary software, restricted-access, or non-public data environments. But the majority are not, and this can have severe reputational consequences for the researchers and their discipline.

To increase the rate of replicability in Political Science and other social sciences:

- A practice in many graduate school programs is asking students to do a 'replication study'; that is, choosing a published article from the literature and replicating the results.
- Many academic journals now require authors whose work is accepted to make available not only the dataset from which the results were produced but also the exact statistical coding to be inspected by viewers and readers of the article.
- Pre-registration of research projects is proposing a research design before you even open the dataset. The purpose of which is three-fold. One, establish your research as truly exploratory (rather than confirmatory); two, avoiding accusations *ad hoc* p-hacking; and three, stake your claim to the research idea. Essentially, you post the design of your research in advance of collecting and analysing the data. Some academic journals have started asking for pre-registrations.
- Academic publishing continues to distinguish itself from other sorts of publication by the peer-review process in which reviewers of the research focus on how the results are produced and whether they are communicated accurately.

CONFLICT OF INTEREST

A related element of potential research misconduct is a **conflict of interest** in which the researcher may have substantial incentives to 'find the right result'. This conflict is a contest of the researcher's interest in conducting rigorous, objective, scientific research, and incentives for that same research to produce a particular outcome. In other fields, such as chemistry, physics, biology, and pharmacy, the conflicts of interest can be quite substantial, with laboratory funding and access as well as potential patents on the line. For Social Scientists, there are fewer financial incentives – although access to greater funding or pay rises/bonuses are not insubstantial – other incentives or interests may be in advancing one's own career or the career of one's student, being the first to 'discover' something, promotion, reputation, or other personal considerations. Any conflict of interest can give rise to the appearance of compromising the researcher's judgment in conducting an investigation or reporting results. Clearly, this is to be avoided.

Justice

Finally, participants have the **right to service**. Very often, our research is normatively driven. That is, we are investigating a question because we feel that the answer to this question can provide some ways of alleviating a problem or promoting a solution. Right to service means that whatever normative or practical benefit is derived from the study should be made available to all of the participants. In the language of ethics, **justice** demands a distribution of benefits and burden of research.

This is a noble although sometimes unachievable goal. Perhaps we find that cities in which new drivers – getting their first driver's licence – are automatically enrolled to receive their voting materials without even having to request them show higher levels of aggregate youth participation in local and national elections. While it seems justified to demand this be adopted elsewhere (as we see voting in a democracy as a civic and ethical good), we can at best advocate for this on the basis of our research but we cannot independently 'distribute the benefits' of our research.

This is not a moot question. A great deal of development studies have historically been able to convince or persuade national governments of poorer countries to allow a wide variety of studies in which developmental outcomes (at the individual, family, local level) are compared across groups randomly given a social, economic, or political advantage and others that are not. Despite any potential finding, for example, having books at home is good for kids' academic achievement or having access to a small breakfast before school aids educational attainments, the benefits, in order to be distributed, require scaling such provisions at a national level. Very often, this is too demanding on already strained national budgets and is not done.

In a ghastly version of this, the Tuskegee Syphilis Study ran for 40 years in Alabama (1930s–1970s). African American men were not informed if they had tested positive for syphilis in order to see what happened if it was left untreated. We now know that the outcomes are an increase in the probability of disability and early death. Against nearly all ethical considerations, this continued even after a treatment – and subsequently a cure – for syphilis had been developed. That is, the actual goal was never to provide the benefit of treatment or the cure, but simply to study the effects of the disease when left untreated.

A Modest Proposal

The temptations to skip ethical considerations or make choices that do not hermetically seal us off from charges of unethical behaviour are real and numerous. There are the ethical considerations of, as we have discussed here, data collection, analysis, and presentation, but also the 'unspoken' ones of individual motivation. This is a constant and tenuous struggle. There is a very real incentive to be first or to out-publish others in your (sub-)field. Publication bias has a profound effect – ethically – on science as it is practised. To be first, or the most-cited, or 'known' is not merely about scientific reputation but also the primary means to improving one's job, location, pay, or level. These are strong incentives.

Other incentives to ethical shortcuts – such as making analytical choices so that results appear greater than they would be otherwise or presenting results as more substantial or impactful than the data suggests – can be otherwise be seen as potentially noble. You are investigating climate change, poverty, sex trafficking, and want the results to be a reason for people to take action, to listen and be motivated, to 'make something right'. This speaks directly to the debate of whether the ends justify the means or whether the means, however frustrating one finds them, are inviolable.

However, the reason for ethical behaviours and choices is not merely for one's own reputation, they fortify or undermine one's discipline. Inasmuch as we need to hear from expert voices, disciplinary reputation affects everyone under that disciplinary umbrella. That is, our subjective and ethical choices can benefit one's own research but also the reputation of what your discipline produces. Those same choices can harm them as well.

Thus, the linchpin of scientific research is not the approach chosen, the data available, or the aims of the research but rather the researcher herself. The performance of scientific research rests on the training, knowledge, experience, and skills of the researcher. Nearly all Social Scientists have had some level of training in the ethics of conducting research. Most have confronted one or many of the issues discussed above, whether a question of data quality and origin, how to safeguard participant anonymity, or the delivery of an accurate description of their research results to others. These ethical issues are paramount for the simple reason that another human is submitting themselves to the measure and/or manipulation by another person.

All the ethical issues that arise in these types of research require a sensibility toward others – again, from participants in the data collection process to the audience members of our findings – in the form of being both honest and humble. We must put others before ourselves. We must prioritize the safety of others before our publications. We must not mislead or misrepresent what it is we are doing and finding. To a very high degree, the academic community uses its reputational sanctions and rewards to maintain research integrity and individual adherence to ethnical research norms. However, this is a function of both training – exposure to the key elements and their conceptual importance – as well as the experience of why it matters in practice.

We have reached the end. It is now incumbent on you, my dear reader, to align yourself with this ethical responsibility. It will serve you – and others – well. It is also therefore time for me to pass the torch to you. I leave you with a final thought. Any challenge, any problem you face, will contains elements that emanate from you. This is natural although often unnoticed. Recognize this and make the effort to get out of your own way. Put yourself in alignment with the solution. In this way, you will move more swiftly and accurately to where it is that you want to be.

End of Chapter Summary

- Social Science struggles to remain neutral as we seek to understand things that are both important and personal to many people.
- It is imperative to consider and rigorously employ ethical guidelines for our Social Science research.

- Ethical issues are paramount in research for the simple reason that another human is submitting him/herself to manipulation by another person.
- Ethical considerations, particularly anonymity (right to privacy), benefit both the respondent and the research. For the respondent, the ability to answer honestly with no fear of reprisal. For the researcher, greater confidence that we are getting honest answers (i.e., better data), thus more confidence in our analysis and most importantly, conclusions.
- Research is conducted under a trifold rubric of ethical behaviour:
    o Beneficence: protecting people from harm
    o Respect for persons: autonomous agents
    o Justice: distribution of benefits and burden of research.
- By law, all subjects must agree in the form of informed consent which consists of their voluntary participation and knowledge of the intent of the study.
- All subjects have the right to privacy, including both anonymity and confidentiality.
- All subjects have the right to service including the distribution of benefits and burden of research.

Glossary

- The **deontological approach** refers to a rigorous focus on the means of an investigation rather than the ends.
- The **consequentialist approach** refers to a investigative focus on the ends – producing a meaningful result – with less attention to the means.
- **Beneficence** is protecting people from harm in an investigation.
- The **potential for harm** refers to the possibility for individuals to suffer physical, psychological, emotional, or legal harm by participating in an investigation.
- An **informed consent** document tells potential participants about their voluntary participation, the direction, the nature, and intended outcome of an investigation.
- Individuals have a **right to privacy** including protection for their personal data.
- **Respect for persons** refers to handling and securing data.
- **Anonymity** refers to data collection and analysis in which the identities of the participants are unknown.
- **Confidentiality** refers to data collection in which the researcher(s) know who the participants are but make personally identifiable data unavailable to others to thwart identification.
- The **General Data Protection Regulation** (GDPR) is legislation at the European Union (EU) level that imposes privacy and security obligations on any organization in the EU that collects data on individuals.

- **Ethics Committees** are university bodies that review proposed research for ethical violations.
- **Replication** of research – reproducing exiting results – is a means to underscore the validity of the results.
- A **conflict of interest** refers to divergent incentives for an actor.
- A **right to service** refers to all participants and potential beneficiaries share any practical benefit derived from a study.
- **Justice** is the ethical distribution of benefits and burden of research.

Questions

1. One means of thinking about the ethics of research is imagining that you had to explain your research choices to others. Not in the annoying way of trying to bore them from listening or overwhelming them with academic jargon, but explaining to them in straightforward language the choices you make to achieve your research. Does the audience matter? That is, would it matter if your audience was your friends, your academic advisor, a group of university students at another university, a group of potential funders for your research, to a person you looked up to, to your parents? If so, why?
2. In discussing beneficence, we note that the subjects of a data collection project need be made aware of the intent of the study. This, however, does not include the method to collect these data. That is, if the data collection instrument is an experiment, there is no need to mention the actual treatment – or effect – introduced in the treatment group and excluded from the control group. If the instrument is a survey, which questions will be used to capture the variables of interest. Is this ethical? If so, why? If not, why not?
3. It is common for data collectors – in the form of individual researchers, experimental labs, online/telephone/in person survey companies – to pay respondents. There are in fact a growing number of survey companies that keep thousands of respondents on a literal payroll who are paid to be survey participants. However, subjects cannot be coerced into participation. This distinction has created some debate as to the ethical question of 'To what extent are respondents, who may rely on this income, being coerced?' Do you think this is an important distinction? Remember, most survey respondents – but not all – do already receive payment for participation.
4. In 1971, Prof. Philip Zimbardo designed and conducted an experiment that quickly became famous and is now referred to as the 'Stanford Prison Experiment'. As a psychologist, he wanted to examine individuals' behaviour when placed into roles of either prisoner or guard, particularly whether they would assume these 'roles' partially or fully, including the exhibition of in-group norms and out-group rejection. Using 24 undergraduate volunteers from Stanford University who responded to a newspaper ad, he gave all of them preliminary psychological

exams and briefed them on what was going to happen. After telling them that they were free to leave at any time, he randomly assigned them the role of guard or prisoner in a fake campus-based prison he had built in the basement of an on campus building. Neither set of subjects were given specific instructions or training other than their role assignment. It was designed to run for two weeks. Within 6 days, he had to stop the entire experiment. After an initial uncertainty about what they were to do, the 'guards' began to exhibit sadistic tendencies. On the second day of the experiment, there was a prison 'rebellion' which was brought under control by the 'guards' who then more fully took on the profiles of prison guards. They began a privilege system used to interfere with the solidarity of prisoners, cultivating distrust. They reported becoming increasingly paranoid about the prisoners and their intentions and as a result extended the privilege system to all aspects of prisoners' days, including going to the restroom and eating. Unlike the guards, the prisoners were put into situations purposely meant to cause disorientation, degradation, and depersonalization. Prisoners began to experience emotional disturbances, depression, and learned helplessness. Within days of the outset, two prisoners had to be removed due to emotional trauma. The 'prisoners' used their prison number instead of their names to address the visiting 'chaplain' and when asked how they planned to leave the prison, they became confused. Like the obedience experiments (1963), they show how individuals assume roles under the right circumstances, even if the roles are arbitrarily assigned. This experiment seems fraught with potential ethical issues and many have called this one of the most unethical experiments conducted. Given key elements of ethical considerations above (*informed consent*; *right to privacy*; *right to service*), to what extent did this experiment violate informed consent, voluntary participation, minimizing harm to participants, deception, anonymity, and justice?

5. As pointed out above, Big Data has introduced a number of new challenges to ethical considerations of Social Science research. In a case in which individuals' personal data was hacked, researchers jumped on the opportunity to use the data to publish. Poor and Davidson (2016, see below for the link) ask, 'When the exact data you wanted but couldn't get presents itself to you thanks to hackers, can you use the data?' Do you feel stronger defending or attacking the use of hacked data and why?

6. Academic researchers Gill and Spirling (2015) used diplomatic cables released by Private Manning to WikiLeaks (https://doi.org/10.1093/pan/mpv005). How does this case compare to the case of Patreon in Question 5? What is the same and what is different? Would you act differently than these researchers?

7. In a famous case of non-replicability, two highly-esteemed Economists – Carmen Reinhart and Kenneth Rogoff – promoted a 2010 paper entitled 'Growth in a Time of Debt' (www.nber.org/papers/w15639) that was used widely by public officials and others to undermine public spending in the name of *holy* growth. A graduate student – Thomas Herndon – sought to replicate what amounted to an Excel spreadsheet's worth of data and could not. Some have argued that

this was a substantial ethical breach. A summary is here: www.bbc.com/news/magazine-22223190. To your mind, was the authors' response to this controversy sufficient? What is the responsibility of the authors, the universities, and of the discipline toward such breaches?

Annotated References and Further Reading

Desai, Tanvi Felix Ritchie, and Richard Welpton. 2016. 'Five Safes: Designing Data Access for Research.' Economics Working Paper Series1601. https://doi.org/10.13140/RG.2.1.3661.1604
Safe Projects, Safe People, Safe Data, Safe Settings, Safe Output.

Gill, M., and A. Spirling. 2015. 'Estimating the severity of the WikiLeaks U.S. diplomatic cables disclosure' *Political Analysis* **23(2): 299–305. https://doi.org/10.1093/pan/mpv005**
This is an academic article on Private Manning's release of classified diplomatic cables.

Iphofen, Ron. 2009. *Ethical Decision-Making in Social Research. A Practical Guide.* **London: Palgrave Macmillan.**
A great guide to integrating ethics into our research projects.

King, G. 1995. 'Replication, replication' *PS: Political Science and Politics* **28(3): 444–452. https://doi.org/10.2307/420301**
The clearest and strongest push for the importance of disciplinary replication.

Kramer, Adam D.I., Guillory, Jamie E., Hancock, Jeffrey T. 2014. 'Emotional contagion through social networks' *Proceedings of the National Academy of Sciences* **Jun 2014, 111 (24): 8788–8790. https://doi.org/10.1073/pnas.1320040111**
One of the studies that enrolled Facebook users without their knowledge.

Poor, N., and R. Davidson. 2016. 'The ethics of using hacked data: Patreon's data hack and academic data standards' *Data and Society* **Case Study 03.17.16. https://bdes.datasociety.net/wp-content/uploads/2016/10/Patreon-Case-Study.pdf**
This is the article on the Patreon hack.

Political Science Replication Initiative: https://projects.iq.harvard.edu/psreplication/home
An example of the importance of replicability in Political Science.

Vilhuber, L. 2020. 'Reproducibility and replicability in economics' *Harvard Data Science Review* **2(4). https://doi.org/10.1162/99608f92.4f6b9e67**
A recent and unsettling account of the state of replication in the social sciences. While political science and sociology fare well, economics does much more poorly.

Signposts to the Accompanying Digital Resources

Data used in this chapter

- www.visualcapitalist.com/terms-of-service-visualizing-the-length-of-internet-agreements/
- The General Data Protection Regulation (GDPR): https://gdpr.eu/
- The American Political Science Association. *A Guide to Professional Ethics in Political Science. Second Edition* (2008). www.apsanet.org/imgtest/ethicsguideweb.pdf. This is a comprehensive compendium of ethical considerations of modern Political Science research that represents a code of ethical conduct in Political Science.
- American National Election Surveys Restricted Data Access Application: https://electionstudies.org/data-center/restricted-data-access/

INDEX

Note: Figures, tables and images are indicated by page numbers in bold print. The letters '*Ref*' after a page number indicate information in an 'Annotated References and Further Reading' section.

Adcock, Robert and Collier, David 63*Ref*
additive indexes 356, 366
Agenda-Setting theory 41–2, 69
Aiken, Alexander C. 392*Ref*
aims of this book 1–2, 9, 22
Aitken, Alexander C. 392*Ref*
Akaike's Information Criterion (AIC) 404
Almond, G.A. and Verba, S. 179
Almond, Gabriel A. and Genco, Stephen J. 102*Ref*
alternative hypothesis 241, 257
American National Election Survey (ANES) 469–70
American Political Science Review 53, 91
analysis 68–71
   case selection 69–70
   choice of 78–80
   ethics 468–72
   levels 68–9
   units 69
Anderson, Christopher J. and Guillory, Christine A. 433, 438*Ref*
Application Programming Interface (API) 453
Argentina (CPI and PCI) 274–5
autocorrelation 381, 383, 390
Autoregressive Integrated Moving Averages (ARIMA) 383

Ballotpedia (website) 430
bar charts 127–**8**
Bates, Robert H. 82*Ref*
Bayes, Thomas 444
Bayesian statistics 443, 444–50, 459
   Bayes' Theorem 447–8, 460
   Bayesian ratio/factor 450
   and Central Limit Theorem (CLT) 446–7
   confidence intervals 446
   example: national referendum to expand use of renewable energy 448–50

   and hypothesis testing 445–6
   limitations 450
   subjectivity 445, 450
Baysian Information Criterion (BIC) 404
Benoit, K. et al 461
Bessel's correction 120
Best, Linear, Unbiased, Estimator (BLUE) 199, 402
bias
   in Data Science 455
   and personal preferences 87
   in politics 88–9
Big Data 47, 451, 452
   ethical considerations 467–8
   see also Data Science (Machine Learning)
binary logistic regression 393–417
   cumulative density function (CDF) 399, 401, 415
   democracy or not and HDI **400**
   discrete change 398, 415
   error term 396
   example of binary logistic regression: Voting in the Last Election 402–414, **406**
   Ideal Types 409, 415
   interpretation: regression coefficients 405–8, **406**
   logits, odds and probabilities **409**
   odds ratio 406–8, 415
   likelihood ratio chi-squared (χ^2) test 404, 415
   Model Fit **404**
   predicted probabilities 408–414, 415
      graphic equalizer 409–**410**
      voting and age **410**–411
      voting, age and 'close to party' 411–**12**
      voting, age, 'close to party' and far left, centre and far right **413**–14
   Statistical Significance **405**
   Wald test 404

linear solution **398**
marginal effect 398, 406, 409, 415
Maximum Likelihood Estimation (MLE) 401–2
natural log 'e' **396**
natural log of the odds (link function) 396
natural log transformations 397
normal probability and cumulative density functions 400
probabilities **399**
probability density function (PDF) 399, 415
bivariate regression 189–214, 318
   assumptions 210–211
      exogeneity 211
      independence of observations 211
      linearity 210
      multicollinearity 210
      multivariate normality 210–211
   best regression line **195**–9, **196**, **199**
      Ordinary Least Squares (OLS) regression 199
      string method **197**
   coefficient of determination (R^2) 202–4
      examples 203–4
   deterministic relationships 193
   error term ε 190, 193–5, 213
   intercept (alpha α) 190
   model fit (goodness of fit) 203, 213
   modelling (Voice and Accountability and corruption perceptions) 204–210, 213
      step one research question 205
      step two identify variables 205
      step three 3scatterplot 205–**6**
      step four calculate regression equation 206–8
      step five coefficient of determination 209
      step six interpretation 209
   random (stochastic) components 194, 213
   regression coefficient/slope (beta) 190, **191–2**, 193
   regression equations 190
      examples with Voice and Accountability 199–202, **200**
         global militarization **201**
         life expectancy **200**
         press freedom 201–**2**, 214
   residual (μ) 193
   squared differences 198
   systematic components 194, 213
black swan theory 35–6
Blandlot, René 436
Box-Steffensmeier, Janet M. et al 82*Ref*
Brambor, T. et al 368*Ref*

Carlin, George 126
case studies and small-n studies 71, 72–4, 77
   degrees of freedom 73, 81
      example: Electoral Turnout **74**
   external validity 74
   internal validity 72–4
cases: definition 110, 132
categorical regression models 414, 415
causation/causality 37–8, 93
   causal claims 454
   causal identification 98
   causal inferences 16, 24
   causal mechanisms 96–7
   and computers 94
   and correlation 37–8, 96, 179–80, 181
   deterministic causality and probabilistic explanation 457
   importance in Political Science 95
   limit on discovery 97
   and measurement 95–6
   and prediction 456–8
   'proving' causal relations 95, 98
censored data 430, 437
Central Limit Theorem (CLT) 261–87
   and Bayesian statistics 446–7
   description/definition of CLT 266, 285
   normal distribution 263–6, **264**–**6**, 285
      68-95-99.7% rule 264–6, 282
   sampling distributions 262–3, 446–7
      probabilities of rolling two dice 262–**3**
      standard error 267, 285
   Z-distribution and Z-scores 267–84, 285
      standard deviations **272**–3
      tables 269, **270–71**
      uses of Z-scores
         comparisons of interval-level variables 273–5
         correlation of CPI and PCI (Argentina and Turkey) **274**–6
         determining expected probability of different outcomes, CPI and PCI scores 273, 276–84, **276**, **278–83**
central tendency and dispersion **124**–6
certainty 16–18, 95
   and uncertainty 18, 335, 444
chi-squared (χ^2) test for independence 239, 245–55
   degrees of freedom (*df*) 246
   distribution 246–**7**, **247**, **249**
   example: political gender parity 250–55
      chi-squared (χ^2) distribution **254**
      cross-tab: Egalitarian Democracy and Political Power of Women **251**
      Expected Values of Egalitarian Democracy and Gender Power **253**
      test of independence 252–3, 254–5
      variables 250–51
   formula 245

level of confidence (α) 246–8, **247**
classical hypothesis testing 240–58
  steps one and two: null and alternative hypotheses 241
  step three: test statistic 241
  step four: critical or rejection region 241
  step five: interpretation 242
  chi-squared (χ^2) test for independence 245–55
  statistical significance 244
  Type I and Type II errors 244–**5**, 257
cluster samples 225
coefficient of determination (R^2) 202–4, **203**, 324, 459
common sense 19, 38
Comparative Politics 431
complement of an event 230, 236
conceptual congruence 90–91
conceptualization 52–4, 151–**2**
  'conceptual stretching' 53
  connotation 52–3
  denotation 53
  'Ladder of Abstraction' 53
confidence intervals 446
connotation 52–3
constructivism 20
context in modelling 432, 433, 435
control 14, 21
controlled comparisons 152–5, **153**, 157
correlation 167–82
  calculating 171–2
  and causation 37–8, 179–**80**, 181
  challenges
    non-linearity 178
    number of observations 177–8
    outliers 178
    shape of distributions 178
    symmetry 177, 178, **179**
    truncated range 178
  and linearity 170–**71**
    deviations 170
    summary 170
  measure of strength and direction of relationship 167, **168–9**
  Pearson's correlation coefficient 168
  positive/negative 168, 183
  and theory 179
  Voice and Accountability
    corruption perceptions **173**, **174**
    democratic political culture **180**, 181, **195**
    global militarization **173**, **175**, **203**
    internet access **166–7**
    life expectancy at birth **173**, **174**, 203
    mean level of DPC **196**, **197**
    press freedom **173**, **176**, **202**, **203**
    renewable energy consumption **173**, **175**

Corruptions Perceptions Index (CPI) 273, 274, 286, 287
count outcomes 431, 437
Cramer's V. 155
critical thinking 93
critical value 241, 257
critical/rejection region 241
Cronbach's alpha 356, 366
cross-national differences 434–5, 435–6
cross-tabulation **138**–9, 156, **162**
  see also measures of association
crowdsourcing 453
cumulative density function (CDF) 399, 400, 401, 415

Dahlgren, P. 165
Dalton, Russell and Wattenberg, Martin 403, 416*Ref*
data 47–63
  Big Data *see* Data Science (Machine Learning)
  censored 430, 437
  change to evidence 89
  comprehensive and sufficient 62
  conceptualization 52–4, 59–60
  consistency with theory/hypothesis 70
  converting into information 6, 459
  data availability 54–6
  definition 47, 62, 132
  incomplete data 6
  level-1 and level-2 data 432
  measurement error 59–61
  NxK design 50, 62
  operationalization 54, 55, 59–60
  organizing **50**
  purpose 47–8
  quality of data 48–51, 93
  and research question (difference) 66
  suitability 70
  trace data 456
  transforming 50–51, 426, 456
  used in this book 5
  validity and reliability 56, **57–8**
  see also data collection; datasets; variables
data collection 68, 81
  ethics 465–8
  'level' of and research question 71
  and reactivity of data 452
Data Science (Machine Learning) 443–4, 451–9, 460
  Big Data 451, 452
  ethical considerations 467–8
  and complementarity 453–4
  and data collection 452, 453
  data-driven 455, 460
  digital trace data 453, 460
  mass collaboration 453, 460

model building 453
online data and internet access 456–7
and prediction 454–7
Supervised/Unsupervised Machine Learning 453, 460
user preferences 456
data-driven approaches 455, 460
datasets 50, 110, 132
   Dataset of 25 Most Populated Countries **109**–111
      levels of measurement 111–12
      source materials 110–111
   digital trace data 453
deductive reasoning 30–31, 43
degrees of freedom 73, 81, 258
democracies and elite schisms 448
democracies and non-democracies distribution 226, 395
democracy and internet access 138–55, 162
   conceptualization and operationalization 151–**2**
   conditional probability 232–4
   correlations: magnitude and direction **169**
   cross-tabulation **138**
   and economic performance (controlled comparisons) 152–5, **153**
   interpretation **149**–51
   means comparison 162–5, **163**
democracy, measures of 54–5
democracy and political gender parity 250–55
democratic political institutions and democratic political culture 98, 179–81, **180**, **195**
Democratic Republic of Congo 150
Dennett, Daniel 12
denotation 53
dependent variables: definition 38, 39, 43
Desai, Tanvi Felix Ritchie and Welpton, Richard 480Ref
descriptive inferences 15, 24
descriptive statistics 21, 23, 25, 107, 108, 221
deterministic confirmation 17, 24
Diamond, Jared and Robinson, A. 160Ref
Dickens, David R. and Fontana, Andrea 20
digital trace data 453, 460
distribution of political power 259
dummy variables *see* multiple regression, dummy variables
Durbin-Watson test 383
Durkheim, Emile 25Ref

early election calling in Europe 229–**30**
Easton 179
ecological fallacy 70
egalitarian democracy index 259
Einstein, Albert 34

empirical approaches 71–7
   case studies and small-n studies 72–4
   experimental approach 71, 74–6
   internal and external validity **77**
   large-N quantitative studies 72, 76–7, 224
endogeneity 385, 390
epistemology 18, 24
Erasmus students' place of birth **113–15**, 130
   pie chart 126–**7**
error terms 190, 193, 194, 195, 213
Esping-Andersen, Gøsta 160Ref
ethics 463–81
   anonymity 468, 469–70, 477
   beneficence 465, 467–8, 477
      potential for harm 465, 477
   confidentiality 469, 477
   conflict of interest 474, 478
   data protection and security 468–70, 477
   deontological and consequentialist approaches 464, 477
   ethical codes 466
   ethics committees 471, 477
   informed consent 465–6, 477
      example 466–7
   institutional responsibility for standards 470–72
   justice 474–5, 478
   morals and ethics 464
   and proritizing others 476
   replicability 473–4, 478
   reporting and presentation 473, 475–6
   research transparency 472
   respect for persons 468, 477
   Review Boards 471
   right to privacy 468, 477
   right to service 274–5
   training for researchers 476
EU support among European voters **222**, 223
EU support for unification 306–8, **342**
   Eastern and Western respondents 344–5
   and attitudes to immigration 345–51, **346**
      Eastern and Western respondents 359–62, **360**, **361**
   and income 362–5, **363**, **364**
   gender differences **367**
Eurobarometer 466
European Election Studies 466
European national-level income inequality 390–92, **390–91**
European Parliamentary (EP) elections turn-out 121, **122–3**, 130
   histogram **129**
European Social Survey 66, 125, 128, 180, 224, 306, 308, 403, 422, 466
Evans, M.D.R. et al 388, 392Ref

exogeneity 390
experimental approach 71, 74–6, 77
　external validity 75–6
　internal validity 75
explanation of relationships 13–14, 16, 23
　see also theories

F-test 326
factor analysis 357–8, 366
falsifiability of theories 35–6
Farr, James et al 102*Ref*
feminism 20
Ferguson, Michaele L. 20
Fisher, Ronald A. 250, 258*Ref*, 444, 445
fitted values 382, 390
Freedom House
　Cabinet Composition and Electoral
　　Systems 158
　Cabinet Composition and Electoral Systems
　　(Eastern Europe) **159**
　Cabinet Composition and Electoral Systems
　　(Western Europe) **159**
　'Global Freedom Scores' 55, 157
　internet freedom **158**
frequentist approaches 444, 445–6, 450

Galton, Sir Francis 70, 91
Garring, John 102*Ref*
Gauss-Markov theorem 388, 390
Geddes, Barbara 44*Ref*
Geertz, Clifford 74
gender theory 20
General Least Squares (GLS) 383
generalization 11
　and inference **15**, 220
German elections: voting and education
　14–15, 16, 32
Gide, André 94, 102*Ref*
GIGO (garbage in, garbage out) 48, 93
Gill, Jeff 446, 461*Ref*
Gill, M. and Spirling, A. 480*Ref*
Gill and Spirling 479
Gini Index 265
Goldacre, Ben 292
Goodman and Kruskal's Gamma **146**–8,
　156, 162
　direction **148–9**
　formula 252
　magnitude 148
Goodman and Kruskal's Lambda 140, 143,
　143–6, **144–5**, 156, 162
Gosset, W.S. **298**
Gould, Stephen Jay 368*Ref*
graphs 126–30
　bar charts 127–**8**

histograms 128–**9**
nominal- and ordinal-level graphing 155–6
pie charts 126–**7**
scatterplots 165, **166**, **166–7**, 182
Gross Domestic Product (GDP) 268–**9**
Gross National Product 92

Hardy, M.A. 368*Ref*
Hausman, Jerry A. 392*Ref*
Hawking, Stephen 98
Hay, Colin 20
Heisenberg, Werner 8*Ref*
Herndon, Thomas 479
heteroscedasticity 381, **383**, 389
Hidden Figures (film) 193
Hindmann, Matthew 165
histograms 128–**9**
Hoekstra, R. et al 461*Ref*
Hoffman, Bert 165
Holland, P.W. 102*Ref*
homoscedasticity 381, **382**, 389
Hug, Simon 430, 438*Ref*
Human Development Index 92, 328,
　328–35, 395
Human Flight and Brain Drain (HF/DB) 328,
　328–35
hypotheses 38–42, 43
　definition 43
　example: Agenda Setting 41–2
　good hypotheses 40–41
　　directional 41
　　general 40–41
　　and strong theories 40
　null hypotheses 39
　see also classical hypothesis testing; infer-
　　ence for interval-level variables
hypothesis testing 445–6
　and null hypotheses 445

Ideal Types 409, 415
independent events 234, 236
independent variables: definition 38, 39, 43
inductive fallacy 35
inductive reasoning 30, 43
inequality and democracy 51–6, 88, 95–6
inference 14–16, 23, 219–35, 236, 336
　causal 16
　descriptive inferences 15
　and generalization **15**, 220
　inferential statistics 21, 23, 25, 49, 444
　logic of inference 220, 221, 236
　and predictions 16
　and samples 49, 228
inference for interval-level variables 289–313
　changing intervals 292–4
　confidence intervals 290–95, 299

binomial probability confidence intervals
    294–6
    example: World Values Survey, Feeling
        of Happiness 295–**6**
    margin of error 299
point estimates 289, 290, 311
standard error 290
t-test 297–302
    difference of means t-test 305–9, 312
        examples
            European unification 306–8
            European unification: Eastern European
                respondents 308–9
    hypothesis testing 289, 303–5
        example: E-Government Index 303–5
        steps 303
    one- and two-tailed tests 309–**310**
    Student's t-distribution **298**
    t-distribution **297**
        Standard Normal 298, 299
    t-distribution table **300**–**301**, 311
    t-score 297
    t-value 297–8, 312
inferential statistics 107, 219, 221, 228, 236
Inglehart, Robert 97
institutions and culture 97, 98
instrumental variables 387, 390
interaction terms *see* multiple regression,
    interaction terms
intercept (α) 190, 343
interest in politics 351–**2**
International Relations (IR) 13, 20, 86, 131, 431
interpretivist approaches 18, 24
interval-level variables 111, 119–21
    central tendency and dispersion 119, 124–6
    graphing 128–**9**
    measure of dispersion: standard deviation
        119, 120
    sample mean 119
    see also inference for interval-level variables
interviews 452, 460
intuitive mind 1
Iphofen, Ron 480*Ref*
Item Response Theory (IRT) 358, 366
Iversen, Gudmund 461*Ref*

Jackman, Simon 63*Ref*
James, William 34
Johnson, Katherine **193**
joint distribution 138, 156
Jones, Bradford S. 438*Ref*
journals 474
Judea, Pearl and Mackenzie, Dana 8*Ref*

Kendall's Tau 155
King, Gary 439*Ref*, 480*Ref*

King, Gary et al 8*Ref*, 10, 71
Klotz, Irving M. 439*Ref*
Kohli, Atul et al 44*Ref*
Kramer, Adam D.I. et al 467, 480*Ref*
Kuhn, Thomas 26*Ref*

Lakatos, Imre 35
Laplace, Pierre-Simon 17, 444
large-N quantitative studies 72, 76–7, 224
last stop image **99**
Lec, Stanislaw Jerzy 457, 461*Ref*
level of confidence (alpha) 246, 258, 322
levels of analysis 68–9, 81
levels of measurement
    definition 132
    example from dataset of most populated
        countries 111–12
    see also interval level variables; nom-
        inal-level variables; ordinal-level
        variables
Lewis-Beck, M.S. et al 392*Ref*
Lijphart, Arend 71
likelihood ratio chi-squared (χ^2) test 404, 415
Likert Scale **116**–**17**, 124
linearity 372–3
literature review 67–8, 81
log-linear transformations 375–**6**, 389
logits 397, 398, 415
Long, Scott 416*Ref*
Loveless, Matthew and Rohrschneider,
    Robert 339*Ref*

McAdam, Doug et al 78, 79
McCombs, Max and Shaw, Donald 41
McGrayne, Sharon Bertsch 462*Ref*
Machine Learning *see* Data Science (Machine
    Learning)
McLuhan, Marshal 11
marginal effect 398, 406, 409, 415
mass collaboration 453, 460
materialism and post-materialism 97, 98
math skills 4–5
mathematics as 'language of nature' 92–3
Maximum Likelihood Estimation (MLE)
    401–2, 421
mean 126, 133
means comparison 162–5, **163**,
    183–7, **184**
    utility 163–5, **164**
measurement error 59–61, 380, 389
    systematic/non-systematic 59, 63
measurement strategy 68
measures of association
    (bivariate) regression 189–214
    interval-level variables 161–87
        correlation 167–82

interval- by interval-variables: scatterplot 165, **166**, **166–7**, **167**
means comparison 162–5, 183–7, **184**
nominal- and ordinal-level variables 137–59
   controlled comparisons 152–5, **153**, 157
   cross-tabulation **138**–9
   graphing **155**–6
   interpretation 149–51
   zero-order relationships 152, 157
measures of central tendency and dispersion 112, **124**–6, 132, 402
   outliers 130
   skew 130–**31**
median 119, 124, 126, 132, 133
Mencken, Harry Louis 98, 102*Ref*
methodology 66
methods section in research design 65, 68, 78
minimum log likelihood 402
mixed methods 79
mode 124
model fit (goodness of fit) 203, 213, 324–6
model specification 385, 389, 390
modelling 28–30
   Spitfire **29**
Mood, Carina 416*Ref*
Morgan-Jones, Edward and Loveless, Matthew 433, 439*Ref*
Morozov, Eygeny 165
Morton, Rebecca B. and Williams, Kenneth C. 82*Ref*
Muller, E.N. and Seligson, M.A. 179
multi-level modelling 432–5
   and cross-national differences 434–5, 435–6
   cross-sectional data 432, 437
   cross-unit heterogeneity 433
   dummy variables 433–4
   and hierarchical linear modelling (HLM) 435–6, 437
   individual-level data 432, 433
   level-1 and level-2 data 432
   pooled analysis 432, 437
multicollinearity 210, 377, 378, 379, 455
multinomial logit 425, 437
   four types of political participation **427**
   interpretation 427–30
     digital participation 428–30
     vs. traditional participation **429**
     non-traditional participation 428
   transforming data 426
   types of political participation 425–**6**
multiple regression
   additive indexes 356, 366
     Cronbach's alpha 356, 366
   analytical abilities 318
     control 318

description 318, 337
inference 318
assumptions
   diagnostic check-up, need for 371–2
   error term is well-behaved 380–83
     autocorrelation (serial correlation) 381, 383, 390
     Autoregressive Integrated Moving Averages (ARIMA) 383
     Durbin-Watson test 383
     fitted values 382–3, 390
     General Least Squares (GLS) 383
     heteroscedasticity 381, **383**, 389
     homoscedasticity 381, **382**, 389
     meaning 381
     Multivariate Normality 381
     Ordinary Least Squares (OLS) 383, 388
     spatial autocorrelation 382, 390
   fixed in repeated samples 386–8
     Hausman test 387
     instrumental variable estimation 387, 390
     measurement error 386, 389
     proxy variables 387–8, 390
   importance of assumptions 372
   mean of error term is zero (exogeneity assumption) 384–6, 390
     endogeneity 385, 390
     omitted variable bias 384, 390
   uncorrelated independent variables 376–80
     high correlation 377, **378**, 379
     multicollinearity 377, 378, 379
     corrections 379
     types of variation **377–8**
     Variance Inflation Factor (VIF) test 378, 389
   underlying linearity 372–6
     resolving non-linearity 374–6
       log-linear transformations 375–**6**, 389
     scatterplots of Left/Right placements **373–4**
base/reference categories 343, 350, 353
dependent variables with two outcomes **394**–5
dichotomous dummy variables 343–8
   difference of t-test 344–**5**
   example: European unification 344–7
   and immigration **346**, **347**
   statistically significant variables 348
dummy variables 341–56, 365, 366
elements 319–26
   inferential additions 321–4
     p-value 322–**3**, 337
     software output example **323**

standard error 321–2
t-scores 321
model fit (goodness of fit) 324–6
  adjusted R^2 324–5, 337
  F-test 326, 337
  nested models 325
  regression coefficients (partials) 320–21, 323–4, 337, 358
  standardized regression coefficients 320–21, 337
example: national level income inequality 390–92
  scatterplot: error terms and fitted values **391**
  table: income inequality in Europe **390–91**
factor analysis 357–8, 366
flexibility and versatility 432
interaction terms 358–65, 366
  centring 364
  dichotomous dummy variable : EU support for unification 359–62, **360**
    immigration and West/East interaction **361**
  interval-level variables example 362–5, **363**
    immigration and income interaction **364**
  problems 365
  when to use 359
Item Response Theory (IRT) 358, 366
limitations 353–4
modelling 326–35, 337–9
  Steps 326–35
    one: research question 326, 327
    two: identify variables 326, 327–8
    three: Pearson's Product Moment Correlation Coefficient 326, **328**–9
    four: regression equation 326, 329–34
      output: CPI **330**
      output: p-values **332**
      output: regression coefficients **330**
      output: t-test statistics **331**
    five: model fit 326, **334**
    six: interpretation 326–7, 334–**5**
ordinal dummy variables 351–4, **352**
  difference between each category **353**
  with different reference categories **354**
  ordinal-level variables as interval-level variables 354–**5**
  ordinal-level variables reshaped to a lower level variable **355**
polychotomous nominal-level dummy variables 348–51, **349**
  changing the reference category **350**–51
power of multiple regression 341

reasons for use 341–2
robustness testing 379–80
spurious relationships **319**
variables to include 318–19
see also binary logistic regression
multivariate normality 381, 389
mutual exclusivity 231, 236

NxK design 50, 62
N-Ray affair 436
new methods 79–80
Neyman-Pearson hypothesis testing 445, 446, 447
Niemi, R. et al 368*Ref*
nominal-level variables 112–16
  central tendency and dispersion **124**–6
  graphing 126–7
  variation ratio 114–15, 133
non-normative statements 40
non-systematic measurement errors 59, 63
non-traditional political participation 91, 356
Normal distribution 263–6, **264–6**, 285, 402, 447
normative approaches 12, 13, 24
Norris, P. 179
null hypotheses 39, 240, 241, 257, 444, 445
  and hypothesis testing 445

objectivity 12, 24, 40, 87, 463
  and Bayesian statistics 445
observation 30
odds ratio 406–8, 415
omitted variable bias 384, 390
online research
  and access to internet 456–7
  ethics 467–8
ontology 18–19, 24
operationalization 54, 63, 151–**2**
ordinal regression model (ORM) 420–24, 437
  cutpoints 421, 437
  example distribution of ordinal-level dependent variable **421**
  interpretation **422**–4
    Likelihood Ratio chi-squared (χ^2) 423
    odds ratios 423
    predicted probabilities for 'very interested', age, 'close to party' and ideology **424**
  political interest **422**
  proportional odds assumption 421, 437
ordinal-level variables 111–12, **116–**19, **117, 118**
  central tendency and dispersion **124**–6
  generating median 116–17
  graphing 127–**8**

see also ordinal regression model (ORM)
Ordinary Least Squares (OLS) 199, 383, 388, 398–9, 402
outliers 130, 133

parameter 222, 236
parsimony of theories 34
partials 320
patterns 6
Pearson, Karl 187*Ref*, 250, 258*Ref*, 444
Pearson's *r* 168
peer-review 8, 12
peer-reviews 474
Perestroika Movement 91
Phi 155
Picasso, Pablo 2
pie charts 126–**7**
plausibility 31–3
　clarity of concepts 32–3
　consistency 32
　and credibility 32
　and variable elements 32
Poincaré 2
Poisson regression model 431, 437
Political Corruption Index (PCI) 273, 274, 286, 287, 341
　multiple regression 326–35
Political Economy 131
political efficacy 357
political ideology: left-right self-placement 124–5, 128, **129**, 135, **373**, **374**
political interest 422–4
political participation
　changes 60–61
　digital participation 428–30
　forms of 402–3, 425–**6**
　non-traditional political participation 91, 356, 428
political questions 86
'Political Science Replication Initiative' (article) 480*Ref*
political values 88–9
Polity IV Project 55
Poor, N. and Davidson, R. 480*Ref*
Popper, Karl 26*Ref*, 35
populations 49, 62, 221–3, **222–3**
positivist approaches 12–13, 18, 24
post-communist media systems 96–7
post-positivism 19
postmodernism 19, 20
pre-registration of research projects 474
predicted probabilities 408–414
prediction 14–15, 454–6
　and confidence 411
　and explanation 454–6
　and inferences 16, 454

prediction models and causal models 456
　and target variable 455
　use of 458
predictive and causal models 455–6
Press Freedom Index (PFI) 328, 328–35
principal components analysis 357
probabilistic confirmation 17, 25, 100
probabilistic reasoning 446
probability assumption 220–21
probability density function **247**
probability samples 224, 225
probability theory 228–34, 235
　classical method 229, 236
　conditional probability 232–4, 236
　　Bayes' Theorem 447–8
　　example: democracy and internet access 232–3
　　order of events 233
　intersection/joint probability 231
　posterior probability 448
　probabilities of rolling two dice 262–**3**
　probability and independence 234–5
　relative frequency method 229
probability density function (PDF) 399, 415
Probit 397
Proportional Reduction of Error (PRE) 141, 143, 150, 156, 402
proxy variables 387–8, 390
Przeworski, Adam and Teune, Henry 73
Psychology 92
publishing 474
Putnam, Robert 97, 98, 179

qualitative and quantitative studies 71–2, 100
Quality of Government dataset 172, 286
　'Conflict Intensity' 286, 291
　E-Government Index 303–4
　'Ethnic Fractionalization' 286, 291, 299
quantification in Political Science 91–3
questions, clarity of 5

random variables 263
randomization 49, 223–8, 236
range 118, 119, 124, 125, 127, 128, 130, 132
ratio-level variables 111
reactivity of data 452
reasons for studying statistics 2–3
Reinhart Carmen and Rogoff, Kenneth 479
relative frequencies 113, 133
reliability 56, 57–8, 63
　inter-coder reliability 58
　of measurements 59
　split test 56
　test/re-test 56, 58
replication 11–12, 14, 23, 24, 88, 473–4, 478

replication studies 474
research design 65–82
   analysis 68–71, 81
   checklist 77–8
   and conceptualization 53
   data collection 68
   empirical approaches 71–7
   guided by theory 28
   importance in Political Science 89
   literature review 67–8, 78, 81
   methods section 65, 68, 78, 81
   minimizing limitations 62
   research questions 65–8
   theory section 67–8, 78
research questions 65–8
   conditions 67
   and data (difference) 66
   and level of data collection 71
research skills 4
residual (μ) 193
robustness testing 379–80
Rohrschneider, R. 179
Rutherford, Ernest 85

sample mean 119
sample standard deviation 120
samples/sampling 49, 63, 220–21, 236
   and case selection 69–70
   and Central Limit Theorem (CLT) 262–3, 446–7
   distributions 262, 263, 266–7, 285
   and populations 221–3, **222–3**, 446
     and Big Data 451
     example **222–3**
   prediction 454–6
   probability samples 224, 225
   problems 454–7
   random sampling 454
   randomization 49, 223–8
   sampling frame 222, 236
   size of sample 226, **227**, 266, 371
   for surveys 224–5
   see also central limit theorem (CLT)
Sartori, Giovanni 53
Scarborough, W.J. et al 55
scatterplots 165, **166–7**, 182
Schmidt, Manfred G. 160*Ref*
scientific research/methods 9–16, 22, 24
   characteristics of scientific research 10–11
   as a convention 2
   key principles 10–16, **23**
     1. transparent and replicable description 10, 11–13, 23
     2. explanation of relationships 10, 13–14, 23, 137–8
     3. making appropriate inferences 10, 14–16, 23

   and knowledge 18–20
   objectivity and subjectivity 12
   in Political Science 10, 11, 13, 20, 85–7
     objectivity 87–8
     reasons for scientific approach 86
   and quest for certainty 16–18
   and statistics 3, 21–3, 93
   subjectivity 68, 78
Scott, James 79
Sen, Amartya 92
serial correlation 381, 383, 390
Shirky, C. 165
Shmueli, G. 462*Ref*
significance level (α) 246
significance testing *see* classical hypothesis testing
skew 130–**31**, 133
Snijders, T.A.B. and Bosker, R.J. 439*Ref*
social capital 98
social movements and resistance study 78–9
'social trust' (fake) survey 116–19
   bar chart 127–**8**
Sociology 92
software for statistics 4, 5, 120, 423
   multiple regression **323**
Somers' D. 155
Soviet Communism collapse 179–80
spatial autocorrelation 382, 390
spurious correlations 37–8, 43
standard deviation 119, 133
Standard Normal distribution 297, 399
standardization 268–9
statistical abilities 3–4
statistical literacy 2–3
statistical significance 221, 244, 255, 257
statistics 21, 25, 76–7
   external validity 77
   internal validity 76–7
   limitations 165
   in Political Science
     challenges
       causation 93–100
       conceptual congruence 90–91
       definitions and measurement 90
       quality of data 93
       quantification 91–3
     importance 89–90, 99
   and science 3, 21–3
   uses of 2, 3, 4, 6–7, 23
Stein, M. 103*Ref*
stratified samples 225
strikes 91
structuralism 19
student performances 435
subjectivity 12, 24, 87
   in scientific research/methods 68, 78

substantive significance 221, 236, 252, 257
surveys, samples/sampling for 224–5
systematic measurement errors 59, 63
systematic samples 225

Tanzania 150
test statistic 241, 257
Theocharis, Y. and Van Deth, J.W. 60–61, 403, 417*Ref*, 425, 439*Ref*
theory 13, 17, 27–38
  and causal claims 454
  and causation 37–8, 94
  and correlation 179
  definition 43
  as explanations of relationships 28, 29
  and hypotheses 38–42, 43
  inductive and deductive reasoning 30–31
  and modelling 28, 29
  negative and positive heuristic 35
  plausibility 96
  in Political Science 88–9
  and proof 98
  role of theory 28–**30**
    model 30, 31
    as simplifications 29
  strong theories 31–7
    definition 43
    falsifiability 35–6, 43
    fertility (accumulating evidence) 33, 34
    parsimony (leverage) 34, 43
    plausibility 31–3
    strong and weak (not right or wrong) 31, 33, 94, 98
  theory section in design 67–8, 78
theory-developing/building 15, 30
Tobit model 430, 437
trace data 456
transforming data 50–51, 426
transparency 11, 12, 14, 23, 24, 472
Transparency International 273
truncated data 430, 437
Tufte, Edward R. 134*Ref*
Turing, Alan 444
Turkey (CPI and PCI) 274–5
Tuskegee Syphilis Study 475
Twitter 457
Type I and Type II errors 244–**5**, 257

Unemployment Rate (UNEMP) 328, 328–35
union of events 230, 236
United Nations Development Programme (UNDP) 92
units of analysis 69
univariate descriptive statistics 108–134
  graphing 126–31

V-Democracy dataset 250, 251, 273
validity 56, 57–8, 63
  construct validity 56
  face validity 56
  internal and external 71, 72, 81
  of measurements 59
value of education 3–4
value of studying politics 86
variables
  and data/datasets 109–111
  definitions 50–51, 63, 132
  dependent/independent 38–9, 43, 152
  levels *see* interval-level variables; nominal-level variables; ordinal-level variables; ratio-level variables
  relationships
    at heart of scientific study 137–8
    magnitude and direction 139, 141, 157
    summarizing 107, 108, 109
  see also data
Varian, H. 462*Ref*
variance 112, 133
variance inflation factor (VIF) test 378, 389
variation ratio 114–15, 133
Verba, Sidney et al 60
Vilhuber, L. 473, 480*Ref*
Voice and Accountability
  and Corruptions Perceptions Index (CPI) 204–210, 326–35
  description 135, 328
  interval-level variable 111
voting and levels of education 14–16, 32, 66, 70, 100
voting practices 403

Wald test 404
Watts, Alan 1
Weber, Max 12, 40
Wilkinson, Richard and Pickett, Kate 187*Ref*
women, attitudes about role of 55–6
Wonnacott, Thomas H. and Wonnacott, Ronald J. 215*Ref*
World Bank 152
World Governance Indicators 55
World Values Survey 55, 91

Yule's Q(Gamma) 140–43, **141**, **142**, 156, 162

zero-order correlation coefficients 320
zero-order relationships 152, 157
Zhang, W. et al 165
Zimbardo, Philip 478